PRESIDENTIAL LEADERSHIP

POLITICS AND POLICY MAKING

ELEVENTH EDITION

D1622980

GEORGE C. EDWARDS III
TEXAS A&M UNIVERSITY

KENNETH R. MAYER
UNIVERSITY OF WISCONSIN, MADISON

STEPHEN J. WAYNE
GEORGETOWN UNIVERSITY

ROWMAN & LITTLEFIELD
Lanham • Boulder • New York • London

To Carmella, Susan, and Cheryl

Executive Editor: Traci Crowell
Assistant Editor: Deni Remsberg
Higher Education Channel Manager: Jonathan Raeder
Interior Designer: Rosanne Schloss

Credits and acknowledgments for material borrowed from other sources, and reproduced with permission, appear on the appropriate pages within the text.

Published by Rowman & Littlefield
An imprint of The Rowman & Littlefield Publishing Group, Inc.
4501 Forbes Boulevard, Suite 200, Lanham, Maryland 20706
www.rowman.com

6 Tinworth Street, London SE11 5AL, United Kingdom

British Library Cataloguing in Publication Information Available

Library of Congress Control Number: 2019949888

ISBN 9781538136089 (pbk. : alk. paper) | ISBN 9781538136096 (ebook)

∞™ The paper used in this publication meets the minimum requirements of American National Standard for Information Sciences—Permanence of Paper for Printed Library Materials, ANSI/NISO Z39.48-1992.

Brief Contents

Contents

★ ★ ★

Tables, Figures, and Photos

★ ★ ★

TABLES

FIGURES

PHOTOS

Preface

The presidency is both a much-praised and a much-damned institution. During the early 1960s, many thought presidential power was the key to change and saw the presidency as the major innovative force within the government. People looked to the president to satisfy an increasing number of their demands for public policy. By the late 1960s and early 1970s, however, many of the same people saw presidential power as a serious problem. Scholars blamed presidents and their excesses for involvement in the war in Southeast Asia and for Watergate and other scandals. Restrain the "imperial" presidency became the cry.

Presidents Gerald Ford and Jimmy Carter responded to this plea by attempting to deimperialize the office. Ford opened the White House to opposing views; Carter initially reduced the White House staff's size, status, and perquisites. Both were careful not to exceed their constitutional and statutory powers.

Growing institutional conflict between Congress and the presidency and within the executive branch raised questions about the possibility of effective governance. Worsening economic conditions, increasingly scarce resources, and a series of foreign policy crises produced a desire for more assertive leadership. Some observers saw the presidency as imperiled; weakness, not strength, its problem. Disappointment in presidential performance replaced fear of presidential abuses.

The Reagan presidency led scholars once again to reevaluate the workings of the system and the role of the president within it. Ronald Reagan's ability to achieve some of his major policy goals at the beginning of his administration indicated that stalemate need not paralyze the government. However, his leadership style gave rise to fears, particularly in the Iran-Contra affair, of power improperly exercised.

During the George H. W. Bush and Bill Clinton presidencies, the need for change, accompanied by the difficulty of achieving it within a divided government, reemerged. Both presidents were frustrated in their attempts to govern, particularly within the domestic arena, and the public expressed its own disillusionment—first in defeating Bush and then in putting the Republicans in power in both houses of Congress for the first time in forty years. Yet, in the midst of defeat, Clinton rejuvenated himself, his presidency, and his party, winning the 1996 presidential election and reaching agreement with Congress on a balanced budget, proving once again that divided government works during periods of economic prosperity, social tranquility, and world peace—when the government does not face increased demands, and especially when hundreds of billions of dollars of unexpected revenues are predicted for the treasury's coffers.

George W. Bush campaigned on bringing change to Washington. The narrowness of his election in 2000, and the unusual nature of its resolution, denied him any claim to a mandate, but he moved quickly to pass the largest tax cut in a generation, a major change in federal education policy, and, in his third year, a substantial increase in Medicare benefits. However, it was the terrorist attacks on September 11, 2001, that transformed his presidency by placing a premium on decisive action and focusing attention on the president's roles as crisis manager, national security director, and commander in chief.

Bush interpreted his close but clear reelection victory in 2004 as a public confirmation of his policies and actions during his first term and his proposals for the second, including Social Security, immigration, tax, tort, and bankruptcy reform; a national energy policy; and a continuation of his deregulatory policies within the private sector of the economy. He was much less successful in obtaining congressional support for major policy change in his second term, however, and his public approval ratings declined sharply. His lack of success in achieving his policy initiatives, combined with widespread discontent with the administration's handling of the occupation of Iraq and its response to the devastation of Hurricane Katrina, undermined the public's assessment of the president's competence. Charges of the abuse of executive power and misleading the public about the threat posed by Iraq further diminished the public's confidence in Bush's presidency and also raised significant questions about his own trustworthiness.

Beset by scandal and inaction, Republicans lost control of Congress in 2006 and the White House in 2008 in an election in which both Democratic and Republican candidates criticized the Bush administration for its heavy-handedness, deficit spending, and failure to anticipate, much less react to, the severe economic problems that began to surface at the end of 2007. The result was a substantial victory for the Democrats and their presidential candidate, Barack Obama.

President Obama acted quickly to stem further economic deterioration by supporting a stimulus and reinvestment bill of almost $800 billion, strengthening regulation of large investment and banking firms and increasing accountability for the funds the government provided them, and giving direct relief to people who lost their jobs, were threatened with foreclosure of their homes, and were without adequate health insurance. He also supported reinvestment in America's infrastructure, schools, and policies to promote energy efficiency.

Obama promised policy and political change, but achieving that change within a constitutional system that divides powers, a political system that represents diverse and often competing constituencies, and an increasingly interdependent world in which no country can effectively act alone is an enormous challenge. In addition, the country was, and is, highly polarized. Despite his rhetorical skill, Obama found that he could not move the public to support his policies, nor could he win bipartisan support in Congress. He was, however, able to achieve many of his legislative goals in his first two years as a consequence of Democratic control of Congress. After the Democrats suffered huge losses in the 2010 midterm elections, Obama's legislative initiatives and policy successes dwindled significantly.

The president won reelection in 2012, but divided government persisted. The debt limit, the budget, health care, and presidential decisions regarding immigration and environmental protection continued to divide the parties and threatened to immobilize the government. Facing divided government and partisan polarization with limited resources poses an extraordinary test of leadership for the president.

Donald Trump ran an unusual presidential campaign in 2016, emphasizing issues such as immigration and international trade, which he claimed harmed the employment prospects of the working class, and promising to undo much of what Barack Obama had done. Losing the popular vote by a sizeable margin—but winning in the electoral college—he has never had the support of a majority of the public. Using social media to declare his views, his public pronouncements please his base but irritate many others. The most polarizing president of the modern era, he routinely attacks the news media and those who oppose him, often in harsh terms.

Although Republicans had majorities in both houses of Congress, the president found it difficult to get things done. For example, after protracted efforts, his party could not pass health-care legislation. Once the Democrats won the House in the 2018 midterm elections, Trump's legislative agenda ground to a halt. The president was also slow to fill positions in the bureaucracy and was widely criticized for a chaotic and uninformed decision-making style. Many observers raise questions about the appropriateness of his temperament, knowledge, and skills for leading the country. There is little doubt that he has found the presidency a difficult and frustrating job.

This book is about the leadership dilemma that presidents face and their institutional, political, and personal capacities to meet it. We posit two models of presidential leadership: one in which a strong president dominates his environment as a director of change, and one in which the president has a more limited role as facilitator of change. In the director-of-change model, presidents lead the nation by creating opportunities to move in new directions and leading others where they otherwise would not go. In the facilitator model, presidents work, bargaining and pleading, at coalition building to further the attainment of their goals and the goals of their constituencies. Effective facilitators recognize and exploit opportunities for change already present in their environments. These models provide perspectives that we employ to better understand leadership in the modern presidency and evaluate the performance of individual presidents.

We offer no simple formula for success, but we do argue that the first step is for presidents and citizens alike to understand the nature of presidential leadership in a pluralistic system in which separate institutions share powers. We believe that effective, responsible presidential leadership can play a vital role in providing the coherence, direction, and support necessary to articulate and achieve national policy and political goals.

We thank our friends at Rowman & Littlefield, especially our editor Traci Crowell and assistant managing editor Janice Braunstein for the help they have provided us in the development, editing, and marketing of the eleventh edition of this book and the political scientists whose insightful comments and suggestions helped us improve this volume.

We also want to acknowledge and thank our respective wives, Carmella Edwards, Susan Mayer, and Cheryl Beil, for their patience, encouragement, and help. It is to them that we dedicate this book.

George C. Edwards III
Kenneth R. Mayer
Stephen J. Wayne

About the Authors

George C. Edwards III is University Distinguished Professor of political science and Jordan Chair in Presidential Studies Emeritus at Texas A&M University. He is also a Distinguished Fellow at the University of Oxford and has held appointments at Oxford, Sciences Po-Paris, the US Military Academy, Peking University, Hebrew University in Jerusalem, and the University of London. A leading scholar of the presidency, he has written or edited twenty-six books on American politics. He is also the editor of *Presidential Studies Quarterly* and general editor of the *Oxford Handbook of American Politics* series.

Among his recent books, *On Deaf Ears: The Limits of the Bully Pulpit* examines the effectiveness of presidential leadership of public opinion; *Why the Electoral College Is Bad for America* evaluates the consequences of the method of electing the president; *Governing by Campaigning* analyzes the politics of the Bush presidency; *The Strategic President* offers a new formulation for understanding presidential leadership; and *Overreach* analyzes presidential leadership during the Obama presidency. *Predicting the Presidency* shows how understanding the context of a presidency allows us to predict the success of a president in winning support from the public and Congress for his initiatives and also explores the possibilities for exploiting the potential support of those predisposed to follow the president's lead. His latest book, *The Bungler*, focuses on the leadership of Donald Trump.

Professor Edwards has served as president of the Presidency Research Section of the American Political Science Association, which has named its annual dissertation prize in his honor and awarded him its Career Service Award. A member of Phi Beta Kappa and a Woodrow Wilson Fellow, he has received the Decoration for Distinguished Civilian Service from the US Army and the Pi Sigma Alpha Prize from the Southern Political Science Association. He is also a member of the Council on Foreign Relations. He has spoken to three hundred universities and other groups in the United States and abroad, keynoted numerous national and international conferences, done several thousand interviews with the national and international press, and can be heard on National Public Radio.

Professor Edwards also applies his scholarship to practical issues of governing, including advising Brazil on its constitution and the operation of its presidency, Russia on building a democratic national party system, Mexico on elections, and

Chinese scholars on democracy. He also authored studies for the 1988, 2000, and 2016 US presidential transitions.

Kenneth R. Mayer is a professor of political science and affiliate faculty at the Robert M. La Follette School of Public Affairs at the University of Wisconsin, Madison. He is the author or editor of twenty-two books, including *With the Stroke of a Pen: Executive orders and Presidential Power*, which won the Richard E. Neustadt Award from the Presidency and Executive Politics section of the American Political Science Association for the best book on the American presidency. He is also the author of *The Political Economy of Defense Contracting* and coauthor of *The Dysfunctional Congress? The Individual Roots of an Institutional Dilemma* (with David T. Canon). He coedits a best-selling reader for introductory American government classes, *The Enduring Debate: Classic and Contemporary Readings in American Politics* (with David T. Canon and John J. Coleman).

He teaches courses on the presidency, American government, election law, and campaign finance. He was the inaugural Fulbright Distinguished Chair in Political Science at the Australian National University, the first Distinguished Chair position in the Pacific region, and returned to Australia as part of the US State Department Public Speaker Program to give a nationwide series of lectures on the 2012 presidential election. An award-winning teacher, he also regularly serves as an expert witness on voting rights, campaign finance, and redistricting cases in both state and federal courts.

Stephen J. Wayne is a well-known author and lecturer on American presidents and the presidency. A professor of government–emeritus at Georgetown University, he taught courses on the American presidency, US elections, and psychology and politics. A presidential and a Washington-based "insider" for fifty years, Wayne has written or edited twelve books, many in multiple editions, and authored numerous articles, chapters, and reviews that have appeared in professional journals, scholarly compilations, newspapers, and magazines. In addition to *Presidential Leadership*, his best-known works include *The Road to the White House*, now in its eleventh edition, *Is This Any Way to Run a Democratic Election?* and *Personality and Politics: Obama for and against Himself*.

Professor Wayne is frequently quoted by White House journalists, regularly appears on television and radio news shows, and has been interviewed in documentaries on the presidency and political leadership. He lectures widely at home and abroad to international visitors, college students, federal executives, and business leaders. He has testified before Congress on the subject of presidential elections and governance and before the Democratic Party and Republican Party advisory committees on the presidential nomination processes.

1

Introduction

The White House, where the president faces the most challenging
responsibilities in American politics.

Pgiam/iStock

N o official in American government commands the attention, stirs the imagination, and generates emotions as much as the president. The presidency has
become the driving force in a system designed for balanced government, the
prime initiator and coordinator among separate and independent institutions sharing power, the foremost mobilizer among disparate and competing interests, and the
principal communications link among a multitude of groups and individuals. It is a
many-faceted, dynamic office—with a plethora of responsibilities, a variety of roles,
and an impressive range of powers.

Within the presidency, the president is clearly the chief. Executive officials look
to the office for direction, coordination, and general guidance in the implementation of policy; members of Congress rely on it for establishing priorities, exerting
influence, and providing services; the leaders of foreign governments turn to it for
articulating positions, conducting diplomacy, and flexing muscle; and the general

public looks to it for enhancing security, solving problems, and exercising symbolic and moral leadership—a big order, to be sure.

Unfortunately for most presidents, these expectations often exceed their abilities to meet them. It is not simply a question of skill or personality, although both contribute to the capacity to do the job well. The challenge is the system, particularly its constitutional, institutional, and political structures. The Constitution divides authority; institutions share power; and parties usually lack cohesion and a sustained policy thrust.

This context presents a challenge to the president's political leadership. President Harry Truman, writing to his sister, reflected on his job:

> Aside from the impossible administrative burden, he has to take all sorts of abuse from liars and demagogues. . . . The people can never understand why the President does not use his supposedly great power to make 'em behave. Well, all the President is, is a glorified public relations man who spends his time flattering, kissing and kicking people to get them to do what they are supposed to do anyway.[1]

To accomplish their goals, presidents rely on leadership. Leadership is perhaps the most commonly employed concept in politics. Politicians, pundits, journalists, and scholars critique and analyze public officials, attributing both success and failure to the quality of their leadership. When times are bad, as people often perceive them to be, the reflexive call is for new—and better—leadership.

Yet, the American political system is not a fertile field for the exercise of presidential leadership. Most political actors are free to choose whether to follow the chief executive's lead; the president cannot force them to act. At the same time, the sharing of powers established by the Constitution prevents the president from acting unilaterally on most important matters and gives other power holders different perspectives on issues and policy proposals. Thus, the political system compels the president to attempt to lead while inhibiting his (or her) ability to do so.

When asked about his first seven years in office, Barack Obama sounded a lot like Truman:

> [W]hat I didn't fully appreciate, and nobody can appreciate until they're in the position, is how decentralized power is in this system. When you're in the seat and you're seeing the housing market collapse and you are seeing unemployment skyrocketing and you have a sense of what the right thing to do is, then you realize, "Okay, not only do I have to persuade my own party, not only do I have to prevent the other party from blocking what the right thing to do is, but now I can anticipate this lawsuit, this lobbying taking place, and this federal agency that technically is independent, so I can't tell them what to do. I've got the Federal Reserve, and I'm hoping that they do the right thing—and by the way, since the economy now is global, I've got to make sure that the Europeans, the Asians, the Chinese, everybody is on board." A lot of the work is not just identifying the right policy but now constantly building these ever shifting coalitions to be able to actually implement and execute and get it done.[2]

To some extent, these difficulties have always been present in America, but the gap between expectations and performance seems to have widened. Disenchantment with the political system has increased, confidence in the institution of the presidency has declined, and the popularity of each president has plummeted at one time or another during the course of his administration. Exercising effective presidential leadership has thus become more difficult—but no less vital if the American system is to work.

EXPLORING PRESIDENTIAL LEADERSHIP

This book is titled *Presidential Leadership* because it focuses on just that—leadership. We address the capacity of chief executives to fulfill their tasks, exercise their powers, and utilize their organizational structures. It is a book about political leadership—about public opinion, group pressures, media coverage, and presidential salesmanship before, during, and after elections. It is also a book about policy leadership; institutions and processes; and priority setting, coalition building, and governmental implementation. Finally, it is a book about personal leadership, incumbents in office and their goals, national needs, and the formal and informal ways of accomplishing presidential objectives.

The exercise of influence is central to our concept of leadership, as it is for most political scientists. We want to know whether the president can influence the actions and attitudes of others and affect the output of government. It is important to distinguish between attempts to lead and leadership itself. Both concepts are of primary interest in this book, and we devote much of our effort to exploring the relationship between the two.

To guide our analysis, we find it useful to refine the concept of leadership by contrasting two broad perspectives on the presidency.

The Director Model

A common perspective on presidential leadership is the president as the *director* of change. In this view, the president creates opportunities to move in new directions and leads others where they otherwise would not go. The president is out in front, establishing goals and encouraging others inside and outside of government to follow. Accordingly, the president is the moving force of the system and the initiator of change.

The notion of a dominant president who moves the country and the government by means of strong, effective leadership has deep roots in our political culture. Those chief executives whom Americans revere—from George Washington to Franklin D. Roosevelt—have taken on mythical proportions as leaders. Even though both the public and commentators are frequently disillusioned with presidential performance and recognize that stalemate is common in the political system, Americans eagerly accept what appears to be effective presidential leadership as evidence on which to renew their faith in the leadership potential of the presidency. After all, if presidential leadership works some of the time, why not all the time?

Perhaps faith in the potential of presidential leadership persists because such a view simplifies political analysis. Because broader forces that may influence changes in policy are complex, and perhaps even intractable, focusing primarily on the individual as leader eases the burden of explaining policy change. Faith in presidential leadership also simplifies the evaluation of the problems of governing. If it is reasonable to expect the White House to create opportunities for change, then failures of leadership must be personal deficiencies. If problems arise because the leader lacks the proper will, skills, or understanding, then the solution to our need for leadership is straightforward and simple: Elect presidents who are willing and able to lead. Because the system is responsive to appropriate leadership, it will function smoothly with the right leader in the Oval Office. The blame for unsuccessful leadership lies with the leader rather than the opportunities for change in the leader's environment.

The Facilitator Model

Conversely, what if presidential leadership is not preeminent in American government? What if presidential leadership has less potential than holders of the conventional wisdom believe and the president actually operates at the margins in leading the country? What if the national preoccupation with the chief executive is misplaced and belief in the impact of the individual leader is largely a myth—a product of a search for simple solutions in an extremely complex, purposefully inefficient system in which the founders' handiwork in decentralizing power defeats even the most capable leaders?

If this is the case, the public should expect less of its presidents and be even less surprised when they are not successful in leading. To understand better the presidency and the engines of change, we should focus less exclusively on the president and devote more attention to the context in which the president seeks to lead. If there are significant limits on presidential leadership, it follows that major changes in public policy require more than just the "right" person in the job and will not necessarily turn on a president's leadership qualities.

The second perspective, then, is less heroic than that of the director. Here, the president is primarily a *facilitator* of change. Facilitators understand the opportunities for change in their environments and fashion strategies and tactics to exploit them. Rather than create constituencies to follow them, they reflect and sometimes clarify, intensify, or channel their constituencies' aspirations, values, and policy views. Instead of persuading others to support them, they skillfully work at the margins of coalition building, perhaps influencing a few critical actors, to obtain support for their initiatives.

It is important not to underrate this role. The facilitator is *not* simply one who seizes opportunities as they present themselves and invites people to do what they already want to do. Change is not inevitable, and facilitators make things happen that otherwise would not. Effective facilitators are skilled leaders who must recognize the opportunities that exist in their environments, choose which opportunities to pursue, when and in what order, and exploit them with skill, energy, perseverance, and commitment.

The president's dependency on existing opportunities implies a critical interdependence between leaders and followers, which we miss when we focus only on the pinnacle of power. Moreover, there are many influences on followers and potential followers and many obstacles to influencing them. The president is an important agenda setter,[3] for example, but there are other key influences on the agenda as well.[4] Thus, we need to devote more attention to thinking about politics from the bottom-up as well as the top-down and to the context in which the president seeks to lead.

It does not follow, of course, that we may never attribute failures of presidential leadership to the White House or that presidents have no control over the outcome of their relations with other political actors. The president may be a vital centralizing force, providing direction and energy for the nation's policy making. However, the facilitator presidential model does imply that a better understanding of presidential leadership is necessary in order to think sensibly about the role of the chief executive within the nation's political system.

Models in Perspective

The director reshapes the contours of the political landscape to pave the way for change, whereas the facilitator exploits opportunities presented by a favorable configuration of political forces. The director creates a constituency to follow his (or her) lead, whereas the facilitator endows his (or her) constituency's views with shape and purpose. The range and scope of the director's influence are broad, whereas those of the facilitator are narrower.

The two perspectives are not neat categories; we employ them simply to aid our understanding of leadership by exploring its possibilities. Once we understand the possibilities of leadership, we are in a better position to assess both the performance of presidents and the opportunities for change. Equally important, we will be better positioned to *explain* the success or failure of presidential leadership.

The leadership types also reflect, but do not precisely mirror, different thrusts in the scholarly literature on the presidency. Richard Neustadt's *Presidential Power*, widely considered to be the most influential book on the presidency, focuses on the president as center of government and the one who must lead if leading is to be done.[5]

Other scholars see the presidency differently. Charles O. Jones, for example, argues that "The president is not the presidency. The presidency is not the government. Ours is not a presidential system."[6] One of the authors of this book argues that presidential influence is "at the margins" of American politics and emphasizes the importance of the political environment in which the president operates.[7] Stephen Skowronek finds presidents constrained in important ways by the historical context in which they serve, but he also sees them as the major force in causing fundamental political change.[8]

The question is not whether presidents matter. Of course they do. The question is *how* they matter—how do they bring about change? It is not sufficient to conclude that the environment is sometimes receptive to change and at other times not. This viewpoint simply begs the question of whether presidents are able to influence the environment to *create* the opportunity for change.

The questions we ask about the presidency determine what we will learn about it. Thus, it is important that we ask the right questions. In the remainder of this chapter, we briefly examine different approaches that scholars have employed to study the presidency, focusing on what each approach helps us understand about the presidency—and what questions each tends to overlook. In the final section, we discuss how we will explore the dilemmas of presidential leadership.

APPROACHES TO STUDYING THE PRESIDENCY

There are many approaches to studying the presidency, ranging from concern with the constitutional authority of the office to dealing with the personality dynamics of a particular president. By *approaches* we mean orientations that guide us to ask certain questions and employ certain concepts in answering them. In this section, we focus on four of the principal approaches employed by political scientists who study the presidency. The categories we use are neither mutually exclusive nor comprehensive.

We present these approaches not to create an ideal typology of scholarship on the presidency but to increase sensitivity to the implications of different approaches for what is studied, how it is studied, and what types of conclusions may be reached. Similarly, our focus is on approaches, rather than the works of individual authors or a comprehensive review of the literature.[9]

Legal

The oldest approach to studying the presidency, what we shall term *the legal perspective*, concerns the president's formal powers. Legal researchers analyze the Constitution, laws, treaties, and legal precedents to understand the sources, scope, and use of the president's formal powers, including their legal limitations.[10] Because of the significance of the founders' intentions and because these powers have changed over time, the legal approach has a historical orientation.

With its emphasis on the historical development of the office and the checks and balances in the Constitution, the legal perspective also lends itself to discussion of the president's place in our system of government, both as it is and as scholars think it ought to be. Thus, there is often a clear prescriptive or normative element in these studies.

The range of issues involving presidential authority is great. Illustrations from recent decades include the president's authority to

- use emergency powers to construct a border barrier with funds not appropriated for that purpose;
- restrict entry into the United States from specific countries;
- authorize domestic intelligence surveillance in the absence of a statutory delegation;
- establish the Deferred Action against Childhood Arrivals program;
- make long-term recess appointments;
- exercise the line-item veto;
- impound funds appropriated by Congress;
- issue executive orders and proclamations;
- freeze federal hiring;
- use the pocket veto during brief congressional recesses; and
- use signing statements to in effect partially veto provisions of statutes.

Other topics include the constitutionality of the legislative veto, the role of the comptroller general in triggering budget reductions, and numerous claims of executive privilege such as those proposed by Bill Clinton to prevent his senior aides from testifying in the probe of his relations with White House intern Monica Lewinsky, the refusal of George W. Bush to allow aides to testify about the firings of US attorneys, and the refusal of Barack Obama to release internal Justice Department memos regarding a failed effort to stem the flow of firearms into Mexico.

Foreign policy issues also have important legal dimensions. These have included the exclusive power of presidents to recognize countries; detention of prisoners and suspected terrorists without recourse to the courts by George W. Bush; waging the Vietnam War without explicit congressional authorization by Lyndon Johnson and Richard Nixon; using troops in invasions of Grenada by Ronald Reagan and Panama by George H. W. Bush and to occupy Haiti and bomb Bosnia and Kosovo by Bill Clinton; terminating a defense treaty with Taiwan by Jimmy Carter; Carter's settling of Iranian assets and hostage issues; and, more generally, presidents employing executive agreements as substitutes for treaties.

Although the legal perspective has a deservedly honored place among American political scientists—the United States prides itself on the rule of law—it also has its limitations. Legal analysis cannot explain most of what the president does. The Constitution, treaties, laws, and court decisions affect only a small portion of the president's behavior. Most of the president's relationships with the public, Congress, the White House staff, and the bureaucracy do not easily fall within the purview of the legal perspective. Instead, informal or extraconstitutional powers explain this behavior. Similarly, because the legal perspective is heavily government centered, scholars adopting it largely ignore topics such as press coverage of the presidency, the public's evaluation of the president, and other relationships that involve nongovernmental actors.

It is equally significant that the legal perspective, although it requires rigorous analysis, does not lend itself to explanation of presidential behavior. Studies of the boundaries of appropriate behavior do not explain why actions occur within those boundaries or what their consequences are. Moreover, the heavy reliance on case studies by scholars employing this approach inevitably makes the basis of their generalizations somewhat tenuous.

Thus, although studies that adopt the legal perspective make important contributions to our understanding of American politics, they do not answer many of the questions that entice most people to study the presidency. For answers to these questions, we must turn to alternative approaches.

Institutional

A second approach to the study of the presidency focuses on it as an institution in which the president has certain roles and responsibilities and is involved in numerous structures and processes. Thus, the structure, functions, and operation of the presidency become the center of attention. These concerns are broad enough to include agencies such as the Office of Management and Budget (OMB) and units in the White House such as the legislative liaison operation. Scholars following this approach move beyond formal authority and investigate such topics as the formulation, coordination, promotion, and implementation of the president's legislative program; the president's relationships with the media and interest groups; or the president's decision-making processes.[11] This focus gives much of its literature a historical perspective and also lends itself to evaluations of the success of institutional arrangements.

The institutional approach plays a crucial role in helping us to understand the presidency. Although at one time many institutional studies emphasized formal organizational structure and rules, such as organization charts of the White House or budgetary process procedures, in recent years the behavior of those involved in the operation of the presidency has received more attention. This change in focus has increased the utility of institutional research. It is, after all, necessary to collect empirical data about what political actors are doing before we can discuss the significance of their behavior, much less examine analytical questions of relationships such as those pertaining to influence. By seeking to identify patterns of behavior and studying interactions, such as those between the White House and Congress, the OMB, or the media, institutional research tells us not only what happens, but more significantly, it also helps us to understand why it happens. When scholars examine presidential efforts to influence the media, for example, they are looking at typical, and potentially significant, behavior that may explain patterns of media coverage of the White House.

Historical institutionalism and American political development scholars are also interested in the presidency as an institution but reach beyond the confines of the policy process and presidential agendas' success to explore the broader significance of the presidency in American politics. They view the presidency from the standpoint of the political system and focus on modes of governance, the institutionalized authority relations that underpin and legitimate them, and the sources of tension that destabilize them over time and contribute to fundamental political change. Researchers seek to understand the ways in which presidential action facilitates or impedes this change and to document the signature elements of new governing configurations, the factors behind their coalescence, and the location of the presidency within them. One central goal of such scholarship is to understand why successive episodes of political development have, on balance, tended to reinforce and deepen the relative authority of presidents.[12]

The "New Institutionalism" is yet another mode of scholarship that makes useful contributions to the broad institutional approach. It is grounded in rational choice theory and focuses on questions of the origins and effects of institutions, emphasizing challenges for the president such as the transaction costs arising from efforts to get subordinates to act as he or she wishes (principal–agent issues). It assumes individuals want to maximize benefits for themselves and that outcomes of institutions (including organizational design) have roots in individual behavior. Basic features of the political system provide the opportunities, capabilities, incentives, and interests that drive political actors to behave in predictable ways.[13]

New Institutionalism encourages students of the presidency to think of presidents in impersonal terms, as institutional actors whose institutional locations structure their incentives in particular ways and whom we can thus expect to behave in a characteristic manner—a presidential manner—regardless of who they are.[14] The goal of those applying this approach is to simplify the complexity of presidential studies and focus on one crucial factor influencing presidential behavior.

There are two principal limitations to focusing on the presidency as an institution. Many scholars have emphasized description at the expense of explanation. We know a great deal more about how presidents have organized their White House staffs, for instance, than about how these arrangements have affected the kinds of advice they have received.[15] In other words, we know more about the process than about its consequences. This lack of understanding in turn provides a tenuous basis for the prescriptive aspect of some institutional research. We cannot have confidence in recommendations about presidential advisory systems, for example, until we understand their effects.

The second limitation of some institutional studies is that they may downplay, or even ignore, the significance of political skills, ideology, and personality in their emphasis on organizations and processes. Indeed, the implicit assumption that underlies the often extensive attention scholars devote to structures and processes is that they are very significant. However, this assumption may not always be justified. It may be that the worldview a president brings to the White House or the political environment in which the president operates influences decisions more than the organization of the advisory system or decision-making procedures.

Similarly, ideology, party, and constituency views may be more important than the White House legislative liaison operation in influencing congressional votes on the president's program.

Political Power

In the political power approach to the study of the presidency, scholars do not examine institutions but rather the people within them and their relationships with each other.[16] These authors view power as a function of personal politics rather than formal authority or position, although they often find that the context of a presidency is the key to understanding a president's success.[17] They find the president operating in a pluralistic environment in which there are numerous actors with independent power bases and perspectives and interests different from his. The president must marshal resources to persuade others to do as he wishes; a president cannot rely on expanding the institution's legal authority or adjusting its support mechanisms.

The president's need to exercise influence in several arenas leads those who follow the power perspective to adopt an expansive view of presidential politics that includes both government officials, such as members of Congress, the bureaucracy, and White House staff, and those outside of government, such as the public, the press, and interest groups. The dependent variables in studying presidential interactions (what authors are trying to explain) are wide-ranging and may include congressional or public support for the president, presidential decisions, press coverage of the White House, or bureaucratic policy implementation.[18] Because this approach does not assume presidential success or the smooth functioning of the presidency, the influence of bureaucratic politics and other organizational factors in the executive branch is as important to investigate as behavior in more openly adversarial institutions such as Congress.

Power is a concept that involves relationships between people, so this approach forces researchers to try to explain behavior and seek to develop generalizations about it. However, it also slights certain topics. The emphasis on relationships does not lead naturally to the investigation of presidential accountability, the president's unilateral powers, or the day-to-day operation of the presidency.

Some commentators are bothered by the top-down orientation of the power approach—that is, viewing the presidency from the perspective of the president.[19] They feel that this neglects the question of examining the presidency from the perspective of the American political system and that it carries the implicit assumption that the president should be the principal decision maker in American politics. These critics argue that such premises are too Machiavellian and that analyses of power must include an evaluation of the goals and means of presidents.

Psychological

Perhaps the most fascinating and popular studies of the presidency are those that approach the topic from the perspective of psychological analysis. Some of these take the form of psychobiographies of presidents;[20] others attempt to categorize presidents on the basis of selected personality dimensions.[21] The authors of all these works base their analyses on the premise that personality is a constant and that individuals may displace their personality needs onto political objects and that these displaced needs become unconscious motivations for presidential behavior.

We need to take what goes on inside a person's head into account if we are to understand that person's behavior. A psychological perspective forces us to ask why presidents behave as they do and to look beyond external factors, such as advisers, Congress, the media, and interest groups, for answers. If individual presidents' personalities did not affect them, presidents would neither be very important nor merit much attention.

Psychological analysis also has a broader application to the study of the presidency. Presidents and their staffs view the world through cognitive processes that affect their perceptions of why people and nations behave as they do, how power is distributed, how the economy functions, and what the appropriate roles of government, presidents, and advisers are. Cognitive processes also screen and organize an enormous volume of information about the complex and uncertain environment in which presidents function. Objective reality, intellectual abilities, and personal interests and experiences merge with psychological needs (such as those to manage inconsistency and maintain self-esteem) to influence the decisions and policies that emerge from the White House. Cognitive processes simplify decision making and lessen stress, especially on complex and controversial policies such as going to war. Group dynamics may also influence decision making, limiting the appraisal of alternatives by group members. Efforts to sort out the impact of these factors are only in their early stages, but there is little question that we cannot claim to understand presidential decision making until those efforts succeed.[22]

Psychological studies can sensitize us to important personality and cognitive traits that influence presidential behavior. Nevertheless, such studies, especially those that emphasize personality, are probably the most widely criticized research on the presidency.[23] A fundamental problem is that they often display a strong tendency toward reductionism; that is, they concentrate on personality to the exclusion of most other behavioral influences. As a result, they convey little information about the institution of the presidency or the relationships between psychological and institutional variables. Psychological studies are especially likely to fall prey to a failure to consider alternative explanations for behavior.

A related drawback is that psychological studies tend to stress the pathological aspects of a presidency and do so in a highly subjective fashion. Scholars, like others, are drawn quite naturally to investigate problems. Their principal interest often becomes the relationship between the personality flaws of presidents and what the authors feel to be some of their most unfortunate actions in office. This focus reinforces the reductionist tendency, because it is usually not difficult to find plausible parallels between psychological and decisional deficiencies.

The lack of systematic data is also a problem for psychological studies. It is difficult both to discern unconscious motivations or cognitive processes and to differentiate their effect from that of external factors. Often, authors must rely on biographical information of questionable validity about the behavior and environment of presidents, stretching back to their childhoods.

Summary

The legal, institutional, power, and psychological approaches have advantages and disadvantages for understanding the presidency. Each concerns a different aspect of the office and concentrates on certain variables at the expense of others. We need to carefully determine what it is they want to investigate before selecting an approach, because not all approaches are relevant to answering particular questions. Although the power and psychological approaches are stronger in their concern for explanation, the legal and institutional orientations are better at providing broad perspectives on the presidency. In this book, we employ all four approaches to provide a comprehensive examination of the presidency. In Appendix A, we discuss appropriate methods for making the best use of these approaches.

OUR APPROACH

This book explores the president's leadership problems and the attempts by recent chief executives to overcome them. It does so by examining multiple facets of the presidency within the context of its political and policy-making roles. Our orientation is eclectic. Instead of adopting a particular perspective, the book presents several. Instead of imposing a single thesis, it will discuss many of the hypotheses, generalizations, and conclusions that scholars of the presidency have advanced.

The reason for utilizing a variety of approaches and presenting a broad body of research findings is that there is no one generally accepted theory of the presidency or single conceptual framework within which to study the office (other than, perhaps, Richard Neustadt's volume on presidential power)[24] that has commanded the attention and acceptance of most presidency scholars. As we have seen, work within each of a number of approaches to studying the presidency has something to teach us.

Despite an abundance of literature on the presidency, our understanding of how that institution works is not complete. There are fewer testable hypotheses about the presidency than about Congress and less cumulative knowledge than about the Supreme Court and its decisions.

Why is this so? What factors have conditioned the methodology, shaped the content, and limited the findings of so much of the presidency literature? Three stand out: (1) the view that each president (and administration) is relatively unique, (2) the difficulty of obtaining firsthand information on the internal operation of the institution at or near the time that the operation is occurring, and (3) the absence of a comprehensive theory of presidential behavior. Together these factors have impeded the ability of scholars to do rigorous, analytic, empirical research on the presidency.

The personalities of individual presidents and their staffs, the particular events and circumstances of their times in office, and the specific problems and actions of their administrations have led many scholars to treat each presidency and the times in which it operates as if it were unique. Emphasizing the differences rather than the similarities between presidencies makes the identification of patterns and relations more difficult and, in turn, makes it harder to generalize. Description rather than analysis and speculation rather than generalization too often characterize studies of the presidency.

The relatively closed character of the institution has contributed to the problem. The presidency is not easy to observe from a distance and, up close, the view may be partial and even biased. Public pronouncements and actions tell only part of what happens and why—and usually only the part that the people in power wish to convey. Inside information is difficult to obtain. Decision makers, particularly those at the top of the executive bureaucracy, are not readily accessible. Their busy schedules, combined with their natural reluctance to reveal information that may be embarrassing, sensitive, or in other ways controversial, often make them unwilling, unresponsive, or unreliable sources.

Nor is dependence on journalistic accounts usually satisfactory. Journalists tend to be event oriented and deadline driven. They do not usually employ a time frame or perspective that is sufficiently broad or historical to permit generalizations, particularly on the institutional and behavioral aspects of the office. In addition, time pressures may force journalists to rush to conclusions before they have had an opportunity to collect information from all relevant sources.

The third factor that contributes to the problem is the absence of an overall theory that explains presidential behavior. Unlike other areas in political science—such as individual voting behavior, in which there is a body of theory that explains and predicts who votes and why—the presidency literature has not produced a comprehensive explanation of why presidents do what they do. Although we have made substantial progress in predicting the consequences of presidential actions regarding Congress and the public, there are many other important areas of the presidency.

The nature of these problems suggests that when examining the institution and exploring the president's leadership opportunities and problems, we should cast our net as broadly as possible. Thus, we examine a set of critical relationships—the relationships between presidents and those whose support they need in order to do their job—rather than focus on a single theme, which might exclude important information.

To function effectively, a chief executive must win election, build and maintain popular support, make decisions, and present, promote, and implement policies. Each of these requirements involves reciprocal relationships in which presidents influence, and are influenced by, others. That is why we must examine both sides of these relationships rather than focus exclusively on the president.

Relationships provide a conceptual framework for studying presidential leadership, as they enable us to explain the behavioral causes and consequences of presidential activities. By stressing relationships, however, we do not suggest that legal powers, informal roles, institutional structures, or psychological factors are unimportant. Indeed, we firmly believe that we cannot understand the presidency without an extensive knowledge of these matters. This is the background that we provide here. Our point of departure is a discussion of these matters within the context of presidential relationships, rather than vice versa. We should not view powers, roles, structures, and personality as ends in themselves. Rather, they are important for what they contribute to the president's ability to formulate, establish, and implement policies.

A PREVIEW

In order to understand the challenges of contemporary presidential leadership, it is necessary to gain perspective on the institution and its development. We do that in the next chapter, where we present an overview of the creation of the office and its evolution, with particular emphasis on the powers of the president and the growth of presidential policy-making roles, advisory and administrative structures, and the office's political and public dimensions.

The next five chapters concern the relationship between the president and the public. In chapters 3 and 4, we discuss nomination politics and the general election. Here, the focus is on the interaction between presidential candidates, the electorate, and the implications of this interaction for governing—what an administration tries to do, when, and to what effect. In chapter 5, we turn to presidents in office and their relations with the general public, and in chapter 6, we focus on the key question of the president's attempts to lead the public. In chapter 7, we examine the communications link between the incumbent and the news media. In each of these chapters, we explore leadership problems tied to communication with the public: winning electoral support, gaining job approval, and obtaining favorable media coverage. Presidents engage in a perpetual campaign to woo, win, and maintain the hearts and minds of the body politic. But are they usually successful?

In chapters 8 and 9, we analyze the relationship between the institution and the people in it—specifically, interactions among the president, senior White House advisers, and others who wish to affect presidential decisions. Here, we direct attention toward decision making at the presidential level: the institutional environment, combined with the incumbent's personal style, conditions, presidential discretion, and, ultimately, presidential choices.

In chapters 10 through 12, we turn to the interactions that the president must have with the executive branch, Congress, and the judiciary, respectively, to achieve policy objectives. Promoting programs in Congress, implementing them in the bureaucracy, and adjudicating them in the courts are necessary if presidential leadership is to be effective.

After scrutinizing presidential relations, we then discuss the formulation of public policy in and by the presidency. Chapters 13 and 14 concern domestic and national security policy making, respectively. In each chapter, we identify the key questions regarding the relevant policies and detail and assess the processes for dealing with them.

Currency is important in presidential politics, especially in the tumultuous era of Donald Trump. We cover his presidency in depth, including boxed material throughout the book that focus on the many distinctive aspects of the forty-fifth president.

Having explored the critical relationships between the president and the public, the presidency itself, the other branches, and the policy-making process, we end with appendices, one of which discusses another important but different kind of relationship: that of the president and methods of political science. Another appendix provides background on succession, tenure, and removal, including a discussion of the Clinton impeachment. We also list relevant constitutional provisions on the presidency, plus historical data on elections.

SELECTED READINGS

Edwards, George C., III. *The Strategic President: Persuasion and Opportunity in Presidential Leadership*. Princeton, NJ: Princeton University Press, 2009.

———. *Predicting the Presidency: The Potential of Persuasive Leadership*. Princeton, NJ: Princeton University Press, 2016.

Edwards, George C., III, and William G. Howell. *The Oxford Handbook of the American Presidency*. New York: Oxford University Press, 2009.

Edwards, George C., III, John H. Kessel, and Bert A. Rockman, eds. *Researching the Presidency*. Pittsburgh, PA: University of Pittsburgh Press, 1993.

Edwards, George C., III, and Stephen J. Wayne, eds. *Studying the Presidency*. Knoxville: University of Tennessee Press, 1983.

Neustadt, Richard E. *Presidential Power*. New York: Free Press, 1990.

Skowronek, Stephen. *The Politics Presidents Make*. Cambridge, MA: Harvard University Press, 1993.

2
The Powers of the Presidency

★　★　★

President Donald Trump signs the executive order halting immigrants from some Muslim-majority countries from entering the United States.

I n 1952 during the Korean War, President Harry S. Truman responded to an impending nationwide strike of steel workers by placing most of country's steel manufacturers under federal government control. Citing his authority under the "Constitution and laws of the United States, and as Commander in Chief of the armed forces," Truman asserted that the president had the inherent emergency authority to prevent disruption of vital wartime steel production even if it meant seizing private property.[1]

The steel companies sued and, in one of the most important Supreme Court decisions on presidential power in US history, won. In the landmark case *Youngstown Sheet and Tube v. Sawyer* (1952), the Supreme Court rejected the notion that the president had such sweeping emergency powers. Associate Justice Robert Jackson's concurring opinion, which remains one of the most important jurisprudential statements about the president's constitutional power, began with an observation about the ambiguities of that power:

> A judge, like an executive adviser, may be surprised at the poverty of really useful and unambiguous authority applicable to concrete problems of executive power as they actually present themselves. Just what our forefathers did envision, or would have envisioned had they foreseen modern conditions, must be divined from materials almost as enigmatic as the dreams Joseph was called upon to interpret for Pharaoh. A century and a half of partisan debate and scholarly speculation yields no net result but only supplies more or less apt quotations from respected sources on each side of any question. They largely cancel each other.[2]

Two decades later the renowned legal scholar Charles Black echoed this view, writing that "the history of presidential power is the resolution of doubtful questions that remain doubtful."[3]

It seems odd that some of the nation's best legal minds believe that the president's powers are ambiguous or that the Constitution does not give clear answers to questions of what presidents can or cannot do. But as a thought exercise, consider a few questions: Can presidents refuse to carry out a law they consider unconstitutional? Can a president unilaterally reshape immigration policy by declaring that broad categories of undocumented immigrations will not be deported? Do President Trump's ongoing worldwide business operations violate the constitution's Emoluments Clause? Can the president violate the law in order to protect the nation against a threat to its survival? Does the pardon power allow presidents to pardon themselves?

There are no "short answers" to these questions. The long answers involve careful analysis of the specific facts of each case, will usually take the form of "sometimes yes, sometimes no, but it depends," and will almost always generate disagreement. The answers also require thinking about inherent contradictions of executive power, how the framers attempted to resolve them, and why the explicit text of the Constitution cannot answer all of the questions that arise about the nature of that power. Some of these questions do not have clear answers at all. "Ultimately there is no conclusive answer to the question of how far the executive power reaches. Even after two hundred years of precedent and judicial opinion, the nature and scope of presidential power remain astonishingly ambiguous."[4]

THE CONSTITUTIONAL DESIGN

When the framers assembled in Philadelphia and agreed to replace the Articles of Confederation with a new constitution, they quickly settled on an overall plan with three branches of government—legislative, executive, and judicial. Designing the "national executive" proved to be one of the most difficult problems, because there were no precedents for placing an executive in a republican government, and there were widespread fears that such an office would inevitably evolve into tyranny. Another reason creating the presidency was difficult was that the nature of executive power was not quite clear to the framers and embodied both ambiguities and contradictions.

What is the "executive power?" What does it mean, to "execute" the laws or serve as a "chief executive"? It appears simple enough: the executive is the one who *executes*—carries out, administers, implements, enforces—the law. In this limited conception, the executive is an agent of whomever has the authority to write those laws. In a common formulation, the legislature exercises its legitimate authority by enacting laws, and the executive administers those laws in the manner that the legislature intended and instructs. The executive merely wields power as the agent of, and in the name of, the legislature.[5]

But that formulation is indeed simplistic, as it renders the executive itself superfluous. An executive who does nothing but implement precisely what a legislature instructs is not an executive but, rather, a "clerk" (in Richard Neustadt's famous formulation).[6] In a system based on the separation of powers, such an office is just an extension of the legislature and defeats the whole purpose of establishing an independent executive. The Articles of Confederation took this form, famously lacking an executive branch and relying on state governments to enforce federal laws. It was a profoundly dysfunctional system, whose failures prompted the Constitutional Convention.

A viable executive, then, requires independent powers, as well as discretion in the exercise of those powers. The British political theorist John Locke is usually regarded as the first to examine executive power in a constitutional government (defined here as the exercise of authority with constraints and within the rule of laws). Locke saw the need for the executive to carry out the will of the legislature. But he allowed a degree of discretion in the exercise of powers, an ability to protect the public generally and, when necessary, an inherent authority to act when the law is silent.[7] Most controversially, Locke also argued that the executive has the ability to act *contrary* to the law when doing so is necessary to protect the public good; this is known as the prerogative power. The prerogative power creates an immediate problem for democratic principles: if the executive has the ability to act against laws, how can the executive power be limited to what the law allows? Are there any barriers that keep a viable executive from abusing its power?

These questions pose the central problem of executive power that the framers confronted: constructing an office with enough power to be effective, but with sufficient checks to prevent the president from becoming a tyrant. It is a problem that is at once difficult and in tension with itself:

> The daunting task for the framers was to figure out how to create a democratic executive. None had ever existed before in their world, certainly not on the scale that these thoughtful men in Philadelphia were attempting. How, they repeatedly asked themselves, do you have a chief magistrate who is competent and powerful and yet accountable and responsible in the exercise of power?[8]

The framers never did resolve the question of what the executive power was, and they devoted most of their attention to the specifics of what express powers the executive would have. The result was an ambiguous structure in which constitutional language lacks the clarity or specificity necessary to resolve every dispute about presidential authority that might arise. The framers spent considerable time debating how the office should be structured—a single or plural executive, term of office, eligibility, method of election—and what specific powers the office should have. Giving the president the appointment power, a qualified veto, the role of commander in chief, and the ability to "receive ambassadors and other public ministers" adds some dimension to the president's authorities, but these allocations do not answer the fundamental question of what, precisely, "the executive power" is.

Harris, Sidney/CartoonStock.com

The most prominent passage about executive power in the *Federalist* is Alexander Hamilton's oft cited, "Energy in the executive is a leading character in the definition of good government."[9] Hamilton goes on,

> It is essential to the protection of the community against foreign attacks; it is not less essential to the steady administration of the laws; to the protection of property against those irregular and high-handed combinations which sometimes interrupt the ordinary course of justice; to the security of liberty against the enterprises and assaults of ambition, of faction, and of anarchy.

But this discussion does not provide much clarity about what the executive power consists *of*; rather, it gives examples of what the power can be useful *for*. And while Hamilton insisted that "energy" is crucial to an effective executive, critics have pointed out that he never actually defines what it means, or why it was so important.

Is the executive power limited to carrying out the will of Congress?[10] If so, the president is merely the agent of Congress, able only to do that which Congress explicitly instructs or authorizes. But that cannot be correct, because the Constitution gives the president *independence* from Congress: elected via a separate process, not routinely answerable to legislators and able to block Congress from acting through the veto, and constructed in a way that ensures that the president can operate in a separate sphere. Even more, the Framers clearly intended the executive (and the judiciary) to act as an independent check on the legislative power; in turn, the judiciary and legislature would act as an independent check on the executive.[11] Madison's famous dictum, that "ambition must be made to counteract ambition"[12] requires that each branch have means to resist encroachment by the other branches, which means that each has a reserve of independent authority and discretion.

The Constitutional Convention

Although the Constitution's framers saw the need for an independent executive endowed with its own authority, they did not begin with a consensus on the form this executive should take or the powers it should possess. At the outset of their deliberations, they had to answer three basic questions: (1) Should one person or several individuals hold the office? (2) What combination of functions, obligations, and powers would yield an energetic, yet safe, executive? And (3) what checks were needed to protect against the abuse of executive power?

A Single Executive?

The first of these questions was resolved early in the convention after a short, but pointed, discussion. James Wilson, a delegate from Pennsylvania, argued that only a single individual could combine the characteristics of "energy, dispatch, and responsibility." Critics immediately charged that such an executive would be dangerous—"the foetus of monarchy," in the words of Edmund Randolph of Virginia.

In denying the allegation that what they really wanted was a king, Wilson and James Madison contrasted the powers of their more limited executive with those of a king. As the debate intensified, Madison proposed that the delegates establish the institution's authority before deciding on the number of executives, a move that constituted one of the most astute parliamentary maneuvers of the Constitutional Convention. Wilson had previously declared that the prerogatives of the British monarch were not a proper guide for determining the executive's domain, as they were too extensive. The American executive, in his view, should possess only executive authority—the power to execute laws and make those appointments that had not otherwise been provided for. The convention accepted Wilson's delineation, which made it safe to entrust the office to a single individual. Only later did the framers detail executive powers.

Presidential Powers

Wilson was primarily responsible for this elaboration as well. As a member of the committee charged with taking propositions approved by the convention and shaping them into a draft constitution, he detailed the executive's powers with language taken from the New York and Massachusetts constitutions. Surprisingly, his enumeration engendered little debate. The powers were not particularly controversial, and couching them in the language of two state constitutions made them even more palatable to the delegates. Thus, the framers quickly and quietly adopted most of these powers.

Achieving agreement on the checks to secure and restrain the executive was more difficult. Abuses by past executives—particularly British monarchs and colonial governors—combined with the excesses of contemporary legislatures made the maintenance of an institutional balance essential. The problem was how to preserve the balance without jeopardizing the independence of the separate branches or impeding the lawful exercise of their authority.

In the end, the framers resolved this problem by checking those powers that they believed to be most dangerous (the ones that had been subject to greatest abuse during the colonial era, such as appointments, treaty making, and declarations of war), while protecting the general sphere of authority from legislative encroachment (in the executive's case, by a qualified veto). The provisions for reeligibility and a short term of office also encouraged presidential responsibility. Reappointment was the principal motive for good behavior. Impeachment was the ultimate recourse for those executives who flagrantly abused their authority.

The traditional weapon used to defend executive authority was the veto. Theoretically it could function to protect those executive powers threatened by the legislature, but in practice colonial executives had frequently employed the veto to prevent the enactment of laws they opposed. Herein lay its danger. The compromise was to give the president the veto but allow two-thirds of both houses to override it.

In summary, the relative ease with which the constitutional delegates empowered the presidency indicates that they had developed a consensus on the bounds and sub-stance of executive authority. In deciding which of these powers to give to the new institution, the framers turned to the tenets of balanced government, as articulated by the French theorist Charles de Montesquieu in his often-quoted treatise *The Spirit of the Laws* and practiced to some extent in the states of Massachusetts and New York.[13] The founders accepted those powers that conformed to the basic division of authority; they rejected those that, actually or potentially, threatened the institutional balance.

Limiting Abuses

Fears of potential abuse led to differing opinions on how best to constrain the branches without violating the principle of separate spheres of authority. The major-ity of the delegates opted for sharing powers, particularly in foreign affairs and principally with the Senate. This broad decision, which they reached toward the end of the convention when the pressures to compromise were greatest, exacerbated the fears of those who believed that the Senate would come to dominate the president and control the government.

Many of the opponents of the Constitution saw the sharing of powers as far more dangerous than the general grant of executive authority specified in Article II. Although each of the president's powers engendered some objection during the ratification debate, the most sustained criticism was directed at the president's rela-tionship with the upper chamber. In the end the proponents of the Constitution prevailed, but the debate over the efficacy of shared powers between the executive and legislative branches has continued through the years.

The debate at the Convention, however, did not resolve the central dilemmas of executive power, settle the foundational question of how much discretionary authority the president would have as Chief Executive, or conclusively address how presidential authority can be checked. By combining elements of both an office subordinate to Congress and an office with its own reservoir of authority, the fram-ers expressed the "ambivalence of executive power"[14] (see box 2.1, "Can a Sitting President Be Indicted?").

Box 2.1 ★ Can a Sitting President Be Indicted?

In his March 2019 report, Special Counsel Robert Mueller found evidence of extensive Russian efforts to influence the 2016 presidential election but no con-spiracy or coordination with these efforts by the Trump campaign. Mueller also detailed ten instances in which the president engaged in conduct designed to frustrate the investigation and declined to say that it was clear that the president had not violated the law.[15]

(continued)

Box 2.1 ★ Continued

Mueller declined to indict the president or even allege that he had committed the crime of obstruction of justice. A key reason was that opinions by the Department of Justice's Office of Legal Counsel (OLC) in 1973 and 2000 concluded that a sitting president *cannot* be prosecuted or even charged with a crime.[16]

What is the basis for the position that a sitting president cannot be tried for a crime? The answer stems from the president's position in our constitutional system. Although the Constitution says nothing about presidential immunity from criminal charges, the president's unique position as the singular head of a branch presents several difficulties for subjecting them to criminal liability while in office.

First, prosecuting presidents would interfere with their ability to carry out the office's constitutional responsibilities; being subject to a criminal trial would be "so onerous that a President may not be able fully to discharge the powers and duties of his office if he had to defend a criminal prosecution."[17] Immunity is also necessary to preserve the executive branch's independence (except for the constitutionally specified impeachment and removal process). Yale Law Professor Akhil Amar poses a hypothetical case in which a South Carolina prosecutor indicted Abraham Lincoln in March 1861 and forced him to stand trial in Charleston.[18] Such a situation, he concludes, would be constitutionally intolerable, allowing a locality to incapacitate a national executive.

In addition, prosecution is a plenary executive function (meaning that only executive officials can carry out a federal prosecution). As a result, any prosecutor would be under presidential control, and subjecting a sitting president to a criminal trial would make the president "prosecutor and defendant in the same case."[19]

Finally, trying a president in a criminal court could give twelve randomly selected jurors the power to remove a president.

Ultimately the OLC concluded that subjecting a president to criminal prosecution would jeopardize the unique constitutional role of a chief executive. Similarly, the OLC concluded that charging the president with a crime—even if actual prosecution was delayed during a term—presented a risk that a president would be unable to govern.[20]

The OLC opinion argues that when the president has broken the law, impeachment and removal is the only constitutional remedy.[21] Alexander Hamilton argued in *The Federalist* that a president is liable for criminal punishment in ordinary courts only after impeachment and removal.[22] John Adams and Thomas Jefferson held the same view.

Some legal scholars question the OLC position. Can a president who shoots and kills someone in plain view truly be immune? "Surely," argues Lawrence Tribe, "there must be an exception for *that* kind of case: Having to wait until the House of Representatives impeaches the alleged murderer and the Senate removes him from office before prosecuting and sentencing him would be crazy. Nobody seriously advocates the OLC mantra of 'no indictment of a sitting president' in that kind of case."[23] If the policy is not absolute, then the question is what sorts of behavior should leave the president liable for indictment and prosecution.

OLC opinions do not have the binding precedential character of a Supreme Court ruling or other authoritative statement. They reflect policy, not legal mandates. The question of presidential immunity from criminal indictment has never been subjected to court review, though the Court has held that presidents are not immune from civil litigation while in office (*Clinton v. Jones* in 1997).

Interpreting Article II

Article II of the Constitution establishes and empowers the presidency. Section 1 specifies the method of election and eligibility (supplanted by the Twelfth Amendment, which changed the way that presidential electors cast their ballots for the president and vice president), prohibits Congress from altering the president's compensation while in office, and prescribes an oath. Section 2 sets out specific powers, Section 3 specifies a series of obligations, and Section 4 allows for impeachment and removal from office of the president, vice president, and all other civil officers of the United States.

In 1,023 words, a combination of authorizations, limits, and duties, the Constitution created what is now the most powerful democratic office in the world.

Vesting Clause

The ambiguities of executive power are revealed in the first sentence of Article II, the Vesting Clause: *The executive power shall be vested in a President of the United States of America.* The language seems to imply a general grant of authority, specifying that whatever the "executive power" is, it is to be exercised by the president. But there is a problem: the text of Article II does not define "the executive power," and we need to know that if we are to fully understand the scope of presidential constitutional authority. To be sure, there are powers delineated in the remainder of the Article, but does this mean that the executive power is limited to what is specifically mentioned there? Does the vesting clause constitute an assignment of a general executive power to the president, or is it merely a description of the powers that follow?

Article II provides no clear answer, and the distinction between a description and a grant is important. A descriptive interpretation would mean that the president could only do what the Constitution explicitly permitted, while a general grant would imply a broader concept of executive authority that includes powers not specifically described.

In parsing the language, one approach compares the vesting language in Article I and Article II. Article I begins (emphasis added): *All legislative powers **herein granted** shall be vested in a Congress of the United States.* These words clearly state that the powers of Congress are not legislative powers generally, but are limited to those specified in the rest of Article, most of which are in section 8. Article I also includes other language not found in Article II: a set of explicit limits describing things that Congress may not do in section 9, and the "necessary and proper" clause in section 8 which grants implied powers.[24]

The provenance of these differences is uncertain. The phrasing emerged from the Committee on Style that put the final touches on the draft Constitution and was written by Pennsylvania delegate Gouverneur Morris. The wording may or may not have been intentional, but it had the effect of "[admitting] an interpretation of executive power which would give to the President a field of action much wider than that outlined by the enumerated powers."[25] Richard Pious argues that it was purposeful, and

> sufficiently ambiguous so that no one could say precisely what it meant. It was possible that the words referred to more than the specific powers that followed and might confer a set of otherwise unspecified executive powers: the power to

give orders to department secretaries, and the power to remove officials who did not follow presidential policies. When Morris and his allies used the term "The Executive Power," they were seeking deliberately to build into the Constitution an open-ended clause that might later expand the powers of the presidency.[26]

For years, scholars have debated whether these linguistic differences matter. Two noted constitutional scholars, Steven Calabresi and Saikrishna Prakash, argue that the distinctions are crucial and signify that the vesting clause "must be read as conferring a general grant of 'the executive power' to the president."[27] Two other noted constitutional scholars, Lawrence Lessig and Cass Sunstein arrive at the opposite conclusion, contending that "the framers intended the Vesting Clause to vest constitutionally little more than the enumerated executive powers. It says *who has the executive power*, not what that power is."[28] Yet another noted authority maintains that the difference is substantively unimportant.[29] This disagreement about what the first sentence of Article II means confirms what Justice Jackson wrote in *Youngstown*: disputes about executive power produce "more or less apt quotations from respected sources on each side of any question."

It was not until 1890 that the Supreme Court weighed in on the matter, holding in *In re Neagle* that the president indeed had implied authority to carry out "the rights, duties, and obligations growing out of the constitution itself" even in the absence of specific constitutional or statutory warrants.[30] If the Constitution vested a power in the president, it also vested the implied authority necessary to effectuate that power. Over the next century, other Court decisions identified many other inherent powers that flow from the president's general executive authority: control over classified information, general responsibility for diplomacy and foreign affairs, and the ability to remove officials.

Powers and Duties

The structure and powers of the office are set out in the remainder of Article II. The list of explicit powers, identified in table 2.1, is brief. The first column shows powers assigned to the president alone. The commander in chief power makes the president the highest-ranking military official, although the full authority over the military is shared between the president (who commands it) and Congress (who establishes and regulates it and has the power to declare war). Presidents can require subordinate officials to provide written opinions, something designed to ensure a degree of accountability and establish a chain of authority. Presidents may make recess appointments to executive branch positions when the Senate is not in session and cannot confirm them, with the officials serving until the end of the subsequent congressional session; this was more of a concern when Congress met only a few months out of the year.[31] The president can call Congress into an extraordinary session outside of the legislature's normal schedule (Harry Truman was the last president to do this, in 1948) and set the adjournment date if the two chambers disagree (no president has done this). Presidents may grant pardons and reprieves for people who have committed federal crimes.

Several presidential powers are shared with Congress: The power to make treaties and appoint Supreme Court Justices and other officials requires Senate approval—majorities in the case of appointments, two-thirds approval for treaties. The president may veto legislation, though Congress can override with two-thirds vote in both chambers.

Table 2.1 Article II Assignment of Explicit Constitutional Powers and Obligations

Powers	Shared Powers	Obligations (What the President "Shall" Do)
• Commander in Chief • Require opinions in writing from principal officers • Grant reprieves and pardons • Make recess appointments • Call Congress into special session on "extraordinary occasions" • Set adjournment of Congress when House and Senate disagree on the date	• Make treaties with 2/3 Senate concurrence • Nominate ambassadors, Supreme Court Justices, and other officers as established by Congress, with advice and consent of Senate • Veto subject to congressional override (Article I, § 7)	• "From time to time" give Congress information on State of the Union • Recommend "necessary and expedient" legislation • Take care that the laws be faithfully executed • Take oath of office • Receive ambassadors and other public ministers • Commission officers

And the president is obligated (through the use of the imperative "shall," although it is up to the president to determine what this means) provide information on the state of the union, recommend legislation, take care that the laws be faithfully executed, commission officers, and take the oath of office.

On paper, these powers and duties may not appear to amount to much and, notably, have not changed at all since 1787. The explicit grants of constitutional authority available to Donald Trump are no different from those that were available to George Washington. Contemporary presidents are far more powerful than Washington, because that language has been interpreted in different ways, government capacity has grown, and presidential action serves as precedent for subsequent presidents, incrementally expanding power over time.

The Constitution leaves key terms undefined, and virtually all of the grants of power require substantial interpretation. The power to receive ambassadors and public ministers, for example, is expressed as a "shall," indicating that it is a presidential duty. Hamilton considered it a matter of diplomatic protocol rather than a substantive power, "more a matter of dignity than of authority."[32] But the clause is almost universally interpreted as granting the president the sole discretion to conduct diplomacy and officially recognize foreign governments. More controversially, some read it as evidence that the president is solely responsible for foreign policy. The power's expansion from the limited literal textual grant was a matter of historical precedent and defined, beginning with Washington, by "post ratification theory and practice."[33]

Another example of a presidential duty is the "take care" clause obligating the president to faithfully execute the laws. It also leaves open many questions. As with the vesting clause, the language can be read as requiring the president to adhere to congressional intention in carrying out enacted laws, making the president subject to congressional will in how the laws are administered.[34] Or it could be a confirmation "that the President possesses unique powers with respect to the execution of the law" by giving the office the sole control over administration.[35] Or it could mean that the president merely lacks the royal prerogative to unilaterally suspend laws or refuse to carry them out (which would also fit with the qualified nature of the veto, which can be overridden by Congress). Yet another interpretation is that the structure of the take care clause—which does not say that the president "shall faithfully execute the laws" but, rather, that the president "shall take care that the laws be faithfully executed"—"necessarily carries with it the authority to perform actions necessary and proper to the accomplishment of the duty," which includes the power to supervise executive branch agencies.[36] Which interpretation is correct? The Constitution does not say.

What appears to be an arcane and highly technical debate over how to parse constitutional syntax becomes more important when we consider whether the *laws* referred to in the take care clause include the Constitution as well as those that Congress enacts. If presidents have a duty to take care that the *Constitution* be faithfully executed, that would give them a role in determining what the Constitution means, and it might justify extraordinary action necessary to protect the constitutional structure itself. (See box 2.2 for a discussion of whether the president can refuse to carry out an unconstitutional law.)

Box 2.2 ★ Donald Trump Agrees: The President Can Refuse to Obey or Implement Unconstitutional Laws

On August 2, 2017, Donald Trump signed a bill leveling sanctions against Iran, North Korea, and Russia. At the same time, he issued a statement saying that Congress had included "a number of clearly unconstitutional provisions," including displacing the president's exclusive right to recognize foreign governments and their territorial boundaries; granting Congress the ability to change the law outside the constitutionally required process; directing subordinates in the executive branch to undertake certain diplomatic initiatives; and prohibiting the president from receiving certain ambassadors.

In other words, the president was claiming the right to ignore provisions of the law that he considered unconstitutional. He was not the first to do so.[37] Thomas Jefferson pardoned everyone convicted under the Sedition Acts, thus nullifying the statute.[38] Andrew Jackson asserted that the president has a co-equal role to the courts in assessing the constitutionality of a law. Andrew Johnson refused to obey the Tenure in Office Act and was impeached, at least in part, for violating it. (Sixty years later the Supreme Court agreed with Johnson that the law was unconstitutional.) William Howard Taft viewed the budget power as a central executive function that Congress could not limit. He instructed his cabinet secretaries to ignore a statute prohibiting them from preparing budget documents for the president to review, ordering them to submit them anyway.[39]

Ronald Reagan refused to abide by some provisions of the Competition in Contracting Act of 1984, which required the president to refer certain contract award protests to the Comptroller General (which is part of Congress).[40] The Obama administration concluded the president did not have to follow a 2003 law requiring the president to submit legislation if cost increases occurred in Medicare.[41]

Clearly, no one would expect the president to enforce a law ordering the immediate summary execution of a defense contractor CEO for overcharging the Pentagon and prohibiting federal court review. Such a law would be an absurdly obvious violation of the Constitution's ban on bills of attainder and guarantees

Box 2.2 ★ Continued

of due process.[42] Thus, presidents have an independent ability to determine the constitutionality of a law.[43]

Presidential review is another instance of an important constitutional question that does not have a clear answer. In many instances presidential defiance will lead to legal and political blowback, depending on how Congress, the courts, and the public respond. In others, it will be celebrated. The power of review is a matter of "[powers] that are not so much separated as duplicated and distributed, so that concurrent approval is necessary for action."[44]

The presidential oath of office, which is the only oath whose language is explicitly stated in the Constitution, requires presidents to swear or affirm that they "will, to the best of my ability, preserve, protect and defend the Constitution." This could reasonably be read as imposing a duty to enforce constitutional obligations and to consider the Constitution as included among the laws that shall be faithfully executed. But, again, the text itself does not say which interpretation is correct.

The vagueness and gaps in the language were not accidental. Instead, "the provisions dealing with the presidency were purposely left sketchy, with the intention that the presidents themselves (beginning, the framers expected, with George Washington) would fill in that outline."[45]

THE IMPORTANCE OF PRECEDENT: EARLY CONTROVERSIES AND CONTEMPORARY APPLICATIONS

Because Article II reflected the tensions in the framers' different views of executive power, and the inherent "ambivalence" of the concept, it was inevitable that history and precedent would flesh out the realities of that power. Washington was keenly aware of this, writing to Madison shortly after his inauguration, "as the first of everything, *in our situation* will serve to establish a Precedent, it is devoutly wished on my part, that these precedents may be fixed on true principles."[46]

Not surprisingly, disputes arose immediately, and if many of them appear to the modern observer to be anachronistic or even quaint, they reflect the same uncertainties and tensions seen in modern disputes. These events also show that all presidents—even those who had expressed much more limited views of the executive power—acted in ways that expanded that power, by setting precedents and pragmatic application of the *theory* of executive authority to the "concrete problems of executive power as they actually present themselves" that Justice Jackson considered in his *Youngstown* opinion. Later in this chapter we will consider whether this pattern of expansion via precedent poses a problem for separation of powers if the process is a one-way ratchet of ever increasing power.

The Presidential Title

Perhaps the first major disagreement was what to call the president. Although seemingly trivial, the issue reflected a "struggle over the nature of the office" and a symbolic statement of whether the president was to be regarded as loftier than, or answerable to, Congress.[47] Vice President John Adams wanted a "superior title," lest the country suffer "the Contempt, and Scorn of the Derision of all Europe."[48]

Calling the president merely "the president," in Adams's view, "made him think of the president of a fire company or a cricket club."[49] A joint congressional committee recommended that no titles be added to what was already in the Constitution ("President of the United States"). The House agreed, but at Adams's urging the Senate recommended that the president be addressed as "His Highness, the President of the United States of America, and Protector of their Liberties." Members of the House refused to go along, and in the interest of comity the Senate acceded. In the end, "President of the United States" it was.[50]

The issue of the president's title arose again after William Henry Harrison died shortly after taking office in 1841. His death led to uncertainty over what happens when the vice president assumes the office because of a president's death or removal. The relevant language in Article II, section 6 is hazy:

> In Case of the Removal of the President from Office, or of his Death, Resignation, or Inability to discharge the Powers and Duties of the said Office, the Same shall devolve on the Vice President.

The text is unclear whether "the Same shall devolve on the Vice President" refers to the "Office" of the president (in which case the vice president would become the president) or merely the "Powers and Duties of the said Office" as a stand-in. The common view at the time was that the vice president was merely a caretaker who would exercise the powers of the office until the next election.

Nevertheless, Vice President John Tyler insisted on taking the oath of office, demanded that he be addressed as "the president," moved into the White House, and considered himself a fully empowered and legitimate chief executive. "That Tyler was wrong in his reading of the original intentions of the Constitution," writes Corwin, "is certain,"[51] but no other official or institution was in a position to authoritatively challenge him. Tyler's assumption of the presidency in the face of congressional opposition (some legislators took to calling him "His Accidency") became known as the Tyler Precedent and legitimized the next seven vice presidents who succeeded a president who died in office: Millard Fillmore (Taylor), Andrew Johnson (Lincoln), Chester A. Arthur (Garfield), Theodore Roosevelt (McKinley), Calvin Coolidge (Harding), Harry Truman (Franklin D. Roosevelt), and Lyndon Johnson (Kennedy). This ambiguity was not authoritatively settled until the 25th Amendment was ratified in 1967. It specifies that "in case of the removal of the President from office or his death or resignation, the Vice President shall become President."

The Removal Power
A broad removal power is most consistent with a strong executive, making subordinate officers directly answerable to the president. When Congress established the first three executive departments in 1789 (Foreign Affairs, Treasury, and War), legislators spent considerable time debating the nature of the president's appointment power. Article II was clear about the president's ability to nominate officials who assumed office upon Senate approval. However, it said nothing about the power to *remove* those officials, and some legislators insisted that if Senate approval of presidential nominees was required to put them in office, Senate approval was also required for the president to remove them. Alexander Hamilton said as much in *Federalist* 77, that "consent of that body would be necessary to displace as well as to appoint."

Congress debated whether the president could remove a confirmed official and whether even putting that authority into legislation violated separation of powers by having Congress redundantly authorize powers the president already had. The House inserted language into a bill creating the Foreign Affairs department acknowledging that the Secretary of State could be removed by the president, thus appearing to recognize the presidents' removal power, and the Senate did the same on a tie vote broken by Vice President Adams. But constitutional scholar David Currie notes that "there was no consensus as to whether he got that authority from Congress or from the Constitution itself."[52]

Congress moved in the other direction with the 1867 Tenure in Office Act, which required Senate approval for any cabinet removal, and prohibited the president from dismissing any Senate-confirmed appointment until a replacement had been confirmed. President Andrew Johnson vetoed the Act, citing the 1789 debate in claiming that it infringed upon the president's constitutional powers, but Congress overrode the veto the same day. Johnson continued to insist it was unconstitutional, writing in his 1867 message to Congress: "I am entirely persuaded that under such a rule the President cannot perform the great duty assigned to him of seeing the laws faithfully executed."[53]

That summer, Johnson fired Secretary of War Edward Stanton, in an act fully intended to provoke a constitutional confrontation with Congress. He got his wish: the dismissal, which violated the Tenure in Office Act, became one of the formal charges when the House impeached him in 1868.[54] Johnson avoided conviction and removal in the Senate by a single vote.

Within the space of eighty years, Congress had first concluded that presidents had broad authority to dismiss executive officials and then that they did not, impeaching and nearly removing a president who insisted he did.

The scope of the president's removal power was formally addressed in 1926, when the Supreme Court weighed in. In *Myers v. United States* (1926) the Court held that the president had constitutional authority to remove any appointees, because the power to remove is central to the president's authority to control the executive branch. Less than ten years later, however, the Court pared back this ruling, ruling in another case that Congress *could* limit the president's removal power in certain types of agencies: those that, in the words of the Court, carried out "quasi-legislative" or "quasi-judicial" functions; see *Humphrey's Executor v. United States* (1935). So, the sequence of authoritative rulings on whether there are any limits to the president's removal power, the first two from Congress and the last two from the Supreme Court, are no, yes, no, and yes.

Humphrey's Executor allowed Congress to create many "independent" agencies whose heads serve fixed terms and typically can only be removed for cause (examples include the Securities and Exchange Commission, the Federal Reserve, and the Federal Trade Commission), because the agencies are designed to be insulated from political influences.[55] The Federal Reserve, which controls monetary policy and has significant authority over the direction of economic policy, is governed by a seven-member Board of Governors, who serve fixed fourteen-year terms. The president appoints the governors, subject to Senate confirmation. The terms are staggered, so one opens up every two years; this means that under most circumstances, a one-term president will appoint at most two governors, and a two-term president four. The statute establishing the Fed specifies that governors serve until their term is up and a successor has been confirmed, unless "sooner removed for cause by the President."[56] There is no precise definition in the statute of what a proper cause for removal would be, but the general understanding is that it does not permit dismissing a member of the Board of Governors because that member did not follow the president's directives.[57]

Nevertheless, the underlying dispute about the nature of the removal power has not disappeared. Some legal scholars continue to insist that the legal question is far from settled and that executive branch officials whom the president cannot remove (such as the heads of independent agencies) are flatly unconstitutional. According to this line of argument, the Supreme Court opinions limiting the president's removal powers (such as *Humphrey's Executor*) were wrongly decided. Even after two centuries of practice, the nature of the president's removal power remains "one of the oldest and most venerable debates in US constitutional law."[58]

The Neutrality Proclamation

Only a few years after collaborating on the *Federalist Papers*, Alexander Hamilton and James Madison became embroiled in a contentious dispute over presidential power. In 1793, shortly after war broke out between France and Great Britain, President Washington issued a Neutrality Proclamation, in which he declared that American citizens were not to become involved in the hostilities (by, for example, participating in the seizure of French or British ships) and that the US government would not protect them in the event that they did. The proclamation had the effect of nullifying a 1788 treaty between the United States and France. Washington convened his cabinet to consider the question, as Congress was in recess when the issue arose. His advisors recommended not calling Congress into special session, so Washington issued the proclamation on his own authority.[59]

The proclamation triggered a dispute between Hamilton and Madison over the president's authority to issue it. Nothing in the Constitution explicitly authorizes independent presidential declarations of policy. Following up on his *Federalist* writings advocating for an energetic executive,[60] Hamilton argued that the president had an inherent general foreign policy power. In his view, the Neutrality Proclamation did nothing but inform citizens of the current state of relations between the United States and France and Britain, which would last until Congress could make its own determination as to the existence of war or peace.[61] As such, the president had done nothing to encroach upon the congressional war power. Madison disagreed, strongly so, and attacked Hamilton's theory of presidential power as nothing more than a justification for the president employing the royal prerogatives of the British monarch.

Congress subsequently affirmed US neutrality and authorized the prosecution of violators. But the proclamation established the precedent of the president making unilateral declarations of policy "to state strong and binding positions for the nation,"[62] especially in foreign affairs. Such declarations quickly became routine. By 1823, when James Monroe declared the Western Hemisphere off limits to European powers, this far more expansive declaration generated almost no controversy.

Today, something like the Neutrality Proclamation, in which the president issues a statement declaring government policy, would be completely unexceptional. Even more, such declarations are now expected, and a president who declined to make statements of policy or define what the United States would consider to be threats to national security would be considered irresponsible and negligent.

The Louisiana Purchase

Thomas Jefferson was an ardent opponent of Hamilton's expansive view of presidential authority and led the Democratic-Republican Party that ejected the Federalists from power in the 1800 election. Once in office, however, he adopted a more aggressive view of presidential authority and with his decision to execute the

Louisiana Purchase went far beyond even his own view of the president's constitutional powers.

Most schoolchildren know the Louisiana Purchase—the land purchased from France in 1803, which doubled the size of the United States—as a historic moment. Joseph Ellis called it "one of the most consequential executive actions in all of American history."[63] Less well known is that the deal posed a constitutional problem, since "the authority to buy territory and simply to incorporate it into the new Republic is nowhere to be found among the enumerated powers of either the president or of Congress."[64] Some of Jefferson's advisors insisted that the power to acquire territory was a basic function of any sovereign nation with or without any explicit constitutional language, but Jefferson doubted that the government—much less the *president alone*—had the constitutional authority to incorporate new territory, and he had to be dissuaded from the idea of seeking a constitutional amendment.[65]

A treaty to acquire the territory had been negotiated in France before Jefferson's envoy, James Monroe, had approval to do so, as Napoleon's offer to sell all of Louisiana was only communicated to Monroe after he had arrived in France in April 1803. The Senate eventually ratified the treaty—thus establishing an important precedent governing territorial expansion—but Jefferson is now regarded as abandoning his constitutional scruples in favor of a "national interest" view of executive power. He discussed his concerns in language that Abraham Lincoln would revisit sixty years later:

> The Executive in seizing the fugitive occurrence which so much advances good of their country, have [sic] done an act beyond the Constitution. The Legislature in casting behind them metaphysical subtleties, and risking them-selves like faithful servants, must ratify & pay for it, and throw themselves on their country for doing for them unauthorized what we know they would have done for themselves had they been in a situation to do it.[66]

In other words: regardless of what the Constitution said, the national interest demanded it, and Jefferson could only hope that the public would understand and agree that it was the right thing to do.

The Veto

The veto—the ability to disapprove a bill and return it to Congress—is a formidable tool that gives the president enormous bargaining power. By wielding it, the president can prevent Congress from passing laws unless it can muster two-thirds majorities, something that rarely happens with controversial legislation. Its existence is indicative of the ambiguities of executive power, for although the veto is exercised as a presidential act, it is, and always was understood by the framers to be, a legislative power, thus blurring the boundaries between the executive and the legislature (this is one reason it is included as part of Article I, not Article II).[67]

A common view of the framer's understanding of the veto is that it should be used to protect the presidency from legislative encroachment and protect the office's constitutional powers. Although this use of the veto was emphasized in the Constitutional Convention, from the beginning the framers understood the utility of the veto as a defense against bad laws as well. Hamilton defended it as "an additional security against the enaction of improper laws . . . to guard the community against the effects of faction, precipitancy, or of any impulse unfriendly to the public good, which may happen to influence a majority of that body."[68]

The first presidents used the veto sparingly, but did not limit its use to constitutional matters. Washington vetoed two bills, a congressional apportionment bill that he considered unconstitutional and a military appropriations bill that he though was unwise (Congress removed the language that Washington found objectionable, and Washington signed the revised legislation). Madison vetoed seven bills, three for policy reasons; Monroe one; and Adams, Jefferson, and John Quincy Adams none. Between 1789 and 1828, presidents had vetoed ten bills, without a single override.

Andrew Jackson changed the mix, vetoing twelve bills, more than the first six presidents combined, and was open about substituting his judgment on policy issues for congressional sentiment even as he couched his objections in constitutional language. Jackson routinely inserted himself into legislative deliberations by announcing his intention to veto a bill while Congress was still deliberating (considered "almost revolutionary" at the time, but now utterly routine).[69]

One prominent presidential scholar argues that Jackson was the first president to veto a bill—the establishment of the Second Bank of the United States in 1832—for political purposes related to the upcoming presidential election.[70] And although the Supreme Court had previously ruled that the Bank was constitutional, Jackson did not consider himself bound by that ruling, insisting that the president had a right to make an independent judgment of constitutionality. Johnson was also the first to regularly use the pocket veto—refusing to sign a bill presented to him within ten days of the end of a congressional session at which point the bill dies—wielding it seven times. Jackson's use of the veto triggered a Senate censure, a charge by Senator Henry Clay that Jackson "wished to ascend the throne," and efforts to amend the Constitution to allow Congress to override a veto by simple majorities.[71]

Cartoon of Andrew Jackson depicting him wearing the ermine robes and crown of a king and stepping on a shredded copy of the Constitution. Author unknown, probably published in 1832 or 1833.

The role of the veto changed again after the Civil War, becoming less of a constitutional defense mechanism and more of a routine instrument of policy disagreement. The frequency went up: Andrew Johnson vetoed 29 bills, Grant 93, and Cleveland 414. In the seventy-six years between 1789 and 1865, presidents had vetoed 59 bills. Over the next seventy-six (1866–1942), they vetoed 1,662. Objections to the basis of the veto exercise vanished, and although there might be questions about the president's judgment regarding a specific veto, there was no longer controversy over the president's right to veto legislation for any reason. Presidential justifications changed as well, and the veto is now universally recognized as a basic policy tool that presidents use to influence congressional deliberation.[72]

The key to this evolution is that the constitutional language of the veto power has not changed at all. That language imposes no boundaries or conditions for the veto, and presidents have always been able to veto legislation for any reason—because they think it is unconstitutional, bad policy, damaging to their political interests, or because signing would benefit political opponents. But the ways in which presidents have used the power have changed dramatically, and there is no way to understand that evolution solely by looking at the constitutional text.

These examples from the eighteenth and early nineteenth centuries—a time not usually associated with aggressive presidential assertions of authority—show that even the first few presidents acted in ways that broadened the scope of that authority and provided vital precedents for future presidents who expanded that power further.

The Prerogative Power

John Locke famously argued that the executive power contained within it an inherent right to act in the absence of formally authorized powers granted by the law (what Pious calls the "soft" prerogative)[73] and even *against* those powers in an emergency (the hard prerogative). If the survival of the government or the nation is at risk, the theory posits, the executive must be able to act in the emergency to do what is necessary to preserve them, even if it entails violating the law.

We have seen examples of both earlier in this chapter: The Neutrality Proclamation and the Louisiana Purchase are cases of presidents acting without explicit authority (soft prerogative), although their actions are within widely accepted doctrines of implied powers. In other cases, presidents went well beyond what the law allowed and even acted in the face of clear prohibitions.

In the spring of 1861, Congress was in recess. After the Confederacy seceded and Southern troops fired on Ft. Sumter, Lincoln took a number of actions that exceeded the president's constitutional authority and amounted to the exercise of prerogative power:

- blockading southern ports in the absence of a congressional Declaration of War;
- suspending habeas corpus, a power explicitly assigned to Congress;
- increasing the size of the Army and Navy without any legislation;
- expending funds with no authorization or appropriation;
- censoring the mail.[74]

Later that year, Lincoln refused to obey an order from the Chief Justice of the Supreme Court to release a civilian held in a military prison under a ruling that Lincoln's *habeas* suspension was invalid.[75]

Many of Lincoln's Civil War acts, such as suspending *habeas corpus* and unilaterally expanding the size of the military, fell into the category of "hard" prerogative, since they involved powers assigned to other branches. Lincoln defended his exercise of power using the classic justification for prerogative: the gravity of the situation. "Was it possible to lose the nation and yet preserve the Constitution?" he asked. To his own question he replied, "I felt that measures otherwise unconstitutional might become lawful by becoming indispensable to the preservation of the Constitution through the preservation of the nation."[76]

Similarly, he justified his suspension of *habeas* rights and refusal to obey a court order to release a prisoner as necessary, since Congress was not in session and its ability to meet threatened:

> Are all the laws *but one* to go unexecuted, and the Government itself go to pieces lest that one be violated? Even in such a case, would not the official oath be broken if the Government should be overthrown when it was believed that disregarding the single law would tend to preserve it? . . . it can not be believed the framers of the instrument intended that in every case the danger should run its course until Congress could be called together, the very assembling of which might be prevented, as was intended in this case, by the rebellion.[77]

Lincoln's exercise of emergency powers was drastic enough to constitute "the paragon of all democratic, constitutional dictatorships"[78] and made him "the clearest example of a constitutional dictator."[79]

Ninety years later, the Supreme Court's 1952 *Youngstown* decision rejected the notion that the president has generalized emergency powers, holding that all presidential actions must be traced to constitutional or statutory provisions. However, Congress has delegated specific powers to the president that go into effect when the president declares a national emergency. An example is the Emergency Banking Act of 1933, which authorized a wide range of banking, currency, and financial regulations "[d]uring time of war or during any other period of national emergency declared by the President."[80] Another is the International Emergency Economic Powers Act, a 1977 law that gives the president authority to regulate international economic transactions during a declared national emergency (ironically, the IEEPA was designed to scale back presidential emergency authorities created during World War I).

Because most of these statutes contained no termination provisions, the number of national emergencies proliferated. A congressional investigation in 1973 found 470 different statutes authorizing the president to declare emergencies, and some of those declarations had been in effect for decades.(including one of Truman's Korean War emergency proclamations).[81]

In response, Congress passed the National Emergencies Act in 1976, which set some limits on president's delegated emergency powers. A presidential emergency declaration can last only one year (though it can be renewed), and Congress can rescind an emergency by a Joint Resolution.[82] The president still has almost unlimited discretion in determining that a national emergency exists, even when a statute includes guidance on what constitutes an emergency situation. Jimmy Carter's 1979 declaration of a national emergency with respect to Iran, issued after the American embassy in Teheran was overrun and allowing the president to freeze Iranian assets, has been renewed thirty-eight times, by every president since then.[83] Most national emergencies since then have involved trade sanctions, export controls, and freezing other nations' assets in the United States.

Donald Trump has pushed the boundaries of these powers. After a month-long federal government shutdown from December 2018 to January 2019 that occurred over an impasse between the president (who insisted that Congress provide funding for a wall on the US-Mexico border) and Congress (which refused to appropriate the funds for it), the president declared a national emergency in February 2019, claiming that doing so allowed him to use military funding to start wall construction in the absence of a congressional authorization.[84] It was the first time since the National Emergencies Act that a president attempted to use emergency power for a purpose Congress had explicitly refused to fund. Within a month both the House and Senate voted to rescind the declaration but failed to override the president's veto.[85] A coalition of states, environmental groups, and the House of Representatives filed several lawsuits asking federal courts to overturn the use of funds under the emergency declaration. In May 2019, a federal judge blocked the transfer of funds as exceeding the president's delegated authority.[86] Trump has even claimed the authority under the IEEPA to order American firms to stop doing business in China.[87]

Executive Privilege

In 1792, Congress requested documents from the president regarding a failed military mission in which American forces suffered nearly 100 percent casualties (the St. Clair expedition). It is considered the first congressional investigation into executive branch activities.

Washington turned over the information Congress requested, but he claimed that a president had the right to withhold information from Congress if disclosure was not in the public interest.[88] Later in his term, when Congress asked for information provided to diplomats and treaty negotiators, Washington withheld some documents from the Senate and refused a House request altogether, citing the need for confidentiality and preserving "the boundaries fixed by the Constitution between the different departments."[89]

Every president since has held to Washington's view, based on the idea that the right to shield information is necessary for the president to carry out the executive function, which in turn requires confidential advice.[90] But the Constitution is silent on the question of whether the president can keep information secret; the notion of executive privilege must be inferred from the general grant of executive authority (some scholars argue that the reason secrecy is not mentioned in Article II is that the Framers saw the authority as so obvious an executive power that mentioning it would be superfluous).[91] "Nowhere in the Constitution," the Supreme Court has held, "is there any explicit reference to a privilege of confidentiality, yet to the extent that this interest relates to the effective discharge of a President's powers, it is constitutionally based."[92]

Although this doctrine—known as "executive privilege"—is noncontroversial in theory, in practice the precise boundaries are more contested. Under what circumstances can the president refuse a congressional *demand* for information? The Supreme Court has upheld the validity of executive privilege, but it has also said that it must give way when another branch requires the information in order to carry out *its* constitutional functions (*United States v. Nixon* in 1974). The Court required Nixon to turn over White House tapes to prosecutors in that case. Later cases limited the president's ability to claim executive privilege to direct discussions with senior aides and made it harder for presidents to apply the privilege to departmental or agency communications. However, there is still ambiguity into the scope of the privilege:

> Many significant issues remained unresolved, including whether the President has to have actually seen or been familiar with the disputed matter; whether the presidential privilege encompasses documents and information developed by, or in the possession of, officers and employees in the departments and agencies of the executive branch outside the Executive Office of the President; whether the privilege encompasses all communications in which the President may be interested or if it is confined to a particular type of presidential decision making; and precisely what kind of demonstration of need can overcome the privilege and justify the release of privileged materials.[93]

In 2019, Donald Trump refused to turn over an unredacted version of the Special Counsel Report on Russian interference to the House of Representatives, provide documents from former White House Counsel Don McGahn, or release records on adding a citizenship question to the 2020 Census, citing executive privilege.[94] In doing so, Trump has gone much farther than other presidents in refusing *all* congressional subpoenas or document demands. These refusals have precipitated a constitutional confrontation between the Executive Branch and Congress, between a presidential claims of secrecy and Congress's authority to conduct oversight and investigations. The dispute will almost certainly be adjudicated by the courts, but it may take years to resolve.

ACCOUNTING FOR GROWTH IN PRESIDENTIAL POWER

The contemporary presidency bears little resemblance to that which the framers of the Constitution had artfully designed in 1787 in Philadelphia, even though the formal powers are the same. Their executive had less practical authority, less functional responsibility, and no explicit institutional structure or operating procedures. Of course, their Constitution was designed for different times.

There is no single explanation for why presidential power grew, but we can outline some major themes. First, government became larger and exercised increasing responsibilities over a growing nation. With government doing more, presidents had an incentive to assert control over these new capabilities. As Congress established federal agencies, it delegated to the president the discretion to administer these new functions. Second, presidents themselves articulated new theories of presidential power, offering arguments that explained and justified new conceptions of the office. Third, the courts became more accommodating to the executive, recognizing new (and often implicit) powers and frequently deferring to presidential action. Finally, the presidency benefited from new organizational capabilities, particularly the establishment of the Executive Office of the President in 1939.

Increase in the Size of Government
If the president is to direct the executive branch, the amount of power that designation conveys will be related to the size of the executive branch. Trump oversees a government with over $4 trillion in expenditures; hundreds of agencies, departmental units, bureaus, commissions, and quasi-official organizations; a dedicated Executive Office staff; 2.7 million civilian federal employees; and a military budget

larger than the defense budgets of next eight largest countries combined. As a result, he wields far more administrative power than early presidents, who had a few thousand government employees, a handful of departments with minimal programmatic functions, and a budget 0.001 percent the size of the 2019 total.[95]

Presidential authority is not limited to what the Constitution provides; the president also gets authority from statutes, when Congress directs the president to do something or establishes a new executive branch agency with its own statutory responsibilities. From the creation of the Department of Interior in 1849, the Federal Reserve in 1913, the Department of Defense in 1947, Medicare in 1964, the Department of Homeland Security in 2002, or the Affordable Care Act in 2010, new agencies and programs offer opportunities for the president to guide implementation and shape policy. Since no legislation, no matter how long or detailed, can specify every aspect of administration, new programs inevitably leave significant discretion to the president. More administrative capacity means there is more to do, and more to control.

It is therefore not a coincidence that most of the dramatic expansions of presidential power occurred alongside expansions in the scope of government and often resulted from competition between the president and Congress over who would control the expanded executive branch. The first regulatory agency, the Interstate Commerce Commission, was established in 1887 to regulate railroads.[96] The Civil Service was established in 1883, a recognition that increasing complexity of government administrative functions required a more neutral work force. By the turn of the century, increased government expenditures prompted a close look at government budget processes, leading to the establishment of the Bureau of the Budget in 1921. All of these agencies offered new opportunities for presidential leadership.

Franklin Roosevelt enlarged the president's role in economic affairs. On coming into office in the midst of the Great Depression, he initiated a series of measures to deal with the domestic crisis and persuaded Congress to enact them. He also maintained the posture of an international leader, maneuvering the country's entrance into World War II and participating in summit conferences to win the war and plan the peace. In addition, he made the critical decision to develop the atomic bomb.

Many observers mark the beginning of the modern presidency, characterized by presidential activism in a variety of policy-making roles, in the era of Franklin Roosevelt. His successors have institutionalized many of the practices that Roosevelt initiated or continued, and Congress has required others. America's expanding role in the world and the growth of government services since the New Deal have increased the president's prominence and also created new demands on the office. More recently, the vulnerability of the United States to terrorist attacks has contributed to both the public's psychological dependence on the president and the security responsibilities of the chief executive.

The president is often considered the most powerful person in the world, not because the formal authority of the office is greater than that of other national leaders (it clearly is not) but because the president sits atop a government that has more capacity to influence national and global events than that of any other nation.

Presidential Theories

The nineteenth century was an era of mostly forgettable presidents who did not dramatically affect the office, periodically interrupted by those who did (Jefferson, Jackson, Lincoln). Congress did not check Lincoln's assertion of power during the Civil War, although it did review and then approve it. After the war, however, the legislature reasserted its

In 1940, critics of FDR's decision to run for a third term insisted he was breaking a constitutional norm.

authority. Throughout the remainder of the nineteenth century, Congress, not the president, dominated the relationship between the branches. In fact, when Woodrow Wilson, then a professor of politics (and the only president to have a PhD), wrote a book on the American political system in the mid-1880s, he titled it, *Congressional Government*.

Wilson wrote at the end of an era. By the time he became chief executive, the president's roles in both foreign and domestic affairs had expanded (and Wilson revised his book). Demands for a more activist government had encouraged President William McKinley and, especially, President Theodore Roosevelt to work more closely and harmoniously with Congress in fashioning major policy initiatives.

Stewardship Doctrine

Theodore Roosevelt (1901–1909) and his successor William Howard Taft (1909–1913) articulated two very different theories of presidential authority. Roosevelt, often regarded as the first truly activist president who asserted a broad policy-making authority in foreign and domestic affairs, promoted what became known as the "stewardship theory" of the presidency. Writing in his autobiography after his political career had ended, Roosevelt argued that the president "was a steward of the people":

> I declined to adopt the view that what was imperatively necessary for the Nation could not be done by the President unless he could fund some specific authorization to do it. My belief was that it was not only his right but his duty to do anything that the needs of the Nation demanded unless such action was forbidden by the Constitution or by the laws. Under this interpretation of executive power I did and caused to be done many things not previously done by the President. . . . I acted for the common well-being for our people, when ever and in whatever manner was necessary, unless prevented by direct constitutional or legislative prohibition.[97]

Assuming an assertive posture in both foreign and domestic affairs, Roosevelt expanded the president's policy-making roles. He sent the navy halfway around the world (and then requested appropriations from Congress to return it home); he announced a corollary to the Monroe Doctrine, further involving the United States in hemispheric activities; he helped instigate a revolution in Colombia; and he quickly recognized the independence of insurgents on the isthmus of Panama and entered into an agreement with them to build a canal. He was the first president to travel outside the United States (to Mexico and Panama) and the first to help settle a war, for which he won the Nobel Peace Prize. Within the domestic sphere, Roosevelt busted trusts, crusaded for conservation, and mediated a major coal strike. He was also instrumental in pushing Congress to enact important legislation, including the Pure Food and Drug Act, the Meat Inspection Act, and the Hepburn Act regulating railroads.

Caretaker Doctrine

In contrast, William Howard Taft, Roosevelt's successor, expressed a much more restrained conception of executive authority, taking almost the precisely opposite position. Unlike Roosevelt, who argued the president can do anything that is not specifically prohibited, Taft, who took a faculty position at Yale Law School after leaving the presidency in 1913, wrote

> The true view of the Executive function is, as I conceive it, that the president can exercise no power which cannot be fairly and reasonably traced to some specific grant of power or justly implied and included within such express grant as proper and necessary to its exercise. Such specific grant must be either in the Federal Constitution or in an act of Congress passed in pursuance thereof. There is no undefined residuum of power which he can exercise because it seems to him to be in the public interest . . . his jurisdiction must be justified and vindicated by affirmative constitutional or statutory provision, or it does not exist.[98]

Taft took a different view when he was president, insisting that the "executive power" included a broad range of authority, including the right to compile a centralized presidential budget even when Congress passed a law specifically prohibiting him from doing so (Taft instructed his cabinet officials to ignore the law), and issued an executive order that had the effect of nullifying a law.[99] Justice Jackson highlighted the inconsistency between Taft's behavior as president and his later more restrained view of executive power, noting in his *Youngstown* concurrence that "a Hamilton may be matched against a Madison. Professor Taft is counterbalanced by Theodore Roosevelt. It even seems that President Taft cancels out Professor Taft."

Modern Views

Roosevelt's stewardship theory has prevailed. With the exception of the three Republican presidents of the 1920s (Harding, Coolidge, and Hoover), twentieth century occupants of the Oval Office have assumed active political and policy-making roles. Woodrow Wilson and Franklin Roosevelt, in particular, expanded Theodore Roosevelt's initiatives in international and domestic affairs. After World War II and the emergence of the United States as a global superpower, there was no alternative to an active presidency. Even presidents who tried to scale back the size of government, such as Reagan or Trump, still relied heavily on the aggressive use of presidential power to pursue their policy goals.

At times these doctrines go too far and are eventually repudiated. During the presidency of George W. Bush, a number of his advisors advanced an even broader view of presidential authority. Several key appointees in the Department of Justice (DOJ) were adherents of the "Unitary Presidency" theory, which in its strongest form argues that all executive authority is exercised by the president *alone*, to the point that no other institution—not Congress, not the courts—can restrict in any way what presidents may do within the ambit of their own authority, especially in foreign affairs.[100] After 9/11, some DOJ officials argued that the president could ignore federal statutes prohibiting torture of suspected terrorists and that it would unconstitutional for Congress to try to stop torture if the president determined it was necessary.[101]

These latter positions were extreme and were subsequently withdrawn by a later Assistant Attorney General in the Office of Legal Counsel who concluded that they were "legally flawed, tendentious in substance and tone, and overbroad" and written with an "unusual lack of care and sobriety in their legal analysis."[102]

The evolution of these different doctrines among presidents, as they extended from Jackson, to Lincoln, to Roosevelt, Taft, and Bush are tied to the underlying disputes about the proper role of the president in our constitutional system, and "the struggle between two conceptions of executive power: that it ought always to be subordinate to the supreme legislative power, and that it ought to be, within generous limits, autonomous and self-directing . . . Nor has this struggle ever entirely ceased, although on the whole it is the latter theory that has prospered."[103]

Jurisprudential Doctrines

When disagreements arise over presidential authority, it is often left to the courts to settle them. At times, these disputes pose crucial issues of major constitutional importance, and presidents sometimes lose, but judicial doctrines of executive power frequently work in the president's favor.

Judicial Deference

First, courts are frequently reluctant to order the president to act (or not act) out of deference to presidential determinations and actions. In other words, courts frequently begin with the assumption that a presidential action is valid when there are ambiguities, are reluctant to second-guess presidential reasoning, and will generally defer to executive branch interpretations of a statute. This deference is greater in foreign affairs and national security, in large part because courts acknowledge that presidents have greater expertise and information than judges. In January 2018, for example, the Supreme Court upheld Donald Trump's ban on travel from primarily Muslim countries, voting 5–4 that Congress had given the president the authority to set conditions for entry into the United States. The Court discounted statements by the president that suggested the ban was motivated by religious animosity, holding that the congressional delegations "[exude] deference to the president in every clause."[104]

Congressional Precedents

Second, the Supreme Court has ruled that some questions of presidential authority can be resolved by looking how Congress has responded to similar presidential actions. In simplest terms, if the president has exercised a particular power over a long period of time without congressional objection, it be read as a congressional *acceptance* that the president in fact has that power.

The most famous Supreme Court case that supports this notion is *United States v. Midwest Oil Co* (1915). The case arose out of a decision by President Taft to prohibit private oil drilling on government-owned lands, even though federal law explicitly permitted it. Taft issued a proclamation declaring the land off limits, and that was that. An oil company sued, arguing that Taft's proclamation had nullified a statute and thereby exceeded his constitutional authority.

But the Court held that the president had such authority, because there was a long tradition of similar presidential actions, and Congress had never objected. Because Congress had not objected, the Court reasoned, it must have agreed that such presidential actions were valid. In this decision, the Court established the "acquiescence doctrine," which accepted precedent itself as a basis of presidential authority:

> Both officers, law-makers, and citizens naturally adjust themselves to any long-continued action of the Executive Department—on the presumption that unauthorized acts would not have been allowed to be so often repeated as to crystallize into a regular practice. That presumption is not reasoning in a circle but the basis of a wise and quieting rule that in determining the meaning of a statute or the existence of a power, weight shall be given to the usage itself—even when the validity of the practice is the subject of investigation.[105]

Judicial Reticence

Third, the courts will sometimes decline to become involved at all. *Marbury v. Madison* is famous mostly for establishing the principle of judicial review (something that is not explicitly mentioned in the Constitution), but it also created the "political questions" doctrine, which puts some disputes beyond the court's reach, either because they are a matter for one branch or the other or because the Court lacks any standard for resolving them. In foreign policy disputes over presidential actions on treaties, use of military force, or even the definition of what a war is and when it begins and ends, the Supreme Court has refused to consider claims, leaving them entirely to the president and Congress.[106] This reticence works in the president's favor, since Congress is generally reacting to what a president has already done, and Court deference leaves the presidential act in place by default.

Institutional Capacity

The structure of the modern presidency also developed during Franklin Roosevelt's tenure. In 1939, FDR created the Executive Office of the President. Prior to that time, presidents had depended largely on their department heads for administration and advice. The rapid expansion of government during the New Deal stressed this advisory structure far beyond its capacity.

When Franklin Roosevelt took office and expanded the president's domestic policy role, he needed more information, more expertise, and more staff. At first, he depended on personnel provided by the executive departments, but when that did not prove satisfactory, he turned to a small group of experts to advise him on how to make the organizational structure of the executive more responsive to his needs. The group, headed by Louis Brownlow, a noted student of public administration, issued a report that urged the creation of a separate presidential office.[107] In 1939, Congress approved the act that established the Executive Office of the President (EOP). Today, the approximately dozen elements of the Executive Office of the President employ a combined staff of about 1,800 and provide the president with a staff directly responsive to his interests. This staff extends to every aspect of presidential administration: national security, budgets, legal advice, policy coordination, scheduling, dealing with Congress, press relations and communications, political and strategic advice; all enhance the president's reach and ability to monitor, direct, and assimilate information from executive branch agencies.

The president's closest aides are located in the White House Office. Having no constitutional or statutory authority of their own, their influence is dependent on their access to the president. The White House Office is also flexible, able to accommodate changing needs by adding political and policy advisors, communications aides, and others as demands for their services arise.

Whereas the White House functioned as a personal extension of the president, the Bureau of the Budget (later the Office of Management and Budget) became an institutional extension of the presidency. It coordinates key aspects of policy making in the departments and agencies, imposing a presidential perspective on the executive branch in the process. More broadly, presidential policy processes have become institutionalized. Officials have developed mechanisms for preparing the budget, formulating a legislative program, building support in Congress, advising the president whether to sign or veto legislation, and evaluate proposed regulations; succeeding administrations have continued these processes over time. Chapter 8 discusses these structures in more detail.

Unilateral Action

The presidential actions we have seen throughout this chapter follow a pattern. Presidents, beginning with Washington, have acted to fill in constitutional silences and ambiguities, claimed the authority to make policy without any explicit constitutional authorization, wielded implied powers, and asserted control of government. Through a combination of precedent, judicial acceptance of presidential authority, and the growth of government, presidents became much more powerful.

A key element of that growth occurred through *unilateral action*, or the ability to act alone, solely on the basis of presidential authority. Washington's Neutrality Proclamation, the Louisiana Purchase, and Lincoln's actions at the beginning of the Civil War are instances where presidents took the initiative to act, without waiting for congressional approval. Much of the time Congress eventually ratified these actions retroactively, but in other instances presidents never obtained explicit congressional approval or acted in the face of legislative opposition.

The president, by virtue of the office's unitary character, is able to act quickly, unlike Congress, which is not always in session, requires majorities in order to act, and is frequently riven by partisan and sectional disputes that make decisive action difficult. Because Congress often has difficulty reaching agreement and because the courts are deferential to executive action, the power to act unilaterally comes with a vital presidential advantage: even when the authority of the president to do something is ambiguous, the president can still act first and leave it up to Congress or the courts to respond. Unilateral action is a form of Hamilton's energy in the executive, and he identified the advantages of the first move: "Decision, activity, secrecy, and dispatch will generally characterize the proceedings of one man, in a much more eminent degree than the proceedings of any greater number."[108]

Many of the unilateral actions described in this chapter follow this pattern. At the time they occurred, the Neutrality Proclamation, the Louisiana Purchase, and Tyler's insistence that he became *president* upon the death of William Henry Harrison (instead of "acting president") pushed executive power beyond what was at the time considered valid. But the decisions stood, in large part because opponents could not generate sufficient support to counteract them. They had the effect of filling in gaps and ambiguities of constitutional language and establishing precedent for future acts. Other examples followed a similar pattern, with presidents acting and their decisions usually standing: Lincoln's Emancipation Proclamation, Roosevelt's establishment of the Executive Office of the President, Truman desegregating the armed forces, Kennedy creating the Peace Corps, Reagan instituting a new system for evaluating the cost-effectiveness of regulations.

Some unilateral action occurs when Congress delegates authority to the president, such as the emergency authorities delegated via the National Emergencies Act (described earlier in this chapter). Another example is tariffs, or duties imposed on imports. Although the Constitution explicitly gives Congress the power to set tariffs,[109] Congress gave the president limited authority to act in its stead in 1934, "hoping that the president would pursue a trade agenda in the interest of both the domestic economy and foreign policy."[110] In general, the president must find that imports hurt US industry in order to impose tariffs. In 1977, Congress also gave the president discretion to respond to economic emergencies that constitute an "unusual and extraordinary threat," via the International Economic Emergencies Powers Act (IEEPA).[111]

Limits

In 2012 and 2014, Barack Obama established a new immigration enforcement policy that suspending removal proceedings for certain noncitizens who were illegally present in the United States. Relying on *prosecutorial discretion*, or the executive power to determine who will be investigated and prosecuting for breaking the law, Obama declared that those who were brought here as children illegally and met certain conditions would not be subject to deportation proceedings (a program called Deferred Action Against Childhood Arrivals, or DACA).[112] In 2014, these protections were extended to undocumented immigrants whose children were US citizens or who qualified under DACA for deferred prosecution (called Deferred Action against Parents of Americans and Lawful Permanent Residents, or DAPA).[113] Critics attacked what they saw as an unconstitutional nullification of immigration law by a president who simply refused to enforce it in violation of his "take care" duty, and who used unilateral action to undermine clear congressional intent. A federal court blocked DAPA, and when the Supreme Court declined to overturn that decision, the Obama Administration suspended the program.[114]

In 2001, George W. Bush established a military tribunal process to try suspected terrorists outside of the federal judiciary. Detainees would be tried in military courts, using rules different from what is permitted in civilian criminal trials and without the ability to appeal convictions or challenge their detentions. In a series of landmark decisions, the Supreme Court denied the president the authority to cut off detainees' access to the courts and required more robust protection of constitutional rights.[115] Congress weighed in as well, prohibiting the use of coercive interrogation techniques.

In the first two years of his term, Trump experienced an unprecedented string of court losses, as many of his unilateral actions—from the use of emergency powers to violations of the Administrative Procedure Act, a 1946 law that imposes requirements on agency rule making—were overturned by lower federal courts. The Supreme Court might reverse these lower court decisions, as it did for the immigration ban that lower courts rejected.[116] But the consistency of the legal setbacks—an analysis found that the Trump Administration lost 93 percent of the lawsuits filed against its deregulatory actions between 2017 and 2019—suggests that courts will insist on adherence to basic procedural and administrative law requirements, even for presidential actions.[117]

These unilateral actions, and many hundreds of others, began as a presidential decision based on a claim of constitutional or statutory authority. They frequently provoked a backlash from critics who insist that when unilateral actions are unconstitutional, they constitute an abuse of power. Some of the acts, particularly the steel seizure, military tribunals, elements of Obama's immigration enforcement policy, and some of Trump's unilateral actions, were blocked by the courts. But many were not, and some of the lower court decisions were temporary.

Incentives to Act

The ability to act unilaterally is intertwined with the incentive to do so. A presidents is uniquely positioned, as the country's only nationally elected official, to exert broad influence over government, and the unitary nature of the office means that presidents are far less able than legislators to escape blame for policy failures. "Unlike legislators, presidents are held responsible by the public for virtually every aspect of national performance. When the economy declines, an agency falters, or a social problem goes unaddressed, it is the president who gets the blame, and whose popularity and historical legacy are on the line. All presidents are aware of this, and they respond by trying to build an institutional capacity for effective governance."[118]

An important result from this argument is that all presidents will engage in unilateral action to align government policy with their own preferences. Thomas Jefferson, who believed in a small central government, did so, as did Abraham Lincoln and FDR. Jimmy Carter and Ronald Regan, Bill Clinton and George W. Bush, and Barak Obama and Donald Trump did as well, even though their policy preferences were all very different. The structure of the presidency and incentives that shape presidential behavior provide presidents with the motive and opportunity to take unilateral action to put their stamp on policy and government outputs.

Trump was particularly critical of Obama's use of executive orders and other forms of unilateral action during the 2016 campaign, claiming "right now, Obama goes around signing executive orders. He can't even get along with the Democrats, and he goes around signing all of these executive orders. It's a basic disaster. You can't do it."[119] As president, though, Trump highlighted the number of executive orders he had signed in arguing that his hundred days had been historically productive, signing more executive orders (30) than any president since Franklin Roosevelt.[120] Trump's inconsistency is typical of presidents, who (going back to Jefferson) view executive power quite differently once they are in office.

THE ULTIMATE CHECK: IMPEACHMENT AND REMOVAL

Alexander Hamilton was confident that the electoral college would prevent a corrupt person from being chosen president.[121] That optimism did not answer the question of what to do if a president failed to carry out the duties of office, abused executive powers, acted in a corrupt fashion once in office, or served as an agent of a foreign power. Most of the Framers agreed on the need for some way to remove a president under what Madison called a "nightmare scenario."[122] The result was an impeachment and removal process divided between the House and Senate. Article II, section 4, provides that "The President, Vice President and all civil officers of the United States, shall be removed from office for impeachment for, and conviction of, treason, bribery, or other high crimes and misdemeanors." The House has the sole power of impeachment—the official act of bringing charges against a president—and the Senate then conducts a trial, removing the president by a 2/3 vote.[123]

The definition of treason and bribery may be evident enough (treason, in fact, is the only criminal offense defined in the Constitution). What constitutes "other high crimes and misdemeanors" is far less apparent, and Congress has the "last word in defining what constitutes an impeachable offense."[124] No matter how deeply one digs into the historical record or the debates of the constitutional convention, no clear answer emerges: there was no debate at all at the Constitutional Convention over the meaning of "high crimes and misdemeanors."[125] Impeachable offenses go beyond criminal violations and include acts that threaten the integrity of the governing process or abuse the powers of office. At the same time, impeaching a president *solely* for violating the law is too broad, since some presidents find themselves on the wrong side of a federal court decision holding that they have gone beyond the office's constitutional or statutory powers. A criminal act or violation of the law, then, is neither a sufficient nor a necessary condition for impeachment.

If there is a consensus on the question of what constitutes an impeachable offense, it is that impeachment is a momentous step that challenges core constitutional values, balancing the risk that the impeachment power might be misused against "[denying] the nation any lawful means of swiftly removing a disastrous leader."[126] It is, in the end, a question Congress determines by political deliberation.

The Articles of Impeachment against Andrew Johnson charged him not only with violating the Tenure in Office Act (which attempted to restrict his firing members of his cabinet) but also of attempting to "bring into disgrace, ridicule, hatred, contempt and reproach the Congress of the United States . . . and to excite the odium and resentment of all the good people of the United States against Congress" (Article X).[127] All of this language, however, obscured the true reason for Johnson's impeachment (which some insist would have made a much stronger case for his removal): his abysmal record in handling Reconstruction.[128] The Senate fell a single vote shy of convicting and removing Johnson from office.

In 1974, the House Judiciary Committee approved articles of impeachment against Richard Nixon, citing obstruction of justice, perjury, illegally using law enforcement and intelligence agencies to violate the rights of his political opponents, and refusing to comply with congressional subpoenas. Nixon resigned before the House took further action.[129] In 1998, the House impeached Bill Clinton for perjury and obstruction of justice regarding his affair with Monica Lewinsky; the Senate fell far short of the two-thirds majority required to convict.[130]

You can read more about the Johnson, Nixon, and Clinton cases in Appendix B, "Nonelectoral Succession, Removal, and Tenure".

In 2019, some House Democrats pushed for an impeachment investigation of Donald Trump, arguing it was justified by the results of the Mueller investigation and the president's repeated refusals to obey congressional subpoenas and demands for documents.[131] House Speaker Nancy Pelosi had resisted pressure to support those proceedings, opting for less drastic congressional investigations. This changed in September 2019, after new allegations that the president was using his office to solicit foreign interference in the 2020 election.[132] A whistleblower claimed that Trump used military aid to pressure Ukraine to investigate former Vice President Joe Biden, one of the leading contenders for the Democratic presidential nomination. Pelosi announced that the House would begin a formal impeachment inquiry with several House committees looking into this claim, investigating whether Trump had similar conversations with other foreign leaders, and whether they White House had moved transcripts of this and other phone calls to a highly classified National Security Council computer system designed for highly classified intelligence information (and not routine diplomatic phone calls) in an attempt to hide evidence of the conversations.[133]

WAR POWERS

The story so far is one of a steady growth in presidential power over the last century, as increased institutional capacity, government growth, and evolving doctrines all expanded the president's ability to shape outcomes and affect policy.

In 1973, historian Arthur Schlesinger argued in *The Imperial Presidency* that the president had become far too powerful, validating fears that the executive had turned into the very thing the framers feared: an unaccountable office, operating without constitutional checks, not subject to any restraints.[134] Schlesinger was reacting not only to Watergate, a web of criminal activities and obstruction of justice in which the famous burglary of Democratic National Committee headquarters was only the most visible strand, but also to Lyndon Johnson's and Richard Nixon's escalation of the Vietnam War without congressional permission, presidential secrecy, and what amounted to total functional control of foreign policy. Watergate was just latest example of a long pattern of executive aggrandizement in which presidents expanded their powers, and neither Congress nor the courts were willing or able to stop them.

Few areas of constitutional authority have been seen more growth in presidential power, and generated more controversy, than war powers—the authority to commit US military forces and initiate military action—and there is no policy area that has seen such a large growth in the presidential ability to dictate national security policy. Louis Fisher, a longtime Congressional Research Service scholar, argues that presidential dominance over the use of force vastly exceeds anything the framers intended and the Constitution justifies. The result, in his view, is a system in which the president has the ability to initiate military action anywhere, at any time, for any purpose, with Congress unable to stop it and the courts refusing to referee. Congress's explicit constitutional authority to declare war and regulate the armed forces is thereby rendered meaningless.[135]

Disputes over the war power stem from the manner in which the Constitution splits authority. Congress has the constitutional power to "raise and support armies . . . provide and maintain a navy . . . make rules for the regulation of land and naval forces," and, most notably, "to declare war."[136] The president is "commander in chief of the Army and Navy of the United States."[137] Corwin called the overall allocation of foreign affairs powers an "invitation to struggle" between Congress and the president shaped through precedent, mostly to the benefit of the president.[138]

The origins of the constitutional language are well known. The framers intended that the president not have a general war-making power, because that was reminiscent of the royal prerogatives from which the framers were distancing themselves. To make it more difficult for the country to go to war, Congress was given the power of war and peace. The early drafts of the Constitution gave Congress the power to *make* war, which was changed to *declare* war to give the president the authority to repel sudden attacks in an emergency.[139] The contours were seemingly clear, with Congress making decisions about when to engage in conflict and the president given control of the military once they had been employed in a war-fighting capacity.

But over time, presidents began blurring the distinction between declared wars and other uses of military power, by employing military force in more limited capacities. "At first narrowly confined" to the framer's intent, writes Fisher, "the scope of presidential action gradually widened."[140] Some of this was a function of necessity, such as Lincoln's wartime actions, but presidential war powers were increasingly recognized by the Courts[141] and strengthened by the president's growing ability to shape public opinion in support of these missions.

By the middle of the twentieth century, the "use of force" had been sufficiently divorced from "declared wars" that the president could, as commander in chief, order the military to engage in attacks without any congressional approval. Presidents have relied on extraconstitutional authorities, including international law, the United Nations, and humanitarian emergencies as justification for military force. Although there is no authoritative count covering all years since 1789, one source identified 383 instances of presidential uses of military force without advance congressional approval between 1945 and 2000.[142]

Truman ordered US troops into the Korean War in 1950 without waiting for congressional approval (in fact, he did not even consult congressional leaders before committing troops and never did ask for approval), citing the United Nations as authority. Lyndon Johnson expanded US troop presence in Vietnam, again without a formal declaration of war. George H.W. Bush deployed hundreds of thousands of US troops in the Middle East in 1990 in response to Iraqi President Saddam Hussein's invasion of Kuwait. Although the attack did not begin until Congress had authorized hostilities, Bush based the troops and assembled an international coalition to fight well before Congress had deliberated. In April 2017, Donald Trump ordered a strike on an air base in Syria, launching fifty-nine cruise missiles in retaliation for Bashar Al Assad's use of chemical weapons against Syrian civilians.[143]

A key presidential advantage in the use of force is that a presidential order to launch an attack will normally be carried out quickly (with "dispatch"), putting Congress in a reactive stance. The president issues the order, and it many cases the mission will be over long before Congress could even convene, much less weigh in.

Congress attempted to restore its authority with the War Powers Resolution, enacted over Nixon's veto in 1973.[144] The law requires the president to withdraw troops within sixty days in any deployment where hostilities had occurred or were imminent, unless Congress had specifically approved that deployment. It also requires the president to consult with Congress "in every possible instance" prior to committing US troops and to report all troop commitments to Congress.

Every president has considered the law an unconstitutional infringement on the president's Commander in Chief authority. It has done little to slow the pace of presidential uses of force, and has never been invoked to require the president to withdraw troops at the sixty-day deadline. Presidents have reported troop commitments as required by the Act but have cited provisions that do not start the sixty-day clock.[145]

In April 2019, Congress passed a joint resolution requiring Trump to end US involvement in a conflict in Yemen, the first time Congress had taken such an action under the Act.[146] The president vetoed it, and the Senate failed to override.[147]

The War Powers Resolution is considered the high-water mark of congressional efforts to restore Congress' role in the use of military force. However, it has done little to constrain presidents. Other tools of congressional control, particularly the power of the purse, are similarly inefficient as they require affirmative legislative action which will be subject to a presidential veto.

CONCLUSION

The argument laid out in this chapter is that the explicit constitutional language in Article II does not—and cannot—resolve every question about executive power, explain why modern presidents are so vastly more powerful than their predecessors, or account for the gap between powers and expectations. Explaining that growth, and interpreting the practical meaning of constitutional warrants requires careful analysis of structure and practice, as well as recognition of what many scholars have identified as the fundamental tensions and ambiguities of executive power. Presidential authority derives from constitutional text, to be sure, but it also derives from historical practice, institutional capabilities, expectations, and ongoing struggle among the coordinate branches of national government about the nature of government power and their own roles in our constitutional system.

Joseph Story, a prominent nineteenth-century legal scholar, professor at Harvard Law School, and a Supreme Court Justice, wrote in his classic work on the Constitution:

> What is the best constitution for the executive department, and what are the powers, with which it should be entrusted, are problems among the most important, and probably the most difficult to be satisfactorily solved, of all, which are involved in the theory of free governments.[148]

The problems Story noted confronted the framers: how to construct an executive that was both powerful and accountable, energetic and democratic, independent but constrained by the rule of law. These are also the problems Justice Jackson addressed in 1952, and the unresolved problems occupying contemporary observers.

Given the lack of clear definitions of executive authority, and the inability of even the framers to specify what it is or how far it extends, things can hardly be otherwise. But recognizing that ambiguities and gaps exist does not mean that there are no working definitions or limits to executive power. It does mean, however, that the answers will often be unclear and will emerge from a political and legal process that is a function of context, stakes, and contested theories of power.

The contradictions of executive power continue to define the presidency. As the historian Jeremi Suri describes it, the president occupies a position that is unparalleled in its ability to bring to bear all of the authority that government has to offer: vast military power, a tremendous institutional capacity, and doctrines that justify an expansive reach of presidential action. At the same time, those powers and authorities are insufficient to effectively carry out the duties of the office or meet public expectations.

> In its extremes of power and responsibility, the US presidency is the most talked about and least understood office in the world. Presidents are elected to accomplish big things, but they spend most of their time focusing on problems that do not serve, and frequently contradict, their larger agenda. Presidents command the most powerful military in the world, but they repeatedly confront the frustrating limits of what they can achieve by force. . . . Presidential power is awesome and pathetic at the same time.[149]

Under these circumstances, the Framer's apparent strategy of using Article II to specify some general rules of structure, and rely on subsequent practice and disputes to flesh out the details of executive power, may have been the only real option in creating an office that had never existed before and that continues to pose challenges to our understanding of government power and the nature of constitutional limits.

DISCUSSION QUESTIONS

1. Democrats tend to be suspicious of executive power when the president is a Republican and less concerned about it when the president is a Democrat. The pattern is reversed for Republicans, who dislike executive power when the president is a Democrat but largely support it with a GOP White House. Donald Trump was highly critical of Obama's use of executive orders to make policy but pointed to his own use of unilateral action as evidence of policy effectiveness. To what degree are disputes over the legality of presidential action merely a proxy for disputes over policy and partisanship?

2. What would be the likely reaction to a president who adopted Taft's "caretaker" theory of the presidency, announcing that no action would be taken unless it was explicitly authorized by clear constitutional language? Consider the specific case of a president who announced that no military action or attacks would take place without congressional approval. Do you think the public would accept this as a welcome departure from presidents aggressively pushing the limits of action? Or do you think the public would view it as an abdication of presidential responsibility and a justification for not doing anything?

3. Given that the constitutional language on presidential authority has not changed since 1787, while the nature of the job has changed so dramatically, is it time to consider revising the language in Article II?

WEB EXERCISES

1. Go to the US Department of Justice Office of Legal Counsel Opinions page (https://www.justice.gov/olc/opinions). This is where DOJ attorneys publish memoranda on the legality of presidential actions. How long does it take you to find an opinion that concludes the president may ignore a statute or demand for action that the OLC considers unconstitutional?
2. The Federalist Papers nos. 67–77 consist of Alexander Hamilton's views of the presidency and executive power. These essays are available here: https://www.congress.gov/resources/display/content/The+Federalist+Papers. Can you identify examples where Hamilton's theory of executive power have become obsolete? How much of his analysis is applicable to the modern presidency?
3. Has Donald Trump's use of unilateral action—executive orders, memoranda, etc.—differed from his predecessors' use? The American Presidency Project tracks unliteral actions: https://www.presidency.ucsb.edu/documents/presidential-documents-archive-guidebook/executive-orders-jq-adams-1826-trump-2018. Do the raw numbers give us an accurate picture of how presidents wield the authority of the office? If not, what else do we need to know?

SELECTED READINGS

Belco, Michelle, and Brandon Rottinghaus. *The Dual Executive: Unilateral Orders in a Separated and Shared Power System*. Stanford: Stanford University Press, 2017.

Bessette, Joseph M., and Jeffrey K. Tulis. *The Constitutional Presidency*. Baltimore: Johns Hopkins University Press, 2009.

Corwin, Edward S. *The President: Office and Powers, 1787–1957*. New York: New York University Press, 1957.

Fisher, Louis. *Presidential War Power*, 3rd ed. Lawrence: University Press of Kansas, 2013.

Mayer, Kenneth R. *With the Stroke of a Pen: Executive orders and Presidential Power*. Princeton: Princeton University Press, 2001.

Rozell, Mark J. *Executive Privilege: Presidential Power, Secrecy, and Accountability*, 2nd ed. Lawrence: University Press of Kansas, 2002.

Rudalevige, Andrew. *The New Imperial Presidency: Renewing Presidential Power after Watergate*. Ann Arbor: University of Michigan Press, 2006.

Shane, Peter M. *Madison's Nightmare: How Executive Power Threatens American Democracy*. Chicago: University of Chicago Press, 2009.

Suri, Jeremi. *The Impossible Presidency: The Rise and Fall of America's Highest Office*. New York: Basic Books, 2017.

Thach, Charles C. *The Creation of the American Presidency: A Study in Constitutional History*. Baltimore: Johns Hopkins University Press, 1923.

Tribe, Lawrence and Joshua Matz. *To End a Presidency: The Power of Impeachment*. New York: Basic Books, 2018.

3

The Nomination Process

Donald Trump celebrates his victory in the New Hampshire primary.

Rick Friedman/Polaris/Newscom

Presidential elections occur in two phases. In the first, political parties choose a nominee who will run under the party label. In the second, the nominees (in practice, the Democratic and Republican tickets) run against each other. Both require considerable time, money, and effort and require candidates to get organized years before the election process starts.

The extended quest for the nomination heightens public expectations but frequently proves divisive, accentuating intraparty factions that the successful nominee must try to unify. The campaign encourages personality politics by focusing on the candidates' qualifications and experience; a theatrical style of presentation designed to energize as it informs; a barrage of media advertising on television, radio, and online; and news coverage that emphasizes the contest over public policy. The tougher the competition within the nomination process, the greater the likelihood that the candidates will engage in negative campaigning, highlighting their opponents' undesirable qualities and the most controversial policy stands they take. This negativism often creates cynicism within the party and the electorate, which the winning candidate and party must overcome if they are to govern successfully.

The evolution of the nomination process is largely a story of managing these demands and responding to changing notions of democratic legitimacy. New processes and strategies have been a function of necessity, capabilities, demands from within the parties, and, of course, actual election success. The current system began in the 1970s, but both parties have continually tweaked the rules since, a process that continues today.

THE EVOLUTION OF THE NOMINATING SYSTEM

When the Framers created the presidential election process, they did not devote any attention to the question of narrowing down the pool of potential presidents in the manner of the modern primary system. The reason is simple: they did not envision a government based on political parties. With no political parties, there was no need for a nomination process, no need for president-vice president combinations, and no distinction between the selection process (who would be considered for the office) and the election process (who was chosen). The delegates to the Constitutional Convention assumed that potential presidential and vice presidential candidates would all be well qualified, with no need for screening, winnowing, or campaigning.

However, political parties emerged almost immediately as competing factions coalesced around disagreements over federal government powers. The original electoral college design would not survive this development. Once political parties arose, the notion of the electoral college making an independent judgment was constrained by the parties' desire to choose nominees whose views were consistent with their own. Such a choice required a nomination process, to present a presidential and vice presidential slate to the electoral college.

When Washington declined to stand for a third term in 1796, rival blocs of congressional party leaders met informally to promote their preferred candidates (John Adams for the Federalists, Jefferson for the Republicans).[1] In 1800, with Congress split along partisan lines, members of each party advanced presidential and vice presidential candidates as a set (Adams and Charles Pinckney for the Federalists, Jefferson and Aaron Burr for the Democratic-Republicans).

For the next few decades, congressional caucuses comprised of legislators from each party selected most presidential tickets. This system was, in theory, efficient (since members of Congress were already together in Washington, DC), feasible (as it did not require travel or communication over long distances), and politically expedient (since a nominee who had the support of congressional members from a state was likely to get votes from electors chosen in that state). In practice, it was less than ideal. Allowing members of Congress to choose whom the electors would consider ran up against the Framers' concern about presidential independence from the legislature. Critics argued that it was unrepresentative, secretive, and unconstitutional, giving it the pejorative nickname "King Caucus."

The caucus process also proved increasingly inefficient, with legislators frequently absent and even attacking its legitimacy. It also failed to produce winning candidates: In 1824, a fracture in the Jeffersonian Democratic-Republican Party led to four separate party tickets, with Andrew Jackson and John Quincy Adams ignoring the caucuses to run on their own.[2] Although Jackson won both the popular and electoral college vote, his lack of an outright majority threw election into the House, which selected Adams.

The fracture of 1824 proved the death-knell of the caucus system. State party organizations were becoming more influential in the nomination process, and candidates solicited their support directly. Doing so helped candidates extend their appeal beyond Washington, DC. The broadening of political support meant that caucuses no longer served a legitimating function or as a way of unifying national parties. They were replaced by a more decentralized mode of nomination, one that was consistent with the increasingly sectional composition of the parties and better able to unite the parties for the general election: national nominating conventions.

The Anti-Masons, a small but active third party, held the first convention in 1831, with delegates from state-level party subsidiaries choosing its nominees. In 1832, the Democratic Party—they had dropped "Republican" from the name—followed suit with a nominating convention of its own. Thereafter, party conventions became the dominant method of selecting nominees.

Delegates from state party organizations, invariably chosen by party "bosses" for their loyalty, assembled at a national convention where they set party platforms and chose presidential nominees. Conventions provided a mechanism for negotiating agreements and mobilizing support. By brokering interests, conventions helped unite conglomerations of state party organizations into a national coalition for the general election. The convention system also buttressed the position of state party leaders and gave them control over their organizations.

By the late nineteenth century, the convention process was showing signs of strain amid demands for broader rank-and-file participation. The "smoke-filled room" conjured images of party bosses deciding among themselves who would win the nomination, with little regard for what the party members wanted. The corruption of party machines, typified by George Washington Plunkitt of Tammany Hall, the archetype of a crooked but powerful party boss,[3] prompted reform efforts to reduce their power.

At the beginning of the twentieth century, several states changed their mode of selection to primary elections to permit greater public participation. Between 1905 and 1916, twenty-five states enacted some form of popular election of delegates to national conventions, with some states allowing the electorate to vote for "instructions" about whom delegates were expected to support.[4] This movement, however, was short-lived. Low voter turnout, the costs of holding elections, and opposition from party leaders to a process that reduced their clout persuaded several states to make their primaries advisory only—or even discontinue them entirely. The number of primaries declined after World War I, as did the percentage of delegates selected in them.

The impact of primaries was further muted because state party leaders still controlled most delegations attending nominating conventions. Primaries were an opportunity for candidates to demonstrate public support to party leaders, rather than a mechanism for amassing delegates. Running in too many of them was a sign of weakness, indicating that a candidate lacked both national recognition and elite support. The rules in many states did not translate primary victories into delegate wins.[5] In 1952, Tennessee Senator Estes Kefauver won twelve of the fifteen Democratic primaries but still lost the nomination to Illinois Governor Adlai Stevenson.[6]

The growth of television in the 1950s presented new opportunities for candidates to demonstrate their popular appeal and go around party leaders. Dwight

D. Eisenhower (1952), John F. Kennedy (1960), and Richard M. Nixon (1968) used this new medium to overcome doubts that a general, a Catholic, or a once-defeated presidential candidate could be elected president. The success of their campaigns generated public pressure to make nomination processes more participatory.

These forces reached a peak in 1968.[7] That year, President Lyndon Johnson dropped out of the race after barely defeating Minnesota Senate Eugene McCarthy in the New Hampshire primary. When Vice President Hubert Humphrey entered the race with the support of Democratic party leaders, it was too late to appear on the ballots of any remaining primaries. McCarthy and Robert Kennedy (who entered the race just before Johnson dropped out) continued to rack up primary wins. The nomination battle had become a referendum on the Vietnam War, a fight between establishment choice Humphrey and renegade McCarthy.

The 1968 convention in Chicago was a disaster for the Democrats. Humphrey was nominated, demonstrating that party leaders could select whomever they wanted regardless of what Democratic voters thought. Open disputes on the convention floor, platform fights, and Chicago police beating antiwar protesters in the streets showed a party in disarray. The combination of party fracture, convention conflict, anti-war sentiment, and massive street protests proved devastating, with everything broadcast live to a nationwide audience. Humphrey never recovered from the convention debacle and went on to lose narrowly to Richard Nixon in the general election.

In the midst of the convention chaos, delegates called for a review of party nomination rules. It seemed to be a technicality, but it led to "the greatest systematic change in presidential nomination procedures in all of American history."[8]

The reforms, recommended by the ensuing McGovern-Fraser Commission[9] stripped party officials of control over who the delegates were or which candidate they supported; that would be determined by voting, in either primary elections or local party meetings (caucuses) open to public participation. Candidates would win the nomination by appealing to voters over a long series of elections and caucuses. The new rules increased the percentage of delegates selected in binding contests from 49 percent in 1968 to 81 percent in 1980 for the Democrats, and a similar increase for Republicans.[10]

Opening the nomination process to broad participation, however, did not resolve the underlying question of how to nominate a candidate who has the support of the party and also who can win the general election. One of the justifications for party leaders controlling the process was that it would prevent an ideologically extreme candidate from winning the nomination; this was a lesson the Republican party took from 1964, when Arizona Senator Barry Goldwater secured the nomination through careful grassroots organization, only to fight a portrayal as an extremist and lose the election in a landslide to Lyndon Johnson.[11]

THE NOMINATION SYSTEM TODAY

Candidates seeking a major party nomination run in a series of elections and caucuses around the country that occur between (roughly) January and June of an election year. The modern nomination process has led to more primary contests, more candidates running in them, and more appeals to wider groups of voters. However, the system has also contributed to unequal influence among the states (states with earlier elections have more say in weeding out candidates), factionalism within parties, and advantages for candidates with more name recognition and financial resources. The modern primary process has also become one of continuous tinkering, as the parties adjust their rules in response to the demands of coalitions within the party and to electoral defeat.

Primaries and Caucuses

Most states have chosen to select delegates to the national convention in presidential primaries. In these elections, voters go to the polls and cast ballots just as they do in the general elections held in November. Some states (Iowa, most notably) use a caucus system to select delegates, in which voters record their preferences in meetings held around the state. Primaries are more like the general election and, especially in large states, they require large-scale media spending and mobilization efforts. In caucus states, voters must show up at a fixed time and attend an open meeting lasting several hours to cast a vote, and they often vote publicly rather than by secret ballot. Caucuses test candidates' ability to organize and are a measure of the intensity of their supporters. Caucuses may also give more influence to activists, preserving their role as a possible counterweight to candidates with more traditional bases of support.

Because attending a caucus requires greater time commitment than voting in a primary election, participation is much lower than voter turnout in primaries. Except for Iowa, where intense media coverage of the first major contest of the season usually boosts turnout to about 20 percent, only about 5 percent of the voting age population shows up for caucuses. Overall, turnout in presidential primaries is about 25 percent, although it varies from state to state; in contrast, turnout in general elections has been about 55 percent in the past few presidential elections.

Some states changed their rules for 2020. At least seven states that held caucuses to select delegates in 2016 have shifted to primaries (Alaska, Colorado, Idaho, Minnesota, Nebraska, Utah, and Washington) . The Iowa Democratic Party proposed new rules for its caucus in response to concerns about low participation and the time required to count the votes. The intent was to allow Iowa voters to register their preferences by phone in "virtual" caucuses held during the week preceding the actual caucus, giving voters who cannot attend the caucus meetings an opportunity to take part.[12] When national Democratic Party officials concluded that phone voting was insecure and vulnerable to hacking, the plans for remote participation were abandoned.[13]

Allocating Delegates

Parties set the rules and formulas that award delegates to candidates based on the results in state contests. The Supreme Court has held that the parties have rights to determine their own internal rules, and they may either refuse to seat convention delegations from states that violate those rules or reduce the size of offending state delegations.[14]

Each party determines how many delegates are at stake nationwide and how many are allocated to each state. In 2020, the Republican nomination contest will have 2,550 delegates (with 1,276 needed to win the nomination), and the Democratic contest will have 4,532 (with 2,267 needed to win). Both parties set state delegation size based on population and the overall support the party has within the state. The number of Republican delegates from each state is adjusted according to the number of Republican elected state and federal officeholders in the state. The Democratic

Party adjusts delegate allocations based on the presidential vote in the past three election cycles.[15]

The parties differ in how election results translate into delegate allocations for each candidate: Democratic rules prohibit winner-take-all elections, where the candidate finishing first wins all of a state's delegates (whether they received 80 percent or 30 percent of the vote), while Republican rules allow them in later stages. Winner-take-all elections give the candidate with the most votes a huge boost in delegates awarded and usually reduce the time it takes for a candidate to clinch the nomination by amassing a majority of a party's delegates. But winner-take-all rules may also backfire by exaggerating delegate counts for a candidate who wins narrowly or who wins with less than 50 percent of the vote in a multi-candidate race. Proportional allocation rules result in delegate allocations more consistent with the actual vote shares but can also drag out the process.

The Caucus and Primary Calendar

Although political parties shape their own decision rules, state laws control election processes. When state legislatures enact primary elections or caucus procedures, the laws usually apply to both major parties; as a result, Republican and Democratic Party practices tend to move in parallel.[16]

States are free to choose the date on which they hold their primaries or caucuses, although party rules can set permissible windows. In 2008, both Michigan and Florida moved their presidential primaries to January, outside the window established by both parties. In response, the Republicans cut each state's delegation by half, and the Democrats cut the delegations to zero (although the party later restored half of each delegation). Both states moved their primaries back into the permissible window in 2012.

Iowa is the opening contest, holding a caucus in either January or February. The New Hampshire primary is next. Although candidates do not have to win Iowa and New Hampshire to gain the nomination, doing poorly in both (by finishing out of the top three, as a rule) will almost always doom a campaign. These early contests serve a crucial role in narrowing the field, so candidates begin their campaigns many months—often a year or more—before the primary season starts.

States that hold their contests first have outsize influence, as the results establish frontrunners, narrow the field, and generate buzz and momentum as candidates head into the rest of the schedule. With so much attention paid to the early contests, more states have moved their primaries up. In 2016, 56 percent of Democratic and 65 percent of Republican delegates were chosen by the end of March. In 2020, 70 percent of Democratic and 69 percent of Republican delegates will be chosen by then.[17]

Between 1972 and 1992, California held its presidential primary at the beginning of June, usually well after the races had been decided. Even though it was the most populous state with the largest delegation, it played little role in determining who won either party's nomination. Because of this lack of influence, a state law moved the date to the beginning of March starting in 2000, and then to early February in 2008. But the long gap between an early primary and the November general election, and the costs of running a separate presidential primary, prompted legislators to move the presidential primary back to June 2012 to align it with primaries for state offices. However, the countervailing concern about a lack of influence has again proven decisive, and California moved its primary back to early March in 2020.

Frontloading forces candidates to begin their quest for their party's nomination earlier and earlier to raise money, gain media attention, and set up their campaign organizations. A compressed, frontloaded calendar benefits better-known, -financed, and -organized candidates, because there is less time for unknown candidates to break through, create momentum, and be taken seriously.

In an effort to leverage early-stage influence, a number of states hold their contests at the same time in early March, on a day dubbed "Super Tuesday" (in 2020 it will take place on March 3). Many of these states are in the South, and the intent was to boost the chances of conservative Democratic candidates. It has not had the desired effect, as most conservative Democratic voters have migrated to the Republican Party since the 1980s.[18]

Superdelegates

Not all delegates are formally bound to a specific candidate. Jimmy Carter's loss to Ronald Reagan in 1980 led some Democrats to conclude that renominating him was a mistake. The result "seemed to confirm all of the critics' worst fears about the system wrought by McGovern-Fraser" by excluding party leaders from the process.[19] The Democratic nomination system had produced two outsiders who lost in landslides (McGovern in 1972 and Carter in 1980), and party professionals wanted to take back some of the power they had lost. As a result of this pressure, in 1984 the Democratic party created a new category of Democratic delegates, Party Leaders and Elected Officials (PLEOs)—superdelegates—who were not pledged to any candidate and could vote for whomever they thought would be the strongest nominee. The number has varied between about 14–19 percent of the delegate total. In theory, superdelegates could prevent the nomination of a candidate who might be popular with primary constituencies but is certain to lose in November, or resolve a deadlock if no candidate had won a majority of delegates heading into the convention.

PLEOs were an issue in both 2008 and 2016. In 2008, as noted below, Hillary Clinton found herself in an unexpectedly competitive primary battle with Barack Obama. She hoped to persuade enough superdelegates to support her that she could overcome Obama's lead among pledged delegates, backing away only when it became clear that the move would trigger a backlash. In 2016, Bernie Sanders' supporters argued that superdelegates, who overwhelmingly supported Clinton, were reversing the judgment of voters, insisting that the Democratic Party was unfairly putting its thumb on the scales to deliver the nomination to Clinton.

Stung by Clinton's loss to Trump, which Democratic officials attributed in part to Sanders supporters abandoning Clinton in November, the party moved to reduce the influence of superdelegates in 2020.[20] Under the new rules, PLEOs vote only if pledged delegates do not nominate a candidate on the convention's first ballot.[21] It represents the biggest change to nomination processes since superdelegates were created in the 1980s.

THE ELECTORAL ARENA

Until the mid-twentieth century, the quest for the nomination was an internal party affair, run by insiders; today, it is not. Campaigns need hundreds of staff and volunteers at their headquarters and thousands in the field. Most senior campaign advisers are professional consultants—pollsters, media strategists, grassroots organizers, accountants, lawyers, and, increasingly, tech experts—not the party leaders who once selected the nominees and ran their campaigns. Today, candidates must build their own organizations, manage their own campaigns, craft their own messages, and find ways to appeal to the party's multiple primary constituencies.

By activating the most committed partisans, primaries and caucuses can exacerbate cleavages within the party and motivate candidates to take more extreme positions. The process can also be divisive if candidates wind up attacking each other as they try to win the nomination. The candidate who remains at the end of this process might be weakened, with effective negative strategies telegraphed to the other party. Candidates in a large pool might have trouble standing out, possibly splitting key constituencies and leaving a path open for someone who might win by appealing to a small number of primary voters.

Campaign Finance

Running for president is expensive. Candidates must create organizations in key states, provide logistics for everything from office space to a campaign airplane, purchase advertising, and hire strategists, advisors, and a large network of staffers. In recent cycles, all of this money has come from private donors, who can make contributions directly to candidate campaign committees as well as fund independent efforts to support (or oppose) candidates.[22]

Until the mid-1970s, candidates of both parties depended almost exclusively on large contributions from private donors to finance their campaigns. This dependence, combined with spiraling campaign costs, secret and sometimes illegal contributions, and sparse public information about who gave how much to whom (and what they might have received in return) raised questions about the democratic character of American elections.

Federal Law

In 1974, concern over rising costs and the corruption of Richard Nixon's 1972 campaign led to the Federal Election Campaign Act in 1974; it remains the foundation of the regulatory environment. The Act imposed contribution limits, disclosure requirements, public subsidies for presidential campaigns, and spending limits. Opponents challenged the law as violating the First Amendment's free speech and free association provisions. In the landmark case of *Buckley v. Valeo* (1976) the Supreme Court invalidated spending limits but upheld contribution limits and disclosure requirements.

By the early 1990s, a series of regulatory changes allowed political parties to raise funds for "party building" and state-level activities (colloquially called "soft money") without the limits that applied to contributions to candidates. Soft money quickly became a vehicle for parties to raise large amounts—nearly $200 million in 1996 and $500 million in 2000—raising questions about ethics, legality, and equity.

President Clinton went to great lengths to extend White House hospitality to big Democratic soft money donors in 1996. Major contributors were invited to sleep in the Lincoln Bedroom, have coffee with the president, and ride on Air Force One. Republicans, not to be outdone, invited donors to have dinner with President George W. Bush and Vice President Dick Cheney, gave them access to cabinet officials and congressional leaders, and provided them with VIP treatment at the 2000 Republican National Convention.

The 2002 Bipartisan Campaign Reform Act eliminated soft money, forcing parties to raise all funds in accordance with federal contribution limits, but doubling contribution limits to candidates. Candidates responded by raising historically large amounts. In 2008, Barack Obama spent $391 million during the primaries; he and Hillary Clinton spent a combined $635 million, obliterating all previous records.[23] By this time, candidates benefitted from the ability to raise money online, as internet technologies became an efficient and flexible way to raise very large sums very quickly even from small donors. The presidential public funding system (see endnote 21) became irrelevant, as the funding levels and spending limits were far too low to attract participation when candidates could easily raise ten or twenty times as much money on their own.

In 2010, the Supreme Court opened the door to corporate election expenditures in its *Citizens United* decision.[24] The Court ruled that groups of individuals—even corporations—had a First Amendment right to spend money supporting a candidate, as long as they were independent of a candidate's campaign (an appeals court later overturned contribution limits on independent efforts based on this decision). Thus were super PACs (Political Action Committees) born: independent expenditure groups that supported candidates and that could accept unlimited contributions from individuals and corporations. Super PACs can raise large amounts of money from a handful of contributors (or even one), and they frequently support a single candidate. Such "single candidate super PACs" spent an estimated $300 million in the 2016 presidential primaries.[25] It is now routine for candidates to benefit from super PACs organized to benefit their campaigns or to have to deal with super PACs organized to oppose them.

The changes in campaign finance laws, and recent Supreme Court jurisprudence, have dramatically increased the amount of money candidates can raise, and how much they must raise in order to run a competitive campaign. Table 3.1 shows candidate and super PAC primary spending in 2016.

The Importance of Money

Money is vital to candidates. It buys recognition for lesser-known candidates at the outset of the nomination process. To remain competitive with front-runners, Republicans Steve Forbes (1996), Mitt Romney (2008), and a host of Republican hopefuls in 2016, and Democrats Howard Dean (2004), Barack Obama (2008), and Bernie Sanders (2016) relied on aggressive early fundraising or self-contributions to promote themselves as viable alternatives to more heavily favored candidates.

Early money is important for several reasons. The press and potential donors view it as a sign of a candidate's viability; it provides a way for candidates to break through with advertising and media attention; and the public may see it as an indicator of broad-based support. For front-runners, aggressive fundraising can discourage rivals from coming forward. Incumbent presidents running for reelection follow this strategy to avoid challenges to their nomination. Donald Trump, who created his 2020 reelection committee the day he was inaugurated, raised over $10 million within a few months of taking office; by April 2019, his campaign had raised over $93 million, nearly as much as all Democratic candidates combined. Bernie Sanders was first among Democratic candidates, raising $21 WWmillion over the same period.[26]

At the same time, spending money too quickly and too early can be a mistake. If the race remains competitive after the first wave of primaries, a campaign that burns through its money can find itself in a financial bind. Hillary Clinton confronted this problem in 2008. She was counting on early victories to clinch her nomination and

Table 3.1 Presidential Nomination Expenditures, January 1, 2015–June 30, 2016 (in millions of dollars)*

	Candidate Organization	Outside Groups	Total
Republicans			
Bush, Jeb	35.4	87.0	122.4
Carson, Ben	62.5	5.3	67.8
Christie, Chris	58.7	21.6	80.3
Cruz, Ted	86.3	27.5	113.8
Fiorina, Carly	11.3	3.9	5.2
Gilmore, Jim	0.4	—	0.4
Graham, Lindsay	5.8	3.5	9.3
Huckabee, Mike	4.3	2.9	7.2
Jindal, Bobby	1.4	3.0	4.4
Kasich, John	19.3	20.9	40.2
Pataki, George	0.5	—	0.5
Paul, Rand	12.3	5.3	17.6
Perry, Rick	1.8	1.9	3.7
Rubio, Marco	50.7	49.3	100.0
Santorum, Rick	1.4	0.2	1.6
Trump, Donald	71.1	44.8[†]	115.5
Walker, Scott	8.6	2.3	10.9
Democrats			
Clinton, Hillary	230.2	12.3	242.5
Lessig, Lawrence	1.2	—	1.2
O'Malley, Martin	6.2	0.4	6.6
Sanders, Bernie	227.4	6.1	233.5
Webb, Jim	0.8	—	0.8
Others			
Johnson, Gary	0.9	—	0.9
Stein, Jill	0.6	—	0.6
Totals			
Republicans	381.7	279.4	661.1
Democrats	465.8	18.8	484.6
Others	1.5	—	1.5
Total	**849.1**	**299.2**	**1,147.2**

* Includes only candidates who raised and spent more than $100,000.
† Trump was the only presidential candidate for whom outside groups spent more in opposition to his nomination candidacy ($44.1 million) than for him ($0.4 million).

Note: Due to rounding, totals may differ slightly from those of the Federal Election Commission and Center for Responsive Politics.

Sources: For Candidate Organizations: "Presidential Campaign Finance Summaries," Federal Election Commission, January 1, 2015–June 30, 2016, http://classic.fec.gov/press/bkgnd/pres_cf/pres_cf_Even.shtml. For nonparty groups: "2016 Outside Spending, by Candidates: Primary Election Expenditures Only," Center for Responsive Politics, https://www.opensecrets.org/outsidespending/summ.php?cycle=2016&disp=C&type=P.

did not anticipate that Obama would be a credible rival. As a result, by February even her main supporters worried that she had spent too much too fast, focusing too much on consultants and not enough on infrastructure and organizing.[27] Clinton had to loan her campaign over $13 million just to stay competitive in larger primary states holding elections in March, and she was never able to catch Obama in the delegate chase.

Finally, money is not everything, as Donald Trump demonstrated in 2016. At the beginning of the primary season, before the first votes were cast, Trump ranked ninth in the amount of money he had raised, lagging behind everyone but second tier candidates Mike Huckabee, Rick Santorum, and James Gilmore. Jeb Bush had outraised every GOP candidate, with $35 million plus another $124 million raised by his super PAC. He dropped out on February 21 after disappointing finishes in Iowa, New Hampshire, and South Carolina.

Despite running an atypical campaign with an unusually small budget, Trump benefited from massive free media coverage (as distinguished from campaign advertising, or "paid media"), which reached millions of viewers and kept him in the news even though he rarely ran campaign ads. Between social media (especially Twitter) and news coverage, Trump earned the equivalent of $2 billion worth of free media in the early primaries and in the range of $5 billion over the entire election cycle.[28]

Polling, Positioning, and Tracking Delegates

One of the first questions serious candidates ask themselves is whether they can identify a core of support within the party large enough to propel them to victory. The answer is a function of who candidates think their supporters will be: to what demographic groups, ideological blocs, or types of voters will they appeal? It is also a function of who the other candidates are: will multiple candidates attempt to appeal to the same groups—liberals, conservatives, moderates, rural, suburban, men, women, young, elderly—or will a candidate have a clear lane?

In 2016, Senator Bernie Sanders (I-VT) was the only major candidate to challenge Hillary Clinton for the Democratic nomination. He presented himself as the progressive alternative, a message that resonated with his enthusiastic supporters. In 2020, most observers give him lower chances, mainly because he will be only one of several candidates competing for the progressive mantle. Democratic primary voters will have other options, making it harder for him to generate the same breadth of support as he received in 2016.

Similarly, the large number of Republican candidates in 2016 may have eased the way for Donald Trump. All seventeen candidates claimed to be the best conservative choice, giving Republican primary voters many alternatives. Republicans split their support in the early phases of the campaign. Trump did not receive a majority of the vote in any primary until April 19, when the race was down to three candidates (Trump, Ted Cruz, and John Kasich) and Trump won 59 percent of the vote in the New York primary. By then, his delegate lead was insurmountable, and he ran the table in the remaining contests.

In the weeks and months leading up to the primaries, and during the season, polls are a primary method of tracking how candidates are doing. John F. Kennedy in 1960 was the first candidate to hire a pollster in his quest for the nomination, and since then polls have become ubiquitous in both campaigns and in the media. Campaigns use polls to hone messages, identify where they are competitive, and test the effectiveness of campaign tactics. Candidates also rely on focus groups, a collection of individuals brought together and asked to discuss and react to a variety of real and hypothetical campaign appeals.

As the primary season unfolds, reporters and other observers track how candidates are amassing delegates in each state primary or caucus. Some analysts—including prominent forecasting operations such as FiveThirtyEight—use sophisticated models to evaluate how candidates are doing based on election results, delegate counts, polls, and voter demographics.[29]

News Coverage

How candidates are doing in state and national polls affects the amount and tone of news coverage. In general, candidates doing well receive the most coverage, which helps them raise money, attract volunteers, and extend their appeal. A lack of media attention, particularly in the early stages of the nomination process when less is known about the candidates, can be fatal.

Since the mid-1950s, television has been the primary vehicle candidates use to communicate campaign appeals and leadership imagery to voters. Before then, candidates relied on party literature, print journalism, and radio. Although television remains the major medium for election news, the internet is rapidly becoming a supplementary source of news for most voters, and a primary source for many.[30]

The early nomination contests receive the most attention. Naturally, candidates who do well in them benefit enormously from positive news coverage. Barack Obama's surprising win over John Edwards and Hillary Clinton in Iowa in 2008, a state in which African Americans constituted only 4 percent of voters, made him the Democratic front-runner overnight. Similarly, in 2016, Donald Trump's victory in New Hampshire and wins in many of the primaries conducted on Super Tuesday made him the Republican front-runner, while Hillary Clinton's Super Tuesday victories reinforced the perception that she would be the Democratic nominee.

The disproportionate amount of news coverage they received throughout the nomination period boosted both Trump's and Clinton's status. Donald Trump received more coverage than all his Republican opponents combined. Hillary Clinton was in the news twice as often as Sanders. Trump's controversial rhetoric, emotional appeals to disaffected Americans, and primary victories against his better-financed Republican opponents generated his coverage. Clinton's coverage was the result of her lead in the polls, endorsements from party leaders, and significant fundraising.

Journalists believe that they have the responsibility to present other sides, perform fact checks on candidates' statements and political ads, and raise questions about candidates' personal motives and tactics. In performing its watchdog role, the press rarely accepts what candidates say as the truth but treats it as spin. Candidates understand this orientation and try to affect the coverage they receive. Their advisers orchestrate events, prepare and rehearse their speeches, and pretest public reactions to their words, phrases, and appeals.

In the past, most candidates spoke and acted in accordance with media and public expectations of accepted electoral behavior. Candidates who deviated from this norm were criticized and put on the defensive. Donald Trump abandoned this conventional approach during the 2015–2016 election cycle. He campaigned as an antiestablishment candidate, appealed to the emotions of discontented Republicans and Independents, and did so with unusually heated and sharp-edged rhetoric. He ridiculed his opponents with demeaning names and descriptions. He also used the news media as a foil, insisting that their coverage was biased and untrue—fake news. The public's growing distrust of the news media, particularly among Republicans, reinforced Trump's approach and contributed to the amount of press coverage he received. Trump adopted a press strategy that worked well for him in the primaries and general election, although it presented problems for his presidency.

There is another way that campaigns try to influence media coverage: by routinely leaking opposition research to reporters. Once this information becomes public, candidates reinforce it with advertising using the same themes. The decline in press resources devoted to investigative reporting has increased reliance on campaigns as a source of information. Critical reporting and commentary also tend to be more negative than positive, at least until the race is over.

The press fits the story of the campaign into a horse race format. News coverage focuses on who is ahead and who is behind, who is on track and who is not, and on who "wins" debates. Election results are interpreted based on how well a candidate was expected to do rather than the actual results. Winning is usually good news and provides more favorable coverage, unless a candidate does not meet expectations. Losing is bad news, discouraging supporters and donors. In the year before caucuses and primaries are held, the press evaluates candidates based on polls and fundraising results. Once the elections start, reporters focus on the winners and losers in the early contests through Super Tuesday and then, increasingly, on the number of pledged delegates a candidate has accumulated as the contest progresses and the finish line approaches.

Primary Debates

Candidate debates showcase the candidates on the same stage, highlight their telegenic and communication skills, and give primary voters an immediate basis of comparison. Primary debates have been common feature of the nomination process since 1980, although there were earlier cases in which presidential candidates faced each other in ad hoc affairs.[31] In 1980, a New Hampshire newspaper offered to host a televised debate between Ronald Reagan and George Bush but was told that it could not sponsor the event unless it invited all of the Republican candidates. Reagan offered to pay the costs to keep it one-on-one but secretly invited the other candidates to participate without informing Bush until the debate was under way. The Bush campaign, ambushed, insisted on the original two-candidate arrangement. In the resulting impasse the moderator asked to have Reagan's microphone cut. Reagan's thundering response, *"I am paying for this microphone!"* triggered cheers from his supporters and became the most memorable part of the debate (if not the entire primary season).[32]

Debates are also known for slip-ups that can doom a campaign. In the 2012 Republican primaries, former Texas governor Rick Perry had been leading in most polls through September 2011. He fell behind eventual nominee Mitt Romney, a decline attributed in part to his support for in-state tuition for undocumented immigrants. Then, in a widely watched November 2011 debate, he stumbled when listing the three federal agencies he wanted to eliminate: after naming the Departments of Commerce and Education, he could not name the third (it was the Department of Energy). "What's the third one here? Let's see . . . I can't. The third one, I can't. Sorry. Oops." Pundit Chris Cillizza called it a performance that "will go into presidential debate folklore of one of the most awkward moments ever."[33] Perry's support quickly fell to the single digits, his fundraising dried up, and he dropped out of the race after finishing fifth in Iowa.

The importance of primary debates is enhanced by the large audiences they often attract, the amount of news coverage they receive, and the enthusiasm they generate among supporters of particular candidates. Debates can be especially important in primaries, as partisan cues are absent in these intramural contests and voter attachments can be weaker than in general elections.[34]

Debates provide information to the electorate and spark interest in the campaign. Twenty-four million people watched the first Republican presidential debate in 2016 and sixteen million the first Democratic one. Press coverage afterwards was extensive.

At the same time, debates can highlight conflicts and give candidates more opportunities to attack each other, creating potential vulnerabilities for whomever wins the nomination. In 2012, for example, there were twenty-seven Republican primary debates and multi-candidate forums held between May 2011 and February 2012. After the nominee Mitt Romney lost in November, GOP leaders concluded that the large number of debates led to attacks on Romney and pushed him to take ideologically extreme positions that hurt him in the general election.[35] The head of the Republican National Committee called the large number of debates "an embarrassment and ridiculous" for the party.[36] In the 2016 primaries there were far fewer Republican debates—twelve—even though more candidates were running.

Debates fit into the news media's horse race frame, which focuses on winners and losers rather than on the substance of policy proposals. That framing satisfies a key journalistic objection: making the news interesting to attract viewers (and, not coincidentally, industry profits and recognition for correspondents). The new, the unexpected, and the controversial are newsworthy, while the old and anticipated are not. Press coverage frequently focuses on "zingers" and digs that the candidates can direct towards rivals, or on memorable comments (such as Reagan's in 1980).

Kevin Dietsch/UPI/Alamy Stock Photo

Hillary Clinton and Bernie Sanders in a 2016 Democratic primary debate.

Even more, campaigns try to affect how viewers perceived the debates, by offering post-debate commentary and analysis in a setting called the "spin room," an open recognition that everyone is trying to shape perceptions. How reporters and pundits react can shape how viewers react.[37]

In the 2016 Republican primaries, there were so many candidates (seventeen) that it was impossible to include all of them in candidate debates. To manage, candidates were divided into two groups, with the ten candidates running best in recent polls invited to a prime-time debate and the others relegated to an "undercard" debate broadcast a few hours earlier. The candidates were arranged on stage based on their polling, with the most popular at the center and the lowest-ranked on the sides. This arrangement all but guaranteed that the second-tier candidates would never be able to break out of the pack, and all of them had dropped out by February 2016.

The format worked to Donald Trump's advantage, as the other candidates had little time for detailed explanations of policy and struggled to present themselves in the face of Trump's unconventional comments and asides ("Lyin' Ted" Cruz, "Low Energy" Jeb Bush, "Little Marco" Rubio). Some initial hopefuls, such as Wisconsin Governor Scott Walker, never were able to find their footing in debates and lost opportunities to introduce themselves to national audiences. After a disappointing debate performance in September in which he spoke less than any other candidate, and with polls showing fewer than 1 percent of viewers saying he won, Walker ended his campaign.[38]

The rules for Democratic primary debates changed for the 2020 election, partly in response to the large field that has emerged (as of mid-2019, twenty-three Democrats had declared[39]), and partly in response to criticisms that the party had limited the number of 2016 debates to help Clinton. Twelve debates are planned. The rules for the first two debates specified that candidates had to reach 1 percent support in the polls or raise money from at least 65,000 individual donors to participate.[40] Twenty candidates qualified, so the debate was split over two nights with randomly selected candidate lineups for each. Beginning with the third debate, held in September, the qualification thresholds doubled (2 percent in the polls and 130,000 individual donors), and only ten candidates qualified.

Campaign Advertising

Promotion through advertising on radio, television, and the Internet remains an important communications tool of election campaigns. Although political ads have their limits, they provide information, create an image, and highlight salient issue positions. Campaigns test the ads before they air them to make sure that they will achieve their desired effect on their targeted audience. About half the funds in a campaign budget are usually spent on advertising.

In recent nomination contests, hundreds of thousands of ads have been aired and placed online by candidate organizations, political parties, and nonparty groups supporting or opposing particular candidates. In the 2015–2016 nomination cycle, over $500 million was spent on more than 600,000 ads, many more ads than in 2012 when only the Republicans had a competitive nomination process.[41] Most of the Democratic ads in the Clinton-Sanders contest were paid for by their campaigns. Sanders accepted no political action committee (PAC) contributions, and Clinton's supporters created only one large super PAC supporting her candidacy. For the Republicans, however, candidate-oriented nonparty groups did most of the advertising, and most of it was negative.

It is difficult to measure the impact of advertising on the outcome of the primaries. Groups supporting Jeb Bush spent the most on advertising in 2016, and he did poorly. Ted Cruz and Marco Rubio spent more than Trump and lost. Trump depended on free media coverage of his rallies and speeches rather than on ads, and he won.

Digital Communications

Campaign strategies have adapted to new technologies: television changed the way that candidates ran and also rewarded new skills and candidate characteristics. Digital technologies—the Internet, digital media, and social media—have revolutionized the way that candidates assimilate information, how they organize their campaigns, how they present themselves to voters and the appeals they make, and how they target messages to supporters and potential supporters.

In 2000 John McCain became the first major party candidate to solicit contributions online. In the aftermath of his surprising victory over George W. Bush in the New Hampshire primary, he raised $5 million through his campaign's website. In 2004 Democrat Howard Dean created a campaign blog to raise money and communicate with his supporters.[42] Dean demonstrated the potential of digital media, but his campaign's failure to turn out backers in Iowa and New Hampshire cast doubts about the effectiveness of the internet as a mobilizing tool.

In 2008, the Obama campaign eliminated these doubts. Obama's web operation began even before his official declaration of candidacy in 2007. Moved by his keynote address to the 2004 Democratic National Convention, several college students had already set up blogs to pass the word about him and drum up support for a potential presidential run. Obama's advisers took advantage of these blogs, encouraged others to start their own, and eventually incorporated the most successful ones into the campaign's digital operation, creating a huge database to identify and target potential supporters. Field organizers had access to data that enabled them to determine which people to contact and what appeals to make.

At first, Republicans lagged the Democrats in digital communications. Their 2012 nomination contest was conducted in a fairly traditional manner, emphasizing war chests, television advertising, campaign rallies, and personal contact by volunteers.

The growth of the online news sources and social media forced candidates for the 2016 Republican nomination to devote more resources to the new technologies. Ted Cruz had the largest operation, using electronic voter lists to target potential supporters in key states. For a time, his campaign also hired a private firm to design psychologically based appeals to certain groups of voters. Although Donald Trump considered digital campaigning overpriced and overrated, he also engaged strategists to solicit small contributions and identify and screen invitees to his rallies. He also personally tweeted daily comments that were magnified by tens of millions of Twitter followers who supported his candidacy. Trump's tweets became newsworthy and personalized his campaign against his Republican political opponents. He used the same tactics in the general election.

Both major Democratic candidates, Hillary Clinton and Bernie Sanders, followed the Obama playbook, with Clinton initially advantaged by her fundraising lead. Once the Sanders campaign took off, almost beating Clinton in Iowa and winning in New Hampshire, tech experts who supported him quickly designed a data operation relying on social networking for voter outreach and fundraising.

The utility of these digital campaigns in energizing supporters, soliciting donations, and expanding enthusiasm and voluntarism have affected the nomination process in a variety of ways: encouraging early starts; incorporating the personal data available on Facebook and other social sites into integrated banks of information; targeting online advertising to groups with common interests; using YouTube, Instagram, Snapchat, and other visually oriented websites to campaign virally; and interacting with news sites to direct and project the campaign's message.

Personal Contact

Personal contact is necessary in nomination campaigns, particularly at the beginning of the process. Candidates open offices and often spend considerable time in the states that hold the first caucuses and primaries, especially Iowa and New Hampshire.

For candidates who are not as well known, getting started is difficult. Unless a campaign can attract and train a large number of volunteers early, it will have to depend on paid staff and outside groups to check voter registration lists, establish phone banks, go door to door, and organize a get-out-the-vote (GOTV) drive on Election Day. The use of outside groups to perform these activities has blurred the line between candidate organizations and candidate- oriented super PACs and the noncoordination rule that the law requires. As the election approaches, GOTV activities become more important.

Strong organizations are key to turnout in caucus states. The public phases of the campaign along with organized field operations are essential in primaries. Much of the public remains uninformed and uninvolved, despite extensive news coverage of nomination contest. Only 35 percent of eligible voters participated in the 2016 presidential nominations, and in only one state, New Hampshire, did a majority of the electorate participate.[43]

STRATEGIES AND TACTICS

The nomination strategies candidates pursue depend on their status at the beginning of the nomination process: front-runners, candidates in the middle of the pack who believe they can win, or candidates with remote chances running to promote a cause or make a point. Strategies also depend on how many candidates are running: a race with two or three plausible contenders will look different than one with 10 or 15 candidates and no clear favorite.

Front-Runners

A front-runner has all the initial advantages: national recognition, fundraising strength, experience, key endorsements, and rank-and-file voter support. With these assets, the front-runner's main task is to stay in front and maintain leads. Status and position make it easier to raise money and build an organization, but they can also raise expectations and generate critical coverage by a news media interested in reporting on a competitive race as long as possible.

The main risk to front-runners is a failure to meet expectations: an upset loss, or even winning by a smaller-than-expected margin, can puncture the aura of invincibility and open a path for another candidate. Hillary Clinton's third place finish in Iowa in 2008 signaled vulnerability, as did her narrow win in 2016 over Bernie

Sanders. Most of the time, a front-runner can overcome a single defeat but will find it more difficult to survive a string of setbacks.

When front-runners have the support of party leaders, they usually win and often wrap up the nomination quickly. Incumbent presidents running for reelection have the strongest hands: since 1972, no president seeking renomination has failed to win it, and only Gerald Ford (1976), Jimmy Carter (1980) and George H.W. Bush (1992) faced internal party opposition. Tellingly, they all went on to lose. This pattern suggests that potential challenges to Donald Trump's 2020 re-nomination are longshots, barring developments risking the president's base. Jeb Bush publicly urged a Republican to step forward, but by mid-2019, only former Massachusetts Governor William Weld and former Congressman Joe Walsh (R-IL) had announced a challenge to Trump.[44]

At the same time, support from party leaders is no guarantee of success. Candidates supported by party elites often win the nomination but go on to lose in November (Hillary Clinton in 2016, Bob Dole in 1996), and sometimes the support of party elites is not enough to win the nomination (Jeb Bush in 2016, Hillary Clinton in 2008). Outsiders sometimes win the nomination against the wishes of party elites and go on to win in November (Donald Trump in 2016, Barack Obama in 2008, Jimmy Carter in 1976).

Front-runners' greater recognition and resources give them more flexibility and greater survivability if they sustain one or two early defeats. Over time, however, disappointing performances weaken candidates and raise doubts about their electability. Republican Jeb Bush in 2016 and Democrat Hillary Clinton in 2008 illustrate the story of the odds-on favorite weakening over the course of the race and eventually dropping out.

The post-reform Democratic Party has had less control over the nomination process than Republican Party leadership has had over theirs. Democratic primaries give more opportunities for non-front runners to appeal to the party's rank-and-file. The 2016 primaries were an exception, in which Democratic leaders were almost unanimous in their support of Hillary Clinton, leading some Sanders supporters to claim that party elites had stolen the nomination from him.

Front-runners do not generate the attention and excitement that come-from-behind candidates do. Their nomination victories are largely routine affairs that confirm the expectations of party leaders and partisan supporters. Primaries with upstarts doing well or front-runners stumbling prove much more newsworthy.

Non-Frontrunners

Non-frontrunners face the difficult hurdle of establishing their credentials as viable contenders. At the outset, the key is recognition. Non-frontrunners may get initial notice through news coverage if they do better than expected in early primaries and caucuses. They can achieve crucial momentum—the public perception that they are doing well—by winning, exceeding expectations, or rising in the polls.

Jimmy Carter in 1976, Barack Obama in 2008, and Donald Trump in 2016 are examples of successful non-frontrunner strategies. In 1976, Carter began his campaign as an unknown southern governor without much campaign money or organizational support. He concentrated his efforts in Iowa and New Hampshire, hoping that press attention would help establish him as a viable candidate and counting on early success to facilitate fundraising, organizational strength, and continued media attention. He was right—it did.

Barack Obama also focused on doing well in Iowa and New Hampshire, which he hoped would demonstrate that an African American could win in predominately white states, would show that a Clinton victory was not inevitable, and would prove that it was possible to organize an army of volunteers using the internet as a primary communications tool. Since Clinton had the support of party leaders and a lead in the polls, the best strategy for Obama was to identify and attract new voters. His campaign outworked and out-organized his competitors, and his unexpected victory in Iowa propelled him to national competitiveness, which he leveraged into a fundraising juggernaut.

Donald Trump's victory also fits into the category of an upset victory by a non-frontrunner. You can read about it in box 3.1.

Box 3.1 ★ Upsetting the Odds: Trump's Insurgent Victory

Donald Trump declared his candidacy on June 16, 2015 in a flashy entrance at Trump Tower in New York City. He immediately generated controversy with a promise to build a wall on the US-Mexico border for which Mexico would pay and a claim that Mexico was sending criminals into the United States.

Political and party professionals considered him a vanity candidate. He was given little chance to do well in Iowa (as a New Yorker), Florida (given that Jeb Bush and Marco Rubio were running), or among conservatives (as he had contributed to Democrats over his life, including Hillary Clinton). He was unpopular among Republican voters (with 57 percent having an unfavorable view of him in June 2015), and he was "the first candidate in modern presidential primary history to begin the campaign with a majority of his own party disliking him."[45] Even though Trump quickly jumped out to a narrow lead in national polls, the large number of experienced candidates and his relatively low support (typically between 20 and 30 percent of Republican voters) prompted most observers to still not take him seriously.[46]

The other Republican candidates insisted that Trump was unelectable; in particularly sharp words, Marco Rubio called him a "con man,"[47] and Jeb Bush tweeted that he was "unhinged."[48] When Wisconsin Governor Scott Walker ended his presidential campaign in September 2015, he said he was dropping out to clear the field. "I encourage other Republican candidates to do the same so that voters can focus on a limited number of candidates who can offer a positive, conservative alternative to [Trump]."[49]

Initially, Trump said he would self-fund his campaign. He eventually accepted donations from individuals but not from nonparty groups, asserting his independence from special interests. Some of the $20 million he lent his campaign for expenses was funneled back to his businesses, including Trump Towers where his headquarters was located and Trump Air for his plane travel. Although he advertised less than his opponents, Trump received much more media coverage. His unconventional rhetoric, daily tweets, enthusiastic rallies, and debate performances countered the negative tone of the coverage he received.

Trump made an emotional appeal to Republicans and Independents disaffected with the economic and social changes that the country had experienced: the Great Recession, loss of manufacturing jobs, growing income inequality, fear of terrorism, and social changes sparked by America's growing multiculturalism and LGBT tolerance.

Trump rejected political correctness, promoted his business acumen and wealth with a "can't be bought" claim, and offered simple generic solutions to job

(continued)

Box 3.1 ★ Continued

losses, immigration, US involvement in international conflict, and a host of other partisan issues such as Obamacare, tax reform, and defeat of the Islamic State of Iraq and Syria (ISIS). His appeal struck a responsive chord among about one-third of the Republican electorate despite the opposition of much of the party's political establishment that deemed him impulsive, lacking in knowledge, and not sufficiently faithful to the party's traditional conservative policy positions.

Early on, Trump turned his media attention and boisterous rallies into a popular vote lead. He finished a close second in the Iowa caucus and then won handily the first two primaries in New Hampshire and South Carolina. On Super Tuesday, he won six of seven Republican primaries, primarily in the South and Southwest.

With Trump building his momentum and gaining an increasingly large lead in convention delegates, it looked as if he could be nominated on the first ballot of the Republican convention. This threat, which establishment Republicans feared would result in a landslide loss to the Democrats, promoted many of them to endorse Ted Cruz, who was in second place. Nonparty groups also launched an anti-Trump campaign and spent millions criticizing his candidacy.

Trump's victories continued in primary states. After he swept the April mid-Atlantic primaries, only Ted Cruz and John Kasich remained in the race. Behind in the delegate count, Cruz attempted a last-ditch tactic, naming Carly Fiorina, one of the initial GOP candidates, as his running mate if he won the nomination. Ronald Reagan had tried a similar move in 1976 against President Ford but had failed to attract additional support. Cruz also failed. After losing badly to Trump in Indiana, Cruz dropped out of the race at the beginning of May; Kasich did so a day later. Trump had won.

Despite the opposition of his more experienced and better-funded Republican opponents and the negative commentary of most traditional news media, Trump had generated an enthusiastic base by recognizing and building on the anger and discontent of a portion of the Republican electorate. His "tell-it-like-it-is" rhetoric, populist and chauvinistic policy appeals, personal assertiveness, self-confidence, and distinctive leadership style became a tonic that enthused Republican voters. Trump had waged an unconventional campaign and achieved a surprising victory a month before Hillary Clinton clinched the Democratic nomination.

Pulpit Candidates

Some candidates run not because they realistically believe they have a chance to win but because they want to have their voices heard by party leaders and voters. Democrats Jesse Jackson 1984 and 1988 and Bernie Sanders in 2016, Republicans Pat Robertson in 1988 and Ron Paul in 2008 and 2012 fit into this category of using the campaign as a podium (Sanders unexpectedly became a contender, showing that the strategy can work in surprising ways). In each case, these nontraditional candidates used the campaign as a "bully pulpit" to articulate their political philosophy and show that others in the party coalition share their views. In doing so, the candidates hope for greater influence in the party. To the extent that pulpit candidates attract press coverage and some popular support, they can achieve their objectives.

THE CONVENTIONS

The national party conventions held in the summer of election years formally signify the transition to the general election campaign. Prior to the 1970s-era reforms, conventions served deliberative functions: formulating party platforms, settling on the rules, approving the credentials of delegates, and often determining who was selected as the nominee. Now, these decisions are settled well in advance, and the nominee has been known for months. Traditionally, the "out" party—the one that does not hold the White House—goes first, while the incumbent party holds its convention last.

Conventions have become highly orchestrated affairs designed for television. They are rarely newsworthy. Because of the careful scripting, the major networks now usually broadcast only an hour of prime-time coverage, although cable news, C-SPAN, and network digital sites offer much more. The controversy around the Trump campaign changed this calculus in 2016, as interest rose at the prospect of what could be the first deadlocked convention in over sixty years.[50] But an improbable attempt to block Trump's nomination was quashed on the first day of the convention.

The absence of any real news puts the burden on party leaders, convention planners, and the nominee's communications team to design and produce an entertaining show. The goal is to energize delegates, engage viewers, present the candidate in a positive light, and launch the general election campaign. Conventions rely on speeches by noteworthy people, film clips that highlight party leaders and key policies, and high-production-value video biographies of the soon-to-be nominated presidential and vice presidential candidates. Another component is pageantry: the banners, cheers, and enthusiastic demonstrations on behalf of the nominee.

Don Mennig/Alamy Stock Photo

Hillary Clinton accepting the Democratic presidential nomination at the Democratic Convention in Philadelphia.

Events are carefully scheduled and sequenced to build momentum. Typically, each successive night of the three- or four-day convention includes increasingly prominent speakers during prime time. The 2016 Democratic National Convention featured Michelle Obama as the keynote speaker on the first night, Bill Clinton on the second, and Barack Obama on the third. The Republican convention posed more of a challenge, as former presidents George W. Bush and George H. W. Bush declined to attend, as did 2012 nominee Mitt Romney and 2008 nominee John McCain. Ohio Governor John Kasich refused to attend even though the convention was held in Cleveland. The result was a "roster of speakers [including] D-list celebrities like Scott Baio."[51] Even with the potential drama, viewership was about the same in 2016 as it was in 2012.

Most Americans do not watch much of the conventions, and those who do tend to be more committed partisans who look to the conventions to reinforce their political attitudes. Conventions rarely convert the undecided. The high point is usually the candidate acceptance speeches: in 2016, about thirty-five million people watched Donald Trump's speech, compared to about thirty-four million who watched Clinton's.[52] However, conventions still serve a mobilizing and educational function. Public opinion surveys have found that public interest and political knowledge increase during conventions, in part because even people who do not watch the conventions read news accounts about them. As Harvard political scientist Thomas Patterson noted in September 2016:

> Although conventions are no longer the deliberative events they once were, they remain a key moment in the presidential campaign. The television ratings are smaller than in the era when Americans' viewing choices were limited to the three broadcast networks, but they are large by today's standards. More than 25 million Americans watched the 2016 conventions on the average night, and the presidential nominees' lengthy acceptance speeches drew more than 30 million viewers. In an era of ten-second sound bites and thirty-second political ads, it's hard to argue that the conventions somehow fail to serve the voters' interests and needs.[53]

Candidates usually get a post-convention "bounce" in public opinion polls reflecting the positive setting of the convention and the activation of partisan supporters. The relative standing of the nominees after the conventions indicates who has the advantage going into the general election campaign. It is not, however, a foolproof predictor of who will win. In 2016, Clinton enjoyed a large bounce after the Democratic convention (which followed the Republican convention), and opened September 2016 with a lead over Trump. It did not last.

THE INFLUENCE OF THE NOMINATION ON THE GENERAL ELECTION AND ON GOVERNANCE

The nomination process affects the conduct, strategy, and position of the candidates going into the general election. Nominees benefit from popular enthusiasm among partisans, a campaign staff that has been tested, and messages that have resonated with the base. All these structural and operational components will be expanded in the general election.

On a personal level, the lengthy primary process can raise the nominee's knowledge of the issues and the ability to campaign effectively. Refining policy stands, polishing debate performances, and routinizing interactions with the public and the news media are all critical skills. Experience can be a good teacher.

There are downsides, however. Candidates and their staffs can be exhausted by the end and campaign funds depleted. Intramural attacks can weaken the nominee heading into the general campaign. Candidates must unify the party after potentially contentious primaries and reach out to opponents to overcome factional divisions.

The conventional wisdom is that a divisive primary—candidates attacking each other, exposing fault lines within the party, forcing the nominee to move to the ideological edges to hold the base—hurts the nominee in the general election.[54] The hypothesis seems reasonable enough, and there are notable examples. Ted Kennedy's challenge to Jimmy Carter for the 1980 nomination and Pat Buchanan's challenge to George H. W. Bush in 1992 are the last two times an incumbent president failed to win reelection. There are counterexamples, however. The hard-fought 2008 Democratic primary, in which Hillary Clinton and Barack Obama went to the wire, did not keep Obama from winning the general election (although some Clinton supporters wound up voting for McCain).[55] It is not clear, moreover, whether divisive primaries lead to a divided party and November losses or whether divisive primaries are a *consequence* of an already divided party

In 2016, both Clinton and Trump faced fractured parties. Many Sanders supporters were deeply unhappy with what they saw as a deliberate effort by Democratic leaders to deny Sanders the nomination and insisted that Clinton was too closely tied to wealthy backers and Wall Street. By the time Clinton had clinched the nomination in early June, 60 percent of Sanders supporters had an unfavorable view of her.[56] When Sanders endorsed Clinton on the first night of the Democratic convention, some of his delegates booed.[57]

The Republican primary was also divisive, with Trump and Republican leaders trading unusually acerbic language. In May 2016, many Republicans criticized Trump after he attacked a federal judge presiding over a lawsuit against him (Trump claimed he would not get a fair trial from a biased judge "of Mexican heritage").[58] Some of Trump's primary opponents, including Jeb Bush, Lindsey Graham, Carly Fiorina, Ted Cruz, and John Kasich, would not commit to supporting him if he won the nomination. Ted Cruz conspicuously refused to endorse Trump in a prime-time convention speech, telling convention delegates that they should "vote their conscience," to a torrent of "boos and taunts."[59] But Trump's selection of former Indiana Governor Mike Pence as his running mate strengthened Trump's standing among Republican conservatives.[60]

The 2016 presidential nomination process produced one candidate (Hillary Clinton) who had the near unanimous support of Democratic party leaders and another (Donald Trump) who won the nomination against overwhelming opposition among Republican party leaders.[61] Even so, postelection surveys showed that Republican voters were just as loyal to Trump (87 percent said they voted for him) as Democratic voters were to Clinton (89 percent said they voted for her).[62]

Nominees almost always adjust in the transition from the primary fight to the general election. The electorate is larger, more ideologically moderate, and less apt to be engaged than the activists and strong partisans who supported the nominee in the primaries. Building a larger electoral coalition may require softening policy stances initially directed toward partisans, and political lore holds that candidates must "move to the center" to pick up moderates and independents. It is not clear that this advice holds in today's highly politicized political environment, as both

Democrats and Republicans have relied on "base-maximizing" strategies in the last twenty years in an effort to mobilize supporters. In an age of rough partisan parity, party turnout is crucial to success.

CONCLUSION

The nomination process has changed significantly over the years as parties developed, notions of democratic legitimacy evolved, and both candidates and party leaders adapted to new environments. On the whole, the trend has been one of increasing democratization, expanding public participation and requiring candidates to solicit support from voters rather than party elites.

Throughout all of the changes, the goal has been consistent: choosing candidates who have the support of the most engaged partisans *and* who appeal to the broader electorate that participates in the general election. There is no fail-safe method of achieving this, however. At times, a candidate whom partisan voters enthusiastically support proves unacceptable to the general electorate; at other times, a candidate whom party professionals support overwhelmingly cannot generate enough support among voters. In the modern environment, the side that loses the general election— Republicans in 2012, Democrats in 2016—takes a close look at their own nomination rules to fix problems that party leaders think played a role in the loss.

Opening the process and reducing the power of party elites makes the system more representative, a normatively positive feature. But it comes at a cost. Openness can create and expose internal divisions in the party, splitting key constituencies and rewarding candidates who adopt negative strategies. A lengthy primary season requires candidates to raise enormous amounts of money and gives inequitable advantages to states holding their primaries and caucuses earlier. Huge fields— seventeen Republicans in 2016 and more than twenty Democrats in the 2020 cycle—can create a volatile campaign environment in which candidates struggle for footholds.

The nomination process also effects governance. Nominees generally have to appeal to their party's activists, who have the strongest ideological beliefs and are most likely to vote. These activists will remember the pledges the nominee made and expect the winner to fulfill them. This relationship increases democratic accountability but also makes it more difficult for the president to compromise. Core supporters may interpret flexibility as having sold-out, which can make the president's leadership tasks more difficult in polarized times.

DISCUSSION QUESTIONS

1. How will the record size of the Democratic 2020 candidate pool affect the strategies of individual candidates? Which of the candidates are frontrunners? Outsiders? Pulpit candidates?
2. Assess Donald Trump's 2016 campaign from the time he declared his candidacy until the time he clinched the nomination. Do you think the result would have been the same if there were fewer candidates? How did Trump—an outsider and newcomer—defeat so many experienced challengers?
3. Why is the vice presidency considered a stepping stone to a party's nomination? What advantages and disadvantages do contemporary vice presidents have in their quest to be the next nominee of their party?

WEB EXERCISES

1. Examine the 2020 state delegate assignments for both the Republican and Democratic nomination processes (https://www.thegreenpapers.com/P20/) and evaluate the allocations for more Republican states (Texas, Utah, South Carolina) and more Democratic states (California, New York, Illinois). Do the differences in the percentage of total delegates each state has for the Republican and Democratic contests seem material to you? Can you propose a different allocation formula?
2. Compare the social media feeds of candidates running in 2020 (you can do a search on Twitter or Instagram). How do the candidates' use of these communication channels differ?
3. The Center for Responsive Politics has initial fundraising data for 2020 candidates (https://www.opensecrets.org/2020-presidential-race). Can you conclude anything about the fate of contenders using this data? What lessons do you apply given what occurred in 2016?

SELECTED READINGS

Caesar, James W. *Presidential Selection: Theory and Development*. Princeton: Princeton University Press, 1979.

Cohen, Marty, David Karol, Hans Noel, and John Zaller. "Party versus Faction in the Reformed Presidential Nominating System," *PS: Political Science and Politics*, October 2016, pp. 701–708.

Costa, Robert. "Donald Trump and a GOP Primary Race Like No Other." In *Trumped: The 2016 Election that Broke All the Rules*, edited by Larry Sabato, Kyle Kondik, and Geoffrey Skelley. Lanham, MD: Rowman & Littlefield, 2017.

FairVote.org. *Delegating Democracy: How Parties Can Make Their Presidential Nominating Contests More Democratic*. Center for Voting and Democracy, 2008. https://www.fairvote.org/delegating-democracy.

Kamarck, Elaine. *Primary Politics: Everything You Need to Know about How America Nominates Its Presidential Candidates*. Washington, DC: Brookings Institution Press, 2018.

Lepore, Jill. "How to Steal an Election: The Crazy History of Nominating Conventions." *New Yorker*, July 4, 2016.

Patterson, Thomas E. "News Coverage of the 2016 Presidential Primaries: Horse Race Reporting Has Consequences." Faculty Research Working Paper Series RWP16-050, Harvard University, July 2016.

Sides, John, Michael Tesler, and Lynn Vavreck. *Identity Crisis: The 2016 Presidential Election and the Battle for the Meaning of America*. Princeton: Princeton University Press, 2018.

4

The Presidential Election

Jessica Rinaldi/The Boston Globe via Getty Images

Donald Trump celebrates his victory on election night.

Winning the nomination was only half the battle for Donald Trump. Victory in the general election was the real prize. Running for the general election is an ambitious undertaking. It requires the candidate and his or her aides to organize a substantial campaign operation, raise many millions of dollars, communicate with the public, obtain news coverage, commission polls, engage in presidential debates, and encourage his or her supporters to go to the polls. Ultimately, he or she has to win the votes of nearly seventy million Americans. All of this activity takes place within the framework of the electoral college.

THE ELECTORAL COLLEGE

When voters go to the polls every fourth November to select the president, they are not actually voting for the presidential candidates. Instead, they vote for the electors who subsequently choose a president. All that the Constitution says of this stage of the election process is that "each state shall appoint, in such manner as the legislature

74

thereof may direct, a number of electors, equal to the whole number of Senators and Representatives to which the state may be entitled in Congress." (Appendix C contains the constitutional provisions relating to presidential elections.)

The Origins of the Electoral College

The framers created the electoral college to solve one of their most difficult problems: how to protect the president's independence and, at the same time, fashion an electoral system that would be consistent with a republican form of government. They had no theory or model of selecting the executive to follow and struggled with their decision until the end of the Constitutional Convention.[1]

Selection by Congress?

Perhaps the most prominent criterion the constitutional delegates applied to evaluating schemes for selecting the president was limiting the potential for cabal, intrigue, faction, and corruption in the selection of the chief executive. The framers feared selection by the legislature, as occurred in Britain. Moreover, the delegates did not want the president to be dependent on the legislature for election. How could the executive's independence be preserved if election and reelection hinged on the president's relations with Congress?

Selection by the Public?

Although some prominent delegates supported selecting the president by direct election, many framers worried about giving the public a direct say in choosing the president. Some feared "mob" rule. Others thought voters would lack the necessary information about distinguished leaders in other parts of the country. In addition, some delegates were apprehensive that a president selected with the legitimacy of a broad popular vote would be too powerful.

Concern about National Elections

Some of the framers were also worried that the size of the country and the state of its communication and transportation systems would preclude holding and effectively monitoring the voting in a national election. Sectional distrust and rivalry aggravated this problem, because the states were to conduct the election of federal officials.

Slavery

Slavery also played a role. An earlier compromise allowed states to count three-fifths of the slaves living within them in calculating the basis for their representation in the House of Representatives—and thus for electoral votes. However, the slave population would not count with direct election of the president by the people because slaves could not vote. Thus, some delegates were concerned that direct election of the president would cause a reduction in the relative influence of the South because of its large nonvoting slave population. The electoral college obviated this problem.[2]

Short-Term Concerns

There were also short-term concerns. The decision about the electoral college came near the end of the Constitutional Convention, when delegates were tired and impatient. They also had a need to avoid additional conflict as they took the Constitution to the states for ratification. Everyone knew that George Washington would be the first president, so the framers were content to defer further decisions about presidential selection.

Contemporary Relevance
The motivations behind the creation of the electoral college are simply irrelevant today: legislative election is not an option; there is little danger that the president will be too powerful if directly elected; voters have extraordinary access to information on the candidates; there is no justification at all for either electors or state legislatures to exercise discretion in selecting the president; defending the interests of slavery is unthinkable; and the short-term pressures have long dissipated.

Deciding on Electors
In the end, the framers created the electoral college, a body of electors charged with the task of voting for the president and vice president. The framers allowed the states to decide how to select the electors, and many states used the state legislatures for this purpose in the early years of the Republic. In those states, there was no general election to choose the president.

So great was the sectional rivalry, so parochial the country, and so limited the number of people with national reputations that the delegates feared that electors would vote primarily for candidates they knew, candidates from their own states. To prevent the same states, particularly the largest ones, from exercising undue influence in the selection of both the president and vice president, electors were given two votes each but could not cast them both for inhabitants of their own state.

The framers expected the electors to exercise discretion in selecting the president. They were not agents of a political party, as parties did not exist in 1787 when the Constitution was written. It did not take long for parties to develop, however, and soon electors were selected by parties and expected to support their parties' candidates. Many of the framers expected no candidate to receive a majority of the electoral vote, forcing the House of Representatives to choose the president (discussed below).

How the Electoral College Works
Each state's representation in the electoral college is equal to its representation in Congress. As a result, every state is guaranteed a minimum of three electoral votes: two matching the number of its US senators and one or more corresponding to the number of representatives it has in the US House of Representatives. In the twenty-first century, with fifty states in the Union, the electoral college consists of 538 persons: 435 corresponding to the number of representatives, 100 to the number of senators, and an additional 3 for the District of Columbia under the Twenty-third Amendment to the Constitution. Appendix D shows how each state cast its electoral votes in the 2016 presidential election.

The electors gather in their state capitals in December to cast their electoral votes. These votes are then sent to Congress. If one candidate receives a majority of the electoral votes, that candidate is declared the winner.

If no candidate wins a majority of the electoral votes, as happened in 1800 and 1824, the House of Representatives chooses the president. In such an election, each state's House delegation receives one vote, which would allow the seven smallest states, with a population of about 6 million, to outvote the six largest states, with a population of about 133 million. It is virtually impossible to find any defenders of this constitutional provision, which is the most egregious violation of democratic principles in American government.

If, as would be likely, there is no majority in the electoral college vote for vice president when a presidential candidate also lacks a majority, the Senate chooses the vice president by majority vote. The Senate would probably select a vice president from the same ticket as the person the House chose as president, but it does not have to do so. The Senate has selected the vice president only once, in 1837, when it chose Richard M. Johnson to serve in that post.

Violating Political Equality

Political equality lies at the core of democratic theory. Robert Dahl, the leading democratic theorist of the twentieth century, included equality in voting as a central standard for a democratic process: "Every member must have an equal and effective opportunity to vote, and all votes must be counted as equal."[3] Indeed, it is difficult to imagine a definition of democracy that does not include equality in voting as a central standard.

A popular misconception is that electoral votes simply aggregate popular votes. In reality, the electoral vote regularly deviates from the popular will as expressed in the popular vote—sometimes in such a way as to deny the presidency to the people's preferred candidate. Popular votes do not equal electoral votes—the former express the people's choice, while the latter determine who is to be the people's president.

Unit-Vote System

The percentage of electoral votes received by a candidate nationwide rarely coincides with the candidate's percentage of the national popular vote for several reasons, the most important of which is the winner-take-all (or unit-vote) system.[4] All states except Maine and Nebraska have a winner-take-all system in which they award *every* electoral vote to the candidate who receives the most popular votes in that state. In effect, the system assigns to the winner the votes of the people who voted *against* the winner.

The operation of the winner-take-all system effectively disenfranchises voters who support losing candidates in each state. In the 2000 presidential election, nearly three million people voted for Al Gore in Florida. Because George W. Bush won 537 more votes than Gore, however, he received all of Florida's electoral votes. A candidate can win some states by very narrow margins (as Trump did in Michigan, Pennsylvania, and Wisconsin in 2016), lose other states by large margins (as Trump did by more than one million votes in California and New York), and so win the electoral vote while losing the popular vote. Because there is no way to aggregate votes across states, the votes for candidates who do not finish first in a state play no role in the outcome of the election.

In a multicandidate contest such as the ones in 1992, 1996, 2000, and 2016, the winner-take-all system may suppress the votes of the majority as well as the minority. In 1996 less than a majority of voters decided how the electoral votes of twenty-six states would be cast. In 2000, pluralities rather than majorities determined the allocation of electoral votes in eight states, including Florida and Ohio. In 2016, pluralities decided the electoral votes in fourteen states. In each case, fewer than half the voters determined how *all* of their state's electoral votes were cast.

One result of these distorting factors is that there is typically a substantial disparity in almost all elections between the share of the national popular vote a candidate receives and that candidate's percentage of the electoral vote. In 1876, 1888, 2000, 2016, and, arguably, 1960,[5] the candidate who finished second in the popular vote *won* the election.

The unit-vote system also allows even small third parties to siphon more votes from one major-party candidate than the other and thus determine the outcome in a state, as Ralph Nader did in both Florida and New Hampshire in 2000. Indeed, by taking more votes from Gore than from Bush, Nader determined the outcome of the entire election. The results distorted the preferences of the voters because the preferred candidate in both Florida and New Hampshire in a two-person race was Al Gore, not George W. Bush who ultimately won the states.[6]

Allocation of Electoral Votes among States

The Constitution allocates electoral votes to each state equal to that state's representation in Congress. This system of distribution further diminishes the impact of the popular vote in electing the president. First, the number of House seats does not exactly correspond to the population of a state. The populations of some states barely exceed the threshold for an additional seat while those in other states just miss it. In 2010, Wyoming had one representative for 563,626 individuals and Montana had one representative for 989,415 individuals.[7] As the House becomes increasingly malapportioned, the electoral college becomes further skewed in favor of the small rural states, accentuating the difference between the popular vote and the electoral college vote.[8]

The census figures used to determine the number of seats a state has in the House (and thus the electoral votes that match them) may be out of date and thus lead to the overrepresentation of some states and underrepresentation of others. The allocation of electoral votes in the election of 2000, for example, actually reflected the population distribution among the states of 1990, a decade earlier. On the basis of the 1980 census, California was allocated forty-seven electors. The Census Bureau estimate for California's population in 1988, however, would have translated into fifty-four electoral votes in the election of that year. Other high-growth states such as Florida, Texas, and Arizona have also been penalized in recent elections, whereas states with slower growth or population declines have benefited from the lag in reapportionment.[9] As a result, presidential candidates who win high-growth states are penalized while those winning lower-growth states benefit.

In addition, each state receives two electoral votes corresponding to the number of its US senators. When states with unequal populations receive similar numbers of electoral votes, states with smaller populations gain a mathematical advantage. Thus, every voter's ballot does not carry the same weight. That is, the ratio of electoral votes to population varies from state to state, benefiting the smallest states. In the most extreme case, for example, an electoral vote in Wyoming in 2016 corresponded to only 195,167 persons, while one in California corresponded to 713,637 persons. The typical citizen of Wyoming, then, had on average more than three and a half times as much influence in determining an electoral vote for president as the typical citizen of California, and more than three times as much influence as the typical Texan, New Yorker, or Floridian.[10]

The allocation of electoral votes among states overrepresents small states in the electoral college and introduces yet another deviation from voter equality into the election of the American president. Smaller states have a larger percentage of the electoral vote than of the national population.

It is often said that the mathematical advantages of small states are more than compensated by the winner-take-all system of awarding electoral votes to candidates. This system is said to favor large states because the largest prizes in electoral votes are in the most populous states. Inhabitants of the large states thus benefit from candidates courting their votes. However, whether any large state will be courted depends on whether it is "in play" in the sense that either candidate might win the plurality of its votes. In all elections since 2000, for example, the three largest states have not been competitive on the presidential level and have been largely ignored by the candidates.

Faithless Electors

One other factor that can affect the translation of votes into electoral votes is the fidelity of electors. Since the first presidential election, there has been controversy about the proper role of presidential electors. The main point of contention is whether they are to think and act independently or are merely to serve as agents of the people who chose them. Electors who vote for whomever they wish destroy any relationship between the popular vote in their states and their own electoral votes.

Over the years, there have been a number of electors who did not vote for the candidate of their party.[11] In 2016, seven electors voted for someone other than their party's designated candidate. Five of them deserted Hillary Clinton and two chose not to vote for Donald Trump.

Constitutional Consistency?

Some defenders of the electoral college argue that its violations of majority rule are just an example of several constitutional provisions that require supermajorities to take action. For example, it takes the votes of two-thirds of the senators present to ratify a treaty. The framers designed all such provisions, however, to allow minorities to *prevent* an action. The electoral college is different. It allows a minority to *take* an action—that is, to select the president. As such, it is the only device of its kind in the Constitution. Thus, the electoral college does not prevent tyranny of the majority. Instead, it provides the potential for tyranny of the minority.

Electing the Loser of the Popular Vote

The principal consequence of the way the electoral college works is to sometimes elect the person who lost the popular vote. Such an occurrence is especially likely in close contests. Since 1828 there have been twelve presidential elections in which the candidate receiving the most popular votes had a lead of fewer than 3 percentage points over his or her closest competitor (1844, 1876, 1880, 1884, 1888, 1916, 1960, 1968, 1976, 2000, 2004, and 2016). Of these twelve elections, the electoral college has elected the *loser* of the popular vote in five instances: 1876, 1888, 1960, 2000, and 2016 (table 4.1), or 42 percent of the time.

The presidential election of 2016 was the second one in this century in which the popular vote winner lost in the electoral college. Hillary Clinton won almost three million more popular votes than Donald Trump, but he received seventy-seven more electoral votes than Clinton, which gave him an electoral college majority.

The electoral college also caused two other violations of political equality in earlier elections. Too few states allowed popular selection of electors to make reasonable comparisons of candidates' popular vote totals in 1800. What is unequivocally clear, however, is that Thomas Jefferson benefited from the constitutional provision that

Table 4.1 Electoral College Reversal of Popular Vote Winners

Year	Candidate	Popular Votes		Electoral Votes	
		N	%	N	%
1876	Tilden (D)	4,288,546	51.0	184*	50
	Hayes (R)	4,034,311	48.0	185	50
Tilden popular vote margin of 254,235; Hayes winner with electoral vote margin of 1.					
1888	Cleveland (D)	5,534,488	48.6	168	42
	Harrison (R)	5,443,892	47.8	233	58
Cleveland popular vote margin of 95,096; Harrison winner with electoral vote margin of 65.					
1960	Nixon (R)	34,108,157†	49.5	219	41
	Kennedy (D)	34,049,976	49.5	303	59
Nixon popular vote margin of 58,181; Kennedy winner with electoral vote margin of 84.					
2000	Gore (D)	50,996,062	48.4	266	49
	Bush (R)	50,456,169	47.9	271	50
Gore popular vote margin of 539,893; Bush winner with electoral vote margin of 5.					
2016	Clinton (D)	65,677,168	48.0	227	42
	Trump (R)	62,692,411	45.8	304	57
Clinton popular vote margin of 2,984,757; Trump winner with electoral vote margin of 77.					

* The electoral vote results in 1876 were arrived at by a bipartisan election commission, voting along party lines, which awarded twenty disputed electoral votes to Hayes.

† The popular vote totals for 1960 used here are computed by crediting Kennedy with five-elevenths of Alabama's Democratic votes and the unpledged elector slate with six-elevenths.

Note: The election of 1824 also resulted in a reversal of the popular vote winner but through use of the House contingent procedure.

Sources: Congressional Quarterly's Guide to U.S. Elections, 6th ed. (Washington, DC: CQ Press, 2010); Jerrold G. Rusk, A Statistical History of the American Electorate (Washington, DC: CQ Press, 2001); Clerk of the House of Representatives Jeff Trandahl, Statistics of the Presidential and Congressional Election of November 7, 2000 (US House of Representatives, 2001); and Statistics of the Presidential and Congressional Election from Official Sources for the Election of November 8, 2016 (Office of the Clerk, US House of Representatives, Washington, DC, February 22, 2017).

counted slaves as three-fifths of a person for representation in the House and consequently in a state's votes in the electoral college. At least twelve of the electoral votes Jefferson received (he won by eight) were the result of the three-fifths rule.[12] Had there been no electoral college, which accorded slaveholders and their neighbors extra weight in selecting the president, John Adams would have won reelection in 1800.

In addition, the provision for contingent elections in the House of Representatives resulted in the candidate with the most popular votes losing the election in 1824, when the House chose John Quincy Adams over the winner of the popular vote, Andrew Jackson.

Defending State Interests or Distorting the Campaign?
One common justification for the electoral college and its violations of political equality is that it ensures that presidential candidates will be attentive to and protective of states' interests, especially the interests of states with small populations.

In reality, the electoral college discourages candidates from paying attention to most states, because most states are not competitive in presidential elections. The winner-take-all nature of the electoral college weakens the incentive for the candidates of either the majority or minority party in a noncompetitive state to attempt to persuade citizens to go to the polls and support its national ticket. It makes no sense for candidates to allocate scarce resources to states they either cannot win or are certain to win. Moreover, winning a state by a large margin is irrelevant. It does not matter if you win by one vote or by a million votes, you receive the same number of electoral votes.

Candidates focus on competitive states, especially large ones such as Florida and Ohio. Such states are known as *swing* states or *battleground* states.[13] As Barack Obama's 2008 campaign manager wrote, "Most of the country—those who lived in safely red or blue states—did not truly witness the 2008 presidential campaign. The real contest occurred in only about sixteen states."[14]

Candidate Visits
During the presidential general election of 2012, the major party presidential candidates visited just three of the twenty-five smallest states (including the District of Columbia): New Hampshire, Nevada, and Iowa. Barack Obama visited only eight states during the entire general election, and Mitt Romney visited only ten. The states the candidates did visit were competitive states, especially large competitive states such as Florida and Ohio.

The emphasis on campaigning in swing states is not unusual.[15] In 2016, no presidential candidate visited any of the seven smallest states—those with three electoral votes—or the District of Columbia. Of the thirty-seven smallest states—those with eleven or fewer electoral votes, they campaigned in only thirteen. Once again, they focused their attention on large competitive states.

In addition to its failure to encourage candidates to visit small states, the electoral college provides incentives to ignore many larger states during the general election. In 2012 the candidates never campaigned in California, Texas, New York, or Illinois, four of the five largest states. In 2016, among the largest states Hillary Clinton made one stop in Illinois and Donald Trump visited Texas twice.

In the course of overlooking most states, candidates also avoid entire regions of the country. Democrats have little incentive to campaign in the heavily Republican Great Plains and Deep South, and Republicans have little incentive to visit the West Coast and most of Democratic New England.

Contrary to the conventional wisdom, then, the electoral college provides no incentive for candidates to pay attention to small states and take their cases directly to their citizens. Indeed, it is difficult to imagine how presidential candidates could be less attentive to small states than they already are. They go where the electoral college makes them go, and it makes them go to competitive states, especially large competitive states. They ignore most small states; in fact, they ignore most of the country.

Advertising
Candidates reach most voters through television advertising. Technology makes it easy to place ads in any media market in the nation at short notice. Do candidates compensate for their lack of visits to small or noncompetitive states by advertising there?

No. Some voters are bombarded with television advertising; others see none at all. Following a well-established pattern,[16] in 2016, 99 percent of the advertising was done in fourteen battleground states, which included only 35 percent of the population.[17] Similarly, in the 2012 general election, almost all the advertising by the Democrats and Republicans occurred in the swing states.[18]

Voter Turnout

The foregone nature of the election in most states also reduces the incentives for people to vote. As a consequence, turnout in competitive states is usually higher than in the rest of the country.[19]

Preserving Federalism?

In the electoral college, votes are cast by states. Is the electoral college an essential bulwark of federalism? We have already seen that the electoral college does not cause presidential candidates to devote attention to the states as states in general or to small states in particular. Neither the existence nor the powers and responsibilities of state governments depend in any way on the existence of the electoral college. If it were abolished, states would have the same rights and duties they have now.

Federalism is deeply embodied in congressional elections, in which two senators represent each state just because it is a state and in which members of the House are elected from districts within states. Direct election of the president would not alter these federalism-sustaining aspects of the constitutional structure. A leading expert on federalism, Neal Peirce, has said it best: "The vitality of federalism rests chiefly on the constitutionally mandated system of congressional representation and the will and capacity of state and local governments to address compelling problems, not on the hocus-pocus of an eighteenth-century vote count system."[20]

Two of the most important authors of the Constitution, James Wilson and James Madison, understood well both the diversity of state interests and the many protections for states embodied in the Constitution. They saw little need to confer additional power to small states through the electoral college. "Can we forget for whom we are forming a government?" Wilson asked. "Is it for *men,* or for the imaginary beings called *States?*"[21] Madison declared that "the President is to act for the *people* not for *States*"[22] and opposed counting the presidential vote by state (as in the unit rule).[23]

Moreover, Madison did not want candidates to make appeals to special interests. As he proclaimed at the Constitutional Convention, "Local considerations must give way to the general interest."[24] He did not want a presidency that was responsive to parochial interests in a system that already offered minority interests extraordinary access to policy makers and opportunities to thwart policies they opposed. Madison also understood that rivalry was more likely to occur among large states than coalition.[25] The great political battles of American history—in Congress and in presidential elections—have been fought by opposing ideological and economic interests, not by small states and large states.

Protecting Non-State-Based Minority Interests

Does the electoral college ensure a "proper distribution" of the vote, in which the winning candidate receives majority support across social strata, thus protecting minority interests? The evidence is clear that it does not. In 2016, Donald Trump won a *smaller* percentage than Hillary Clinton of the votes of women; African

Americans, Hispanics, and Asian Americans; voters aged eighteen to forty-four; members of labor unions; those with less than $50,000 annual household income; college graduates and those with postgraduate educations; Jews; liberals and moderates; urbanites; or those living in the East and the West.

In 2000, George W. Bush did not win a larger percentage than Al Gore of the votes of women, African Americans, Hispanics, and Asian Americans; voters aged eighteen to twenty-nine or those aged sixty-five or older; the poor; members of labor unions; those with less than $50,000 of household income; those with a high school education or less and those with postgraduate education; Catholics, Jews, and Muslims; liberals and moderates; urbanites; or those living in the East and West.[26]

Thus, neither Trump's nor Bush's votes represented concurrent majorities across the major strata of American society. What actually happened in 2000 and 2016 was that the electoral college elected a candidate supported by white male Protestants—the dominant social group in the country—over the objections not only of a plurality of all voters but also of most "minority" interests in the country.

Consequences of Direct Election

What would be the likely consequences of electing the president by direct election, the same way we elect virtually every other official in the nation?

Campaigning

First, candidates would be much more attentive to small states and minorities. Because every vote counts in a direct election, candidates would have an incentive to appeal to all voters and not just those strategically located in swing states.[27] An extra vote in Massachusetts or Texas would count as much as one in Michigan or Florida.

With these incentives, candidates would find it easy to spread their attention more evenly across the country. Because the cost of advertising is mainly a function of market size, it does not cost more to reach ten thousand voters in Wyoming than it does to reach the same number of voters in a neighborhood in Queens or Los Angeles. Actually, it may cost less to reach voters in smaller communities because larger markets tend to run out of commercial time, increasing the price of advertising.

Direct election of the president also would provide the incentive for candidates to encourage all of their supporters, no matter where they live, to go to the polls, because under direct election every vote counts. Conversely, under the electoral college it does not matter how many votes a candidate receives in a state as long as the number of votes surpasses that any opponent receives. The goal is to win states, not voters.

It is possible, but by no means certain, that some candidates would find it more cost effective under direct election to mobilize votes in urban areas or to visit urban areas where they would receive free television coverage reaching large audiences. Such actions would do nothing to undermine the argument against the electoral college, however. Small states cannot be worse off than they are now, because under the electoral college candidates rarely visit or campaign there. Instead, direct election would provide increased incentives for candidates to campaign in most small states, as well as increased incentives to campaign in many large and medium-sized states. Direct election would disperse campaign efforts rather than deprive small states of them.

Direct election, unlike the electoral college, thus encourages citizens to participate in elections and candidates to take their campaigns to these citizens, enhancing our civic life. Direct election would increase voter turnout and stimulate party-building efforts in the weaker party, especially in less competitive states.

Two-Party System

Some critics of direct election mistakenly claim that it would splinter the two-party system. Their criticism is based on the premise that direct election would require a runoff between the two leading candidates. But it would not. Under the electoral college, victorious presidential candidates—including, most recently, John F. Kennedy (1960), Richard Nixon (1968), Bill Clinton (1992 and 1996), George W. Bush (2000), and Donald Trump (2016)—have received less than a majority of the national popular vote about 40 percent of the time since 1824, and there is no relation between the vote they received and their later success in, say, dealing with Congress. Some of our strongest presidents, including James K. Polk, Abraham Lincoln, Grover Cleveland, Woodrow Wilson, Harry S. Truman, and Kennedy, received a plurality, but not a majority, of the popular vote.

Nor is the electoral college the basis of the two-party system. Single-member districts and plurality election are, and the nation would be one electoral district under direct election. Thus direct election would not splinter the party system.

By contrast, direct election would protect the country from the mischief of third parties. The electoral college's unit rule encourages third parties, especially those with a regional base, because by winning a few states they may deny either major-party candidate a majority of the electoral vote. Such a result was certainly the goal of the racist candidates Strom Thurmond in 1948 and George Wallace in 1968. Moreover, even without winning any states, Ralph Nader inadvertently distorted the vote and determined the outcome of the election in 2000.

Nevertheless, the United States still uses the electoral college system to select the president. Thus, winning the election is about building and maintaining an electoral college majority, not a popular vote victory. Presidential campaigns, then, focus on battleground states.

THE GENERAL ELECTION CAMPAIGN

Presidential candidates have not always actively campaigned. For much of American history, personal campaigning by nominees was seen as demeaning and unbecoming of the dignity of the presidency. Candidates left the campaign task to surrogates. It was not until 1840 that this tradition of nonparticipation was broken when William Henry Harrison made campaign speeches in his home state of Ohio. Though a decidedly mild tactic by modern standards, the appearances "were unprecedented efforts at displaying the candidate to the electorate."[28] It was twenty years before another presidential candidate followed the practice, when Senator Stephen A. Douglas spoke out on the slavery issue as the Democratic nominee in 1860.

Major-party nominees returned to the sidelines until the 1880s, when Republican James Garfield broke tradition by receiving visitors at his Ohio home (in what became known as "front porch" campaigning). Four years later, Republican James Blaine made hundreds of campaign speeches around the country in an effort to rebut accusations that he had profited from a fraudulent railroad deal. Benjamin Harrison, the Republican nominee in 1888, continued the practice of front-porch campaigning, as did William McKinley in 1896. But Democratic nominee William Jennings Bryan's traveling road show in 1896 served as a harbinger of modern campaigns. Bryan traveled 18,000 miles, gave six hundred speeches, and spoke to almost five million people.[29] In 1900 Republican vice presidential candidate Theodore Roosevelt broke Bryan's record, giving nearly 700 speeches in 24 states.[30] Campaigning across the country had become the rule; the last of the front-porch campaigns was staged in 1920 by Warren G. Harding.

In 1932, Herbert Hoover became the first incumbent to actively campaign for reelection. His opponent, Franklin Roosevelt, crisscrossed the country by railroad, appearing before thousands of people and thereby undermining rumors that he had been disabled by polio.

Technological developments changed presidential campaigns. Radio offered the first mass media opportunities, giving candidates the ability to speak to nearly unlimited audiences. Rather than run ads, candidates bought radio time to talk directly to voters through broadcast speeches.[31] Roosevelt's skillful use of radio in 1932 magnified the impact that personal appeals can have for winning the election and leading the country.

The first television spots ran in 1952, when both Dwight D. Eisenhower and Democratic nominee Adlai Stevenson communicated with voters over the new medium. The percentage of households with televisions grew from under 1 percent in 1948 to 34 percent in 1952 and 92 percent in 1968,[32] making television ads a permanent and ubiquitous part of the campaign. Television accelerated personal campaigning by the candidates, and made leadership qualities more important. The focus on visual imagery encouraged candidates to use themes, slogans, and code words in their ads and speeches.

The Internet created new tools and technological opportunities, revolutionizing the ways candidates engage with voters. Candidates, parties, and outside groups create websites to connect with voters and disseminate information, without the limits imposed by thirty-second ads or the cost of mass mailings. Campaigns analyze data on web activity and social media groups, using vast troves of digital information to target communications to the individual voter.

All of these functions are managed by professionals active in election activities and usually with discernible partisan orientations. Advances in communication technologies have increased the size, composition, and complexity of running a modern presidential campaign.

Organization and Operations

Today, running for president requires a large and highly specialized campaign organization. In addition to communications, the campaign must raise money; develop strategy; research and draft speeches and policy positions; schedule travel and events; conduct polls; test themes and slogans; design, evaluate, and place advertising; manage grassroots operations; run vast data analysis operations; and organize get-out-the-vote efforts. In addition, there are accounting and legal requirements; liaison with national, state, and local party committees and other friendly groups; Secret Service coordination; and constant interaction with the news media. Senior campaign officials direct each of these functions.

The following snapshots from previous campaigns highlight these organizational requirements.

2000–2012

The campaigns of George W. Bush in 2000 and 2004 and Barack Obama in 2008 and 2012 were models of well-run and well-coordinated efforts. Each had tightly controlled operations, carefully designed strategic plans, highly centralized decision making, and rapid response to attacks. In contrast, their opponents' campaigns were

Richard Ellis/Alamy Stock Photo

Donald Trump during the 2016 campaign.

not nearly as well orchestrated and well run. Obama's campaigns in particular used data analytics and digital communications to great effect in fundraising, voter targeting, and grassroots organizing. The losers' campaigns were plagued by mixed messages, strained resources, and staff turmoil during periods in which they lost ground to their opponents. Tension among campaign personnel—the natural consequence of ambitious people working long hours under constant pressure—is nothing new, but it does tend to be worse when the nominee appears to be slipping and candidates and staff search for scapegoats.

2016

The Trump and Clinton campaigns of 2016 both had their share of internal dissent. Clinton's campaign organization, modeled on Obama's presidential campaigns, was larger with more paid staff and field offices than Trump's smaller and more fluid staff structure. They both had digital operations that depended on social media platforms, especially Facebook. At the outset, Clinton's campaign had better analytical capabilities than Trump's, although over the course of the campaign his online staff improved their data analysis, targeting potential supporters on Facebook. Still, Trump ran an unconventional campaign, which through September 2016 had spent more on merchandise than on polling or direct mail.[33] Clinton depended heavily on her campaign's grassroots operation, while Trump built a volunteer base from the enthusiasm generated by his rallies.

Financial Resources

Presidential candidates and their outside supporters spent $2.4 billion during the 2015–2016 election cycle.[34]

Raising large sums is easier now than in the past. Individuals can contribute unlimited amounts to independent groups promoting a candidate or issue (super PACs). Laws regulating contributions to political parties have been amended to allow parties to transfer money between state and national committees, in effect increasing individual contribution limits to more than $1 million per person per election cycle.[35] The Bipartisan Campaign Reform Act (2002) doubled individual contributions to candidates and adjusted that amount to inflation. In 2016, the contribution limit to federal candidates was $2,700, with the nominations and general election counting as separate elections.

The Internet has become a major fund-raising tool for candidates, parties, and nonparty groups. Fundraising over email and online is much more efficient than traditional techniques, and even a contribution of a few dollars can exceed the cost of soliciting it. In 2016, Donald Trump received 26 percent of his campaign funds from contributions of $200 or less, more than Hillary Clinton, who raised 16 percent of her contributions in such amounts. In 2012, Barack Obama received almost one-third of his revenue from small donations.[36]

There are differences in how candidates, parties, and independent groups raise and spend money. Although contributions to candidates are limited, the campaign organization has much more flexibility in spending than do nonparty groups. Candidates are charged the lowest rate a television or radio broadcaster charges for political commercials; nonparty groups pay more. Candidates can direct expenditures to their campaign themes and agenda; nonparty groups are not permitted to coordinate their spending with candidates. The non-coordination rule has been difficult to enforce, however, especially when candidates set up their own super PACs and hire the same professional consulting firms to advise them on public relations, event activities, fund-raising, and grassroots and digital operations.

Nonparty groups, particular super PACs, were active during the 2015–2016 election cycle. *Priorities USA Action*, a Clinton super PAC, spent the most, $133.4 million. Jeb Bush's super PAC, *Right to Rise USA* had the second-highest expenditures, $86.8 million

Many troublesome issues can arise from the solicitation and expenditure of such large amounts of private funds. One is the burden of constant fundraising on candidates and their staffs. A second is the effect that big donors and spenders have on election results and on the winners once the election is over. The perception that elected officials are unduly influenced by the individuals and groups that helped them get elected has contributed to the public's distrust of politicians and their ability to govern fairly in the public's interests, not special interests. Although the Supreme Court has concluded that, as a matter of law, independent expenditures cannot be corrupting, a super PAC that spends $100 million supporting a candidate almost certainly has influence over policy in ways that a $2,700 individual contributor to that candidate does not.[37]

At the presidential level, the general election winners usually spend more money than the losers. In 2008, Barack Obama raised and spent more than twice as much as John McCain and the Republican Party and won handily; in 2012, Obama's campaign organization also had a financial advantage but when outside expenditures are included, more was spent by and for Republican Mitt Romney than for Obama. In 2016, Donald Trump contributed $66.1 million of his own money to his campaign for the Republican nomination and general election. Nevertheless, Hillary Clinton raised and spent far more than Trump, and she still lost.[38] Money did not dictate the outcome of that election.

Communications

Candidates air advertising, send digital messages, and hold live events to engage voters, and they try to create or reinforce news as they do so. Repetition is key to reaching people who may be relatively uninterested in electoral politics; reinforcement is essential to maintain consistent imagery; and coordination of the various communication messages is necessary for thematic focus. The goal is to activate partisan tendencies and mobilize voters.

Advertising

Television remains the primary means of communicating with voters, both through paid advertising and "free media" obtained through news coverage, although digital and social media advertising has grown. Over the last few decades, presidential candidates have devoted roughly half of their overall spending to advertising of one form or another.

There were over one million ads on air and online in the 2016 presidential election. Hillary Clinton dominated the advertising, running more than three times as many ads and spending more than three times as much as Trump did.[39] Clinton's defeat raises the question of how effective advertising is in determining voting behavior. Surprisingly, there is not much evidence that presidential campaign ads are very effective in changing voters' minds about the candidates. Ads have more impact on activating voters' existing preferences and encouraging voter turnout.[40]

Radio and television advertising tends to be targeted to different sections of the country and different groups within the electorate. Candidates direct their campaign ads toward the major media markets in the battleground states. Media buyers typically identify stations by their viewers and program format so that the messages fit the audience both demographically and geographically. Far more advertising appears on local stations and cable networks than on national broadcast news, as this allows for more precise geographic and demographic targeting.

Candidates work as hard to destroy their opponent's image as they do to build their own. Negative advertising has a long history: in the 1800 presidential election, supporters of Thomas Jefferson and John Adams went after the opposing candidates with a ferocity notable even by contemporary standards.[41]

Negative TV spots have been used regularly since 1964, when the Johnson campaign ran what is perhaps the most famous negative ad ever. Called "Daisy Girl," it was intended to cast Republican nominee Barry Goldwater as a trigger-happy zealot who would not hesitate to use nuclear weapons against Communist foes. The advertisement begins with a young girl standing in a meadow and plucking petals from a daisy. She counts to herself in a soft voice. When she reaches eleven, she starts counting back to zero. Her voice fades as a stern male voice takes over the countdown. At zero, there is an explosion, the little girl disappears, and a mushroom-shaped cloud covers the screen. President Lyndon Johnson then says in voice-over: "These are the stakes: to make a world in which all of God's children can live, or go into the dark. We must either love each other, or we must die." The ad closed by urging a vote for Lyndon Johnson, with an announcer saying, "the stakes are too high for you to stay home." Notably, it did not mention Goldwater at all.[42]

The "Daisy Girl" Ad, 1964.

Library of Congress, Motion Picture, Broadcasting, and Recorded Sound Division.

The commercial ran only once. Outraged Goldwater supporters filed complaints with the Federal Communications Commission and the National Association of Broadcasters. Their protests only kept the issue alive. The ad itself became news. Parts of it ran on television newscasts, reinforcing the impression the Democrats wished to leave in the voters' minds. It is widely considered to have changed political advertising, ushering in the modern era powerful imagery and metaphorical rather than literal themes.[43]

The use of negative advertising has increased in recent years. Since 2008, more than half the ads run in the presidential campaigns have been negative. Outside groups and political parties sponsor most of the negative ads, but campaign organizations do their share. Half of Clinton's ads in 2016 were negative; Trump relied more on ads that contrasted the candidates than on strictly negative ones.[44] Positive ads are most likely when less is known about the candidates, usually in the early stages of the nomination process or general election. The most negative presidential campaign occurred in 2012. The 2016 campaign was a close second.[45]

Digital Communications

The Internet emerged as a campaign communication vehicle in the 1990s. Bill Clinton's 1992 campaign communicated internally via e-mail, keeping its staff informed on policy and political matters. By 1996, most candidates had websites. John McCain used his to make his first appeal for funds in 2000 after winning the New Hampshire primary. In 2004, Howard Dean created a campaign blog which thousands accessed and on which he and other campaign staff regularly communicated with supporters. Dean raised $27 million online, much of it in the form of small contributions.[46] In

2008, Obama raised $500 million through digital media, and almost $700 million in 2012.[47]

The Obama campaigns hired programmers, statisticians, and bloggers; set up a multipurpose, user-friendly website and encouraged those who accessed it to start their own discussion groups, network with their friends, contribute money, and disseminate information. The campaigns acquired a large database of email and postal addresses, cell phone numbers, and other information, which campaign staff not only used but also made available online to volunteers who solicited funds and made personal contacts. The Obama team also took advantage of YouTube and Twitter, uploading nearly 2,000 video clips that were seen millions of times.

In 2012, Obama's reelection campaign more effectively integrated and analyzed its voting data and targeted different groups with specific communications based on the data it acquired on individuals' friends, associates, interests, and web activities. Volunteers personally contacted 150 million people in their homes or by phone, with follow up calls before the election.

Cognizant of the Democrats' lead in digital capabilities, the Republicans launched their own updated digital operation following the 2008 elections. In 2012, Mitt Romney invested heavily in an app designed to connect tens of thousands of volunteers on election day and use real-time data on voting activity that could direct election-day get-out-the-vote activities in crucial battleground states. The much-hyped but untested system, named ORCA (after the killer whale and a jab at the Obama campaign which had named its main data analytic system Project Narwhal) did not live up expectations: it broke down immediately on election day as volunteers could not log in, the system crashed multiple times, and at one point everything was shut down by the internet service provider because the number of attempts to connect appeared to be a hacking effort.[48]

Donald Trump spent much of his advertising budget on Facebook. He had a staff of over a hundred people engaged in online operations that collected lists of registered voters, gun owners, and others with views that coincided with the candidate's. His campaign bought thousands of Facebook ads, targeting users who matched the demographic or ideological profile of Trump voters.[49] Trump also sent out a near-constant stream of tweets that were magnified by an online group that supported his candidacy. His use of Twitter had a clear effect on news coverage: tweets would generate stories, which would generate responses and subsequent tweets, which would in turn generate more stories. It was an unprecedented use of social media and an extremely effective campaign tool.[50]

Hillary Clinton tried to replicate Obama's digital strategy, engaging and micro-targeting with the huge amounts of data that her campaign had collected. Her strategists depended heavily on analyzing these data, performing simulations, and projecting voting trends among targeted groups. However, her campaign did not advertise online until near the end of the campaign. Similarly, Clinton tweeted, but not to the extent that Trump did, and she recieved nowhere near the amount of news coverage for her online activities that Trump's campaign did.

The initial goal of Trump's digital operation was to expand his electoral base and raise campaign funds. In the latter stages of the campaign when he was behind in the polls, his online operatives added a new strategic objective: suppress the Clinton vote, particularly among liberals, young women, and African American men. His online ads referred to her previous support of the Trans-Pacific Partnership, her accusations against women with whom her husband had affairs, and her 1996 reference to African American males as "super predators."[51] Although Clinton's share of the vote in these demographics was smaller than what Obama received in 2012, it is difficult to know how much of Trump's effort contributed to her declining support.

Presidential Debates

More than any other single campaign event, presidential debates focus public attention and offer candidates a way to communicate to a large national audience—for free. It is estimated that more than half the adult population in the United States watched the first presidential debate between John F. Kennedy and Richard Nixon in 1960, and almost 90 percent of the electorate saw at least one of their debates. Even though less attention has been focused on a single debate since then, the debates still attract millions of television viewers. Eighty-four million people watched the first presidential debate in 2016 on television; an additional thirteen million saw it online. It was the largest debate audience in American electoral history.[52] The second largest audience was the Reagan-Carter debate in 1980, which 80.6 million watched. The second and third 2016 debates had television audiences of 66.5 and 71.6 million, respectively, plus several million more online viewers.[53]

Debates are usually more important to challengers than to incumbents. By appearing on the same stage as their more experienced opponents, they can seem to be their equals. George W. Bush seemed more presidential in 2000 than Al Gore, who sounded and looked overly aggressive in two of their three debates. Similarly, in 2008, Barack Obama's composure, confidence, and knowledge of the issues contrasted sharply, and to his advantage, with the personal attacks that McCain and the Republicans were making against him.

Pictorial Parade/Getty Images

The fourth and final 1960 presidential debate between Richard Nixon and John Kennedy, held in New York City.

Once a debate ends, the news media are preoccupied with evaluating it, focusing largely on the question of who "won" or "lost" and whether a candidate scored a good one-liner or made an embarrassing gaffe. These evaluations can matter to millions of additional likely voters who did not watch the debates but hear and read about them. Campaigns try to influence this coverage with their own "spin doctors," the luminaries who speak to the media following the debate. Polls over the next few days measure any bounce the candidates receive.

Few voters admit that debates actually change their vote, although most say that they are informative. More often than not, debates reinforce existing attitudes rather than change them. Most of the attentive audience roots for the candidate it already supports and sees that candidate's performance in a more favorable light than the opponent's. Supporters tend to discount a weak performance by their favored candidate. Ronald Reagan's loss of focus in his first debate with Walter Mondale in 1984 or George W. Bush's "fuzzy math" encounter with Al Gore in 2000 did not change many minds.[54] Reagan joked about his lackluster performance during the next debate, saying he would not make an issue of Mondale's "youth and inexperience" (even Mondale laughed). Hillary Clinton generally got higher evaluations from the public and the news media in her debates with Donald Trump, but she went on to lose the election.[55]

Despite the popular interest they engender, presidential debates do not seem to matter all that much. They are likely to be pivotal only in very close elections in which influencing a small number of voters can make a difference. In the 1960, 1976, and 2000 elections the debates may have affected the results, as all three were decided by narrow margins. In 1980, the single presidential debate probably increased Reagan's margin of victory. In 2000, debates helped Bush; and in 2008, they benefited Obama, who overcame concerns about his experience and leadership skills. It is much harder to show that the debates were decisive, however, and the 2016 presidential debates did little but harden opinions among the candidates' supporters.

News Coverage

Most of what voters learn about candidates comes from news coverage of the campaign. Today, most people follow presidential campaigns on television (58 percent), although an increasing share of the electorate (38 percent) supplements that coverage with online news.[56] Of the television news sources, cable leads the broadcast networks in viewership. Reliance on print media has steadily declined in recent decades, although the websites of major newspapers receive traffic, especially from younger and more educated voters.[57]

The news sources on which people depend are important because they shape the amount and tone of election coverage. That coverage affects the electorate's understanding and knowledge about the campaign, but usually by reinforcing preexisting partisan attitudes and orientations rather than challenging them. The proliferation of news sources has extended and reinforced this confirmation bias, since viewers can get their news from sources that mirror their own predispositions.

The Horse Race

Journalists need to generate public interest to maximize the size and the stability of their audience. Thus, to be newsworthy, a story must attract attention. Elections lend themselves to attention in part because reporters cover them using a sports frame. The horse race is the dominant story: who is ahead and by how much; what factors can change the race; and what the results will be and they mean for politics and government.

The need to stress the contest affects which issues are covered and how they are covered. Most election news tends to focus on the personality and policy issues that provide clear-cut differences between the candidates, provoke controversy, and can be presented in a straightforward manner. These news stories are not necessarily what the candidates wish to emphasize. Not only does the press shape the campaign, but they can also become part of it as they did in 2016.

In general, substantive policy questions receive less attention than events surrounding the campaign: the motives, strategies and tactics of the candidates, their slips of the tongue, inconsistent policy statements, factual errors, past private behavior—all of which may have little relevance to contemporary issues or job performance. An analysis of the 2016 campaign found that 42 percent of the news coverage pertained to the horse race, 17 percent to campaign controversies, and 7 percent to leadership attributes and deficits. Only 10 percent was devoted to policy, and the rest to other campaign activities.[58]

Negativity

The tone of campaign news coverage is more critical than complimentary. Critical reporting accords with the press's watchdog role to reveal what campaigns want to obscure, unearth what is new and unexpected, and provide balance by telling the other side. Coverage of the 2016 presidential campaign was exceptionally negative. In analyzing the tone of presidential news, Patterson found 71 percent of the 2016 election stories were negative and 29 percent positive.[59]

What effect does this type of coverage have on voters? It generates interest, may increase the level of civic participation, and provides the electorate with information. An overwhelming proportion of the electorate say they have received sufficient information to cast an informed vote, but they also criticize the candidates and the news media for being too negative.[60]

Campaigns see negative strategies as a way to solidify their base. Negative ads energize partisans. From a broader perspective, however, negativism deepens and extends the partisan political divide, damaging the winner's presidential image and weakening support for a new administration. It also makes governing more difficult, particularly when control of the government is divided between parties or when the majority is factionalized on major policy issues.

Polling and Forecasting

Pollsters monitor the electorate throughout the election cycle. The candidates use their own polls to evaluate messages and strategy; they want to know where to focus their campaigns and what to say. The media report polls as news, and an entire cottage industry of forecasters now folds them into complex predictive models (such those developed by *FiveThirtyEight*). Polls fit nicely into the horse race frame into which close elections are cast.

Candidates have always tried to assess the electoral landscape, but reliable statistical methods of analyzing voting behavior did not exist until the twentieth century. All polling is an effort to generate estimates of what the electorate thinks by sampling a small number of individuals. When a sample is representative, a poll of as few as a thousand people can accurately measure the views of the entire country, within a margin of error of a few percentage points. Most of the election polls that the news networks report are national polls, with a margin of error between 2 and 4 percent.

Some early polls failed spectacularly. The most notable gaffes in presidential election polling were in 1936 and 1948, when major surveys predicted that Alfred M. Landon and Thomas E. Dewey, respectively, would win. The error in 1936 was the failure to select a random cross-section of the public to interview and bias in who responded to the survey.[61] In 1948, the polling concluded too soon before Election Day, missing a surge by Truman in the final weeks of the campaign. The samples were biased as well.[62]

Contrary to popular belief, most national polls were accurate in 2016, generally showing Hillary Clinton ahead, although her lead declined in the closing days of the election. The final preelection polls had Clinton ahead by 2–3 percent. She won the popular vote by 2.2 percent. Final polls in the battleground states of North Carolina, Florida, and Pennsylvania were mixed, with Clinton and Trump trading narrow leads. Trump won all three. Most battleground state polls were within the margin of error, and some were dead-heats in late polling.[63] Still, there were surprises: Clinton was well ahead in all Wisconsin polling and in most Michigan polling in the last week of the campaign, but she lost the popular vote in both states. It was the first time that a Republican presidential candidate had won Wisconsin since Ronald Reagan in 1984.

A postelection review conducted by a national association of public opinion researchers concluded that although overall poll accuracy was normal by historical standards, polls underestimated Trump's support in key states. This error was a combination of some voters making up their minds in the last week of the campaign and Trump supporters being less likely than Clinton supporters to respond to pollsters. In states decided by razor thin margins, these effects may have been decisive. The 2016 results did not show a systematic problem with polling methodologies.[64]

Impact of the Campaign

Candidates devote enormous amounts of money and effort to presidential campaigns. In the end, there is a winner, but the question remains about the campaign's contribution to the result. Campaigns are focused on reinforcing and activating supporters and making sure they turn out to vote. Candidates certainly wish to reach Independents and would be happy to convert voters who identify with the other party. As we will see, however, not much conversion occurs, although even a small shift in vote can turn a close election.

VOTING

The purpose of the campaign is to influence and mobilize voters. On Election Day, potential voters have to decide whether to vote, and then they must choose among the candidates.

Voter Turnout

Americans have extended suffrage to all but noncitizens and felons (the latter are disqualified in most states). Nevertheless, voter turnout in the United States is lower than in any other democracy with a developed economy. For years, analysts used the percentage of the voting-age population that votes to measure turnout. A better measure is the percentage of people *eligible* to vote who actually do, which excludes noncitizens and felons from the denominator. Both sets of figures are shown in table 4.2. Looking at the last column of the table, we can see that usually less than 60 percent of the eligible voter population actually vote for president.

There are different bureaucratic requirements potential voters must navigate: registration is a critical one. Although Congress and some states have tried to ease registration procedures, permit it at the time of voting, or make it automatic, 20 percent of the eligible American electorate are still not registered to vote.

An increasing number of states require voters to present government-issued ID before casting ballots. The purported justification for voter ID laws is that they are necessary to prevent voter impersonation at the polls. However, this type of voter fraud is virtually nonexistent, with only a handful of credibly established cases over the past 20 years.[65] Moreover, racial and ethnic minorities are less likely to have such identification and thus are more likely be prevented from voting. Trump asserted, falsely, that millions of illegal votes were cast in the 2016 election, depriving him of a popular vote victory. A commission he created in 2017 to investigate allegations of voter fraud produced no evidence of any irregularities.[66] It was abolished after legal challenges, poor security practices, and state objections to data requests.[67]

A related issue has been the reduction of the period during which people can vote in certain states. Shortened hours may save money for the states but they also reduce turnout, particularly for people with job and/or family obligations that limit their ability to get to the polls or obtain absentee ballots. Similarly, voting on a workday is more difficult for people paid by the hour, without their own transportation, with young children, with disabilities, or who work long distances from their residences. Non-English speakers and others burdened by conditions that make the act of voting more difficult are also less likely to vote.

Age, education, income, and occupational status are closely related to turnout. People who are older, more educated, or farther up the socioeconomic ladder are more likely to vote than people who are younger, less educated, and have less income.[68] Those of Latino heritage also are less likely to vote. Naturally, the stronger

Table 4.2 Voter Turnout in Presidential Elections, 1980–2016

Year	Voting Age Population	Presidential Vote	% VAP Turnout	Voter Eligible Population	% VEP Turnout
1980	164,445,475	86,515,221	52.6	159,635,102	54.2
1984	173,994,610	92,652,680	53.3	167,701,904	55.2
1988	181,995,484	91,594,691	50.3	173,579,281	52.8
1992	190,777,923	104,405,155	54.7	179,655,523	58.1
1996	200,015,917	96,262,935	48.1	186,347,044	51.7
2000	210,721,837	105,375,486	50.0	194,331,436	54.2
2004	220,803,686	122,294,978	55.4	203,483,455	60.1
2008	231,229,580	131,304,731	56.9	213,005,467	61.6
2012	240,926,957	129,070,906	53.6	219,296,589	58.0
2016	250,055,734	136,700,729	54.7	230,585,915	59.3

Note: VAP = voting age population; VEP = voter eligible population
Source: Michael McDonald, "Voter Turnout: 1980–2016," The Elections Project. http://www.electproject.org.

people feel about the election and the stronger their partisan loyalties, the more likely they are to vote. Table 4.3 shows the reported turnout rates of some major components of US society.

Republicans tend to vote with greater regularity than do their Democratic counterparts. Higher Republican turnout has helped that party counter an advantage in the number of registered voters held by the Democrats since the 1930s. Beginning with the 2000 election, both parties have mounted extensive registration and get-out-the-vote drives. In 2004 and 2016, Republican turnout in the presidential election exceeded that of the Democrats, particularly among voters in the key battleground states.[69] An estimated four million people who voted for Obama in 2012 did not vote in 2016.[70]

Partisanship

Scholars have identified three major influences on how people vote. The first, and most important, is party identification. Voters come to the election with preexisting views. They do not see and hear the campaign in isolation but rather observe and

Table 4.3 Reported Turnout Rates, 2016

Category	% Voting
Gender	
Men	59
Women	63
Race/Ethnicity	
White, non-Hispanic	65
Hispanic	48
African American	59
Asian American	49
Age	
18–24	43
25–34	53
35–44	60
45–54	65
55–64	68
65 and over	71
Education	
No high school diploma	34
High school diploma	52
Some college	63
College degree	74
Postgraduate degree	80
Marital Status	
Married	69
Single	49

Source: Martin P. Wattenberg analysis of the 2016 US Census Bureau surveys.

absorb it as part of their daily lives and through the filters of their prior beliefs and attitudes. These attitudes and associations affect perceptions and influence voting behavior.

For most people, party identification simplifies politics by providing a cue for interpreting issues, judging candidates, and deciding how to vote. The stronger this identification, the more compelling the cue is likely to be. People develop political attitudes as they become more aware of politics. Over time, partisan inclinations become firmer and more resistant to change. They constitute an increasingly important influence on voting behavior.

The amount of information known about the candidates also affects the influence of partisanship on voting behavior. In general, the less people know about the candidates, the more likely they are to follow their partisan orientations when voting. Since presidential campaigns convey more information than do other elections, the influence of party is apt to be weaker in these higher-visibility contests than in congressional and state elections. Nevertheless, partisanship has been highly correlated with the presidential vote in the last eight presidential elections. About 90 percent of the public vote for the candidate of the party with which they identify, and most people who say they are independent tend to vote consistently for one party. Moreover, the more polarized the parties become, the more likely people are to vote for their party's candidate.

When party identification is weak or nonexistent, other factors such as the personalities of the candidates and their positions on the issues will be more important. In contrast to party identification, which is a long-term, relatively stable factor, candidate and issue orientations are short-term influences that vary from election to election.

Candidate Images

A second factor that influences voters is their evaluations of the candidates. Voters have long said they value integrity, reliability, and competence,[71] although these assessments depend on whether voters like *either* candidate. Donald Trump made headway against Hillary Clinton with his taunts to "lock her up" because of her use of a private e-mail server while she was secretary of state. He questioned her integrity by constantly referring to her as "crooked Hillary." At the same time, the Clinton campaign emphasized Trump's continuous string of falsehoods.

In the end, Clinton and Trump had the lowest favorability ratings of any major party nominees ever measured.[72] Even many Trump voters did not admire him, and no candidate since 1980 had a lower percentage of voters saying they planned to cast a vote *for* him rather than against his opponent (Clinton).[73] Table 4.4 shows that most people held unfavorable views of both Trump and Clinton and thought they lacked honesty and the proper temperament to be president.

Table 4.5 examines the question of honesty in more detail. The voters for each candidate overwhelmingly saw the other candidate as dishonest. Both candidates, especially Clinton, received only modestly positive evaluations from those who voted for them.

Strength, boldness, and decisiveness are intrinsic to the public's image of the office. During times of crisis or periods of social anxiety, the public especially values these characteristics. In 2004, George W. Bush benefited from the perception of his wartime decisiveness, while John Kerry's image suffered when the Republicans successfully defined him as a flip-flopper.

Table 4.4 Evaluation of the Candidates in 2016

	% of Voters
Opinion of Trump	
Favorable	38
Unfavorable	60
Opinion of Clinton	
Favorable	43
Unfavorable	55
Honest and Trustworthy?	
Trump	33
Clinton	36
Right Temperament?	
Trump	35
Clinton	55

Source: Data from Edison Research as published in "Election 2016: Exit Polls," CNN, November 23, 2016, http://edition.cnn.com/election/results/exit-polls.

Table 4.5 Evaluations of the Honesty of the Candidates by Vote Choice in 2016 (by percentage)

	Extremely Well	Very Well	Moderately Well	Slightly Well	Not Well at All
Clinton					
Clinton voters	9	22	37	20	12
Trump voters	1	1	3	8	88
Third party voters	1	1	12	22	64
Trump					
Clinton voters	2	3	6	14	76
Trump voters	15	31	34	14	6
Third party voters	5	7	16	18	54

Question: "Think about Hillary Clinton [Donald Trump]. In your opinion, does the phrase 'she [he] is honest' describe Hillary Clinton [Donald Trump] extremely well, very well, moderately well, slightly well, or not well at all?"
Source: 2016 American National Election Study.

In 2016, Donald Trump's brash and unfiltered rhetoric contrasted sharply with Hillary Clinton's emphasis on her knowledge and experience. Trump also subtly introduced gender by questioning Clinton's health and stamina while asserting his own macho character—his assertiveness, bullying, and demeaning ridicule of his Democratic opponent. These tactics activated attitudes toward gender and sexism to Clinton's disadvantage, particularly among White voters.[74]

Issue Preferences
The third major influence on voters is their policy preferences. Knowing candidate positions on the issues permits voters to make judgments about the consequences of

electing them. Making such choices requires, first, having positions on issues. Then, voters must know where the candidates stand and vote accordingly. However, the complexity of many issues, the low level of information and awareness that much of the electorate possesses, and the fact that a candidate's policy stands may be too numerous, complex, or insufficiently detailed to understand makes expressing issue preferences through voting difficult.

Ironically, that portion of the electorate that can be more easily persuaded—weak partisans and Independents—tends to have the least information. Conversely, the most committed voters are usually the most informed, and they typically use that information to reinforce their partisanship. Thus, the partisan disposition of the electorate is usually more important than the issues because it shapes views on a multiplicity of issues and aligns them with prior political attitudes. Many people take their cues on where they should stand on the issues from the candidates they already support, usually because of party affiliation.

Contemporary campaign themes are designed to appeal to voters' issue preferences. They promote the campaign's policy agenda and employ symbols, catch phrases, and code words to remind the electorate where the candidates stand and what they will do if elected.

Barack Obama ran in 2008 on a theme of change that so resonated with the electorate that his opponent, John McCain, also had to stress his independence and ability to make his own judgments rather than continue the economic and national security policies of the Bush administration. In 2012, the speed of the economic recovery from the Great Recession was the principal issue for both candidates. In criticizing the tepidness of the economy during Obama's first term, Mitt Romney promised to create six million new jobs, while Obama highlighted the positive trajectory of the economic and middle-class needs and argued his policy approach was more likely to benefit society as a whole.

In 2016, Donald Trump preached a nationalistic and populist catchphrase, "Make America Great Again." Hillary Clinton's "Stronger Together" slogan was designed to unify her multicultural base and contrast her positive message with Trump's appeal to discontented Americans.

According to the exit polls, the most salient policy issues in the 2016 presidential election were the economy (cited by 52 percent), terrorism (18 percent), immigration (18 percent), and foreign policy (13 percent). There was also a high level of dissatisfaction with the federal government (69 percent).[75] Trump's main policy promises were directed to these issues: create jobs, increase homeland security, defeat the Islamic State of Iraq and Syria, prevent illegal immigration by building a wall between the US–Mexican border, and "drain the swamp" in Washington. He did not go into specifics about how he was going to achieve these objectives but voiced confidence that he would be able to do so. The Clinton campaign was more policy oriented and less focused on simple solutions to address these areas of concern.

The conventional wisdom is that economic anxiety explains Trump's surprising victory as well as his ability to attract voters who had previously supported Democrats. Some research, however, shows that a fear of losing status and attitudes about race and immigration better explains the shift among White voters, who were central to Trump's wins in the crucial states of Wisconsin, Pennsylvania, and Michigan.[76]

THE 2016 ELECTION

Donald Trump's election to the presidency in 2016 was one of the biggest surprises in recent American election history. *FiveThirtyEight*'s election day forecasting model gave Trump less than a 29 percent chance of winning; the *New York Times* model gave him a one-in-seven chance.[77] Princeton University neuroscientist Sam Wang, who had accurately predicted the 2012 popular and electoral college vote, gave Clinton a 99 percent chance of winning and said he was so confident in his prediction that would eat a bug on live TV if Trump won more than 240 electoral college votes (he ate a cricket on a November 12 CNN broadcast).[78]

In 2016, partisanship and personality shaped the surprising outcome, as did the political environment in depressed regions of the country. The economic consequences of the Great Recession, the continuation of racial and ethnic polarization, and declining confidence in government, all of which Trump exploited in his campaign, helped energize and mobilize his voters. Clinton's political and personal baggage—including the controversy around her use of a private email server while secretary of state—plagued her candidacy.

Donald Trump's campaign, much as his nomination effort, was characterized by large rallies, emotional appeals to disaffected Americans, nationalistic themes, and unconventional political rhetoric. He called Clinton the most corrupt candidate ever to run for president. In turn, Clinton insisted that Trump lacked the temperament, experience, and judgment to be president.

Trump's campaign was nearly derailed in early October, when the *Washington Post* published a story and recording of Trump speaking about women in vulgar terms to *Access Hollywood* host Billy Bush. Within days, his favorability rating dropped by twelve points and "Clinton opened up her largest lead . . . of the entire campaign."[79] Prominent Republicans criticized Trump in harsh terms, and dozens of Republican governors and members of Congress repudiated him. Some GOP leaders asked him to drop out of the race.[80]

But within a few hours of the story, Wikileaks began releasing the hacked emails of Clinton campaign chairman John Podesta,[81] dumping several batches over the next few days. The emails diverted attention away from the *Access Hollywood* tape, and Republicans who had chastised Trump returned to the fold, mitigating the damage the tape caused to his campaign.

Another pivotal event occurred on October 28, when Director James Comey announced that the FBI had reopened its investigation into Clinton's private email server.[82] It was an unusual step, as the FBI does not normally publicly announce investigations, and it had an immediate effect on Clinton's support. In the last week of the campaign, the story dominated news coverage and renewed the image of Clinton as playing fast-and-loose with classified information on her private server. Clinton's seven-point lead in the polls lead was cut in half, and the shift of three or four percentage points was larger than Trump's margin of victory in key battleground states (Michigan, Pennsylvania, and Wisconsin). Nate Silver of *FiveThirtyEight* concluded that the Comey letter was "probably" decisive in her loss, although others say it is impossible to know.[83]

Finally, the 2016 campaign revealed an unprecedented degree of Russian government attempts to interfere in the election. Box 4.1 describes what is known about those efforts, which involved hacking as well as social media campaigns and advertising.

Box 4.1 ★ Russian Interference in the 2016 Election

Multiple federal investigations found that the Russian government "interfered in the 2016 presidential election in sweeping and systematic fashion."[84] US intelligence agencies concluded that Russian President Vladimir Putin ordered the campaign, which "aspired to help President-elect Trump's election chances."[85] A Senate Intelligence Committee review agreed with these assessments.[86] Robert Mueller's investigation also found conclusive evidence of interference.

The Russian effort had two components. First, units of Russian intelligence services hacked computers at the Democratic National Committee and the Clinton campaign. Intruders (generally pretending to be campaign IT staff or other trusted sources asking recipients to change their account passwords) accessed the Clinton campaign by sending "spearphishing" emails to hundreds of campaign staff and volunteers, including chair John Podesta. Hackers also installed malware on DNC computers. Thousands of DNC and Clinton campaign documents and tens of thousands of emails were stolen, including the campaign's internal modeling and data.[87] The Clinton campaign targeting began within hours of Donald Trump's July 27, 2016 press conference at which he said, "Russia, if you're listening, I hope you are able to find the 30,000 emails that are missing. I think you will probably be rewarded mightily by our press," referring to personal emails that Clinton had not turned over to federal investigators examining her use of a private email server while Secretary of State.[88]

The Russians then strategically released stolen documents and emails, either directly or through Wikileaks. These releases included a document dump that occurred the afternoon the *Access Hollywood* tape was released on October 7, 2017. Kathleen Hall Jamieson found that news coverage of the leak focused on their content (which was embarrassing to Podesta and Clinton) rather than how they had been obtained.[89]

Although the Special Counsel did not find evidence that anyone in the Trump campaign had coordinated with Wikileaks or Russians, the office did identify numerous contacts between the campaign and "individuals with ties to the Russian government."[90]

The second component of the Russian influence effort was a social media campaign conducted by a government-linked company called the Internet Research Agency (IRA), located in St. Petersburg, Russia. The IRA created thousands of fake Twitter and Facebook accounts, posting targeted messages that reached millions of viewers; the agency also purchased thousands of ads on Facebook and Instagram. These ads could be very narrowly targeted to specific groups and were intended to demobilize Clinton supporters or urge them to vote for third-party groups. They ran disproportionately in battleground states such as Wisconsin, Pennsylvania, and Virginia.[91] Well over a hundred million Americans were exposed to content or ads from IRA-backed accounts on multiple platforms.

The Special Counsel charged thirteen individuals and three Russian organizations with crimes relating to hacking and social media activities. As most of these entities or individuals are in Russia, actual prosecution is unlikely.[92]

Is it possible to know what effect these efforts had on the election, or whether they might have been decisive? One analysis concluded it is unlikely, as the Russian activities constituted a tiny share of overall activity on Facebook or Twitter (the $100,000 in Russia-backed ads on Facebook was trivial in the context of the billions spent in the presidential campaign; the 126 million potential Facebook views are, similarly, a miniscule fraction of the 1.1 trillion total Facebook posts over the same period).[93] But Trump won Michigan, Pennsylvania, and Wisconsin by a combined 77,744 votes, and Jamieson argues that the Russian targeting effurts in those states "very likely delivered Trump's victory."[94]

Despite ambiguity about the effects of Russian election interference, there is no doubt that it happened. Mueller summarized his investigation during a May 2019 public statement: "there were multiple, systematic efforts to interfere in our election. And that allegation deserves the attention of every American."[95]

Trump capitalized on the anger many Americans felt with the state of the country. Sixty-two percent of voters said the country was on the wrong track, and the same percentage reported that they felt that the condition of the national economy was either not good or poor. Trump's basic messages—that immigration needed to be strictly controlled, that terrorists had to be dealt with more severely, that trade deals needed to be renegotiated, and that Obamacare was costing too much—all won him substantial numbers of votes. And among the 39 percent of voters who said that what they most cared about was the ability to bring change, Trump won an impressive 83 percent.[96]

The concentration of Trump's supporters in rural areas and small towns that lost manufacturing jobs before and during the Great Recession contributed to his electoral college triumph in three states that traditionally had gone Democratic: Michigan, Pennsylvania, and Wisconsin. Clinton's failure to turn out as many minority votes as Obama had contributed to Trump's narrow victory in these states. Trump won Pennsylvania, Wisconsin, and Michigan by a combined total of 77,744 votes out of nearly 14 million cast, or 0.56 percent of the total presidential vote in the three states.

You can see a breakdown of who voted for Trump and Clinton in table 4.6, and you can read about it in box 4.2.

Table 4.6 Portrait of the American Electorate: 2012 and 2016

	2016 Electorate (%)	2012 Obama (D)	2012 Romney (R)	2016 Trump (R)	2016 Clinton (D)
All	100	52	44	44	50
Party Identification					
Republican	32	6	92	87	9
Independent	27	49	43	47	40
Democrat	41	91	7	8	89
Ideology					
Liberal	33	90	7	6	88
Moderate	26	64	32	33	57
Conservative	41	16	80	84	12
Gender					
Male	47	47	47	47	46
Female	53	56	41	42	53
Race/Ethnicity					
White	76	42	54	53	40
Hispanic	10	69	29	20	74
Black	11	94	4	4	90
Asian	3	53	47	31	74
Age					
Age 18–29	16	59	35	31	61
Age 30–44	23	51	43	37	55
Age 45–64	41	51	46	49	45
Age 65+	20	48	49	51	46

	2016 Electorate (%)	Vote (%)			
		2012		2016	
Category		Obama (D)	Romney (R)	Trump (R)	Clinton (D)
Education					
High School or Less	31	53	45	46	48
Some College	32	50	46	49	44
College or Advanced Degree	30	52	43	38	55
Religion					
Protestant	43	43	54	55	40
Catholic	22	53	44	45	49
Jewish	2	67	29	28	72
Other/None	33	62	33	29	62
Marital Status					
Married	58	43	53	53	41
Unmarried	42	62	34	32	61
Income					
<$30,000	17	63	35	40	53
$30,000–49,999	19	56	42	41	52
$50,000–99,999	30	46	52	49	46
$100,000+ (2012)	n.a.	44	54	n.a.	n.a.
$100,000–199,999 (2016)	24	n.a.	n.a.	48	47
$200,000–249,999 (2016)	4	n.a.	n.a.	47	49
$250,000+ (2016)	6	n.a.	n.a.	46	46

n.a. = not available
Source: American National Election Studies, University of Michigan and Stanford University. ANES 2016 Time Series Study. Ann Arbor, MI: Inter-university Consortium for Political and Social Research [distributor], 2017-09-19, https://doi.org/10.3886/ICPSR36824.v2. Income marginals from Edison Research as published in "Election 2016: Exit Polls," CNN, November 23, 2016, http://www.cnn.com/election/rersults/exit-polls.

Box 4.2 ★ Who Voted for Trump?

Despite the popular view of Donald Trump's election as representing an upheaval in American politics, the pattern of voting among groups within the United States followed standard paths (see table 4.6). These figures come from a nationally representative postelection survey of voters, called the American National Election Study.[97]

Partisans overwhelmingly voted for their parties' candidates, while Independents were more closely split. Similarly, liberals voted for Clinton and conservatives supported Trump. Moderates also broke for Clinton. Once again, there was a "gender gap," with women favoring the Democratic candidate and men the Republican, although by a closer margin. Whites voted for Trump by a

(continued)

Box 4.2 ★ Continued

wide margin, but Hispanics, blacks, and Asian Americans supported Clinton in even larger percentages. Those under forty-five supported Clinton, while older voters went with Trump. Related to this division is that of marriage, with married people supporting Trump and unmarried voting for Clinton. Protestants, especially those who were born again and/or evangelical, flocked to Trump, Catholics were more evenly divided, and minority religions and those without religion voted for Clinton.

Perhaps the most interesting aspect of the election results were divisions among income and education groups, classic measures of class. Low-income ($30,000 per year or less) voters supported Clinton but by a much smaller margin than they voted for Barack Obama in 2012. Many low-income voters switched to Trump. Clinton actually did better than Obama among high-income groups, essentially tying with Trump.

We see the same pattern when we examine education cohorts. Trump did considerably worse than Mitt Romney among voters who were college graduates or had postgraduate degrees. Nevertheless, Trump picked up—and Clinton lost—votes from those with less education, compared to 2012. In the end, these changes in voting patterns were enough to give Trump the victory.

Clinton won nearly three million more popular votes than Trump, winning the popular vote 48 percent to Trump's 46 percent (the ANES survey data show a slightly different result, 50–44, which is a normal variation that occurs in even large-scale surveys). Nevertheless, Trump won where it counted: in the electoral college. He won thirty states with 304 electoral votes. Clinton won twenty states and the District of Columbia with 227 electoral votes. Seven electors did not vote as their states voted. Two abandoned Trump, and five failed to support Clinton. These faithless electors did not affect the outcome of the election.

CONCLUSION

Presidential elections take place within the framework of the electoral college, which determines where candidates campaign and the incentives voters have to vote. Because of the way states choose to allocate their electoral votes and because of the way the Constitution allocates electoral votes to the states, the electoral college can put the candidate who came in second in the popular vote in the White House.

Campaigns are long, expensive, and demanding of the candidate. They require complex organizations, exploitation of the latest technology and social media, constant fund-raising, a broad range of communications with the public, relentless efforts to obtain favorable press coverage, extensive commissioning of public opinion polls, and effective performances in presidential debates. Ironically, most of this effort is aimed at reinforcing and activating those already disposed to support a candidate. Only a small percentage of the public is open to persuasion, but this group may be large enough to decide the election.

One of the presidential candidates' most difficult tasks is mobilizing their supporters to actually vote. Large percentages of eligible voters—up to half—simply skip the election. For those who do vote, partisanship is the most important influence on their votes. Partisanship also filters everything else they see and hear about the candidates. The images that voters have of the candidates' personal qualities are also key influences on their votes, although these images are filtered by partisanship. Finally, voters' issue preferences can affect their choice for president. For issue preferences to be logically related to votes, however, voters must have views on issues and know where candidates stand on them. These conditions are often not met.

The results of the 2016 election were surprising to most political observers. Donald Trump appealed successfully to disaffected voters concerned about the loss of well-paying blue-collar jobs, immigration, crime, terrorism, and trade. He lost traditional Republican support among the more educated but gained voters from white working-class voters who usually support Democratic candidates. Equally important, Trump lost the popular vote but won the election because of the electoral college.

Once the election is over, the winner has to govern. What presidents do in office is the focus of the rest of this book.

DISCUSSION QUESTIONS

1. Explain some of the ways in which advances in communications technology, particularly social media and online platforms, have changed the conduct of presidential elections, the campaigns of candidates and political parties, and the relationship between elections and governing.
2. For many years, political scientists have debated the merits and liabilities of the electoral college, in particular whether the college should be reformed and if so, how. In light of recent presidential elections, do you think that the electoral college has outlived its usefulness? Is it consistent with a democratic electoral process? Does it benefit one major party at the expense of the other? Can and should it be changed? If so, how? If not, why not?
3. Design a campaign strategy for the Republican and Democratic nominees for the next presidential election. In your strategy, discuss the substance and targets of the candidates' basic appeals, how they should project those appeals in paid and unpaid media, the geographic/electoral college strategies they should employ, and whether and how each candidate should treat the current administration and its leadership in the next campaign.

WEB EXERCISES

1. Exit polling data from the 2016 presidential election are available at http://edition.cnn.com/election/results/exit-polls. How does the support of various segments of the population differ from previous elections in this century? What issues were most important to voters? How might the candidates' policy stances have affected the votes they received? How much did evaluations of the candidates' personal qualities affect their vote?
2. Go to the Elections Project at http://www.electproject.org/2016g and observe voter turnout in the states in the 2016 presidential election. Why is the turnout in some states so much higher than in other states? What role do you think the electoral college plays in turnout? What impact would an increase in turnout have on the outcome of the election?
3. The Living Room Candidate, a website maintained by the Museum of the Moving Image (http://www.livingroomcandidate.org/) is an archive of presidential campaign ads since 1952. Look at some ads from different presidential campaigns, making note of how production values and ad strategies have

changed. At what point can you say that ads began to look "modern," in the sense of being similar to ads run in 2012 or 2016? Are there any ads that strike you as particularly persuasive? Any ads that you think might have changed a voter's mind? Any ads that might have changed *your* mind?

SELECTED READINGS

Campbell, Angus, Philip E. Converse, Warren E. Miller, and Donald E. Stokes. *The American Voter*. New York: Wiley, 1960.

Clinton, Hillary Rodham. *What Happened?* New York: Simon & Schuster, 2017.

Edwards, George C. III. *Why the Electoral College Is Bad for America*, 3rd ed. New Haven, CT: Yale University Press, 2019.

Erikson, Robert S., and Christopher Wlezien. *The Timeline of Presidential Elections: How Campaigns Do (and Do Not) Matter*. Chicago, IL: University of Chicago Press, 2012.

Hersh, Eitan D. *Hacking the Electorate: How Campaigns Perceive Voters*. New York: Cambridge University Press, 2015.

Issenberg, Sasha. *The Victory Lab: The Secret Science of Winning Campaigns*. New York: Crown, 2012.

Leighley, Jan E., and Jonathan Nagler. *Who Votes Now? Demographics, Issues, Inequality, and Turnout in the United States*. Princeton, NJ: Princeton University Press, 2014.

Sabato, Larry, Kyle Kondik, and Geffrey Shelley, eds. *Trumped: The 2016 Election That Broke All the Rules*. Lanham, MD: Rowman & Littlefield, 2017.

Sides, John, Michael Tesler, and Lynn Vavreck. *Identity Crisis: The 2016 Presidential Campaign and the Battle for the Meaning of America*. Princeton, NJ: Princeton University Press, 2018.

Troy, Gil. *See How They Ran: The Changing Role of the Presidential Candidate*. New York: Free Press, 1996.

West, Darrell M. *Air Wars: Television Advertising and Social Media in Election Campaigns, 1952–2012*, 7th ed. Los Angeles, CA: Sage/CQ Press, 2017.

5

The President and the Public

Castle Light Images/Alamy Stock Photo

Donald Trump holds a rally with his supporters.

efore his election, Donald Trump had spent his life in public relations, promoting himself, his real estate ventures, and television programs. He knew how to make an impression. Moreover, he had touched a responsive chord with many in the public as he campaigned for office. Thus, he might well have expected to have a favorable relationship with the public once in the White House. Instead, he found himself to be the most polarizing public figure in modern times, experiencing record-low approval ratings. Although he may have benefited from low expectations of his performance, his lack of mastery of public policy and his often indecorous behavior encouraged many in the public to conclude that he was not up to the job of chief executive. Clearly, relating to the public is a difficult job.

"Public sentiment is everything. With public sentiment nothing can fail, without it nothing can succeed."[1] These words, spoken by Abraham Lincoln, pose what is perhaps the greatest challenge to any president: to obtain and maintain public support. Presidents usually make substantial efforts to lead the public. Sometimes their goals have been to gain long-term personal support, while at other times they have been more interested in obtaining support for a specific program. Often, of course, both goals are present.

In this chapter, we explore presidential attempts to understand public opinion and the public's expectations and evaluations of the chief executive. We are interested in identifying and explaining the public's attitudes to deepen our understanding of expectations and evaluations and also of the obstacles the White House faces in measuring public opinion. We focus on presidents attempting to lead public opinion in the next chapter.

UNDERSTANDING PUBLIC OPINION

Presidents need public support, and understanding public opinion can be a considerable advantage to them in gaining and maintaining it. At the very least, presidents want to avoid needlessly antagonizing the public. Thus, they need reliable estimates of public reactions to the actions they are contemplating. They also need to know what actions and policies, either symbolic or substantive, the public wants. By knowing what the public desires, presidents may use their discretion to gain public favor whenever they feel the relevant actions or policies are justified.

In addition, presidents often want to lead public opinion to increase support for themselves and their policies. To do so, they need to know the views of various segments of the public, whom they need to influence and on what issues, and how far people can be moved. Presidents usually want to avoid expending their limited resources on hopeless ventures. Nor do they want to be too far ahead of the public, lest they risk losing their followers and alienating segments of the population. These motivations encourage contemporary presidents to poll the public on a regular basis as well as to have their aides organize groups to test some of their ideas and the rhetoric they use to explain them.

Americans' Opinions

Before a president can understand what opinions the public holds, individual citizens must form opinions. Although Americans are usually willing to express opinions on a wide variety of issues, these responses cannot be interpreted as reflecting crystallized and coherent views. Opinions are often rife with contradictions because the public often fails to give views much thought or consider the implications of policy stands for other issues.[2] For example, national polls show consistently that the American people place a very high priority on controlling government spending. At the same time, however, majorities favor maintaining or increasing expenditures on many domestic programs.[3] In general, Americans are philosophical conservatives but operational liberals. In other words, they like small government in principle but they also like the programs that larger government provides.[4]

Policy making is a complex enterprise, and most voters do not have the time, expertise, or inclination to think extensively about most issues—especially those distant from their everyday experiences, for example, federal regulations, nuclear weapons, and bureaucratic organization. The public can miss the point of even the most determined and straightforward rhetoric. Donald Trump routinely touted the size of the tax cut passed in December 2017, often exaggerating its size. Much of the public missed the message, however. When taxes came due under the new law, only 17 percent of the public thought their own taxes would decrease, while 28 percent thought they would go up.[5]

In his 2010 State of the Union address, President Obama declared that as part of their economic recovery, his administration had passed twenty-five different tax cuts. "Now, let me repeat: We cut taxes," he said. "We cut taxes for 95 percent of working families. We cut taxes for small businesses. We cut taxes for first-time homebuyers. We cut taxes for parents trying to care for their children. We cut taxes for 8 million Americans paying for college." In a televised interview on Super Bowl Sunday, he touted the tax cuts in the stimulus package: "we put $300 billion worth of tax cuts into people's pockets so that there was demand and businesses had customers." (The only tax increases passed in 2009 were on tobacco.)

Shortly afterward, a major polling organization asked, "In general, do you think the Obama Administration has increased taxes for most Americans, decreased taxes for most Americans or have they kept taxes the same for most Americans?" Twenty-four percent of the public responded that the administration had *increased* taxes, and 53 percent said it kept taxes the same. Only 12 percent said taxes were decreased.[6] In July, that figure dwindled to 7 percent of the public.[7] Misperceptions only grew as the midterm elections approached. In September, 33 percent of the public thought that Obama had raised taxes for most Americans.[8] By the end of October, 52 percent of likely voters thought taxes had gone up for the middle class.[9]

In addition, the president was frustrated when

- Seventy-two percent of the public believed the economy was in recession—six years after the recession ended.[10]
- Thirty-four percent of Americans, including 53 percent of Republicans, mistakenly believed the unemployment rate was higher in late 2015 than it was when he took office in 2009—even though the unemployment rate was cut in half.[11]
- Three years after the Affordable Care Act (ACA) passed in 2010, 42 percent of the public was unaware that it was the law of the land.[12]
- Seven years after the ACA passed, six in ten Americans did not know the uninsured rate in America had nearly halved and was at an all-time low; half the public incorrectly thought the ACA provided health insurance to undocumented immigrants; and four in ten incorrectly believed the ACA cut Medicare benefits.[13]
- In mid-2012, after Obama had been almost a full term in office, a majority of the public did not know he was a Christian.[14]

- In mid-2012, 20 percent of the public, including a plurality of Republicans, thought he was not born in the United States and another 25 percent were not sure—even after he released his long-form birth certificate in April 2011.[15]

Before the war with Iraq in 2003, two-thirds of the public expressed the belief that Iraq played an important role in the 9/11 terrorist attacks. After the war, substantial percentages of the public believed that the United States had found clear evidence that Saddam Hussein was working closely with al-Qaeda, that the United States had found weapons of mass destruction in Iraq, and that world opinion favored the United States going to war in Iraq.[16] All of these beliefs were inaccurate, as even the White House admitted. Even more disturbing, in 2012, nine years after the invasion, 32 percent of the public, including 63 percent of Republicans, still believed that Iraq had weapons of mass destruction when the United States invaded.[17]

Conversely, collective public opinion has properties quite different from those of individual citizens. There is evidence that the public holds real, stable, and sensible opinions about public policy, which develop and change in a reasonable fashion in response to changing circumstances and new information. Changes that occur are usually at the margins and represent different trade-offs among constant values.[18]

In short, as the White House attempts to understand American public opinion, it is handicapped by the fact that many people have no opinion on issues of significance to the president and, moreover, that many of the opinions the public does express are neither crystallized, coherent, nor informed. In contrast, it is possible to grasp the essential contours of public opinion, especially where opinions on policies that touch the public directly—for example, on issues such as economic conditions and civil rights—are widely held. Moreover, the president desires to know the distribution of whatever opinions do exist. Under these circumstances, what means can the White House rely on to measure public opinion?

Public Opinion Polls

George Washington invested considerable effort in monitoring public opinion, but his means of doing so, such as traveling around the country on its primitive roads, were inefficient.[19] Today, a common tool for measuring public attitudes is public opinion polling. Whether commissioned on behalf of the White House or by various components of the mass media, polls help the president to learn how a cross section of the population feels about a specific policy, general living conditions, or the administration's performance.

In an attempt to understand public opinion on matters of special concern to them, modern presidents have commissioned their own polls. Franklin D. Roosevelt was the first to pay close attention to polls, which were just becoming scientific during his tenure in office. All presidents since John F. Kennedy have retained private polling firms to provide them with soundings of American public opinion, and in the last seven administrations, pollsters have also played a significant role as high-level political advisers.[20] Donald Trump made his campaign pollster, Kellyanne Conway, counselor to the president. Breaking with tradition, he filed for reelection immediately after taking office, and his campaign has spent heavily on polling since the beginning of his tenure.

Limitations of Polls

Despite their widespread use in the contemporary White House, public opinion polls are not completely dependable instruments for measuring public opinion.

John Angelillo/UPI/Newscom

Donald Trump points to Kellyanne Conway, his campaign pollster, who he then appointed counselor to the president.

An important limitation of polls is that the questions they contain often do not attempt to measure the intensity with which opinions are held. In reality, however, people with intense views will probably be more likely to act on those views to reward or punish politicians than people whose preference for the issue is a matter of indifference.

A related problem with polls is that the questions asked of the public seldom mesh with the decisions that presidents face. In fact, the executive rarely considers issues in the "yes/no" terms presented by most polls. Moreover, evidence of widespread support for a program does not indicate how the public stands on most of the specific provisions under consideration, much less how it balances certain programs with others. Such details do not lend themselves to mass polling because they require specialized knowledge of the issues, which few Americans possess.

Another problem is that responses may reflect the particular wording of the choices that are presented, which is a problem especially for people who lack crystallized opinions on issues. Moreover, if questions are of the "agree/disagree" variety, there may be a bias toward the "agree" alternative. On policies that are very controversial, it may be impossible to ascertain public attitudes without some contamination caused by question wording. For example, a systematic study found that Americans support decreasing immigration in the abstract but actually support increasing it when asked about visas for family reunification, skilled workers, or refugees. (These three categories make up 95 percent of all immigrants.)[21]

The use of the president's name in a question may affect the results. For example, including Donald Trump's name in a question influences respondents to move toward his policies if they generally like him and against his policies if they do not.[22]

Using Polls

Some questions inevitably arise when discussing presidents and polls: How should presidents use public opinion data? Does the use of these data constrain presidents rather than indicate where their persuasive efforts should be focused? By using polls, do presidents, in effect, substitute "followship" for leadership?

Presidents ritually deny that polls influence their decisions. According to President Carter's chief media adviser, Gerald Rafshoon, "If we ever went into the president's office and said, 'We think you ought to do this or that to increase your standing in the polls,' he'd throw us out."[23] Polls do influence White House political strategy, however.

More than any previous administration, the Reagan White House used polling in its decision-making process. Reagan's pollster, Richard Wirthlin, took polls for the president every three or four weeks (more often during a crisis) and met regularly with Reagan and his top aides. Wirthlin's goal was to determine when the nation's mood was amenable to the president's proposals and gauge public reactions to the president's actions. The White House wanted the timing of the president's proposals to be compatible with the political climate so as to maximize the probabilities of achieving its objectives; thus, polls were used to help set the presidential agenda.[24]

Presidents George H. W. Bush and Bill Clinton used their pollsters to perform similar functions, although Bush commissioned only a small number of polls (however, he did use focus groups regularly).[25] President Clinton, in contrast, was very attentive to polls, and his administration had the most comprehensive White House polling operation in history. Within a week of taking office, Clinton directed his aides to begin regular polling on issues, and pollsters were thoroughly integrated into the Clinton White House planning and strategy sessions on legislation. They assessed public support for various policy options (such as how to fund health care or providing clean needles to drug addicts) and tested market phrases for describing proposals ("anticrime" was found to be preferable to "gun control" and helping "working families" was more popular than helping "poor children," for example). In 1998, the White House regularly polled regarding the Lewinsky scandal. Whenever the president gave a speech, pollsters gathered groups of people to watch and register their reactions on a handheld device called a "dial-a-meter."[26]

Despite its claims of disdain for polls and focus groups, the George W. Bush White House had extensive involvement in polling. The White House Office of Strategic Initiatives monitored and analyzed the results of numerous national polls, and it commissioned millions of dollars for its own polls and focus groups. Polls conducted by Republican pollsters at the state level also informed its analyses.[27]

Barack Obama commissioned millions of dollars of polls through the Democratic National Committee. His pollsters and other top advisers met regularly to discuss their latest polling and how to use the results to advance the president's agenda.[28] For example, the White House introduced the words *recovery* and *reinvestment* to rebrand the historic and controversial "stimulus" package in 2009.[29]

Much of the White House's effort to poll the public is designed to frame the president's message most effectively in order to win public support for his policies, such as when President Obama attempted to frame the debate over health-care reform as a campaign against irresponsible insurance companies (polling found that people dislike insurance companies).[30] At other times, the White House may be trying to identify possible pitfalls in its path or to clarify the administration's policies. When polls have revealed that the public was ignorant about an issue, such as President Reagan's education policy or President Clinton's cooperation with the Whitewater investigation, the White House has gone to great lengths to talk about it.[31]

Presidential Election Results

Although presidents cannot always rely on polls to inform them about public opinion, they can, theoretically, gain valuable insights through the interpretation of their own electoral support in the period following the election. In other words, they may be able to learn what voters are thinking when they cast their ballots for president. For such an approach to be useful for a president seeking to understand public opinion, the following conditions must be met:

1. Voters must have opinions about policies.
2. Voters must know candidates' stands on the issues.
3. Candidates must offer voters the alternatives the voters desire.
4. There must be a large voter turnout so that the electorate represents the population.
5. Voters must vote on the basis of issues.
6. It must be possible to correlate voter support with voters' policy views.

As we saw in Chapter 4, these conditions rarely, if ever, occur, making presidential election results a tenuous basis for interpreting public opinion. ●

In addition, voters may be concerned with several issues in an election, but they have only one vote with which to express their views. Citizens may support one candidate's position on some issues yet vote for another candidate because of concern for other issues or general evaluations of performance. When they cast their ballots, voters signal only their choice of candidate, not their choice of the candidates' policies. As Ken Mehlman, George W. Bush's 2004 campaign manager, put it, "This election is a choice—not a referendum."[32] The White House must be cautious in inferring support for specific policies from the results of this process, for the vote is a rather blunt instrument for expressing policy views.

Even landslide elections are difficult to interpret. For example, political scientist Stanley Kelley found that in Lyndon Johnson's victory in 1964, issues gave the president his base of support, and concerns over the relative competence of the candidates won the swing vote for him. In 1972, however, the question of competence dominated the election. Although traditional domestic issues associated with the New Deal were salient, they actually favored George McGovern, not the landslide winner, Richard Nixon.[33] In 1984, voters preferred Walter Mondale to Ronald Reagan on a wide range of important issues, but most voted for Reagan for president.[34]

Mail from the Public

The mail, including both letters and email, is another potential means for the president to learn about public opinion. Although estimates vary and record keeping is inconsistent,[35] there can be no doubt that the White House receives several million communications from the public each year, including more than 25,000 letters, phone calls, and electronic mail messages daily. (The president's email address is president@whitehouse.gov.) The White House staff screen the mail and keep a log summarizing opinion on critical issues. Correspondence that requires a response is forwarded to the relevant agencies.

The president usually reads only a few items from a day's mail, primarily communications from personal friends, prominent and influential citizens, and interest-group leaders. Most also read a small sampling of the week's mail. Although the president may answer a few letters from ordinary citizens, often as a public relations ploy, top White House aides usually answer mail from important individuals and organizations. Lower-level officials and volunteers using computer-designed responses answer the rest.

Even if the president could read more mail, this effort would not necessarily provide a useful guide to what the public is thinking about policy issues, considering that little of the mail focuses on the issues with which the president must deal, particularly at the depth at which the president evaluates options. In addition, those who communicate with the White House are not a cross-section of the American people. Instead, they overrepresent the middle and upper classes and people who agree with the president.

Acting Contrary to Public Opinion

Presidents often find it difficult to understand public opinion, and there is no lack of examples of the White House being surprised by public reaction to events and presidential actions. These range from President Nixon's decision to invade Cambodia in 1970 and Ronald Reagan's efforts to halt increases in Social Security benefits in 1981 to President Clinton's proposal to lift the ban against homosexuals in the military in 1993 and Donald Trump firing FBI director James Comey in 2017.[36]

Even if presidents believe (or, at least, claim to believe) that they understand public opinion on a particular issue, they do not necessarily follow it.[37] Throughout most of Ronald Reagan's tenure in office, polls showed that the public wanted him to lower the federal deficit but not to cut social programs. Moreover, people were willing to decrease planned military spending to accomplish these goals. However, the president refused to act accordingly. President Obama persisted in advocating health-care reform in the face of substantial public opposition. Donald Trump followed this pattern, as you can read in box 5.1.

Presidents offer several rationales for not following public opinion. President Nixon claimed that he was not really acting contrary to public opinion at all but instead represented the "silent majority," which did not express its opinion in activist politics. Similarly, presidents may argue that their actions are carried out on behalf of underrepresented groups, such as the poor or an ethnic minority, or of a

---

Box 5.1 ★ Donald Trump Keeps His Promises

Donald Trump has attempted to keep a number of his core campaign promises such as building a border wall with Mexico, ending the DACA program that allowed certain illegal immigrants who entered the United States as children to receive work permits and avoid deportation, cutting taxes for the wealthy, deporting illegal immigrants, increasing defense spending, decreasing domestic spending, repealing the Affordable Care Act (ACA), and overturning regulations designed to protect the environment. None of these policies enjoyed the support of a majority of Americans, and many of them, especially health-care reform and ending DACA, were extraordinarily unpopular.[38]

future generation. Advocates employ this kind of rationale today on behalf of efforts designed to decrease the burden of debt for future generations by paying down the national debt and environmental protection policies designed to preserve a healthy and rich natural environment for others to share.

Presidents have also wrapped themselves in the mantle of the courageous statesman following his principles and fighting the tides of public opinion. For example, President Bush told his staff that if the United States had to fight Iraqi leader Saddam Hussein to liberate Kuwait, "it's not going to matter to me if there isn't one congressman who supports this, or what happens to public opinion. If it's right, it's gotta be done."[39] His son articulated the same sentiment regarding the invasion of Iraq. After a year in office, President Obama declared in a televised interview that he would not sacrifice his ambitious goals simply to win a second term in the White House: "I'd rather be a really good one-term president than a mediocre two-term president." He added, "I don't want to look back on my time here and say to myself all I was interested in was nurturing my own popularity."[40]

Presidents often feel (and with good reason) that they know more about policy than most members of the public and that they sometimes must lead public opinion instead of merely follow it. In the words of Gerald Ford,

> I do not think a President should run the country on the basis of the polls. The public in so many cases does not have a full comprehension of a problem. A President ought to listen to the people, but he cannot make hard decisions just by reading the polls once a week. It just does not work, and what the President ought to do is make the hard decisions and then go out and educate the people on why a decision that was necessarily unpopular was made.[41]

PUBLIC EXPECTATIONS OF THE PRESIDENT

When new presidents assume the responsibilities of their office, they enter into a set of relationships, the contours of which are largely beyond their control. The nations with which they will negotiate, the Congress they must persuade, and the bureaucracy they are to manage, for example, have well-established routines and boundaries within which they function, and which set the context of the president's relationships with them.

Public evaluations of the president also occur within an established environment: that of public expectations. The president is in the limelight of American politics. Although this prominence provides the potential for presidential leadership of the public, it is purchased at a high cost. The public has demanding expectations of what presidents should be, how they should act, and what their policies should accomplish. The burden falls on chief executives to live up to these expectations.

Although some presidents may succeed in educating the public over time to alter its expectations, views change slowly, and the changes that do take place usually create more hurdles for the president to overcome. In addition, the static nature of the president's personal characteristics and leadership style and the American political system's inherent constraints on executive power in terms of choosing the most effective policies limit the executive's ability to meet the public's expectations. Frustration, on the part of both the president and the public, is inevitable in such a situation.

High Expectations

The public's expectations of the president in the area of policy are substantial and include the assurance of peace, security, and prosperity. Herbert Hoover wrote prophetically,

> My friends have made the American people think of me a sort of superman, able to cope successfully with the most difficult and complicated problems. They expect the impossible from me and should there arise in the land conditions with which the political machinery is unable to cope, I will be the one to suffer.[42]

In January 2018, the Gallup Poll found that 52 percent of Americans said the person who is serving as president affects their overall happiness.[43]

Table 5.1 shows the results of polls taken shortly before the inaugurations of Presidents Trump, Obama, and George W. Bush. Performance expectations of the new president were quite high and covered a broad range of activities.[44] Clearly, Americans expect the president to do well at the core activities of the presidency. It is worth noting that expectations for Donald Trump were considerably lower than for his two predecessors, one a Democrat and the other a Republican.

Interestingly, there is a substantial gap between the public's expectations of what presidents should accomplish (and for which it will hold them accountable) and the degree of success it expects presidents to have in meeting such expectations. For example, we have seen that most people were optimistic about the Obama presidency at the time of his inauguration (as they were for all recent presidents).[45] At the same time, however, bare majorities expected the president could remove all US troops from Iraq in sixteen months and cut taxes for most Americans, two of his

Table 5.1 Early Expectations of Recent Presidents

Responsibility	Very/Somewhat Confident That the President Can (%)		
	Trump	Obama	G. W. Bush
Work effectively with Congress to get things done	60	89	74
Handle the economy effectively	59	n.a.	n.a.
Defend US interests abroad as president	55	75	n.a.
Manage the executive branch effectively	53	84	77
Use military force wisely	47	71	78
Handle an international crisis	46	73	71
Prevent major scandals in his administration	44	74	77

n.a. = not available

Source: Gallup poll question: "Now I'd like you to think about [. . .]'s ability to handle a number of things over the next four years. Please tell me whether you are very confident, somewhat confident, not too confident or not at all confident that [. . .] can . . . ?" December 7–11, 2016; January 9–11, 2009; January 15–16, 2001. The Gallup Organization. All rights reserved. Reprinted with permission.

Table 5.2 Expectations of Policy Accomplishments for President Trump

Issue	Yes, Will Accomplish (%)
Reduce unemployment and create new jobs	62
Improve the economy	60
Control illegal immigration	59
Keep the United States safe from terrorism	57
Improve education	53
Improve the health-care system	52
Appoint good justices to the US Supreme Court	52
Cut your taxes	51
Improve the way the federal government works	49
Increase respect for the United States abroad	47
Substantially reduce the federal budget deficit	46
Improve conditions for minorities and the poor	44
Reduce the crime rate	43
Heal political divisions in this country	39
Keep the nation out of war	38
Improve the quality of the environment	35
Improve race relations	35

Source: Gallup poll question: "Regardless of which presidential candidate you preferred, do you think the Trump administration will or will not be able to do each of the following?" November 10–11, 2016.

signature campaign issues.[46] The fact that such a juxtaposition of views might be unfair to the president seems irrelevant to many of his constituents.

The case of Donald Trump is less clear. Expectations of his handling major responsibilities have been lower than for other recent presidents (see table 5.2). Nevertheless, the public has held reasonably high expectations of his ability to accomplish his central campaign promises regarding jobs, immigration, and terrorism.

Later in this book, we will emphasize how the president's influence on public policy and its consequences are often limited. Nevertheless, the public holds the president responsible. To quote President Carter, "When things go bad you [the president] get entirely too much blame. And I have to admit that when things go good, you get entirely too much credit."[47] Because the press tends to emphasize bad conditions more than good, the attention presidents receive is usually more negative than positive.

In addition to expecting successful policies from the White House, Americans expect their presidents to be extraordinary individuals.[48] This, of course, buttresses the public's policy expectations. The public desires the president to be honest, intelligent, cool in a crisis, compassionate, strong and decisive, inspiring, and a competent manager and politician. People also expect the president to exercise sound judgment and to possess both a vision for the country and a sense of humor. Substantial percentages also want the nation's leader to have imagination and charisma. Obviously, it is not easy to meet these diverse and somewhat unrealistic expectations.

The public has not only high expectations for the president's official performance but also lofty expectations for its leader's private behavior.[49] Substantial percentages of the population strongly object if a president engages in bad behaviors that are nonetheless very common in American society. For example, when the Watergate tapes revealed that President Nixon frequently used profane and obscene language in his private conversations, many Americans were outraged. Similarly, revelations regarding President Clinton's extramarital affairs and his failure to tell the truth about them, as well as the favorable treatment he accorded political donors, substantially diminished the public's regard for him as a person.

Sources of High Expectations

The tenacity with which Americans maintain high expectations of the president may be due in large part to the encouragement they receive from presidential candidates to do so. As noted in Chapter 4, the lengthy process by which Americans select their presidents lends itself to political hyperbole. For at least one year out of every four, the public is encouraged to expect more from the president than it is currently receiving. Evidently, people take this rhetoric to heart and hold presidents to high standards of performance, independent of the reasonableness of these expectations.

Political socialization also supports high expectations of presidents; for example, schoolchildren often learn American history organized by presidential eras. Implicit in much of this teaching is the view that great presidents were largely responsible for the freedom and prosperity that Americans enjoy. From such lessons, it is a short step to presuming that contemporary presidents can be wise and effective leaders and, therefore, that the public should expect them to be so. Furthermore, commentators may compare contemporary presidents to an ideal president—a composite created out of the strongest attributes (but none of the liabilities) of their predecessors.

Another factor encouraging high expectations is the prominence of the president. As the nation's spokesperson and the personification of the nation, the chief executive is the closest thing Americans have to a royal sovereign. Especially at election time, presidents and their families—even their pets—dominate the news in America. Presidents' great visibility naturally induces people to focus attention, and thus demands and expectations, on them.

Related to the president's prominence is the tendency to personalize. Issues of public policy are often extremely complex. To simplify them, Americans tend to think of issues in terms of personalities, especially the president's. It is easier to blame a specific person for personal and societal problems than it is to analyze and comprehend the complicated mix of factors that really forms the cause. Similarly, it is easier to project frustrations onto a single individual than it is to deal with the contradictions and selfishness in people's own policy demands. At the midpoint of his term in office, President Carter reflected, "I can see why it is difficult for a President to serve two terms. You are the personification of problems and when you address a problem even successfully you become identified with it."[50]

Part of the explanation for the public's high expectations of the president probably lies in its lack of understanding of the context in which the president functions. We shall see in later chapters that the president's basic power situation in the nation's constitutional system is one of weakness rather than strength. However, this fact is widely misperceived by the public, most of whom do not feel that the president has too little power.[51]

Consequences of High Expectations

Do high expectations of our presidents affect the public's evaluations of their performance? Although we lack sufficient data to reach a definitive conclusion, there is

'OK — BRING IN THE NEW GUY...'

© Tony Auth Archive

reason to believe that the wider the gap between expectations and performance, the lower the approval of the president.[52] The fact that Donald Trump underperformed even the modest expectations that Americans had for him helped keep his approval ratings low.[53]

Sometimes the negative impact of high expectations in the public's support for the president is of the chief executive's own making. George H. W. Bush promised, in dramatic fashion, not to raise taxes and to create millions of jobs. When he agreed to a tax increase as part of a deficit reduction agreement with Congress and the jobs failed to materialize, his opponents, and even his friends, wasted no time in criticizing him. Bill Clinton began his administration on a sour note when he announced that he would not be able to provide a tax cut for the middle class as he had promised during the campaign. During his campaign for the presidency in 2000, George W. Bush said the US military should not be involved in peacekeeping operations, but after he became president he ordered its involvement in peacekeeping in Afghanistan and Iraq.

Barack Obama promised that everyone could keep his or her existing health insurance and doctors under his reform proposal. The public withheld its support when the government was not able to keep that pledge. Donald Trump promised that no one would lose his or her health insurance under the reform he would support. When it was clear that millions would lose their health insurance, his approval dropped to historic lows for a new president.

We have, of course, no way to calculate precisely the influence of such unkept promises on the president's standing with the public, and many of them may be of little significance in isolation. However, their collective impact, particularly during periods of some domestic distress, undoubtedly depresses the president's approval ratings. They help to undermine the aura of statesmanship and competence that attracted support in the election campaign. According to Richard Wirthlin, President Reagan's pollster, expectations are the ultimate source of public frustration.[54]

Perhaps presidents should lower expectations, especially at the beginning of their terms, so they will not have to mortgage their reputations and prestige to nuances of governing that they have yet to learn. Nevertheless, the president cannot easily ignore or diminish expectations. Consequently, disappointment is frequent, regardless of who occupies the Oval Office. As Donald Trump declared after a short time in office, "This is more work than in my previous life. I thought it would be easier."[55]

Contradictory Expectations

The contradictions in the public's expectations present an additional obstacle to presidents in their efforts to gain public support. As the focus of contradictory expectations, it is very difficult for them to escape criticism and loss of approval—no matter what they do. Contradictory expectations of presidents deal with either the content of policy or their style of performance. The public's expectations of policy are confused and seemingly unlimited. We want low taxes and efficient government, yet we do not want a decrease in most public services. We expect plentiful gasoline, but not at a higher price. We want economic inflation to be controlled, but not at the expense of higher unemployment or interest rates. We want a clean environment, yet we support industrial development and energy production.

It is true, of course, that the public is not entirely to blame for holding these contradictory expectations. Presidential candidates often enthusiastically encourage voters to believe that they will produce the proverbial situation in which the people can have their cake and eat it too. In the 1980 presidential campaign, Ronald Reagan promised, among other things, to slash government expenditures, substantially reduce taxes, increase military spending, balance the budget, and maintain government services. Similarly, in 1992, Bill Clinton promised to increase social services while lowering taxes on most Americans—a feat he was not able to accomplish. George W. Bush promised a large tax cut, debt reduction, and substantial expenditure increases for defense and Medicare. The deficit, in fact, ballooned during his presidency.

Our expectations of presidential leadership style are also crucial in our evaluation of the president. The public wants a president who embodies a variety of traits, some of which are contradictory:

1. We expect the president to be a leader—an independent figure who speaks out and takes stands on the issues, even if the views are unpopular. We also expect the president to preempt problems by anticipating them before they arise. Similarly, we count on the president to provide novel solutions to the country's problems. To meet these expectations, the president must stay ahead of public opinion, acting on problems that may be obscure to the general populace and contributing ideas that are different from those currently in vogue in policy discussions.

   In sharp contrast to our expectations for presidential leadership are our expectations that chief executives be responsive to public opinion and that they be constrained by majority rule, as represented in Congress. The public overwhelmingly wants Congress to have final authority in policy disagreements with the president, and it does not want the president to be able to act against majority opinion.[56]

These contradictory expectations of leadership versus responsiveness place presidents in a no-win situation. If they attempt to lead, they may be criticized for losing contact with their constituents, being unrepresentative and, at worst, acting like demagogues. Conversely, if they try to reflect the views of the populace, they may be reproached for failing to lead, following the polls, and settling for the easiest, rather than the optimal, solution to a problem.

2. We expect our presidents to be open-minded politicians in the American tradition and thus exhibit flexibility and willingness to compromise on policy differences. At the same time, we expect presidents to be decisive and to take firm and consistent stands on the issues. These expectations are also incompatible, and presidents can therefore expect to be criticized for being rigid and inflexible when they are standing firm on an issue. Critics will disparage presidents for being weak and indecisive when they do compromise or change their policy proposals.

3. We want the president to be a statesman—to place the country's interests ahead of politics—yet we also want a skilled politician who exercises loyalty to his political party. A president who acts in a statesmanlike manner may be criticized for being an ineffective idealist who is too far above the political fray and insufficiently solicitous of party supporters. Jimmy Carter began his term on such a note when he attempted to cut back on "pork barrel" water projects. A president who emphasizes a party program, however, may be criticized for being a crass politician who lacks concern for the broader national interest; this happened to Bill Clinton when he proposed an economic stimulus plan in his first year in office that contained billions of dollars for projects designed to please Democratic constituents around the country.

4. We like our presidents to run open administrations. We expect a free flow of ideas within the governing circles in Washington, and we want the workings of government to be visible, not sheltered behind closed doors. At the same time, we want to feel that the president is in control of things and is providing a rudder for government. If presidents allow internal dissent among their aides and this becomes visible to the public, critics will complain that the White House is in disarray. However, if presidents should attempt either to stifle dissent or to conceal it from the public, critics will accuse them of being isolated, undemocratic, unable to accept criticism, and desirous of muzzling opposition.

5. Finally, we want our presidents to be able to relate to the average person in order to inspire confidence in the White House and promote compassion and concern for the typical citizen. However, we also expect the president to be above the crowd—to possess characteristics far different from our own and to act in ways that are beyond the capabilities of most of us. To confuse the matter further, we also expect the president to act with a special dignity, befitting the leader of the country (and the free world) and to live and entertain royally, with much pomp and circumstance. In other words, presidents are not supposed to resemble the average person at all.

On the one hand, if presidents seem too common, opponents may disparage them for being just that. One only has to think of the many political cartoons of Harry Truman, Gerald Ford, George W. Bush, and Donald Trump that implied they were really not up to the job of president. On the other hand, if presidents seem too different, appear too cerebral, or engage in too much pomp, they will likely be denounced as snobbish and isolated from the people and as too regal for Americans' tastes. The Nixon White House evoked such criticisms about the president and his aides because of its seeming isolation and formality, while Barack Obama was often criticized for being too dispassionate and analytical.

PUBLIC APPROVAL OF THE PRESIDENT

The most visible and significant aspect of presidents' relations with the public is their level of approval. Presidents' efforts to understand and lead public opinion and their efforts to influence the media's portrayal of them are aimed at achieving public support. This support is related to their success in dealing with others, especially Congress. A high level of public approval increases the chances of the president receiving support in Congress for his programs.[57]

Whether they base their judgments on perceptions encouraged by the White House, the media, or other political actors or on detached and careful study, people constantly form and reform opinions about presidents and their policies. The impact of foreign and domestic policies also affects opinions, sometimes quite directly. In this section, we examine issues, the president's personality and personal characteristics, and dramatic international events as possible influences on presidential approval. In addition, there are certain less dynamic factors in the form of predispositions that citizens hold, such as political party identification and the positivity bias, which may strongly influence their evaluations of the president. Political party identification, in particular, not only directly affects opinions of the president but also mediates the impact of other influences.

Levels of Approval

Presidents cannot depend on the public's approval. Presidents Nixon, Ford, Carter, George W. Bush, and Obama did not receive approval from 50 percent of the public on the average (see figure 5.1). Donald Trump has never won the approval of even a bare majority of the public. Even Ronald Reagan, often considered the most popular of recent presidents, averaged only 53 percent approval. George H. W. Bush achieved a high average approval, 61 percent. Yet when he needed the public's support the most, during his campaign for reelection, the public abandoned him. He received only 38 percent of the popular vote in the 1992 presidential election. The fact that Bill Clinton enjoyed strong public support during his impeachment trial, helping him obtain an average approval level of 55 percent, should not mask the fact that he struggled to obtain even 50 percent approval during his first term and did not exceed such a yearly average until his fourth year in office.

Party Identification

Motivated reasoning is a central concept in the study of political behavior. It refers to the confirmation bias (seeking out information that confirms prior beliefs), a prior attitude effect (viewing evidence consistent with prior opinions as more compelling than evidence that is inconsistent with them), and the disconfirmation bias (challenging and dismissing evidence inconsistent with prior opinions, regardless of their objective accuracy). Motivated reasoning may distort a person's perception of

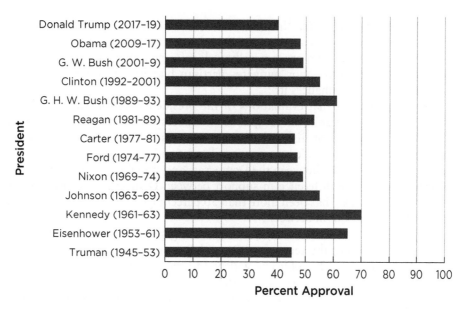

Figure 5.1 Average Levels of Presidential Approval
Source: George C. Edwards III with Alec M. Gallup, *Presidential Approval* (Baltimore, MD: Johns Hopkins University Press, 1990); updated by the authors from Gallup poll data.

new information and the conclusions he or she reaches about it. Most people seek out information confirming their preexisting opinions and ignore or reject arguments contrary to their predispositions. When exposed to competing arguments, they typically accept the confirming ones and dismiss or argue against the opposing ones.[58]

Partisan identification is a primary anchor of political behavior and the basis for much motivated reasoning.[59] Partisan leanings significantly influence perceptions of conditions and policies and interpretations and responses to politics. Partisans display a selective pattern of learning in which they have higher levels of knowledge for facts that confirm their worldview and lower levels of knowledge for facts that challenge them.[60] Thus, party identification has strong independent effects on perceptions and thinking about politics.[61] Moreover, these consequences occur over a wide range of policies and political phenomena, including the presence of weapons of mass destruction in Iraq,[62] assessments of the economy,[63] energy policy,[64] presidential approval,[65] performance in presidential debates,[66] belief in political conspiracies,[67] and the Watergate and Lewinsky scandals.[68]

Partisans' tend to discount or reject uncongenial information. Even the most basic facts are often in contention between adherents of the parties,[69] such as whether inflation, tax rates, or the budget deficit had risen or fallen, whether there were weapons of mass destruction in Iraq, or whether the number of people with health insurance increased under Obamacare.[70] In June 2017, 42 percent of Republicans—but 76 percent of Democrats—accepted the widely reported consensus judgment within the intelligence community that Russia interfered in the 2016 election.[71] Similarly, partisans frequently credit a president of their own political party for perceived policy successes and blame a president of the opposite party for perceived failures.[72]

As Adam Berinsky states, "In the battle between facts and partisanship, partisanship always wins."[73] Partisan bias and the misperceptions it causes are often most prevalent among those who are generally well informed about politics.[74] Political knowledge neither corrects nor mitigates partisan bias in perception of objective conditions. Instead, it enhances it.

It is not surprising that evaluations of the president's performance reflect the underlying partisan loyalties of the public. Members of the president's party are predisposed to approve of his performance, whereas members of the opposition party are predisposed to be less approving.[75] Independents (those without explicit partisan attachments) fall between the Democrats and Republicans in their levels of approval. The average difference in support between Democrats and Republicans over the past forty years has been more than 50 percentage points, a very substantial figure. Independents fall in between.

The public has been especially polarized along party lines in recent decades (see table 5.3). During the tenures of Ronald Reagan and Bill Clinton, the gap between Democrats and Republicans widened to more than 50 percentage points. Polarization increased even more in George W. Bush's presidency, with a partisan gap often exceeding 70 percentage points in his second term[76] and averaging 61 percentage points in his entire tenure.

The fact that the public had been polarized under his predecessor was of little comfort to Barack Obama. It merely showed the stability of the partisan divide and indicated the difficulty of reaching those identifying with the opposition party. After a month in office, Obama averaged 89 percent approval from Democrats but only 28 percent approval from Republicans.[77] During his tenure, the gap grew to an average of 70 percentage points. Polarization increased even more once Donald Trump entered the White House, as you can read in box 5.2.

Table 5.3 Partisan Job Approval of Presidents (ranked from largest to smallest party gaps, in percentage)

President	Average Approval among Republicans	Average Approval among Democrats	Average Party Gap
Trump*	85	8	77
Obama	13	83	70
G. W. Bush	84	23	61
Clinton	27	82	55
Reagan	83	31	52
Nixon	75	34	41
Eisenhower	88	49	39
G. H. W. Bush	82	44	38
Kennedy	49	84	35
Ford	68	37	31
Johnson	44	71	27
Carter	30	57	27

* 2017–2018
Source: Gallup Poll

Box 5.2 ★ Donald Trump and Public Disapproval

Donald Trump's initial job approval was the lowest in the history of polling, dropping below 40 percent after only two months in office. His average approval for his first year was 38 percent, 11 percentage points lower than the next lowest modern president (Bill Clinton at 49 percent). In his second year he averaged 40 percent approval, again the lowest ever. Indeed, he has never registered a job approval rating above 50 percent.[78]

Low approval decreases the chances of large gaps between the parties by compressing the differences in approval. Nevertheless, the differences between Democrats and Republicans in approval levels averaged 77 percentage points in his first two years in office. Although his political base maintained its approval, approval rates among Democrats were very low—in the single digits. Only about a third of Independents approved of his performance.[79]

Nevertheless, motivated reasoning has given the president a firm foundation of support. At a campaign rally in January 2016, Trump boasted "I could stand in the middle of 5th Avenue and shoot somebody and I wouldn't lose voters."[80] There is some truth to his claim. His approval ratings, although low overall, have been remarkably stable. His base has stuck with him.

Despite the strong impact of partisanship on presidential approval, it is not the only factor that affects the public's evaluations of the president. As we shall see, developments that conflict with a group's partisan predispositions increase the volatility of approval.[81]

Positivity Bias

Another predisposing factor is the "positivity bias," which one authority defined as the tendency "to show evaluation of public figures and institutions in a generally positive direction."[82] Americans have a general disposition to prefer and to expect positive relationships more than negative ones and to perceive stimuli as positive rather than negative. Thus, they tend to have favorable opinions of people.

Although the positivity bias should encourage presidential approval throughout a president's tenure, it is likely to be especially important at the beginning, when no record exists. As presidents perform their duties, citizens obtain more information and thus a more comprehensive basis for judging them. Moreover, as time passes, people may begin to perceive greater implications of presidential policies for their own lives. If the public views these implications unfavorably, it may be more open to, and pay more attention to, negative information about the president.

A related factor may affect public approval early in a president's term. As people have little basis on which to evaluate the president, they may turn elsewhere for cues. A new chief executive is generally treated favorably in the press. Moreover, there is excitement and symbolism inherent in the peaceful transfer of power, the inaugural festivities, and the prevalent sense of "new beginnings." All this creates a positive environment in which initial evaluations of elected presidents take place, buttressing any tendency toward the positivity bias.

There was little evidence of a positivity bias for Donald Trump, however. Political polarization encourages those identifying with the opposition party to evaluate the president negatively, and the fact that Trump did not win the popular vote only inflamed his opponents further. Moreover, his early actions such as the travel ban on citizens of some Middle Eastern countries were highly controversial and generated much critical press reaction.

The Persistence of Approval

We have seen that presidents typically begin their initial terms with the benefit of substantial support from the public, but how long does this honeymoon last? Conventional wisdom indicates that it does not last long. The thrust of the argument is that the president will soon have to begin making hard choices, which will inevitably alienate segments of the population. Additional support for this view comes from a revealing response by President Carter in 1979 to a reporter's question concerning whether it was reasonable to expect the president to rate very highly with the American people. The president answered,

> In this present political environment, it is almost impossible. There are times of euphoria that sweep the Nation immediately after an election or after an inauguration day or maybe after a notable success, like the Camp David Accords, when there is a surge of popularity for a President. But most of the decisions that have to be made by a President are inherently not popular ones. They are contentious.[83]

Despite the reasonableness of these expectations, presidential honeymoons are not always short-lived. Examining shifts in presidents' approval ratings reveals that although declines certainly do take place, they are neither inevitable nor swift. Eisenhower maintained his standing in the public very well for two complete terms. Kennedy and Nixon held their public support for two years, as did Ford (after a sharp initial decline). Johnson's and Carter's approval losses were steeper, although Johnson's initial ratings were inflated by the unique emotional climate at the time he assumed office. (The same was true, of course, for Ford.)

Reagan's approval ratings were volatile, but he stood at 64 percent approval at the time of his second inauguration, 13 thirteen percentage points higher than when he began. Bush maintained very high levels of public support until about the last year of his tenure. Clinton sank in the polls soon after taking office but enjoyed higher average levels of approval in his fourth through eighth years than for any of his first three years. George W. Bush rose to extraordinary heights in the polls after the 9/11 terrorist attacks and enjoyed strong support for the next two years before his approval plummeted. Barack Obama left office with a 59 percent approval rating, 11 percentage points higher than his average.

Thus, honeymoons are not necessarily fleeting times during which the new occupant of the White House receives a breathing period from the public. Instead, the president's constituents seem to be willing to give a new chief executive the benefit of the doubt for some time. It is up to each president to exploit this goodwill and build solid support for his administration in the public. This is why the first few months are often critical for setting the tone of the administration, shaping the president's reputation, and establishing a popular base.

In particular, President Clinton's rocky early months in office made it more difficult for him to obtain the public's support. Similarly, the controversy attending Barack Obama's early proposals to deal with the economic crisis, stimulate the economy, and reform health care kept his approval ratings low throughout his first term in office. Donald Trump's early tenure was marked by missteps and controversy, resulting in low approval and no honeymoon at all. His low approval ratings persisted with little variance throughout his tenure.

Long-Term Decline

In addition to examining approval levels within presidential terms, we also need to look for trends in public support across presidents. As shown in figure 5.2, from 1953 through 1965, with the single exception of 1958, at least 60 percent of the public, on average, approved of the president. At that time, support from two out of three Americans was not unusual. Starting in 1966, however, approval levels changed dramatically. Since that time, presidents have obtained support from even a bare majority of the public less than half the time.

Personality or Policy?

One factor commonly associated with approval of a president is personality. In common usage, the term *personality* refers to personal characteristics, such as warmth, charm, and humor, which may influence responses to an individual on a personal level. It is not unusual for observers to conclude that the public evaluates presidents based more on style than substance, especially in an era in which the media and sophisticated public relations campaigns play such a prominent role in presidential politics.[84] The fact that Americans pay relatively little detailed attention to politics and policy adds further support to the view that the president's personality plays a large role in the public's approval or disapproval. In other words, some argue that members of the public evaluate the president by how much they like him as a person.

Personality may buttress presidential approval, but it is not a dynamic factor. In other words, it cannot explain shifts in the president's standing with the public. Sharp changes in approval have occurred for presidents whose public manners have remained unaltered. Although the impressions the public holds of the president's personality form early and change slowly, factors such as what the public feels ought to

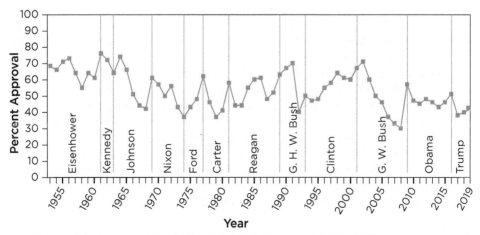

Figure 5.2 Average Yearly Presidential Approval, 1953–2019
Source: George C. Edwards III with Alec M. Gallup, *Presidential Approval* (Baltimore, MD: Johns Hopkins University Press, 1990); updated by the author.

be and the way people evaluate what they see can change more rapidly. "Cleverness" can also be viewed as "deceit," "reaching down for details" as "a penchant for the trivial," "evaluating all the alternatives" as "indecisiveness," "charm" as "manipulation" or simply "acting common" (or, even worse, "vulgar"), and "staying above politics" as "naiveté." The contradictory expectations that people hold about the president help to set the scene for these changing interpretations of presidential behavior, allowing the public to switch emphasis in what it looks for in a president and how it evaluates what it sees.

In addition, Americans appear to compartmentalize their attitudes toward the president and seem to have little difficulty in separating the person from the performance. Dwight Eisenhower was unique among modern presidents in that his public standing preceded, and was independent of, his involvement in partisan politics. He was a likable war hero who had recently been a principal leader in the highly consensual policy of defeating Germany in World War II. His image following the war was so apolitical that both parties approached him about running for president. Nevertheless, the public evaluated Eisenhower as a partisan figure. Thus, the public may "like" a president but still disapprove of the way he is handling his job. The public typically liked Jimmy Carter but disapproved of his performance as president.[85] In Bill Clinton's case, compartmentalization also occurred—but in reverse. Most Americans believed that he engaged in behavior of which they disapproved, yet a clear majority approved of the president's performance in office throughout his second term.[86]

Personal Characteristics

Much of the commentary on presidents in the press and other forums focuses on their personal characteristics, especially integrity, intelligence, and leadership abilities. When the public is asked about such job-related characteristics, its responses are clearly related to its evaluations of the president.[87] Assessments of characteristics such as the president's integrity, reliability, and leadership ability may change as new problems arise or in relation to the president's past performance. Certain characteristics may become more salient in response to changing conditions. For example, when the Iran-Contra affair became news, President Reagan's decision-making style became a prominent issue. Many people came to evaluate his focus on the "big picture" and detachment from the details of governing in a less positive light. Similarly, George W. Bush's decisiveness became less attractive as his decisions regarding the war in Iraq lost favor with the public.

Donald Trump has suffered in the polls because many Americans view him negatively. A Gallup poll in July 2017 found that a clear majority of the public disapproved of his handling the job of president. Most of these people responded that their disapproval was based on his job-related character traits. They felt he did not act in a presidential fashion, had a bad temperament, and was arrogant and obnoxious. Moreover, they judged that he did not know what he was doing. Still others emphasized that in their view he was untrustworthy and racist or sexist.[88] A Fox News poll found the public considered the president to be unstable, dishonest, and a bully.[89] Other polls have shown similar findings.[90]

Issues

Ultimately, the public cares about presidents because of issues of public policy. For an issue to have a significant influence on presidential evaluation, it must be salient to people; the people must hold the president responsible for it, and they must make their evaluation in terms of the president's performance regarding the issue. Obviously, perceptions of reality, sometimes influenced by interest groups,[91] mediate each of these components of assessment.

Salience of Issues

For most of his first term in office, George W. Bush stood high in the polls despite the public's low rating of his performance on a wide variety of issues, ranging from abortion to the economy. How could the public approve of a president who was considered to be doing a poor job on so many issues? The answer is that it evaluated the president primarily in terms of other issues, especially foreign policy, on which it approved of his performance.

If a matter is not salient to people, it will be unlikely to play a major role in their evaluations of the president. Understanding presidential approval, then, requires identifying what is on the minds of Americans. One cannot assume that people always judge the president by the same benchmarks. In fact, people generally have only a few issues that are particularly important to them and to which they pay attention.[92] The importance of specific issues to the public varies over time and is closely tied to objective conditions such as unemployment, inflation, international tensions, racial conflict, and fatalities during war.[93] Increasing fatalities and other issues are likely to be salient to different groups in the population at any given time. For example, some groups may be concerned about inflation, others about unemployment, and yet others about a particular aspect of foreign policy or race relations.[94]

The relative weights of values and issues in evaluations of the president also vary over time. Valence or style issues are values—such as patriotism, morality, or a strong national defense—on which there is a broad consensus in the public and that are more basic than a position on a specific policy. The president's articulation of valence issues, directly and in the symbols the White House employs in speech and actions, can affirm the values and beliefs that define citizens' political identities. Valence issues can be powerful instruments for obtaining public support, because presidents often prefer to be judged on the basis of consensual criteria with which they can associate themselves.

Research has found that values are relatively constant over time and that policy debates are rarely single-valued. Some values become more salient and some less so in making such trade-offs.[95] For example, antigovernment and anti-welfare attitudes give way to concerns for health and compassion if it is discovered that children are going hungry. Similarly, in the debate over abortion, the salience of values represented by "life" and "choice" varies substantially among citizens.

Finally, within an issue area, the bad news may outweigh the good in capturing the public's attention. People weigh negative information more heavily than positive—that is, bad news is more salient to them.[96] If the economy slumps, for example, this downturn may be more salient to the public than if the economy grows at a moderate rate. Thus, it is possible that presidents may be punished in the polls if the economy is not doing well yet not be comparably rewarded for prosperity.[97] It may be that an issue comes to the public's attention only when it reaches a certain threshold level, which usually means that there is a problem.[98] This, in turn, may provide the basis for more vocal, and thus more salient, opposition to the president.

Responsibility

Even if a matter such as the economy is salient to the public, it is not likely to affect people's evaluations of the president unless they hold him responsible for it.[99] Furthermore, the more the public attributes responsibility for an issue to the president, the more the issue is likely to affect evaluations of his performance.[100]

Despite the prominence of the chief executive, there are several reasons why people may not hold the president responsible for all the problems they face personally or for some problems that they perceive to be confronting the country. Most people do not politicize their personal problems, and most of those who are concerned about personal economic problems, such as credit card debt, do not believe the government should come to their assistance.[101] There is also evidence that people do not necessarily exaggerate the importance of the president or ignore contextual and institutional factors beyond his control.[102] In addition, some people may feel that those who preceded the president or who share power with him are to blame for important problems. Few people blamed Barack Obama for the economic turndown in 2009.

Presidential Performance

For an issue that is salient to the public and for which it holds the president accountable, the quality of the president's performance on that issue should become a factor in presidential approval. Many observers assume that, for example, if unemployment is rising, the public will evaluate the president negatively. Perhaps this is true, but perceptions may not follow directly from objective indicators of the economy's performance.

The unemployment level was virtually the same in summer 1984 as it was in summer 1992, yet the public evaluated the economic performance of President Reagan and President Bush (respectively) quite differently. Reagan was rewarded for bringing the level down, whereas Bush suffered the consequences of economic stagnation.

The public may be less harsh in its evaluations of presidents who are struggling with difficult situations, even if they are not meeting with short-term success. Franklin D. Roosevelt may have enjoyed the public's tolerance in 1933 and 1934 not only because he could not be held responsible for the Great Depression but also because he was seen as doing the best that could be done under trying circumstances. Jimmy Carter's standing in the public benefited for several months from favorable public perceptions of his handling of the Iranian hostage crisis, despite the fact that the hostages were not freed during this period.

In addition, a substantial body of evidence supports the argument that the political attitudes of Americans are more influenced by what they see as important national issues than by their personal experience. Focusing on the most often-discussed issue area, the economy, will clarify the point.

The conventional view is that people's evaluations of the president are affected strongly by their personal economic circumstances. That is, they are more likely to approve of the president if they feel they are prospering personally. In recent years, an impressive number of studies have found that when people evaluate government performance or individual candidates, personal economic circumstances are typically subordinated to other, broader considerations.[103] More specifically, it appears that citizens evaluate the president on the basis of broader views of the economy

rather than simply their narrow self-interests. In other words, rather than asking what the president has done for them lately, citizens ask what the president has done for the nation.[104]

Furthermore, people typically differentiate their own circumstances from those of the country as a whole. For example, polls regularly report that people are much more satisfied with their personal lives than with the way things are going in the nation.

Rally Events

To this point, we have examined factors that may affect presidential approval systematically over time, yet sometimes public opinion takes sudden jumps, as in the case of the 18 percentage point increase George H. W. Bush received in the polls after the Persian Gulf War began in January 1991. Even more dramatically, George W. Bush went from 51 percent in the Gallup poll on September 10, 2001, to 90 percent on September 22. The cause for this change, of course, was the great national outpouring of patriotism in response to the terrorist attacks on September 11, much of which focused on the commander in chief.

One popular explanation for these surges of support involves "rally events." John Mueller, in his seminal definition, explained the concept as an event that is international, directly involves the United States (and particularly the president), and is specific, dramatic, and sharply focused. Such events confront the nation as a whole, are salient to the public, and gain public attention and interest.[105]

The theory behind attributing significance to rally events is that the public will increase its support of presidents in times of crisis or during major international events, at least in the short run, because at such times they are the symbol of the country and the primary focus of attention. Moreover, people do not want to hurt the country's chances of success by opposing the president. The president, meanwhile, has an opportunity to look masterful and evoke patriotic, consensus-building reactions among the people.

Conversely, there is also reason to expect the potential for the public rallying around the flag to be limited. Studies of American public opinion regarding national security have found little inherent deference to the president as an individual.[106] More than patriotic fervor is involved in rallies, as those who rally are the most disposed to support the president in the first place,[107] and those most politically aware are less likely to make a sudden switch in their judgments regarding the president.[108]

Individual citizens seem to respond to criticism from members of both parties, especially from the president's party, and praise from members of their own party in evaluating military incursions abroad. Interestingly, press commentary by members of Congress following the typical incursion tends to be critical of the president, making a rally less likely. Conflicts involving substantial incursions of ground forces such as the US invasions of Grenada, Panama, Afghanistan, and Iraq in both 1991 and 2003 may be partial exceptions because in the short run they tend to evoke less credible criticism and more credible praise relative to less extensive uses of force.[109]

The preponderance of evidence indicates that the rally phenomenon rarely appears and that the events that generate it are highly idiosyncratic and do not seem to differ significantly from other events that were not followed by surges in presidential approval. Moreover, the events that cause sudden increases in public support are not restricted to international affairs, and most international events that would seem to be potential rally events fail to generate much additional approval of the president. Rather than being a distinctive phenomenon, a rally event seems to be simply an additional force that pushes potential supporters over the threshold of approval. For a rally to sustain support for the president, it requires the event that produced the rally to remain as the most salient issue for the public and for the president's response to receive widespread support. When people turn their attention to more divisive issues, the president's standing in the polls inevitably declines.

CONCLUSION

A president's relations with the public are complex. All chief executives need the support of the people in order to play an effective leadership role, yet they have a difficult time obtaining it. Expectations are high and contradictory, and the public's desires are frequently difficult to ascertain. Although the public appears to award or withhold its support of the chief executive based largely on job performance, its perceptions of issues and the president's actions may be hazy. Just how the public reaches its conclusions about the president's performance is not well understood.

In theory, however, there is ample opportunity for the president, directly and through the press, to influence public perceptions. We examine their efforts to do so in the next chapter.

DISCUSSION QUESTIONS

1. Private public opinion polls commissioned by the White House have become common. Should presidents take so many polls? How should they use the results?
2. Do presidents suffer politically from public expectations that are contradictory and unreasonably high? If so, how would you advise a president to deal with this problem? Illustrate your answer with examples from the presidencies of Barack Obama and Donald Trump. What were the public's expectations when they were elected and how successful have they been in meeting them?
3. Presidents try hard to win public approval but often fail. Is there anything they can do to remain high in the public's esteem? Does partisan polarization make their quest hopeless?

WEB EXERCISES

1. Go to https://www.whitehouse.gov/the-press-office/2017/02/28/remarks-president-trump-joint-address-congress and read President Trump's first address to a joint session of Congress. Did he set expectations too high with his promises?
2. Select a prominent issue that interests you. Search http://www.gallup.com/home.aspx or http://www.people-press.org to find out where the public stands on the issue. Then go to https://www.whitehouse.gov to see where the president stands on that issue. Does the president's stand match that of a majority of the public? If not, should the president change his policy to be consistent with public opinion?
3. Check the president's public approval since he took office at https://news.gallup.com/poll/203207/trump-job-approval-weekly.aspx. Given the discussion in this chapter, why does the president have this level of public support? How do you explain the fluctuations during his presidency?

SELECTED READINGS

Druckman, James N., and Lawrence R. Jacobs. "Presidential Responsiveness to Public Opinion." In *The Oxford Handbook of the American Presidency*, edited by George C. Edwards III and William G. Howell. Oxford, UK: Oxford University Press, 2009.

Gronke, Paul, and Brian Newman. "Public Evaluations of Presidents." In *The Oxford Handbook of the American Presidency*, edited by George C. Edwards III and William G. Howell. Oxford, UK: Oxford University Press, 2009, pages 232–253.

Heith, Dianne J. *Polling to Govern: Public Opinion and Presidential Leadership*. Stanford, CA: Stanford Law and Politics, 2004.

Jacobs, Lawrence R., and Robert Y. Shapiro. *Politicians Don't Pander*. Chicago, IL: University of Chicago Press, 2000.

Jacobson, Gary C. *A Divider, Not a Uniter: George W. Bush and the American People*, 3rd ed. New York: Longman, 2011.

Simon, Dennis M. "Public Expectations of the President." In *The Oxford Handbook of the American Presidency*, edited by George C. Edwards III and William G. Howell. Oxford, UK: Oxford University Press, 2009, pages 135–159.

Waterman, Richard C., Carol L. Silva, and Hank C. Jenkins-Smith. *The Expectations Gap Thesis: Public Attitudes Concerning the Presidency*. Ann Arbor: University of Michigan Press, 2014.

Wood, B. Dan. *The Myth of Presidential Representation*. New York: Cambridge University Press, 2009.

6

Leading the Public

★　★　★

President Obama uses the bully pulpit to try to obtain the public's support.

D onald Trump expected the public to be responsive to his leadership. He was soon to be disappointed. Indeed, he is the least popular new president in the history of polling. Moreover, many of his policies have been as unpopular as well. His recurrent use of Twitter to reach his supporters helped solidify his base but did little to expand his level of support beyond this core. In addition, his many false or inaccurate statements reinforced the view among his opponents that he was unfit to be president. Leading the public, then, was to be one of the president's greatest challenges.

All presidents devote a large portion of their time to obtaining public support for themselves and their policies. They believe it will increase their chances for success in Congress—and at the ballot box. They promote their programs through hundreds of speeches and public statements each year and frequently employ Air Force One to speak before audiences around the country.

If public support can be a useful leadership resource for presidents, are they in a position to call on it when needed? Commentators on the presidency often assume that the White House can persuade or even mobilize the public, provided the president is a skilled enough communicator. Various presidents have agreed. In the words of Franklin Roosevelt, "All our great Presidents were leaders of thought at times when certain historic ideas in the life of the nation had to be clarified." His cousin Theodore Roosevelt had earlier observed, "People used to say of me that I . . . divined what the people were going to think. I did not 'divine.' I simply made up my mind what they ought to think, and then did my best to get them to think it."[1]

Just how useful is the "bully pulpit"? Ultimately, we want to know whether presidents can direct change by imposing their priorities on the national agenda and creating and mobilizing a constituency to follow their lead. We should not assume that presidents are successful in influencing the public; we need to examine the obstacles to leadership as well as the president's efforts at persuasion.

DIRECT OPINION LEADERSHIP

The most recognizable technique employed by presidents to lead public opinion is to seek the public's support directly. At first glance, it seems that the president has some significant advantages in his attempts to lead the public. As by far the most visible political figure in the country, the president is well positioned to gain the public's attention. Moreover, no one else can as credibly claim to speak authoritatively for the whole nation and present statements in the context of the symbolic trappings of the White House. Nevertheless, there are a number of important constraints on the White House's ability to move the public.

Presentation Skills

All presidents since Truman have sought media advice from experts on lighting, makeup, stage settings, camera angles, clothing, pacing of delivery, and other facets of speechmaking. Despite this aid and the experience that politicians inevitably gain in public speaking, presidential speeches aimed at leading public opinion directly have typically been less than impressive. Not all presidents are effective speakers, and not all look good under the glare of hot lights and the unflattering gaze of television cameras. Only Kennedy, Reagan, Clinton, and Obama mastered the art of speaking to the camera.

Presidents not only have to contend with the medium; they also must concern themselves with their messages. It is not clear what approach works best. Many of the most effective speeches seem to be those whose goals are gaining general support and image building rather than gaining specific support. They focus on simple themes rather than complex details. Calvin Coolidge used this method successfully in his radio speeches, as did Franklin Roosevelt in his famous "fireside chats."[2] The limitation of such an approach, of course, is that general support cannot always be translated into public backing for specific policies.

There is no magic associated with certain leaders, and the "charisma" and personality of leaders are not the keys to successfully leading the public. Even George Washington, who was better positioned than any of his successors to dominate American politics because of the widespread view of his possessing exceptional personal qualities, did not find the public particularly deferential.[3]

Public's Predispositions

No matter how effective presidents may be as speakers or how charming their personalities, they still must contend with the predispositions of their audience. We know that humans have strong tendencies toward *motivated reasoning*. As we saw in chapter 5, this concept refers to tendencies in all people to distort the way they process information. Thus, most people seek out information confirming their pre-existing opinions and ignore or reject arguments contrary to their predispositions. When exposed to competing arguments, they typically accept the confirming ones and dismiss or argue against the opposing ones.

Those who pay close attention to politics and policy, the very people who might pay the most attention to the president's messages, are likely to have well-developed views and strong partisan attachments and thus be less susceptible to persuasion. Better-informed citizens possess the information and sophistication necessary to identify the implications of messages. They are best able to construct ostensibly reasonable counterarguments and rebuttals to evidence that they are emotionally inclined to resist and thus reject communications inconsistent with their values. In the typical situation of competing views offered by elites, reinforcement and polarization of views are more likely than conversion among attentive citizens.[4]

It may seem that those with less interest and knowledge present the most potential for presidential persuasion because they have fewer commitments to policies and less information to challenge the president's views. However, these people are also less likely to be aware of the president's messages, even when there is substantial public debate, limiting the president's influence.[5] To the extent that such people do receive the president's messages, they will also hear from the opposition how the president's views are inconsistent with their predispositions. Moreover, even if their predispositions make them sympathetic to the president's arguments, many people lack the understanding to see that the president's messages are consistent with their own underlying values.[6]

Partisanship

We have seen that partisan identification is a primary anchor of political attitudes and behavior and the basis for much motivated reasoning. Thus, it is not surprising that party cues influence opinion.[7] When the president speaks, he clarifies where the political parties stand, cutting through the complexity of policy debates. Members of the public use the cues of presidents and other party elites to align their partisanship and their issue stands, usually bringing the latter in line with the stances of their party's leaders.[8] In other words, when party leaders debate an issue, they activate the public's partisan predispositions and thus strongly influence people's policy preferences—both *for* and *against* the president.[9] (Of course, the strength of a person's partisanship should mediate partisan-motivated reasoning.[10]) Party cues may also encourage attentive individuals to produce arguments supporting the correctness of their party's position.[11]

In times of highly polarized politics—such as the United States is experiencing in the twenty-first century—the incentive to be loyal to one's own party and maximize differences with the opposition party is especially strong.[12] Polarized environments intensify the impact of party endorsements on opinions, decrease the impact of substantive information, and, ironically, stimulate greater confidence in those—less substantively grounded—opinions.[13] Moreover, increased confidence in their opinions makes people even less likely to consider alternative positions and more likely to take action based on their opinions, such as attempting to persuade others.[14]

When presidents take stands with which their co-partisans already agree, they reinforce those views. When Donald Trump supported tax cuts, repealing Obamacare, and weakening environmental protection, he was acting consistently with the views of most Republicans. He did not need to convince them that they should change their views.

Maintaining preexisting support or activating those predisposed to back him can be crucial to a president's success. Important policies usually face substantial opposition. Often opponents are virulent in their criticism. Presidents quite naturally believe they must engage in a permanent campaign just to maintain the status quo. Such efforts may require reassuring supporters as to one's fundamental principles, strengthening their resolve to persist in a political battle, or encouraging them to become more active on behalf of a candidacy or policy proposal.

Partisan polarization and motivated reasoning should also increase the prospects of presidents winning new support from their co-partisans as the latter bring their policy views in line with their partisan and ideological predispositions. Such change is most likely to occur on views that are not strongly held. People can resolve dissonance by shifting their own view on issues that are not central to them. Crystallized opinions on matters such as abortion or racial and ethnic attitudes, however, are not as likely to change.[15]

Elite signaling does not encourage people to change their minds by reasoning about an issue. Instead, signaling provides cues to people that serve to short-circuit their reasoning processes, trigger motivated reasoning, and thus shape how they process information provided by different sides, including largely ignoring arguments from the opposition.[16] Thus, when a party leader voices a strong opinion on an issue, many people will just accept that view. In effect, people replace a difficult question such as "How do I feel about corporate taxation?" with an easy question, "How does my party answer this question?" Some work has found that party cues encourage motivated reasoning to produce arguments supporting the correctness of their party's position.[17] Either way, the signaler is showing supporters where their predispositions should take them on a particular matter.

Motivated reasoning, then, may provide an opportunity for the president as leader of his party. When the president signals his views on issues, identifiers with his party should be responsive to those signals. These cues help his co-partisans cut through the complexity of policy debates and reach a conclusion. Of course, the strength of a person's partisanship should moderate partisan-motivated reasoning.[18] In addition, those who lack information or knowledge of the parties' traditional issue positions are likely to be less constrained in following a president of their party, because political knowledge is highly correlated with the levels of ideological constraint and issue consistency.[19]

Two scholars used a novel survey experiment in January 2017 and found that when told that President Trump supported a liberal policy, Republicans were substantially more likely to endorse this policy compared to the same question with no mention of Trump's position. The same was true, to a smaller extent, when Republicans were informed that Trump supported a conservative policy. Low-knowledge respondents, strong Republicans, those who approved of Trump, and self-described ideological conservatives were the most likely to respond to the treatment condition in *both* a liberal and a conservative direction. These results paint a picture of partisans who emphasize group attachment over issue positions.[20]

Motivated reasoning cuts two ways, however. Just as it may aid presidents' leadership of their co-partisans, it should encourage identifiers with the out party to *oppose* the administration's policies. Their predispositions are likely to be a difficult barrier to overcome. In an environment of high partisan polarization, there is little potential for the president to increase support for his initiatives. Thus, although the president has a potential to sway opinions among his base, he also is likely to create a backlash among his detractors.

Loss Aversion

A distinct type of predisposition is the preference for avoiding loss, which encourages people to place more emphasis on avoiding potential losses than on obtaining potential gains.[21] In their decision making, people place more weight on information that has negative, as opposed to positive, implications for their interests. Similarly, when individuals form impressions of situations or other people, they weigh negative information more heavily than positive. Impressions formed on the basis of negative information, moreover, tend to be more lasting and more resistant to change.[22]

Risk and loss aversion and distrust of government make people wary of policy initiatives, especially when they are complex and their consequences are uncertain. Since uncertainty accompanies virtually every proposal for a major shift in public policy, it is not surprising that people are naturally inclined against change.[23] Further encouraging this predisposition is the media's focus on political conflict and strategy, which elevates the prominence of political wheeler-dealing in individuals' evaluations of political leaders and policy proposals. The resulting increase in public cynicism highlights the risk of altering the status quo.

Jim West/Alamy Stock Photo

Members of the public show their disagreement with repealing the Affordable Care Act at a congressional town hall meeting.

The predisposition for loss aversion is an obstacle for presidential leadership of the public. Most presidents want to leave some substantial change at the core of their legacies. Yet, those proposing new directions in policy—and Donald Trump is all about change—encounter a more formidable task than advocates of the status quo. Those opposing change have a more modest task of emphasizing the negative to increase the public's uncertainty and anxiety to avoid risk.[24] In addition, fear and anger, which negative arguments presumably evoke, are among the strongest emotions and serve as readily available shortcuts for decision making when people evaluate an impending policy initiative.[25]

An excellent example of this phenomenon is public opinion regarding the Affordable Care Act (ACA), often known as Obamacare. As we will see later in this chapter, President Obama had a difficult time obtaining support for his signature legislative achievement. Indeed, he could not win majority support. However, when Republicans and President Trump tried to make major changes in the ACA in 2017, the public suddenly became more enthusiastic about the policy and strongly opposed the proposed changes.[26]

Misperceptions

Another limitation on presidential persuasion is the fact that people are frequently *misinformed* (as opposed to uninformed) about policy, and the less they know, the more confidence they have in their beliefs. Thus, they resist correct factual information. Even when others present them with factual information, they resist changing their opinions.[27] Moreover, the tendency to process information with a bias toward their preexisting views means that those who are most susceptible to misinformation may reject the corrections that they receive.[28] Interestingly, misperceptions are often most prevalent among those who are generally well informed about politics. Political knowledge neither corrects nor mitigates partisan bias in perception of objective conditions. Instead, it enhances it.[29]

The increasing array of media choices means that individuals are less likely to encounter information that would correct misperceptions. The advent of right-wing talk radio and Fox News, the influence of social sites such as Facebook, Twitter, and Reddit, and the mainstreaming of conspiracy sites such as InfoWars allow partisans to live in their separate informational and misinformational bubbles and, in some cases, to allow real news to be rendered as false—and false news to be rendered as true.

Other psychological factors also increase the likelihood that corrections will fail to undo the effects of misperceptions. Negations (i.e., "I am not a crook") often reinforce the perception they are intended to counter.[30] In addition, even if people initially accept corrections debunking a false statement, they may eventually fall victim to an "illusion of truth" effect in which people misremember false statements as true over time.[31] Finally, misleading statements about politics continue to influence peoples' beliefs even after these statements have been discredited.[32] Thus, our findings in the previous chapter that the public was uninformed about Barack Obama's actions on taxes and health-care reform, the state of the economy, and unemployment—or even whether he was born in the United States—are not surprising.

Source Credibility

A related matter of perception is the credibility of the source. Because the president's credibility mediates his influence as a persuader,[33] the public must view the president as a credible source if he is to lead public opinion.[34] Individuals interpret a policy, ranging from war to the budget deficit, in light of their opinions concerning the policy's sponsor.[35] The president typically enjoys high levels of approval from his co-partisans, and they are more likely to be influenced by White House cues.[36] However, many others, especially identifiers with the opposition party, are unlikely to find him a credible source on a variety of issues, especially those on which opinion is divided and on which he is the leader of one side of the debate. Indeed, people whose party is out of power have almost no trust in a government run by the other party.[37] High levels of polarization exacerbate this pattern and pose a severe credibility problem for the chief executive.

Public Attentiveness and Understanding

If the president is going to lead the public successfully, the public must receive and understand his messages. Those who are unaware of a message are unlikely to know the president's positions. The president cannot depend on an attentive audience, however.[38] If attempts to lead the public fall on deaf ears, they are unlikely to be successful.

It seems reasonable to assume that because the president is so visible and speaks on such important matters, he will always attract a large audience for his speeches. Wide viewership was certainly common during the early decades of television. Presidential speeches routinely attracted more than 80 percent of those watching television, an audience no one network could command.[39]

Things have changed, however. The White House finds it increasingly difficult to obtain an audience for its views—or even airtime on television to express them. Audiences for presidential speeches and press conferences have declined steadily since the Nixon administration in the early 1970s.[40]

The audience for Donald Trump's inaugural address (table 6.1) was more than six million persons smaller than the audience for Obama's in 2009. His first message to a joint session of Congress drew 4.7 million fewer viewers than Obama's eight years earlier. He drew even fewer viewers when he addressed the nation about immigration during the government shutdown in January 2019. Only a small fraction of the nation's 330 million people watch a presidential address.

Paradoxically, developments in technology have allowed the president to reach mass audiences, yet further developments have made it easier to for these same audiences to avoid listening to the White House. Cable television, networks that run only entertainment programming, and streaming services provide alternatives that make it easy to tune out the president.[41]

Television is a medium in which visual interest, action, and conflict are most effective. Unfortunately, presidential speeches are unlikely to contain these characteristics. Only a few addresses to the nation—such as President George W. Bush's address to a joint session of Congress on September 20, 2001—occur at moments of high drama.

The public's general lack of interest in politics constrains the president's leadership of public opinion in the long run, as well as on any given day. Although they have unparalleled access to the American people, presidents cannot make much use of it. If they do, their speeches will become commonplace and lose their drama and interest. That is one reason why presidents do not make formal speeches to the public on television very often—only a few times a year.[42]

Beginning with Richard Nixon, most recent presidents have turned to radio and midday addresses to supplement their prime-time televised addresses,[43] although

Table 6.1 Subjects and Audiences for Donald Trump's Nationally Televised Speeches

Date	Venue	Topic	Audience Size
January 20, 2017	Capitol	Inaugural Address	30.6 million
January 31, 2017	White House	Nomination of Neil Gorsuch to Supreme Court	32.4 million
February 28, 2017	Joint Session of Congress	Overview of Administration	47.7 million
August 21, 2017	Ft. Myer, Virginia	Afghanistan	27.6 million
November 15, 2017*	White House	Asian Trip	n.a.
January 30, 2018	Joint Session of Congress	State of the Union Message	45.6 million
April 13, 2018†	White House	Bombing of Syria	n.a.
July 9, 2018	White House	Nomination of Brett Kavanaugh to Supreme Court	25.6 million
January 8, 2019	White House	Immigration	39.6 million
January 19, 2019*	White House	Immigration/ Shutdown	n.a.
February 5, 2019	Joint Session of Congress	State of the Union Message	46.8 million

* Not delivered in primetime
† Short statement.
Source: Nielsen Company.

media coverage of these addresses has diminished over the years.[44] To increase the visibility of his radio addresses, Barack Obama recorded them for digital video and audio downloads from venues such as YouTube and iTunes. As a result, people could access them whenever and wherever they wanted. Donald Trump has made much less use of radio addresses, concluding that they do not attract a large enough audience.

In addition to the challenge of attracting an audience for the president's television appearances, the White House faces the obstacle of obtaining television coverage in the first place. Traditionally, presidents could rely on full network coverage of any statement they wished to make directly to the American people or any press conference they wished to be televised. The networks began to rebel against providing airtime in the 1970s and 1980s when one or more of them occasionally refused to carry an address or a prime-time press conference held by Presidents Ford, Carter, Reagan, or Bush. Bill Clinton encountered so much resistance from the networks to covering his speeches and press conferences that he held only four evening press conferences in his eight years in office (only one of which all the networks covered live) and made only six addresses on domestic policy, all of them in his first term.

In the two months following the terrorist attacks on the United States on September 11, 2001, George W. Bush received plenty of prime-time coverage for his speeches and a press conference. By November 8, however, most networks viewed the president's speech on the US response to terrorism as an event rather than news and did not carry it. Nearly a year later, on October 7, 2002, Bush made his most comprehensive address regarding the likely need to use force against Saddam Hussein's regime in Iraq. Nevertheless, ABC, CBS, NBC, and PBS chose not to carry the president's speech, arguing that it contained little that was new. Similarly, the Obama White House requested prime-time airtime to announce its new policy toward Cuba on December 17, 2014, but the networks rejected the request.

In addition, for the president to lead opinion, people must perceive accurately the view offered by the White House. Yet, we have seen that different people perceive the same message differently. With all his personal, ideological, and partisan baggage, no president can assume that all citizens hear the same thing when he speaks. Partisanship is especially likely to bias processing perceptions, interpretations, and responses to the political world.

The public can miss the point of even the most pointed rhetoric. Nine months after the president signed the 2017 tax bill, 60 percent of Americans underestimated the size of personal tax cuts, which Trump had touted as a great Christmas gift to the public.[45] Similarly, only 40 percent of the public knew the stock market had risen substantially in 2017, despite the president's frequent references to it. Partisan filters were at play here. Although 67 percent of Trump voters correctly said that the stock market had risen, just 35 percent of Hillary Clinton voters said the same.[46] In March 2018, despite Trump's frequent boasts about the strength of the economy, many people did not agree. Democrats in particular thought the economy was in worse shape than before the president took office.[47]

Focusing Attention

The White House not only wishes to have the public receive its messages, but it also wants to focus the public's attention on its priorities.[48] Given the protracted nature of the legislative process and the president's need for public support at all stages of it, sustaining a message can be as important as sending it in the first place. Moreover, the impact of communications tends to decay rapidly, and people tend to rely on the most recent message (and the most recent events) when forming their attitudes.[49]

Keeping the public focused requires frequent repetition of the president's views.[50] As former White House public relations counselor David Gergen put it, "History teaches that almost nothing a leader says is heard if spoken only once."[51] According to President George W. Bush, "In my line of work you got to keep repeating things over and over and over again for the truth to sink in, to kind of catapult the propaganda."[52]

Nevertheless, despite the enormous total volume of presidential public statements, they are dispersed over a broad range of policies, and wide audiences hear only a small portion of the president's remarks. The president rarely concentrates a televised address on an issue before Congress and actually makes few statements on even significant legislation. In addition, the president faces strong competition for the public's attention from previous commitments of government, congressional initiatives, opposing elites, and the mass media.[53]

Of equal consequence, the president often provides competition for himself as he addresses other issues, some of which are on his own agenda and others that events and others force upon him. Donald Trump is not a focused communicator. He rarely sticks to a script, whether it is for a theme week in the White House, an address to a rally or organization, or a discussion with congressional leaders.

The president often veers off topic and may undermine the message he intended to send. For instance, Trump's news conference with Senate Majority Leader Mitch McConnell on October 23, 2017, was orchestrated to project GOP unity on taxes. However, the president falsely accused his predecessors of not calling on the families of fallen soldiers, which set the White House on the defensive and dominated the national media for several days.

The Reagan White House was successful in maintaining a focus on its top-priority economic policies in 1981. It molded its communication strategy around its legislative priorities and focused the administration's agenda and statements on economic policy to ensure that discussing a wide range of topics did not diffuse the president's message.[54] In contrast, the Clinton administration blurred its focus by raising a wide range of issues in its first two years in office. The president later lamented that in the beginning of his tenure,

> I gave almost no thought to how to keep the public's focus on my most important priorities, rather than on competing stories that, at the least, would divert public attention from the big issues and, at worst, could make it appear that I was neglecting those priorities.[55]

Sustaining such a focus is very difficult to do, however, as there are many competing demands on the president to act and speak, which divert attention from his priorities. After 1981, President Reagan had to deal with a wide range of noneconomic policies. As Barack Obama's communications director, Daniel Pfeiffer, put it, "In the White House, you have the myriad of challenges on any given day and are generally being forced to communicate a number of complex subjects at the same time."[56] Although the White House had a daily communications plan on what message to tell they country, most of the time the staff had to rip it up in the first morning meeting to deal with an unexpected crisis that had popped up overnight.[57] Thus, according to the president's senior adviser, David Axelrod, the sheer volume of crises overwhelmed the message.[58]

Presidents only rarely repeatedly go public regarding even their most significant legislative proposals.[59] Commentary cascades from the White House, of course. One official estimated that the White House produces as many as five million words a year in the president's name in outlets such as speeches, written statements, and proclamations.[60] The number of presidential statements regarding a prominent policy can exceed two hundred in a year.

Wide audiences hear only a small proportion of the president's comments, however. Comments about policy proposals at news conferences and question-and-answer sessions and in most interviews are also usually brief and made in the context of a simultaneous discussion of many other policies. Remarks to individual groups and written statements may be focused, but the audience for these communications is modest. In addition, according to David Gergen, nearly all of the president's statements "wash over the public. They are dull, gray prose, eminently forgettable."[61]

Televised Addresses

The largest audiences, of course, are for the president's nationally televised addresses, but most of the comments in these addresses are made in the context of remarks about many other policies. There is little opportunity to focus on one issue area, especially in domestic policy. Bill Clinton made twenty-eight nationally televised addresses. Ten of these addresses were of a general nature, including his inaugural and State of the Union messages. Another nine announced US military interventions, and three dealt with his impeachment problems. The president made only six national addresses on legislation before Congress, four of them in 1993, one in 1994, and the last one in June 1995. In the remaining five and a half years of his presidency, he never again made a nationally televised address on legislation, except for his obligatory State of the Union addresses!

George W. Bush delivered thirty-three nationally televised addresses but used them even less than his predecessors to speak to the country about his initiatives. Almost all of his nationally televised addresses either were general addresses or related to the war on terrorism. Regarding other initiatives, he made one address on his decision regarding stem cell research in 2001, one on his nomination of John Roberts to the Supreme Court in 2005, and one on immigration reform in 2006.

Barack Obama delivered thirty nationally televised addresses, including both his inaugural addresses, his acceptance of the Democratic nomination in 2012, six State of the Union addresses, his Farewell Address, and his overview of his new administration in 2009. Of the remaining nineteen speeches, three were not delivered in prime time, and the three commercial broadcast networks did not carry another. Two of the speeches were memorials to shooting victims. In eight years, he spoke on only four domestic policy matters, one of which was the oil spill in the Gulf of Mexico. Several of the foreign policy speeches were announcements of actions, such as the end of the Iraq War, the death of Osama bin Laden, troop cuts in Afghanistan, and renewed relations with Cuba. There was no chance to use televised speeches to focus public attention on issues on which he needed to mobilize support.

Table 6.1 showed that Donald Trump has rarely addressed the nation on a specific issue. When he has done so, as in his discussion of a trip to Asia in 2017 or his announcement of bombing of Syria in 2018, his presentation may be short or not in prime time. The only times the president has addressed the nation about a matter before Congress in primetime were short presentations on his nominations of Neil Gorsuch and Brett Kavanaugh to the Supreme Court and on immigration policy during the 2018–2019 government shutdown.

Studies have found that the president lacks the capacity to guide public attention both directly through his messages and indirectly through the media.[62] Indeed, there is evidence that much of the president's rhetoric is in response to public concerns rather than a cause of them.[63]

Increasing the Salience of Popular Issues

Instead of seeking to bring new issues to the public's attention, presidents may make appeals on policies that already have public support in an attempt to make them more salient to the public and thus encourage members of Congress to support White House initiatives to please the public.[64] Indeed, presidents rarely appeal to the public about an initiative likely to face widespread opposition, instead making the case for initiatives that the public already favors.[65]

In 2001, George W. Bush made large tax cuts a top priority of his presidency. Although most people were not clamoring for tax cuts, the president's Republican base was enthusiastic, there was little organized opposition to the principle of the policy, many people found the prospect of lower taxes attractive, and the budget surplus in 2000 made tax cuts plausible. Bush traveled extensively to speak on behalf of his tax-cut initiative, focusing on states in which he had done well in the presidential election. His objective was not to convince more skeptical citizens of the soundness of his proposals. Instead, his goal was to demonstrate preexisting support for himself and his policy in the constituencies of potential swing votes in Congress. In 2003, the president seemed to be following the same strategy as he campaigned for another tax-cut proposal. His travel seemed designed to work at the margins to convince moderate senators of both parties that his tax-cut proposal enjoyed public support in their states.

Exploiting existing support for an issue by making the issue more salient to the public requires that (1) the president's initiative be popular, (2) the president has the ability to increase the salience of issues among the public, and (3) the president has the time and energy to take his case to the public.

Some presidential initiatives do have public support, but many do not. Ronald Reagan's efforts to decrease government spending on domestic policy, increase it on defense policy, win support for the Contras, and reduce regulation all typically lacked majority support. Bill Clinton's proposals for stimulating the economy, reforming health-care reform, intervening in Haiti, and enacting NAFTA (North American Free Trade Agreement) faced at least plurality opposition once their opponents responded to them. George W. Bush's most ambitious proposals in his second term, reforming Social Security and immigration policy and maintaining troops in Iraq, confronted a similar lack of popular support. Barack Obama's signature policy, health-care reform, was never popular with the public. Many of Donald Trump's policies, including building a border wall with Mexico, increasing defense spending, repealing the ACA, and overturning regulations designed to protect the environment, lacked the support of a majority of Americans.

'You're fired!'

We know little about the president's success in increasing the salience of issues, but there is reason to be cautious about attributing influence to the White House. Bill Clinton sought to start national discussions on affirmative action and Social Security, trying to develop a consensus on how to reform them. He even participated in roundtables with citizens to discuss the policies. The president's goal was laudable, but there is no evidence that he succeeded in stimulating national discussions, much less forging agreement on solutions.

The hurdles that the White House faces in presenting its case, overcoming the public's predispositions, attracting an audience, obtaining airtime, and sustaining a communications focus encourage presidents to rely on more subtle methods of opinion leadership.

FRAMING ISSUES

The president is interested in not only what the public thinks about a policy but also *how* it is thinking about it. Policy issues are usually complex and subject to alternative interpretations. Both issues within the direct experience of citizens, such as poverty, health care, and racial inequality, as well as those more remote from everyday life, such as arms control and international trade, are susceptible to widely different understandings.

The crux of the decision regarding which side to support in the debate over abortion is the relative weight given to the two well-known values: the life of the unborn and the right of the mother to choose to have the child. Similarly, the parties contending over the minimum wage often seem to be talking past each other. Advocates of increasing the minimum wage focus on *equity*: it is important to pay those making the lowest wages at least enough to support a minimally acceptable lifestyle. Opponents of increasing the minimum wage, on the other hand, focus on *efficiency*: raising the cost of labor puts businesses that employ low-wage earners at a disadvantage in the marketplace and may cause some employers to terminate workers in order to reduce their costs. Each side emphasizes different values in the debate in an attempt to frame the issue to its advantage.

The sheer complexity of most issues combined with the competing values that are relevant to evaluating them create cognitive burdens for most people. They lack the time, interest, and ability to search their memories for all the considerations that might be relevant to evaluating an issue or public official. Instead, they simplify their decisions by employing short cuts,[66] focusing on the dimensions they deem to be most important for their evaluations. In this decisional process, people are likely to weigh most heavily the information and values that are most easily accessible. Recent discussion by political leaders is one factor that determines their accessibility.[67]

The cognitive challenges of citizens are an opportunity for the White House. Although the president will have little impact on the values people hold, by defining and simplifying a complex issue through *framing*, the president attempts to define what a public policy issue is about.[68] He hopes to influence which attitudes and information people incorporate into their judgments of his policies and performance,[69] setting the terms of the debate on his proposals and thus the premises on which the public evaluates them. In the process, the president attempts to show the public that his position is consistent with its values. As one leading adviser to Ronald Reagan put it, "I've always believed that 80 percent of any legislative or political matter is how you frame the debate."[70]

It is not clear whether an issue frame interacts with an individual's memory so as to *prime* certain considerations, making some more accessible than others and therefore more likely to be used in formulating a political preference, or whether framing works by encouraging individuals to think deliberately about the importance of considerations suggested by a frame.[71] In either case, the frame raises the priority and weight that individuals assign to particular attitudes already stored in their memories.[72]

The president may also attempt to prime perceptions of objective circumstances such as the level of economic prosperity. Similarly, presidents try to prime people to view them in terms of positive characteristics such as strength, competence, and empathy.[73] An additional potential advantage for the president is that framing and priming—because they are relatively simple—are less susceptible to distortion by journalists and opponents than direct persuasion on the merits of a policy proposal.[74]

Presidential Framing

Instead of trying to persuade the public directly on the merits of a proposal, then, the White House often uses public statements and the press coverage they generate to articulate relatively simple themes. Public opinion research may have identified these themes as favoring the president's positions.[75] For example, on the eve of the vote in the House on a climate change bill, President Obama shifted his argument for the bill to emphasize its potential economic benefits. "Make no mistake," he declared, "this is a jobs bill."[76] Climate change is a controversial topic, but everyone is for jobs, especially in a period of high unemployment.

Attempts to frame issues are as old as the Republic.[77] Each side of a political contest usually attempts to frame the debate to its own advantage. Byron Shafer and William Claggett argue that public opinion is organized around two clusters of issues, both of which are favored by a majority of voters: social welfare, social insurance, and civil rights (associated with Democrats) and cultural values, civil liberties, and foreign relations (associated with Republicans). Each party's best strategy is to frame the choice for voters by focusing attention on the party's most successful cluster of issues.[78] John Petrocik has found that candidates tend to campaign on issues that favor them in order to prime the salience of these issues in voters' decision making.[79] Similarly, an important aspect of campaigning is activating the latent predispositions of partisans by priming party identification as a crucial consideration in deciding for whom to vote.[80]

Framing Policies

Portraying policies in terms of criteria on which there is a consensus and playing down divisive issues are often at the core of efforts to structure choices for both the public and Congress. The Reagan administration framed the 1986 tax reform act as revenue-neutral, presenting the choice on the policy as one of serving special interests or helping average taxpayers. Few people would choose the former option. Federal aid to education had been a divisive issue for years before President Johnson proposed the Elementary and Secondary Education Act in 1965. To blunt opposition, he successfully changed the focus of debate from teachers' salaries and classroom shortages to fighting poverty and from the separation of church and state to aiding children. This frame changed the premises of congressional decision making and eased the path for the bill.[81]

Similarly, Richard Nixon articulated general revenue sharing as a program that made government more efficient and distributed benefits widely. He deemphasized the distributional aspect of the policy, which redistributed federal funds from traditional Democratic constituencies to projects favored by Republicans' middle-class constituents.[82] Dwight Eisenhower employed the uncontroversial symbol of national defense during the Cold War, even when it came to naming legislation, to obtain support for aiding education (the National Defense Education Act) and building highways (the Interstate and Defense Highway Act).

At other times, the president must try to frame choices in an atmosphere inflamed by partisanship. Independent Counsel Kenneth Starr accused President Clinton of eleven counts of impeachable offenses, perjury, obstruction of justice, witness tampering, and abuse of power. The White House fought back, accusing Starr of engaging in an *intrusive* investigation motivated by a *political vendetta* against the president. The basic White House defense was that the president made a mistake (*personal failing*) in his *private* behavior, apologized for it, and was ready to move on to continue to do the people's business of governing the nation. Impeachment, the president's defenders said, was grossly *disproportionate* to the president's offense. The public found the White House argument compelling and strongly opposed the president's impeachment.

Ronald Reagan understood instinctually that his popular support was linked to his ability to embody the values of an idealized America. He continually invoked symbols of his vision of America and its past—an optimistic view that did not closely correspond to reality but did sustain public support. He projected a simple, coherent vision for his presidency that served him well in attracting adherents and countering criticism when the inevitable contradictions in policy arose. For example, he maintained his identification with balanced budgets even though he never submitted a budget that was even close to balanced and his administration was responsible for more deficit spending than all previous administrations combined. More broadly, Reagan employed the symbols of an idealized polity to frame his policies as consistent with core American values.[83]

Reframing Policies

Sometimes presidents try to increase the public's support for a policy by adding new attributes to it, making the issue salient to a wider segment of the public and thus adding to a supportive coalition.[84] In other words, the president attempts to reframe a policy that people have evaluated principally in some terms so that they will evaluate it in other terms. If a new group cares about the second set of attributes, it may add a crucial component to the president's coalition.

To obtain support for using the budget surplus to pay down the national debt rather than for funding a tax cut, Bill Clinton urged Congress to "save Social Security first." Framing the issue of paying down the national debt as being for or against this popular policy increased the salience of the issue to the public and made it difficult for Republicans to argue that Congress should use the surplus to fund a tax cut.

Similarly, in 1984, Ronald Reagan failed to win congressional support for additional MX missiles when the debate focused on the utility of the missiles as strategic weapons. He was more successful the next year, however, after the terms of the debate changed to focus on the impact of building the missiles on the arms control negotiations with the Soviet Union that had recently begun in Geneva. Senators and representatives who lacked confidence in the contribution of the MX to national security were still reluctant to go to the public and explain why they were denying American negotiators the bargaining chips they said they required.

Despite the success of Clinton and Reagan in these examples, it is usually difficult to frame a policy as central to the success of another, popular policy. Presidents are rarely in a position to make such claims.

Framing of Self

Presidents try to frame themselves as chiefs of state, nonpartisan leaders personifying both the government and the nation's heritage. They frequently appear on television welcoming heads of state or other dignitaries to the White House, dedicating federal projects, speaking before national groups, or performing ceremonial functions, such as laying a wreath at the Tomb of the Unknowns in Arlington National Cemetery or lighting the national Christmas tree. Foreign travels provide additional opportunities for presidents to present themselves as statesmen, dealing with the leaders of other nations on matters of international importance.

While engaging in these and other functions, presidents often make appeals to patriotism, traditions, and US history (and its greatness) to move the public to support them, thus reminding people of their common interests. They also frequently invoke the names of revered leaders of the past who made difficult decisions on the basis of high principles, such as Abraham Lincoln or Harry Truman, and then relate themselves or their decisions to these paragons.

According to Pat Buchanan, who served Ronald Reagan as the White House director of communications, "For Ronald Reagan the world of legend and myth is a real world. He visits it regularly and he's a happy man there."[85] In his 1965 autobiography, Reagan described his feelings about leaving the military at the end of World War II: "All I wanted to do ... was to rest up awhile, make love to my wife, and come up refreshed to a better job in an ideal world."[86] The reader would never realize from this that Reagan never left Hollywood while serving in the military during the war! However, in politics, perceptions are as important as reality; consequently, many people responded positively to the president's vision of history and his place therein.

Presidents also make gestures to show that they are really "one of the people." President Carter made considerable use of this technique in his desire to be seen as a people's president. At his inauguration, he chose to walk (instead of ride) down Pennsylvania Avenue from the Capitol to the White House after taking the oath of office. He conducted a "fireside chat" over national television, seated before a blazing fire and dressed casually in a sweater instead of a suit. He also staged the first press conference in which private individuals could call in from around the country and directly ask him questions, and he held many town meetings where local citizens could question him. Most subsequent presidents have adopted the town meetings format and other means for meeting with average citizens.

Limits to Framing

Despite its potential advantages, framing issues successfully is a challenge for the White House. The president faces committed, well-organized, and well-funded opponents who provide competing frames. When there is elite consensus, and thus only one set of cues offered to the public, the potential for opinion leadership may be substantial. However, when elite discourse is divided, generating conflicting messages, people respond to the issue according to their predispositions, especially their core partisan and ideological views.[87]

The Trumps welcome the president of China, Xi Jinping, and his wife, Peng Liyuan, for a state visit to the United States.

Occasions in which elite commentary is one-sided are rare. Consensual issues tend to be new, with few people having committed themselves to a view about them. Most issues that generate consensual elite discourse arise from external events, like surprise attacks on the United States such as the terrorist assaults on September 11, 2001, or its allies, such as the invasion of Kuwait in 1990. Thus, the president's greatest chance of influencing public opinion is in a crisis (which attracts the public's attention) in which elites articulate a unified message. At other times, most people are too inattentive or too committed to views to be strongly influenced by elite efforts at persuasion.[88]

Similarly, when people can choose their sources of information, as almost everyone can, they are unresponsive to opinion leadership.[89] Many factors condition the impact of framing,[90] and most systematic studies of real-world conditions have found that the public is not very responsive to elite frames.[91] Even what appears to be successful framing may not be,[92] and issue frames seem to have modest effects on how the public later evaluates politicians.[93]

A fundamental limitation on presidential framing and priming is the public's lack of attention to politics, which restricts its susceptibility to taking cues from political elites. There are widely varying levels of interest in and information about politics and public policy.[94] Even if their predispositions make them sympathetic to the president's arguments, less interested and informed citizens may lack the understanding to make the connection between the president's arguments and their own underlying values. Moreover, the more abstract the link between message and value, the fewer people who will make the connection.[95]

In addition, for the president to frame issues for the public, people must perceive accurately the frame offered by the White House. There is reason to believe, however, that different people perceive the same message differently. The media is of little help, as it is unlikely to adopt uniformly or reliably the White House's framing of issues. Moreover, with all his personal, ideological, and partisan baggage, no president can assume that all citizens hear the same thing when he speaks. Partisanship is especially likely to bias processing perceptions, interpretations, and responses to the political world.[96]

We know very little about the terms in which the public thinks about issues. Although frames may evolve over decades,[97] presidents do not have the luxury of such a leisurely perspective. Chief executives need public support during their tenures, usually in their first terms when they are more likely to have majorities in Congress. In addition, the White House must advocate the passage of many proposals at roughly the same time, further complicating its efforts to structure choice on any single issue.

Most presidents seek a strong, clear narrative to help them connect with the public and explain the essence of their administrations. Franklin D. Roosevelt's "New Deal" is perhaps the best-known modern example. The lack of a positive narrative, of course, invites opponents to construct a less flattering portrayal.

Although Donald Trump is a master of branding, despite vigorous efforts to frame issues in ways that would win widespread support for himself and his policies he has not been able to establish a positive narrative for his administration.[98] There have always been counter frames that many people found more compelling than those offered by the White House. Trump promoted lower taxes as agents of economic growth, but more people saw them as giveaways to the wealthy and a cause of exploding deficits. He advocated restricting immigration in terms of protecting the country from gangs and terrorists, job losses to "illegal aliens," amnesty for lawbreakers, and assaults on American values. Opponents, however, saw unfairness to Dreamers and other "undocumented immigrants," a loss of needed workers, a barrier to uniting families, religious discrimination, and racism.[99]

According to the president, he needed to renegotiate international trade agreements to protect American jobs and lower the trade deficit. Others saw the same policy as limiting the sale of US services, manufactured goods, and agricultural products abroad and raising the cost of living for nearly everyone. When US intelligence agencies concluded that Saudi Arabian Crown Prince Mohammed bin Salman ordered the murder of journalist Jamal Ahmad Khashoggi, Trump argued that the United States should take no action such as limiting arms sales because of the loss of jobs, the need to keep the price of oil low, and Saudi Arabia's cooperation in resisting Iran. Opponents, including some Republicans, argued that the president had made outlandish claims regarding new jobs and that Saudi-led OPEC raised the price of oil shortly after the incident.

PUBLIC RELATIONS

In its efforts to mold public opinion, the White House employs public relations techniques modeled after those of commercial advertising firms. One indicator of the importance of public relations to contemporary presidents is the presence of advertising specialists and those with television backgrounds in the White House. More broadly, the White House invests a substantial amount of staff, time, and energy into focusing the public's attention on the issues it wishes to promote and encouraging the public to see its proposals for dealing with those issues in a positive light. A count in the second term of the George W. Bush presidency found that the number of White House communications staff outnumbered the economic and domestic policy staff. If one includes all those who worked on the presentation of the president and development of his communications, a conservative estimate is that there were 350 people on the president's staff working on communications.[100]

A focus on public relations may influence the substance, presentation, and especially the timing of policy. Being human, all presidents are subject to the temptation to do the most popular thing.[101] The potential for subordinating substance to style is clearly present. Top Reagan aide and public relations specialist Michael Deaver freely admitted that he had little interest in matters of public policy and argued "image is sometimes as useful as substance."[102]

A focus on public relations also encourages running the White House like an advertising agency. A close observer of the Reagan administration found that a single focus permeated staff meetings of top White House officials: how the topic under discussion would play in the media.[103] Advertising stresses a uniform image, and attempts to achieve this orientation can be a centralizing force in an administration. However, an emphasis on "team play" may discourage dissent because it might cloud the president's image. The Nixon and George W. Bush White Houses were especially concerned with message discipline, and critics charged each with being unduly closed to alternative views. Both administrations also found it difficult to maintain message discipline, however.[104]

Spreading the Word

The primary goal of White House public relations efforts is to build support for the president and his policies. Part of this job is "getting the word out" about the president, his views, and his accomplishments. The president, of course, carries much of this burden and appears in many venues. Bill Clinton even appeared on MTV within six weeks of taking office in an attempt to reach a more youthful audience, and Barack Obama appeared on network late-night shows, ESPN, and *The Daily Show* and *The Colbert Report*. The White House also places representatives of the administration (the vice president, cabinet members, and senior White House staff) on television programs such as the Sunday interview shows and weekday morning news shows. Similarly, the White House provides or clears speeches for officials to give at university commencement ceremonies and in other visible settings.

The president is his own best publicity agent, however. Donald Trump knows this instinctively. In the *Art of the Deal*, he wrote:

> One thing I've learned about the press is that they're always hungry for a good story, and the more sensational the better . . . . If you are a little different, or a little outrageous, or if you do things that are bold or controversial, the press is going to write about you.
> Even a critical story can be valuable.[105]

Thus, the press covers what he says or tweets because the statements are outrageous, controversial, unnerving, appalling. In end, the president has set the national agenda and also the terms and tone of the debate.

The president's aides may also try to stimulate favorable articles on the First Family and is happy to provide photographs portraying the president as family oriented, a pet owner, or the like. For example, Reagan White House aides ghostwrote, under the president's name, a story on keeping physically fit and had it published in a popular Sunday newspaper magazine supplement. The idea was to make the point subtly that Ronald Reagan was not too old for the job. Likewise, the White

House paid close attention to the president's image, trying to portray him as busy and engaged in important decision making rather than remote and passive, as critics charged.

Reaching the television audience for news is especially important to the White House, and the president's staff builds his schedule around efforts to do so. As one press aide put it, "Whenever possible, everything was done to take into account the need for coverage. After all, most of the events are done for coverage. Why else are you doing them?"[106]

Most recent White Houses have adopted a "rolling" announcement format in which they alert the press that they will be making an announcement (such as a legislative initiative) in coming days, sparking stories on the upcoming news. Then they make the announcement, generating yet additional stories. Finally, the president travels around the country repeating the announcement he just made, obtaining both local and network coverage of his media events. The exception to this pattern is Donald Trump, whose press operation has been less well organized than those of his predecessors and who does not like to travel.

Presidents and their aides tailor the messages they wish to transmit to the public to the needs of the press. The Reagan White House was especially skilled at providing vivid pictures and effective sound bites for the television news. Similarly, the president and his aides time announcements so that reporters can meet their papers' deadlines. Those made too late in the evening will not appear in the next morning's newspapers.

If the White House wants to decrease the coverage of an event, it can wait until after the evening news programs or weekends to announce it. Then, it might be buried among the next day's occurrences. (In the age of twenty-four-hour news channels, however, a cable channel is likely to pick it up.) The White House can also order administration officials to avoid appearing on interview programs or holding press conferences. The White House can make an announcement right before a press deadline, decreasing the opportunity for reporters to obtain unfavorable reactions. Finally, the president can discourage coverage of a divisive issue by acting away from reporters and cameras such as when President Obama quietly signed an order allowing federal funds to be used for international groups that promote abortion. Similarly, President Trump signed a controversial bill allowing states to strip family planning funds from abortion providers, including Planned Parenthood, but he did so behind closed doors and issued no statement regarding his action. He employed the same tactic when he signed a regulation eliminating an expansion of retirement savings accounts.[107] Similarly, Trump directed the Pentagon to ban transgender people from joining the military and pardoned a politically radioactive convicted former sheriff on a Friday night as a Category 4 hurricane was about to slam into the Texas coastline.

Alternately, the president might take another newsworthy action at the same time as an unpopular one.[108] President Clinton timed his firing of Federal Bureau of Investigation (FBI) director William Sessions so that it would cut into the news coverage of a speech on his policy on homosexuals in the military, and he vetoed a ban on late-term abortions on a heavy news day dominated by the funeral of Commerce Secretary Ron Brown. George W. Bush announced his proposal for a Department of Homeland Security just as the Senate Judiciary Committee began hearings on failures of the FBI regarding preventing terrorist attacks.

The White House tries to avoid associating the president with bad news. When the United States pulled the marines out of Lebanon, it was announced after President Reagan flew to his California ranch for a vacation and was not available for questions.[109] It was preferable to let a subordinate serve as the lightning rod.[110] Similarly, when a US plane collided with a Chinese aircraft in April 2001, the White House was determined to keep George W. Bush away from the issue so that he would not appear to be emotionally involved or to be the negotiator with the Chinese. Secretary of State Colin Powell took the lead—but the White House did not want Powell on television to take the credit when he succeeded in winning the crew's release.[111] The general rule of thumb is that the president delivers good news, but bad news comes from his staff or other administration officials.

Presidents may also try to avoid being caught up in controversies. Presidents Reagan and both Bushes addressed the annual Washington antiabortion rally by phone, even though it was held only a short distance from the White House. They wanted to avoid being seen with the leaders of the movement on the evening news. Similarly, President Clinton left a recorded message for those participating in a 1993 gay rights rally in the capital.

Conversely, the White House loves good news, which it tries to distribute over time so that each incident receives full coverage. The president does not want bad news to drive out the good, yet this does happen. The first major piece of legislation that President Clinton signed was the popular Family Leave Act. Coverage of the signing ceremony was diluted, however, by media attention focused on Kimba Wood's withdrawal from consideration as attorney general.

Media Events

In addition to general efforts to publicize the president, the White House often stages "media events" in hope of obtaining additional public support. No administration was more attentive to the potential of media events than Ronald Reagan's. His press secretary, Larry Speakes, kept a sign on his desk that read, "You don't tell us how to stage the news, and we don't tell you how to cover it." Michael Deaver carefully scripted every second of the president's public appearances, right down to placing tape on the floor to show Reagan where to stand for the best camera angles.[112] Deaver was clear about the importance of appealing to television: "You get only 40 to 80 seconds on a given night on the network news, and unless you can find a visual that explains your message you can't make it stick."[113]

The George W. Bush White House was also skilled at using the powers of television and technology to promote the president. "We pay particular attention to not only what the president says but what the American people see," said Office of Communications Director Dan Bartlett. Thus, the White House hired experts in lighting, camera angles, and backdrops from network television to showcase the president in dramatic and perfectly lighted settings. In May 2003, at a speech in Indianapolis promoting his economic plan, White House aides went so far as to ask people in the crowd behind Bush to take off their ties so that they would look more like the ordinary people the president said would benefit from his tax cut. For a speech that the president delivered in the summer of 2002 at Mount Rushmore, the White House positioned the platform for television crews off to one side so that the cameras caught Bush in profile, his face perfectly aligned with the four presidents chiseled in stone.[114]

Perhaps the most elaborate White House event was Bush's speech aboard the *Abraham Lincoln* announcing the end of major combat in Iraq. The Office of Communications choreographed every aspect of the event, including positioning the aircraft carrier so that the shoreline could not be seen by the camera when the president landed, arraying members of the crew in coordinated shirt colors over Bush's right shoulder, and placing a banner reading "Mission Accomplished" to capture the president and the celebratory two words perfectly in a single camera shot. It also specifically timed the speech so that the sun would cast a golden glow on Bush. One of the president's aides proclaimed, "If you looked at the TV picture, you saw there was flattering light on his left cheek and slight shadowing on his right. It looked great."[115]

At times, media events can be used quite cynically. When President Reagan was under fire for not supporting civil rights, he paid a visit to a black family who had had a cross burned in their front yard. However, the White House did not mention that the cross burning had occurred five years earlier. When the president's pollster found that the public overwhelmingly disapproved of the administration's reductions in aid to education, Michael Deaver arranged for Reagan to make a series of speeches emphasizing quality education. As Deaver later gloated, public approval of the president regarding education "flip-flopped" without any change in policy at all.[116]

J. Scott Applewhite/AP Images

George W. Bush uses the background of the USS *Abraham Lincoln* to announce the end of the war in Iraq.

Some of the emphasis on media events is the White House's response to the nature of the media (which we will examine in chapter 7). According to Larry Speakes, the White House press spokesman during most of Ronald Reagan's tenure in the White House,

> We knew that television had to have pictures to present its story. . . . So when Reagan was pushing education, the visual was of him sitting at a little desk and talking to a group of students, or with the football team and some cheerleaders, or in a science lab. Then we would have an educators' forum where the president would make a noteworthy statement. We learned very quickly that the rule was no picture, no television piece, no matter how important our news was.[117]

Operating on similar premises of the value of combining pictures with words, President Obama announced his timeline for withdrawing troops from Iraq before thousands of US Marines at Camp Lejeune, North Carolina. When he ordered thirty thousand additional troops to Afghanistan, he did so in a prime-time speech to the cadets at West Point. President Trump delivered a national address on the war in Afghanistan before an audience of troops at Ft. Myer, Virginia. Obama traveled to Tucson, Arizona, in 2011 to speak at a memorial service for those killed in a shooting. Pictures of the president as First Mourner made the story, and his speech was nationally televised.

The Digital White House

Although technological change has made it more difficult for the president to attract an audience on television, other changes may have increased the White House's prospects of reaching the public. Teddy Roosevelt gave prominence to the bully pulpit by exploiting the hunger of modern newspapers for national news. Franklin D. Roosevelt broadened the reach and immediacy of presidential communications with his use of radio. More recently, John F. Kennedy and Ronald Reagan mastered the use of television to speak directly to the American people. Barack Obama positioned himself as the first Internet president.

The Obama White House regularly alerted the president's millions of followers on Twitter, Facebook, and other platforms and lists of supporters accumulated during his campaign and the Democratic Party's own lists. It also produced and distributed many more videos than any past administration. The administration created a White House blog offering short stories accompanied by photos and videos, streamed live events, and provided podcasts of speeches, remarks, events, and briefings. The administration also held regular question-and-answer Webcasts with policy officials on whitehouse.gov. In addition, the White House introduced *West Wing Week*, a video blog consisting of six-to-seven-minute compilations that appeared each week on the White House's website and on video-sharing sites. The White House also hosted an animated page, made a video on BuzzFeed, and scheduled Obama to appear on the Internet show *Between Two Ferns* and on the comedy website *Funny or Die*. White House assistants even encouraged the president and others to pose for "selfies" and other funny pictures.[118]

The Trump White House has a less organized digital public relations effort than Obama's. However, it began a massive ad campaign on Facebook in 2018, and it included videos on the president's Twitter account. Indeed, Donald Trump is probably the world's most prominent user of social media. You can read more about his tweeting in box 6.1.

Box 6.1 ★ Donald Trump as First Tweeter

Donald Trump is the first president to rely on social media as a primary means of communicating with the public. According to one journalist, "His musings in bursts of 280 characters or less . . . have become a fixture of American life, driving cable news coverage and punctuating the political discourse."[119] The president has sent thousands of tweets (you can find them at www.trumptwitterarchive. com/archive), and he carefully crafts his messages. According to former White House director of message strategy Cliff Sims, "He's meticulous with not just the words that he wants to use but the punctuation."[120]

The president is firm in his belief that Twitter is essential to his success: "let me tell you about Twitter. I think that maybe I wouldn't be here if it wasn't for Twitter. . . . Twitter is a wonderful thing for me, because I get the word out."[121]

The president does indeed spread his message. He had sixty-four million followers on @realdonaldtrump in September 2019 and twenty-seven million on @potus. He had twenty-four million likes on Facebook and fourteen million followers on Instagram. Although many of these followers are duplicates, the president has the potential to directly reach tens of millions Americans completely on his terms.

Most people do not encounter the president's messages on their Twitter feed, however. In a Gallup poll in May 2018, only 8 percent of the sample—30 percent of Twitter users—followed Trump on Twitter. Of that 8 percent, 55 percent reported reading all or most of his tweets. That represents about 4 percent of the population. Another 2 percent said they read some of his tweets.[122] Another poll found that just 14 percent of Trump voters and 11 percent of Americans as a whole say they learn about something Trump has posted on Twitter because they saw it on the site.[123]

Nevertheless, half the public reports seeing, reading, or hearing "a lot" about the president's tweets, and another quarter say they encounter "a fair amount" of information about them.[124] Two-thirds of his voters and 64 percent of all Americans say they are more likely to come across them in a news story.[125] Thus, despite the use of the technology of social media, the president is actually still dependent on the media to convey his case to the public.

The most important question is how people respond to the president's tweets. Despite Trump's affection for tweeting, the public is less appreciative. A poll in March 2017 found that 50 percent of registered voters disapproved of his tweeting while only 16 percent approved. Even 51 percent of Trump voters thought he should be more cautious.[126] Later polls found about two-thirds of the public disapproving of the president's use of Twitter.[127]

By large margins, the public finds the president's tweets "misleading."[128] A series of polls taken in 2017 found that only a fifth of the public thought Trump's tweeting was "effective and informative." More than two-thirds felt it was "reckless and distracting." Even Trump voters had mixed reactions.[129] Similar percentages saw Trump's use of Twitter as a "risky" way to communicate.[130] Indeed they were. For example, his efforts to have his travel bans upheld were undermined by his repeated tweets suggesting that the measures were intended to block Muslims from entering the country.

Moreover, the public oppose personal attacks in tweets, such as the president's attack on the hosts of MSNBC's *Morning Joe*, Joe Scarborough and Mika Brzezinski.[131] On June 29, 2017, Trump tweeted, "I heard poorly rated @Morning_ Joe speaks badly of me (don't watch anymore). Then how come low I.Q. Crazy Mika, along with Psycho Joe, came to Mar-a-Lago 3 nights in a row around New Year's Eve, and insisted on joining me. She was bleeding badly from a face-lift. I said no!" A few days later, he posted a doctored video clip showing him bashing the head of a figure representing CNN. It is hardly surprising that the media gave

(continued)

Box 6.1 ★ Continued

substantial attention to these posts, which were so clearly outside the norms of civility—let alone the norms for a president.

Often, the president's tweets distract from the administration's core message. For example, the White House declared a policy focus (workforce development, technology, energy, and infrastructure) for each week in June 2017. The president made 163 tweets on Monday through Friday of those weeks. Only twelve (7 percent) of the tweets addressed the subject of the White House's focus.[132] The others were distractions.

Often the president used tweets to respond to criticism and to denounce his opponents. However, if you emphasize dissensus and division, you are weakly positioned to attract broad support. If you react to criticism by demeaning others, you are likely to end up demeaning yourself. If you spend your time defending unpresidential behavior, you inevitably focus attention on that behavior.

It is not surprising, then, that the public overwhelmingly thinks the president should stop tweeting.[133] A January 2018 poll found that only 11 percent of the public felt Trump's use of Twitter was helping his presidency. Sixty-six percent it was hurting it. Only 21 percent of Republicans said his tweets were helping, while twice as many, 43 percent, thought they were hurting.[134]

Limitations

Although technology provides the potential for the White House to communicate more effectively with greater numbers of people, there are obstacles to realizing that potential. Americans increasingly read and view material that matches their political beliefs. Moreover, the algorithms of search engines and social media guide people toward material that is likely to reinforce their views. Ideological insulation poses a new challenge for White House communications, a challenge that cannot be overcome by simply communicating in different venues.

Twitter conversations around political issues often quickly polarize into disconnected groups, with people citing different information sources to make their case.[135] Thus, although the Internet offers new opportunities for the president to reach the public, it also fragments the president's audience, making it more difficult to reach those predisposed to oppose the president with unfiltered messages. Moreover, the opposition is able to exploit the same tools and audience characteristics to challenge the White House and reinforce the tendencies of its adherents. In addition, most presidential communications to the public go to true believers, not to the broader pool of potential supporters. The most balanced conclusion is that the impact of the new media on the president's ability to govern is marginal.

Information Control

George W. Bush's press secretary described the Bush White House as "engaging in spin, stonewalling, hedging, evasion, denial, noncommunication, and deceit by omission."[136] There are less direct ways, then, for influencing public opinion than appealing to the public directly. Many of these less savory techniques fall under the category of information control. The goal is to influence public opinion by controlling the information on which the public bases its evaluations of chief executives and their policies and which it analyzes to determine if there is cause for concern. If the public is unaware of a situation or has a distorted view of it, then presidents may have more flexibility in achieving what they desire—which often is public passivity as much as public support.

Withholding Information

Classifying information under the rubric of "national security" is frequently used to withhold information. Most people support secrecy in handling national security affairs, especially in such matters as defense plans and strategy, weapons technology, troop movements, the details of current diplomatic negotiations, the methods and sources of covert intelligence gathering, and similar information about other nations. However, there has been controversy over the amount of information classified and whether the president and other high officials have used classification strategies to influence public opinion. An official might withhold crucial information from the public in order to avoid embarrassment. Yet, this may hinder the public's ability to evaluate an official's performance and ask fully informed questions of public policy. In an attempt to increase or maintain support, an official may provide a distorted view of reality. The Bush White House ordered the CIA not to release the reservations and nonconforming evidence in the full National Intelligence Estimate of October 2002 before the US invasion of Iraq,[137] and it kept classified the evidence of how badly things were going in Iraq in the years immediately after the invasion.[138]

There are other means of withholding information besides classification. One of the highest priorities of the George W. Bush administration in 2004 was to pass a prescription drug bill under Medicare. Many members of Congress were concerned about the program's cost, especially at a time of record budget deficits. Medicare's chief actuary, a nonpartisan official, concluded that the bill would cost considerably more than the administration projected. Thomas Scully, the presidentially appointed administrator of the agency overseeing Medicare, ordered him not to provide to Congress the most recent estimates of the cost of the bill while Congress considered it.

Similarly, the administration was notable for placing political constraints on scientific findings, ranging from public health reports of the US surgeon general to studies on climate change by the Environmental Protection Agency (EPA) and NASA. The White House even refused to open an email message from the EPA so that there would be no official record of the agency's official conclusion that greenhouse gases are pollutants that must be controlled.

The Trump administration removed, altered, or made less accessible information on climate change on websites across the federal government and declined to collect important information—such as the health effects of strip-mining mountaintops for coal, research into offshore drilling, gender pay disparities, and student loan payments—that would contradict its policies.[139] It also stopped publishing online the ethics waivers granted to appointees who would otherwise be barred from joining the government because of recent lobbying activities. In addition, the White House issued a blanket ban on oversight requests sent by Democratic members of Congress, constraining their ability to evaluate the government's performance.[140] Famously, the president has broken with tradition and refused to make his tax returns public.

Withholding information may not always advance an administration's priorities. Lyndon Johnson was determined to limit disclosure of his decision to order an expanded combat mission for US troops in Vietnam in April 1965. He then resisted explaining and defending the policy.[141] These actions contributed to a credibility gap when his decisions became obvious to all. During the Tet holiday in the spring of 1968, the North Vietnamese launched a massive attack against US and South Vietnamese forces. US intelligence and military officials, including the president, anticipated this attack, prepared for it militarily, and rapidly defeated it. Yet, Tet was the turning point in support for the war, as the nation was shocked by the scale of the attack. President Johnson and military leaders had led the nation to believe that we had been so successful that such an attack would not be possible.[142] Moreover, he failed to explain what had happened, what the administration knew and what it was doing beforehand, and how the Tet affected long-term US goals. Media reports focusing on the spectacular reinforced the public's shock and gave the appearance of a major setback and proof that US policies had failed.[143]

Obfuscation

Presidents and their aides may also attempt to obscure or distort the truth in order to confuse or mislead the public. President Eisenhower regularly gave purposefully ambiguous answers at his press conferences.[144] When George Bush agreed to accept "tax revenue increases" as part of the 1990 budget agreement with Congress, his announcement was so confusing that it took officials in Washington several days to determine whether he meant increases resulting from increased economic growth, a cut in capital gains taxes, or an increase in tax rates—and his press secretary refused to define the president's terms, in large part because of Bush's campaign promise not to raise taxes. Bill Clinton carried semantic hairsplitting to new heights with his arguments regarding smoking marijuana (he claimed he did not inhale), dodging the draft, raising campaign funds within the White House, and, of course, the nature of his relationship with White House intern Monica Lewinsky.[145]

Distortion

Distortion comes in many forms. One of the most common is to provide impressive statistics without going into the details of how they were compiled. For example, Reagan's budget director, David Stockman, admitted "rigging the [budget] numbers to the point that even we couldn't understand them."[146]

In the selling of the 2003 tax cut, the catch phrase used by the George W. Bush administration was that "92 million Americans will receive an average tax cut of $1,083." That sounded, and was intended to sound, as if every American family would get about $1,083. Although it was true that those who received tax cuts averaged about $1,100, the administration omitted the fact that fifty million citizens would receive no tax cut at all, and about half of those American families who would receive a tax cut would get less than $100. The $1,083 number was inflated by the very big tax cuts received by a few wealthy people.[147]

It is not only what goes into compiling a "fact" that is important for public evaluation but also the context of events in which the so-called fact occurs. For example, in 1964, Lyndon Johnson went before Congress to ask for a resolution supporting retaliation against North Vietnam for two "unprovoked" attacks on US ships in the Gulf of Tonkin. The Gulf of Tonkin Resolution was subsequently passed, marking a watershed in the nation's military actions in Vietnam. The public might have been less enthusiastic in its backing of military reprisals, however, if it had known that the United States had been supporting covert South Vietnamese operations against North Vietnam for several years and that, moreover, there was considerable reason to doubt that the second attack had ever occurred! As President Johnson later said privately, "For all I know, our Navy was shooting whales out there."[148]

In his first address to a joint session of Congress, Donald Trump declared, "ninety-four million Americans are out of the labor force," implying that unemployment was much higher than the standard unemployment rate indicated.[149] (He had often made the same claim.) Although the Bureau of Labor Statistics reported such a figure, 93 percent of those persons did not want a job at all. Most people out of the labor force are the retired, students, stay-at-home parents, or the disabled. There were about 7.5 million people looking for work at the time of the president's address.

Attempts to distort information are not always successful. For example, by 1967, two-thirds of the American people felt that the Johnson administration was not telling them the whole truth about the Vietnam War, and in 1971, a similar percentage felt the same way about the Nixon administration.[150] Out of such attitudes emerged a credibility gap and low levels of popular standing for these presidents.

Prevarication

The most extreme form of information control is lying. The range of subjects about which presidents have lied is great, ranging from U-2 spy plane flights over the Soviet Union and the nation's attempts to prevent the election of Marxist Salvador Allende as president of Chile to the US military situation in Vietnam and the Watergate cover-up.[151] Bill Clinton lied about his relationship with Monica Lewinsky (which he later admitted in a plea bargain with the special prosecutor). White House press secretaries have often misled the press regarding imminent US military actions.[152]

The war with Iraq presented a number of opportunities to lie to the public. The administration repeatedly implied that there was a link between al-Qaeda, the 9/11 attacks, and Iraq. It was not until September 18, 2003—months after the war started—that President Bush conceded the United States had no evidence of any Iraqi involvement in the attacks. President Bush also continually claimed that Saddam Hussein had reconstituted his nuclear weapons program and was potentially "less than a year" away from possessing nuclear weapons, placing the United States in immediate peril. This allegation was a powerful argument that deposing Saddam Hussein was important for US national security. However, the evidence on which it was based was wrong. Even at the time the president made the claims, the evidence was questionable, including the assertions that Iraq had purchased uranium oxide, "yellowcake," from Niger and that aluminum tubes shipped to Iraq were intended to be used as centrifuges to create the fissile material necessary for a nuclear bomb. One of the keys to broad public support for an invasion of Iraq was the fear that the US mainland could be attacked. Thus, the possibility of Iraq using unmanned, drone airplanes to deliver chemical or biological weapons—a possibility raised by President Bush in his important October 7, 2002, speech—provoked serious concern. However, the US air force had discounted this possibility in its assessments of Iraq's capabilities.[153]

The president and other administration officials, most notably Vice President Cheney, often made statements that in hindsight were wrong.[154] The president may well have believed his statements, although he did not reveal the tenuous basis for his inferences about the threat that Iraq posed to the United States. Nor did he clarify the lack of evidence of any role of Iraq in the 9/11 attacks.

Barack Obama made the clear and sweeping promise that after his health-care reform bill became law everyone would be able to keep their health insurance plan if they chose to do so. This was not true, primarily because the law bolstered coverage and mandated a robust set of benefits, whether someone wanted to pay for it or not.

Donald Trump has received an extraordinary amount of attention and criticism for his lack of veracity. You can read more in box 6.2.

Box 6.2 ★ Donald Trump's Uneasy Relationship with the Truth

Donald Trump has a unique relationship with the truth. His level of untruthfulness—or at least inaccurate statements—is unprecedented in scope, audacity, and frequency. Fact checkers have concluded that the president has made thousands of false or misleading claims,[155] far more than any of his predecessors. The *Washington Post* reported that Trump averaged 15 false claims a day in 2018,[156] and 8,158 false or misleading claims in his first two years in office.[157]

Presidents of both parties are typically very sensitive about saying anything that is not true and go to great lengths to avoid it. President Trump is different. He says whatever is convenient at the moment. He claimed to have built a wall on the border with Mexico, although no wall had been built. He claimed the largest tax cut, the best economy, and the highest defense spending in history, although these assertions were clearly untrue. He declared that steel plants have opened in response to his tariff policy, that the United States has the most liberal immigration laws in the world, that the United States pays most of the budget of NATO, and that defense contracts with Saudi Arabia are responsible for tens of thousands of jobs in the United States. All these and many others are simply untrue.

Part of the explanation for the president's falsehoods is that he refuses to accept some established facts. He does not seem be believe that people are capable of objectivity.[158] Moreover, he relies heavily on instinct. As he put it, "I have a gut, and my gut tells me more sometimes than anybody else's brain can ever tell me."[159] Finally, the president does not read—books, studies, or memos—so he is likely to be poorly informed.[160]

Whatever the reason, he has persistently rejected clear evidence regarding a wide range of issues. He has resisted accepting the unanimous conclusions of intelligence officials that Russia interfered in the 2016 presidential election or that Prince Mohammed bin Salman was responsible for the death of journalist Jamal Khashoggi. The president also continues to deny human contribution to climate change, contrary to the nearly unanimous view of the scientific community.

There often appears to be a method to his mendacity, as the president seems to say whatever is expedient. Sometimes the motivation is simply to make himself look good, such as his exaggerations of the size of his electoral victory in 2016 and the crowds at his inauguration, the number of times he has appeared on the cover of *Time* magazine, or the success of his policies. At other times Trump simply wants to avoid personal embarrassment, such as the many iterations of what he knew about payoffs to Stormy Daniels.

A few days before the 2018 midterm elections, the president claimed he was moving rapidly to have Congress pass a 10 percent middle-class tax cut (and not one for businesses). Of course, he never proposed such a bill, and Congress was out of session anyway. Equally suspect were his claims that a caravan of asylum seekers traveling across Mexico was an "invasion" posing a looming threat to America. He even promised to sign an executive order ending the constitutional right to citizenship for children born in the United States to undocumented immigrants. The president dropped all these matters right after the election.[161]

(continued)

Box 6.2 ★ Continued

Most frequently, however, he prevaricates in his arguments regarding the nature of problems facing the nation, policy options, and the character and competence of political opponents. Typically, he offers no evidence. Often, his assertions and explanations are so convoluted that it is difficult to understand what he means. Untethered from the burden of objective proof, the president says whatever he thinks will help him win. His narratives often have so many layers of unsubstantiated content that it is difficult to address them clearly.

Trump even brags about prevaricating. In a meeting with campaign donors in Missouri, the president admitted to intentionally lying to Canadian Prime Minister Justin Trudeau. The president inaccurately claimed that the United States had a large trade deficit with Canada. When Trudeau disagreed, Trump said, "Wrong, Justin, you do." Later, in recounting his meeting to the donors, he added, "I didn't even know. . . . I had no idea. I just said 'You're wrong.'"[162] Despite acknowledging that he "had no idea" about the trade balance, he asserted his claim anyway—and to a head of state of America's close ally and largest trading partner—demonstrating his disdain for objective reality and telling the truth.

Whether the president's frequent falsehoods are the result of his general ignorance of public policy, a desire to make himself look good, sloppiness in doing reality checks on his thoughts, or a well-developed cynicism, it did not take long for the public to conclude that he was untrustworthy. After only three months in office, 59 percent of the public felt his administration regularly made false claims. Only 35 percent did not.[163] In September 2018, only 34 percent of the public thought he was trustworthy.[164] By December 2018, 71 percent of the public thought the president regularly made misleading claims. Forty-nine percent thought these claims were "flat-out" false, while 22 percent saw them as exaggerations. Seventy-one percent of the public thought it was never acceptable for a president to say things that are false.[165] In the unkindest cut of all for Trump, in December 2018, 59 percent of registered voters had little or no trust in Trump's denial of collusion with Russia in the 2016 presidential election.[166]

The public's evaluations of Trump's truthfulness is a fragile foundation for gaining its support. The president was convinced that his base would believe whatever he told them, and he may have been right. Yet for everyone else, he risked losing credibility. Why would you follow someone you cannot believe?

One thing is clear: The American people resent being lied to. Most feel it is unacceptable for the government to lie—even to achieve foreign policy goals (although it is acceptable to confuse an enemy).[167] When an administration is seen as being untruthful, it loses credibility—a precious resource in White House efforts to lead the public.[168]

Information Control and National Security

Information control is most common in the national security area because it is difficult for the public to challenge official statements about events in other countries, especially military activities, which often are shrouded in secrecy. It is much easier to be skeptical about domestic activities that American reporters can scrutinize and to which they can provide alternative views. In addition, people can relate many domestic policies to their own experiences more easily than they can relate to most foreign and military policies. When official statements fail to correspond to people's experiences, the stage is set for skepticism.

Officials deny information not only to a foreign adversary but also to the American public. In virtually all the examples involving national security policy, from the U-2 flight over the Soviet Union to the secret bombing of Cambodia, the "foreign adversary" knew the truth. Only the American public was left in the dark.

SUCCESS OF OPINION LEADERSHIP

We have seen that presidents invest a great deal of effort and employ a wide range of techniques to lead the public. How successful are they in using the "bully pulpit" to move the public to support their policies?

The answer is: not very successful.[169] As we noted, even George Washington did not find the public particularly deferential.[170] Even Franklin D. Roosevelt, the president often considered the greatest politician of the twentieth century, faced constant frustration in his efforts to move the public to prepare for entry into World War II, and his failure to persuade the public regarding his plan to pack the Supreme Court effectively marked the end of the New Deal.[171]

Ronald Reagan

Ronald Reagan offers a best-test case for modern presidential leadership of the public. He displayed formidable rhetorical skills and went to unprecedented lengths to influence public opinion. Both his supporters and detractors frequently commented on his unusual rapport with the public and often termed him the "Great Communicator." Was he able to function as a director of public opinion?

Reagan knew better. In his memoirs, he reflected on his efforts to ignite concern among the American people regarding the threat of communism in Central America and to mobilize them behind his program of support for the Contras:

> For eight years the press called me the "Great Communicator." Well, one of my greatest frustrations during those eight years was my inability to communicate to the American people and to Congress the seriousness of the threat we faced in Central America. . . .
>
> Time and again, I would speak on television, to a joint session of Congress, or to other audiences about the problems in Central America, and I would hope that the outcome would be an outpouring of support from Americans. . . .
>
> But the polls usually found that large numbers of Americans cared little or not at all about what happened in Central America—in fact, a surprisingly large proportion didn't even know where Nicaragua and El Salvador were located—and, among those who did care, too few cared enough about a Communist penetration of the Americas to apply the kind of pressure I needed on Congress.[172]

Numerous national surveys of public opinion have found that support for regulatory programs and spending on domestic policy increased, rather than decreased, during Reagan's tenure. Conversely, support for increased defense expenditures was decidedly lower at the end of his administration than when he took office. In each case, the public was moving in the opposite direction to that of the president.[173] Indeed, there was a movement away from conservative views almost as soon as he took office. According to one scholar, "Whatever Ronald Reagan's skills as a communicator, one ability he clearly did not possess was the capacity to induce lasting changes in American policy preferences."[174] As press secretary Marlin Fitzwater put it, "Reagan would go out on the stump, draw huge throngs and convert no one at all."[175]

Bill Clinton

Bill Clinton was an articulate, knowledgeable, energetic, and experienced communicator who came to office with an explicit theory of governing by going to the public. Nevertheless, he was repeatedly disappointed in the results of his efforts at public leadership. Health-care reform was to be the centerpiece of the Clinton administration. In September 1993, the president delivered a well-received national address on the need for reform. Yet the president was not able to sustain the support of the public for his bill. The White House held out against compromise with the Republicans and conservative Democrats, hoping for a groundswell of public support for reform. It never came. In the meantime, opponents of the president's proposal launched an aggressive counterattack, including running negative television advertisements. As the figures in table 6.2 show, by mid-July 1994, only 40 percent of the public favored the president's health-care reform proposals, and 56 percent opposed them. The bill did not come to a vote in either chamber of Congress.

George W. Bush

No issue was more important to George W. Bush's presidency than the war with Iraq. In the late summer of 2002, the White House decided to remove Saddam Hussein from power and aggressively sought the public's backing. The context in which Bush sought this support was certainly favorable. There was a lack of organized opposition to going to war. In surveys stretching back to the end of the Gulf War in 1991, majorities of the public had generally supported US military action on behalf of regime change in Iraq. Most Americans felt that Iraq had developed or was developing weapons of mass destruction; many concluded that if left alone, Iraq would use those weapons against the United States within five years; and most believed that Saddam Hussein sponsored terrorism that affected the United States. A little more

Table 6.2 Support for Clinton's Health-Care Reform

Date of Poll	Favor (%)	Oppose (%)	Don't Know (%)
September 24–26, 1993	59	33	8
October 28–30, 1993	45	45	10
November 2–4, 1993	52	40	8
November 19–21, 1993	52	41	7
January 15–17, 1994	56	39	6
January 28–30, 1994	57	38	5
February 26–28, 1994	46	48	5
March 28–30, 1994	44	47	9
May 20–22, 1994	46	49	5
June 11–12, 1994	42	50	8
June 25–28, 1994	44	49	8
July 15–17, 1994	40	56	5

Source: Gallup poll question, "From everything you've heard or read about the plan so far . . . do you favor or oppose President Clinton's plan to reform health care?"

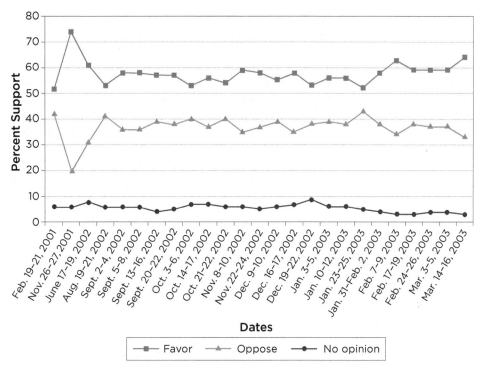

Figure 6.1 Public Support for Invasion of Iraq

Source: Gallup Poll question, "Would you favor or oppose sending American ground troops to the Persian Gulf in an attempt to remove Saddam Hussein from power in Iraq?" © The Gallup Organization. All rights reserved. Reprinted with permission.

than half of the public took the additional inferential leap and concluded that he was directly involved in the September 11, 2001, terrorist attacks.[176]

Figure 6.1 shows that public support for the invasion of Iraq did not change in response to the administration's blitzkrieg.[177] Instead, it stayed within a narrow range throughout the fall and winter until early February 2003. At that point, it increased 5 percentage points in response to Secretary of State Colin Powell's presentation of evidence against Iraq to the United Nations. In the month following Powell's speech, support for an invasion drifted downward until the middle of March, when the president issued the final ultimatum to Saddam Hussein that marked the beginning of a rally in support of war.

Barack Obama

Barack Obama entered the presidency with an impressive record of political success, at the center of which were his rhetorical skills. In college, he concluded that words had the power to transform: "with the right words everything could change—South Africa, the lives of ghetto kids just a few miles away, my own tenuous place in the world."[178] Nevertheless, the president was constantly frustrated in his efforts to obtain support for his major initiatives if they were not already popular with the public. Daniel Pfeiffer, his communications director, recalls, "despite all this talent, one of Barack Obama's greatest frustrations during his time in the White House was his inability to use rhetoric and reason to better tell the story of his presidency."

Thus, in a memo to the White House staff, Pfeiffer wrote what he viewed as the essential truth about modern political communication: "The presidential bully pulpit was dead."[179]

The biggest legislative battle of the Obama administration was health-care reform. Substantially changing any policy that dealt with 17 percent of the nation's GDP was going to be difficult. Doing so in a context of highly polarized partisan politics, enormous budget deficits, and broad skepticism about government activism only made matters worse for the White House. Nevertheless, the president forged ahead. Yet despite the president's efforts to address the public's misgivings in speeches, news conferences, town hall-style meetings, and interviews, the public did not respond. Instead, the public displayed a lack of support for Obama and what it perceived as his health-care plan (see table 6.3). Despite all his and his administration's efforts, the president never obtained majority—or even plurality—support for health-care reform. He could not create an opportunity for change.[180]

Donald Trump

President Trump came to office with a long background in promoting his business interests. Nevertheless, he has been frustrated by his inability to lead the public. The most important legislative focus in the early months of his term was health care. Yet, the public opposed every version of health-care reform the president supported. Equally important, the ACA, which the president wanted to replace, became more popular than ever and majorities opposed the White House's efforts to repeal it. Moreover, for the first time since 2007, a majority (60 percent) of Americans felt it was the federal government's responsibility to make sure that all Americans have health-care coverage. In other words, the public was moving in the opposite direction of the president and pushing back vigorously against his initiatives.[181]

Table 6.3 Support for Obama's Health-Care Plan

Date of Poll	Favor (%)	Oppose (%)	Don't Know (%)
July 22–26, 2009	38	44	18
August 20–27, 2009	39	46	15
September 10–15, 2009	42	44	14
September 30–October 4, 2009	34	47	19
October 28–November 8, 2009	38	47	15
November 12–15, 2009	42	39	19
December 9–13, 2009	35	48	17
January 6–10, 2010	39	48	13
February 3–9, 2010	38	50	12
March 10–14, 2010	38	48	13
April 1–5, 2010	40	44	16
July 8–11, 2010	35	47	17
September 9–12, 2010	38	45	17

Source: Pew Research Center for the People and the Press poll question, "As of right now, do you generally favor or generally oppose the health care proposals being discussed in Congress?"

Table 6.4 Approval of Republican Tax Plans

Dates of Poll	Favor (%)	Oppose (%)	Unsure (%)
2017			
November 7–13	25	52	23
November 29–December 4	29	53	18
December 6–11	26	55	18
2018			
January 5–9	32	52	16
February 2–5	39	47	14
March 3–5	36	50	14
March 16–20	38	47	16
June 14–17*	39	46	15

Question: "Do you approve or disapprove of the Republican tax plan?" (registered voters).

* "Do you approve or disapprove of the 2017 tax law passed by Congress and signed by President Trump?" (registered voters).

Source: Quinnipiac University Poll.

The next major initiative of the Trump administration was a tax cut for individuals and businesses. Tax cuts are typically not difficult sells, as people naturally prefer to have more discretionary income. Nevertheless, at no time did the Republican tax proposals obtain the support of a majority—or even a plurality—of the public (table 6.4). People did not accept the president's narrative that the tax cuts would benefit the typical family, stimulate the economy, and pay for themselves.[182]

Immigration has been the defining issue of Donald Trump's presidency, with his emphasis on tough border security and strict enforcement of US immigration laws. Nevertheless, the public has not followed the president's lead. Instead, majorities of the public

- oppose attempts to deport all illegal immigrants;
- oppose decreasing legal immigration;
- are more concerned that deportation efforts will be overzealous than that dangerous criminals will be overlooked;
- say the nation's top immigration priority should be to allow illegal immigrants to gain legal status;
- oppose ending the Deferred Action for Childhood Arrivals program;
- believe legal immigration into the United States is a boon for the country;
- believe immigrants take jobs that Americans do not want;
- oppose the president's travel bans from certain countries; and
- oppose restricting Syrian refugees from entering the United States.

Most notably, the public opposed building a wall along the Mexican border (table 6.5).[183]

Table 6.5 Support for Building a Wall between the United States and Mexico

Date	Support (%)	Oppose (%)	Unsure (%)
2016			
November 17–20	42	55	3
2017			
February 2–6	38	59	3
February 16–21	37	60	3
March 30–April 3	33	64	3
April 12–18	33	64	3
May 4–9	33	64	3
September 21–26	37	60	3
December 6–11	36	62	2
2018			
January 5–9	34	63	3
February 2–5	37	59	4
April 6–9	40	57	3
June 14–17	39	58	4
August 9–13	38	58	4
December 12–17	43	54	2
2019			
January 9–13	43	55	2
January 25–28	41	55	4
March 1–4	41	55	5

Question: "Do you support or oppose building a wall along the border with Mexico?" (registered voters)
Source: Quinnipiac University Poll.

The difficulty presidents have in moving public opinion poses a direct challenge to the faith that many have in the broad premise of the potential of presidential leadership of the public. Yet it is consistent with important and wide-ranging works on public opinion, including studies by James Stimson,[184] Benjamin Page and Robert Shapiro,[185] and Benjamin Page and Marshall Bouton.[186] They find that the public's collective policy preferences generally are stable and change by large margins only in response to world events. Even on foreign policy, Page and Bouton find that there are often large gaps between public opinion and the views of leaders, and the two are not converging. Thus, there is little evidence of opinion leadership.[187]

CONCLUSION

Presidents are not content to follow public opinion. In their search for public support, they invest substantial time, energy, ingenuity, and personnel in techniques that include directly appealing to the public, framing issues, attempting to increase the salience of issues, employing public relations techniques, and exercising information control. They seek the public attention and its support, but there is no guarantee of success in these efforts. The public's predispositions and lack of attention are difficult obstacles to overcome, and presidents often fail to achieve their desired effects. Even those who are considered "great communicators" are not able to move the public much on their own; they cannot reshape the contours of the political landscape to pave the way for change. Instead, they are facilitators who depend on the public moving at its own pace to provide opportunities to accomplish their goals.

Because the president rarely speaks directly to the American people as a whole, the White House is dependent on the press to transmit its messages. In the next chapter, we examine the president's relations with the media to see whether it can aid the White House in its efforts to lead the public.

DISCUSSION QUESTIONS

1. Leading the public is difficult to do, and presidents employ many techniques to influence public opinion. What are the most useful approaches to obtaining the public's support? How successful has President Trump been in framing issues to his advantage?
2. People's predispositions play a crucial role in their response to the president. Is there any way for the president to alter these predispositions?
3. How could a president increase public attention to his pleas for support?

WEB EXERCISES

1. Go to https://www.whitehouse.gov/briefing-room/speeches-and-remarks. Then go to https://www.whitehouse.gov/briefing-room/statements-and-releases. On how many topics does the president communicate in a typical day? Would it serve the president better if he focused his speeches, remarks, statements, and releases on only high-priority issues?
2. Choose an issue that has been on the White House's agenda for some months and determine the president's stand on the policy. Then go to some major polling sites, such as www.gallup.com and www.pewresarch.org, and search for public opinion on the issue. Has public opinion followed the president's lead?

SELECTED READINGS

Canes-Wrone, Brandice. *Who Leads Whom?* Princeton, NJ: Princeton University Press, 2006.
Edwards, George C., III. *On Deaf Ears: The Limits of the Bully Pulpit.* New Haven, CT: Yale University Press, 2003.
———. *Governing by Campaigning*, 2nd ed. New York: Pearson Longman, 2007.
———. *The Strategic President: Persuasion and Opportunity in Presidential Leadership.* Princeton, NJ: Princeton University Press, 2009.
———. *Overreach: Leadership in the Obama Presidency.* Princeton, NJ: Princeton University Press, 2012.

———. *Predicting the Presidency: The Potential of Persuasive Leadership*. Princeton, NJ: Princeton University Press, 2016.

———. *The Bungler: The Leadership of Donald Trump.* Forthcoming, 2020.

Farnsworth, Stephen J. *Spinner-in-Chief: How Presidents Sell Themselves and Their Policies*. Boulder, CO: Paradigm, 2008.

Kernell, Samuel. *Going Public*, 4th ed. Washington, DC: CQ Press, 2007.

Tulis, Jeffrey K. *The Rhetorical Presidency*. Princeton, NJ: Princeton University Press, 1987.

7

The President and the Media

Official White House Photo by Benjamin Applebaum

President Trump speaks to the press in the Oval Office.

H aving exploited media coverage in his campaign for the presidency, Donald Trump expected a favorable press once he took office. It was not long before he found himself to be at war with the media, however. He branded criticism of his actions as "fake news" and tweeted responses to stories almost on a daily basis. He also disparaged individual journalists, often in ways that drew bipartisan condemnation. Despite the fact that media stories were often fed by Trump's own White House staff, which leaked incessantly, the problems were not his, he claimed. The problem was with the biased and dishonest fourth estate.

Despite all their efforts to lead public opinion, presidents do not directly reach the American people on a day-to-day basis. It is the news media, or press, that provide people with most of what they know about chief executives, their policies, and their policies' consequences. The media also interpret and analyze presidential activities, including even the president's direct appeals to the public. Thus, relations with the press are an important aspect of the president's efforts to lead public opinion.

Presidents whom the media portray in a favorable light will face fewer obstacles in obtaining public support than those who are treated harshly by the media.

Bill Clinton took office with an antagonistic attitude toward the national media, which he planned to bypass rather than use as part of his political strategy. After a rocky start in his press relations, Clinton's orientation changed. He found that he could not avoid the national press, which remains the primary source of news about the federal government. "I did not realize the importance of communications," he confessed, "and the overriding importance of what is on the evening television news. If I am not on there with a message, someone else is, with their message."[1] Clinton even hired David Gergen, who had been a communications adviser in Republican administrations, as a top aide.

In this chapter, we examine the nature and structure of presidential relationships with the press, emphasizing both the context of these relationships and the White House's attempts to obtain favorable coverage through holding press conferences and providing services for the press. We also focus on the substance of the news media's coverage of the president, discussing the controversial issues of leaks to the press and of superficiality and bias in the news. Finally, we consider the evidence regarding the important, but generally overlooked, question of the effects of press coverage of the White House on public opinion.

A president fitting the director model will receive favorable press coverage and reliably use the press to advance his interests. In contrast, facilitators will experience a more adversarial relationship, one characterized by more negative coverage and a constant struggle by the White House to obtain both space and sympathetic treatment in the media.

THE EVOLUTION OF MEDIA COVERAGE

Today, we are accustomed to turning to our newspapers, television sets, or even the Internet to learn almost immediately about what the president has said or done. Things have not always been this way: Before the Civil War, newspapers were generally small, heavily partisan, and limited in circulation. Between 1860 and 1920, however, a number of changes occurred that permanently altered the relationship between the president and the press.

Several technological innovations—from the electric printing press, the telegraph, the typewriter, and the telephone, to Linotype and wood pulp paper—made it both possible and economical to produce mass-circulation newspapers carrying recent national news. Aside from the sales efforts of the newspapers themselves, the increasing literacy of the population helped to create a market for these papers.

The Civil War, efforts to regulate the economy and fight trusts, and the nation's expanded role in world affairs during the Spanish-American War and World War I kindled interest in the activities of the government in Washington. The renewed prominence of the presidency following an era of congressional ascendancy also increased attention to national affairs.

Reporters first obtained space in the White House in 1896,[2] but it was Theodore Roosevelt who made the greatest strides in exploiting the new opportunities to reach the public provided by the mass-circulation press. He took an activist view of the presidency and used the White House to dramatize himself and the issues in which he was interested. He sought and gained extensive access to the press in order to forge a more personal relationship with the American people. Establishing a casual and candid relationship with journalists, he floated trial balloons, leaked stories, and held informal press conferences (some while receiving his daily shave). For the next century, news about the president played an increasingly prominent role in the printed and electronic press, both in absolute terms and relative to coverage of Congress or the national government as a whole.[3] Donald Trump has dominated the news more than any previous president.[4]

Presidents have found that they need the press because it is their primary link to the people. The press, in turn, finds coverage of the president indispensable in satisfying its audience and reporting on the most significant political events. The advent of radio and television only heightened these mutual needs.

Unlimited goodwill has not characterized the history of relations between the president and the press. President George Washington complained that the "calumnies" against his administration were "outrages of common decency" motivated by the desire to destroy confidence in the new government.[5] John Adams was so upset at criticism in the press that he supported the Sedition Act and jailed some opposition journalists under its authority.

Thomas Jefferson, certainly one of America's greatest defenders of freedom, as president became so exasperated with the press that he argued, "[E]ven the least informed of the people have learned that nothing in a newspaper is to be believed." He also felt that "newspapers, for the most part, present only the caricature of disaffected minds. Indeed, the abuses of freedom of the press have been carried to a length never before known or borne by any civilized nation." These observations, we should note, come from the man who earlier had written, "[W]ere it left to me to decide whether we should have a government without newspapers or newspapers without a government, I should not hesitate to prefer the latter."[6]

More than two centuries later, things have changed very little. Although all presidents have supported the abstract right of the press to criticize them freely, while in office most have found this criticism uncomfortable. They have viewed some of the press as misrepresenting (perhaps maliciously) their views and actions, failing to perceive the correctness of their policies, and dedicated to impeding their goals. For example, as the Iran-Contra scandal unfolded, Ronald Reagan complained of the press circling the White House like "sharks." A quarter-century earlier, John F. Kennedy, a favorite of the press, exulted in the potential of television for going directly to the people when he told journalist Ben Bradlee, "when we don't have to go through you bastards, we can really get our story to the American people."[7]

President Clinton, who expressed a desire to punch columnist William Safire in the nose for calling Hillary Clinton a "congenital liar," complained, "you get no credit around here for fighting and bleeding. And that's why the know-nothings and the do-nothings and the negative people and the right-wingers always win. Because of the way people like you [the press] put questions to people like me."[8]

No matter who is in the White House or who does the reporting, presidents and the press always struggle for dominance. Presidents are inherently policy advocates and want to be able to define a situation and receive favorable coverage. They will naturally assess the press in terms of how it aids or hinders their goals. The press, conversely, has the responsibility of presenting and assessing what is really going on. Although the press may fail in its efforts, it will assess itself on those criteria. Presidents want to control the amount and timing of information about their administrations, while the press wants all the information that exists without delay. As long as their goals are different, presidents and the press are likely to be adversaries. Donald Trump is no exception, as you can see in box 7.1.

RELATIONS BETWEEN THE PRESIDENT AND THE PRESS

To understand presidential relations with the press, we must understand the journalists with whom the White House deals and the ways in which the president's staff try to influence them. Because of the importance of the press to the president, the White House goes to great lengths to encourage the media to project a positive image of the president and the administration's policies. These efforts include coordinating

---

Box 7.1 ★ Donald Trump as Media Adversary

Donald Trump wasted no time in expressing his hostility to the media. He frequently dismissed unfavorable coverage as "fake news," and on February 17, 2017, after less than a month in office, he tweeted, "The FAKE NEWS media (failing @ nytimes, @NBCNews, @ABC, @CBS, @CNN) is not my enemy, it is the enemy of the American People!"

White House officials say Trump objects more to the tone of questions than the substance, saying he feels disrespected when reporters pepper him with questions in front of guests, particularly when a foreign dignitary is visiting.[9] Yet there seems to be more at work.

Trump has been open and explicit about his strategy. When asked by veteran *60 Minutes* reporter Lesley Stahl why he kept attacking the press, he responded: "You know why I do it? I do it to discredit you all and demean you all, so when you write negative stories about me no one will believe you."[10]

Sometimes the president's antagonism with the press has caused him to lose all sense of decorum. We saw in the previous chapter that he tweeted disparaging comments about the hosts of the MSNBC program *Morning Joe*, claiming that one, Mika Brzezinski, was bleeding badly from a face-lift when he saw her in Mar-a-Lago. On July 2, 2017, the president posted a doctored video clip showing him bashing the head of a figure representing CNN. It is hardly surprising that the media gave substantial attention to this post, which was clearly outside the norms of civility—let alone the norms for a president.

The president called April Ryan of American Urban Radio Networks a "loser"; replied to Abby Phillip of CNN by saying, "You ask a lot of stupid questions"; dismissed a query from Yamiche Alcindor of PBS as "racist"; and told Cecilia Vega of ABC News, "You're not thinking—you never do." (All four reporters are women of color.)[11] He also told Jim Acosta of CNN that he was "a rude, terrible person" and barred another reporter, Kaitlan Collins of CNN, from a Rose Garden event after aides deemed her questions "inappropriate."[12]

Sometimes the president's criticism of the press descends to the absurd. On January 29, 2019, the nation's top intelligence officials testified in open congressional hearings, which were televised on C-Span, and the director of national intelligence submitted a forty-two-page public statement regarding threats to US national security. Their testimony generated stories about their contradicting what the president has said about the state of affairs with regard to Iran, the Islamic State (also known as ISIS), and North Korea. Trump predictably lashed out at his own appointees the next day, tweeting that they were "wrong" and "extremely passive and naïve." He also suggested that they might need to "go back to school." Still, he needed to defuse embarrassing stories, so he claimed

(continued)

Box 7.1 ★ Continued

the media had fabricated a conflict, claiming the officials later told him they were "totally misquoted"[13]—despite the fact that their testimony was available for anyone to see in its entirety.

On May 26, 2018, Trump accused the *New York Times* of using an unnamed source "who doesn't exist" in a story on negotiations between the United States and North Korea. In reality, however, the *Times* accurately reported on a press briefing arranged by the White House, which insisted that the official not be named. The White House was not available for comment on the president's mischaracterization.[14] The president has also criticized journalists for not asking questions about their stories, yet it is more typical that they ask the questions but receive no answer.[15]

The president's antagonism has caused bipartisan concern about undermining one of the cornerstones of democracy. In August 2018, the Senate unanimously passed a resolution declaring that "The Press Is Not the Enemy of the People."

Equally important, the president has not persuaded the public to distrust the press. The Quinnipiac University Poll has regularly asked registered voters whom they trust more to tell them the truth about important issues, President Trump or the news media. The news media has always won majority support on this question, with little variance over time (table 7.1). We find similar responses when pollsters asked whether people trusted Trump or their "favorite news source" more? People overwhelmingly chose their favorite news source (table 7.2).

Table 7.1 Trust in Trump vs. Media

Poll Dates	*Trust Trump (%)*	*Trust Media (%)*	*No Opinion (%)*
2017			
February 16–21	37	52	10
March 2–6	37	53	10
May 4–9	31	57	12
May 17–23	34	53	13
August 9–15	37	55	9
August 17–22	36	54	10
October 5–10	37	52	11
November 7–13	34	54	12
2018			
April 20–24	37	53	10
June 14–17	36	53	11
July 18–23	34	54	12
September 6–9	30	54	16
November 14–19	34	54	12
2019			
April 26–29	35	52	13

Question: "Who do you trust more to tell you the truth about important issues: President Donald Trump or the news media?" (registered voters)
Source: Quinnipiac University Poll.

(continued)

Box 7.1 ★ Continued

Table 7.2 Trust in Favorite News Source

Poll Dates	Favorite News Source (%)	Trump (%)	No Opinion (%)
October 15–17, 2017	65	26	9
January 8–10, 2018	58	29	14
July 19–22, 2018	62	28	10

Question: "Who do you trust more: Your favorite news source or Donald Trump?"
Source: Marist poll for 2017; NPR/*PBS NewsHour* poll for 2018.

However, there is a strong partisan tilt to the responses. For example, in the November 14–19, 2018, poll, 75 percent of Republicans chose Trump while 89 percent of Democrats selected the media, as did 53 percent of Independents.[16] In the same poll, respondents were asked which came closer to their view: "the news media is the enemy of the people, or the news media is an important part of democracy?" Republicans were split, with 44 percent choosing "enemy of the people" and 42 percent selecting "an important part of democracy." Democrats and Independents were not similarly torn. Ninety-two percent of the former and 72 percent of the latter said the news media was "an important part of democracy."

the news, holding press conferences, and providing a range of services such as formal briefings, interviews, photo opportunities, background sessions, travel accommodations, and daily handouts.

The White House Press Corps

Who are the reporters that regularly cover the White House? This elite contingent represents diverse media constituencies, including daily newspapers, weekly news magazines, wire services, newspaper chains, television and radio networks, the foreign press, and "opinion" magazines. In recent years, many blogs and web-only news sites have obtained White House press credentials. In addition, photographers, columnists, television commentators, and magazine writers are regularly involved in White House–press interactions. Hundreds of journalists have White House regular press credentials. Fortunately, not everyone shows up at once (there are only forty-nine seats in the White House briefing room). About 125 reporters and a dozen photographers regularly cover the White House, although the total increases when an important announcement is expected.

The great majority of daily newspapers in America have no Washington correspondents, much less someone assigned to cover the White House. The same is true for almost all of the country's individual television and radio stations. These papers and stations rely heavily on a national news service or, if part of a network or newspaper chain, their chain's Washington bureau for news about the president.

The Presidential Press Operation

White House relations with the media occupy a substantial portion of the time of a large number of aides. About one-third of the high-level White House staff are directly involved in media relations and policy of one type or another, and most staff members are involved at some time in influencing the media's portrayal of the president.[17]

Press Secretary

The president's press secretary is the person in the White House who daily deals directly with the press, making announcements regarding policies, responding to the actions and criticisms of others, and commenting on breaking news. According to Marlin Fitzwater, press secretary to Presidents Reagan and Bush, "The press secretary stands between the opposing forces, explaining, cajoling, begging, sometimes pushing both sides toward a better understanding of each other."[18]

The central function of press secretaries is to serve as conduits of information from the White House to the press. They must be sure that clear statements of administration policies have been prepared on important policy matters. The press secretaries usually conduct daily press briefings, giving prepared announcements and answering questions. In forming their answers, they do not always have specific instructions on what to say or not say. Instead, they must be able to think on their feet to ensure that they accurately reflect the president's views. Sometimes these views may be unclear, however, or they may be views that the president may not wish to articulate. Therefore, press secretaries may seem to be evasive or unimaginative in public settings. They also hold private meetings with individual reporters, where the information they provide may be more candid and speculative.

To be effective in the conduit role, the press secretary must maintain credibility with reporters. Credibility rests on at least two important pillars: (1) truth and (2) access to (and respect of) the president and senior White House officials. Press secretaries who are viewed as not telling the truth or (like President Clinton's first press secretary, Dee Dee Myers) as being too distant from the top decision makers (and therefore not well informed) will not be effective presidential spokespeople because the press will give less credence to what they say.

Presidential press secretary Sarah Huckabee Sanders briefs the White House press.

MediaPunch Inc./Alamy Stock Photo

Credibility problems have arisen for several press secretaries because of these perceived deficiencies. Sean Spicer, Donald Trump's first press secretary, ran into credibility problems the first day of his tenure when he defended the president's obviously false claims regarding the size of the crowd at his inauguration. Spicer became a recurring source of mockery on *Saturday Night Live*. Nevertheless, his daily briefings became one of the most highly rated programs on daytime TV, reaching 4.5 million viewers. President Trump liked the large audience, even if his spokesperson's performance was less than ideal. By June, however, the White House was frequently refusing to allow the daily briefing to be televised.

Press secretaries also serve as conduits from the press, sometimes explaining the needs of the press to the president. For example, all of Lyndon Johnson's press secretaries tried to persuade the president to issue advance information on his travel plans to the press. When he refused, they provided the information anyway (and then had it expunged from the briefing transcript so the president would not see it). Press secretaries also try to inform the White House staff of the press's needs and the rules of the game, and they help reporters gain access to staff members.

Press secretaries typically are not involved in substantive decisions, but they do give the president advice—usually on what information the White House should release, by whom, in what form, and to what audience. They also advise the president on rehearsals for press conferences and on how to project the proper image and use it to political advantage.

Coordinating the News

Since the time of William McKinley and Theodore Roosevelt, the White House has attempted to coordinate executive branch news. Presidents have assigned aides to clear the appointments of departmental public affairs officials, to keep in touch with the officials to learn what news is forthcoming from the departments, and to meet with them to explain the president's policy views and try to prevent conflicting statements from emanating from the White House and other units of the executive branch. Specialists have had responsibility for coordinating national-security news. Of course, such tactics do not always work. President Ford wanted to announce from the White House the results of the successful effort to rescue seamen from the *Mayaguez*, but he found, to his disappointment, that the Pentagon had already done so, making any presidential announcement anticlimactic.

Coordinating the news from the White House itself has also been a presidential goal. Presidents have sometimes monitored and attempted to limit the press contacts of White House aides who have annoyed their bosses by using the media for their own purposes. President Reagan, for example, instituted a policy midway through his administration that required his assistant for communications to approve any interview requested by a member of the media with any White House official. Aides monitored all requests and entered them on a computer, so the White House could keep tabs on whom reporters wanted to see. Because members of the White House press cannot wander through the East Wing or West Wing on their own, the only way to speak to aides without administration approval was to call them at home, a practice discouraged by presidential assistants and generally avoided by reporters. Recent presidents have also made substantial efforts to control which administration officials appear on major news programs, including the weekday and Sunday morning news shows. To influence both the topics and the responses provided in interviews, the White House only allows officials who receive its permission to appear on these shows.

Recent administrations have also made an effort to coordinate publicity functions within the White House and to attempt to present the news in the most favorable light, such as preventing two major stories from breaking on the same day, smothering bad news with more positive news, and timing announcements for maximum or minimum effect (discussed in chapter 6).

Attending to the News

All recent presidents have read several newspapers each day, especially the *New York Times*, the *Wall Street Journal*, and the *Washington Post*, and most have also been very attentive to television news programs. Lyndon Johnson had a television cabinet with three screens in order to watch all three commercial networks at once. Even this was not enough to satisfy his thirst for news. He also had Teletypes installed in the Oval Office that carried the latest reports from the wire services, which he monitored regularly. Barack Obama was a voracious consumer of opinion journalism.[19] Donald Trump reads the same papers as his predecessors along with the *New York Post*, the *New York Daily News*, and the *Financial Times*, and he also religiously views news on cable television, especially Fox News, and on Internet outlets such as Breitbart.

President Nixon rarely watched television news and did not peruse large numbers of newspapers or magazines, but he was extremely interested in the press coverage of his administration. He had his staff prepare a daily news summary of newspapers, magazines, television news, and the news wires. Often, this summary triggered ideas for the president, who gave orders to aides to follow up on something he read.[20] The news summary also went to White House assistants. Subsequent presidents have continued the news summary, altering it to meet their individual needs, and have circulated it to top officials in their administrations. The Carter White House instituted a separate magazine survey and even began producing a weekly summary of Jewish publications after it became concerned about a possible backlash within the American Jewish community against the administration's Middle East policy.

The Presidential Press Conference

The best-known direct interaction between the president and the press is the formal press conference. The large number of reporters covering these press conferences and the settings in which they take place (such as the East Room in the White House) have inevitably made them more formal than in the days when Franklin D. Roosevelt held forth from his desk in the Oval Office. Beginning with Harry Truman, presidents have typically undergone formal briefings and dry runs in preparation for questions reporters might ask.

Since every word they say is transmitted verbatim to millions of people, modern-day presidents cannot speak as candidly as FDR could. Nor can they speculate freely about their potential actions or evaluations of people, events, or circumstances. Instead, they must choose their words carefully and, as a result, their responses to questions are often not enlightening. In addition, the increased number of reporters attending press conferences has meant a wider range of questions and thus less likelihood of covering any one subject in depth.

The White House saw the televised presidential press conferences as an opportunity "to jump over the press and go directly to the people."[21] Thus, presidents often opened with a carefully prepared statement that gave them an opportunity to reach the public on their own terms. They have also used questions as a vehicle to say something that they had planned ahead of time. Moreover, they can call on a friendly reporter for a "soft" question and ignore others. They may declare that they will not entertain questions on certain topics, and they may also evade questions with clever rhetoric or a simple "no comment." They may even attack the questioner.

The artificial nature and increasingly low ratings of press conferences have discouraged the networks from broadcasting them. Until the end of George H. W. Bush's tenure, the networks would preempt programs for a live, prime-time televised presidential press conference almost without question. In June 1992, however, all three major networks refused to run one of President Bush's press conferences on the grounds that it was mostly a campaign event. Since that time, the major television networks have been less than eager to give up their regular entertainment programming to cover presidential press conferences.

The trend is clearly in the direction of holding fewer formal press conferences. Franklin Roosevelt held about seven a month, whereas Ronald Reagan held only about one every two months. President George H. W. Bush virtually abandoned formal, prime-time press conferences in favor of frequent, brief, informal morning sessions with reporters, which he often called on short notice. President Clinton held just four evening press conferences in his eight years in office, only one of which received live coverage on all the networks (CNN and C-SPAN did provide coverage for all, however) and all in his first term. George W. Bush also held only four during his tenure, as did Barack Obama (all in his first year).[22] President Trump has not held any prime-time press conferences.

Instead of full-blown press conferences, presidents have turned to remarks in controlled settings such as less formal press conferences in the briefing room and events at the White House, especially sessions with visiting foreign leaders. In the latter, they may answer a few questions from the press—but far fewer than they would have answered at a traditional press conference. President Trump frequently engages in short question-and-answer sessions with reporters.

Services for the Press
In order to get their messages across to the American people and to influence the tone and content of press presentation of those messages, presidents provide services for the press.

Briefings
Traditionally, the White House provides briefings for the press each weekday, usually in the morning, and at other times as the situation requires. In these daily briefings, reporters receive information about appointments and resignations, decisions of the president to sign or not to sign routine bills and explanations for these actions, and the president's schedule (appointments, meetings, future travel plans, and availability to the press). More significant from the standpoint of the press, the briefings provide presidential reactions to events, the White House "line" on issues and whether it has changed, and a reading of the president's moods and ideas. Reporters obtain this information through prepared statements or answers to their queries. (Responses to the latter are often prepared ahead of time by the White House staff.) The daily briefings, of course, also provide the press with an opportunity to have the president's views placed on public record, which eases the burdens of reporting.

President Trump holds a joint press conference with Prime Minister Theresa May of the United Kingdom.

Usually, the president's press secretary or the press secretary's deputy presides over these briefings, although sometimes the president participates. White House staff members and executive branch officials with substantial expertise in specific policy areas, such as the budget or foreign affairs, sometimes brief the press and answer questions at the daily briefing or at special briefings, especially if the White House is launching a major publicity campaign.

News briefings were a can't-miss ritual of the early days of the Trump administration, as the president made news with his efforts to change the course of public policy. Television ratings for the briefings were unusually high. After a few months, however, the administration reacted negatively to the bad publicity it often received, the mocking of the press secretary on *Saturday Night Live*, and challenging questions from the press. The briefings became shorter, less informative, and less accessible. Moreover, the White House refused to allow live broadcasts of some of the briefings. By 2018, briefings were rare. On January 22, 2019, President Trump tweeted that he had directed White House press secretary Sarah Sanders "not to bother" with the briefings because he believed that reporters were rude to her and that most members of the media would not cover the administration fairly. The president's aides also said briefings were less necessary because the president was eager to speak for himself.[23]

There are also more private briefings. After the protracted decision-making process that climaxed with President Obama's December 1, 2009, announcement of sending an additional thirty thousand US troops to Afghanistan, the White House briefed the *New York Times*, the *Washington Post*, and the *Los Angeles Times* on the policy discussions. In early December, each newspaper carried behind-the-scenes stories on the process, all reflecting Obama as a deliberative and tough-minded manager.[24]

Backgrounders

One of the most important services for the press is the *backgrounder*. The president's comments to reporters may be "on the record" (remarks may be attributed to the speaker); "on background" (a specific source cannot be identified but the source's position and status can, such as a "White House source"); "deep background" (no attribution); or "off the record" (the information reporters receive may not be used in a story). For purposes of convenience, we shall term all sessions between White House officials (including the president) and the press that are not "on the record" as "backgrounders." All recent presidents, especially Lyndon Johnson and Gerald Ford, have engaged in background discussion with reporters, although President Nixon's involvement was rare. Some presidents, especially Dwight Eisenhower and Richard Nixon, have relied heavily on their principal foreign policy advisers to brief reporters on foreign affairs.

The most common type of White House discussion with reporters on a background basis is a briefing. In a typical background briefing, a senior presidential aide, such as the director of the Office of Management and Budget or the president's national security assistant, explains a policy's development and what the administration expects it to accomplish. Interestingly, the White House does not appear to stress the substance of policy and seldom makes "hard" news statements in background briefings because this would irritate absent members of the press. The briefings do play an important role in preparing the news media for legislative and administrative initiatives, presidential trips, and important speeches, however. The George W. Bush administration targeted many backgrounders for specific reporters—for example, the *New York Times* for a story on foreign policy.

Backgrounders have a number of advantages for the White House. Avoiding direct quotation allows officials to speak on sensitive foreign policy and domestic policy matters candidly and in depth, something domestic politics and international diplomacy would not tolerate if speakers were held directly accountable for their words. The White House hopes such discussions will help it communicate its point of view more clearly and serve to educate journalists and make them more sympathetic to the president's position in their reporting. Moreover, they can use background sessions to scotch rumors and limit undesirable speculation about presidential plans and internal White House affairs. An impressive performance in a background session can also display the administration's competence and perhaps elicit the benefit of the doubt in future stories. Reporters have generally been happy to go along with protecting the identities of "spokespeople" and "sources" (although an experienced observer can identify most of them) because the system provides them more information than they would have otherwise.

The White House may also aim backgrounders at the public (in the form of trial balloons, which it can disclaim if they meet with disapproval) or at policy makers in Washington. They may also be directed at other countries. For example, to discourage the Soviet Union's support of India in its war with Pakistan, Henry Kissinger told reporters in a backgrounder that the Soviet policy might lead to the cancellation of President Nixon's trip to Moscow. Because the statement was not officially attributed to Kissinger, it constituted less of a public threat to the Soviet Union, while it simultaneously communicated the president's message.[25]

In addition to official backgrounders, White House aides may provide reporters information "on background." Reporters tend to view middle-level aides as the best sources of such information because they have in-depth knowledge about the substance of programs and are generally free from the constraints of high visibility. Most interviews with White House staff are made on this basis because presidents are generally intolerant of staff members who seek publicity for themselves. Sometimes an aide will say more than his or her superiors would like in order to prod the president in a particular policy direction or cast doubt on a rival in the administration. Self-serving propaganda is a common feature of these sessions.

Interviews

Modern presidents give hundreds of interviews during their tenures. Barack Obama particularly favored televised interviews as a means of reaching the public in an unmediated form. Donald Trump also gives many interviews, preferring to speak for himself and believing he is his own best press agent.

Interviews with the president and top White House staff members are a valuable commodity to the press, and sometimes the White House uses them for its own purposes. For example, President Nixon traded an exclusive interview with *Time* for a cover story on him. Similarly, in order to obtain an interview with President Ford, even the venerable Walter Cronkite agreed to use only questions the president could handle easily. At other times, the White House may give exclusives to a paper such as the *New York Times* in return for getting a story in which it is interested located in a prominent place in the paper.[26]

In 2012, President Obama held his "first completely virtual interview" as part of an event hosted by Google+. He joined a "hangout" and took questions through YouTube on everything from unemployment to streamlining the federal government. He also held town-hall meetings on Facebook, Twitter, and LinkedIn. These virtual interviews were part of a larger effort by the White House to connect directly to Americans without going through the traditional news media.

Cultivation

Recent presidents, with the exceptions of Richard Nixon, Jimmy Carter, and George W. Bush, have regularly cultivated elite reporters and columnists, the editors and publishers of leading newspapers, and network news producers and executives with small favors, social flattery, and small background dinners at the White House. (Nixon turned these chores over to top aides; Carter was neither interested in, nor skilled at, cultivation; the George W. Bush White House cultivated reporters with information but not frequent social occasions.)[27]

Presidents frequently invite television network anchors to a meal at the White House before delivering major addresses to the nation such as the State of the Union message. The first phone call ABC network anchor Peter Jennings received after landing his job was from Ronald Reagan.[28] George W. Bush and Barack Obama held off-the-record meetings with TV anchors, columnists, and top White House correspondents to learn what they were thinking and to ensure that the presidents' own points of view would be represented in the media.[29] Obama also held meetings with representatives of niche online outlets. Despite his critical rhetoric regarding the media, Donald Trump has cordial interactions with many reporters and is generally accessible to the press, including those papers he excoriates such as the *New York Times* and the *Washington Post*.[30]

Since the 1960s, the White House has had first, a designated person and then, an office for media liaison to deal directly with the representatives of news organizations, such as editors, publishers, and producers, in addition to the press office that deals with reporters' routine needs.

Servicing the Local and Specialty Press

Once the Washington press has reported on an issue, it tends to drop it and move on to the next one; however, repetition is necessary to convey the president's views to the generally inattentive public. Moreover, the Washington press tends to place more emphasis on the support of, or opposition to, a program than on its substance, although the White House wants to communicate the latter. The Washington- and New York–based national media also have substantial resources to challenge White House versions of events and policies and to investigate areas of government not covered by briefings or press releases. As a result, the White House seeks to cultivate the local as well as the national media.

The White House invites local editors, reporters, and news executives to Washington for exclusive interviews and briefings by the president and senior administration officials. Recent presidents have also arranged to be interviewed from the White House by television and radio stations through satellite hookups, and some White House occupants provide briefings for the local press using the same technology. The White House may also send administration briefing teams around the country to discuss the president's policies with local media representatives and provide press releases, speeches, other documents, and audio clips for local media. The Obama White House made a concerted effort to tap into alternatives to the mainstream national media, including Spanish-language magazines, newspapers, television and radio stations, and those oriented to African Americans.

Presidents meet frequently with journalists representing local media during their trips around the country, and they receive substantial local coverage.[31] These efforts enable the White House to tailor messages for specific groups and reach directly into the constituencies of members of Congress while reinforcing its policy message. Naturally, presidents hope to create goodwill and to receive a sympathetic hearing from journalists who are grateful for contact with the White House and, perhaps, susceptible to presidential charm. The impact may be heightened because people are more likely to trust local television stations as a news source than any other major media outlet, and local TV news has more viewers on average than cable and network news programs.[32] (Indeed, Clinton ran ads in twenty key states from the summer of 1995 until the Democratic convention a year later to reach the public through these stations.[33])

Additional Services

There are many additional services that the White House provides for the press. It gives reporters transcripts of briefings and presidential speeches and daily handouts containing a variety of information about the president and his policies, including advance notice of travel plans and upcoming stories. (These items are also available to the general public at the White House's website.)

Photographers covering the president are highly dependent on the White House press office, which provides facilities for photographers on presidential trips and arranges photo opportunities to make sure they will produce the most flattering shots of the president (for Johnson, his left profile). President Reagan even prohibited impromptu questions from reporters at photographing sessions. Moreover, the official White House photographers provide many of the photographs of the president that the media uses. Naturally, these are screened favorably to feature the president's "warm," "human," or "family" side. These photos please editors and the public alike.

When the president goes on trips, whether at home or abroad, the White House travel and press offices make extensive preparations for the press. These preparations include arranging transportation and lodging for the press, installing equipment for radio and television broadcasting, obtaining telephones for reporters, erecting platforms for photographers, preparing a detailed account of where and with whom the president will be at particular times, providing elaborate information about the countries the president is visiting, forming pools of press members to cover the president closely (as in a motorcade), and scheduling the press plane to arrive early so the press can cover the president's arrival.

As many of these services suggest, the press is especially dependent on the White House staff in covering presidential trips, particularly abroad. There are usually fewer sources of information on such trips, and access of the press to the principal figures it wishes to cover is limited. Thus, the president's aides are in a good position to manage press coverage to their advantage. Coverage of foreign trips is generally favorable, although less so than in the past now that reporters with expertise in foreign affairs have started to accompany the president. The press will point out the relationship of the trip and its goals and accomplishments to the president's domestic political problems. (It is interesting that foreign travel does not seem to increase a president's approval ratings.)[34]

Even in Washington, however, reporters are very much in a controlled environment. Reagan aides went so far as to have the motor of the president's helicopter revved to prevent him from hearing questions shouted by the press as he left for a weekend at Camp David. Similarly, when presidents wish to avoid the press during their reelection campaigns, they can simply hold no formal press conferences at all.

Managing the News

Reporters may not freely roam the halls of the White House, interviewing whomever they please. In one of its first acts, the Clinton White House even barred reporters from the area behind the press room, where the offices of the press secretary and communications director are located (it changed this policy after a few months). Reporters are highly dependent on the press office for access to officials, and about half of their interviews are with the press secretary and his or her staff. Much of their time is spent waiting for something to happen or watching the president at formal or ceremonial events. Because most news stories about such occurrences show the president in a favorable light, the press office does everything possible to help reporters record these activities.

The White House can use briefings, press releases, and the like to divert the media's attention from embarrassing matters. Reagan's aides adopted a strategy of blitzing the media with information to divert its attention after the press raised questions about the president's sleeping through Libyan attacks on US forces off the coast of Africa.[35] To avoid publicity about illegal transfers of arms to Nicaragua, the Reagan White House spearheaded a drive for an "Economic Bill of Rights."[36]

More frequently, the White House, by adopting an active approach to the press, gains an opportunity to shape the media's agenda for the day. Through announcements and press releases, it attempts to focus attention on what will reflect positively on the president. Such information frequently generates questions from reporters and subsequent news stories. Representatives of the smaller papers, who have few resources, are more heavily dependent on White House–provided news than are the larger news bureaus, including the major networks. Thus, the former are the most likely to follow the White House's agenda. Moreover, since White House reporters, especially the wire services, are under pressure to file daily "hard news" reports, the White House is in a strong position to help by providing information—much of it trivial, some of it personal, and all of it designed to reflect positively on the president. As a Ford official put it, "You can predict what the press is going to do with a story. It is almost by formula. Because of this they are usable."[37]

The White House has a special advantage in managing the news on national security issues. In the case of Iraq and weapons of mass destruction, the media amplified the administration's voice through straightforward transmissions of White House, Pentagon, and official administration statements, validating the administration's messages in the process. The conventions of breaking stories tied journalists to leading with the "news," which meant reporting the president's assertions about the threat that Iraq posed because it had such weapons. There were few critical voices, and the press only rarely covered them. The pressure among journalists to be first with a story increases the potential for White House manipulation inherent in this deferential approach, as concerns for accuracy give way to career interests.

Presidents have undoubtedly hoped that the handouts, briefings, and other services they and their staffs provide for reporters will gain them some goodwill. They also want to keep reporters interested in the president's agenda because bored journalists are more negative in their reporting and may base their stories on trivial, embarrassing incidents such as President Ford stumbling while getting off a plane or Bill Clinton getting a $200 haircut while on one.

In addition, the White House controls a commodity of considerable value to the press: information on the president's personal life. Most reporters are under pressure to provide stories on the minutiae of presidents' lives, no matter what they do. Some White House aides have found that the provision of such information can co-opt journalists or sidetrack them from producing critical stories. Some reporters will exploit the opportunity to please their editors instead of digging into more significant subjects; others reciprocate their favorable treatment by the White House with positive stories about the president.

The White House has been less successful when wielding the stick. The Obama administration soon grew weary of Fox News's unrelenting and often vitriolic criticism and limited the appearances of some top officials on some Fox News shows. More visibly, it excluded *Fox News Sunday* with Chris Wallace—which it had previously treated as distinct from the network—from a round of presidential interviews with Sunday morning news programs in mid-September 2009. In late October, the White House tried to exclude Fox from a round of interviews with the executive-pay czar Kenneth R. Feinberg. When Fox's television news competitors refused to go along, the White House relented,[38] and Fox's access soon returned to normal.[39]

Early in the Trump presidency, the White House did not allow journalists from certain organizations to enter the West Wing office of the press secretary for a scheduled briefing. Representatives of the barred news organizations made clear that they believed the White House's actions were punitive.[40] Normal practices resumed with the next briefing, however. In October 2017, Trump threatened to use the federal government's power to license television airwaves to target NBC in response to a report by the network's news division that he contemplated a dramatic increase in the nation's nuclear arsenal. (In fact, the networks themselves—and their news departments—do not hold federal licenses.)[41] In November 2018, the administration suspended the White House credentials of CNN correspondent Jim Acosta after an intense verbal clash with the president at a news conference earlier in the day, citing a false accusation about Acosta "placing his hands" on a White House intern who tried to take his microphone. CNN sued, and Acosta's pass was restored.

PRESS COVERAGE OF THE PRESIDENT

In addition to the chief executive's efforts to influence the media, there is another side of this relationship we must examine: the content of the news. Ultimately, it is the written and spoken word that concerns the president. Leaks of confidential information and what the White House sees as superficial or biased reporting exacerbate the tensions inherent in relations between the president and the press. Presidents commonly view the press as a major obstacle to their obtaining and maintaining public support. Most administrations criticize the media for its trivial coverage, for its distortions, and for violating confidences. The White House feels that this type of reporting hinders its efforts to develop public appreciation for the president and his policies.

Leaks

After some time in office, Bill Clinton made it a rule not to say anything sensitive in a room with more than one aide. If he did, he felt, he might as well speak directly to the AP.[42] Barack Obama hated leaks,[43] and his Department of Justice formally investigated a substantial number of them. At a rally on November 4, 2016, just before Election Day, Donald Trump proclaimed, "Boy, I love reading those WikiLeaks!" After less than a month in office, however, he assailed leaks that led to the departure of his national security adviser, Gen. Michael Flynn. "The press should be ashamed of themselves" for running stories based on leaks, Trump told reporters at a press conference on February 16, 2017.[44]

Leaks bedevil most presidents. Sometimes, they are potentially quite serious, as when leakers disclosed the US negotiating strategy for nuclear disarmament talks during the Nixon administration. When the *Pentagon Papers* (on decision making in the war in Vietnam) were leaked to the public, President Nixon felt that there was a danger that other countries would lose confidence in our ability to keep secrets and that information on the delicate negotiations then in progress with China might also be leaked, endangering the possibility of rapprochement.[45] At other times, leaks are just embarrassing—for example, when they reveal internal dissent in the administration to the public. President Johnson feared that leaks would signal what he was thinking and he would lose his freedom of action as a result.

Who leaks information? The best answer is "everybody." Presidents themselves do so, sometimes inadvertently. As Lyndon Johnson once put it, "I have enough trouble with myself. I ought not to have to put up with everybody else too."[46] Once John F. Kennedy ordered Secretary of State Dean Rusk to find out who had leaked a story on foreign policy only to discover that the culprit was the president himself.[47]

Top presidential aides may also reveal more than they intend. When a leak regarding President Reagan's willingness to compromise on his 1981 tax bill appeared in the *New York Times*, White House aides tracked down the source of the story and found it to be budget director David Stockman.[48] A year earlier, a leak revealing secret Central Intelligence Agency (CIA) arms shipments to Afghan rebels was attributed to the office of the president's chief national security adviser.[49]

Most leaks, however, are deliberately planted. As one close presidential aide put it, "99 percent of all significant secrets are spilled by the principals or at their direction."[50] Presidents are included in those who purposefully leak. For example, *Newsweek* used to hold space open for the items John Kennedy would phone to his friend Benjamin Bradlee right before the magazine's deadline.[51]

There are many reasons for leaks. The White House often uses them as trial balloons to test public or congressional reaction to ideas and proposals or to stimulate public concern about an issue. Both the Ford and Carter White Houses used this technique to test reaction to a tax surcharge on gasoline. When the reaction to these proposals turned out to be negative, both administrations denied ever contemplating such a policy. President Clinton's task force on health-care reform engaged in a series of leaks regarding a wide range of health policy options.

At other times, aides leak information to reporters who will use it to write favorable articles on a policy. Or, as the Clinton White House often did, the administration may leak an exclusive story on relatively modest proposals, such as plans to renovate schools or to crack down on truants, to one news organization. This technique encourages that organization to give it added coverage as an exclusive story and forces the competition to play catch-up and give the president two days of favorable publicity instead of only one.[52]

Diplomacy is an area in which delicate communications play an important role. Officials often use leaks to send other nations nuanced signals of friendship, anger, or willingness to compromise. While sending messages to other nations, leaks provide the president with the opportunity to disavow publicly or to reinterpret what some might view as, for example, an overly "tough" stance or an unexpected change in policy. This makes it easier for these countries to respond to US wishes. For example, during negotiations with the Japanese regarding restricting imports, the Reagan administration leaked a story that the talks were going badly to pressure Japan into moderating its position. President Clinton's national security assistant regularly leaked stories to CNN for diplomatic purposes, including using a leak to warn Iraqi leader Saddam Hussein to move his troops away from the Kuwaiti border in 1994.[53] Diplomatic leaks also have the advantage of speed. When President Bush wanted to send a message of US support for Soviet president Mikhail Gorbachev during the attempted coup to remove him, he wanted to use the fastest source available for getting a message to Moscow, so he chose to leak the message to CNN.[54]

People may also use leaks to influence personnel matters. The release of information letting a stubborn official know that the official's superiors wish him or her to leave may force a resignation and thus save the problem of firing the official. Conversely, a leak may make the official's position a public issue, increasing the costs of such a firing. Similarly, the release of information on an appointment before it is made places presidents in an awkward position and can help ensure that they follow through on it or else prematurely deny they have such plans.

Some leaks are designed to force the president's hand on policy decisions. Officials in the Clinton administration who were hostile to welfare reform regularly leaked stories critical of the plan the administration was formulating. They also tried to tie the president's hands by leaking false stories that the president had made a decision, thus hoping to encourage him actually to make that decision to avoid being viewed as flip-flopping.[55] During the India–Pakistan War, President Nixon maintained a publicly neutral stance but really favored Pakistan. When this fact was leaked, there was inevitably pressure to be neutral in action as well as in rhetoric.[56] Conversely, a leak about what Lyndon Johnson was thinking about a decision would generally ensure that he would take no such action.

Leaks may serve a number of other functions. They may make some individuals feel important or help them gain favor with reporters. Officials may also use leaks to criticize and intimidate personal or political adversaries in the White House itself or to protect and enhance reputations. In the Ford administration, White House counsel Robert Hartmann and Chief of Staff Richard Cheney often attacked each other anonymously in the press. Several members of the White House staff attacked Press Secretary Ron Nessen in an effort to persuade the president to replace him. When negotiations with North Vietnam broke down in late 1972, White House aides employed leaks to dissociate the president from Henry Kissinger, his national security assistant.

Presidents sometimes leak information for their own political purposes. By leaking findings about lax security measures regarding the deaths of 241 marines in Beirut in 1983, Reagan White House aides focused press attention on security lapses rather than the criticism of the ill-defined nature of the marines' mission in Lebanon, a mission given them by the president.[57] George W. Bush, through Vice President Dick Cheney, secretly declassified an intelligence estimate and authorized Cheney's aide, I. Lewis Libby Jr., to leak it to fight back against critics of the Iraq war.

In all these cases, government officials were using the press for their purposes, not vice versa. Although reporters may well be aware of being used, the competitive pressure of the news business makes it difficult for them to pass up an exclusive story. Nevertheless, most good reporting, even investigative reporting, does not rely heavily on leaks. Instead, reporters put together stories by bits and pieces.

It is generally fruitless to try to discover the source of a leak. The Reagan administration tried everything from lie detector tests to logging every journalist's interviews on a computer, but nothing stopped the leaking. According to White House Chief of Staff Donald Regan, "In the Reagan Administration the leak was raised to the status of an art form. Everything, or nearly everything, the President and his close associates did or knew appeared in the newspapers and on the networks with the least possible delay."[58]

The Clinton White House made some progress in discouraging leaks when Chief of Staff Leon Panetta began trying to identify who had leaked and then retaliating by leaking a critical story to a major news outlet about the suspect.[59] The Obama administration prosecuted more alleged leakers than all previous administrations combined.[60] In 2013, federal investigators secretly seized phone records for reporters and editors of the AP, probably in response to leaks about the CIA's disruption of a Yemen-based terrorist plot to bomb an airliner.[61] Nevertheless, leaks remain common in press coverage of the president, and the incentives to leak remain as strong as ever.

The Trump White House is no exception to the presence of leaking—and the president's frustration with it—as you can see in box 7.2.

Box 7.2 ★ The Leaky Trump White House

Indiscriminate leaking has characterized the Trump White House. "This is the most porous administration I have observed," said Martha Joynt Kumar, a leading media expert who has studied the media relations of every administration since Gerald Ford's. "The leaks seemingly come from everywhere." Embarrassing details of Trump's calls with foreign leaders, the administration's imperious handling of the National Security Council, the fact that Trump approved an ill-fated military raid in Yemen over dinner with two aides, and seemingly every Trump mood swing and personal foible has leaked, along with endless details about the rivalries and distrust among aides. When Trump berated his inner circle for their missteps at an Oval Office meeting and details of the meeting leaked, White House Chief of Staff Reince Priebus spent much of his afternoon attempting to kill stories about the meeting—a gambit that both failed and also leaked.[62]

Speaking by phone to the widely scorned president of the Philippines, Rodrigo Duterte, Trump himself revealed the presence of two nuclear submarines off North Korea, a highly unusual disclosure. Worse, on May 10, 2017, President Trump met with the Russian foreign minister and ambassador at the White House. During their discussion, he revealed highly classified information regarding an Islamic State of Iraq and Syria plot and the city where the plot was detected by an intelligence gathering partner, providing details that could expose the source of the information and the manner in which it was collected. Officials feared that Russia would be able to determine exactly how the information was collected and could disrupt the ally's espionage efforts.

The information the president relayed had been provided by Israel through an intelligence-sharing arrangement considered so sensitive that details have been withheld from allies and tightly restricted even within the US government. Israel had not given the United States permission to share the material with Russia, and Trump's decision to do so endangered cooperation from an ally that has access to the inner workings of the Islamic State of Iraq and Syria. (The *Washington Post*, which broke the story, withheld most plot details, including the name of the city, at the urging of officials who warned that revealing them would jeopardize important intelligence capabilities.)

After Trump's meeting, senior White House officials took steps to contain the damage, placing calls to the CIA and the National Security Agency, the services most directly involved in the intelligence-sharing arrangement with Israel, and sought to strike the problematic portion of Trump's discussion from internal memos. In separate statements Secretary of State Rex W. Tillerson and national security adviser H. R. McMaster said that the president did not discuss sources, methods, or military operations with the Russians.

However, no news organization reported that he had done so. Trump's advisers refuted charges that were never made. Appearing to undercut his advisers, the president then tweeted to defend his decision to share sensitive information with the Russians, saying that he had an "absolute right" to do so in the interest of fighting terrorism. He did not dispute reports that he might have provided enough details to reveal the source of the information and the manner in which it had been collected.

The revelation also opened Trump to criticism of hypocrisy, given his vocal criticism of Hillary Clinton's mishandling of classified information through her private e-mail. It was also likely to intensify scrutiny about the president's dealings with Russian officials.

The president then tried to turn attention away from whether he had leaked information to finding those who had disclosed what he had done. "I have been asking Director Comey & others, from the beginning of my administration, to find the LEAKERS in the intelligence community," he tweeted on May 16.

Superficiality

A common complaint in the White House is that the press is interested in the superficial layer of politics rather than the meat and potatoes of governing. Woodrow Wilson, one of the first presidents to serve in the era of mass media with a national focus, complained that most reporters were "interested in the personal and trivial rather than in principles of policies."[63] More recently, Jimmy Carter complained to reporters, "I would really like for you all as people who relay Washington events to the world to take a look at the substantive questions I have to face as a president and quit dealing almost exclusively with personalities."[64] Barack Obama criticized the media's preoccupation with conflict and complained that too often press coverage focuses on political winners and losers rather than substance and there reflected a "false balance," in which two opposing sides are given equal weight regardless of the facts.[65]

Brevity and simplicity characterize media coverage of national news in mainline media such as most newspapers and broadcast networks. Editors do not want to bore or confuse their viewers, listeners, or readers. Stories must be few in number and short in length. The amount of information transmitted under such conditions is inevitably limited and insufficient for the president to educate the public about his policies. The substance as well as the amount of media coverage hinders the president's efforts to persuade the public. Rather than focusing on policy issues, the news is becoming more personality-centered, less time-bound, more practical, and more incident-based. About 50 percent of all news stories have no clear connection to policy issues.[66]

News organizations demand information that is new and different, personal and intimate, or revealing and unexpected. Most reporting is about events, actions taken, or words spoken by public figures, especially if the events are dramatic and colorful, such as ceremonies and parades. According to ABC correspondent Sam Donaldson, "A clip of a convalescent Reagan waving from his window at some circus elephants is going to push an analytical piece about tax cuts off the air every time."[67] In such a news environment, there is little time or space for reflection, analysis, or comprehensive coverage.

Human-interest stories, especially those about presidents and their families, are always in high demand. Such stories are novel, and the public can relate to the subjects more easily than to complex matters of public policy such as a presidential tax proposal. Donald Trump's glitzy lifestyle and fashionable wife and daughter naturally generate human-interest stories. Editors expect this type of coverage (which they believe will please their readers), and reporters do not want to risk missing a story. As the Washington bureau chief of *Newsweek* said, "The worst thing in the world that could happen to you is for the President of the United States to choke on a piece of meat, and for you not to be there."[68] When President Bush vomited at a state dinner in Japan, television networks had a field day and ran the tape again and again of the president being taken ill.

The press also has a bias toward conflict.[69] Conflicts between clearly identifiable antagonists (e.g., President Trump vs. Speaker of the House Nancy Pelosi) are highly prized, particularly if there is something tangible at stake such as the passage of a bill or impeachment of the president. As one prominent White House correspondent put it, "Most reporters I know are not passionately political, left or right. Our real ideology is a love of conflict, meaning that we have a bias for stories about, yes, personality feuds, but also about disputes over policy."[70]

In the process of covering such controversies, the press may repeat distortions, half-truths, and even untruths about the president and his opponents and reduce complex matters to black-and-white terms, thus obscuring the real issues that underlay the conflict. The same thing occurs when the media increasingly devote extensive attention to negative ads in presidential campaigns.[71]

President Obama's health-care reform proposal evoked an eruption of anger at town-hall meetings, and this, rather than the substance of the plan, became the story the media presented. After the president convened a low-key town hall in New Hampshire, Fox broke away from the meeting and anchor Trace Gallagher told her audience, "Any contentious questions, anybody yelling, we'll bring it to you."[72]

Scandals involving the president or those close to him receive high-priority coverage in the media, often driving out coverage of news on the president's policies. For example, on April 22, 1994, President Clinton held a press conference on imminent air strikes in Bosnia, which only CNN carried live. On the same day, First Lady Hillary Rodham Clinton held a press conference on the Whitewater investigation, which all the networks carried. When Paula Jones charged President Clinton with sexual harassment (while he was governor of Arkansas), the media devoted extensive coverage to the case, yet even this attention paled in comparison to the frenzy of coverage devoted to the president's sexual relationship with a White House intern, Monica Lewinsky. No policy issue received as much attention, especially on television, until the Senate acquitted the president more than a year later. Indeed, one-seventh of the network news in 1998 focused on the scandal.[73]

Chuck Kennedy/KRT/Newscom

President Bill Clinton denies having had sex with Monica Lewinsky, an issue that launched a frenzy of press coverage.

Most of the White House press activity comes under the heading of the "body watch." In other words, reporters focus on the most visible layer of the president's personal and official activities and provide the public with a step-by-step account. They are interested in what the president is going to do, how his actions will affect others, how he views policies and individuals, how he presents himself, and whose stars are rising and falling, rather than in the substance of policies or the fundamental operations of the executive branch. Coverage of the consideration of both President Obama's and President Clinton's massive health-care proposals in 1993–1994 and 2009–2010 focused much more on strategy and legislative battles than on the issues of health care.[74]

Major news organizations spend a great deal of money covering the presidents, including following them around the globe on official business and vacations. Because of this investment and the public's interest in the president, reporters must come up with something each day. Newsworthy happenings do not necessarily occur every day, however, so reporters either emphasize the trivial or blow events out of proportion. While covering a meeting of Western leaders on the island of Guadeloupe, Sam Donaldson faced the prospect of having nothing to report on a slow news day. Undaunted, he reported on the roasting of the pig that the leaders would be eating that evening, including "an exclusive look at the oven in which the pig would be roasted."[75]

Similarly, the White House press often focuses on the exact wording of an announcement in an effort to detect a change in policy, frequently finding significance where none really exists. It often blows presidential slips of the tongue or gaffes out of all proportion.

In its constant search for "news," the press, especially the electronic media, is reluctant to devote repeated attention to an issue, even though this might be necessary to explain it adequately to the public. As a deputy press secretary in the Carter administration said, "We have to keep sending out our message if we expect people to understand. The Washington press corps will explain a policy once and then it will feature the politics of the issue."[76] This is one incentive for the president to meet with the non-Washington press and to address the nation directly on television or radio.

Delving more deeply into the presidency and policy requires not only substantial expertise but also certain technical skills. Washington reporters in general, and White House reporters in particular, do little documentary research. They are trained to conduct interviews and transmit handouts from press secretaries and public information officials rather than to carry out research. Moreover, in-depth research demands a slower pace and advance planning, and journalists tend not to be comfortable with either requirement.

Sometimes, several factors influence coverage of the presidency at the same time. Despite the glamour attached to investigative reporting since the Watergate scandal, not much of it actually takes place, the *New York Times* and the *Washington Post* being exceptions. Most news organizations are unwilling or unable to devote the time and resources necessary for investigative work or engage in the coordination required with other reporters and news bureau staff to cover all leads successfully. The maxim of journalism is to go it alone, and the incentives are generally to get the news out fast—and first. Similarly, the slowness of the process of using the Freedom of Information Act to force the release of documents inhibits its use.

The speed of the modern news cycle also promotes superficiality. Instead of seeking context or disputing a claim, reporters often simply get two opposing quotes and file a he said/she said story. As Peter Baker of the *New York Times* put it, a decade ago a reporter could write for the next day's newspaper. He or she had time to call people, access information, and provide context. Today, you have to file for the web, radio, and perhaps appear on television and a blog. "Even with a well-staffed news organization, we are hostages to the non-stop, never-ending file-it-now, get-on-the-Web, get-on-the-radio, get-on-TV media environment."[77]

Not only does the press provide superficial coverage of the stories it reports, but it also misses many important stories about the presidency altogether because of its emphasis.[78] The implementation of policy, which is the predominant activity of the executive branch, is very poorly covered because it is not fast-breaking news; it takes place mostly in the field, away from the reporters' natural territory, and it requires documentary analysis and interaction with civil servants who are neither famous nor experts at public relations. Similarly, the White House press misses most of the flow of information and options made available to the president from the rest of the executive branch unless a scandal is involved.

In sum, although the president is dependent on the media to disseminate his views, the superficiality of the news is often an obstacle to obtaining public support. The press transmits only limited information to the public and the nature of this information ill-equips people to deal with the ambiguities and uncertainties of most complex events and issues. Moreover, the news provides little in the way of the background and contextual information that is essential for understanding political events. Although the electronic media, especially television, are the most typical source of news for Americans, they do a relatively poor job of providing information to the public. According to CBS network anchor Dan Rather, "You simply cannot be a well-informed citizen by just watching the news on television."[79] Yet, television is the principal source of news for most people.

Bias

Bias is the most politically charged issue in press relations with the president. It is also an elusive concept with many dimensions. Although we typically envision bias as news coverage favoring identifiable people, parties, or points of view, there are more subtle and more pervasive forms of bias that are not motivated by the goal of furthering careers or policies.

Many studies covering topics such as presidential election campaigns, the Vietnam War, and local news conclude that the news media are not biased systematically toward a particular person, party, or ideology, as measured in the amount or favorability of coverage.[80] In the same vein, after six years as President Reagan's press secretary, Larry Speakes concluded that the news media had generally given the administration "a fair shake" and that "they probably gave us a longer honeymoon than we deserved."[81] Lanny Davis, a prominent defender of Bill Clinton during his impeachment and trial, found reporters wrote fair stories if the White House gave them full information.[82] Scott McClellan, a George W. Bush press secretary, concluded that media bias was not a problem and that any liberal bias had minimal impact on the way the public was informed. The "Bush administration had no difficulty in getting our messages across to the American people," he declared.[83]

This discussion of the general neutrality of news coverage in the mass media pertains most directly to traditional television news shows and newspaper and radio reporting. Columnists, commentators, and editorial writers usually cannot even pretend to be neutral. Typical newspaper endorsements for presidential candidates overwhelmingly favor Republicans (1992, 2004, and 2016 were exceptions).[84] News magazines are generally less neutral than newspapers or television because they often adopt a point of view in their stories. Hosts of many cable television and radio shows, such as those on Fox and MSNBC, take an explicitly ideological edge.[85]

In addition, media outlets may give more attention to stories favoring their editorial views and less to those that run counter to them. For example, Democratic-leaning newspapers—those with a higher propensity to endorse Democratic candidates in elections—provide relatively more coverage of scandals involving Republican politicians than scandals involving Democratic politicians, while Republican-leaning newspapers tend to do the opposite.[86] Fox News unfailingly supports President Trump and has devoted less time reporting about the investigation of the Trump campaign's ties to Russia, the president's payment of hush money to conceal his affairs, ethical lapses of administration officials, and other negative stories.[87]

Donald Trump has complained constantly about the press, but he has benefited from strong support from key elements. Most radio political talk shows are conservative and back him. The cable news network with the largest audience is Fox News, which has virtually become a mouthpiece for the administration.[88] In fact, when a story on Democrats on August 28, 2019, was not critical enough to suit his taste, the president complained that day on Twitter that "Fox "isn't working for us anymore!"

Thus, the president has blurred the distinction between the White House and the press. At a rally in Missouri on the eve of the midterm elections, Rush Limbaugh, the conservative host of the political talk show with the largest audience in the country, introduced the president. Then Fox News's Sean Hannity and Jeanine Piro joined the president onstage where each delivered a short speech backing the president. Backstage was Bill Shine, a former Fox executive, who was serving as deputy White House chief of staff in charge of communications.

In addition, a small number of large holding companies are taking over local TV stations, often more than one in the same market. This development has allowed companies to cut costs by consolidating newsrooms that may have once competed against each other—creating a uniformity of news coverage and a significant rightward shift in the ideological slant of coverage.[89] Another study found that in 2016 a pro-Trump right-wing media network using social media as a backbone developed as a distinct and insulated media system, to transmit a hyper-partisan perspective to the world.[90]

Restraints on Bias

A number of factors help to explain why most mass-media news coverage is not biased systematically toward a particular person, party, or ideology. Reporters tend not to be partisan or strong ideologues, nor are they politically aligned or holders of strong political beliefs. Journalists are typically not intellectuals or deeply concerned with public policy. Moreover, they share journalism's professional norm of objectivity. The organizational processes of story selection and editing also provide opportunities for softening reporters' judgments. The rotation of assignments and rewards for objective newsgathering are further protections against bias. Local television station owners and newspaper publishers are in a position to apply pressure regarding the presentation of the news, and, although they rarely do so, their potential to act may restrain reporters.

Self-interest also plays a role in constraining bias. Individual reporters, as opposed to media commentators, may earn a poor reputation if others view them as biased. The television networks, newspaper news services, newsmagazines, and wire services, which provide most of the Washington news for newspapers, have a direct financial stake in attracting viewers and subscribers and do not want to lose their audience by appearing biased, especially when multiple versions of the same story are available to major news outlets. Slander and libel laws and the "political attack" rule, providing those personally criticized on the electronic media with an opportunity to respond, are formal limitations on bias.

There is a tendency of the press to defer to the best-packaged, officially advanced stories, according an advantage to officials with the greatest perceived power to affect the issues at hand, the greatest capacity to use the levers of office to advance their news narratives on a regular basis, and the best communications operations to spin their preferred narratives well. Of the 414 stories on the buildup to and the rationale for the Iraq war presented by ABC, CBS, and NBC from September 2002 through February 2003, only 34 originated outside the White House.[91]

News organizations do not want to be seen as crusaders. Thus, it is difficult for journalists to report and sustain stories opposing the president unless they have credible sources with power in government articulating opposition. Even strong newspapers such as the *Washington Post* and the *New York Times* relied heavily on the Bush administration's assertions about the existence of weapons of mass destruction in Iraq and downplayed stories questioning them. Without some government mechanism such as congressional hearings or a serious election challenge from Democrats, there was nothing to sustain an opposing story on Iraq.[92]

Ultimately, the issue of bias may hang on questions of nuance. As public affairs analyst and former presidential press secretary Bill Moyers put it, "Depending on who is looking and writing, the White House is brisk or brusque, assured or arrogant, casual or sloppy, frank or brutal, warm or corny, cautious or timid, compassionate or condescending, reserved or callous."[93] Given the limitations of language and the lack of agreement on the exact nature of reality, it is almost impossible for the media to please everyone.

Distortion

To conclude that the mainstream news contains little explicit partisan or ideological bias is not to argue that it does not distort reality in its coverage. Even under the best of conditions, some distortion is inevitable as a result of simple error or such factors as lack of careful checking of facts, the efforts of news sources to deceive, and short deadlines. In addition, the focus of stories, such as those on presidency-related scandals, seem to depend on factors such as the number of other stories on the news agenda.[94]

We have already seen that the news is fundamentally superficial and oversimplified and is often overblown, all of which provides the public with a distorted view of, among other things, presidential activities, statements, policies, and options. The emphasis on action and the deviant (and therefore "newsworthy" items), rather than on patterns of behavior, and the implication that most stories represent more general themes of national significance, contribute further to this distortion. Personalizing the news downplays structural and other impersonal factors, which may be far more important in understanding the economy, for example, than individual political actors.

Themes

The press prefers to frame the news in themes and story lines, which both simplify complex issues and events and provide continuity of people, institutions, and issues. Once these themes and story lines have been established, the press tends to maintain them in subsequent coverage. Stories that dovetail with the theme are more likely to be in the news. By necessity, framing the news in this fashion emphasizes some information at the expense of other data, often determining what information is most relevant to news coverage and the context in which it is presented.

George Bush's privileged background gave rise to a greatly distorting media theme of isolation from the realities of everyday life in the United States. Thus, a story that he expressed amazement at scanners commonly used at supermarket checkout lines was widely reported as further evidence of his isolation—even though the story was incorrect. Similarly, once the theme of Bill Clinton's weak political and ethical moorings had been established, even the most outrageous tabloid claims of his past misbehavior received media attention, while stories about his policy stances frequently focused on whether or not he was displaying backbone.

Once the press typecasts a president, news coverage and late-night comedians repeatedly reinforce his image, and a negative image is difficult to overcome. For example, after a stereotype of President Ford as a "bumbler" had been established, his every stumble was magnified as the press emphasized behavior that fit the mold. Ford was repeatedly forced to defend his intelligence, and many of his acts and statements were reported as efforts to "act" presidential.[95] There was a similar theme to the coverage of Vice President Dan Quayle, and as a result, after he misspelled "potato" during the 1992 presidential campaign, it became a widely reported story.

In 1992, the press's predominant theme regarding the presidency was that President Bush was in trouble, so it focused on information that would illustrate the theme. Bush received overwhelmingly negative coverage during the year. Indeed, the television networks' portrayal of the economy became more negative even as the economy actually improved! Similar themes were established for President Carter in 1980 and President Ford in 1976.[96]

Media Activism

Some people may equate objectivity with passivity and feel that the press should do no more than report what others present to it. This simple conveyance of news is what occurs much of the time, and it is a fundamental reason for the superficiality of news coverage. If the press is passive, however, it can be more easily manipulated and even made to represent fiction as fact.

Reporters increasingly feel the necessity of setting the story in a meaningful context. The construction of such a context may entail reporting what was not said as well as what was said, what had occurred before, and what political implications may be involved in a statement, policy, or event. More than in the past, reporters today actively and aggressively interpret stories for viewers and readers. They no longer depend on those whom they interview to set the tone of their stories, and they now regularly pass sweeping (and frequently negative) judgments about what politicians are saying and doing.[97] One of the forces driving this change in journalism is the fact that news is broken regularly via Twitter—often by the newsmakers themselves rather than a reporter. Journalists naturally spend more time doing analysis, reacting to the news and trying to answer the "so what?" and "now what?" questions. It is not surprising that the leading cable news networks—CNN, Fox

News, and MSNBC—spend as substantial a percentage of their airtime hosting commentary about the news as reporting it.[98]

Negativity

Increasingly, the public receives news about the president in a negative context.[99] To meet their needs for a story containing conflict and to serve readers who seem to prefer negative news content,[100] it is routine for reporters to turn to opponents of the president when he makes a statement or takes an action.[101] President Clinton received mostly negative coverage during his tenure in office, with a ratio of negative to positive comments on network television of about two to one.[102] The trend continued in the George W. Bush presidency.[103] Although Barack Obama enjoyed a brief honeymoon with the press,[104] the news soon turned negative for him as well. Coverage of his economic stimulus proposal and his health-care reform plan was more negative than positive,[105] as was coverage of the 2012 presidential campaign.[106] Coverage of the 2016 presidential campaign was also overwhelmingly negative in tone,[107] as has been coverage of Donald Trump as president.[108]

Journalists typically present negative stories in a seemingly neutral manner. Such "objective" reporting can be misleading, however, as the following excerpt from Jimmy Carter's diary regarding a visit to Panama in 1978 illustrates:

> I told the Army troops that I was in the Navy for eleven years, and they booed. I told them that we depended on the Army to keep the Canal open, and they cheered. Later, the news reports said that there were boos and cheers during my speech.[109]

Pat Byrnes/The New Yorker Collection/The Cartoon Bank

"Media at the gate!"

Similarly, an emphasis on scandals in an administration, even if the press presents the stories in an even-handed manner, rarely helps the White House. The coverage of the Monica Lewinsky story seems to be an exception, as President Clinton benefited, at least for most of 1998, from a backlash against media intrusiveness into his private life. Nevertheless, President Clinton received mostly negative coverage during his tenure in office.[110]

Some observers feel that the press is biased against whomever holds office at the moment and that reporters want to expose office holders in the media. Reporters, they argue, hold disparaging views of most politicians and public officials, whom they find self-serving, dishonest, incompetent, hypocritical, and preoccupied with reelection. Thus, it is not surprising that, as part of the "watchdog" function of the press, journalists see a need to expose and debunk them. This orientation to analytical coverage may be characterized as neither liberal nor conservative but, rather, as reformist.[111]

White House reporters are always looking to expose conflicts of interest and other shady behavior of public officials. Moreover, many of their inquiries revolve around the question of whether the official is up to the job. Reporters who are confined in the White House all day may attempt to make up for their lack of investigative reporting with sarcastic and accusatory questioning. Moreover, the desire to keep the public interested and the need for continuous coverage may create in the press a subconscious bias against the presidency that leads to critical stories. In the end, some observers agree with George W. Bush's chief political strategist, Karl Rove, that the press is "less liberal than it is oppositional."[112]

Conversely, one could argue that the press is biased toward the White House. Reporters' general respect for the presidency may be transferred to individual presidents. Framed at a respectful distance by the television camera, the president is typically portrayed with an aura of dignity and as working in a context of rationality and coherence on activities benefiting the public. The press's word selection often reflects this orientation as well. It has only been in recent years that journalists have stopped following conventions that protected politicians and public officials from revelations of private misconduct.

The White House enjoys a great deal of positive coverage in newspapers, magazines, and network news. The most favorable coverage comes in the first year of a president's term, before there is a record to criticize or critics for reporters to interview. Coverage focuses on human-interest stories of the president and on his appointees and their personalities, goals, and plans. The media often picture the president in a positive light as a policy maker dealing with problems. Controversies over solutions typically arise later.[113] President Clinton was not as fortunate in his first year because of especially active congressional critics; his own partisans, who clamored for policies they had been denied during twelve years of Republican presidencies; an inability of the White House to keep its internal dissensions to itself; and the poor performance of the White House public relations staff. Donald Trump began his presidency with a controversial travel ban and never had a honeymoon with the press.

MEDIA EFFECTS

The most significant question about the substance of media coverage, of course, is about the impact it has on public opinion. Most studies of media effects have focused on attitude changes, especially in voting for presidential candidates, and have typically found little or no evidence of influence. Reinforcement of existing attitudes and opinions was said to be the strongest effect of the media.[114] In the words of one expert, "Most media stories are promptly forgotten. Stories that become part of an individual's fund of knowledge tend to reinforce existing beliefs and feelings. Acquisition of new knowledge or changes in attitude are the exception rather than the rule."[115] There are other ways to analyze media effects, however.

Setting the Public's Agenda

The public's familiarity with political matters is closely related to the attention they receive in the mass media,[116] especially in foreign affairs. The media also have a strong influence on which issues the public views as important.[117] "Many people readily adopt the media's agenda of importance, often without being aware of it."[118] Moreover, when the media cover events, politicians comment on them and take action, reinforcing the perceived importance of these events and ensuring more public attention to them.

During the 1979–1980 Iranian hostage crisis, in which several dozen Americans were held hostage, ABC originated a nightly program entitled *America Held Hostage*. On CBS television, Walter Cronkite provided a "countdown" of the number of days of the crisis at the end of each evening's news. Countless feature stories on the hostages and their families were reported in all the media, and the press gave complete coverage to "demonstrations" held in front of the US embassy in Tehran (often artificially created by demonstrators for consumption by Americans). This crisis dominated American politics for more than a year and gave President Carter's approval rating a tremendous, albeit short-term, boost. In the longer term, however, the coverage destroyed his leadership image. Conversely, when North Korea captured the American ship *Pueblo* in 1968, there were many more American captives, and they were held for almost as long as the hostages in Tehran, but there were also no television cameras and few reporters to cover the situation. Thus, the incident played a much smaller role in American politics.

The media's influence on the public's agenda can be to the president's advantage. When the public is already concerned with an issue, the president is likely to respond to the public's agenda. However, when the president devotes attention to issues that are not of great concern to the public, he can influence the public's agenda indirectly through the news coverage he receives.[119]

Media Framing and Priming

At any one time, there are many potential criteria for evaluating the president, ranging from personal characteristics such as integrity to performance on the economy or foreign affairs. In chapter 6, we learned that the concept of priming is premised on the fact that most of the time the cognitive burdens are too great for people to reach judgments or decisions based on comprehensive, integrated information and the consideration of a large number of criteria. Instead, the public takes shortcuts or uses cues. One source of cues is the White House, but another is the mass media.

Media coverage of issues and events may prime the criteria most people select for evaluating the president. In the words of a leading authority on the impact of television news on public opinion, "The themes and issues that are repeated in television news coverage become the priorities of viewers. Issues and events highlighted by television news become especially influential as criteria for evaluating public officials."[120]

The media are more likely to influence perceptions than attitudes. The press can influence the perceptions of what public figures stand for and what their personalities are like, what issues are important, and what is at stake. If the media raise certain issues or personal characteristics to prominence, the significance of attitudes that people already hold may change and thus alter their evaluations of, say, presidential performance, without their attitudes themselves changing. In other words, the media can influence the criteria by which the public judges the president and his policies.[121]

If the media were simply following the White House's lead in priming criteria for evaluating the president, the media's impact would not pose an obstacle to presidential priming. Instead, it would reinforce the White House's efforts. The media, however, typically follow their own course.

When the media began covering the Iran-Contra affair, Ronald Reagan's public approval took an immediate and severe dip as the public applied new criteria of evaluation.[122] The role of George Bush's economic performance in overall evaluations of him decreased substantially after the Gulf War began, and it is reasonable to conclude that media priming effects caused a shift of attention to his performance on war-related criteria.[123] Although the president wanted the public to continue to weigh heavily his foreign policy stewardship in its evaluations of his performance after the war, the public did not comply. Instead, both the media and the public turned their focus to the economy.[124]

Coverage of the Camp David peace accords boosted the impact of President Carter's performance in dealing with foreign countries on overall evaluations of the president.[125] Similarly, experiments found that network news affected his overall reputation and, to a lesser extent, views of his apparent competency. The standards people used in evaluating the president, what they felt was important in his job performance, seemed to be influenced by the news they watched on television.[126]

When the press gave substantial coverage to President Ford's misstatement about Soviet domination of Eastern Europe in a presidential debate, this coverage had an impact on the public. Polls show that most people did not realize the president had made an error until the press told them so. Afterward, pro-Ford evaluations of the debate declined noticeably as voters' concerns for competence in foreign policy making became salient.[127] A somewhat similar switch occurred after the first debate between Walter Mondale and Ronald Reagan in 1984.[128]

Although the public's information on and criteria for evaluating presidential candidates parallel what the media present,[129] the press probably has the greatest effect on public perceptions of individuals and issues between election campaigns, when people are less likely to activate their partisan defenses.

The extraordinary attention that the press devotes to presidents magnifies their flaws and makes them more salient to the public. The prominent coverage of Gerald Ford's alleged physical clumsiness naturally translated into suggestions of mental ineptitude and became a prominent criterion for evaluating the president. In the president's own words, "Every time I stumbled or bumped my head or fell in the snow, reporters zeroed in on that to the exclusion of almost everything else."[130]

Even completely unsubstantiated charges against them may make the news because of their prominence. Familiarity may not breed contempt, but it certainly may diminish the aura of grandeur around the chief executive. In the past, criticism of presidents was restrained by the reluctance of many editors to publish analyses sharply divergent from the president's position without direct confirmation from an authoritative source who would be willing to go on the record in opposition to the president. During the famous investigation of the Watergate scandal, the *Washington Post* verified all information attributed to an unnamed source with at least one other independent source. It also did not print information from other media outlets unless its reporters could independently verify that information.[131] Things have changed, however.

When the story broke about charges that President Clinton had sexual relations with a young White House intern named Monica Lewinsky, virtually all elements of the mass media went into a feeding frenzy,[132] relying as much on analysis, opinion, and speculation as on confirmed facts. Even the most prominent news outlets carried unsubstantiated reports about charges that had not received independent verification by those carrying the story. If another news outlet carried a charge, most of the rest soon picked it up because they did not want to be scooped. For example, the media widely reported unsubstantiated charges that members of the Secret Service had found the president and Ms. Lewinsky in a compromising position. Such reporting helped sensationalize the story, keeping it alive and undermining the president's efforts to focus the public's attention on matters of public policy.

Similarly, the press gave immediate attention to a story on the CBS television program *60 Minutes* that revealed documents regarding President George W. Bush's service in the National Guard. The documents purported to show dissatisfaction with the president's performance—or nonperformance. Upon closer scrutiny, however, it turned out that the documents were forgeries.

In addition to framing evaluations of the president in terms of some criteria rather than others, the media also frames individual issues in certain terms.[133] Once again, the media is not an agent of the White House. For example, the media framed the issue in the debate over President Obama's health-care reform proposal in 2009–2010 as one of strategy and conflict between the president and his opponents rather than emphasizing the consequences of the issue for the nation. Thus, the media did not mirror the president's attempts to frame the issue.[134] In addition, public support for rebuilding the health-care system varied in tandem with changes in media coverage.[135] In general, the media's focus on political conflict and strategy elevates the prominence of political wheeling and dealing in individuals' evaluations of political candidates and policy proposals.[136]

The ideologically driven cable news channels, especially Fox and MSNBC, pose additional challenges for the president. They frame issues in a fashion that is consonant with their underlying principles and provide greatly different accounts of the same events. They denounce bipartisanship and compromise, intensifying motivated reasoning and polarizing their audiences.[137] All this makes it more difficult for the president to present his message in terms that favor his position.

Public Knowledge and Attitudes

Because people receive most of their information on public affairs from the media, it is likely that the media will have a significant influence on the public's knowledge of and views about public policies. Research has found that people are frequently *misinformed* (as opposed to uninformed) about policy, and the less they know, the more confidence they have in their beliefs. Thus, they resist correct factual information. Even when presented with factual information, they resist changing their opinions, including those that were the objects of elite framing.[138]

In recent years, there has been an explosion of media outlets that offer news in a variety of formats and with a variety of viewpoints. We have seen that different news sources provide different levels of information. Unsurprisingly, the media can have a significant influence on what people know.[139] Regular viewers of Fox News were far more likely than viewers of other cable news channels to believe the false claim that President Obama's health-care reform contained "death panels"[140] and that President Obama was not a legal citizen of the United States.[141] Similarly, those who relied on Fox were most likely to hold the misperceptions that there were weapons of mass destruction in Iraq.[142] Fox and CBS, the same two networks whose viewers were most likely to hold misperceptions, had the highest percentage of pro-war commentators on its prime-time evening broadcasts.[143] In addition, the more attention viewers reported giving to Fox News, the higher their levels of misperception. Differences in coverage of the aftermath of the war affected beliefs about whether the effort in Iraq was progressing well or poorly.[144]

There is also evidence that political talk radio, which is overwhelming conservative, misinforms listeners and influences their attitudes,[145] and watching Fox News directly causes a substantial rightward shift in viewers' attitudes.[146] Newspaper candidate endorsements can affects voters' preferences.[147]

Recently, there has been increased attention to the "soft news" found in network news magazines, entertainment news magazines, tabloid news magazines, and talk shows. For audiences who are relatively uninterested in politics and who tune in primarily for entertainment, soft news increases their attentiveness to, and to a smaller degree their knowledge about, some high-profile political issues, including foreign policy crises, that involve scandal, violence, heroism, and other forms of sensational human drama that are amenable to framing as dramatic human-interest stories. One study found that those who consume soft news are more likely to oppose proactive or interventionist foreign policies. It also found that watching soft news affected vote choices in the 2000 presidential election.[148]

Limiting the President's Options

If the media affect mass attitudes about the importance of issues and the president's handling of them, the president has a strong incentive to address those issues—to put them on his agenda. Analysts have found that even in foreign policy, the media more often influence the president's agenda rather than the other way around.[149] (There are, of course, important exceptions, such as health care in 1993–1994.)[150] Former secretary of state James Baker argued that media coverage of issues creates powerful new imperatives for prompt action, making it more difficult for the president to engage in world affairs selectively.[151] This pressure may force presidents to issue policy statements or send troops when they would prefer to let situations develop or encourage other nations to deal with a problem. Bill Clinton complained that television coverage of Bosnia was "trying to force me to get America into a war."[152] In fact, the president did respond to images of atrocities in Haiti, Bosnia, and Kosovo.[153]

Colin Powell recalled, "The world had a dozen other running sores that fall [1992], but television hovered over Somalia and wrenched our hearts, night after night, with images of people starving to death before our eyes." Scenes of children starving in Somalia pressured the United States to send in armed forces to maintain peace and deliver food to the hungry. Things changed after eighteen soldiers were killed in Somalia, however. When scenes of an American soldier being dragged through the streets of Mogadishu were shown on television, Powell reflected, "We had been drawn into this place by television images, now we were being repelled by them." Television coverage now forced President Clinton to begin a troop withdrawal.[154]

Television coverage may limit the president's options even during a crisis. Pictures of Iraqi troops retreating from Kuwait on the "Highway of Death" created an impression of a bloodbath and thus influenced President Bush's decision to end the Gulf War. Bush himself described the "undesirable public and political baggage [that came from] all those scenes of carnage" appearing on television.[155] Similarly, during the 1990 invasion of Panama, the press noticed that a radio tower was standing near the center of Panama City. Reports of the tower led policy makers to order its destruction, although it had no value to the enemy.[156]

Undermining the President

Presidents need public understanding of the difficulty of their job and the nature of the problems they face. The role of the press here can be critical. Watching television news seems to do little to inform viewers about public affairs; reading the printed media is more useful. This may be because reading requires more active cognitive processing of information than watching television and because more information is presented in the newspapers.

We have seen that press coverage of the president is often superficial, over-simplified, and overblown, thus providing the public with a distorted picture of White House activities. This trivialization of the news drowns out the coverage of more important matters, often leaving the public ill informed about matters with which the president must deal (ranging from negotiations over international trade to funding Social Security benefits). The underlying problems that the president must confront may be largely ignored. The preoccupation of the press with personality, drama, and the results of policies does little to help the public appreciate the complexity of presidential decision making, the trade-offs involved in policy choices, and the broad trends outside the president's control. Instead, illustrations of international conflict—scenes of combat or demonstrations, for example—may become the essence of the issue in the public's mind.

In chapter 6, we saw that the president's access to the media is at least a potential advantage in influencing public opinion. However, the president has to compete with other media priorities while attempting to lead the public. The television networks created distractions during President Clinton's 1997 State of the Union message when they delivered the news of the verdict in the civil suit against O. J. Simpson *during his speech*, and the front page of the *Washington Post* the next day led with the story on Simpson, not the story on the president.

Press focus on the president has disadvantages as well. It inevitably leaves the impression that the president *is* the federal government and is crucial to our prosperity and happiness. This naturally encourages the public to focus its expectations on the White House. Another problem arises from the national frame of reference provided by a truly mass media and the media's penchant for linking coverage of even small matters with responses from the president or presidential spokespersons. Media coverage affects how people attribute blame to the president.[157] This is one reason voters regularly punish presidents for events that are not closely connected to their responsibilities, such as the 2010 BP oil spill.

Commentary following presidential speeches and press conferences may influence what viewers remember and may affect their opinions.[158] Although the impact of commentary on presidential addresses and press conferences is unclear, it is probably safe to argue that it is a constraint on the president's ability to lead public opinion. In the words of observers David L. Paletz and Robert M. Entman,

> Critical instant analysis undermines presidential authority by transforming him from presenter to protagonist. . . . Credible, familiar, apparently disinterested newsmen and—women—experts too . . . comment on the self-interested performance of a politician. Usually the president's rhetoric is deflated, the mood he has striven to create dissipated.[159]

The increasing negativism of news coverage of presidents parallels the increasingly low opinions voters have of them. The media impugn the motives of presidents and presidential candidates and portray them as playing a "game" in which strategy and maneuvers, rather than the substance of public policy, are the crucial elements. This coverage fosters public cynicism and encourages citizens to view presidents and other political leaders in negative terms.[160] If politics is a game played by deceptive politicians, a person is less likely to be influenced by the president's arguments.

The framing of issues in terms of strategy and wheeling and dealing may also undermine efforts to change the status quo by highlighting the risk of deferring to people who engage in such maneuvering. In general, the media's focus on political conflict and strategy elevates the prominence of political wheeling and dealing in individuals' evaluations of policy proposals.[161]

Limits on Media Effects

While reviewing evidence of the impact of the media on public opinion concerning the president, it is important to keep in mind the significant limitations on this influence. Characteristics of readers and viewers—including lack of interest in the news, short attention spans, lack of reading ability, selective perception (especially for those who have well-developed political views), general lack of interest in politics, lack of attentiveness to the media when exposed to them, and forgetfulness—limit the impact of the media. Another limitation is the ability of people to reject or ignore evaluations (implicit or explicit) in stories, particularly evaluations that conflict with their own.[162]

The nature of the news message also affects the impact of the media, and the factors constraining its influence are many: the great volume of information available in the news; the limited time available in which to absorb it (especially for television viewers); the superficial coverage of people, events, and policies; the presentation of the news on television and in most newspapers in disconnected snippets; and the lack of guidance through the complexities of politics. As a result, people often do not understand the news and actually learn little in the way of specifics from it.

The lack of credibility of news sources among some readers and viewers further limits the impact of the media. Although people typically trust the media more than they trust Donald Trump, many believe that much of the news they see, hear, or read is biased.[163] Nearly a third of the public believe that traditional major TV and newspaper media outlets regularly report "fake news."[164]

Visuals may also distract from verbal messages. For example, Leslie Stahl of CBS News did a long report on Ronald Reagan during the 1984 presidential campaign in which she criticized him for deceiving the American people with public relations tactics. Instead of the complaints she expected from the White House, however, she received thanks. Reagan's press aides appreciated the pictures of the president campaigning and were not concerned with the journalist's scathing remarks.[165]

CONCLUSION

The mass media play a prominent role in the public presidency, providing the public with most of its information about the White House and mediating the president's communications with constituents. Presidents need the press in order to reach the public, and relations with the press are an important complement to the chief executive's efforts at leading public opinion. Through attempts to coordinate news, press conferences, and the provision of a wide range of services for the press, the White House tries to influence its portrayal in the news.

The president's press relations pose many obstacles to efforts to obtain and maintain public support. Although it is probably not true that press coverage of the White House is biased along partisan or ideological lines or toward or against a particular president, it frequently presents a distorted picture to the public and fails to impart an appropriate perspective from which to view and evaluate complex events. Moreover, presidents are continuously harassed by leaks to the press and are faced with superficial, oversimplified coverage that devotes little attention to substantive discussions of policies and often focuses on trivial matters. This type of reporting undoubtedly affects public perceptions of the president, usually in a negative way. It is no wonder that chief executives generally see the press as a hindrance to their efforts to develop appreciation for their performance and policies in the public.

It is clear that in relation to the press, presidents are facilitators rather than directors. They engage in a constant struggle with the press and cannot depend on it to stress what they feel is most important about their administration or provide favorable coverage in the stories it produces. Presidents vary in their success in using the media to promote their goals, but all are limited in doing so by the nature and independence of this "fourth branch of government."

Before ending this chapter, we feel it is important to put the subject in perspective. Americans benefit greatly from a free press, a fact that should not be forgotten as we examine the media's flaws. The mainstream media are much less biased than the heavily partisan newspapers that were typical early in the nation's history. The same press that provides superficial coverage of the presidency also alerts people to abuses of authority and efforts to mislead public opinion. Citizens successfully hold their government accountable when a robust opposition makes timely information accessible and a healthy media relays this information to the public.[166] For example, information in newspapers led those open to challenging President Bush on the Iraq War (Democrats and Independents) to oppose the war, despite the absence of strong antiwar messages from political elites.[167]

Clearly, the press is an essential pillar in the structure of a free society. Moreover, perhaps the fundamental reason that press coverage is much less than its critics would like it to be is that it must appeal to the general public. If the public, or a sizable segment thereof, demands more substance from the mass media, it undoubtedly will receive it. In short, although mass-media coverage of the presidency is often poor, it could be much worse, and it is probably more or less what the public desires. Thus, the media reflect, as well as influence, American society.

DISCUSSION QUESTIONS

1. It is common to criticize the media for providing the American people with superficial coverage of presidents and their policies. What should the balance be between "hard news" on public policy and human-interest stories such as scandals and personal conflicts? Can the media educate a public that prefers superficial coverage?
2. How can we identify bias when we see it? Were the media biased in covering the various charges of misdeeds levied against President Clinton, the opposition to George W. Bush's invasion of Iraq, or President Trump's frequent false statements?
3. Journalists have become more active in interpreting stories for their viewers and readers rather than depending on those they interview to set the tone for their stories. Is the public better served by this approach to journalism?

WEB EXERCISES

1. Read some White House press releases and briefings for reporters at https://www.whitehouse.gov/briefing-statements. Notice the give-and-take between the press secretary and the journalists. Is the press secretary trying to "spin" the news? Are the questions the reporters are asking fair?
2. Go to http://www.journalism.org/, a site of the Pew Research Center. Use the stories and data there to determine which news sources people use. How does this usage vary by age? Are these sources sufficient to fully inform people about government and public policy? How much bias do people see in news coverage? How are these perceptions related to party identification?

SELECTED READINGS

Baum, Matthew A., and Philip B. K. Potter. *War and Democratic Constraint: How the Public Influences Foreign Policy*. Princeton, NJ: Princeton University Press, 2015.

Cohen, Jeffrey E. *The Presidency in the Era of 24-Hour News*. Princeton, NJ: Princeton University Press, 2008.

——. *Going Local: Presidential Leadership in the Post-Broadcast Age*. New York: Cambridge University Press, 2010.

Eshbaugh-Soha, Matthew, and Jeffrey S. Peake. *Breaking through the Noise: Presidential Leadership, Public Opinion, and the News Media*. Stanford, CA: Stanford University Press, 2011.

Farnsworth, Stephen J., and S. Robert Lichter. *The Nightly News Nightmare*, 3rd ed. Lanham, MD: Rowman & Littlefield, 2011.

Feldman, Stanley, Leonie Huddy, and George E. Marcus. *Going to War in Iraq: When Citizens and the Press Matter*. Chicago, IL: University of Chicago Press, 2015.

Hallin, Daniel C. *The "Uncensored War": The Media and Vietnam*. New York: Oxford University Press, 1986.

Kumar, Martha Joynt. *Managing the President's Message: The White House Communications Operation*. Baltimore, MD: Johns Hopkins University Press, 2007.

8

The Structure of the Presidency

The West Wing of the White House, the center of presidential governing.

The president is not the presidency. Although the president sits at the apex of the executive branch and is formally responsible for almost everything the federal government does, the job is clearly impossible for one person to do alone. No individual could conceivably understand all of the issues a president must address, make and communicate policy decisions to the rest of government, or monitor the vast executive branch without a substantial amount of help. The president (an individual) relies on a large and complex set of organizations comprising the *presidential institution* to effectuate the duties and powers of the office.

By the first part of the twentieth century, chief executives needed their own specialized institutional capability to oversee the executive branch. The story of that growth parallels the growth of presidential power generally. Today, the presidential instruments are the Executive Office of the President and the White House Office, two large and complex institutions in their own right, which extend the president's reach at the same time as they pose their own problems of control.

Presidency scholars debate the best way to approach the office: Should we focus on the individual who happens to be president at any given time? Or should we focus on the institutions in which the president is embedded, which provide the capacity to carry out the functions assigned by the constitution, demanded by the public, and required by other governmental actors? Which gives us more insight into what presidents do: a president's psychological orientation and decision-making style, or the people around the president who provide advice, filter information, and constrain presidential action?

A close examination of the presidential institution allows us to look at regular processes and activities that occur in different presidencies, which are themselves the results of institutional structures and can give us insight into how presidents make decisions and how they carry out the powers and duties of the office. Institutions empower by extending the reach of a president's effective authority and facilitating good decision-making practices. Institutions also constrain by enforcing standards and norms that channel the behavior of individuals and by regularizing the activities that take place within them.

THE DEVELOPMENT OF A PRESIDENTIAL INSTITUTION

A working definition of an "institution" is an organization of individuals that carries out regular functions and that has a set of rules or norms. (A norm establishes expectations of how people *should* behave, enforced with informal sanctions rather than formal discipline.)[1] Business corporations, government bureaucracies, the military, Congress, and universities are examples of large and complex institutions. Each is organized to carry out a set of functions, has a boundary that distinguishes between those inside the institution and those on the outside, and consists of people who operate according to the institution's rules or norms. We can further differentiate the internal organization of these institutions by noting that the individuals within them will have specialized functions. Institutions tend to have an internal hierarchy, which often takes the form of a pyramid with one person or a few people at the top and larger levels below, with the larger tiers involved in the most routine tasks. Authority tends to increase as one moves up the hierarchy.

More important than what institutions are is what they do: they create efficiencies in carrying out large-scale tasks, which makes it easier for groups of individuals to achieve goals than if the same people were relying on individual agreements negotiated one at a time to achieve the same goals, or if a single person tried to carry out every function.[2] Political institutions—a term often synonymous with government agencies—help individuals carry out the functions of government, everything from drafting legislation, awarding military contracts, collecting intelligence, and delivering social security checks. What makes institutions efficient is, in theory, the ability to carry out these functions on a routine basis.

As we shall see, the presidential institution developed over time, in response to the demands placed on presidents and their need to exert control over what the executive branch did. Presidents seek this control because they are held responsible for most of what government does and because it gives them more opportunity to apply their own vision of what government *should* do.

Early History

The Constitution did not explicitly provide for an executive branch administrative structure. There is no mention of a presidential staff, the cabinet, or any specific agencies. Delegates at the Constitutional Convention considered different structures of presidential advice, ranging from an advisory council to assist with appointments, a multiple executive, to Gouverneur Morris's proposal of a "Council of State—composed of the Chief Justice and the heads of [departments] to which the president could submit any matter for discussion."[3] Article II contains only an oblique reference to an administrative hierarchy, giving the president the authority to demand the opinions of subordinate officials in writing.

In the early years of the Republic, the central government (here, defined as people working in the seat of government in the executive departments) was tiny. In 1792, the central staff of the Department of State consisted of thirteen people: the Secretary (Jefferson), five clerks, a translator, a messenger, and five diplomatic officials. Treasury was larger, with roughly ninety-five people, almost all of whom were clerks apart from about seven top staff.[4] In 1801, the entire executive branch consisted of 3,000 employees, but only about 150 were in the departments. The rest were deployed around the country as revenue collectors, customs officials, postmasters and postal workers, territorial officials, district attorneys, and federal marshals.[5] At that size, a president might expect to be able to review most written communications with his senior cabinet appointees, but even then it turned out to be difficult.

The informality of presidentially managed administrative arrangements reflected the limited scale of government activity, the available technologies, and the Framer's concept of "administration." To a contemporary observer administration has a much more formal meaning, but in Washington's time concepts such as "bureaucracy," "standard operating procedures," or "public administration" did not yet exist in the United States. Early government officials "found nothing of the books of their time to guide them."[6] Communication, travel, and record-keeping technologies were in their infancy. "The art of organizing, coordinating, and directing the work of many individuals toward a single end was in fact a 'mystery'."[7]

The basic questions of government administration were similar to what they are now: who controls whom, how is that control exercised, and to what end? George Washington is given credit for establishing a system based on competence, integrity, and deliberation. Still, there were conflicts over of who was to direct executive branch officials, although the intensity of these conflicts was limited by the government's narrow scope. The government did not provide services, administer programs, distribute benefits, or even operate large centralized organizations. Its day-to-day functions focused on mundane matters such as "[land] offices, post offices, and customhouses."[8]

Delegation was uneven: although Washington allowed his department heads to run their agencies as they saw fit, he remained immersed in details, signing individual building contracts and reviewing and approving virtually every personnel decision or document that left the president's office. Washington circulated drafts of important communications, requested information and opinions about policy, issued directives, approved plans, and expressed frustration with the mass of documents and correspondence that he had to deal with. Within months of taking office, he "complained that he had no leisure to read or answer the dispatches that were pouring in upon him from all quarters."[9] Later presidents also protested the minutiae that took up much of their time. James Monroe asked for additional staff in 1825, noting that routine administrative duties prevented him from attending to "matters of higher importance." Congress ignored his request.[10]

The First Presidential Assistants

It is commonly believed that Congress did not provide money for any presidential staff until the 1850s, but that is not entirely accurate. Beginning with the first appropriations for the president in 1789, Congress intended that presidential compensation—paid in a lump sum of $25,000 and not described as a "salary"—would also be used to pay expenses and hire clerks. The reason for the lump sum rather than something more specific was constitutional deference: legislators believed that designating funding for staff or itemizing appropriations would infringe on presidential discretion.[11] Washington hired his nephew Lawrence Lewis as a clerk, paying him out of his own pocket (one reason the distinction between total presidential compensation and presidential salary weakened).

Congress appropriated money for a small dedicated presidential staff in 1857, funding a private secretary, a White House steward, and a messenger. This did little to ease the burdens of administration, as the jobs were considered menial and presidents had trouble filling them. If anything, the quality of the secretaries actually employed by presidents declined once Congress formally recognized the need for a staff. Presidential aides of the era were frequently beset by scandal or were incompetent.[12]

The presidential secretary's role began to expand with the administration of Chester Arthur (1881–1885). Theodore Roosevelt's principal aide, William Loeb Jr., began to deal with the press on a regular basis. Woodrow Wilson's secretary, Joseph Tumulty, controlled access to the president and functioned as a scheduler, political adviser, administrative manager, and public relations aide.

The number of presidential assistants rose during the early part of the twentieth century. Whereas Benjamin Harrison (1889–1893) could place his entire staff on the second floor of the White House, near his own living quarters, William McKinley (1897–1901) constructed a separate group of offices outside the mansion for the president's staff. When the West Wing was renovated and expanded in 1909, the president's aides came to occupy an even larger space near the president's new Oval Office. Presidential staff took on some of the characteristics of the modern White House. The staff began to specialize, with presidents beginning to rely on a single person as liaison to the press or as a key political advisor, a practice that become more formalized beginning with Hoover in the late 1920s.[13]

Evolution of the Cabinet as an Advisory Body

Without a staff, the natural locus of presidential administration was initially the heads of government agencies. The "cabinet" is a term without a precise legal definition, with the meaning more a matter of custom than formality. Nowhere mentioned in the Constitution, the cabinet has come to denote the heads of major executive departments (which are specified in federal law),[14] who collectively provide institutional support for presidential direction of executive branch activities.

There are cases where these secretaries have special legal status, as in the Presidential Succession Act or the Twenty-Fifth Amendment,[15] but the cabinet has "no institutional life apart from the president . . . no legalized group prerogatives, and no collective decision-making authority."[16] There are no meetings, agendas, or decision times other than what the president decides on, no requirement that the president solicit or listen to its advice.

With the 1789 establishment of the first executive departments—the Departments of Treasury, War, and Foreign Affairs—and the appointment of an Attorney General (a separate Department of Justice was not created until 1870), Washington had an able group that included Alexander Hamilton (Treasury), Henry Knox (War), Thomas Jefferson (Foreign Affairs), Edmund Randolph (Attorney General), and Samuel Osgood (Postmaster General). Washington regarded them as presidential assistants as much as subordinates[17] and frequently turned to them for advice. By 1792 meetings were a regular feature of Washington's administration: he convened his cabinet forty-nine times in 1793 and twenty-nine times in 1794 to "request advice . . . build consensus among his secretaries or provide political cover for potentially controversial policy."[18]

Much of this reliance was pragmatic as well as deferential to constitutional boundaries. A president needed informed advice; the question was, who was in a position to provide it? Congress was, Washington concluded, unsuited to the task. An attempt in the summer of 1789 to discuss a treaty on the floor of the Senate went badly, as senators refused to offer any advice. "No Chief Executive would ever again come before Congress for purposes of direct dialogue or inquiry."[19] The Courts were similarly unavailable, as the Supreme Court declared in 1793 that it would not issue advisory opinions or consult on constitutional questions.

Subsequent presidents continued to rely on cabinet deliberations for advice and policy recommendations. For the next 140 years, the cabinet functioned as the president's major advisory body for both foreign and domestic affairs, with positions on controversial proposals thrashed out at cabinet meetings. Presidents also used their cabinets to exercise influence on Capitol Hill. The personal relationships among the individual secretaries and members of Congress frequently put the cabinet officials in a better position than the president to promote the administration's legislative goals. Strong cabinets and weak presidents characterized executive advisory relationships during most of the nineteenth century.

But the significance of the cabinet eventually declined, as other institutions (especially political parties) became more important and pulled cabinet secretaries in different directions and as more specialized White House staffs reduced the need for cabinet advice.

Conflicting Loyalties

Cabinet secretaries often had conflicting loyalties, between the president (to whom they answered formally), Congress (which provided budgets and defined agency missions), and other constituencies (who may have supported their appointment or who benefited from the agency mission). Throughout most of the nineteenth century, Congress, not the president, dominated government administration. Statutes specified departmental structures, jurisdictions, staffing levels, and even operating procedures. Presidents exercised little oversight. Even if presidents were so inclined, they could not do much, as they simply did not have the administrative capabilities or staff to perform the monitoring and supervisorial tasks necessary for effective control.

The autonomy of the departments contributed to the influence of the secretaries who headed them. Because the department heads were the president's principal advisers, they exercised considerable influence over designing the administration's goals and in mobilizing congressional support. With the exception of the Jefferson, Jackson, and Lincoln administrations, the executive branch consisted of strong department secretaries and weak presidents.

The Decline of the Cabinet

This pattern began to change at the outset of the twentieth century as a consequence of the president's growing influence. As that influence increased, the potency of the department secretaries, individually and collectively, began to decline. They lost their privileged position between president and Congress, and their support of administration proposals became less critical to the president's legislative success. The president's efforts to shape public opinion and mobilize partisan support, evident during the administrations of Theodore Roosevelt and Woodrow Wilson, strengthened the chief executive's hand in dealing with Congress. Beginning in 1921, the power to affect executive branch decision making through the budget process also reduced the importance of department secretaries.

As a consequence of these developments, cabinet meetings became more of a forum for discussion than a mechanism for formulating administration policy. Franklin Roosevelt even trivialized the forum. His practice was to go around the table asking each participant what was on his or her mind. Frequently after the session, some secretaries remained to discuss their important business alone with the president without others in attendance. Truman continued Roosevelt's emphasis on one-to-one relationships with his department heads rather than calling on them collectively for advice.

The cabinet enjoyed a resurrection under President Dwight Eisenhower, meeting 230 times during his eight years in office. As president, Eisenhower presided over many of these meetings and used his presence to help forge a consensus on major administration policies and programs. After Eisenhower's presidency, the cabinet functioned less and less as a policy-making or advisory body. Presidents continued to meet with their cabinets, in part because they were expected to do so, but the meetings decreased in frequency.

The increasingly technical nature of policy making contributed to the cabinet's decline; cabinet secretaries are rarely versed in the intricacies of issues outside their substantive policy areas. At best, the need for specialized knowledge limited participation at cabinet meetings to the few individuals who were informed and competent; at worst, it reduced the level of the discussion to the lowest common denominator. Increasing pressure from outside groups has encouraged secretaries to assume more of an advocacy role for their departments (referred to as "going native").[20] Their need to advocate departmental interests and attend to their administrative responsibilities makes it more difficult for them to see problems from the president's perspective or to recommend solutions that accord with the president's priorities rather than their own.

Donald Trump's cabinet appointments highlight the key problem in relying on the cabinet for advice: how to ensure that secretaries advocate policies that are consistent with the president's agenda. Unlike previous presidents, Trump came to office with no government experience and few connections to existing political networks. As a result, most of his cabinet nominations were people with whom he did not have longstanding relationships, were made to satisfy the demands of important political groups and constituencies, and went to people who often had their own ambitions and policy agendas. Secretary of State Rex Tillerson came to Trump's attention during the transition, when former Secretary of State Condoleezza Rice and former Secretary of Defense Robert Gates recommended him. Tom Price, Secretary of Health and Human Services, had little personal history with the president and was much more closely aligned with Vice President Mike Pence, with whom he served in Congress. Attorney General Jeff Sessions and Treasury Secretary Steve Mnuchin became close to Trump early in the campaign and were among the first prominent figures to support him. By mid-2019, Tillerson, Price, and Sessions were gone, along with Secretary of Interior Ryan Zinke, EPA Administrator Scott Pruitt, Secretary of Defense Jim Mattis, Secretary of Homeland Security John Kelly (as well as his successor, Kirstjen Nielsen), Secretary of Veterans Affairs David Shulkin, and UN Ambassador Nikki Haley. It was a historically unprecedented turnover.[21]

Despite the decline in the importance of the cabinet, presidents still must maintain ongoing channels of communication to and from the heads of the executive departments. An office of cabinet affairs within the White House facilitates this flow of information and coordinates the involvement of cabinet secretaries in promoting administration policies in Congress. Table 8.1 lists the major departments, employment in fiscal year 2017, and expenditure levels for fiscal year 2018.

Table 8.1 Cabinet Departments

Department	Year Created	President	Employees FY 2017	Outlays FY 2018 (in billions of dollars)
State	1789	Washington	10,166	26.4
Treasury	1789	Washington	78,734	629.5
Interior	1849	Polk	49,721	13.2
Agriculture	1862	Lincoln	73,231	136.7
Justice	1870	Grant	111,778	34.5
Commerce (formerly part of Department of Commerce and Labor, 1903)	1913	Wilson	35,757	8.6
Labor (formerly part of Department of Commerce and Labor, 1903)	1913	Wilson	14,424	39.6
Defense (consolidated Department of War, 1789, and Department of the Navy, 1798)	1947	Truman	676,840*	656.1
Housing and Urban Development	1965	Johnson	7,697	54.7
Transportation	1966	Johnson	53,568	78.5
Energy	1977	Carter	14,249	27.0
Health and Human Services (formerly part of Department of Health, Education, and Welfare, 1953)	1980	Carter	65,866	1,120.5
Education (formerly part of Department of Health, Education, and Welfare, 1953)	1980	Carter	3,842	63.7
Veterans Affairs	1988	Reagan	342,111	178.5
Homeland Security	2002	Bush	173,326	68.4

* Defense Department employment includes active-duty military personnel.
Sources: Employees—Office of Personnel Management, Sizing up the Executive Branch: Fiscal Year 2017, February 2018; Outlays—Budget of the U.S. Government Fiscal Year 2020, Historical Tables, Table 4.1.

FROM THE BUREAU OF THE BUDGET TO THE EOP

By the beginning of the twentieth century the president's management task was vastly more complicated than it had been a hundred years earlier. The population had grown from 5.3 million in sixteen states in 1800 to 76.2 million and forty-five states in 1900. The economy had moved from an agrarian and mercantile footing to an industrial one. Government had also grown. In 1881 the federal government had 51,000 civilian employees and spent $292 million (or about $7 billion in 2017 dollars). By 1901, the number of employees had grown nearly fivefold to 239,000 and spending rose to $525 million (or $15 billion in 2017 dollars).[22] Congress was firmly in control of the administrative apparatus, much more so than the president, but the rapidly growing capacity of the government pushed presidents to find new ways of asserting their authority over it, often clashing with Congress in the process.

The rise of the budget power, and the establishment of the first major institution of *presidential control*—the Bureau of the Budget (BOB), created in 1921—show how important administrative capacity is to presidents.[23] According to the influential congressional scholar James Sundquist, "the modern presidency . . . began on June 10, 1921, the day that President Harding signed the Budget and Accounting Act," creating the BOB.[24]

The Budget Power

It is a truism about government that virtually everything it does involves spending money. Deciding what the government will spend money *on* is synonymous with deciding what the government will *do*, whether the issue is building up a defense capability or creating an office to enforce civil rights laws. Historically, Congress was completely dominant in budget matters, controlling the purse strings and setting budgets for each department, often negotiating directly with agency officials and not even bothering to involve the president. Agency officials were largely responsible for drafting their own budget requests, which were forwarded to the Treasury Department, thus providing at least the potential for presidential direction. Yet all Treasury did was compile the requests and send them to Congress without revision. This routine made department heads "ministerial agents of Congress rather than representatives of the President."[25]

It was a dysfunctional system that rendered the president superfluous, and it created budget problems since there was no effort to coordinate programs or make sure that spending was related to revenue. Agencies frequently ran out of money mid-year and had to ask Congress for additional appropriations. Overlapping programs and inefficiencies abounded.

Theodore Roosevelt tried to assert control over budget requests, prohibiting agency employees from lobbying Congress for increased expenditures unless the communication went through the agency head. Taft prohibited executive branch employees from responding to congressional information requests without department approval (Congress responded by cutting agency budgets). This constituted an early form of *central clearance*, or routing information and requests through the presidential office for review and approval, or at least making sure that the president knew what the agencies were doing.

President William Howard Taft advocated an "executive budget" in which the president would coordinate agency budgets requests, have the authority to alter those requests, and exercise control over what the executive branch presented to

Congress as an overall budget. Legislators resisted, seeing this as a direct threat to Congress' constitutional authority to make appropriations and undermining their ability to control executive branch activities. Taft created a presidential commission in 1910, the Commission on Economy and Efficiency, which recommended an executive budget controlled by the president. Over congressional objections, Taft submitted such a budget request in 1912; Congress ignored it, but the foundation had been laid for a future president to try again.

The Bureau of the Budget

World War I presented that opportunity. Government spending rose from $712 million in 1916 to $18.25 billion in 1919 (a twenty-six-fold increase), and a 1916 budget surplus of $48 million turned into to a 1919 deficit of $13.4 billion. These changes drove home the reality that existing budget practices were inadequate. Congress responded by passing a Budget Act in 1921, creating the Bureau of the Budget (BOB) in the Treasury Department (as well as the office of the Comptroller General with the authority to audit government finances). Agencies now submitted their budget requests to the BOB, which had the authority to make revisions and recommend administrative efficiencies.[26] For the first time, the president had a dedicated staff with the ability to review and prepare an overall federal budget. The first director, Charles Dawes, quickly established the bureau as an agent of presidential influence, using his staff of forty-five to extend the bureau's reach. Within a few years, the BOB was

White House Historical Association

Taft's original Oval Office in the middle of the new West Wing (White House Museum), which was constructed when the West Wing was renovated in 1909. The museum site writes, "an oval office may have symbolized his view of the modern-day president. Taft intended to be the center of his administration, and by creating the Oval Office in the center of the West Wing, he was more involved with the day-to-day operation of his presidency than were his recent predecessors." http://www.whitehousemuseum.org/west-wing/oval-office-history.htm. FDR renovated the West Wing in 1933, moving the Oval Office to its current location in the southeast corner of the building.

reviewing legislation that had budgetary implications, executive orders, and agency recommendations about whether the president should sign enacted legislation.

The New Deal and the Brownlow Committee

Franklin D. Roosevelt's presidency and the expansion of federal government capacity during the New Deal permanently altered the president's administrative responsibilities. Government grew so large so quickly that it proved impossible for the White House to even keep track of what agencies were doing or what laws were in effect. In one infamous instance illustrating the administrative problem, the Justice Department prosecuted someone for violating a 1933 executive order limiting oil production without realizing that FDR had mistakenly issued another order that deleted enforcement provisions. Government attorneys recognized their mistake just before they were to appear at oral argument before the Supreme Court and had to drop the case.[27]

The administrative job, always difficult for presidents to do with a small staff, had become impossible. FDR relied on a number of White House assistants who were formally employees of executive branch agencies to help him. However, even this arrangement could not keep up with the workload. The government was too large, too complex, and too wide ranging to allow one person, operating without significant staff support, to oversee it. In an attempt to solve the increasingly difficult management problem, FDR created a new presidential commission to study administrative practices.

The President's Committee on Administrative Management was headed by Louis Brownlow and staffed by academics who studied public administration. The committee's key observation in its 1937 report captured the core of the problem: "The president needs help. His immediate staff assistance is entirely inadequate."[28] Noting that the president could not conceivably even monitor the entire federal government, much less direct it, the committee's observation was the same as "that made by President Monroe in 1825, [indicative] of the lack of any substantial progress in meeting the president's staffing needs in the previous 112 years."[29]

The Committee recommended the creation of a formal, dedicated, and permanent presidential staff, far beyond the clerical support that previous staffs had provided.

THE EXECUTIVE OFFICE OF THE PRESIDENT

FDR implemented the recommendation of the Brownlow Committee, creating the Executive Office of the President in 1939 and moving the Bureau of the Budget from the Treasury Department to the White House.[30] The EOP consisted initially of five units—the White House Office, the Bureau of the Budget, a Planning Board, and two departments for personnel management and record keeping. The president would have six administrative assistants. While the office has grown and sub-units have come and gone, the basic organizational characteristic of the EOP has remained the same: a White House Office with the closest presidential advisors, the budget bureau (which became the Office of Management and Budget in 1970), and other specialized units with focused responsibilities, such as the National Security Council (created in 1947) and the Council of Economic Advisors (created in 1946).

The importance of the EOP's creation cannot be overstated. "It is difficult to imagine," writes John Hart in his study of the presidency, "how the presidency could have survived as an effective institution in American government without [it]."[31] It fundamentally transformed the nature of presidential management and radically increased the ability of the White House to monitor executive branch activities, formulate policy, and centralize administration.

The principal objective of the EOP has always been to help presidents perform core presidential tasks, including those involved in their expanded policy-making and policy-implementation roles. The various offices in the EOP have not taken over the administrative responsibilities of the departments and agencies, although they do coordinate interagency projects and impose a presidential perspective on policy making and public relations. The EOP's functions are not exclusively executive, nor is it a single office, but its staffers do work for a single client—the president. Table 8.2 lists the current major units within the EOP and the number of employees for fiscal years 2018 to 2020.

The White House Office (WHO)

The White House Office comprises the staff closest and most accountable to the president. The internal structures and organization have taken regular form, although the specific arrangements vary according to presidential desires. Staff

Table 8.2 Executive Office of the President Staff Levels, 2018–2020

| | Full-Time Equivalents | | | |
| | | | FY 2020 Level | |
Components	FY 2018 Actuals	FY 2019 Estimate	FY 2020 Estimate	FY 2019 to FY 2020 Change
The White House Office	357	450	450	0
Executive Residence	75	96	96	0
Office of Administration	241	248	245	−3
National Security Council and Homeland Security Council	51	58	58	0
Council of Economic Advisers	23	28	28	0
Office of the Vice President	20	25	25	0
Office of Management and Budget	472	480	477	−3
Information Technology Oversight and Reform	124	108	69	−39
Office of National Drug Control Policy	65	65	60	−5
Intellectual Property Enforcement Coordinator	—	—	5	5
Office of Science and Technology Policy	19	33	30	−3
Office of the US Trade Representative	243	278	284	6
National Space Council	2	7	7	0
Council on Environmental Quality	13	24	24	0
Total	**1,705**	**1,900**	**1,858**	**−42**

Source: Executive Office of the President, *Fiscal Year 2020 Congressional Budget Submission*, p. 9.

include top-level advisors, policy and communications specialists, administrative support personnel, and informal advisors who may lack specific portfolios but remain influential. Few of these positions are required by law, and they have emerged because they serve vital functions. Presidents are free to create, abolish, alter, or reorganize most of the advisory units. Even more, presidents make their own decisions about how much deference or attention they will show toward advisors. (The Washington press corps pays close attention to who has the president's ear, who is in or out, and internal power struggles inside the White House.) At times, aides will disagree with each other, and it is left to the president to decide on a course of action. Some presidents are more receptive than others to advisory structures. Trump, by his own admission, trusts his "gut instincts" more than his aides and frequently goes against staff advice.[32] In May 2019, for example, he threatened tariffs on Mexican imports in response to border crossings against the advice of both Treasury Secretary Mnuchin and Special Trade Representative Robert Lighthizer.[33]

The functions of the staff may seem clear enough, in the abstract: assist the president with decision making through information and expertise; provide advice on policy and strategic matters; assist with the president's public leadership role by communicating decisions to the public and other governmental actors; forge relationships with other key institutions, especially Congress; and monitor implementation of presidential decisions throughout the rest of government. Some of this is high drama. However, most staff functions involve far more mundane matters of establishing priorities, analysis, monitoring, follow-up, coordinating the activities of multiple organizations and people, and all while dealing with an unpredictable environment.

In practice, though, these abstract ideals about process almost inevitably give way to the reality that no matter how a White House is organized (and, as we will see, there are some organizational practices that are more likely to facilitate good results than others), presidents and their staffs are often overwhelmed by the magnitude of the job. Trying to keep up with the endless stream of tasks and problems has been compared to holding back the tides, and staffers feel as if they are constantly reacting to events they cannot control. Being in the White House involves long hours, harsh scrutiny and criticism, intense pressure, and almost no margin for error. One account of the Clinton White House put it this way:

> Working for a president turns out to be a lot like looking directly into the sun: a great temptation but debilitating to anyone who tries. It is wrong . . . to think of the president and his staff as striving warriors or visionary leaders. Rather, they are better imagined in a defensive crouch, waiting for the next crisis to erupt and then scurrying to cope as best they can. The White House is a madhouse almost all the time.[34]

The White House Office, in theory, helps presidents avoid this and create order out of chaos. The following are major units inside the White House Office. All have subunits and internal complexity, with numerous lower level staff.

Chief of Staff

The informal organization and operation of Roosevelt's White House was a template for exercising personal control; it was a model that Truman continued. Eisenhower,

President Ronald Reagan with his White House leadership team
(the "Troika") in the Oval Office.

Courtesy Ronald Reagan Library

a career military officer, was used to having a chief of staff to relieve him of routine decisions and give him more time and greater flexibility. He believed that the president should set overall policy and then work behind the scenes to implement it.[35] As a consequence, he set up a more hierarchical staff and was the first to have a formal chief of staff to direct White House activities. As discussed below, Eisenhower also created several other staff structures that have endured.

The chief of staff runs the White House organization, at least administratively, and is typically first among equals.[36] The chief's job is, in a sense, "everything": to manage the overall operations of the White House Office (WHO), coordinate the activities of WHO units, resolve conflicts that do not require presidential attention, and protect the president's time and political interests. Contemporary presidents do not have the time to run the White House from inside the Oval Office, even if they had the inclination, and recent presidents who have tried—Jimmy Carter, most famously—realized that they cannot be everywhere or do everything, and therefore they *need* a chief of staff to perform most administrative and management functions. As Gerald Ford put it:

> I started out in effect not having an effective chief of staff and it didn't work. So anybody who doesn't have one and tries to run the responsibilities of the White House I think is putting too big a burden on the president himself. You need a filter, a person that you have total confidence in who works so closely with you that in effect he is almost an alter ego. I just can't imagine a president not having an effective chief of staff.[37]

Clinton also tried to do without a strong chief of staff, placing an old friend with no Washington experience, Mack McLarty, in the position. Characterized as an intentional installation of a "'weak' chief of staff . . . who did not have a mandate to crack the whip in the manner of most of his predecessors," McLarty presided over a White House so disorganized that the president replaced him with the much more experienced Leon Panetta (who had served in Congress and as Clinton's first director of the Office of Management and Budget). The White House operated much more smoothly as a result.[38]

One of the most important roles of the chief is to control access to the president and mange what gets to the president's desk. Often, chiefs of staff say that the most difficult and important part of their job is to say no, to be the "heavy" who does unpleasant tasks of insisting on order or imposing discipline. Good chiefs function as the president's *alter ego*, and their influence is a function of proximity to the president. They are effective only as long as they have the president's confidence, but they must also be willing to say "no" to the president.[39] Donald Trump's first chief of staff, Reince Priebus, lacked control over access and information and did not have Trump's confidence or trust. Few thought the White House ran smoothly (see box 8.1).

Box 8.1 ★ Donald Trump's Chiefs of Staff

The first iteration of Donald Trump's White House was highly decentralized. A senior advisor, senior policy advisor, counselor, chief strategist, communications director, strategic communications director, the National Infrastructure Council, the Office of Trade and Manufacturing Policy, Oval Office Operations, and Ivanka Trump all reported directly to the president, not to the White House chief of staff. There was little coordination to ensure that the different units were communicating or maintaining consistency with each other. It is little wonder that the White House was so chaotic, despite assurances from the president and spokespeople that everything was working smoothly. Chief of Staff Reince Priebus was never able to establish control of the organization, in large part because he lacked the authority to do so. Priebus was clearly outranked in status and influence by other members of the staff, particularly Ivanka Trump, Jared Kushner, and Kellyanne Conway.[40]

The costs of this organizational inefficiency eventually became too much to bear: "multiple staff divisions were slowing the development of the President's agenda, creating a wave of leaks to news organizations from one staff faction seeking to undermine others, all resulting in poor staff morale and contributing to a drop in his poll numbers."[41]

In July 2017, Trump dismissed Priebus and replaced him with Secretary of Homeland Security John F. Kelly. Kelly, a retired Marine Corps General, moved quickly to establish more order in the White House, insisting on exerting authority over hiring, information, and access to the president.[42] He reorganized the White House into a much more hierarchical structure, and required all White House personnel, even the president's family members, to go through him to get to the president. He imposed controls on the information flow to the president, requiring everything be reviewed by the chief of staff and staff secretary's office before going to the president.[43] The expectation was that his military background and reputation as someone who "won't suffer idiots and fools" would restore order to the White House.[44] Kelly removed a number of controversial White House aides, including Stephen K. Bannon and Sebastian Gorka.

During his time, the retired four-star general had tried in vain to bring some discipline to a freewheeling White House, instituting tighter controls on who was

(continued)

Staff Secretary

The staff secretary, an office first created by Eisenhower, manages the paper flow in the White House (or in the contemporary context, the flow of information), distributes all documents or decisions to those officials whose input is needed, makes sure that the what the president sees is "ready for prime time" and that presidential

John F. Kelly (left), former Trump chief of staff, and Mick Mulvaney, Trump's acting chief of staff (as of 2019).

decisions are communicated to the appropriate staff for follow-up. Staff secretaries frequently define their role as "managing the president's in-box and out-box," coordinating the flood of paper and information that is "like trying to drink out of a fire hose."[50]

Doing the job often involves judgments about who is going to be involved in a decision as it moves through the staff and making sure that they are included as policies are formulated and documents distributed. In the George W. Bush and Obama Administrations, the staff secretary assembled a daily compilation of memos, papers, reports, travel schedules, and other information that staff used to keep track of who was doing what in the White House and where issues stood in the decision-making process.

Managing this might appear to be a trivial job, but it is sufficiently important that people who serve in it often move to other more senior positions in government; Richard Darman was Reagan's first staff secretary and later served as Director of the Office of Management and Budget; John Podesta served as staff secretary for Bill Clinton and later as chief of staff; Brett Kavanaugh was a staff secretary to George W. Bush, and became Trump's second Supreme Court appointment in 2018.

Trump's first staff secretary, Rob Porter, resigned after a year in the position, following allegations of domestic violence made by two of his ex-wives.[51]

Political and Strategic Advisors

A second important category consist of individuals on whom the president relies for overall advice on policy, strategy, or political matters. These individuals are usually selected for their policy expertise or because the president trusts them and has come to rely on their political judgment. Often these aides operate in the background; at other times, they can be high-profile and controversial. These staffers typically go by the title "Senior Advisor to the President," "Counselor," or some variant, and often have portfolios that cross policy or institutional lines.

Apart from individuals who head up specific White House offices, presidents are free to seek advice from anyone, and frequently rely on staff who operate peripherally to these more formal structures or in *ad hoc* groups outside of existing units. Woodrow Wilson relied heavily on Edward M. House, whom he first met only a year before becoming president. As a confidant, House became so close to Wilson that he became "a sort of assistant president" with influence "arguably greater than any single advisor has ever had on an American president."[52] FDR had a "Brain Trust," a group of academics who advised him on economic issues, and he continued to rely on outside advisors throughout his presidency. Clark Clifford served as Truman's White Counsel but advised the president on a wide range of policy issues, including diplomatic and foreign policy matters.

George W. Bush relied heavily on Karl Rove, a longtime campaign consultant who was the main strategist of Bush's 2000 and 2004 presidential election victories, as well as Karen Hughes, who had worked with Bush since his first campaign for governor of Texas in 1994 (she has been described as "the most powerful woman ever to serve in the White House"). Valerie Jarrett, who had known Obama for nearly two decades before his election, was one of a handful of Obama's senior advisors. Both George W. Bush and Barack Obama made extensive use of what are often termed "policy czars," with the use triggering a backlash among critics who argued that overreliance posed problems for separation of powers (as few of them required Senate confirmation).[53]

Donald Trump made a number of controversial advisory appointments to his top staff. He named Stephen K. Bannon, a founding member of the right-wing website Breitbart.com, as Chief Strategist and Senior Counselor to the President. Even more controversial was his installment of son-in-law Jared Kushner as Senior Advisor and daughter Ivanka as First Daughter and advisor. Critics argued that the appointments violated federal anti-nepotism laws that prohibited any public officials from hiring relatives, citing a 1967 law often portrayed as a reaction to John F. Kennedy naming his brother Robert Kennedy as attorney general.[54] The Department of Justice determined that the statute did not apply to the White House and that the president retained broad authority to make staff appointment without regard to limiting statutes.[55]

Communications and Press Office

The communications and press office is one of the most visible in the White House, presenting the administration's public face, usually in the form of a press secretary who gives frequent briefings to the White House press corps. Other staff, such as a communications director, develop overall press and public relations strategies and coordinate speeches and press appearances by presidential staff or cabinet secretaries.

This office has become vital to presidents and central to the function of public leadership. It is primarily engaged in "messaging": identifying effective strategies for presenting policies and strategies and forging relationships with reporters and media outlets in an effort to generate favorable coverage. Modern communications efforts extend well beyond traditional media (television and newspapers). The White House Office now includes staff dedicated to social media and digital media, and Trump is well known for using his private Twitter account (@realDonaldTrump) to reach the public, make presidential statements, and retweet favorable stories.

It is a difficult job: presidents often come to see their political problems as *communication* problems, holding this office responsible for bad press (which may reflect poor strategy, poor presidential decisions, or negative events). Sean Spicer, Trump's first press secretary, often frustrated reporters with evasive and nonresponsive answers and incurred the president's wrath for negative stories. After a few months giving press briefings, he stepped into the background, with Deputy Press Secretary Sarah Huckabee Sanders taking over the day-to-day briefings; she became press secretary in July 2017 when Spicer resigned after Trump brought in a new communications director, Anthony Scaramucci. Scaramucci lasted in the position for only a few days, and was fired after an incendiary interview with a reporter in which he blasted other White House staff.[56]

Sanders has had a contentious relationship with the press, harshly criticizing reporters and refusing to say whether she disagreed with the president's characterization of the press as the "enemy of the people."[57] She suspended the practice of daily White House press briefings, holding only two in the first half of 2019.

Legislative Affairs

A key function inside the White House is working with Congress, either on the president's policy priorities or influencing congressional action on other bills moving through the legislature. Although presidents can take substantial action on their own through unilateral powers or via existing regulatory procedures, large-scale policy change still requires congressional cooperation. At the beginning of an administration, legislative affairs staffers work closely with Senate committees on presidential nominations and confirmations.

Eisenhower was the first president to create a dedicated unit to handle legislative relations (originally called the Office of Congressional Relations). Since then, the office has become more specialized, with some staff devoted to the House, others the Senate, and still others to specific committees or bills as necessary.

Office of Cabinet Affairs

In an effort to coordinate agency activities, Eisenhower created the position of Cabinet Secretariat in 1954. Originally a mechanism for encouraging cabinet secretaries to work with each other,[58] its role has varied, from managing cabinet councils comprised of agency officials and organized by issue rather than agency to a mechanism for managing communications with department heads and monitoring department activities. Its size and importance has declined as the cabinet has become less important as a collective advisory body and policy work has moved to other specialized units. An official named the cabinet secretary typically heads the office.

White House Counsel

The White House Counsel provides legal advice to the president on all matters of White House concern. The counsel is not the president's personal lawyer but, rather, the legal advisor to the White House. Originally comprising a single person with no staff when it was created in 1943, the office began to grow in size and complexity during the Nixon administration, when White House Counsel John Dean hired several assistants as the Watergate scandal grew and Nixon faced impeachment. Until Nixon, White House counsels functioned less as the president's legal advisors than as all-purpose staff members. (During the Kennedy Administration, Theodore Sorensen held the position but was more involved with speechwriting and general policy advice than legal matters.)[59]

Occasionally the office becomes visible when a crisis hits the White House or the counsel becomes involved in controversial policy. One of Clinton's White House counsels, Bernard Nussbaum, was accused of blurring the distinction between advocacy for the presidency and functioning as Clinton's personal lawyer.[60] In January 2002, Alberto Gonzales Jr. advised George W. Bush that the Geneva Conventions on Prisoners of War did not apply to members of Al Qaeda or the Taliban, and he was involved in creating the warrantless National Security Agency surveillance program implemented shortly after 9/11.[61]

The office was in the news often during Donald Trump's first two years. Don McGahn, White House Counsel from Trump's inauguration to October 2018, was active in the nominations of Brett Kavanaugh and Neil Gorsuch to the Supreme Court. He also refused to carry out the president's order to fire Special Counsel Robert Mueller in June 2017; McGahn threatened to resign and additionally refused Trump's demands that he publicly deny press reports about the order to fire Mueller.[62] According to the *New York Times*, Trump wanted to prosecute Hillary Clinton and former FBI Director James Comey; McGahn told the president that the request could trigger "a range of consequences, including possible impeachment."[63]

Support Units

Several units within the White House Office provide ongoing administrative support for the president. Most of these are under the Office of Management and Administration, which handles the full range of services necessary for an organization as complicated as the White House to function: everything from records management and document preservation to staff travel and IT support. Although the Office of Management and Administration's work is often considered mundane, it fills a vital but unsung role. The job, a former head of the office explained, "is like being captain of a minesweeper. As long as you're doing your job, nobody knows you're there. You make one mistake, and there's a hell of an explosion."[64]

Administrative support extends well beyond the White House, with many departments and agencies throughout the government contributing to the everyday needs of presidents, vice presidents, and their spouses, their official residences, and their duties and activities. These include the Department of Defense—the White House Communications Agency (secure communications), the US Air Force (air transportation), the US Army (explosive detection and ground transportation), and the US Navy (helicopter transportation, Marine guards, food, medical facilities, and Camp David, the presidential retreat in Maryland); the General Services Administration (buildings and grounds); the National Park Service (visitors and the fine arts collection); the National Archives (custody of official documents); the Secret Service in the Department of Homeland Security (protection of the president, vice president, and their families as well as those of former presidents); the Commission on White House Fellowships; the US Postal Service; and the State Department (official visits and receptions for foreign dignitaries).

Discretionary Units

The structure of the White House Office is not fixed. The main units have remained stable, but new offices come and go according to presidential style and policy needs or to demonstrate a symbolic commitment to an issue. John F. Kennedy convened a special Executive Committee to advise him during the Cuban Missile Crisis, consisting of "his most trusted advisors" from throughout the government, and accepted counsel from former secretaries of State and Defense.[65] George W. Bush created the Office of Homeland Security in October 2001 as a coordinating office to assist with overall domestic security after 9/11 (at the time there were nearly two dozen agencies throughout the executive branch involved in domestic security spread out over multiple departments).[66] Although key security functions were combined when Congress created the Department of Homeland Security in 2002, the Homeland Security Council still exists as a unit within the EOP. Bush also created the White House Office of Faith-Based and Community Initiatives (renamed the Office of Faith-Based and Neighborhood Partnerships by Barack Obama) a few days into his first term.[67] The goal of this office was to expand the availability of federal funding to religious organizations engaged in social welfare.

Obama created the White House Rural Council in 2011 to develop strategies for improving services and economic policies serving rural communities. Donald Trump dissolved it in April 2017, replacing it with an interagency task force that operated outside of the White House. Trump established several units of his own, including the National Infrastructure Council, the White House Office of American Innovation, and the Office of Trade and Manufacturing Policy

Domestic Policy Units

In addition to these administrative units, other policy-specific advisory offices in the White House Office provide substantive policy formulation, developing broad agendas, crafting specific proposals, and evaluating plans originating in agencies. These structures have become more specialized and institutionalized and are now firmly entrenched in the White House. We discuss them in more detail in chapter 13.

The Office of Management and Budget (OMB)

While the White House Office comprises the president's closest staff, other units in the Executive Office have specialized (and often statutory) functions that assist with monitoring executive branch activities and coordinating policy. Most are congressionally established and cannot be eliminated by presidential action, though presidents are not obligated to pay attention to their work or policy recommendations.

Created in 1970 after Richard Nixon added functions to the Bureau of the Budget and renamed it to recognize its broader responsibilities, the OMB is a vital tool of presidential control. It is the largest unit in the Executive Office, with a staff of about 480 compared to about 450 in the White House Office. Apart from about twenty to twenty-five political appointees, OMB staff are career employees who carry over from one administration to the next.[68]

The most visible of the OMB's functions is the preparation of the president's annual budget request, a continuation of what the BOB did. About eighteen months before a fiscal year begins, the OMB sends initial budget guidance to agencies, outlining presidential priorities. Over the next eight months, agencies submit their requests, which are reviewed by the OMB for consistency with presidential policy, with the president (or White House staff) making final decisions about funding levels. The office ultimately produces the budget document, which is sent to Congress and becomes the starting point for legislative action (see chapter 13 for more on the budget process).

The OMB also plays a central role in regulatory review—analyzing the costs and benefits of federal regulations that agencies plan to issue. This function became increasingly important in 1981, when Reagan issued an executive order requiring agencies to justify new rules by showing that the benefits exceeded costs. Barack Obama ordered the OMB to oversee and reevaluate existing regulatory authority. Donald Trump announced an intention to extend OMB cost-benefit requirements to all executive branch departments, even independent agencies that to date have had more flexibility in proposing rules.[69]

Other responsibilities include issuing guidance on management and efficiency, on information technology and security, and on federal government procurement practices.

The National Security Council (NSC)

Responsibility for national security and foreign policy is spread across multiple federal agencies: the Departments of Defense and State, a myriad of intelligence agencies, the military services, and specialized offices in other federal agencies such as Energy or Treasury (discussed in more detail in chapter 14). The National Security Council (NSC), created in 1947, is designed to help the president integrate and coordinate national security policy and provide independent advice. It is "the highest coordinative and advisory body within the Government in this area."[70] The head of the NSC, formally the Assistant to the President for National Security Affairs but more commonly called the National Security Advisor, is one of the most important national security official in the government.[71]

The council's charge is primarily advisory, but its mandate is broad—to help define goals and priorities; to coordinate and integrate domestic, foreign, and military policies; and to suggest specific courses of action, all within the national security sphere. During the Truman presidency, the council functioned as a forum for discussion and had an important advisory role during the Korean War. President Eisenhower converted it into a planning board for developing general policy positions. Kennedy eliminated the council's policy-making function and reduced its advisory role, turning instead to a presidential assistant for national security affairs and sometimes to an informal group, which he dubbed the Executive Committee of the National Security Council.

For the most part, presidents since Kennedy have preferred a White House–based assistant and staff rather than a department-based council to inform and advise them on national security matters. They have looked to their national security advisor, who functions as a senior White House aide, to coordinate input from the departments and agencies, funnel information to the president, and identify problems that merit presidential attention.

The increasing importance of the national security advisor and NSC staff has allowed presidents to maximize their discretion, exercise more central control, act more decisively, and do so in a manner that is consistent with their basic political beliefs and policy objectives. Unburdened by administrative responsibilities, the national security staff can respond quickly and less visibly, particularly in times of emergencies. Leaks can be minimized, but as Barack Obama, Donald Trump, and almost every contemporary president has discovered, not eliminated entirely.

There is a downside to vesting too much power in, and with it possible dependency on, the White House's national security staff. Presidents may not be attentive to external influences that should be considered in policy formulation and that may affect how those policies are implemented and what the results will be. The ideological and partisan perspectives of the president's staff maybe too narrow; as a consequence, there may be greater likelihood that recommendations the president receives are incomplete, ill informed, or ill advised.

In addition, a strong and visible national security assistant who also serves as a presidential spokesperson, negotiator, and liaison with other governments can generate internal conflict within an administration, particularly if the secretaries of state and defense believe that their roles are being circumvented in the process. Presidents Nixon and Carter relied primarily on their national security advisers, Henry Kissinger and Zbigniew Brzezinski, to perform multiple roles, leading to dissent within their respective state departments and ultimately to the resignations of their secretaries of state. Nixon tried to remove the tension by nominating Kissinger to be secretary of state as well as national security adviser at the beginning of his second term, but when Gerald Ford became president, he disengaged the two positions, and they have remained separate ever since.

The National Security Council system gives the president a centralized staff that can enhance the creativity, decisiveness, and consistency of national security policy. The centralization, however, comes at a potential cost: limited information, unexplored policy alternatives, and tenuous political support, particularly if the policy is viewed as unsuccessful down the road.

The Homeland Security Council (HSC)

Shortly after 9/11, George W. Bush issued an executive order creating an Office of Homeland Security in the EOP, headed by an Assistant to the President for Homeland Security and a Homeland Security Council (HSC), to coordinate activities among the many government agencies involved in protecting US domestic territory.[72] At the time, dozens of federal agencies had some involvement: the Federal Aviation Administration, the Coast Guard, the Federal Emergency Management Agency,

Customs, Immigration, the intelligence community, the Secret Service, and others, spread across nearly every executive department, as well as hundreds of state and local emergency and first responder agencies. The intent of the president's order was to create an NSC-like policy coordination mechanism. When Congress placed many of these offices into the Department of Homeland Security in November 2002, it also established the Homeland Security Council as a statutory body in the Executive Office of the President.[73]

Bush, Obama, and Trump organized the NSC and HSC somewhat differently. Obama placed the Homeland Security Council within the National Security Council staff structure and did not have an official Homeland Security advisor, designating one senior staff member as Assistant to the President for Homeland Security and Counterterrorism. This assistant acted as a Deputy National Security Advisor.[74] Trump, as Bush did, organized the NSC and HSC as parallel organizations, although both were served by the National Security Council staff.

The Council of Economic Advisors (CEA)

The CEA was established by the Employment Act of 1946, as a response to the high unemployment that occurred after World War II. Establishing a policy of promoting "maximum employment, production, and purchasing power,"[75] the act created the CEA and gave it responsibility to advise the president on economic trends. Its primary statutory responsibility is to produce an annual economic report to the president. The Council has declined in influence since the 1970s and has been overshadowed by the head of the Federal Reserve and National Economic Council in the making and promotion of economy policy. The CEA's role in preparing the president's annual economic report makes it more of a purveyor of hard, factual economic data designed to inform policy debates and less of an advisory body.[76]

Other Specialized Offices

Congress has established other offices within the EOP to raise the visibility of an issue or provide an efficient mechanism for presidential control. Examples include the Office of National Drug Control Policy, created by Congress in 1988 and tasked with coordination of federal anti-drug programs, reducing illicit drug use, and opposing efforts to legalize them. The Office has always been controversial, with many questioning its effectiveness; a preliminary fiscal year 2018 budget plan suggested that the Trump administration was planning on reducing its budget by nearly 94 percent, effectively killing the office's mission.[77]

The Office of the Special Trade Representative is responsible for conducting trade negotiations on behalf of the United States, administering trade agreements, and advising the president on trade policy. President Kennedy established the unit in the EOP in 1963 (although Congress authorized its creation in 1962 trade legislation).[78] Its responsibilities have grown as Congress has added responsibility and delegated authority to it.[79]

The 1969 National Environmental Policy Act (NEPA) created the Council on Environmental Quality, which Richard Nixon situated in the EOP.[80] The Council advises the president on environmental policy and assists in coordinating and overseeing agency implementation of NEPA. Trump has shown less interest in the work of the CEQ, reflecting the administration's priority on reducing environmental regulations and expanding production of fossil fuels.

THE CHALLENGES OF CENTRALIZATION

The main trend in the development of the presidential staff has been increasing specialization and complexity, which in turn has led to increased centralization of authority within the White House. Some students of public administration see these changes as necessary to achieve a more responsive federal bureaucracy, one that conforms to the judgment of the electorate as expressed in the last presidential election.[81] Others, however, believe that the changes lead to a rush to judgment by officials driven more by partisan presidential interests than the merits of sound public policy judgments.[82]

Centralization has been driven by presidents' desires to have more control over the executive branch. Presidents can act quickly and decisively, translate their campaign promises into policy proposals, and make sure that the costs of the policy coincide with their budget requests. Moreover, a centralized process in the White House can minimize the pressures of Congress, party, and nonparty groups; encourage a national rather than a parochial perspective; and produce policies that accord with an administration's political beliefs. A centralized system facilitates action and thus demonstrates a president's leadership skills. It also may provide the president more bargaining leverage with Congress and others who stand in the way of achieving the administration's policy goals.

The rise of the presidential institution poses challenges to presidents, even as it has dramatically increased their effectiveness. The first challenge is building winning coalitions in Congress to enact policies created in the White House. The second is the increasing tension between the White House and cabinet agencies, as secretaries resist ceding their own power or object to what they see as inappropriate demands from presidential staff. Finally, centralization increases the demands of managing the institution, which has grown large enough to create internal problems of its own. Presidents and top staff now must devote time and attention to dealing with internal rivalries and organizational management problems, in effect supervising the supervisors. The presidential institution, which was created in large part to help the president monitor the executive branch, now requires its own monitoring.

Creating Coalitions

There are often problems associated with moving too quickly, with too little input from too few sources on too few options. In a constitutional system of separate institutions sharing powers, in a political system with a multiplicity of interested groups and organizations, and in a government in which electoral support must be expanded to convert campaign promises into public policy, centralization often impedes rather than facilitates successful policy outcomes. According to Andrew Rudalevige, congressional support is harder to achieve when the formulation of policy is restricted to a small group within a highly centralized presidency.[83]

The inverse relationship of policy centralization to successful legislative outcomes places contemporary presidents in a dilemma. They can formulate the policy they prefer but may not get it through Congress, or they can consider other interests and perspectives that members of Congress bring to the table that may dilute their policy objectives but improve the chances of passage. Members of Congress are more sensitive to pressures from their constituencies; they tend to take a narrower perspective than do presidents and their advisers. Presidents must remember that coalition building inside and outside of government is the key to successful legislative outcomes.

White House–Cabinet Tensions

The centralization of power in the White House has reduced the role of the president's cabinet. In a top-down system, influential advisers filter and broker ideas and then funnel them to the president. Their influence stems primarily from their control over the information and their access to the president. The senior advisers tend to be advocates as well as mediators. That presidents rely on them enhances their status and influence, not only with the president but also with others who wish to affect the president's policy judgments.

Cabinet secretaries and their principal assistants, who thought they would be advising the president in their areas of expertise, have complained about being left out of the loop or being required by junior White House aides to perform what they consider relatively unimportant and time-consuming functions. The dilemma for presidents is that increasing centralization of authority in the White House *by itself* generates conflict with the executive branch, thus making agencies more suspicions of that centralization. Giving the president more control "alienates the executive branch from the presidential branch and makes that relationship appear more and more an adversarial one."[84]

Presidential Management

The size of the WHO and the EOP and the proliferation and specialization of units within them pose their own challenges to presidential management. Recall that a main driver of presidents' desire to exert some control over agencies is the fact that agencies tend to value their independence: with their own constituencies and policy interests, the people in the agencies may push back against presidents who wish to radically alter missions or priorities.[85]

The desire to centralize authority in the White House is a direct response to the difficulty of gaining control over the executive branch. But as the presidential institution grows, it develops its own tendency toward insufficient responsiveness to presidents, compounded by the high profile of many presidential advisors (who may not have what the Brownlow Committee saw as a crucial quality of a presidential advisor: a "passion for anonymity").

An increasing amount of a president's time—and surely a chief of staff's time—is now spent controlling the White House staff itself, coordinating the activities of a large and wide-ranging institution that can develop its own routines that may conflict with what a president demands. Size alone can present a problem:

> Having long ago surpassed the charmed size of a group government by personal relations, the White House office today can be fairly labeled a bureaucracy. The entourage of presidential confidants envisioned by Brownlow has evolved into a multifunctional firm, replete with diversification of tasks and the recruitment of experts into specialized roles.[86]

But bureaucracies, by their nature, develop their own routines and the people within them their own interests (see chapter 9), complicating the task of exerting control. Presidential delegation to staff, a necessity of contemporary governance, increases the likelihood of that same staff pursuing their own policy interests instead of the president's.

A larger staff, moreover, creates more opportunities for organizational pathologies, whether infighting (different staff blocs competing for the president's attention and undermining each other through public leaks), insulation (in which staff shield the president from negative information or neglect to give their candid opinion), or organizational dysfunction (where staff operate independently without any centralized coordination). Moreover, the larger the organization, the more time a president (or, more properly, a chief of staff) must spend in maintaining and monitoring it.

Transitioning to the Presidency

The size of the presidential institution raises additional questions of where the people who will staff it come from and how the president will structure advisory networks and processes.

Campaign organizations are important not only for winning the election but also for making the transition to government and providing a preview of the new administration and its personnel selections and management style. Candidates' organizational styles and decision-making preferences carry over to how they act as president.

Ronald Reagan and George W. Bush's reliance on their campaign organizations and their reluctance to second-guess their advisers augured the way they operated in the White House. Barack Obama left campaign organization and day-to-day activities to his strategists. He was involved in strategic planning, oversaw the drafting of major speeches, and made tactical decisions when asked to do so by his staff. He tended to surround himself with experts and desired a full range of information before making policy and political decisions. That is also how he operated once in office.

Donald Trump is a contrast with these presidents. His penchant for expressing unvarnished views, demeaning his critics, and constantly remaining in the public eye was distinctive. In common with his predecessors, these patterns were consistent with how he has behaved in office. As we noted earlier, his administration has seen historically high turnover, and many of the staffers imported from the campaign had relatively short and controversial tenures (though others, like Kellyanne Conway, who became senior Counselor to the President after managing the campaign, have remained). One reason for this instability is that Trump abandoned the initial transition effort, firing Chris Christie days after the election and starting over with Vice President Mike Pence in charge.[87]

Campaign personnel are frequently recruited for key administration positions. Many senior aides in recent White Houses served in the inner circles of their presidential campaigns, as did many of their assistants. However, the success with which these campaign personnel have made the adjustment to White House staff has been mixed at best. Carter's, Clinton's, and Trump's senior staff experienced the most difficult and error-prone transitions, while those of the Reagan, George W. Bush, and Obama campaigns had the smoothest and most professional transitions.

THE VICE PRESIDENT AND THE PRESIDENT'S SPOUSE

In recent years, institutional support for the president has been supplemented by the activities of the vice president and the president's spouse. The staffs of both offices have increased in size and specialization as their personal and professional roles have transformed their positions.

First Lady Melania Trump.

The Vice President

For years, the vice presidency was regarded as a position of little importance; in fact, it was the butt of jokes and laments. The nation's first vice president, John Adams, complained, "My country has in its wisdom contrived for me the most insignificant office that ever the invention of man contrived or his imagination conceived."[88] Thomas Jefferson, the second person to hold the office, was not quite as critical. Describing his job as "honorable and easy," he added, "I am unable to decide whether I would rather have it or not have it."[89] Jefferson spent much of his vice presidency at his home in Monticello.

Throughout most of the nineteenth century, the vice president performed few official functions. Other than succeeding to the presidency, the holder of this position had only one designated constitutional job—to preside over the Senate and vote in case of a tie. Nor did eighteenth- and nineteenth-century presidents enhance that job very much. Vice presidents played only a peripheral role within their respective administrations. When Professor Woodrow Wilson published his classic treatise on American government in the 1880s, he devoted only one paragraph to the vice president, writing: "The chief embarrassment in . . . explaining how little there is to be said about it is that one has evidently said all there is to say."[90] John Nance Garner, Franklin Roosevelt's first vice president, offered perhaps the bluntest description in his much-quoted (but probably apocryphal) refrain that the office was "hardly worth a pitcher of spit."

Were Adams, Jefferson, and Garner alive today, they would have to reevaluate their comments. The position of vice president has increased enormously in importance and visibility. Roosevelt's sudden death, Eisenhower's illness, and Kennedy's assassination focused attention on the vice president and generated a debate that resulted in a constitutional amendment on presidential disability and vice presidential selection should the position become vacant (see Appendix B). Presidents now do more to prepare vice presidents, in the event that succession becomes necessary.

Eisenhower was the first of the modern presidents to upgrade the vice president's role. He invited Richard Nixon, his vice president, to attend cabinet, National Security Council, and legislative strategy meetings, and during Eisenhower's illness Nixon presided over these sessions.[91] In addition, Eisenhower sent Nixon on a number of well-publicized trips for the administration.

Lyndon Johnson was also involved in a variety of activities as John F. Kennedy's vice president. He helped coordinate administration efforts to eliminate racial discrimination and promote exploration of outer space; participated in legislative lobbying efforts, joining Kennedy at the White House breakfasts for congressional leaders; and also traveled abroad on behalf of the administration. Still, Johnson was not enamored with his job, telling biographer Doris Kearns:

> Every time I came into John Kennedy's presence, I felt like a goddamn raven hovering over his shoulder. Away from the Oval Office, it was even worse. The Vice Presidency is filled with trips around the world, chauffeurs, men saluting, people clapping, chairmanships of councils, but in the end, it is nothing. I detested every minute of it.[92]

Despite their own experiences as vice presidents, neither Johnson nor Nixon added new responsibilities to that office during their presidencies, although they did have their vice presidents perform a variety of ceremonial, diplomatic, and political roles.

Nelson Rockefeller, Gerald Ford's vice president, was given an important policy-making role—to shape the Ford administration's domestic policy goals and prepare the president's agenda for his 1976 campaign. Rockefeller's proposals, however, clashed with those of other Republicans within the administration and Congress. Coming under increasing criticism from GOP leaders and senior White House staffers, Rockefeller announced his intention not to seek the vice presidency in 1976 and subsequently removed himself from an active advisory role.

Whereas Rockefeller failed to realize the potential of the office, Walter Mondale did. The first vice president to have an office in the West Wing of the White House, Mondale saw President Carter on a regular basis. He had *carte blanche* to attend any conference, see any paper, and participate in any decision in which the president was involved. Carter also provided opportunities for Mondale to shape policy and facilitate congressional relations. Mondale headed a presidential priority-setting group, lobbied on key bills, and helped establish a public liaison operation in the White House. His staff was integrated with Carter's.[93]

When President Reagan wished to emphasize his concern with crisis management, drug enforcement, and government relations, he appointed his vice president, George H. W. Bush, to head committees studying these issues. Bush also served as the president's envoy, visiting North Atlantic Treaty Organization (NATO) countries, making a fact-finding trip to Lebanon, and attending the funerals of several foreign policy leaders. However, Bush was not a member of Reagan's inner circle, nor did he assume a general policy-making role.

Dan Quayle played a similar role in the first Bush administration. Although Quayle was more visible than George H. W. Bush as vice president, he was not a major adviser to Bush. The president even considered dropping him from the ticket in 1992 but chose not to do so out of fear of alienating conservative Republicans to whom

Quayle appealed. Bush sent Quayle on a number of foreign missions, appointed him to chair a committee overseeing space exploration (as Lyndon Johnson had done during the Kennedy administration), and relied on him as a liaison to the Republican Party, outside groups, and members of Congress.

Vice President Al Gore had considerably more policy and personal influence in the Clinton administration, participating in the selection of cabinet and subcabinet secretaries, reviewing the drafts of presidential speeches, and, in his most important responsibility, directing the National Performance Review project, the administration's effort to "reinvent government." Gore lunched regularly with the president, attended political strategy sessions, and had regular input into most major policy decisions, especially in the areas of the environment, science, and technology. A principal link to organized labor, Senate Democrats, and the Democratic Party, Gore also played a prominent role in foreign affairs as a personal representative of the president. Clinton seldom made a major policy decision without consulting Gore, although he did not always follow the vice president's advice.

Dick Cheney exercised more power in this position than any other vice president before him. He presided over the Bush transition and led a key task force on energy policy and another to coordinate the administration's response to future terrorist attacks. With the president out of town on 9/11, Cheney directed White House operations. For much of the Bush presidency, he functioned as the president's principal adviser and policy enforcer.

Bush delegated considerable operational authority to Cheney, whose experience as Ford's chief of staff, a member of the Republican leadership in Congress, and secretary of defense during the senior Bush's administration gave him knowledge and experience that few, if any, in the administration could match. He had a staff of approximately ninety people working out of three offices (in the West Wing, the Eisenhower Executive Office Building, and the Senate).[94] He also served as a spokesman for the administration on the Sunday talk shows, as a liaison to business, political, and veteran groups and Republican Party leaders, as well as a frequent diplomatic representative for the country.

Cheney involved himself in a range of policy matters, frequently behind closed doors. He was particularly active in forging a policy for combating terrorism at home and abroad. His office drafted the orders that extended CIA and military discretion on methods for obtaining information from those suspected of aiding and abetting terrorist activities. He was also a forceful advocate of using military force in Afghanistan and Iraq.[95]

Cheney's vice presidency was controversial, however. He received criticism for the secretive manner in which he and his aides operated, the way in which they were able to circumvent normal channels of government decision making, and the power they exercised behind the scenes.

Partially in reaction to these criticisms, Barack Obama's vice president Joseph Biden said that he would model his office on that of Mondale, not Cheney. An influential negotiator and adviser, Biden played a key role in negotiations with congressional party leaders during the budget debate of 2010, the deficit and debt limit discussions of 2011, and the resolution of fiscal crisis at the end of 2012. His recommendation of fighting terrorism abroad with Special Forces, drones and other advanced technologies, and enhanced on-the-ground intelligence became US policy during the first term of the Obama administration. The president asked him to play a key role in designing new gun legislation after the school shooting in Newtown,

Box 8.2 ★ Vice President Mike Pence

Vice President Mike Pence plays an unusually influential role in the Trump Administration, taking on a wide range of substantive responsibilities and serving as one of the president's most important advisors and most loyal spokespersons. His extensive political history—six terms in the House of Representatives and one as Governor of Indiana—provide him with a depth of experience few others in the White House have.

Pence headed the Trump transition effort once Trump fired the first transition director, Chris Christie. That position gave him substantial influence over appointments, and he was instrumental in bringing in key members of the initial national security team, including United Nations Ambassador Nikki Haley, CIA Director Mike Pompeo, and Director of National Intelligence Dan Coats (Pompeo became Secretary of State in March 2018, and Haley left the UN ambassadorship in December 2018).[96] His transition duties generated controversy. Trump fired National Security Advisor Michael Flynn in February 2017, after reports of undisclosed meetings with Russian officials and lobbying on behalf of foreign governments surfaced and the Acting Attorney General warned the White House that Flynn was vulnerable to blackmail.[97] Publicly, the official reason for Flynn's dismissal was that he had misrepresented those contacts to the vice president, but critics questioned how carefully Pence had vetted Flynn and whether he should have been aware of Flynn's entanglements with foreign governments.

As vice president, Pence has traveled abroad extensively, and his public remarks are taken as authoritative statements of foreign policy. When Trump notably became the first president to decline to publicly endorse Article 5 of the NATO treaty (which commits all members to mutual defense), the vice president made such a commitment two weeks later.[98] But the Pence has at times faced resistance in promoting Trump Administration's policy to skeptical and unreceptive international audiences,"[exacerbating] already tense relationships between the US and allies by simply repeating Trump's threats and grievances in a different tone."[99]

Pence is active in legislative liaison, helping the White House monitor congressional activities and legislative liaison. He has also helped smooth over tensions in White House–Congressional relations, assuaging legislators unhappy over surprise policy announcements and reversals.[100] He has been a regular attendee at a weekly policy lunch hosted by Senate Majority Leader Mitch McConnell (R-KY), something that Richard Cheney did as George W. Bush's vice president.[101]

As President of the Senate, Pence has often cast tie-breaking votes on key legislation, casting the deciding vote on confirming Secretary of Education Betsy DeVos and on allowing debate to begin on the effort to repeal the Affordable Care Act. As of September 2019, Pence had cast thirteen tie-breaking votes as vice president, the most in the first two and a half years of an administration since John Adams in 1789–1791.[102]

Connecticut. He was also active as an administration spokesperson, party advocate, and personal representative of the president with foreign governments and domestic groups. (See box 8.2 for the vice presidency of Mike Pence.)

The President's Spouse

The president's spouse has the potential to become an important component or point of controversy in the contemporary presidency. Although the Constitution does not acknowledge any role for them, presidential spouses have performed social and ceremonial functions from the time the government first began to operate. Initially and throughout the nineteenth century, spouses avoided involvement in policy matters and, to a slightly lesser extent, in politics. Even though they were expected to stay out of the limelight, some presidential wives became controversial, Rachel Jackson and Mary Todd Lincoln in particular.

At the beginning of the twentieth century, and with the development of a White House press corps, spouses became more visible but not necessarily more influential. The exception was Edith Wilson after her husband suffered a major stroke in the fall of 1919. She made decisions in his name, shielded him from the press and the public, and may have even forged his signature to legal documents and legislation.[103]

Eleanor Roosevelt established an important communications link between her husband, who had been physically disabled by polio and moved with great difficulty, and the American people during FDR's twelve years in office. Mrs. Roosevelt traveled across the country, monitored public opinion, and reported the country's mood to the president. She was an advocate for the poor and an early supporter of civil rights. She also wrote a column, entitled "My Day," which appeared in newspapers around the country.[104]

Jackie Kennedy and "Lady Bird" Johnson supplemented the policy interests of their husbands with their concerns about American history, culture, and landscaping. Mrs. Kennedy was instrumental in the restoration of the Lafayette Park area across from the White House and the preservation and restoration of the White House interior. Mrs. Johnson cared deeply about the environment and worked to enhance the beautification of Washington in parks and along public highways.

Betty Ford and Rosalyn Carter spoke out on health care issues and family-related concerns. Mrs. Carter was the first spouse to attend a cabinet meeting.[105] Nancy Reagan played the role of a spokesperson, spearheading the administration's antidrug policy with her "Just Say No" campaign. In addition, Mrs. Reagan was involved in internal White House matters, particularly as they pertained to staffing and travel of her husband. She was instrumental in the removal of several key aides who she believed were serving the president poorly. Barbara Bush and Laura Bush served as advocates for literacy; Hillary Rodham Clinton, for universal health care, human rights, and family values; and Michele Obama for health and physical fitness issues.

Mrs. Clinton's involvement in the development and marketing of the administration's health reform proposal, however, went well beyond advocacy. She had an office on the policy floor of the West Wing in addition to the suite of offices in the East Wing that is normally reserved for the First Lady. As chief architect and lobbyist for the administration's health-care reform proposal, she testified before Congress and attended negotiating sessions with congressional leaders. Her policy advocacy embroiled her in partisan politics. Her alleged involvement in the firing of personnel in the White House Travel Office, combined with the disappearance of some of her legal records (Mrs. Clinton was the first presidential spouse to be subpoenaed to testify about her activities before a federal grand jury), added to her image as a partisan and raised questions about the proper role for a presidential spouse.

Melania Trump has adopted a more reserved role, opting initially to stay in New York at the beginning of 2017 rather than move to the White House (she cited a desire to keep the president's youngest son in his school). She has "remained private and minimally involved" in the administration.[106] Her main public position has been her anti-bullying campaign "Be Best," announced in May 2018 but with sporadic follow up in its first year.[107]

People who admired the Eleanor Roosevelt–Hillary Rodham Clinton model saw the presidential spouse as a valuable partner who could help the administration in a variety of ways, from performing ceremonial duties and meeting with government leaders, workers, or the general public, to making policy and even exercising political leadership. A spouse may be in a unique position to say what the president does not want to hear—and what other advisers might be fearful of saying.

Others, however, point with some trepidation to the unique relationship that the president's spouse enjoys with the president. The fact that spouses cannot be fired makes them less vulnerable to the usual constraints on and criticism of presidential advisers. Moreover, it places them in a position to impose their own views on others and be more persuasive with the president, given the intimacy and time spent together. These dangers, however, may be partially offset by the visibility of the spouse and the desire not to be a source of negative press attention and commentary.

CONCLUSION

The singular nature of the president—a purposeful decision by the Framers to vest the executive power in a lone individual, rather than a council or some other sort of collective body—enhances "energy, dispatch, and responsibility,"[108] As the sign on Harry Truman's Oval Office desk famously said, "The buck stops here." That accountability creates public expectations of leadership and focuses public displeasure on the president when things go poorly. Taken together, these give presidents a powerful incentive to seek meaningful control over what the institutions of government do. The need for control is the foundation for the development of administrative capacity, as this capacity is what gives presidents the ability to extend their reach, to control more.

And yet it was immediately obvious that presidents needed some sort of support and could not do the job alone. Whereas early presidents could get by with one or two clerks to deal with the affairs of state (and complained about how the demands of office left them little time to think about high-level policy), by the early twentieth century it was obvious that the degree of support presidents had was entirely inadequate to the needs of contemporary administration. Government was growing, expanding its reach into a wider range of economic and social policies, *doing* more. While Congress maintained the primary authority over the creation of those capabilities through establishing new agencies, the executive power to administer those functions gave the president substantial discretion in how to carry out those functions, if he could find a way to exercise it.

The presidential institution—the Executive Office of the President and its component parts, the White House Office, the National Security Council, the Office of Management and Budget, and others—provide that capability. The precise structure of that institution has not been constant, and subunits have come and gone as new responsibilities arise or become obsolete. But the pattern is clear enough: the White House has become more powerful, specialized, and politicized. It has developed an independent capacity to advise and inform the president, to formulate and prioritize policy, to orchestrate and oversee department and agency input, and to build public and congressional support. Senior presidential aides have become more important, prestigious, and visible; they are also subject to more press scrutiny and criticism. In contrast, the department secretaries have lost some of their notoriety and status, access to the president, and influence over policy development.

The presidential institution is now a permanent fixture, and it is difficult to envision a modern presidency operating without it. At the same time, though, the size of the institution confronts contemporary presidents with a dilemma: they need a large, functionally differentiated staff to carry out the duties of office, yet that institution can create its own political problems, and presidents must spend an increasing amount of time trying to control their own staff. Presidents who try to manage things alone or rely excessively on their own instincts will inevitably fail, but presidents who rely on powerful staff (especially a strong chief of staff) put themselves at the mercy of that same staff, who may pursue their own ambitions rather than the president's. From an organizational standpoint, that is the modern contradiction of presidential governance.

DISCUSSION QUESTIONS

1. It is often said that a key function of the presidential staff is to compensate for the president's weaknesses: a well-functioning staff can prevent problems from occurring by anticipating presidential behaviors that are hurting the president's interests and channel that behavior into more productive forms. But presidents often resist this, objecting to what they see as attempts to "handle" them. Is there anything a staff can do when a president objects to efforts to control him (or her)? Where does Trump fit into this process?

2. A hierarchical White House—now taken as a given as the only way to organize the institution—is hardly the sort of nimble structure that characterizes more innovative companies and organizations (think of high-tech firms such as Amazon or Google). Is there any reason the White House *has* to be organized this way? Is it even possible to envision a flatter or more fluid organization?

3. Assume that the president-elect has asked you to prepare a memo on how the White House Office should be organized and staffed. Think about what structures you would recommend, how you would organize the various units in the White House, and what units you would eliminate and create. What kinds of people would you appoint to top positions? What problems do you foresee that the staff might face in their first year? Which contemporary White Houses would you cite as the most and least effective during their first year? Are there any common problems?

WEB EXERCISES

1. Go to Donald Trump's Twitter feed (https://twitter.com/realDonaldTrump). One way of understanding the president's tweets is that they allow him to communicate directly with the public with no intermediate filters. Working through a series of presidential tweets, can you identify those that staff might have objected to if they had had the opportunity to filter? What do you conclude about the importance (or lack thereof) of trying to monitor presidential communications?

2. Here are some links to online versions of presidential schedules (others are available online if you search for them by president):
   a. Obama: https://obamawhitehouse.archives.gov/blog#today
   b. Reagan: https://reaganlibrary.gov/digital-library/daily-diary

Examine a sample of schedules: How much time do presidents devote to substantive policy meetings? How much to symbolic and public activities? When do presidents have time to analyze or deliberate on issues and policy? What can you conclude about how presidents spend their time?

3. The American Presidency Project shows total employment in the White House as far back as Coolidge. The data (http://www.presidency.ucsb.edu/data/eop.php) show that the number of staff in recent years is *lower* than it was in the 1970s. Is it possible that the staff is too small to effectively carry out the president's responsibilities? What would be the advantages and disadvantages to increasing the size of the staff?

SELECTED READINGS

Burke, John P. *The Institutional Presidency: Organizing and Managing the White House from FDR to Clinton*, 2nd ed. Baltimore, MD: Johns Hopkins University Press, 2000.

—— *Honest Broker? The National Security Advisor and Presidential Decision Making*. College Station: Texas A&M University Press, 2009.

Goldstein, Joel K. *The White House Vice Presidency: The Path to Significance, Mondale to Biden*. Lawrence: University Press of Kansas, 2016.

Kumar, Martha Joynt, and Terry Sullivan, eds. *The White House World: Transitions, Organization, and Office Operations*. College Station: Texas A&M University Press, 2003.

Lewis, David E. *The Politics of Presidential Appointments: Political Control and Bureaucratic Performance*. Princeton, NJ: Princeton University Press, 2008.

Rudalevige, Andrew. *Managing the President's Program: Presidential Leadership and Legislative Policy Formulation*. Princeton, NJ: Princeton University Press, 2002.

Sullivan, Terry. *The Nerve Center: Lessons in Governing from the White House Chiefs of Staff*. College Station: Texas A&M University Press, 2004.

Walcott, Charles E., and Karen M. Hult. *Governing the White House: From Hoover through LBJ*. Lawrence: University Press of Kansas, 1995.

Woodward, Bob. *Fear: Trump in the White House*. New York: Simon and Schuster, 2018.

9

Presidential Decision Making

Donald Trump involved in decision making, the core responsibility of the president.

The essence of the president's job is making decisions—about foreign affairs, economic policy, and literally hundreds of other important matters. The task is a difficult one, and there are many obstacles to making rational decisions. Donald Trump found that he had to work much harder at the job than he had anticipated. He also learned that issues such as health care were far more complex than he had realized. Nevertheless, Trump shares with every president what Barack Obama said about his foreign policy goal, and that is to "not do stupid stuff."[1]

Leadership in the area of decision making is of a different nature than in the other arenas of presidential activity. Presidents need to ensure that they have before them a full range of options and the appropriate information necessary for evaluating them. The president's leadership requires the establishment of a working relationship with subordinates and an organization in the White House that serves presidential decision-making needs. Often, presidents have to persuade their own appointees in the

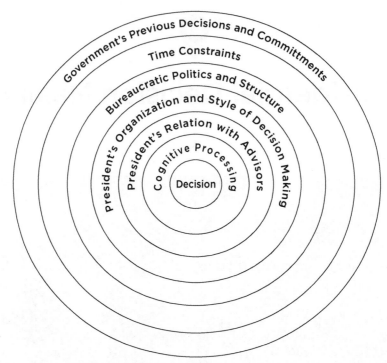

Figure 9.1 Influences on Presidential Decision Making

White House and the bureaucracy to provide the options and information that they require. However, these appointees have many incentives not to do so. Lack of time to consider decisions and previous commitments of the government may constrain a president's decision making, as may the president's own personal experiences and personality.

Presidents fitting the director model would have a full range of options and information at their disposal and be relatively unencumbered by environmental constraints on their range of choices. Presidents in the facilitating mode, conversely, would be more subject to the influence of contextual factors, more dependent on their environment for options and information, and thus more constrained in their decision making.

Figure 9.1 is a graphical representation of the influences on presidential decision making. In the outer circles are the broad contexts in which decisions take place; in the inner circles are the more immediate influences.

PREVIOUS COMMITMENTS

The first step in understanding presidential decision making is to recognize that presidents operate under severe constraints in their decision making, no matter what their approaches to making decisions are. As John Kennedy's aide Theodore Sorensen observed,

> Presidents rarely, if ever make decisions . . . in the sense of writing their conclusions largely on a clean slate. They make choices. They select options. They exercise

judgments. But the basic decisions, which confine their choices, have all too often been previously made by past events or circumstances, by other nations, by pressures or predecessors or even subordinates.[2]

Thus, the president's decisions usually fall within parameters set by prior commitments of the government that obligate it to spend money, defend allies, maintain services, or protect rights.[3] When Donald Trump took office in January 2017, he was not able to start from scratch and consider how best to allocate federal expenditures. Almost the entire federal budget was already committed before he took the oath of office. He could not choose, for example, to end health care for the indigent or eliminate the navy. These public services were embodied in law.

The president is also constrained by the institutional capabilities of the executive branch, which are also products of past decisions. For example, the option of airlifting aid to a country experiencing famine is a viable one because the air force has a well-established airlift capability. However, rapidly allocating federal police officers to a city experiencing a crime wave is not feasible because the national government does not have a large police force. Similarly, President Obama was dependent on BP to cap its oil well that was spilling millions of gallons of crude into the Gulf of Mexico because the federal government has no capability for doing this.

TIME CONSTRAINTS

The diverse obligations of the president and his top aides impose severe constraints on the amount of time they can devote to generating and evaluating options and information. According to a Jimmy Carter aide, "When the President asks to see all the potential alternatives, it is an impossible request [because] . . . it involves too much time."[4]

Overloaded advisers may rely on others, who may be equally overloaded, to bring crucial information to the attention of the president. Several of President Harry Truman's advisers believed there would be a serious danger of Chinese intervention in the Korean War if the president attempted to reunite all of Korea under a noncommunist government. However, no one went to him to argue that he should reverse his decision allowing General Douglas MacArthur to invade communist North Korea. Each person thought that someone else would do it.[5]

The president and his advisers rarely have the luxury of anticipating new issues. According to Jim Baker, secretary of state for President George H. W. Bush, due to the demise of the Soviet Empire, the unification of Germany, the 1989 massacre in Tiananmen Square in Beijing, the Middle East peace process, and the civil wars in Central America, the administration paid little attention to Iraq prior to the invasion of Kuwait.[6] As former White House aide Jim Cicconi put it, "I can recall many instances when a White House [tried] long-term planning. In no instance that I can recall did it ever work. The White House is inexorably tugged toward the here and now, the immediate. It is the nature of the place."[7]

Fighting terrorism was not the highest priority for the George W. Bush administration in early 2001. A cabinet-level meeting did not approve an antiterrorism plan until a week before the 9/11 attacks, and there was no further discussion among the president and his top advisers about al-Qaeda before the attacks. The president's chief adviser on terrorism never briefed him on the plan. The secretary of defense was focused on placing personnel in the Department of Defense and reviewing defense policy, and the Treasury Department was more concerned with high-level international fraud and the laundering of drug money than with terrorist financing.[8] Thus, the president did not make the organizational reforms necessary to combat terrorism before the 9/11 attacks.[9]

Similarly, CIA Director George Tenet declared that the CIA was too busy fighting al-Qaeda in 2002 to devote time to producing a high-quality national intelligence estimate on Iraq's possession of weapons of mass destruction (WMDs) before the United States invaded in March 2003.[10]

The same problem of time constraints arose when it came to postwar planning for the war in Iraq. The president was consumed with the prewar diplomatic effort, as was the Secretary of State Colin Powell. Because Powell saw securing the United Nations' authorization for the war as the basic building block for a successful postwar situation, he did not get deeply involved in the internal debate on post-Saddam governance. Secretary of Defense Donald Rumsfeld's prime concern was with in-depth planning for the invasion, reflecting later that "I wasn't able to give it the time it needed."[11] As a result, the official policy for postwar governance was not decided until days before the invasion of Iraq and remained vague even then.

Sometimes deadlines make it necessary for the president and his aides to cease the consideration of information and options and make a decision. In the words of President Ronald Reagan's budget director David Stockman,

> I just wish that there were more hours in the day or that we didn't have to do this so fast. I have these stacks of briefing books and I've got to make decisions about specific options. . . . I don't have time, trying to put this whole package together in three weeks, so you just start making snap judgments.[12]

Because of such time limits, the less controversial parts of elaborate policies often receive inadequate attention.

ORGANIZATION AND STYLE OF DECISION MAKING

Each president is unique and has broad discretion in structuring the decision-making process in the White House. There are many ways to do this, and each has consequences for the effectiveness of the advisory system. In this section, we explore the ways in which the organization and style of the presidential advisory process can affect the president's consideration of options and information.

White House Organization

There is no ideal organization for the White House that is appropriate for every president. Political scientist Alexander George came to this conclusion:

> There appears to be no single structural formula by which the chief executive and his staff can convert the functional expertise and diversity of viewpoints of the many offices concerned with international affairs into consistently effective policies and decisions.[13]

We may confidently add that this is also true for domestic policy decisions.

The organization of the White House will inevitably reflect the personality and work habits of the incumbent. Moreover, the chief executive's personal style will dominate any organizational scheme, no matter what the organizational charts may say. If presidents have a penchant for acting without adequate study, they will defeat any advisory system they may have established in the White House. According to an experienced presidential aide, "The nature of the man is absolutely crucial and decisive, altogether overriding the issue of organization."[14] Henry Kissinger added that the influence of a presidential assistant "derives almost exclusively from the confidence of the President, not from administrative arrangements."[15]

Although the style and priorities of recent presidents have differed, the structure and functions of their White Houses have remained relatively constant (as we saw in chapter 8), with individual presidents adding their own personal touch, usually at the beginnings of their terms in office. For example, the priority that Barack Obama gave to new policy initiatives led him to set up a relatively large number of policy-making offices at the start of his presidency.

Presidents may simultaneously use several approaches to organizing their decision making, depending on their level of interest in a policy area, their policy priorities, and the strengths and limitations of their principal advisers in each policy area. For example, President Gerald Ford employed a hierarchical model of centralized management for foreign policy, whereby he concentrated responsibility in Henry Kissinger's hands. In economic policy, he employed a managed multiple advocacy system in which collegial discussions among a wider range of advisers occurred. In the area of domestic policy, where he did not want to undertake policy initiatives, he delegated responsibility to Vice President Nelson Rockefeller and dealt with issues on an ad hoc basis.[16] George H. W. Bush employed much the same structure in each of these policy areas.

Thus, it is possible to overemphasize the formal aspects of White House organization. As Kennedy aide Theodore Sorensen commented, "to ascribe to . . . form and structure a capacity to end bad decisions—is too often to overlook the more dynamic and fluid forces on which presidential decisions are based."[17] Nevertheless, organization does make a difference.

The Hub and Spoke

There are two main models for organizing the staff: the first is a decentralized model, often likened to the "spokes of a wheel" with the president at the hub and staff oriented around the president in a loose and informal structure. This model is most closely associated with Franklin Roosevelt, who supervised the staff himself, giving out assignments, receiving reports, and generally coordinating activities. Roosevelt purposely blurred the lines of authority and overlapped assignments to encourage competition among his aides in order to maximize his information and extend his influence.

Kennedy consciously attempted to emulate Roosevelt's model but without the internal competition Roosevelt had generated. Ford, Carter, Clinton, and Trump (see box 9.1) all tried at first to run their White Houses in this mode, but they had to alter their organizational schemes to establish more hierarchical systems headed by a chief of staff to coordinate the flow of White House business. Someone has to be responsible for scheduling appointments, coordinating the paper flow, following up on decisions, and giving status reports on projects and policy development.[18] Ford reflected,

> I started out with the concept that any cabinet member or top executive in the administration could have direct access to me. In effect, that undercut the role of the chief of staff. I shortly found out that was impractical. A president doesn't have

that much time every day to meet with the various cabinet officers and other top people. You've got to have the chief of staff as a sort of filtering spot. I changed the policy . . . within two months.[19]

Carter, similarly, found his initial hub-and-spoke staff arrangement unworkable. Even with his prodigious reading ability and willingness to take large briefing books to the White House residence at day's end, he could not keep up. In his first year in office, he wrote that "the backlog of paperwork was mountainous. This is my biggest headache, trying to keep current with routine work and still have time for long-range strategic decisions."[20] Internal battles and mixed messages from presidential aides added to the difficulties in the Ford and Carter White Houses and eventually led both presidents to designate a chief of staff to coordinate activities and look out for their political interests.

Box 9.1 ★ Donald Trump's Fractious White House

Many observers, including those from a range of political persuasions, criticized Donald Trump's early White House as lacking the proper organization and discipline. The president was operating as the center of many spokes. As we saw in chapter 8, a senior adviser, senior policy adviser, counselor, chief strategist, communications director, strategic communications director, the National Infrastructure Council, the Office of Trade and Manufacturing Policy, Oval Office Operations, and Ivanka Trump all reported directly to the president rather than through the White House chief of staff. People were frequently walking into the Oval Office without appropriate preparation and staffing. There was typically poor vetting of presidential decisions.[21]

In addition, there was intra-White House conflict. Trump seems to not only tolerate feuds within his team but actually fuel them, playing one aide off another. According to his deputy press secretary, the president "likes that type of competition and encourages it." In addition, however, the president also often humiliates his aides both in public and in private, apparently believing that competition and criticism keep his aides humble and assure loyalty. It is doubtful that he is correct.

Moreover, freewheeling behavior is likely to discourage cooperation, distract from careful analysis, and leave aides uncertain of his confidence in them, thus undermining their ability to do their jobs. Leaks, which Trump detests and considers disloyal, were a symptom of a lack of order: staff used them to discredit their opponents inside the White House and grab the president's attention.

To bring order to the White House, the president named former marine general John Kelly to serve as his chief of staff. Kelly took control of White House personnel decisions and communications to the president, including phone calls. Most important, the new chief of staff organized briefing papers with relevant information and different viewpoints on the cost and benefits of decisions. But this as Bob Woodward characterized it, "was a fantasy."[22]

Within a year, the president had unleashed himself from the processes and constraints that Kelly sought to impose on him. Trump told some aides, such as his national security adviser, John Bolton, and his chief economic adviser, Larry Kudlow, that they should report to him directly rather than through Kelly and did not bend to limits on the persons who could call him directly. Trump, at times, went to extreme lengths to get around his chief of staff, such as by conducting government business on his unsecured personal cell phone.[23]

The president replaced Kelly at the end of 2018. Indeed, the Trump administration has had by far the highest turnover of top-tier staff of any recent president, about two-thirds in the first two years. Many of these position have had more than two occupants.[24] This instability has detracted from a disciplined decision-making process. The chief culprit is the president himself.

The Hierarchical Model

The other model of White House organization is the much more bureaucratic "hierarchical" model, with the president at the apex and a pyramid below with a well-defined chain of command and lines of authority, restricted access to the president, and much less freewheeling improvisation. The hierarchical model requires much more delegation on the president's part and much less direct presidential involvement in routine activities.

The hierarchical mode was initiated by Dwight Eisenhower, who came to the White House after a career in the military and preferred tight administrative control and staff efficiency to the freewheeling style of Truman and Roosevelt. He created the position of chief of staff to oversee the White House and the staff secretary to manage the flow of paperwork. All presidents since his tenure have eventually adopted some version of the hierarchical model.

Presidents need their staff to give them time to focus on priorities and reflect on questions of basic strategy. The president's staff also needs to screen issues so that only those requiring the president's direct involvement will arrive on his desk. If he attempts to solve all the problems that come to the White House, the president will spread his attention and that of his advisers too thinly, wasting time and scarce resources. In addition, the more the president does, the more problems will arise for which others will hold him accountable. Presidents Ford, Carter, and Clinton all tended to become involved in relatively minor matters and were criticized, in some cases even by their own aides, for lacking the appropriate breadth of vision and understanding that are necessary to shape and guide the government.

Most presidents prefer for the principal advisers to reach agreement on a recommendations on routine matters. This process saves time and the cost of overruling senior officials. On major issues, however, presidents typically like to have alternatives.

Hierarchical staff organizations save the president's time and promote thorough evaluation of the options, yet many observers of the presidency are concerned that a centrally managed system may aggravate the proclivity toward isolation that White Houses usually evidence over time. A hierarchy that screens information may also distort it and insulate the president and those around him from both public and private criticism. Important decisions may also be made before they even reach the president. This insulation occurred during Reagan's second term, when Chief of Staff Donald Regan unduly restricted the flow of people and paper into the Oval Office and isolated the president. The risk is that sufficient weight will not be given to countervailing views, and bad policy decisions and poor political judgments can result.

We should not assume that presidential aides can easily "capture" the president, however. Even in the Richard Nixon administration, which boasted a "palace guard" around the president, whatever isolation occurred in the Oval Office had the full concurrence and encouragement of the president. The president used his staff to serve his own needs and to keep out those individuals he did not want to see. As long-time presidential adviser Clark Clifford put it, "In the end, every President gets the advice—and the advisers—that, in his heart, he really wants."[25] Moreover, we lack systematic evidence that Nixon's chiefs of staff provided the president with a distorted view of the issues with which he dealt.

The Form of Advice

Different presidents prefer to receive advice in different forms. Presidents Nixon and Carter preferred to reach their decisions on the basis of written memoranda discussing the pros and cons of various options. In contrast, most recent presidents, including Donald Trump, Barack Obama, and George W. Bush, have used memos to focus the discussion but frequently explored the issues with advisers in relatively open settings. President Reagan had a more detached style, reading less than other recent presidents and instead talking directly to a small number of aides.

There are advantages and disadvantages to both the verbal and paper approaches. The latter requires that options that go to the president be thoroughly "staffed out"—that is, that relevant officials comment on them following a careful analysis. This analysis decreases the chances that verbal fluency will overwhelm cool analysis and that a fleeting and superficial consensus will leave crucial assumptions unexamined. It also makes it more likely that recommendations will be translated into specific operational terms and that advisers will rigorously evaluate the consequences of the options they present to decision makers.[26]

Reviewing advice on paper saves the president time and protects the confidentiality of communications. It may also provide an outlet for those who find it difficult to express themselves directly to the president in order to articulate their views. It is not unusual for the most vociferous critic out of the president's presence to become the meekest lamb when meeting the president personally. People's oral skills often desert them when in the Oval Office. As Henson Moore, deputy chief of staff during the George H. W. Bush administration, put it, "It's just something about the Oval Office; there's something about the aura of the power of a president that people just won't say what really needs to be said to a president."[27]

WDC Photos/Alamy Stock Photo

President Obama receiving both oral and written advice.

However, face-to-face discussions with advisers may provide the president with information that is not reflected in the written word. Direct confrontation between advocates of diverse positions allows the participants to pinpoint their critiques of each other's positions and raise relevant follow-up points. Oral discussions also provide opportunities for advisers to highlight the most important points and crucial nuances in arguments and for presidents to learn the intensity of officials' views and the confidence with which they hold them. This process may alert the chief executive to the level of support he may expect from officials who oppose his ultimate decision. In addition, some ideas, especially those that are highly sensitive, can be best, or perhaps only, advanced personally and informally in the give-and-take of conversation.

For reliance on oral communication to be effective, the president must not dominate the discussion. If he does, he may not devote sufficient attention to the advice he receives and may influence that advice by his comments. According to Hamilton Jordan, Carter's White House chief of staff,

> I had learned . . . that if I wanted to change his mind or challenge him on something that was important or complicated, it was best to do it in writing. If I went into his office to argue with him, armed with five reasons to do something, I would rarely get beyond point one before he was aggressively countering it. I seldom got to the second or third point.[28]

When personally confronted, President Carter may have gone on the defensive; written differences of opinion were perhaps easier for him to accept.

Multiple Advocacy

Closely related to the form in which presidents receive advice is the range of options they receive and the effectiveness with which those options are presented. The president needs to hear a wide range of options, vetted by neutral parties who have no personal stake in them. He should not be dependent on a single channel of information, as occurred, for example, when the president and other high officials, including the Joint Chiefs of Staff, relied on the CIA's estimates of the success of the 1961 invasion of Cuba at the Bay of Pigs. Only the CIA evaluated the Bay of Pigs plan—the briefers were also the advocates—with disastrous consequences. As CIA Director Allen Dulles put it, "It isn't your job to say, 'Well, that's a rotten plan I've presented'."[29]

Subordinates may exaggerate the evidence in support of their favored options. Officials in the George W. Bush administration who supported invading Iraq made assertions about the existence of WMDs that went beyond the evidence. The CIA itself was too assertive about the evidence of WMDs in the *President's Daily Brief* (the highly classified intelligence report the president receives each morning) and in the National Intelligence Estimate on Iraq it produced in the fall of 2002.[30]

Quality decision making requires more than simply presenting the president with a diversity of views. It is also necessary that an effective advocate represent each point of view. This is not always the case, however, because differences exist among advisers in persuasive skills, intellectual ability, policy expertise, power, status, standing with the president, and analytical staff support. These disparities may distort the decision-making process by giving some viewpoints an undue advantage. As Theodore Sorensen observed, "The most formidable debater is not necessarily the most informed, and the most reticent may sometimes be the wisest."[31]

Costs

Presidents need advice that gives them a manageable amount of useful information that relates to real-world options. Multiple advocacy forces a large number of issues to the top—that is, to the president. Debate and give-and-take on issues require a substantial commitment of time on the part of both the president and his staff, and time is a scarce commodity in the White House. According to a Ford assistant, "We don't have time to make sure all the advisors have access to the President."[32]

A multiple advocacy system also requires that the president want to hear the effective presentation of a wide range of views. The president may not be interested in hearing much about some issues. Some presidents may simply not want to hear the effective presentation of a wide range of views. Bill Clinton and Barack Obama are notable for typically examining issues from every angle, although this sometimes led to policy drift. Obama was careful to include representatives of an array of opinions and often sought information from expert advisers to senior officials. He also insisted on being offered more than one viable option.[33]

In order for debate among advisers and the chief executive to be useful, the president must be able to accommodate the interpersonal tensions inherent in an advisory system of close give-and-take. However, not all presidents possess this tolerance. Ronald Reagan hated conflict, as did Richard Nixon, whose personality was not amenable to dealing with oral confrontations. Thus, Nixon conducted as much business as possible by memos. In fact, his aversion to open disagreement both affected the quality of his decision-making process and led him to alter policy decisions to achieve consensus. According to national security assistant Henry Kissinger,

> So much time, effort, and ingenuity were spent in trying to organize a consensus of the senior advisers that there was too little left to consider the weaknesses in the plan or to impose discipline on the rest of the government.[34]

Multiple advocacy also runs a considerable risk of increasing staff conflict. Presidents must engage in the delicate balancing act of being in firm control of the process of decision making while encouraging free and open discussion. This balancing is difficult enough to accomplish while they are considering options. It is even more of a challenge after they decide on a course of action, because it is not uncommon for both winners and losers among presidential advisers to be less than gracious and turn to backstabbing and leaking information to the press.

Process Manager

Some political scientists have suggested that the president needs a process manager to balance the resources of his advisers and strengthen the weaker advocates, ensure that all options are articulated and have effective advocates, set up additional channels of information, arrange for independent evaluations of decisional premises and options when necessary, and generally monitor the decision-making process and identify and correct any malfunctions. This delicate role can easily be undermined if the custodian is also a policy adviser, presidential spokesperson, enforcer of decisions, administrative operator, or watchdog for the president's power stakes. He or she must remain an "honest broker" who is concerned with the process of advising the president. This adviser must also keep his or her own staff small so that it will not become specialized and circumvent established channels of advice.[35]

Devil's Advocate

In some decision-making situations, an adviser may adopt the role of "devil's advocate" in order to provide a challenge to the dominant point of view. The devil's advocate may relieve some of the stress of decision making because officials feel they have considered all sides of an issue, and there may be some public relations benefits for publicizing the fact that the president considered a full range of views. Decision makers may also benefit from listening to and rebutting challenges to their course of action, and those who are least enthusiastic about a decision may be more willing to join in a consensus view if there was prior debate.

Nevertheless, the devil's advocate does not necessarily improve the quality of White House decision making. Because the devil's advocate is playing a role and is not a true dissenter, he or she is unlikely to persist in opposition or try to form coalitions or employ all resources to persuade others. Such an advocate is not really engaged in a truly competitive struggle. Moreover, officials may discount ahead of time the comments of someone who persistently plays the devil's advocate role. Nonetheless, if devil's advocacy is not routinized, there is no assurance that it will operate when needed to provide balance to an argument.

Presidential Participation

In his classic study of presidential power, Richard Neustadt alerted future presidents that they would need information, including tangible details, to construct a necessary frame of reference for decision making.[36] Presidents cannot assume that any person or advisory system will provide them with the options and information they require. As Barack Obama said, "What I know concerns me. What I don't know concerns me even more. What people aren't telling me worries me the most."[37] Thus, the president must be actively involved in the decision-making process, setting the tone for other participants, maintaining the integrity of the advisory system, and reaching out widely for options and information. When presidents fail to follow these principles, the consequences may be profound.

Maintaining the Process

Despite their different styles, all presidents need a systematic process for decision making, and it is up to the president to maintain that process. Failure to do so may lead to the haphazard consideration of options and information. Early in his tenure, Barack Obama was insensitive to organizational issues, and the White House advisory and policy development process suffered from disorganization and distortion in the personnel and options included in important discussions.[38]

In general, the George W. Bush White House lacked a process to ensure that the right questions—such as the consequences of actions—were asked and answered or that alternatives were considered.[39] Even many of the leading policy makers and advisers complained that the policy process was dysfunctional.[40] Secretary of Defense Donald Rumsfeld felt that the president did not always receive, and may not have insisted on, a timely consideration of his options before he made a decision. Rumsfeld also found the National Security Council (NSC) meetings often to be disorganized, decisions to be poorly summarized, and discussion papers late in arriving to the participants.[41]

Vice President Cheney's office sometimes diverted information from the president[42] or took information and options directly to Bush without the normal interagency review.[43] Some officials injected raw, unvetted intelligence directly into discussions regarding the war in Iraq.[44] Senior officials also sometimes used back channels and informal meetings for real decisions, short-circuiting debate and inter-agency reviews.[45]

In meetings of top officials, the secretaries of state and defense generally did not comment on each other's statements or views,[46] so the president missed the benefit of serious, substantive discussion between his principal advisers. Moreover, the president did not force a discussion or support his national security assistant in efforts to intervene to compel the secretary of defense to answer critical questions about the war in Iraq. Nor did the president press for resolution of differences or contra-dictions in evaluations and recommendations among his advisers.[47] We will see later that the president also did not push his top officials to focus on the basic premises of US policy.

Probing Questions

Presidents need to ask probing questions to ferret out weaknesses in arguments and proposals. Moreover, advisers will anticipate such questions when they take options and information to the president. This expectation will make proposals better before they reach the Oval Office.[48]

Barack Obama had a reputation for asking probing questions that challenged the assumptions of alternatives.[49] In 1986, in contrast, President Ronald Reagan approved a proposal to sell arms to Iran in hopes of obtaining the release of American hostages held in the Middle East without insisting on thorough staff work on the initiative. In the end, the policy was a failure and undermined the nation's strongly asserted position of refusing to trade arms—or anything else—for hostages. In addi-tion, the president's standing fell substantially in the polls, diminishing his political clout. The situation became even worse when the diversion of funds to the Contras came to light, and Reagan had to endure a year of congressional hearings and a critical investigation by a special commission examining his handling of the matter.

A series of books written by top officials in the Reagan administration reveal that the president was a peculiarly detached decision maker. He had strong views on the basic goals of public policy but left it to others to implement his broad vision. Aides prepared detailed scripts on index cards for his use in meetings. Reagan's detachment and lack of mastery of policy details hindered his evaluation of policy options, a process he left to others. As he explained in his memoirs, "Because I was so concerned about getting the hostages home, I may not have asked enough ques-tions about how the Iranian initiative was being conducted."[50]

Two of the most important events of the past generation have been the September 11, 2001, terrorist attacks on the United States and the US invasion of Iraq in 2003. The terrorist attacks caught the country by surprise. The United States invaded Iraq on the premise that it possessed substantial stocks of WMDs. In both cases, there were serious problems with the information the president received. The George W. Bush White House portrayed the president and his top advisers as consumers of imprecise intelligence, making the best decisions they could in a murky world of secret plots and illicit programs.

There is another view, however. President Bush often described himself as an instinctual decision maker,[51] a view shared by other close observers.[52] A drawback to relying on instincts is acting impulsively rather than delving deeply into a range of possible options. Gut reactions also discourage investing time in soliciting and cultivating the views of others and asking probing questions of advisers.

There is a range of views of whether Bush was intellectually passive, lacking inquisitiveness, and resisting reflection, as some have charged.[53] To the extent it was true, it would have also discouraged tough questioning and thorough analysis. Rather than complicated, rigorous policy analysis of what policies should be, his intellectual curiosity focused on reaching the bottom line of a solution and knowing what he needed to do to sell and implement his policies.[54] Such an approach may not do justice to issues such as terrorism that are laced with subtlety and nuance.

When the CIA briefed the president on August 6, 2001, about the threat from al-Qaeda, he did not follow up with questions, instructions, or discussions with his top advisers.[55] When the president expressed dismay at the CIA's information regarding Iraq's possession of WMDs following a briefing on December 21, 2002, CIA Director George Tenet replied that the case was a "slam dunk." Instead of pushing the CIA to reexamine its data or to obtain better information, Bush relied on Tenet's reassurance.[56] Bush later concluded, "In retrospect, of course, we all should have pushed harder on the intelligence and revisited our assumptions. But at the time, the evidence and the logic pointed in the other direction."[57] It is at such times that reassessments may be most crucial.

Actually, the White House never requested any intelligence estimate on Iraq before the invasion; Democrats on the Senate Intelligence Committee requested a National Intelligence Estimate. When the CIA produced the estimate, the White House did not engage in a thorough assessment of the evidence.[58] Indeed, Bush often failed to ask experts and relevant officials probing questions, including what they thought about an issue.[59] For example, after the president met with David Kay, the chief US weapons inspector, who reported on the lack of evidence of WMDs, Bush seemed disengaged. "I'm not sure I've spoken to anyone at that level who seemed less inquisitive," Kay recalled.[60] Even when it came to going to war, he made the decision early without systematic, rigorous internal debate of the pros and cons of doing so.[61] He also did not ask the opinion of some of his chief advisers.[62] Thinking you already know where your advisers stand, as Bush did,[63] is not the same as having them debate an issue in front of you.

Similarly, well-placed officials in the administration were skeptical about the intelligence on WMDs in Iraq, but an effective expression of these views apparently did not reach Bush,[64] at least partly because he did not encourage dissent. In fact, the president's emphasis on expressing certainty and optimism[65] rather than engaging in substantive policy debate regarding Iraq discouraged officials from reconsidering policy, even when it was clear that it was failing.[66] Shades-of-grey analysis is incompatible with certainty.

Bush's lack of inquisitiveness, failure to ask probing questions, and lack of interest in rigorous policy analysis discouraged coherent discussions about policy and led to carelessness in evaluating options. Top officials never systematically discussed disbanding the Iraqi army or de-Baathification of the Iraqi public service[67] or the controversial questions regarding detainees and electronic surveillance.[68] In retrospect, the president concluded he should have insisted on more debate on such decisions.[69]

The president's approach also delayed reaction to realities, such as the insurgency in Iraq, and deterred advice that ran counter to his instincts.[70] Thus, in the president's words, it "took four painful, costly years" to change US military policy in post-invasion Iraq.[71]

At this point, the president changed his approach to decision making. He initiated "deep dives" with national security specialists in which he actively probed and questioned analysts and dug into the details of policy.[72] He also authorized a thorough review of US policy in Iraq. "I wanted to challenge every assumption behind our strategy and generate new options," he reported. After gathering facts and options from inside and outside the administration, he challenged assumptions and weighed all the options carefully.[73] Ultimately, he decided to support the "surge" option, which proved to be successful.

Reaching Out

Bill Clinton was blindsided by the negative congressional and public response to his proposal to lift the ban on homosexuals in the military. He saw the issue as one of discrimination, but many others saw it in other terms—as an issue of morality, of military readiness, or both. By not seeking other perspectives, the president subjected himself to a firestorm of criticism and had to backtrack on his policy. Similarly, at the end of his administration, Clinton issued a large number of pardons, bypassing the normal vetting process for pardons. He was widely criticized for pardoning people who had used family and political connections to get their cases to the Oval Office.

One reason the George W. Bush White House was so slow to recognize the disaster occurring in New Orleans in the wake of Hurricane Katrina is that it was primarily dependent on one line of communication about conditions in the flooded city. It took the president some days to realize that the levees had been breached and acknowledge the terrible conditions of people trapped at the convention center—or even that there were people there at all.[74] Much of the rest of America knew these facts, however, and never forgave the president for his reaction to the worst natural disaster in a century. Bush also did not consult people outside the White House on Iraq and relied heavily on his national security assistant to drive the reevaluation of US strategy in Iraq.[75] Once again, the president suffered the loss of the public's confidence.

Donald Trump's decision-making style stands alone among modern presidents. His admirers applaud his approach while his detractors condemn it. You can read more about the president's approach in box 9.2.

Box 9.2 ★ Donald Trump as Decision Maker

Donald Trump entered the White House with a public persona partially derived from his reality television program, *The Apprentice*, in which he authoritatively barked "you're fired" to underperforming contestants. This weekly ritual became a trademark for Trump, one he often employs in comments as president. The impression left with viewers is one of a decisive decision maker in full command of his field.

The reality is different. Although the president makes decisions, he prefers one-page memos with bullet points to simplify his decision making. He freely admits that he does little background reading on issues.[76] Trump's intellectual passivity and lack of knowledge does not aid him in asking probing questions. The exception seems to be immigration policy, where he has strong views and is heavily engaged in policy making.[77] He also seems to have been atypically systematic in his 2017 decision to ramp up the US effort in Afghanistan.

On the other hand, he does not have rigid views on many issues. He meets with many people, seems willing to listen to advisers on some issues, and sometimes

(continued)

Box 9.2 ★ Continued

changes his mind after hearing their views. It is not clear that he routinely gathers his advisers for open discussion of issues. However, the president has turned to another group of advisers—from family, real estate, media, finance, and politics—many of whom he consults at least once a week. Many of these persons are not experts in public policy.[78]

The White House has experienced substantial chaos and mismanagement, as we saw in box 9.1. The president has not shown much sensitivity toward following a systematic decision-making process.[79] For example, John Bolton, his third national security adviser, cut to a bare minimum meetings in which top national security officials presented and vetted options for the president. Instead of synthesizing and transmitting views across the government to the president, he functioned as an arbiter of what he believed the president needed to hear.[80]

Nor is Trump particularly interested in systematic analyses. The Treasury department never produced a detailed analysis of the impact of the 2017 tax cut, releasing only a one-page appraisal of the nearly five-hundred-page bill. The president has never appointed a science advisor or consulted with scientists in decisions such as those regarding the environment, nuclear proliferation, and food safety.[81] Regarding trade, his Director of Trade and Industrial Policy Peter Navarro summarized his advisory role: "My function, really, as an economist is to try to provide the underlying analytics that confirm his intuition."[82] In other words, Trump's aide was working to bolster the president's instincts, not to inform his beliefs. When asked by Gary Cohn, the director of the National Economic Council, why he thought the trade deficit was a problem for the country—contrary to the view of most economists, Trump replied, "I just do."[83] When his advisors told him Iran was not in violation of the 2015 nuclear agreement with the US and its major European allies, the president rejected their more informed views,[84] as he did with intelligence agencies' views on Iran, North Korea, and Russia—seemingly trying to bully them into acquiescence.[85]

Lacking command of issues, the president makes many decisions largely based on his instincts instead of careful deliberation. As he put it, "I have a gut, and my gut tells me more sometimes than anybody else's brain can ever tell me."[86] His gut has led him to making impulsive decisions, without organized review from relevant parties and policy experts.[87]

Examples include:

- imposing strict tariffs on steel and aluminum imports;
- withdrawing from the Paris agreement on climate change;
- banning travel from citizens of several Middle East nations;
- promising that North Korea threats against the United States would be met with "fire and fury";
- prohibiting transgender people from serving in the military;
- agreeing to a nuclear summit with North Korea;
- ordering an extraordinarily expensive overhaul of nuclear weapons;
- precipitating the longest government shutdown in US history;
- removing US troops from Syria;
- cutting forces in Afghanistan by half; and
- launching a Space Force.

In response to criticism of his impulsive and uninformed decisions, Trump tweeted a description of himself as a "genius . . . and a very stable genius at that!" Whatever one may think of the president's mental abilities (and few think he is a genius), most experienced observers agree that although everyone needs a foundation of values and beliefs, they also need good advice and analysis to test them against.

Secrecy

Because only decision makers directly responsible for a policy are normally consulted on sensitive matters, fewer advisers contribute to secret deliberations than to debate on more open issues. This reduces the range of options that are considered in a secret decision and limits the analysis of the few options that are considered. For example, the secrecy of President Johnson's "Tuesday lunch group," which made the important decisions on the Vietnam War, prevented an advance agenda. Thus, decisions were made without a full prior review of the options.

Secrecy also makes it easier for those directly involved to dismiss (intentionally or unintentionally) the dissenting or offbeat ideas of outsiders as the products of ignorance. This is unfortunate because secret information is often inaccurate or misleading. President Kennedy wished he had not been successful in persuading the *New York Times* not to publish the plans for the Bay of Pigs invasion; afterward, he felt that publicity might have elicited some useful critiques.

RELATIONSHIPS WITH ADVISERS

Presidents require the services of personal aides to carry out their duties. Because they must rely heavily on their aides and work closely with them, they naturally choose people of similar attitudes and compatible personalities. Moreover, strong personalities, and most presidents have them, create environments to their liking and weed out irritations.

Disagreeing with the President

Many—perhaps most—people have found it difficult to stand up to a president and disagree with him. For example, several of President Reagan's top aides had doubts about his economic policies even in 1981 but did not relay them to the president until after the program was enacted. At times, advisers may be strong advocates of a position before a meeting with the president yet will completely switch their arguments during the meeting if they learn the president has accepted the opposite view. It was because of this phenomenon that President Kennedy often absented himself from meetings of his advisers during the Cuban missile crisis—he wanted the participants to feel free to speak their minds.

Sometimes advisers find it difficult to disagree with the president due to his strong, dynamic, or magnetic personality. These traits are certainly not unusual in successful politicians, especially presidents. For example, former White House assistant Chester Cooper wrote that President Lyndon Johnson often polled his foreign policy advisers one at a time to hear their views on the Vietnam War. Each dutifully would respond, "I agree," even though Cooper, and undoubtedly others, did not. Cooper even dreamed of answering no, but he never did.[88] Other Johnson administration officials reported a similar tendency for those around the president to tell him what they thought he wanted to hear about the war rather than what they really thought.[89]

One reason for the reluctance of presidential aides to challenge the president is that they are completely dependent on him for their jobs, their advancement, and the gratification of their egos through his favor. Cabinet members are nearly as dependent, although they may also have support in Congress or from interest groups. Because aides usually desire to perpetuate their positions, they may refrain from giving the president "unpleasant" information or from fighting losing battles on behalf of their principles. Even Nixon's White House chief of staff, H. R. Haldeman, felt that in order to survive in his own job, he could not fight sufficiently to counter the dark side of the president's character.

"*All those in favor say 'Aye.'*"
"*Aye.*"   "*Aye.*"   "*Aye.*"
"*Aye.*"   "*Aye.*"

Thus, presidents often find it difficult to evoke critical responses from staff members. Barack Obama was aware of the potential of aides' stifling dissent, not telling him bad news and telling what they thought he wanted to hear. He wanted pushback and dissent but found it difficult to obtain.[90] According to Gerald Ford,

> Few people, with the possible exception of his wife, will ever tell a President that he is a fool. There's a majesty to the office that inhibits even your closest friends from saying what is really on their minds. They won't tell you that you just made a lousy speech or bungled a chance to get your point across. . . . You can tell them you want the blunt truth; you can leave instructions on every bulletin board, but the guarded response you get never varies.
>
> And yet the president—any president—needs to hear straight talk. He needs to be needled once in a while, if only to be brought down from the false pedestal that the office provides. He needs to be told that he is, after all, only another human being with the same virtues and weaknesses as anyone else. And he needs to be reminded of this constantly if he's going to keep his perspective.[91]

Discouraging Advice

An executive who "punishes" those aides who present options or information he dislikes may reinforce the reluctance of advisers to disagree with the president. Lyndon Johnson was such a person. He forced top aides and officials who dissented on Vietnam to leave his administration, and he went so far as to reduce contact with such key people as Secretaries of Defense Robert McNamara and Clark Clifford and Vice President Hubert Humphrey. In response to a cautionary memo from Humphrey about Vietnam, Johnson said, "We don't need all these memos" and excluded him from his inner circle.[92]

Johnson's press secretary, George Reedy, observed that the Johnson White House had an inner political life of its own. Consequently, the staff carefully studied the president's state of mind to gain and maintain access to him. They wanted to be around when there was good news to report and discreetly absent when the news was bad in hopes that someone else would receive the blame.[93] Naturally, this gamesmanship served to distort Johnson's view of reality.

Richard Nixon had little interest in hearing critiques of his weak points, and those who attempted to criticize him did not maintain their influence for long. Even as secure and personable a president as Franklin Roosevelt is reported to have permitted only staffers who would not challenge him. Bill Clinton was generally open to a range of views, but he had a hot temper, which he frequently unleashed at aides. John F. Kennedy's national security adviser, McGeorge Bundy, banished Richard Goodwin from meetings on Cuba after Goodwin dissented on the Bay of Pigs invasion.[94]

The dampening effect of behavior like that of Johnson, Nixon, or Clinton on discussions even outside the Oval Office can be substantial. Aides may be fearful of presidential punishment or tirades, and therefore remain silent lest they provoke the president to anger. Johnson's Office of Congressional Relations chief Lawrence O'Brien and Vice President Hubert Humphrey were in constant contact for months before they became aware of each other's views on Vietnam. Because President Johnson equated criticism with disloyalty, even the highest officials in the White House kept their dissent to themselves.

George W. Bush

There was a similar phenomenon in the George W. Bush White House, which put a premium on loyalty and team play. As a result, at least some officials did not deliver bad news to the president or sugarcoated it in order to remain in the president's good graces.[95] When the administration publicly rebuked and undermined Army Chief of Staff General Eric K. Shinseki after he testified to Congress that it would take several hundred thousand troops to stabilize Iraq after the invasion, it sent a chilling message through the military and discouraged other generals from requesting troops.[96]

The Bush administration also employed more subtle tactics to influence the information intelligence agencies presented to it. Officials, especially Vice President Richard Cheney and his chief of staff, Scooter Libby, persistently asked the CIA questions regarding Saddam Hussein's ties to terrorists. Some analysts chafed at this constant drumbeat of repetitive questions. More importantly, despite no obvious pressure to change answers, officials' questions and visits to CIA headquarters created an environment that subtly, but unmistakably, influenced the agency's work. As the president's commission on intelligence failures regarding Iraq concluded, "it is hard to deny that intelligence analysts worked in an environment that did not encourage skepticism about the conventional wisdom." There are many opportunities for bias when the evidence is fragmentary and uncertain, which can be expressed in caveat, nuance, and word choice. Moreover, reeling from its failure to predict the 9/11 attacks, the CIA could not assess intelligence free of the administration's assumptions and the obvious context that the United States was going to war. The vice president's characterization of uncertain and ambiguous intelligence as facts skewed the balance of considerations the analysts were weighing. Some skeptical CIA officials were shunted aside while more hawkish officials found it easy to get their reports to the attention of the CIA leadership and other high officials, who did not want to hear skepticism. There was widespread acceptance of weak intelligence. A Department of Energy edict to scientists not to talk to the media about aluminum tubes suspected (wrongly) of being part of a nuclear weapons program prevented them from challenging the CIA's analysis and sent fear throughout the department's nuclear labs.[97]

Need for Secrecy

Presidents with heightened fears of security leaks may place loyalty above competence, independence, or openness among their advisers. They may also control the information flow tightly and keep everyone, even insiders, in the dark. One of the reasons why President Johnson relied so heavily on a group of five or six high officials (called the "Tuesday lunch group") to advise him on the Vietnam War was that he felt the larger NSC leaked too much information. According to Secretary of State Dean Rusk, "The Tuesday luncheons were where the really important issues regarding Vietnam were discussed in great detail. This was where the real decisions were made. And everyone there knew how to keep his mouth shut."[98]

Concern for Public Opinion

Ironically, one inhibition on freedom of dissension in the White House and the upper levels of the bureaucracy is public opinion. If the president allows an open discussion of policy views, there will inevitably be disagreement, which the press may present as evidence that the president is not in control and the White House lacks a sense of direction—or even that it is in disarray. Thus, by being open the president may lose some public support, but by being closed to options and information he may make poor decisions.

Encouraging Dissent

Not all presidents discourage dissent, however. George H. W. Bush was a secure decision maker who was well informed, knowledgeable, experienced, and involved in decision making. He wanted to hear a wide range of options, and he worked at maintaining civility and openness in discussion. Similarly, Dwight Eisenhower established an environment in which his advisers felt free to challenge his views. Barack Obama followed the same pattern.

Groupthink

Psychologist Irving Janis argued that another factor discouraging disagreement among presidential advisers is a psychological phenomenon he termed *groupthink*. Groupthink refers to the conformist thinking that may result when people are intensely involved in small, cohesive decision-making groups, such as those formed during crisis situations. According to Janis, the stress of a crisis generates a desire for unity among policy advisers that, in turn, reduces their uncertainty over the proper course of action and helps to preserve their emotional well-being. The advisers' desire for unanimity overrides their motivations to appraise situations and policy alternatives realistically. They suspend critical opinions and produce a consensus.[99] The groupthink effect may have influenced a number of high-level administration decisions.

The ill-fated decision by almost all of President Kennedy's advisers to support an invasion of the Bay of Pigs in Cuba in 1961 is one illustration that Janis used to support his thesis. Other examples of conformist—and incorrect—decision making include the failure to anticipate the Japanese attack on Pearl Harbor, the North Korean attacks on South Korea that began the Korean War, and the initial thinking on Vietnam at the beginning of the Johnson administration.

Staff Rivalries

Feuding and infighting for power and access to the president among ambitious aides are also obstacles to rational decision making. This rivalry takes several forms. One of the most common techniques is to attack rivals by leaking to the press that they are out of favor with the president or not competent to carry out their duties. Sometimes the leaks place competitors for power in a context that is favorable but will displease the president, who may prefer having credit and publicity for himself rather than his aides.

In recent years, the Nixon, Ford, Reagan, and Trump administrations stand out for the extent of their internal feuding and infighting. One high-level Reagan aide disclosed how he and other White House officials tried to undercut Secretary of State Alexander Haig: "In a classic case of Washington infighting, we threw virtually every booby trap in his way that we could, planted every story, egged the press on to get down on him."[100]

Anthony Scaramucci was named White House communications director in July 2017. The same week he falsely claimed that White House Chief of Staff Reince Priebus had leaked a document. Then, in a vulgarity-laced interview with the *New Yorker*, Scaramucci railed against Priebus and Stephen K. Bannon, the president's chief strategist, calling the former a "f***ing paranoid schizophrenic." He also claimed Trump would ask Priebus to resign soon. It appears that the president encouraged Scaramucci's jihad, keeping with his pattern of subjecting Priebus to both private and public indignities.[101] Priebus lost his job the next day. Scaramucci himself was gone within a few more days.

This widespread feuding encourages self-interested behavior by presidential advisers, which may distort their vision and cause them to overextend their arguments and present unbalanced discussions of options and their consequences to the president. There is also a tendency for competing advisers to seek to aggrandize influence and monopolize the counsel on which presidents base decisions, thereby providing insufficient information, analysis, and deliberation for decisions. Staff rivalry also detracts from the efficiency of White House operations, as it wastes time and lowers morale. Moreover, feuding in the White House can embarrass the president if it is covered in the press (which it inevitably is).

High officials in Washington know that their ability to interact effectively with the bureaucracy depends on being known for their effectiveness with the president. Former Secretary of State Dean Rusk argued that "the real organization of government at higher echelons is . . . how confidence flows down from the President."[102] To maintain their reputations for effectiveness with the president, officials may not strongly advocate positions that they consider sound if they feel the president is unlikely to adopt their proposals. An official does not usually want to be known as someone whose advice the president rejected.

Loss of Perspective

An additional potential hindrance to sound advice for the president is the loss of perspective by White House aides. Because working in the White House is a unique experience, a narrowing of viewpoints can easily occur. Especially for top aides, the environment is luxurious, secure, and heady; the exercise of power is an everyday experience. The potential for isolation is real, and therefore the chief executive must fight these insulating tendencies. President Johnson was very sensitive about the risk that his aides might lose perspective, so he closely controlled the use of White House perks and stripped his staff of pretensions with a "merciless persistency."[103]

Role Conceptions

Advisers' conceptions of their jobs influence their delivery of information and options. President Eisenhower's secretaries of defense, Charles Wilson and Neil McElroy, considered themselves managers of the department and did not become heavily involved in disputes over foreign policy or strategic doctrine. By contrast, Secretary of Defense Robert McNamara adopted an aggressive stance as an adviser; yet McNamara's colleague, Secretary of State Dean Rusk, did not consider it his job to participate in policy disputes with his colleagues or the president. In fact, many observers thought that Rusk failed to present effectively State Department views on important foreign policy issues.

Similarly, Secretary of State Condoleezza Rice did not see it as her role to criticize prominent officials with whom she disagreed such as Vice President Cheney or Secretary of Defense Donald Rumsfeld.[104] Her predecessor as George W. Bush's secretary of state, Colin Powell, met privately with the president to express concerns about war in Iraq rather than speaking frankly in front of other senior advisers who were pressing forward with battle plans. Powell and Secretary of Defense Donald Rumsfeld frequently disagreed but did not confront each other face to face.[105]

Maintaining Morale

With all the long hours and stress that those at the top of government experience, morale becomes even more important than it is in other organizations. The presidents has a role in maintaining the morale of his subordinates.

Donald Trump demands absolute loyalty from those who serve him. This requirement is not unusual, but the fact that he does not always offer it in return is. He seems to prefer a management style in which even compliments can come laced with a bite, and where enduring snubs and belittling jokes, even in public, is part of the job.[106] During a lunch with UN ambassadors, he jokingly polled the room on whether they thought UN Ambassador Nikki Haley, seated next to him, was doing a good job. "How do you all like Nikki?" he asked. "Otherwise, she can easily be replaced." (Trump followed his jest with a reassurance: "No, we won't do that. I promise.")[107]

In July, the president bluntly told an interviewer that he would not have nominated Jeff Sessions for attorney general if he had known that he would recuse himself from the investigation of Russian collusion with the Trump presidential campaign.[108] A few days later he publicly called him "beleaguered" and questioned why the Justice Department was not investigating Hillary Clinton. The next day, the president tweeted again, criticizing Sessions for having a "very weak position" on an investigation into Clinton. He even went so far to claim in an interview that Sessions, his earliest endorser among Senate Republicans, had backed his candidacy only because he saw the big campaign rallies and wanted a piece of the action.[109] Trump also attacked the acting FBI director, Andrew McCabe, and later tweeted to complain that Sessions had not fired him. This style of interaction with subordinates is unlikely to lift subordinates' morale.

Impact of the Decision-Making Process

Presidents Eisenhower and Johnson both faced the decision of military intervention in Vietnam (in 1954 and 1964–1965, respectively). Eisenhower chose not to intervene, whereas Johnson eventually sent more than a half million American troops. How did the two presidents' decision-making processes affect their decisions?

Eisenhower, who had headed organizations of enormous size and complexity as a military commander, was sensitive about the impact of the structure of advisory systems on the process of analyzing policies and making decisions. His system produced spirited, open debate; his aides would challenge the president, often tenaciously, even though he openly expressed his own opinions. He was exposed to diverse views (rather than "loaded" presentations of options), sharply-focused alternatives, and advice separated from parochial interests. In addition, he supplemented his formal advisory system with an informal, fluid process of consultation that interacted with, and reinforced, the formal system.

Eisenhower was clearly in charge and kept his options open. He reasoned explicitly about the means and ends, the trade-offs, and the consequences of options, and he thought strategically, viewing issues as parts of more comprehensive patterns. In this way, he set the tone for decision making in his administration.

Johnson, in contrast, was insensitive to the impact of advisory structures. His advisory system was organizationally chaotic, marked by an absence of regular meetings and routinized procedures, shifts in the membership of advisory and decision-making groups, a reliance on out-of-channel advocacy, weak staff work, and other impediments to rigorous policy analysis.

Johnson's heavy reliance on informal advising by a few people and a lack of systematized staff work left many policy disagreements unresolved and unexamined. Frequently, options were neither coherently assembled nor carefully considered, and there was a lack of broad strategic debate in which the underlying assumptions of policy could be questioned. Policy differences at all levels were typically not sharply stated or directly analyzed, and there was a lack of forums in which contradictory views could be clarified, studied, and debated. The views of most dissenters were not rejected after discussion; instead, they were simply not discussed. The lack of systematic policy analysis and the reliance on a few advisers left the upper and lower levels of the foreign policy community separated, and the impact of advice became more a function of skill and resources in bureaucratic politics than the logic of the argument.

In many ways, the president was his own worst enemy. He immersed himself in detail rather than focusing on broad policy questions, and he was insulated from confrontation with his advisers' views. Johnson failed to press for additional alternatives or question incisively the options presented to him. Continuing the pattern of his years in the Senate, he remained preoccupied with searching for consensus within and probing for areas of agreement rather than disagreement. His personal interactions with his advisers encouraged a narrowing rather than a broadening of options, and his intolerance of disagreement had a chilling effect on the range of advice he received.

In sum, Eisenhower was a planner and conceptualizer, whereas Johnson was an individualistic political operator. Eisenhower was preoccupied with analyzing policy; Johnson, with the politics of making it. Each constructed an advisory system to meet his needs. At least in the case of Vietnam, these advisory systems, as well as the people who composed them and the presidents themselves, made a difference in the options the president chose.[110]

Presidents Lyndon Johnson (left) and Dwight Eisenhower (right) had very different approaches to organizing their advisory processes.

Yoichi Okamoto, LBJ Library Photos

COGNITIVE PROCESSING

Presidents and their advisers, no matter how accomplished, are human beings, subject to the same tendencies and limitations as less prominent people. They bring to office views about the nature of the problems the country faces and appropriate policies to deal with them. They also have cognitive needs that condition their processing of information, evaluating options, and making decisions.

Impact of Worldviews

Presidents and their aides bring to office sets of beliefs about politics, policy, human nature, and social causality—in other words, beliefs about how and why the world works as it does. These beliefs provide a frame of reference for evaluating policy options, for filtering information and giving it meaning, and for establishing potential boundaries of action.[111] Beliefs also help busy officials cope with complex decisions to which they can devote limited time, and they predispose people to act in certain directions. Although sets of beliefs are inevitable and help to simplify the world, they can be dysfunctional as well.

We learned in chapter 5 that motivated reasoning may distort a person's perception of new information and the conclusions he or she reaches about it. Most people seek out information confirming their preexisting opinions and ignore or reject arguments contrary to their predispositions. When exposed to competing arguments, they typically accept the confirming ones and dismiss or argue against the opposing ones. These biases toward continuity result from the physiology of human cognitive processes and are reinforced from thinking a certain way. They are difficult to combat. Consequently, there is an unconscious tendency to see what we expect to see, which distorts our analytical handling of evidence.

Identification of Problems

Worldviews may distort the identification of a problem that requires attention. Surprise attacks by one country on another—unfortunately, not a rare occurrence—perhaps most dramatically illustrate this phenomenon.[112] The George H. W. Bush White House was surprised when Iraq invaded Kuwait in 1990, even though it had obtained substantial evidence of a massive military buildup on the Kuwaiti border. As Secretary of State Jim Baker put it, no one believed that Saddam Hussein would attack because an attack made no sense from the perspective of those who calculated his interests.[113]

It is natural to assume that foreign leaders are rational as Americans understand rationality, so Americans frequently misread the intentions of other countries. The United States did not anticipate the Soviet Union's invasion of Afghanistan because we knew it would be a mistake. We could not believe Mikhail Gorbachev was serious about reforms because we knew they would undermine the stability of the USSR and thus his position. It did not occur to us in 1941 that Japan thought we would be willing to fight and lose a limited war, and we could not believe Nikita Khrushchev would place Soviet missiles in Cuba.[114] We were surprised by the Indian nuclear weapons test in 1998 because it did not seem in India's best interests.[115] The United States and Israel were surprised by Egypt's attack on Israel in 1973, because both countries assumed Egypt would not attack until it had rebuilt its air force.[116]

The George W. Bush administration operated on several basic premises regarding the aftermath of the war in Iraq, such as that

- Iraqis would greet Americans as liberators;
- Iraq's infrastructure would be in serviceable condition;
- the Iraqi army would remain in whole units capable of being used for reconstruction;
- the Iraqi police were trustworthy and professional, capable of securing the country; and
- there would be a smooth and rapid transition for Iraq to become a democratic nation.

Each of these premises was faulty, but the administration made no systematic evaluation of them before the war and was slow to challenge them, even in the wake of widespread violence.[117] As Stephen Headley, the president's national security adviser, put it, "We never connected it up. . . . I don't know why. It seems in retrospect, very clear."[118]

At other times, worldviews may encourage policy makers to *assume* problems rather than subject their premises to rigorous analysis. Because after 9/11 the Bush White House was highly risk adverse[119] and because it was certain that Saddam Hussein possessed WMDs and was a threat to the United States, the administration never organized a systematic internal debate within the administration on the fundamental questions of whether Iraq actually possessed WMDs, whether the Iraqi threat was imminent, whether it was necessary to overthrow Saddam and, if so, the likely consequences of such an action. Instead, it focused on the question of how to invade successfully.[120] As the national intelligence officer for the Middle East put it, the Bush administration "went to war without requesting . . . any strategic-level intelligence assessments on any aspect of Iraq."[121] Moreover, it does not appear that either the president or his national security assistant studied closely the National

Intelligence Estimate made before the war at Congress's request or followed up on the dissents and caveats in the assessment.[122]

It is not surprising, then, that the weakness of the data on Iraq never called into question the quality of basic assumptions. Officials did not interpret the absence of evidence of WMDs as evidence of their absence. Instead, US officials viewed Saddam Hussein's efforts to remove any residue from his old programs to develop WMDs as efforts to *hide* the weapons rather than destroy them.[123] Moreover, it seemed implausible that Saddam would risk destruction of his regime if he actually met international demands regarding WMDs.[124] We did not account for his own view that he could not be too open about his compliance for fear of showing weakness in a dangerous part of the world.[125] In addition, officials remembered that the United States had underestimated Iraq's progress in developing nuclear weapons in the late 1980s and early 1990s and inferred that Iraq had WMDs because it had such a complex organization dedicated to concealing them.[126] In other words, they saw what they expected to see.

In the 1960s, top US officials shared a consensus that

- a communist-free Vietnam was important to the security and credibility of the United States;
- Vietnam was a critical testing ground for the ability of the United States to counter communist support for wars of national liberation;
- stopping communism in Vietnam was critical for US credibility;
- the North Vietnamese would give in to US coercion;
- communism was a world conspiracy;
- South Vietnam would fall to North Vietnam without American aid; and
- if South Vietnam did fall to the Communists, the rest of Southeast Asia would follow.

These premises molded the decisions about US participation in the Vietnam War. This doctrinal consensus made it difficult to challenge US policy and foreclosed policy options such as not escalating the fighting. As a result, "no comprehensive and systematic examination of Vietnam's importance to the United States was ever undertaken within the executive branch. Debates revolved around how to do things better and whether they could be done, not whether they were worth doing."[127]

Options

The worldviews of top decision makers also affect the options they raise to deal with issues and the choices they make. President Reagan believed that the Soviet Union would enter into serious negotiations with the United States only if it were facing an overwhelmingly powerful military force. Consequently, Reagan believed he had no choice but to increase military spending substantially, which he did.

In a crisis, a president's view of a problem and the need to respond to it decisively may foreclose alternatives that do not put a premium on rapid and decisive action. For example, in the period directly preceding the actual fighting in the Persian Gulf War, General Colin Powell, then chairman of the Joint Chiefs of Staff, wanted to consider the option of continuing economic sanctions against Iraq. President George H. W. Bush, however, told him that there was no time to try such a strategy.[128]

Managing Inconsistency

The environment in which the president operates is complex and uncertain, characteristics with which the human mind is not comfortable. People prefer stable views to a continuous consideration of options. About a month before the commencement of hostilities in the Gulf War, George H. W. Bush told an interviewer, "I've got it boiled down very clearly to good and evil. And it helps if you can be that clear in your own mind."[129]

Presidents have to find a level of consistency with which they are comfortable and that is compatible with their intellectual capacities and psychological needs. This may be a difficult task. Decision makers often experience stress as they try to cope with the complexity of decisions, especially in times of crisis. Warren Harding, Ronald Reagan, and sometimes George W. Bush had difficulty analyzing complex policy issues.[130] They dealt with these difficulties by delegating to others much of the responsibility for sorting out the issues and presenting viable options.

These presidents also depended on developing clear-cut (some would say "simplistic") cognitive frameworks for making decisions. These frameworks helped them simplify reality and gave their decisions the appearance of consistency. Once Reagan came to an "understanding" of an event, he did not want to deal with facts that challenged his understanding. As Secretary of State George Schultz put it, "no fact, no argument, no plea for reconsideration would change his mind."[131]

Similarly, Secretary of Defense Robert Gates reported that when George W. Bush had strong convictions on an issue, such as Iraq, he could not be persuaded to change his mind.[132] Richard Clarke, a former antiterrorism top adviser to Bush, said that the president "looked for the simple solution, the bumper sticker description of the problem."[133] Former treasury secretary Paul O'Neill was even more critical, declaring that he never heard Bush "analyze a complex issue, parse opposing positions, and settle on a judicious path."[134]

We have seen in Box 9.2 that Donald Trump had well-established views on a number of issues. Arguments from aides on matters on which the president had developed decades of opinions were pointless. He just did not want to hear views contrary to his own.[135]

Bill Clinton enjoyed grappling with tough policy problems and synthesizing large amounts of data. His elaborate study of an issue could have a political downside, however. It took him longer than promised to design his legislative proposals, the proposals themselves were subject to continuing shifts in emphasis and content, and they were difficult to explain to the American people, which was necessary to build support for them in Washington. Moreover, throughout the process, the president appeared indecisive and inconsistent.

There is widespread agreement about the importance of identifying and examining the major assumptions underlying policy options and evaluating alternatives in the light of these assumptions.[136] Yet we have seen that it is difficult to do this, especially when the truth is implausible and the actions of other leaders are unexpected and self-defeating. Moreover, it is not possible to examine all assumptions, and some of policy makers' assumptions are likely to be correct.

However, decision makers can ask what it would take to disprove their premises and what evidence should be present if their views are correct. They can also focus on the key assumptions of a policy choice in order to carefully scrutinize the information they use to support those assumptions and force themselves to consider alternative explanations for behavior. Reflecting on the war in Iraq, George

George W. Bush was decisive but sometimes failed to examine the core premises of a policy.

W. Bush's national security assistant Condoleezza Rice lamented, "we had not—I had not—done a good enough job of thinking the unthinkable."[137]

Inference Mechanisms

People often simplify reality to deal with the world's complexities and resolve uncertainty by ignoring or deemphasizing information that contradicts their existing beliefs. To do this, they employ inference mechanisms that operate unconsciously and that may have as great an influence on a person's judgments as objective evidence. Consequently, most policy makers remain unreceptive to any major revision of their beliefs in response to new information, especially if they have had success in the past with applying their general beliefs to specific decisions or have held their beliefs for a long time. Moreover, they are unlikely to search for information that challenges their views or options contrary to those they advocate. Instead, they tend to incorporate new information in ways that render it comprehensible within their existing frames of reference. In other words, they rationalize it to support their previously held beliefs.

This rationalization process, combined with the stake presidents have in their previous decisions, explains why it is so difficult for them to change those decisions or even to reconsider them unless circumstances force them to do so. A good example of this phenomenon is the Clinton administration's failure to consider the changing role of the American military in Somalia in 1993. It took a tragic confrontation between US troops and Somalis backing a local warlord to force the administration to confront the issue and ultimately to terminate the mission. Unless presidents make it clear that they really want to hear criticism within their administration, they may not become aware of it until they see it on the news. Advisers find it extremely diffi-cult to tell presidents what they do not wish to hear.

Ascribing Negative Consequences

There are various devices that presidents use to manage inconsistency. One is to ascribe very negative consequences to alternatives such as showing weakness. Presi-dent Johnson and his top aides did not contemplate the option of disengaging from the war in Vietnam because they considered such a move would weaken the United States' position within the international community. Johnson was also haunted by the political price Harry Truman paid for "losing" China when it went communist in 1949.[138]

Similarly, Ronald Reagan would never consider the option of negotiating about his Strategic Defense Initiative ("Star Wars") because he saw it as an instrument to protect the United States against enemy attack. George W. Bush feared that if America failed to take action against terrorists and those states that harbored them, it would encourage further attacks by its inaction. In an address on October 7, 2001, he stated, "Failure to act would embolden other tyrants, allow terrorists access to new weap-ons, new resources, and make blackmail a permanent feature of world events."[139]

Inferring Impossibility

Officials may also employ selective information to make inferences that a particular situation could not possibly occur. If policy makers accept this inference of impos-sibility, there is no need for them to consider information pointing to the opposite conclusion. Most officials believed that the Japanese could not attack Pearl Harbor. Because they were not expecting an attack, American officials did not notice the signs pointing toward it. Instead, they paid attention to signals supporting their cur-rent expectations of enemy behavior. Similar behavior inhibited policy makers from anticipating the North Korean attacks on South Korea in 1950 that precipitated the Korean War, the massive Tet invasion of South Vietnam by the North in 1968, and the Iraqi attack on Kuwait in 1991.

Engaging in Wishful Thinking

Another means of reducing inconsistency and thereby decreasing the pressure to consider alternatives is similar to what we commonly term *wishful thinking*. Secre-tary of State George Shultz has described his boss, Ronald Reagan, as engaging in wishful thinking regarding issues and events, sometimes rearranging facts and allow-ing himself to be deceived—for example, when he insisted that he had not traded arms for hostages in the Iran-Contra affair.[140] Wishful thinking also played a prom-inent role in decision making about the ill-fated invasion of Cuba at the Bay of Pigs at the beginning of the Kennedy administration and the lack of adequate planning for the US peacekeeping operation in Iraq in 2003 following the war.

A form of wishful thinking occurs when information inconsistent with ongoing policy is deemphasized and policy makers conclude that undesirable conditions are only temporary and will ameliorate in response to current policy. Officials used this type of reasoning to garner support for the continued escalation of the Vietnam War. All that was needed to force the enemy to succumb, they argued, was to keep up the pressure. Thus, they resisted rigorous evaluation of their military strategy.[141] However, the continued bombing in Kosovo and Serbia did achieve its desired effect—forcing Slobodan Milošević from power.

Employing Analogies

Reasoning by analogy is yet another means of resolving uncertainty and simplifying decision making. The conclusions supported by this type of reasoning seem to have strength independent of the available evidence, probably because the analogies simplify and provide a coherent framework for ambiguous and inconsistent information.

Metaphors and similes simplify a complex and ambiguous reality by relating it to a relatively simple and well-understood concept. If policy makers then use one figure of speech as the basis of an analogy, the possibilities for error are considerable. The "domino theory"—which held that the United States must prevent countries from falling to the communists because a chain reaction would occur and the countries would fall one after another, like falling dominoes—was part of the theoretical underpinning for the Vietnam War. The simplistic nature of the simile indicates how much room exists for differences between that view and reality.[142] McGeorge Bundy, President Johnson's national security assistant, later concluded that the simile of the domino was inadequate and a "preventor of discourse," but it was powerful enough during the war that it led him to disregard analyses that challenged the theory.[143]

Discrediting Sources

Discrediting the source of information and options is another means of reducing the complexity and resolving the contradictions with which policy makers must deal. At first, President Johnson handled the critics of his Vietnam policy quite well, inviting them to his office and talking to them for hours. However, as opposition increased and polls indicated a dip in his popularity, he responded to criticism by discrediting its source. He maintained that Senator William Fulbright (the chairman of the Senate Foreign Relations Committee) was upset at not being named secretary of state; the liberals in Congress were angry at him because he had not gone to Harvard, because the Great Society was more successful than Kennedy's New Frontier, and because he had blocked Robert Kennedy from the presidency; columnists were said to oppose him so as to make a bigger splash; and young people were hostile because they were ignorant.

Avoiding Information

At other times, presidents may simply avoid information they fear will force them to face disagreeable decisions that complicate their lives and produce additional stress. Richard Nixon is a classic example. In his memoirs, he wrote of putting off a confrontation with his own attorney general, John Mitchell, because of Mitchell's hypersensitivity and his own desire to remain ignorant about Mitchell's involvement in Watergate in case it would prove harmful for him to know about it. Referring to Nixon's ability to engage in self-delusion and avoid unpleasant facts, White House Chief of Staff H. R. Haldeman argued that the "failure to face the irrefutable facts, even when it was absolutely clear that they were irrefutable, was one of our fatal flaws in handling Watergate at every step."[144]

Each of the cognitive processes that reduce uncertainty and complexity can be a reasonable response to a situation. The point is that people have a tendency to rely on them, not only by conscious choice but also because of their need for certainty and simplicity. In each of the examples cited, the president and his advisers made use of an inference mechanism that diverted their attention from vital information and led them to ignore appropriate options. Potential actions that policy makers considered disastrous would have been far less so than those that they took, situations they thought to be impossible actually occurred, results they hoped for from policies never materialized, their inferences were based on inappropriate analogies, and they rejected worthwhile criticism. Thus, the inference mechanisms that top decision makers employ to manage inconsistency may jeopardize sound policy judgments.

At the same time, it is important to recognize the interplay between motivation and cognition. Many people can tolerate at least some inconsistency, and there are other motives aside from consistency that drive behavior, including accuracy, fairness, efficiency, accountability, ideological biases, and time pressure. Consequently, presidents and their advisers have a variety of cognitive strategies available to them and may choose to face the facts rather than simplify them if they have sufficient motivation and intellectual curiosity. Understanding which motivations are operative in a given situation remains one of the most intriguing questions of presidential politics.

PERSONALITY

Presidents cannot escape being themselves. Their personal experiences and social interactions within the environment in which they live and the genes they inherit from their parents combine to shape their personalities, which in turn condition their beliefs and behavior. Personality is not the only factor that affects judgment, but it is always present and potentially relevant.

Political scientists have had problems in studying how personality affects performance, however. For one thing, personality is not directly observable. It is inferred from words and actions, and that inference is inherently speculative. Nor does a president's personality affect every decision and action in the same manner. All the other factors we discuss in this chapter also may have an impact. Nevertheless, we need to be broadly sensitive to the influence of personality on presidential decisions.

James David Barber's *Presidential Character* was one of the most widely read books ever written on the presidency.[145] He began with the premise that the president bears "intense moral, sentimental, and quasi-religious pressures." Thus, it was important for the president not allow these pressures to distort his thinking.

For Barber, self-esteem underlies character. The better people feel about themselves, the more likely they will be able to accept criticism, think rationally, and learn on the job. Thus, he maintains that the degree and quality of presidents' emotional involvement in an issue are powerful influences on how they define the issue itself, how much attention they pay to it, which facts and persons they see as relevant to its resolution, and what principles and purposes they associate with the issues. Some presidents with low self-esteem, Barber argues, demonstrate *rigidification* in which they persevere in disastrous policies when opponents threaten their self-esteem, especially their power and rectitude.

Many critics have found Barber's claims problematic.[146] First, they do not necessarily agree with his classifications of the personality traits of individual presidents.[147] If one does not correctly identify a president's personality, any analysis its consequences will fail.

Equally important is the tendency to reductionism in which Barber typically accords greater weight to personality than to other factors in explaining presidential behavior. The president operates at the vortex of many competing forces, ranging from public opinion and the party divisions in Congress to the nation's foreign policy commitments and his own ideological predispositions. Barber typically accords greater weight to personality than to other factors in explaining presidential behavior.

Was it rigidification or his political philosophy of individualism that discouraged Herbert Hoover from aggressively advocating welfare policies? Was Lyndon Johnson defending his ego against harsh criticism, or was he responding to his worldview, formed partly by domestic politics and opposition charges of the "loss" of China during the Truman presidency? At the very least, we need to consider such explanations.

Moreover, one could argue that neither Hoover nor Johnson had displayed rigidity in their long careers prior to facing these issues. And what are we to make of Hoover relaxing his views on the federal role in the economy in 1932 and Lyndon Johnson reversing his escalation of the war in late 1968? Was Richard Nixon rigid regarding the Watergate cover-up, or was he remarkably flexible in his efforts to hide his violation of the law and maintain his office?

In addition, Barber does not consider the possibility of ego controls. Many people learn to control and regulate the expression of their personal needs and anxieties. For example, we are all familiar with people who learn to control their tempers. Such defenses help them to realistically appraise situations and deal with them more effectively. Is it not possible that the disciplined politicians who become president also have some resources of self-control?

White House Photo by Pete Souza

Stress is inevitable in the presidency. Here President Obama, surrounded by his top national security officials, watches the military raid to capture Osama bin Laden in the White House situation room.

BUREAUCRATIC POLITICS AND STRUCTURE

A primary source of options and information for the president is the bureaucracy. It is not always a neutral instrument, however. Individuals and the agencies they represent have interests of their own to advance and protect and may not necessarily view issues from the president's perspective.

Organizational Parochialism

Government agencies have a tendency toward homogeneous attitudes. People who are attracted to working for the government are likely to support the policies carried out by their agencies, whether they are in the fields of medical research, agriculture, or national defense. Naturally, agencies prefer hiring like-minded people. Within each agency, the distribution of rewards creates further pressure to view things from the perspective of the status quo. Personnel who do not support established organizational goals and approaches to meeting them are unlikely to be promoted to important positions. Moreover, all but a few high-level policy makers spend their careers within a single agency or department. Even with the introduction of the Senior Executive Service (SES) in 1978, very few career SES officials have moved across agency lines.[148] Because people want to believe in what they do for a living, this long association strongly influences the attitudes of bureaucrats.

An additional factor encouraging homogeneous views is the relatively narrow range of each agency's responsibilities. Officials in the Department of Education, for example, do not deal with the budget for the entire national government but only with the part that pertains to their programs. It is up to others to recommend to the president what is best allocated to education and what should go to national defense, health, or housing. With each bureaucratic unit focusing on its own programs, there are few people to view these programs from a wider, national perspective.

Influences from outside an agency also encourage parochial views among bureaucrats. When interest groups and congressional committees support an agency, they expect continued bureaucratic support in return. Because these outsiders generally favor the policies the bureaucracy has been carrying out all along (and which they probably helped initiate), what they really want usually is to perpetuate the status quo.

Where You Stand Depends on Where You Sit

The combination of these factors results in a relatively uniform environment for policy making. Intra-organizational communications pass mainly among people who share similar frames of reference and reinforce bureaucratic parochialism by their continued association.

The influence of parochialism is strong enough that even some presidential appointees, who are in office for only short periods of time, are "captured" and adopt the narrow views of their bureaucratic units. As President Nixon observed, "it is inevitable when an individual has been in a Cabinet position or, for that matter, holds any position in Government, [that] after a certain length of time he becomes an advocate of the status quo; rather than running the bureaucracy, the bureaucracy runs him."[149] The dependence of such officials on their subordinates for information and advice, the need to maintain organizational morale by supporting established viewpoints, and the pressure from their agencies' clienteles combine to discourage high-ranking officials from maintaining broad views of the public interest. Thus, parochialism can lead officials to see different faces on the same issue.

In May 1990, President George H. W. Bush faced a judgment about cutting off agriculture credit guarantees to Iraq. To the deputy national security adviser, this action provided an opportunity to show displeasure with Iraq's clandestine weapons program and threats toward Israel; to the Department of Agriculture, it was a decision about the fate of a controversial program that helped agribusiness; and to the State Department, cutting off credit guarantees represented a turn away from a strategy of constructive engagement that could influence Iraqi behavior toward the Arab-Israeli peace process. To the Treasury Department, the judgment was a threat to Iraq's readiness to continue paying its debts; to the Defense Department, it was an occasion to reevaluate the posture of its central command; and to the president's congressional adviser, it was an opportunity to remove an irritant in relations with Capitol Hill.[150] In other words, policy makers in different bureaucratic units with different responsibilities saw the same policy in a different light and reacted differently to it.

A president can benefit from a diversity of views among the organizational units, but the White House must recognize that each view is likely to be articulated from a biased perspective.

Maintaining the Organization

As a result of parochialism in the bureaucracy, career officials come to believe that the health of their organization and its programs is vital to the national interest. In their eyes, this well-being depends, in turn, on the ability of the organization to fulfill its missions, secure the necessary resources (personnel, money, and authority), and maintain its influence. Organizational personnel can pursue their personal quests for power and prestige, the goals of their organization, and the national interest simultaneously without perceiving any role conflicts. Moreover, policy makers in different organizational units are prone to see different faces on the same issues due to their different organizational needs.

The single-mindedness of policy makers who are attached to various agencies causes them to raise options and gather information that support the interests of their organization and avoid or oppose those that may challenge those interests. In this way, the goals of maintaining an organization may actually displace the goals of solving the problems for which the organization was created. As one former high White House official wrote, "For many cabinet officers, the important question was whether their department would have the principal responsibility for the new program—not the hard choices that lay hidden within it."[151]

Reinforce Essence

Within most organizations, there is a dominant view of the essence of the organization's mission and of the attitudes, skills, and experience that employees should have to carry it out. Organizations usually propose options that they believe will build up and reinforce their essential aspects. For example, during the Vietnam War, the air force lobbied for strategic bombing and deep interdiction, even though its bombing campaigns had not enjoyed unqualified success in previous wars. One way to promote this goal was to argue for bombing as a central feature of US policy in order to show its utility. The lack of success only reinforced the air force's efforts to step up the bombing even further; its commanders never admitted that it was not accomplishing its objectives.

Organizations will also vigorously resist the efforts of others to take away, decrease, or share their essence and the resources deemed necessary to realize it.

Secretary of Defense Robert Gates complained about the resistance to a shift from piloted aircraft to less expensive, and less glamorous, surveillance vehicles in the wars in Iraq and Afghanistan. The air force allowed only those officially rated as pilots to sit at the remote controls of its unmanned reconnaissance vehicles, a policy that Gates said limited how many of these aircraft it could deploy. (The army allows enlisted personnel and noncommissioned officers to apply for those jobs.) Throughout the George W. Bush administration, the air force was also not eager to use pilots in low-tech fixes such as inexpensive aircraft fitted with surveillance gear.[152]

Gates also criticized the Pentagon bureaucracy for a narrow commitment to buying new generations of conventional weapons, which kept it from rapidly developing equipment that would save lives in Iraq and Afghanistan. He had to force the bureaucracy to accept systems to detect improvised bombs and heavily armored transports to protect troops.[153]

In their struggles over roles and missions, bureaucrats may distort the information and options they provide to senior officials. For example, during the Vietnam War, the air force and navy were each concerned that the other might encroach on its bombing missions; the navy was also concerned about justifying the high cost of its aircraft carriers. Thus, the two branches competed in their efforts at air warfare. The aspect of this inter-service competition that was most damaging to the accuracy of the perceptions of high-level decision makers concerning the degree of American success in the war was the battle over the relative effectiveness of each service's air warfare. Each service was concerned about future budgets and missions and felt it could not let the other get the upper hand. Thus, each branch exaggerated its own performance and expected the other to do likewise.

The US Army, photo by Air Force Master Sgt. Jerry Morrison

Robert Gates had extensive experience at high levels of government. He frequently found that bureaucratic politics inhibited effective policy making.

Although the FBI recognized terrorism as a major threat in the 1990s, it was not able to make the cultural change from a police agency to an intelligence agency. It did not reallocate resources to counterterrorism; it downplayed the role of analysis, especially strategic analysis; it did not ensure its analysts access to information; it did not build an effective intelligence collection effort; and it maintained "woefully inadequate" information systems.[154] Thus, the agency was not in a position to provide the president with the information he needed on terrorists in the United States. Even after the 9/11 terrorist attacks, the bureau's resistance to change forced the director to issue a warning that he would not tolerate bureaucratic intransigence.

Budgets

Budgets are another vital component of the strategies necessary to maintain an organization. This is true for grant-awarding agencies as well as for agencies with large operational capabilities such as the military services and the Department of Agriculture. Because the staff within governmental organizations generally believe that their work is vital to the national interest and because conventional wisdom stipulates that a larger budget enables an organization to perform its functions more effectively, units will normally request an increase in funding and fight any decreases. The size of a group's budget not only determines the resources available for its services but also serves as a sign of the importance that others attach to the organization's functions.

Agency personnel also examine any substantive proposal to ascertain the agency's impact on the budget and will rarely suggest adding a new function to their responsibilities if it must be financed from monies already allocated for ongoing activities. Moreover, components of large organizations, such as units in the military or the Department of Health and Human Services, are concerned about maintaining or increasing their percentage of the larger unit's budget.

Autonomy

An organization's staff members are likely to raise and support options that give them autonomy. In their view, they know best how to perform their essential mission. Consequently, they tend to resist options that would place control in the hands of higher officials or require close coordination with other organizations. This desire for autonomy helps explain why several agencies independently gather and evaluate national security intelligence from their own perspective. As Richard Nixon complained after being disappointed by the intelligence reports he received, "Those guys spend all their time fighting each other."[155]

Because organizations seek to create and maintain autonomous jurisdictions, they rarely oppose each other's projects. This self-imposed restraint reduces the conflict between organizations, and correspondingly reduces the options and information available to the president. In dealing with their superiors, the leaders of an organization often guard their autonomy by presenting only one option for a new program. The rationale is that if higher officials are not permitted to choose among options, they also cannot interfere with the organization's preference. Once an agency of government has responsibility for a program, however, it has a tendency to evaluate it positively.

Organizational and Personal Influence

To achieve the policies they desire, organizations and individuals seek influence. In pursuing power, officials may further distort the processes of generating options and gathering information for the president.

Deferring to Expertise

One way for organizations to increase their influence is to defer to one another's expertise. The operations of all large-scale organizations, including governments, require a considerable degree of specialization and expertise. Those who possess this expertise, whether within executive agencies or on congressional committees, naturally believe that they know best about a subject in their field and therefore desire primary influence over the resolution of issues in their subject area. Because each set of experts has a stake in deference to expertise (each receives benefits from it), reciprocal deference to expertise becomes an important theme in policy making. One result of this reciprocity is that fewer challenges to expert views are aired than might otherwise be the case.

In the prelude to the Bay of Pigs invasion, the Joint Chiefs of Staff were bureaucratically cautious about dissecting the CIA's most cherished enterprise.[156] The secretaries of state and defense were also passive.[157] For several decades, there was an implicit agreement between the Departments of State and Defense that each would stay out of the other's affairs. Thus, during the Vietnam War, the State Department often took no part in shaping war policies and refrained from airing many of its views. Contributing to this restraint was Secretary of Defense Robert McNamara's adamant belief that the State Department should not challenge the military's appraisal of the actual progress of the war. He thus deliberately blocked the flow of information on the war. As a result, policy makers had to defer to Defense Department assessments, which were often inaccurate and biased toward military rather than political solutions. During the Iraq war and its aftermath, Secretary of Defense Donald Rumsfeld resisted other members of the NSC reviewing military plans.[158]

Although deference to expertise is not always a satisfactory way of resolving conflicts in policy making, it is often the only possible course of action. Governmental agencies are the sole source of data and analysis on many issues. As their work becomes increasingly specialized, it becomes harder to check their information and evaluations. This problem is exacerbated by a need for secrecy on most national security policies, which makes it necessary to limit even further the number of participants in the policy-making process.

Producing Unanimity

If disagreements exist among the experts in an organizational unit, efforts to produce an appearance of unanimity can reduce the experts' recommendations to broad generalizations. A record of agreement on the least disputed common denominators usually fails to mention many controversial points, which may be crucial to the ultimate success of the policy at issue. When compromise positions reach the president in a form that suggests a unified consensual judgment, they can give him a false sense of security because he may lack an awareness of the potential problems buried within the recommendations.

Inhibiting Innovation

The imperative of consensus can also stifle innovative thinking. For example, the George H. W. Bush administration launched a strategic review of foreign policy early in its first year. Bureaucratic units that had vested interests in established policy produced the papers. As Secretary of State Jim Baker put it, "In the end what we received was mush," with potentially controversial and interesting ideas omitted in the name of bureaucratic consensus.[159] To avoid a similar situation in designing a military strategy for the twenty-first century, Secretary of Defense Donald Rumsfeld in the George W. Bush presidency excluded uniformed military and most civil servants in the Defense Department from the group that devised the strategy.

Stifling Dissent

To take full advantage of deference to expertise and increase their influence further, organizations seek to prevent their own experts from disseminating conflicting information and options. Contrary information and evaluations are believed to undercut the credibility of a unit's position. Moreover, by presenting several real options, a unit increases the range of possible policy decisions and commensurately decreases the probability that the option favored by the unit's leaders will be selected. Thus, the Joint Chiefs of Staff rarely disagree in their recommendations. Similarly, the relevant departments never presented President Carter with real options on welfare reform, in part because they were afraid he would select an alternative they opposed. No one would insist to the president that reform would be costly, because they feared he would then reject their reform efforts.[160]

For bureaucrats interested in their own careers, the prospect of a deferred promotion, or even dismissal, makes them reluctant to report information that undercuts the official stands of their organizations.[161] The example of the Foreign Service officers who frankly (and accurately) reported on the strength of the communists in China during the late 1940s was not quickly forgotten in the bureaucracy. They were driven from the Foreign Service for allegedly holding procommunist sympathies. More than forty years later, in 1992, then CIA Director Robert Gates announced that many within the CIA felt that intelligence reports were still being tailored to please superiors.

Creating the Illusion of Competition

Experts can create an illusion of competition when they agree to compare their preferred action to unfeasible alternatives. Lyndon Johnson's advisers have been criticized for juxtaposing, in 1964, their favored option of bombing North Vietnam against two phony options: in effect, destroy the world or scuttle and run. Barack Obama criticized his advisers for a lack of viable options for the US role in Afghanistan.[162]

Bureaucratic Structure

The structure of administrative organizations is one of the factors that both aids and impedes the flow of options and information to higher-level decision makers.

Hierarchy

Most bureaucracies have a hierarchical structure, whereby the information on which decisions are based usually passes from bottom to top. At each step in this ladder of communication, personnel screen the information from the previous stage. Such screening is necessary because the people at the top—presidents—cannot absorb all the detailed information that exists on an issue. They must have subordinates summarize and synthesize the information as it proceeds upward. The longer the communication chain, the greater the chance that judgments will replace facts, nuances or caveats will be excluded, subordinates will paint a positive face on a situation to improve their own or their organization's image, human error will distort the overall picture, and the speculations of "experts" will be reported as fact.

Screening, summarizing, and human error are not the only pitfalls in the transmission of information. When subordinates are asked to transmit information that can be used to evaluate their performance, they have a tendency to distort it in order to put themselves in the most favorable light. For example, many of the military's assessments of damage done to Iraqi forces and weaponry in the Gulf War turned out to be erroneous, having been inflated substantially by soldiers in the field.[163]

Challenges of Coordination

Even in a hierarchical executive branch, the president cannot assume that information will be centralized. There was a great deal of information pointing to the impending Japanese attack on Pearl Harbor, for example, but it was never fully organized. Similarly, there were many warnings about the possibility of terrorist attacks before September 11, 2001, but most did not reach the president.

No one brings forward all the political, economic, social, military, and diplomatic considerations of a policy in a recognizable manner for the president's deliberation, because the bureaucracy that is relevant to any policy is too decentralized and too large to coordinate it effectively. Moreover, the amount of information available is so vast that it cannot be collected, stored, retrieved, and analyzed in a single database or even a network of linked databases. Table 9.1 lists the intelligence agencies that provide the White House with national security intelligence. Trying to coordinate the information flow from such a decentralized system is a massive task. In an effort to centralize the analysis of intelligence, in 2004 Congress created a new position of "national director of intelligence."

Coordinating Intelligence and the 9/11 Attacks

Before the 9/11 terrorist attacks, the FBI and the CIA did not adequately share the information they collected, did not assess the warning signs as a whole, and were slow to react to the significance of the intelligence they had obtained about the possibility of an attack. They also failed to comprehend the ominous rise of Osama bin Laden and his al-Qaeda network. Two years before the 9/11 attacks, the CIA suspected two of the hijackers of being terrorists and believed they held visas to enter the United States or that they were already in the country. However, the agency did not place the men on the government's terrorism watch list or notify the FBI that they might be in the United States. An FBI informant penetrated the circle of the two men but never received the CIA's information that they might be in al-Qaeda. The FBI failed to grasp the significance of a July 2001 communication sent from an agent in the bureau's Phoenix office that identified a pattern of Middle Eastern men, some with extreme anti-American beliefs, who were receiving pilot training at flight schools in the United States. The FBI also did not connect the Phoenix communication with the arrest in August 2001 of Zacarias Moussaoui, who was later indicted for complicity in the hijackings. The FBI and CIA did not assess the potential threat posed by Moussaoui in light of the heightened fears of a terrorist attack in the summer of 2001.[164]

Officials in the Department of Justice misunderstood and misapplied procedures for sharing information between intelligence and criminal investigations of the department, limiting sharing of information. Thus, the FBI did not tell the US Attorney's office about Moussaoui because it felt it lacked probable cause to search his computer. The FBI also did not tell other agencies what it thought Moussaoui

Table 9.1 Agencies with Responsibility for National Security Intelligence, 2020

Director of National Intelligence
Central Intelligence Agency
Department of Defense
National Security Agency
National Geospatial-Intelligence Agency
National Reconnaissance Office
Defense Intelligence Agency
Army Intelligence and Security Command
Office of Naval Intelligence
Air Force Intelligence, Surveillance, and Reconnaissance Agency
Marine Corps Intelligence Activity
Department of State
Bureau of Intelligence and Research
Department of Treasury
Office of Terrorism and Finance Intelligence
Department of Justice
Counterterrorism Division, FBI
Counterintelligence Division, FBI
Directorate of Intelligence, FBI
WMD Directorate, FBI
Terrorist Screening Center, FBI
Office of National Security Intelligence, DEA
Department of Energy
Office of Intelligence and Counterintelligence
Department of Homeland Security
Office of Intelligence and Analysis
Domestic Nuclear Detection Office
United States Secret Service
United States Immigration and Customs Enforcement
Coast Guard Intelligence

was up to, and no one acted on the general report its agents wrote. More broadly, no one organized law enforcement, immigration, visa, and intelligence information related to the hijackers to allow any agency to detect trends and patterns in their activities. No one was firmly in charge of managing terrorist information and able to draw relevant intelligence from anywhere in the government, assign responsibilities across agencies, track progress, and quickly bring obstacles up to the level where they could be resolved.[165]

As a result, in the words of the 9/11 Commission, "the system was blinking red" before the terrorist attacks, but no one connected the dots to identify the immediate threat. No one ordered domestic agencies to harden the borders, fortify transportation systems, target electronic surveillance, marshal state and local law enforcement, or warn the public. "The terrorists exploited deep institutional failings within our government,"[166] and President Bush did not make the organizational reforms necessary to combat terrorism more effectively until after the 9/11 attack.[167]

In addition, in some instances no one has responsibility for providing critical information. As the 9/11 Commission put it,

> The September 11 attacks fell into the void between the foreign and domestic threats. The foreign intelligence agencies were watching overseas . . . the domestic agencies were waiting for evidence of a domestic threat from sleeper cells within the United States. No one was looking for a foreign threat to domestic targets.[168]

Coordinating Intelligence and the Underwear Bomber

Umar Farouk Abdulmutallab was a Nigerian Islamist who attempted to detonate plastic explosives hidden in his underwear while on board a flight from Amsterdam to Detroit on December 25, 2009. The National Security Agency intercepted al-Qaeda operatives in Yemen talking about using a Nigerian man for an attack, and Abdulmutallab's father warned American diplomats in Nigeria about his son's radicalization in Yemen.

Nevertheless, security agencies could not integrate and understand the intelligence they possessed. Neither the State Department nor the National Counterterrorism Center (NCTC) discovered Abdulmutallab's US visa until it was too late. The NCTC draws on streams of information from more than eighty databases and twenty-eight computer networks across the government. Intelligence analysts were stymied, however, by computer systems that they could not easily search automatically—and repeatedly—for possible links. Using the search tools and databases they had, it was difficult for analysts to conduct dynamic searches to "connect the dots," which involve looking for multiple variables and terms scattered across databases. Further complicating the effort, many of the records in intelligence databases contained additional information in the form of written comments or notes attached to the main record. The notes and comments were not indexed, and so the kinds of keyword searches that analysts performed could not locate them. It is often these subsets of information that contain the nuance, context, and interpretation that might be crucial to connecting the dots.

Compensating for Hierarchy

The president may attempt to compensate for the problems of hierarchy by sending personal aides or outsiders to assess a situation directly and propose options. However, the person assigned to the task, more than the situation itself, may determine the nature of the resulting report. Moreover, the president cannot bypass senior officials very often without lowering their morale and undercutting their operational authority.

President Kennedy's chief White House national security assistant, McGeorge Bundy, ordered that cables to the State Department, the CIA, and the Pentagon be sent directly to the White House, and not just to the Washington headquarters of those departments, where they could be summarized and analyzed for transmittal to the president. However, this practice did not correct any distortion that may have gone into the cables in the first place, and someone still had to summarize and synthesize the tremendous volume of information before it reached the president. President George Bush discovered the same problems when he asked for direct information channels from the field.

Standard Operating Procedures

Organizations use routines or standard operating procedures (SOPs) to gather and process information in a methodical fashion. However, the character of the SOPs may delay the recognition of critical information, distort the quality of information, and limit the options presented to policy makers.

Collecting and Processing Information

Organizational routines masked signs forecasting the 1974 leftist coup in Portugal. Officials from the intelligence services of the CIA, the Defense Department, and the State Department testified after the event that their routines failed to focus much attention on Portugal and they could not shift personnel rapidly to a new area of concern.

One reason that other agencies could not benefit from the FBI's information on possible terrorists before 9/11 is that the bureau did not produce intelligence reports like those other agencies routinely write and disseminate.[169] In the case of the Cuban missile crisis, several weeks before the president was aware of the missiles there was already a good deal of information in the US intelligence system pointing to the presence of the missiles. However, the time required by SOPs to sort out raw information and verify it delayed recognition of the new situation.

Distorting Information

SOPs affect not only if and when information is collected but also the substance of the information. In Vietnam, the military's concentration on the technical aspects of bombing caused it to substitute a set of short-run physical objectives for the ultimate political goals of the war. Military reports emphasized physical destruction per se rather than the political impact of such destruction. The enemy's capacity to recruit more men or rebuild a structure never seemed to enter into the calculations.

Structuring the Process

SOPs give disproportionate weight to information entering the system from regular channels. For example, the United States was highly dependent on the shah of Iran and Savak, his secret police organization, for information about that nation. Up until a few months before the shah was deposed, they reported to the CIA and President Carter that there was no likelihood of revolution. The White House rejected more pessimistic reports from journalists and others outside the regular flow of information.

SOPs structure the process of decision making by preselecting those who will be asked for advice and predetermining when they will be asked. There are routine ways of invading foreign countries and determining agency budgets. Some people will be involved at earlier stages than others, and some will be viewed as having more legitimate and expert voices in policy discussions. When Lyndon Johnson limited his circle of personal advisers on the Vietnam War to a half-dozen top officials, those at a lower rung in the foreign policy hierarchy found it harder to have their dissent heard. In addition, there was little opportunity for others in the cabinet to challenge the war policy because they were not located in the proper decision-making channels.

Proposing Options

SOPs also affect the nature of the alternatives proposed by bureaucratic units. Bureaucracies typically propose their standard ways of doing things rather than innovative solutions to problems. These standard policies may not be appropriate for the problem at hand, as when military commanders attempted to transplant to Indochina the operational methods of conventional warfare that had been successful in the European battle theaters of World War II instead of developing a strategy more appropriate for fighting a counterinsurgency effort in the jungles of Vietnam.[170] The 9/11 Commission complained of the narrow and unimaginative options for countering al-Qaeda that the bureaucracy presented to Presidents Clinton and George W. Bush.[171]

Avoiding SOPs

As a result of problems with established routines, presidents often create special task forces of "outside" experts to develop new programs, as President Clinton did with his health-care proposal. Such bodies, when brought together for a new purpose, are less likely than established agencies to be blinded by SOPs.

CONCLUSION

Presidents face an enormously difficult and complex task in making decisions on a wide range of issues. They must work within the parameters of the national government's prior commitments and are further constrained by the limited time they can devote to considering options and information on any one policy. In addition, they face a number of other potential hazards in reaching decisions. The struggling facilitator, not the dominating director, is the description that generally matches the process of presidential decision making.

There are a variety of ways for presidents to organize the White House and acquire advice, but not all are equally useful in ensuring that presidents are presented with a full range of options, each supported with effective advocacy. Moreover, presidents may experience problems if their aides are reluctant to present candid advice, which may be aggravated by the aides' desire to increase their own influence and by the presidents themselves.

Bureaucratic politics also plays a role in determining the options and information that presidents receive and the forms in which these are presented. Agencies and their personnel inevitably have narrower perspectives than the White House and will desire to maintain and expand their programs, status, and influence. Those ambitions often bias the options and information presented to the White House. The ways in which bureaucratic units collect, process, and transmit options and information, and the secrecy that sometimes accompanies the process, may further distort what the president perceives.

It is important that presidents remain sensitive to the many obstacles to effective decision making and attempt to avoid or compensate for these obstacles as much as possible, while realizing that perfectly rational decision making is unattainable.

DISCUSSION QUESTIONS

1. It is convenient to argue that the president should examine all the options regarding an important policy issue, yet is it really possible for presidents to evaluate a wide range of options on all the policy questions with which they must deal? What do you think presidents really do? Do conservative presidents, for example, often consider liberal options and vice versa? Give examples of contemporary presidents to support your answers.

2. We have seen that organizational parochialism may bias the information that bureaucratic units provide to the president. Is there a solution to this problem? Is it possible for committed, expert managers to run government agencies and still take a broad view of public policy and provide the president with information he may not want to hear?

3. A critical step in presidents' decision making is evaluating the consequences of the various options before them. How well can the White House do this? Is it possible to predict the consequences of choices that have not yet been made, such as levying sanctions against a country or cutting taxes for certain groups?

WEB EXERCISES

1. Go to the White House website, https://www.whitehouse.gov/articles. Look at the wide range of issues with which the president must deal in just one week. How much can one person know about all these issues? Is there a way for presidents to be better informed?

2. Go to the White House website (https://www.whitehouse.gov) and type in a policy area that interests you (such as "education," "defense," or "health") in the search box. How might the president's decisions on the issue have been different had there been no previous commitments restraining him? Were these previous commitments aids or hindrances to good policy?

SELECTED READINGS

Allison, Graham, and Philip Zelikow. *Essence of Decision: Explaining the Cuban Missile Crisis*, 2nd ed. New York: Addison Wesley Longman, 1999.

Burke, John P. "Organizational Structure and Presidential Decision-Making." In *The Oxford Handbook of the American Presidency*, edited by George C. Edwards III and William G. Howell. Oxford, UK: Oxford University Press, 2009.

Burke, John P., and Fred I. Greenstein. *How Presidents Test Reality: Decisions on Vietnam, 1954 and 1965*. New York: Russell Sage Foundation, 1989.

George, Alexander L., and Juliette L. George. *Presidential Personality and Performance*. Boulder, CO: Westview, 1998.

Halperin, Morton H., and Priscilla A. Clapp. *Bureaucratic Politics and Foreign Policy*, 2nd ed. Washington, DC: Brookings Institution, 2006.

Hult, Karen M., and Charles E. Walcott. "Influences on Presidential Decision-Making." In *The Oxford Handbook of the American Presidency*, edited by George C. Edwards III and William G. Howell. Oxford, UK: Oxford University Press, 2009.

Janis, Irving. *Groupthink*, 2nd ed. Boston, MA: Houghton Mifflin, 1982.

Jervis, Robert. *Perception and Misperception in International Politics*. Princeton, NJ: Princeton University Press, 1976.

National Commission on Terrorist Attacks on the United States. *The 9/11 Commission Report*. New York: Norton, 2004.

Pious, Richard M. *Why Presidents Fail: White House Decision Making from Eisenhower to Bush II*. Lanham, MD: Rowman & Littlefield, 2008.

Saunders, Elizabeth N. *Leaders at War: How Presidents Shape Military Interventions*. Ithaca, NY: Cornell University Press, 2013.

10

The President and the Executive Branch

★ ★ ★

President Donald Trump meets with his cabinet.

Donald Trump came to Washington to generate change. A number of his nominees to cabinet-level posts took extreme positions on policies within their purview. Soon, the president was complaining about leaks and resistance from the bureaucracy, aimed he said at undermining his initiatives. He fired the director of the FBI, apparently because he would not bend to his wishes regarding Russia's role in the 2016 presidential election. At the same time, his administration was unusually slow to nominate people for the appointive positions in the departments and agencies, personnel necessary to see his policies implemented effectively.

Every president is dependent on the bureaucracy to achieve many of his goals. With divided government common over the past three decades, presidents more than ever turn to the bureaucracy to accomplish changes in policy.[1] Public policies are rarely self-executing, however. They require a staff of experts who have an understanding of the substantive issues, institutional processes, and political implications involved in turning statutes, executive orders, and the like into services and benefits for the nation. These are the people who work in the executive branch. Some are civil servants while others are political appointees, but both groups implement public policy.

The president sits atop the executive branch, the organization of which is illustrated in figure 10.1. As the title of chief executive implies, the president has responsibility for executing or implementing government policies. Implementation includes issuing and enforcing directives, disbursing funds, making loans, awarding grants, signing contracts, collecting data, disseminating information, analyzing problems, assigning and hiring personnel, creating organizational units, proposing alternatives, planning for the future, and negotiating with private citizens, businesses, interest groups, legislative committees, bureaucratic units, and even other countries.

Because policy implementation is extremely complex, we should not expect presidents to accomplish it easily or exactly as they desire. Indeed, presidents are often frustrated in their efforts to meet their constitutional responsibilities to see that the laws are "faithfully executed." President Jimmy Carter complained, "Before I became president, I realized and I was warned that dealing with the federal bureaucracy would be one of the worst problems I would have to face. It has been even worse than I had anticipated."[2]

In this chapter, we examine presidents' efforts, in conjunction with their subordinates in the executive branch, to implement public policies. Presidents fitting the director model would dominate this process and ensure that policies are executed as they wish; presidents in the facilitator mold will face just as great a challenge in leading the executive branch as in leading those who are not directly in their chain of command. We will find that, despite the unquestioned importance of implementation, it receives relatively low priority in the White House. We will also find that presidents face an uphill fight in implementing the policies for which they are responsible. Thus, we focus on the obstacles to effective policy implementation, including communication, resources, implementers' dispositions, bureaucratic structure, and executive follow-up, to better understand the difficulties the president faces.

LACK OF ATTENTION TO IMPLEMENTATION

Policy implementation has had a low priority in most administrations. Presidents have many obligations, of which implementing policy is only one. They must develop policies, make decisions, promote legislation, defuse or contain controversies, and court the public, to name only the most obvious tasks. Moreover, presidents—even former governors—generally lack experience in administration on the scale of the federal government and tend to find other tasks more compatible with their skills and interests.

Foreign affairs are always a top priority of the chief executive because of their importance, the president's unique constitutional responsibilities to deal with them, and the strong interest in international relations that many presidents bring to office. Besides, presidents often feel they can accomplish more in the international arena than at home, where they must wrestle over domestic issues with an unresponsive Congress or a recalcitrant executive branch. Ceremonial functions performed in the

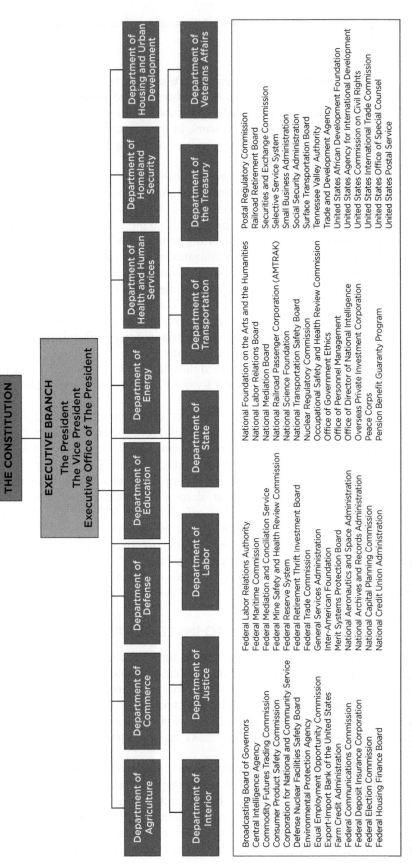

Figure 10.1 Organization of the Executive Branch
Source: United States Government Manual, 2019.

role of chief of state are traditions maintained by the president to broaden public support. All these activities typically take priority over implementation.

In addition, the incentives to invest time in implementation are few. Presidents have only a short time in office, and in their first terms they must constantly think about reelection. This temporal imperative encourages a short-run view in the White House, whereby presidents are more likely to try to provide the public with immediate gratification through passing legislation or giving speeches than with efforts to implement policies. As one Office of Management and Budget (OMB) official put it,

> The people in the White House are there for such a short time. The pressure is on making some impact and getting some programs passed. There is not enough time or reward in thinking carefully about effectiveness and implementation. The emphasis is really on quantity, not quality. The President could never be reelected on the effectiveness theme. "We didn't do much, but it is all working very well." Do you think a President could win with that?[3]

Presidents know that they will receive little credit if they manage policies well, because it is very difficult to attribute effective implementation to them personally. Moreover, to most people, the functioning of government is seldom visible. When they pay attention to government at all, both citizens and the press are most interested in controversial scandals, the passage of new policies, or ceremonial functions. Policies such as Social Security reform or taxation, which can have a direct effect on people's lives, attract their attention; yet even here, the press and public are mainly concerned with the enactment of policies, not the process of their implementation. Although implementation directly influences the effectiveness of policies, this fact seems insufficient to entice the mass public and the press that caters to it to turn their attention to policy implementation. As a result of these incentives, presidents devote a comparatively small amount of their time to the task.

Similarly, policy makers devote too little consideration to problems of implementation in the formulation of policies.[4] Again, the proper incentives are missing. According to a Carter aide, "We all believe there should be more planning. The President has stressed the need for more caution. But when we fall behind, the President will impose a deadline. It is still a political system; and political systems are interested in results, not implementation."[5] As an assistant to President Ronald Reagan commented, "It's unfortunately true that the management of the bureaucracy becomes one of the lowest priorities of almost every administration that comes to this city. Every administration pays a heavy price for it before it's over."[6]

The George W. Bush administration is a good example of paying the price. Its failure to plan adequately for the occupation of Iraq and to anticipate the insurgency that followed the toppling of Saddam Hussein cost it the public's trust. The president's hope to rely on Iraqi institutions such as the military and the police, to remove US troops rapidly, to share the burden with allies, and to pay for reconstruction with Iraqi oil money but avoid massive reconstruction proved illusory.[7] As one commentator put it, "The Bush administration had goals for Iraq, but no coherent strategy for accomplishing them. Its policy was based on a combination of naïveté, misjudgment, and wishful thinking."[8] Similarly, the administration lacked a finished plan to guide its response to a disaster such as Hurricane Katrina.

Bush's successor, Barack Obama also paid a heavy price for failing to devote sufficient attention to implementation issues. The rollout of the Affordable Care Act, the signature policy achievement of the Obama presidency, was a policy and political disaster for the administration. People trying to sign up for health insurance in October 2013 overwhelmed the Department of Health and Human Services (HHS) computers, causing them to crash. Naturally, this irritated millions of citizens and delayed their obtaining health insurance. It also provided Republicans the basis for vocal criticism and stalled the Democrats' momentum they had gained from the unpopular Republican-led shutdown of the federal government.

Massive budget deficits have placed a premium on using scarce public funds efficiently, however. Early in his tenure, President Bill Clinton launched a "National Performance Review" under Vice President Al Gore that emphasized cutting red tape, making government agencies more responsive to the needs of their clients, and cutting wasteful spending.[9] George W. Bush instituted his own performance-rating initiative, the Program Assessment Rating Tool or PART. Barack Obama also committed his administration to efficiency and effectiveness in government programs. The White House launched Performance.gov to track progress on the administration's efforts to create a more effective, efficient, and responsive government and to share best practices across the government.

Despite these effort, problems remain. The official who oversaw Bush's effort acknowledged that PART failed to achieve its main goals and received only cursory attention from policy makers. "There was frustration after eight years . . . that not enough agencies or program managers were actually using the results of the assessments to manage. Nor was Congress—or, frankly, the administration—using the results to make significant budget decisions." He added, "You will never design a tool that will remove politics from the equation."[10]

COMMUNICATION OF PRESIDENTIAL DECISIONS

The first requirement for the effective implementation of presidential decisions or policies for which the president is responsible is that the individuals who are to implement a decision must know what they are supposed to do. Thus, presidents must transmit their decisions and implementation orders to the appropriate personnel. Naturally, these communications need to be accurate and their implementers must accurately perceive them. Implementation directives must also be clear. If they are not, implementers may be confused about what they should do and will have the discretion to impose their own views on the implementation of policies (views that may differ from those of the president). Consistency in the communication directives is also crucial. Contradictory decisions confuse and frustrate administrative staff and constrain their ability to implement policies effectively.

Transmission

Before subordinates can implement a presidential decision, they must be aware that the president has made a decision and issued an order to implement it. This process is not always as straightforward as it may seem. Ignorance or misunderstanding of decisions frequently occurs. Although the executive branch has established highly developed lines of communication throughout the bureaucracy, this does not guarantee that communications will be transmitted successfully.

Orders Not Communicated

The 9/11 terrorist attacks presented many challenges to the US government. Among them was the seemingly simple task of communicating orders. On the most basic level, the president found it difficult to speak with top officials in Washington because the phone line to the White House shelter conference room kept cutting off.

Even when the president's message was clear, his orders did not get through. Although the president and vice president ordered the North American Aerospace Defense Command (NORAD), which is responsible for defense of the nation's airspace, to shoot down planes suspected of having been hijacked, the order was not passed to the pilots in the skies over New York and Washington. One commander did not pass along the order "because he was unaware of its ramifications," while two other officers said "they were unsure how pilots would, or should, proceed with this guidance." As the chairperson of the 9/11 Commission put it, "When the president of the United States gives a shoot-down order, and the pilots who are supposed to carry it out do not get that order, then that's about as serious as it gets as far as the defense of this country goes." Perhaps even worse, an Air National Guard unit in Washington was operating under permissive rules of engagement that would have allowed pilots to shoot down planes, but the president, the vice president, and the military chain of command were unaware of this.[11]

There were also communication gaps between NORAD and the Federal Aviation Administration (FAA), which tracked the hijacked flights. They were unable to share information quickly or coherently as the terrorist attack unfolded, which prevented armed fighter jets from being scrambled fast enough. As a result of these communication problems, the last of the four hijacked planes had crashed before the vice president ordered the shoot downs. NORAD had nine minutes' notice on the first plane and did not know of other planes. In addition, within minutes of the second impact in New York, the FAA's Boston center instructed its controllers to inform all aircraft in its airspace of the events and to advise heightened cockpit security. It also asked for a similar alert nationwide. Neither occurred.[12]

Ignoring Directives

Sometimes aides and other officials ignore presidential directives with which they disagree, primarily to avoid embarrassment for their chief. Such orders are generally given in anger and without proper consultation. For example, President Richard Nixon especially liked to let off steam by issuing outrageous orders. At one time, he instructed Secretary of State William Rogers to "fire everybody in Laos"; another time, he ordered everyone in the State Department to take lie detector tests. White House Chief of Staff H. R. Haldeman and other aides close to Nixon ignored these and similar outbursts, knowing the president would view things differently after he calmed down.[13]

Donald Trump is noted more for his impulsiveness than his mastery of policy. Thus, he told the navy that it could not use the high-tech electromagnetic catapults for aircraft carriers it had been developing for years. Instead, the president decreed that it would go back to old-fashioned steam power. He ordered Defense Secretary Jim Mattis to assassinate Syrian President Bashar al-Assad. He repeatedly called for the Department of Justice to investigate Hillary Clinton. In each case, high-level officials shrugged, disregarded the president's comments, and moved on.[14]

The US response to the terrorist attacks on 9/11 suffered from a number of problems in transmitting presidential orders.

On other occasions, resistance from officials may have saved the president from serious criminal charges. The Mueller investigation into Russian interference in the 2016 presidential election reported,

> Our investigation found multiple acts by the President that were capable of exerting undue influence over law enforcement investigations, including the Russian-interference and obstruction investigations. The incidents were often carried out through one-on-one meetings in which the President sought to use his official power outside of usual channels. . . . The President's efforts to influence the investigation were mostly unsuccessful, but that is largely because the persons who surrounded the President declined to carry out orders or accede to his requests.[15]

Discretion in Interpreting

In most instances, implementers have considerable discretion in interpreting their superiors' decisions and orders.[16] Instructions from the White House are rarely specific, and personnel at each rung in the bureaucratic ladder must use their judgment to expand and develop them. Obviously, this process invites the distortion of communications. Moreover, the further down in the bureaucracy presidential implementation directives go, the greater the potential for distortion becomes. In addition, subordinates may interpret the communications of their superiors in a manner that furthers their personal interests and those of their agencies rather than the goals of the president. Interest groups will also attempt to influence the interpretation of implementation orders at intermediate and low decision-making levels.

It is for these reasons that observers of the federal bureaucracy often recommend that presidents and other high officials make every attempt to commit their directives to writing (in detail where possible), use personalized communications where appropriate, and show persistence in attempting to convey their orders accurately to those who actually implement the policies. In an unusual move, Barack Obama personally wrote clear instructions for implementing his decisions regarding the war in Afghanistan.[17]

Decentralization

In general, the more decentralized the implementation of a public policy, the less likely it is to be transmitted accurately to its ultimate implementers. Decentralization usually means that a decision must be communicated through several levels of authority before it reaches those who will carry it out. The more steps a communication must traverse from its original source, the weaker the signal that is ultimately received will be. A president can tell his secretary of state to go to another country and deliver a policy pronouncement to its prime minister with little concern that the message will be inaccurately transmitted. However, he cannot have the same confidence about messages aimed at caseworkers in a Social Security office or soldiers in the field. Here, the distance between the White House and the implementers is too great.

Moreover, the distance is increasing. Paul Light showed that a "thickening" of government has occurred over the past few decades. There are now more steps than ever through which information must flow to reach the individuals who actually implement a policy. As one frontline manager put it recently, "By the time an idea gets down here, it has been translated, reworked, and bureaucratized to the point where we just can't do it."[18]

In late 1983 and early 1984, President Reagan ordered reconnaissance flights over Lebanon. By the time the troops in the Middle East who were to implement the orders received them through the chain of command, however, they had been changed—undermining US efforts to negotiate peace. In fact, the Pentagon canceled the flights at the very time when US policy was to stand firm in Lebanon and then resumed the flights later, at a time when US policy was to move toward withdrawal.[19]

Indirect Communication

Some presidents lack a personality that is suited to direct communication. Richard Nixon, who feared rejection and confrontation, adopted an indirect administrative style to avoid possible unpleasantness. He spoke elliptically to those who disagreed with him to avoid being rebuffed and typically failed to issue unambiguous orders directly to his subordinates. He did not like to say no personally or to discipline recalcitrant officials. When he found opposition within his administration, he tried to accomplish his objectives without his adversaries' awareness or he had intermediaries deliver either written or verbal orders. The president shunned personal efforts at persuading or inspiring subordinates.[20]

Nixon's unwillingness to communicate directly with his subordinates fostered an environment in which discipline and cohesion were often low. It also revealed a disunity in his administration that others could exploit, further eroding cohesion. Officials in positions of power, such as Secretary of State William Rogers, could increase their discretion by implementing orders with which they disagreed only when transmitted personally to them by the president—which they rarely were.[21] Secretary of State Donald Rumsfeld engaged in similar behavior during the George W. Bush administration.

The press also may serve as a means of more straightforward presidential communication. Individuals in the White House often believe that because most high-level bureaucrats read the *New York Times* and the *Washington Post*, they can communicate with these officials about policy matters more rapidly through news stories than through normal channels. The White House also uses other media outlets, such as television, newsmagazines, and specialized publications, to send messages to government officials.[22] Such messages may indicate a policy decision or position, or they may signal that an official White House statement was issued merely to appease special interests and should not be taken literally. However, the information provided in a story or as a response to a reporter's question is unlikely to be sufficient for guiding the implementation of a complex policy, and indeed, it may even be in error. Still, it is to the nuances contained in such communications that ears in Washington are often most attuned.

Clarity

If officials are to administer policies as presidents desire, White House implementation directives must be clear. However, the instructions it transmits to implementers are often vague and do not specify when or how a program is to be carried out. Lack of clarity provides implementers with the leeway to give new meaning to policies, which sometimes inhibits the intended change or brings about unintended consequences.

The lack of clarity about interrogation techniques in the George W. Bush administration set the stage for abuses in a number of prison settings.[23] Similarly, the president was not clear about who would hold power in Iraq in the aftermath of the US invasion. According to Undersecretary of Defense for Policy Douglas Feith, "there was not a common, clear understanding of what the President wanted done."[24] "Ambiguous guidance delivered in ad hoc meetings replaced carefully documented deliberations involving the principals."[25] Thus, the White House sent mixed signals to US officials, which gave them substantial discretion and led to what many observers felt were disastrous policies.

Presidential decisions vary in specificity, and the White House often articulates them in policy statements expressing a sentiment or intention. They may indicate in general terms that certain actions should be taken but not specify exactly who should take them or when or how they should take them.[26] One of Barack Obama's first acts as president was to send a memorandum to federal agencies ordering them to be as responsive as possible to Freedom of Information Act requests. The sentiment was genuine, but it is easy to see how much discretion this left for officials to interpret the order.

Complexity of Policy Making

There are several explanations for the lack of clarity in many implementation orders. Perhaps the most important is the sheer complexity of policy making. Both President George W. Bush and Secretary of Defense Donald Rumsfeld held contradictory beliefs about the issue of postwar governance in Iraq. They did not wish to engage in nation building but were also uneasy about setting up a provisional government of exiles.[27] These contradictions made it difficult for them to send clear orders to subordinates.

In addition, when they establish policy, neither presidents nor members of Congress have the time or expertise to develop and apply all the requisite details for how it will be carried out. They have to leave most (and sometimes all) of the details to subordinates (usually in the executive branch). Thus, although it is the president's responsibility to implement the policies of the national government no matter who initiates them, the White House must delegate much of this responsibility to others.

Consensus Building

The difficulty in reaching consensus on policy goals also inhibits clarity in implementation directives. In the United States, we share wide agreement on the goals of avoidance of war, equal opportunity, and efficiency in government, but this consensus often dissolves when specific policy alternatives are under consideration. Lyndon Johnson once said, "If the full implications of any bill were known before its enactment, it would never get passed."[28]

Coalition Building

Imprecise decisions make it easier for presidents to develop and maintain winning coalitions. Different people or groups can support the same policy for different reasons, as each may hold its own conception of the goal or goals the program is designed to achieve. Ambiguous goals also may make it less threatening for groups to be on the losing side of a policy conflict, which may reduce the intensity of their opposition.

Program Start-Ups

The problems of starting up a new program may also produce confusion in the implementation instructions. Often, the passage of a new policy is followed by a period of administrative uncertainty in which a considerable time lag occurs before any information on the program is disseminated. This period is followed by a second phase in which rules are made but are then changed quickly as high-level officials attempt to deal with unforeseen problems of implementing the policy and of their own earlier directives.

Discrete Decisions

Presidents seldom make a single, comprehensive decision covering a wide range of interrelated issues. More often, they decide a series of questions discretely and send a series of diffuse and, on some occasions, contradictory guidelines to the bureaucracy. Thus, no official receives just one order, but rather a stream of orders.[29]

Congressional Blame Avoidance

A cynical yet realistic explanation for the lack of clarity in federal statutes is that Congress does not want them to be detailed. It would rather let the executive branch agencies provide the specifics, not because of the latter's expertise but because the agencies can later be assigned the blame for rules that turn out to be unworkable or unpopular. One law affecting almost every college and university in the United States is Title IX of the Education Act Amendments of 1972, which states that "no person in the United States shall, on the basis of sex, be excluded from participation in, or be denied the benefits of, or be subject to discrimination under an education program or activity receiving Federal financial assistance." Such broad language allows Congress to sidestep many touchy questions and leave resolution to the president and his appointees. Moreover, individual members of Congress can gain credit with their constituents by intervening on their behalf regarding the application of regulations. In addition, if the goals are not precise, others cannot hold Congress accountable for the failure of its policies to achieve them. This imprecision adds to the president's burden in guiding the bureaucracy.

Restricting Discretion

Sometimes, Congress makes efforts to restrict the discretion of implementers. The Voting Rights Act reduced the discretion of local voting registrars by limiting the use of literacy tests and similar voter qualification devices. In some cases, the administration of voting registration was physically taken over by federal officials so that local officials could not inhibit voter registration. Congress has also invested a great deal of time in specifying eligibility requirements for government benefits, ranging from social services and agricultural subsidies to grants for state and local governments.

It is generally easier for the president to reduce the discretion of officials via orders to stop doing something rather than instructions to start something. For example, an absolute ban on providing funds for abortions for poor women is more likely to be unambiguous and to be noticed if it is violated than an order to begin implementing a new policy. The implementation of most policies, however, requires positive actions rather than prohibitions. Moreover, in general, a series of positive actions extending over a long period of time and involving the technical expertise of numerous people throughout a bureaucratic hierarchy is necessary to implement a policy. The complexity of such policy making means it is very difficult for a president to communicate and enforce rules that effectively reduce the discretion available to most policy implementers.

Vague policy decisions often hinder effective implementation, but directives that are too specific may also adversely affect implementation. Implementers sometimes need the freedom to adapt policies to suit the situation at hand. A myriad of specific regulations can overwhelm and confuse personnel in the field and may make them reluctant to act for fear of breaking the rules. Apparently, this is what occurred in the Federal Emergency Management Agency (FEMA) as it tried to help the victims of Hurricane Andrew in 1992. During spring and summer 1993, President Clinton gave the same agency clearer direction and a shorter time frame in which to provide emergency assistance to Midwest flood victims, and the agency responded with greater dispatch and efficiency—which worked to the president's advantage.

Strict guidelines may also induce a type of goal displacement in which lower-level officials become more concerned with meeting specific requirements than with achieving the basic goals of the program. By rigidly adhering to the letter of a regulation, they may become so bogged down in red tape that the purpose of the rule is forgotten or defeated. Conversely, implementers sometimes simply ignore rigid regulations.

Consistency

Inconsistency as well as vagueness in guidance from the president may provide operating agencies with substantial discretion in the interpretation and implementation of policy, which they may not exercise to carry out a policy's goals. For example, before it was split into two agencies following the 9/11 terrorist attacks, the Immigration and Naturalization Service was often confronted with inconsistencies: the agency was supposed to exclude illegal immigrants but allow necessary agricultural workers to enter the country; it had to carefully screen foreigners seeking to enter the country but facilitate the entry of foreign tourists; and it had to find and expel illegal aliens yet not break up families, impose hardships, violate civil rights, or deprive employers of low-paid workers. As James Q. Wilson pointed out, "No organization can accomplish all of these goals well, especially when advocates of each have the power to mount newspaper and congressional investigations of the agency's failures."[30]

Similarly, the Forest Service is supposed to both help timber companies exploit the lumber potential in the national forests and preserve the natural environment. After the 2010 BP oil spill in the Gulf of Mexico, we learned that the Minerals Management Service, which regulated offshore drilling, had a dual role of both fostering and policing the industry—collecting royalty payments from the drilling companies while also levying fines on them for violations of law. It was split into two agencies the next year.

Many of the factors that produce unclear communications are also responsible for inconsistent directives. The complexity of public policies, the difficulties in starting up new programs, and the multiple objectives of many policies all contribute to inconsistency in policy communications. Another reason why decisions are often inconsistent is that the president and top officials constantly attempt to satisfy a diverse set of interests that may represent views on both sides of an issue. Consequently, policies that are not of high priority to the president may simply be left to flounder in a sea of competing demands.

RESOURCES

If the president lacks the resources necessary to carry out policies, implementation is likely to be ineffective. Important resources include money; staff of sufficient size and with the proper skills to carry out its assignments; and the information, authority, and facilities necessary to translate written proposals into functioning public services.

Money

Sometimes the problem the president faces in implementing policy and delivering services is simply a lack of money. From repairing the nation's transportation infrastructure to providing health care for the uninsured, from enrolling children in Head Start to buying new weapons systems, a program's budget determines the amount and often the quality of the service that government can provide.

Opponents of a policy may try to sabotage it by denying the funds necessary to implement it effectively. After the Affordable Care Act was passed in 2010, most Republican governors declined to create their own state insurance exchanges, forcing the federal government to take at least partial responsibility for creating marketplaces serving thirty-six states. However, the statute included no money for the development of a federal exchange, and Republicans blocked funding attempts. The lack of funds forced the Department of Health and Human Services (HHS) and other agencies to cobble together HealthCare.gov by redirecting funds from existing programs. The work of designing the federal health exchange, and of helping states that wanted to build their own, became fragmented, with no one taking the broad view.[31]

Staff

Certainly, an essential resource in implementing policy is staff. "Big government" is often under attack, so it may seem surprising to learn that a principal source of implementation failure is inadequate staff. Although more than four million military and

Table 10.1 Federal Civilian Employment

Federal Bureaucracy	No. of Employees*
Executive Departments	
Defense (Military Functions)	758,000
Veterans Affairs	393,800
Homeland Security	201,700
Justice	119,600
Treasury	89,500
Agriculture	83,700
Health and Human Services	76,500
Interior	61,800
Transportation	55,200
Commerce	112,000†
State	36,800
Labor	15,600
Energy	15,500
Housing and Urban Development	7,800
Education	4,000
Larger Non-cabinet Agencies	
US Postal Service	584,914
Social Security Administration	61,700
Corps of Engineers	23,100
National Aeronautics and Space Administration	17,200
Environmental Protection Agency	12,400
Tennessee Valley Authority	10,000
General Services Administration	14,200

* Figures are for 2020.
† Numbers inflated by temporary workers for the 2020 census.
Source: Budget of the United States Government, Fiscal Year 2020: Analytical Perspectives (Washington, DC: US Government Printing Office, 2019), Tables 7.1 and 7.2.

civilian personnel work full-time for the federal executive branch (see table 10.1), and therefore for the president, there are still too few people with the requisite skills to do an effective job implementing many policies. We must evaluate the bureaucracy, not only in terms of absolute numbers but also in terms of its capabilities to perform desired tasks.

Size

The federal government provides a wide range of services—from national defense and immigration control to the maintenance of recreational facilities—through its own personnel. Each of these areas, and others like them, is labor intensive, and thus the quality of the services the bureaucracy provides is directly related to the size and skill of the staff available to the relevant agencies over which the president presides. However, there is substantial evidence that many agencies and departments are woefully understaffed.[32]

After thousands of people were sickened by tainted eggs, peanut butter, and spinach, Congress passed a sweeping food safety law in 2010 that gave the Food and Drug Administration (FDA) new powers to prevent additional outbreaks. However, lawmakers have not provided enough money for the mission. Although 80 percent of the nation's drug supply and a large percentage of its medical devices and food are now imported, the FDA lacks the personnel and computer systems to identify, much less inspect, the plants producing these items. Similarly, at a time when the use of low-cost generic drugs is one of the few ways to rein in skyrocketing health-care costs, the FDA has a backlog of hundreds of applications to bring new generic products to the market. In addition, the FDA has the equivalent of just six full-time inspectors to monitor three million shipments of cosmetics imported each year.

Because of lack of personnel, it takes the Social Security Administration well over a year to process claims for disability insurance. There is a shortage of epidemiologists who are trained to recognize and investigate the outbreak of infectious disease. The Securities and Exchange Commission lacks the personnel to police companies and markets and thus protect investors against abuses in the marketplace such as occurred with Enron and the lending practices that led to the financial crisis in 2008. After the invasion of Iraq in March 2003, the United States had too few troops to devote to fighting the Taliban in Afghanistan and to prevent looting and violence in Iraq after the invasion. The Pipeline and Hazardous Materials Safety Administration is chronically short of inspectors. This situation leaves much of the regulatory control in the hands of pipeline operators. The Fish and Wildlife Service lacks the personnel to evaluate the requests for species to be protected. There are too few US Immigration and Customs Enforcement agents to track the foreign visitors who overstay their visas or to identify, much less deport, more than a small percentage of the estimated 200,000 convicted criminal aliens in the United States.

Although staff size can be critical for almost every policy, it is more critical for some than for others. Insufficient staff is especially critical to implementation when the policy involved imposes unwelcome constraints on people, whether the requirements are those of grant policies, regulatory policies, or criminal law. Because such policies generally involve highly decentralized activities, sufficient staff must be available to monitor this behavior. It is much easier for the chief executive to implement a policy, such as Social Security, that distributes benefits that recipients desire. It requires more personnel to enforce limitations on people than to write checks to them.

Moreover, the lack of staff makes compliance data difficult to obtain. Thus, the president and his subordinates often have to rely on information about compliance from those who are doing the complying, such as those running schools, hospitals, pipelines, and mines. Quite naturally, this system of information raises questions about effective implementation. It should come as no surprise to us, then, when state and local governments misspend federal grants or hazardous wastes pollute the environment.

The fear of creating a totalitarian bureaucratic monolith and the pressures to allocate personnel to more direct services, such as the provision of agricultural expertise to farmers, keep the staff available to monitor implementation small. In addition, the scarcity of payroll funds, coupled with the irresistible urges of policy makers to provide public services (at least in form), ensures that staff size will often be inadequate to implement the programs. Moreover, in an age when "big government" is under attack, there are strong political incentives to downsize the bureaucracy.

Federal programs rely heavily on state agencies for their implementation. This reliance, however, does not solve the president's problem of lack of staff at the federal level; it merely transfers the problem to the states. Because this shortage of personnel exists at every level of government, delegating the implementation of a policy to a lower level rarely alleviates the problem.

Moreover, state governments may be hostile to a president's programs. A number of states declined to expand their Medicaid programs as the Affordable Care Act envisioned. Some states refused to educate the public about the law. Congressional Republicans sent so many burdensome queries to local hospitals and nonprofits gearing up to help consumers navigate the new system that at least two such groups returned their federal grants and gave up the effort. (When the White House tried to enlist stars in the National Football League [NFL] to help promote the law, the Senate's top two Republicans sent the league an ominous letter wondering why it would "risk damaging its inclusive and apolitical brand." The NFL backed off.)

The federal government also contracts with private-sector companies to provide many goods and services, but this approach is not appropriate for many federal government programs, ranging from fighting wars to prosecuting crimes.

Sometimes presidents turn limited staff size to their advantage. For example, the Reagan administration decreased staff in areas such as antitrust, civil rights, and environmental protection in an effort to reduce enforcement activities to which it was opposed.[33] The Trump administration has attempted a similar strategy regarding the

Environmental Protection Agency, immigration judges and those conducting clearance interviews of refugees overseas, consumer finance protection, and other areas to which it is not sympathetic. Reductions in staff have meant less monitoring of pollution and slower screening of applications from refugees.

Such a strategy may be useful for stopping an activity, such as regulatory behavior, but it undermines efforts to take the positive actions that Trump may desire.[34] For example, it has not been successful in creating new institutions or reorganizing existing bureaucracies to better serve its populist policy aims.[35]

Skill

The skills of officials are critical to successful policy implementation, and government executives worry about the skills of the federal workforce.[36] The US General Accounting Office reported that the federal government lacked employees with the necessary skills in information technology, science, economics, and management to run government programs soundly. For example, the Pentagon has a critical shortage of engineers capable of managing complex weapons procurement programs.

Skill is especially critical and often in short supply when a government agency is carrying out or regulating highly technical activities. The Nuclear Regulatory Commission has difficulty finding nuclear engineers to monitor the safety of atomic power plants. As oil and gas companies took their drilling operations into deeper and riskier waters, the Mineral Management Service (MMS) had to rely on the expertise of those doing the drilling because it lacked the resources, personnel, training, and technology (as well as the enforcement tools, regulations, and legislation) that are critical to ensuring that offshore drilling is conducted in a safe and responsible manner. The agency frequently adopted industry-generated standards as federal regulations.

The terrorist attacks on September 11, 2001, dramatically showed that personnel with the proper skills are also often in short supply in the executive branch. We learned, for example, that the FBI and intelligence agencies had (and still have) only enough translators (especially in non-European languages) to interpret a small percentage of millions of pages of intercepted conversations. Only a few dozen FBI agents can converse in Arabic. Because the FBI slashed its criminal investigative workforce to expand its national security role after 9/11, it had to struggle to find enough agents and resources to investigate criminal wrongdoing tied to the country's economic crisis beginning in 2008. Many Foreign Service officers in the Department of State lack the linguistic skills appropriate for their overseas postings. The government also lacked personnel with the right skills and capacity to deal with reconstructing Iraq.[37]

Similarly, in the wake of Hurricane Katrina, we learned that five of the eight top FEMA officials came to their posts with virtually no experience in handling disasters and that the agency's ranks of seasoned crisis managers had thinned dramatically. Before coming to FEMA, the director had been head of the International Arabian Horse Association, not usually a training ground for handling emergencies. The appalling performance of this team followed naturally from its background.

Information

Related to staff expertise is information. After the 9/11 terrorist attacks, we learned that the Immigration and Naturalization Service lacked information, such as terrorist watch lists, to prevent terrorists from entering the United States, the Federal

Aviation Administration did not receive information on flight training by suspected terrorists, and the FAA no-fly terrorist list contained the names of only twelve people (the agency did not receive information on terrorists from the FBI, CIA, or State Department).[38]

The Trump administration did not tell key government agencies about its "zero tolerance" immigration policy before publicly announcing it in April 2018, leaving the officials responsible for carrying it out unprepared to handle the resulting separations of thousands of children from their families. The Department of Homeland Security, which apprehends border crossers, and the Department of Health and Human Services, which cares for separated migrant children, were both caught off guard when Attorney General Jeff Sessions announced plans to criminally prosecute anyone who crossed the border illegally.[39]

Difficulty in Hiring

Sometimes, the necessary personnel are very difficult to hire because of the higher incomes, better career opportunities, and greater flexibility that they can enjoy by working in the private sector.[40] At a time of increasing threats of cyberattacks on critical infrastructure, the Department of Homeland Security is having trouble recruiting much-needed computer experts because it cannot match the pay of the private sector (and it also lacks the allure of intelligence agencies).

At other times, the needed staff may simply not exist, even in the private sector, and a government agency must invest in developing the expertise. The federal government's efforts to build a missile shield illustrate this problem. No one really knew how to build such a system, so it is not surprising that frequent failures have characterized the program.

New Policies

Staff skills are especially critical for new policies or those involving technical questions. Routine functions, such as dispersing funds, building roads, training troops, hiring typists, providing building security, or purchasing goods, are relatively straightforward in their operation, and a wealth of information exists on how to carry them out. However, the implementers of policies such as controlling hospital costs or developing a missile shield do not share these advantages: Officials are being asked to meet goals no one has ever met. Thus, it is one thing for Congress or the White House to mandate a change in policy but something quite different for the executive branch officials who work for the president to figure out how to do it. Unsurprisingly, the government lacked people with the appropriate skills to translate the two-thousand-page Affordable Care Act into reality.[41]

As a result, some responsibilities will simply not be met or else will not be met on time. Inefficiency is also likely to characterize the implementation of such policies. Some efforts will prove to be mistakes, and the implementers will have to try again. Moreover, regulations may be inappropriate, causing other government units or organizations in the private sector to purchase equipment, fill out forms, or stop certain activities unnecessarily. For example, before an agency acts to implement a law by ordering costly changes in an industry or its products (automobile emission standards, for instance), ideally the agency should be able to predict the effects of the change on the economic health of the industry in question. Such information, however, is frequently lacking, and the president may be severely criticized as a result.

Contracting Out

One response to limited staff is for the federal government to do most of its work through contracts, mandates to state and local governments, regulations on corporate and individual behavior, provisions of the tax code, and other indirect means. It is not easy to estimate the "true" size of government. One author concluded that well over ten million jobs resulted from federal contracts or as a result of federal mandates to state and local governments.[42] Employing such techniques extends the range of government activity, but it also makes it more difficult for presidents to influence the implementation of policy directly and for others to hold them accountable for it. Contractors have become a virtual fourth branch of government. Spending on federal contracts soared during the George W. Bush administration to more than $400 billion, and the estimated number of contractor jobs is nearly eight million. This total far exceeds the number of people directly employed by the government.[43] Contractors build ships and satellites for the Department of Defense and intelligence agencies, but they also collect income taxes and develop agency budgets, fly pilotless spy aircraft, and take the minutes at policy meetings. They sit next to federal employees at nearly every agency. The number of such jobs decreased under Barack Obama, but there were still 3.7 million contractors and 1.6 million grant employees at the federal level at the end of his tenure.[44]

The contracting explosion raises questions. One argument for contracting out services is that the private sector will provide them at reduced cost because of competition to obtain the contracts. Yet, most contracts have not been put up for full and open bidding, and the intended savings are scarce. Indeed, there are numerous official reports of billions of dollars of contractor waste and fraud, particularly in the rebuilding of Iraq.[45]

Contractors may not save money, and they also may not provide quality services. We learned on September 11, 2001, that the airport security personnel from the private sector carrying out federal policies lacked the training to adequately protect the airplanes from terrorist hijackings.

There is also almost always less public scrutiny of private companies than of government agencies, hiding government programs behind closed corporate doors. Companies, unlike government agencies, are not subject to the Freedom of Information Act. The lack of transparency is particularly problematic for firms exercising inherently government powers, such as providing security for US personnel in Iraq or running prisons there. Some have been charged with abusing the use of force and engaging in illegal interrogations.

Authority

Authority is often a critical resource in policy implementation. Congress vests most of the authority in subordinate executive officials, but they, of course, work for the president. Sometimes, agency officials simply lack the authority, even on paper, to implement a policy properly. For example, the policy being implemented may provide no sanctions against those violating the law, or the agency may lack authority to initiate administrative or judicial actions.

The Mine Safety and Health Administration lacks the power to subpoena mining company documents or to enforce effective penalties for safety violations. Until recently, the FDA lacked the power to order recalls of contaminated food. It also does no testing of drugs and medical devices on its own and must rely entirely on the test results submitted by manufacturers. Often, it even lacks access to potentially

iStock/Dmy To

Coal mining is a dangerous and unhealthy occupation, but the government lacks the power it needs to regulate the health and safety of coal mining.

damaging company documents that reveal a manufacturer's involvement in product liability cases. The FDA also has no power to require drug makers to undertake new safety tests once a drug is approved.

Interests opposed to regulatory policy may try to limit the authority of agencies. For decades, the National Rifle Association has used its influence to limit the authority of the Bureau of Alcohol, Tobacco, Firearms and Explosives (ATF). It has lobbied forcefully against the nomination of directors who it thought might act to implement the law aggressively and pushed Congress to enact restrictions on how the bureau spends money in order to curtail its ability to regulate firearms and track gun crimes. One funding provision, for example, forbids the ATF from using electronic databases to trace guns to owners. Instead, the agency relies on a warehouse full of paper records.

Exercising Authority

When formal authority does exist, observers frequently mistake it for effective authority. However, authority on paper is one thing; authority effectively exercised is quite another. Executive branch officials may be reluctant to exercise authority for a number of reasons. One of the potentially most effective sanctions is the withdrawal of funds from a program. Cutting off funds is a drastic action. It may be embarrassing to all involved and antagonize the implementers of a program whose active support is crucial. Cutting off federal funds from projects also alienates the members of Congress who represent districts that are adversely affected by the elimination of government funds. Requiring states or cities to repay misspent funds can also have severe political consequences. In addition, terminating a project or withdrawing federal funds may hurt most of those whom the policy is designed to aid. Schoolchildren, the elderly, or the poor are often the real victims of cutbacks. If a company loses federal contracts because of racial or sexual discrimination, it may be forced to lay off workers. Those with the least seniority may be the minorities the policy had tried to help. Similarly, cutting off federal funds for the educationally disadvantaged because of misallocation is most likely to hurt students from poor families. Local taxpayers ultimately pay fines for municipalities violating the Safe Drinking Water Act.

The desire for self-preservation keeps many of the president's agencies from withdrawing funds. Agencies such as the Federal Highway Administration and the Department of Education are primarily involved in channeling grants to other levels of government. To survive, they must give away money. If they fail to do so, they may look bad to Congress and superior executive officials and thus weaken future requests for budgets and authority. Thus, they may sacrifice the economic and social objectives of a program to the "maintenance" objectives of the bureaucratic unit.

Authority over Nongovernmental Actors

Although executive officials often lack effective authority over other public officials, they have even less authority over private individuals, groups, and businesses upon whom the successful implementation of policies often depends. Therefore, officials must make their policies attractive to the private sector. As a result of these efforts, for example, rules regarding safety in the workplace may not be issued; if they are, they rarely result in serious penalties for noncompliance. The federal government provided hundreds of billions of dollars to financial institutions in 2008 and 2009 so that they would stay solvent and keep lending to prime the economy. Nevertheless, many of them failed to lend much of their new funds.

Sharing Authority

One of the greatest obstacles to presidential direction of the bureaucracy is that the president shares authority over the bureaucracy. Congress passes the laws that establish and fund the programs that bureaucrats administer. With increasing frequency, courts issue orders that affect government regulations, as we discuss in chapter 12. In addition, agencies have extensive ties with external groups and congressional committees.[46] From one perspective, then, career civil servants have a strong political base from which to resist White House direction, including playing other political actors against each other to diminish presidential influence.[47]

Mobilizing Opponents

At other times, the president's efforts to change the course of policy mobilizes opponents, as when Ronald Reagan's efforts to reduce enforcement activity in the EPA's Office of Water Quality encouraged citizen suits that had the effect of producing lower levels of political control in the long run.[48] More broadly, Reagan's (and to some extent George W. Bush's) efforts to reduce the rigor of EPA regulation reinvigorated a flagging environmental movement and infuriated the EPA's patrons in Congress, who resented what they saw as a blatant attempt to circumvent legislative intent by administrative action.[49]

Facilities and Equipment

Physical facilities may also be critical resources in implementation. Without the necessary buildings, equipment, supplies, and even green space, implementation will not succeed. US troops in Iraq suffered from insufficient supplies of body armor and armored Humvees and trucks to protect them against roadside bombs. National Guard units have only a third of the equipment they need to respond to domestic disasters and terrorist attacks.

Frequently, there is also a shortage of sophisticated equipment. Computers are essential to the implementation of public policy. Nevertheless, the FBI lacks computers at its headquarters that allow it to search its own databases for multiple terms such as *aviation* and *schools*. The FAA's air traffic control centers across the nation depend on aging, outdated equipment in the effort to direct the nation's air traffic. Similarly, the Internal Revenue Service (IRS) lacks the appropriate computer systems to integrate the dozens of databases that contain the information necessary to collect the nearly $4 trillion in taxes that finance the federal government. The Customs Bureau lacks the computer system to monitor properly the flood of people and goods flowing into the United States every day. The computer system the EPA uses to track and control water pollution is obsolete and full of faulty data and does not take into account thousands of significant pollution sources.

Although the president can request funds for new or additional facilities, both the White House and Congress hesitate to increase government spending to do so. In fact, increased spending in one area may come at the expense of decreased spending in another. Moreover, as is the case for staff, Congress often prefers to spread resources over many policies rather than to fund fewer programs adequately.

Internal government procurement rules ("red tape") may add additional burdens to those trying to purchase expensive equipment such as computers. President Obama, voicing his frustration about the tech problems that undermined the rollout of health-care reform, blamed government IT procurement practices. Speaking at a *Wall Street Journal* forum, he declared that his administration needed to "blow up how we procure for IT."[50] The government lacks expertise for procuring IT and and its procedures were too slow, too complex, and too decentralized.

DISPOSITIONS

We have seen that bureaucrats often operate with considerable discretion in their implementation of policy. Laws often permit agency heads wide latitude in influencing the rules, procedures, design, and substance of agency action.[51] This latitude provides implementers with the potential to give new meaning to policies, which may inhibit intended change or bring about unintended consequences.

The fact that bureaucrats hold particular policy views and have discretion in the implementation of policy does not in itself pose problems for presidents. If implementers are well disposed toward a particular policy, they are likely to carry it out as the president intended. Other policies fall within a "zone of indifference." Lacking strong feelings about these policies, bureaucrats should implement them faithfully.

White House Distrust

The core of the tension between the White House and the career bureaucracy is the view that some recent administrations (including those of Bill Clinton,[52] George W.

Bush, and Donald Trump) have brought to Washington: that the bureaucracy is not a neutral instrument. As the author of one prominent study put it,

> It is a rare political appointee . . . who does not take up his or her office convinced that senior career officials are . . . recalcitrant adversaries, saboteurs-in-waiting, obstinately committed to existing programs, and resistant to new policy initiatives.[53]

New presidents and their staff often believe that officials and the agencies they represent have interests of their own to advance and protect and may not necessarily view issues from the president's perspective.[54] If policies are in direct conflict with the policy views or personal or organizational interests of the implementers, they may exercise their discretion, sometimes in subtle ways, to hinder implementation. Moreover, bureaucrats "have resources of organization, time, and information that enable them to pursue those interests with vigor and persistence."[55]

As the size and scope of the federal government have grown since the 1960s, so has distrust, especially among Republican presidents and the general public. Richard Nixon told his cabinet, "We can't depend on people who believe in another philosophy of government to give us their undivided loyalty or their best work."[56] Similarly, Gerald Ford observed,

> There are bureaucratic fiefdoms out in the states or in various regions, and the people who occupy those pockets of power want to do things in their own way. They are pros at it. They have been disregarding Presidents for years, both Democratic and Republican.[57]

Clashing Ideologies

There is plenty of evidence that at times the ideologies of the White House and senior members of the civil service have clashed, although this potential for resistance to presidential initiatives has varied across agencies.[58] It is also the case that executive departments and independent agencies have agendas set by laws that predate the president's arrival in office and that serve as a force for continuity rather than change in response to the White House. In addition, it does not stretch the imagination to consider that how officials exercise their discretion depends to some degree on their dispositions about the policies and rules they administer.[59] National security assistant and Secretary of State Henry Kissinger declared, "The outsider believes a Presidential order is consistently followed out. Nonsense. I have to spend considerable time seeing that it is carried out and in the spirit the President intended."[60]

Hindering Implementation

There is some evidence that the policy predispositions of civil servants are critical to their compliance with their political principals.[61] The EPA maintained and even increased its inspections and citations of violations of environmental regulations in the face of strong efforts by the Reagan administration to constrain the enforcement of environmental protection laws.[62] There was also some resistance to Reagan initiatives in the Civil Rights Division of the Justice Department.[63]

Donald Trump has frequently complained of the "Deep State" of permanent government employees opposing his initiatives. The president was especially critical of officials in the Departments of Justice, Defense, State, and the Interior, intelligence agencies, and the Environmental Protection Agency. He had some reason for concern. One senior official wrote an anonymous op-ed in the *New York Times* declaring he or she was part of the "resistance" inside the Trump administration.[64]

President Carter ordered federal agencies to discourage the development of low-lying areas that were in danger of damage from flooding. Twenty-five months later, however, only fifteen of the seventy-five agencies that had received the directive had issued regulations specifying how they were going to comply with the president's wishes. Forty-six of the agencies had not even taken the first step toward adopting the regulations. The primary reason for this lack of action was not bureaucratic indolence. Instead, it was the opposition of agencies to the substance of the president's order. Similarly, Ronald Reagan's efforts to build up special commando units for unconventional warfare and counterterrorist operations were hampered by the failure of the air force to provide adequate aircraft to deliver the forces and the army to provide the units with the proper equipment.

Organizational Viewpoints

Differences in organizational viewpoints may also impede the cooperation between agencies that is so often necessary in policy implementation. The army requires aircraft, which belong to the air force (at its insistence), to transport troops. However, transporting troops is a low priority for the air force, which is more interested in flying strategic bombers and fighter planes. Thus, it typically does not fight for resources for troop transport planes or choose to allocate its scarce resources to that function, which undermines the ability of the army to carry out its own function.

Similarly, in Iraq, the army had to develop its own aerial surveillance capabilities, relying in part on civilian aircraft, because it felt the air force would not meet its surveillance needs. Secretary of Defense Robert Gates had to challenge the air force "to do more, much more" to send surveillance drones to collect more information on adversaries in Iraq and Afghanistan. He also found that in Afghanistan the marines, although fighting brilliantly, were determined to keep operational control of their units away from the senior US commander in Kabul, placing their organizational desires above accomplishing the overall mission of the war.[65]

There may also be differences in viewpoints among presidential subordinates with different program responsibilities within a single agency. There was intra-agency conflict over the implementation of the National Environmental Policy Act. Secretaries of transportation, for example, had a difficult time getting development-oriented agencies in the department, such as the Federal Highway Administration, to consider seriously the environmental consequences of their projects.

Trade-Offs

Every president makes a different trade-off between loyalty and competence.[66] In general, presidents nominate significantly more loyalists and fewer experienced officers to higher priority departments, indicating the importance of responsiveness, as well as their suspicion of experienced officers. Presidents select more experienced nominees for lower priority departments to assure competence where they are least concerned with responsiveness.[67]

Bureaucratic Responsiveness to the President

Although there is some evidence of bureaucratic resistance to presidential initiatives, there is good reason to expect the career bureaucracy to cooperate with the president's wishes. The professional norms of career civil servants offer political appointees considerable flexibility in directing agencies.[68] According to Francis Rourke, cases of bureaucratic challenge to presidential authority have been "a rare occurrence"[69] and senior bureaucrats usually follow the election returns and defer to the president.[70] "What is surprising," agreed James Q. Wilson, "is not that bureaucrats sometimes can defy the president but that they support his programs as much as they do. The reason is simple: . . . bureaucrats want to do the right thing."[71]

Most studies have found that bureaucracies change their implementation of policy in line with the president's wishes, even in areas of political controversy. These studies cover a wide range of agencies in virtually every aspect of public policy.[72] As Richard Waterman and Kenneth Meier conclude, "All political-bureaucratic relationships are not a cauldron of conflict."[73]

It is also the case that the clashing of beliefs between career managers and political appointees has receded over time as the political views of the permanent bureaucracy shifted to the right and the senior civil service became more centrist. An increasing number of Republicans and Independents have moved into career managerial positions.[74]

Despite their initial suspicion and hostility, political appointees usually develop trust in the career executives who work for them. A "cycle of accommodation" characterizes the relationship between political appointees and career executives. This cycle occurs among most presidential appointees in all recent presidential administrations. Table 10.2 shows the results of surveys of appointees in the Johnson through the Clinton administrations. The figures in the table make clear that regardless of party, ideology, or administration, political appointees find that career executives are both competent and responsive.[75] As Paul Light puts it, "In interview after interview, presidential appointees celebrate the dedication of their bureaucrats."[76]

Similarly, a survey of George H. W. Bush's political appointees found that they relied heavily on careerists for all aspects of their jobs, from formulating policy to implementing it. The political appointees also reported that they found career civil servants helpful in everything from mastering substantive policy details and anticipating policy implementation problems to providing liaisons with Congress and other components of the bureaucracy.[77] In table 10.3, we can see the results from another survey of Bush political appointees. Most found that civil servants brought valuable experience to the job and had good leadership qualities and management skills. Equally important, these political appointees saw senior civil servants as working hard to carry out administration policies. Indeed, they perceived of themselves as less likely to have valuable experience and be good managers than the civil servants who worked for them.

In sum, the bulk of the evidence supports a view that federal bureaucrats are "principled agents."[78] As Joel Aberbach and Bert Rockman point out, there is little evidence to support assertions of recalcitrant career civil servants when there is effective administrative leadership, including open channels of communication, willingness to listen to advice, clear articulation of goals, and mutual respect. Good management is compatible with good politics.[79] It is interesting that research has found that programs administered by careerists did better in PART evaluations under George W. Bush than those administered by political appointees.[80] Indeed, research on the Bush administration found that the level of trust at top levels of an agency affected performance at lower levels and that mutual support between appointees and careerists based on optimistic trust was a more effective managerial strategy than one founded on unsubstantiated distrust.[81]

Table 10.2 Johnson–Clinton Appointees' Perception of Career Civil Servants

	Rating Careerists as Competent (%)	Rating Careerists as Responsive (%)
Party*		
Democratic	92	86
Independent	85	87
Republican	83	78
Ideology*		
Liberal	78	84
Moderate	90	85
Conservative	82	80
Administration		
Johnson	92	89
Nixon	88	84
Ford	80	82
Carter	81	86
Reagan	86	87
Bush	85	83
Clinton	82	78

* Johnson–Carter appointees only.
Sources: Johnson through Carter data: National Academy of Public Administration, Presidential Appointee Project, Leadership in Jeopardy: The Fraying of the Presidential Appointments System (Washington, DC: National Academy of Public Administration, 1985). This table is adapted from Paul C. Light, "When Worlds Collide: The Political-Career Nexus," in G. Calvin Mackenzie, ed., The In-and-Outers: Presidential Appointees and Transient Government in Washington (Baltimore, MD: Johns Hopkins University Press, 1987), p. 158. Reagan through Clinton data: Paul C. Light and Virginia L. Thomas, The Merit and Reputation of an Administration: Presidential Appointees on the Appointments Process (Washington, DC: Brookings Institution and Heritage Foundation, 2000), pp. 9, 31, 32.

Table 10.3 George H. W. Bush Administration Appointees' Perception of Career Civil Servants and Political Appointees

	Agreement of Political Appointees about Civil Servants (%)	Agreement of Political Appointees about Political Appointees (%)
Bring valuable experience to the job	98	82
Have good leadership qualities	59	64
Have good management skills	61	55
Work hard to carry out administration initiatives and priorities	71	100

Source: Adapted from Joel D. Aberbach and Bert A. Rockman, In the Web of Politics: Three Decades of the U.S. Federal Executive (Washington, DC: Brookings Institution, 2000), p. 123.

Why do new administrations persist in the expectation of facing bureaucratic resistance in spite of strong evidence of bureaucratic responsiveness? Part of the answer may be that suspicions of the bureaucracy are fueled by presidential election campaigns, such as those of Jimmy Carter, Ronald Reagan, and Donald Trump, in which the winning candidate runs as a Washington outsider and engages in "bureaucrat bashing." (Many recent presidents, however, have abstained from the temptation to criticize the bureaucracy in their campaigns and praised government employees.) In addition, most political appointees have viewed their positive experience with careerists as somehow unique, believing that their careerists were different from others.[82]

Staffing the Bureaucracy

The president's most straightforward response to implementation problems is to replace personnel who fail to implement policies the way the president desires with people who will cooperate. When presidents succeed in doing this, they can change the way in which a policy is implemented.[83] However, of the more than four million employees in the executive branch, the president and his designees appoint far less than 1 percent. Mid- and upper-level bureaucratic managers outnumber their political counterparts by almost 100 to 1, which places an obvious constraint on the ability of any administration to alter personnel.

Because the White House often distrusts the career bureaucracy, it invests a great deal of energy in its political appointments. A principal responsibility of political appointees is to elicit responsiveness of career officials to their directions.[84] There are more than four thousand political appointees, in addition to the White House staff.

Executive Schedule

First, there are the Executive Schedule appointees, including the secretaries of cabinet departments, the heads of independent agencies and their deputies, and the heads of major departmental or agency bureaus or divisions such as assistant secretaries. There are also nominations for nearly two hundred ambassadors, ninety-four US attorneys, and ninety-four US marshals, and also for many boards and commissions. These appointees are nominated by the president and confirmed by the Senate. There are currently about 1,200 presidential appointees requiring Senate confirmation.[85]

Other Appointees

A second category of political appointees is comprised of about three thousand noncareer senior executives and other officials who are not subject to Senate confirmation. These appointees include those serving in the Executive Office of the President and most senior White House aides, as well as their deputies and key assistants. Members of the Senior Executive Service (SES) serve in the key positions just below the top presidential appointees. Although approximately 90 percent of senior executives are career civil servants, up to 10 percent government-wide may be political appointees. These positions include senior management positions within most federal agencies. There are also hundreds of political appointees in policy-making positions or positions that require a close working relationship with the incumbent officeholder or key political officials. Most hold titles such as "executive assistant" or "special assistant."[86]

Together, these two sets of appointees do much to set the tenor of governing at the federal level and are critical to a president managing the national government. Nevertheless, early in his tenure, Donald Trump has chosen not to fill many of the appointive positions available to him, as you can see in box 10.1.

Box 10.1 ★ Donald Trump Decapitates the Bureaucracy

Donald Trump campaigned for president based in large part on his skill as an executive. Now he is the chief executive of the US government. We shall see later in this chapter that the White House was unusually slow in filling positions throughout the bureaucracy. In February 2017, Trump told Fox News that he was intentionally leaving many slots open, saying,

> When I see a story about "Donald Trump didn't fill hundreds and hundreds of jobs," it's because, in many cases, we don't want to fill those jobs. . . . A lot of those jobs, I don't want to appoint, because they're unnecessary to have. You know, we have so many people in government, even me. I look at some of the jobs and it's people over people over people. I say, "What do all these people do?" You don't need all those jobs.[87]

The president's view that certain positions should not be staffed was an unusual one. Trump did not specify the positions he felt should not be filled. It is quite possible that he did not know the details. More generally, there is a serious question of whether the president's view was a wise one.

More than two years into his presidency, the president had no head of the National Park Service, the Bureau of Land Management, and the US Fish and Wildlife Service, which together oversee more than 480 million acres of land. More than half the key positions in the Departments of Justice and of Homeland Security were unfilled.

As David Lewis points out, presidents need their appointees.[88] Leaving key positions in tax policy, immigration, and infrastructure vacant left the president shorthanded, dependent on an understaffed and inexpert White House. Moreover, career civil service professionals do not have credibility, political support, or the leverage to push the president's agenda. Nor are they well positioned to communicate a president's priorities to federal employees or to obtain the cooperation of other agencies and state, local, and international governments that is often needed to implement policies successfully. To succeed in these tasks requires that officials have a credible claim to be speaking for the administration.

Presidents, especially those who wish to engender substantial change, need appointees to lead the bureaucracy. Without appointees in place, agencies are prone to keep doing what they have always done. Moreover, without appointees in place, the government is less likely to respond effectively to problems that are impossible to anticipate.

Choosing Appointees

After winning election, a president has less than three months to search for a new team to take over the government. Moreover, this selection must be done by the president-elect and the president's aides, all of whom will have been exhausted by the long, arduous election campaign and have many other demands on their time, such as preparing a budget and a legislative program. Presidents tend to move more quickly on nominations for more important positions and for agencies whose ideological leanings he opposes.[89]

Members of the cabinet and other appointees usually have little advance notice of their selection and will be busy wrapping up their other responsibilities and doing preparation on the issues relevant to their new positions prior to their confirmation hearings. As a result, they can devote less time to recruiting their own subordinates than they might like. Thus, there is often slippage in the recruitment of the personnel at the top of the executive branch.

Presidents are also constrained politically in their appointments. Usually, they feel that such appointments must show a balance of geography, ideology, race, ethnicity, gender, and other demographic characteristics that are salient at the time. (Presidents Clinton, George W. Bush, and Barack Obama made substantial efforts to achieve diversity in their cabinet appointments.) Moreover, interest groups keep a watchful eye throughout a president's tenure in office on who is appointed to what position.

The need for Senate confirmation of the most important officials is also a constraint on the president. Although the upper chamber confirms most nominees to the bureaucracy, there are often delays, frustrating the president's efforts to influence policy implementation. If the president's party has a majority in the Senate, confirmations typically go smoothly and expeditiously. However, even the Republican majority in the Trump years was slow to act on the president's nominees, appearing to find some of them more problematic than normal.

Under divided government, there are frequent delays in the president making nominations (anticipating opposition) and in the Senate confirming them. Moreover, rejections are more likely.[90] Nominees to more important positions tend to receive faster confirmations.[91] During the last six years of Barack Obama's tenure, in several instances the senators did not oppose a particular nominee but rather any nominee so as to try to hamper the president's economic policies on prominent issues such as housing, finance, foreign trade, and offshore drilling. In frustration, the president tested constitutional boundaries by making recess appointments while the Senate was technically in session.

Thousands of people seek appointments for themselves, and members of Congress and party officials urge thousands more on an administration. Few are qualified for the available jobs, yet due to political necessity, the president will appoint some less than qualified individuals. Political favors may please political supporters, but they do not necessarily provide the basis for sound administration. Moreover, such appointments may result in incompatibilities with the president that result in politically costly dismissals. To combat this problem, presidents may use patronage strategically. A study of President Obama's appointees found that he was more likely to place appointees selected for non-policy patronage reasons in agencies off his agenda, in agencies that shared his policy views, and where appointees were least able to affect agency performance.[92]

A surprising limitation on personnel selection is that presidents often do not know of individuals who are qualified for the positions they have to fill. Following his election in 1960, John F. Kennedy told an aide, "For the last four years I spent so much time getting to know people who could help me get elected President that I didn't have time to get to know people who could help me, after I was elected, to be a good President."[93] Similarly, one close observer of the Obama White House found it striking how few top Democratic policy makers the new president knew as he selected his cabinet.[94] Thus, presidents often appoint people they do not know to the highest positions in the federal government.

Donald Trump knew few people with expertise in areas of public policy. When it came time to choose a secretary of state, he relied on a gut impulse and selected businessman Rex Tillerson. He did not, however, delve into their foreign policy differences, which became a source of tension and, ultimately, a reason for Tillerson's firing.

In addition, many qualified people do not want to undergo the loss of income and privacy and the partisan criticism that often accompany public service in senior positions. Such reluctance is not new. George Washington had five candidates in a row turn down appointment as secretary of state, so he moved Timothy Pickering from the Department of War to State and then had three turn down nomination as secretary of war. In addition, the first president had two persons, including John Marshall, turn down nomination as attorney general (and Alexander Hamilton turned down nomination as chief justice).[95]

Political Clearance

In the past, early in their terms, presidents did not typically impose their preferences for subcabinet-level officials on those whom they appointed to head the departments and agencies. The reason was partially the lack of organization in the personnel system. In addition, however, there was a concern that because top officials would be held accountable for the agencies' performances, they should be able to appoint subordinates whom they liked and who would complement their own abilities and help them accomplish their jobs. Naturally, top officials generally requested this freedom. High officials also fought to name their subordinates, because if they lost to the White House on personnel matters, their standing within their departments would drop.

Beginning with the Reagan administration, with the exception of George H. W. Bush, recent presidents have insisted on White House clearance of all subcabinet appointments, and, with the exception of Donald Trump, placed a high priority on recruiting minorities and women to high office. Until Donald Trump, the George W. Bush administration made the most systematic effort to politicize the bureaucracy, "both across the wider organization chart and deep down within the bureaucracy."[96] Sometimes, the administration took political clearance to inappropriate lengths such as using political and ideological tests for hiring and promoting career lawyers in the Department of Justice or firing US attorneys whom the White House saw as insufficiently responsive to its political needs.[97]

Donald Trump has taken political clearance, with an emphasis on personal loyalty to the president, to new heights. This process of political clearance, along with complex legal requirements regarding finances, security, and other matters, have slowed presidents' initial appointments. Indeed, President Trump was unusually slow filling important slots in his administration, as you can see in box 10.2.

Box 10.2 ★ Donald Trump Builds an Administration

Donald Trump had an unusually difficult time populating his administration. His pace of making nominations was far slower than any of his recent predecessors.[98] A year into his presidency, he had nominated people for only about half of the key positions requiring Senate confirmation. Hundreds of vital posts in key departments such as Defense and State remained unfilled for many months into his tenure. For the first five months, he had nominated no US attorneys. Why did this happen?

First, Trump did not have an effective transition effort, so he was not ready to make nominations once he was elected.[99] In addition, he lacked the usual pool of qualified people from whom to draw. Most of the Republican establishment

(continued)

Box 10.2 ★ Continued

opposed him in the primaries, so he was not well connected to the "shadow government" of experienced Republican officials who normally would populate a new Republican administration. Moreover, many Republican former national security professionals overtly opposed Trump's election. Others simply did not feel comfortable working for the new president, especially in departments Trump disparaged, and declined to be considered for positions. Combined with the lack of familiarity with the executive branch of Trump and many of his White House staffers, the administration found it difficult to identify appropriate nominees.

Other problems plagued the White House. There were divisions within the White House between the populists such as Steve Bannon and more establishment Republicans that delayed reaching agreement on nominees. Then the president insisted on personally approving all nominations to top positions, and he applied a high standard of loyalty to himself, ruling out many qualified Republicans.

Presidential recruiters must devote a large portion of their resources to vetting and background investigations. This vetting takes time and personnel resources and is a major cause of delays in making political appointments. The Trump White House devoted fewer people to the task of vetting and those it did employ often lacked personnel experience and ran into problems. Moreover, the president often made impulsive decisions to nominate people before vetting occurred. By April 2019, forty announced or forwarded nominations had been withdrawn, far more than occurred under other presidents.[100] These withdrawals included the president's nominees for secretary of defense, secretary of labor, secretary of the Department of Veterans Affairs, director of national intelligence, ambassador to the United Nations, deputy secretary of the treasury, deputy secretary of commerce, secretary of the navy, secretary of the army (two nominees), the Federal Reserve Board (two nominees), director of US Immigration and Customs Enforcement (two nominees), head of the Justice Department's civil division, and a substantial number of other nominees withdrew because of personal or financial issues.

In addition, the Trump administration has had an unusually high turnover in key positions, both in the White House and in the departments and agencies. These vacancies created yet additional stresses on the personnel process, demands the White House had a difficult time meeting.

As presidential terms extend from weeks into months and years, every White House experiences frustrating problems in policy implementation and tends to take a direct interest in personnel matters below the levels of department and agency heads.[101] Moreover, presidents become increasingly effective at managing the bureaucracy because of the information and expertise that they acquire from their on-the-job experience.[102]

Recess and Temporary Appointments

The Constitution gives the president the power to make temporary appointments to positions when the Senate is not in session. These appointments expire at the end of the next session of the Senate. The founders' goal was to maintain the continuity of government during what they expected to be long recesses of the Senate. Beginning in 1981, presidents made hundreds of such appointments, often attempting to bypass opposition in the Senate. The Senate saw these intra-session recess appointments as circumventing its role in advising and consenting to nominations, and in

Ron Sachs/CNP/Newscom

Andrew Pudzer is one of several of Donald Trump's nominees to high-level positions who had to withdraw from consideration.

2007 it began holding pro forma sessions so that there would be no formal recess. Moreover, in *NLRB v. Noel Canning et al.* (2014), the Supreme Court struck down an Obama appointment made during a three-day recess. The result was the effective ending of recess appointments.[103]

For hundreds of jobs requiring Senate confirmation, federal law allows presidents to appoint officials on an acting basis without lawmakers' approval, to keep agencies running. Donald Trump made purposive use of acting positions, even at the Departments of Defense and Homeland Security and the Office of Management and Budget. He felt it made secretaries more "responsive." "I like acting," he explained, "because I can move so quickly. It gives me more flexibility."[104]

At times, a president has nominated an acting official to take over the post long-term. That practice violates the law, the Supreme Court ruled in *National Labor Relations Board v. SW General* (2017). A person who has been nominated for a position cannot hold the same job on an acting basis. This ruling effectively makes it much harder for presidents to have their preferred people running federal agencies when—as was often the case during the Obama administration—the Senate delays voting on nominations, or does not act on them at all.

Limits on the Utility of Appointments

There has been a trend since the 1960s toward politicizing the bureaucracy and emphasizing the White House's operational control of the executive bureaucracy rather than traditional patronage. The number of political appointees at the top of the executive bureaucracy has increased substantially, as has the number of political appointees at lower ranks.[105] Presidents also make efforts to place political appointees in career positions just before leaving office.

Politicizing the bureaucracy has drawbacks, however. No matter how loyal to the president appointees are, they need to know what to do and how to do it once they obtain their positions. Studies have found that the preparation of appointed officials for their jobs, whether defined in terms of management experience, negotiating skills, congressional relations, or personal style, makes a difference. Good preparation for their jobs helps political appointees to mobilize the resources of the career bureaucracy.[106]

In addition, the design of policy implementation must be appropriate to the president's goals. Robert Durant challenges the assumption that presidents and their emissaries know what they are doing when they apply the tools of the administrative presidency. For example, the Reagan administration decreased staff in an effort to reduce enforcement activities to which it was opposed.[107] Such a strategy may have been useful for stopping an activity, such as regulatory behavior, but it undermined the administration's efforts to take more positive actions.[108]

It is difficult to recruit high-quality political appointees to some of the lower sub-cabinet positions, especially with the new financial reporting and divesting requirements and the visible and contentious nature of many confirmation hearings. Those that the president and his designees do appoint sometimes have policy expertise, but many are quite young and few of them have managerial experience.[109]

The short tenure in the same job of typical political appointees[110] diminishes their ability to implement policy effectively, undermining the president's administrative strategy.[111] As administration becomes more politically and substantively complex, it takes appointees more time to learn their jobs and forge the relationships that make effective implementation possible. Appointees with short time horizons also have fewer incentives to deal with large but distant problems and may be more attentive to political and short-term considerations than to long-term program and agency management. Moreover, careerist agency managers believe that their efforts in implementing appointee initiatives may be wasted, reducing their incentive to engage in long-term planning. As a civilian manager in the Department of Defense put it, "We start, we stop, we reverse, but we seldom move ahead for any period of time. One loses interest after a few years."[112]

Layering political appointees at the top of bureaucratic units complicates management and may separate the top executive from the bureaucracy and its services, thus decreasing the executive's opportunities to build personal support within the bureaucracy through communication, consultation, and access. Placing more political appointees at the top also undermines the motivation of the career service because it closes off the most senior positions to them.

The diffusion of responsibility that comes with a large number of decision points in a bureaucracy also increases the number of actors involved in policy implementation. Therefore, the costs of implementing presidential policy also increase because the White House and the president's top appointees have to influence more people in the implementation chain. Having more political checkpoints means there are more obstacles to innovation and barriers to employee involvement, which makes it more difficult to give frontline employees the authority to solve problems.

Despite its frequent use, political clearance is often a crude process. Many policy views fit under a party label. Democrats range from very liberal to very conservative, and the range for Republicans is nearly as great. Moreover, political appointees may be motivated by materialistic or selfish aims and not necessarily be responsive to the president. For example, a person may want the status of an ambassadorship, or a young lawyer may seek experience in the Justice Department or a regulatory agency in hope of cashing in on it later for a high-paying job in the private sector. Political appointees may also remain loyal to their home-state political organizations, interest group associations, or sponsors in Congress—rather than to the White House. There are frequently unclear and tenuous links between White House and political appointees, providing everyone with more discretion.[113]

Equally important, the president's appointees may disagree with him. Even George Washington had problems with his ambassador to France, future president James Monroe, who actively incited French anger over the Jay Treaty.[114] More recently, Richard Nixon ordered Secretary of Defense Melvin Laird to bomb a hideaway of Palestine Liberation Organization guerrillas, a move that Laird opposed. According to the secretary, "We had bad weather for 48 hours. The Secretary of Defense can always find a reason not to do something."[115] Thus, the president's order was stalled for days and eventually rescinded. President Reagan's national security assistant explained that the United States could not employ a strategy involving the selective use of force in order to support diplomatic efforts to keep peace in Lebanon because of the lack of cooperation between the Departments of State and Defense.[116]

Donald Trump has had a large number of conflicts with his own appointees. He harshly criticized Jeff Sessions, his own attorney general, for his decision to recuse himself from the Justice Department's investigation of Russian interference in the 2016 election. The president also derided his secretary of state, whom he described as "dumb as a rock" and "lazy as hell." "I couldn't get rid of him fast enough."[117] The secretary of defense, top military officers, the secretary of commerce, the deputy attorney general, the heads of several intelligence agencies, the director of the FBI, as well as top White House aides have also run afoul of the president for their disagreements with his policies.[118]

It is sometimes difficult to fire recalcitrant appointees. Bill Clinton had disdain for FBI director William Freeh, who was not responsive to the president. Yet, Clinton felt that dismissing Freeh would unleash denunciations by those claiming he was purging an enemy. Moreover, he feared such an act would generate comparisons to Richard Nixon's "Saturday Night Massacre," in which the president fired the Watergate special prosecutor and then had to endure the resignations of the two top officials in the Department of Justice.[119] That is exactly what happened to Donald Trump when he fired FBI director James Comey, who later testified before Congress about the president's inappropriate requests for personal loyalty and to stop an investigation regarding connections between members of the administration and Russia.

Turf fights among appointed officials over jurisdiction are not unusual in the executive branch. According to Richard Nixon, when presidential appointee J. Edgar Hoover directed the FBI, he "totally distrusted the other intelligence agencies—and, whenever possible, resisted attempts to work in concert with them."[120] At one point, the director cut off all liaison activities with the other intelligence agencies, including the Central Intelligence Agency, the Defense Intelligence Agency, and the National Security Agency.

Although recent presidents have placed many people who had favorable attitudes toward their administrations' policies in top career and politically appointed managerial positions, the number of vacancies they can fill remains limited.[121] Thus, filling vacancies is unlikely to be a sufficient strategy to alter the attitudes in the bureaucracy. The president must also influence those who are already holding their jobs.

When President Trump fired James Comey as director of the FBI, the president faced charges of trying to cover up his own misdeeds.

Civil Service

Most executive branch employees rank below appointed officials in the federal hierarchy. Almost all civilian employees are covered by the protection of personnel systems designed to fill positions on the basis of merit. This system protects employees against removal for partisan political reasons. The military has a separate personnel system designed to accomplish the same goals.

If the president or a presidential appointee finds that a civil servant is obstructing implementation of the president's policies, he or she has some potential remedies. Those at the top of the civil service—in the SES—may be transferred and may be demoted more easily than in the past. Although members of the SES compose only a small percentage of the civil service (there are about seven thousand members of the SES), they are among the most powerful members of the career bureaucracy and the most crucial to implementing the president's policies.

A new administration can exercise the option of reassigning SES members to further its policy goals. It appears that President Trump's secretary of the Interior Ryan Zinke reassigned SES members to unfavorable locations and duties unrelated to their expertise to encourage them to resign or at least stop them from challenging the administration's policies.

Those below the SES are more difficult to move. It is possible to dismiss an incompetent or recalcitrant civil service employee, but such action is not common.[122] It takes more time, expertise, and political capital to fire a civil servant than most officials have or are willing to invest in such an effort. Transferring unwanted personnel to less troublesome positions is one of the most common means of quieting obstructive bureaucrats. In President Carter's words, it is "easier to promote and transfer incompetent employees than to get rid of them."[123] Nevertheless, career executives may choose to leave government if a new president marginalizes their role in implementing policy or as they anticipate conflict with a new administration.[124]

Another potential technique that the president can use is to alter the dispositions of existing implementers through the manipulation of incentives. Because people generally act in their own interest, the manipulation of incentives by high-level policy makers may influence their subordinates' actions. Increasing the benefits or costs of a particular behavior may make implementers either more or less likely to choose it as a means of advancing their personal, organizational, or substantive policy interests.

The ability of top officials to exercise sanctions is severely limited, however. Rewards are the other side of the incentive coin, but they are even more difficult for executives to administer than penalties. Individual performance is difficult to reward with pay increases.[125] President Carter once complained that "more than 99 percent of all federal employees got a so-called 'merit' rating."[126] Raises are almost always given across the board, with everyone in the same category of employment receiving a similar percentage increase in salary, regardless of differences in performance.

The Civil Service Reform Act of 1978 created the potential for awarding merit pay increases or bonuses for many managers, supervisors, and top executives in the federal civil service, but Congress has appropriated little money for these raises and few civil servants have received them. Usually, personal performance can be rewarded only by promotions, which are, necessarily, infrequent. There may not be room at the top for qualified bureaucrats. Unlike a typical private business, a government agency cannot expand simply because it is performing a service effectively and efficiently. In addition, presidential subordinates who oppose or are indifferent to a policy are unlikely to employ incentives to further its implementation.

Limiting Discretion

In the absence of positive and negative incentives, the government relies heavily on rules to limit the discretion of implementers. As Vice President Al Gore explained in a report issued by the National Performance Review,

> Because we don't want politicians' families, friends, and supporters placed in "no-show" jobs, we have more than 100,000 pages of personnel rules and regulations defining in exquisite detail how to hire, promote, or fire federal employees. Because we don't want employees or private companies profiteering from federal contracts, we create procurement processes that require endless signatures and long months to buy almost anything. Because we don't want agencies using tax dollars for any unapproved purpose, we dictate precisely how much they can spend on everything from telephones to travel.[127]

Often, these rules end up creating new obstacles to effective and efficient governing, however. For example, in fall 1990, as US forces were streaming toward the Persian Gulf to liberate Kuwait from Iraq, the air force placed an emergency order for six thousand Motorola commercial radio receivers. However, Motorola refused to do business with the air force because of a government requirement that the company set up separate accounting and cost-control systems to fill the order. Ironically, the only way the air force could acquire the much-needed receivers was for Japan to buy them and donate them to the United States!

The White House has sought to constrain the exercise of bureaucratic discretion by requiring clearance of regulations and congressional testimony, limiting agency budgets, and establishing process restrictions on procurement and other spending.[128] The Office of Management and Budget reviews all regulations proposed by executive agencies (see chapter 8), allowing the president to influence or block individual regulations. Agencies must also inform the OMB of upcoming regulations and documents providing guidance on the application of rules, aiding the White House in preempting or altering regulations and their applications before agencies propose them (when the political costs of opposition are less). Finally, the White House requires agencies to provide cost-benefit analyses of their proposed regulations and to have a regulatory policy office run by a political appointee to supervise the development of and evaluation of rules and documents providing guidance to regulated industries. Because cost-benefit analysis is often as much art as it is science, ideological preferences may determine the conclusions, which in turn may be used to resist regulations the administration opposes.[129]

Success in many policy areas often requires less bureaucratic rigidity, not more.[130] In addition, hierarchical control designed to limit bureaucratic discretion seems inappropriate for new approaches to public administration. Rather than being direct service providers or regulators, large elements of the federal service are becoming arrangers and monitors of proxy or third-party government, including services provided by state and local governments, private firms, and charitable organizations. Thus, the success of policy implementation now frequently depends on how adroitly federal agencies operate in nonhierarchical, loosely coupled networks of organizations that cut across the public, private, and nonprofit sectors, where discretion is either shared or shifts entirely to bureaucrats in the private and nonprofit sector.[131]

THE BUREAUCRATIC STRUCTURE

Policy implementers may know what to do and have sufficient desire and resources to do it, but they may still be hampered in implementation by the structures of the organizations in which they serve. Two prominent characteristics of bureaucracies are standard operating procedures (SOPs) and fragmentation, both of which may hinder presidential policy implementation.

Standard Operating Procedures

SOPs are routines that enable public officials to make numerous everyday decisions. They have many benefits for the chief executive. For one thing they save time, and time is valuable. If a Social Security caseworker had to invent a new rule for every potential client and have it cleared at higher levels, few clients would be served. Thus, officials write detailed manuals to cover as many particular situations as they can anticipate. The regulations elaborating the Internal Revenue Code compose the bible of an IRS agent; similarly, a customs agent has binders filled with rules and regulations about what can and cannot be brought into the United States free of duty.

SOPs also bring uniformity to complex organizations. Justice is better served if officials apply rules uniformly, as in the implementation of welfare policies that distribute benefits to the needy or the levying of fines for underpayment of taxes. Uniformity also makes personnel interchangeable. Soldiers, for example, can be transferred to any spot in the world yet still do their job by referring to the appropriate manual, which is a substantial advantage for the commander in chief.

Hindering Implementation

Although in theory SOPs are designed to make implementing policies easier, they may be inappropriate in some cases and even function as obstacles to action. Presidents have had many a plan thwarted by standard government practices. They certainly frustrated President Franklin D. Roosevelt, as he explained,

> The Treasury is so large and far-flung and ingrained in its practices that I find it is almost impossible to get the action and results I want. . . . But the Treasury is not to be compared with the State Department. You should go through the experience of trying to get any changes in the thinking, policy, and action of the career diplomats and then you'd know what a real problem was. But the Treasury and the State Department put together are nothing as compared with the Na-a-vy. . . . To change anything in the Na-a-vy is like punching a feather bed. You punch it with your right and you punch it with your left until you are finally exhausted, and then you find the damn bed just as it was before you started punching.[132]

SOPs may hinder policy implementation by inhibiting change. Because they are designed for typical situations, SOPs can be ineffective in new circumstances. For example, in 1962, the United States discovered the presence of Soviet missiles in Cuba and reacted by blockading the island. President John F. Kennedy was very concerned about the initial interception of Soviet ships, so he sent Secretary of Defense Robert McNamara to check on the procedures the navy was following. McNamara stressed to Chief of Naval Operations George Anderson that the president did not want to follow the normal SOP, whereby a ship risked being sunk if it refused to submit to being boarded and searched, because Kennedy did not want to goad the Soviet Union into retaliation. However, McNamara found Admiral Anderson uncooperative. At one point in the discussion, he waved the Manual of Naval Regulations in the secretary's face and shouted, "It's all in here." To this, McNamara replied, "I don't give a damn what John Paul Jones would have done. I want to know what you are going to do, now."[133] The conversation ended after the admiral asked the secretary of defense to leave and let the navy run the blockade according to established procedures.

More recently, the FAA's protocols for hijackings assumed that the pilot of a hijacked aircraft would notify an air traffic controller that there had been a hijacking, that the FAA could identify the plane, that there would be time for the FAA and NORAD to address the issue, and that the hijacking would not be a suicide mission. As the 9/11 Commission put it, these SOPs were "unsuited in every respect" for the 9/11 terrorist hijackings.[134] In addition, SOPs for the F-16 fighters based at Andrews Air Force base in Washington determined that none were equipped with missiles. Because there was no time to load missiles, the pilots would have had to use their jets as battering rams against the hijackers' planes.

Secretary of Defense Robert Gates found that the Departments of Defense and Veterans Affairs were not good at treating the wounded from the wars in Afghanistan and Iraq and were continuing their routines of focusing on the health needs of older veterans.[135]

Taking Unwanted Action

Sometimes SOPs cause organizations to take actions that superior officials do not desire, as the Cuban missile crisis dramatically illustrates. Despite President Kennedy's explicit order that the initial encounter with a Soviet ship not involve a Soviet submarine, the US Navy, according to established procedure, used its "Hunter-Killer" antisubmarine warfare program to locate and float above Soviet submarines within six hundred miles of the continental United States. Also following standard "Hunter-Killer" procedures, the navy forced several Soviet submarines to surface. Neither the president nor the secretary of defense ordered this drastic action. It came about because it was the programmed response to such a situation. The highest officials, who ostensibly had authority over the navy, never imagined that standard procedures would supplant their directives. Even worse, the commander of a Soviet submarine that the United States forced to surface had discretionary authority to fire its nuclear-tipped torpedo if attacked, and the crew pleaded with him to fire it.[136] Fortunately, he declined to do so. Clearly, SOPs can become deeply embedded in an organization and be difficult to control, even in times of crisis.

New Policies

New policies are the most likely to require a change in organizational behavior and are therefore the most likely to have their implementation hindered by SOPs. For example, in October 1983, 241 US Marines were killed in their sleep during a terrorist attack on their barracks outside Beirut, Lebanon. A presidential commission appointed to examine the causes of the tragedy concluded that, among other factors contributing to the disaster, the marines in the peacekeeping force were "not trained, organized, staffed or supported to deal effectively with the terrorist threat."[137] In other words, they had not altered their SOPs regarding security (which are basic to any military unit) to meet the unique challenges of a terrorist attack.

During the wars in Iraq and Afghanistan, Secretary of Defense Robert Gates found the military services focused on their routines of developing and purchasing equipment for wars of the future, which bore little resemblance to the counterinsurgency wars the United States was actually fighting. Thus, he had to invest time and energy to procure equipment to counter improvised explosive devices (IEDs), mine-resistant ambush-protected vehicles, and drones and get them to Iraq.[138]

Fragmentation

A second aspect of bureaucratic structure that may impede implementation is fragmentation—the dispersion of responsibility for a policy area among several organizational units. The more actors and agencies are involved with a particular policy and the more interdependent are their decisions, the less is the probability of successful implementation.

The resources and authority necessary for the president to attack a problem comprehensively are often distributed among many bureaucratic units. For example, the federal government has had as many as ninety-six agencies involved with the issue of nuclear proliferation. In his 2011 State of the Union address, President Obama pointed out that there are twelve different agencies that deal with exports and there are at least five different agencies that deal with housing policy. The Interior Department is in charge of salmon while they are in fresh water, but the Commerce Department handles them when they are in saltwater. Twelve federal agencies and commissions regulate the financial industry, in addition to regulators in every state.

At least fifteen agencies regulate food safety. Cheese pizzas are the responsibility of the FDA, but pizzas with pepperoni on top fall under the purview of the US Department of Agriculture (USDA). The USDA inspects commercially sold

The success of the attack on a United States Marine Corps barrack in Beirut was made possible by the marines' use of inappropriate standard operating procedures for their defense.

open-faced meat and poultry sandwiches, but the FDA is in charge of those sandwiches if they have two slices of bread. The FDA oversees the safety of eggs still in their shells, but the USDA regulates liquid eggs that are used in industrial food production, while also being responsible for chickens and the grading of eggs for quality.

Duplication

Duplication in the provision of public services is one result of bureaucratic fragmentation. Donald Trump declared, "There is duplication and redundancy everywhere."[139] President Carter complained, "There are . . . at least 75 agencies and 164,000 Federal employees in police or investigative work. Many of them duplicate or overlap state and local law enforcement efforts unnecessarily."[140] Even worse, duplication may spread the government's resources too thinly. As the 9/11 Commission pointed out, there are too few experts in many areas of national security for us to be able to afford duplication of effort.[141]

Working at Cross-Purposes

Bureaucratic fragmentation may also result in two or more agencies working at cross-purposes. The United States is running out of helium-3, a rare gas crucial for detecting smuggled nuclear weapons materials, because one arm of the Energy Department has been selling the gas six times as fast as another arm could accumulate it, and the two arms failed to communicate for years.

Coordinating Policies

The diffusion of responsibility in government makes the coordination of policies difficult—but also essential. When the BP oil spill in the Gulf of Mexico occurred in 2010, we found that there were twenty-four separate offices and agencies with responsibility for making decisions about how to explore, map, preserve, exploit, and manage the ocean within the US territorial waters. This fragmentation led to delays, distractions, and disagreements over how to cap the well and defend the coastline.

In response to Hurricane Katrina, cities and states, the military, the Coast Guard, and the Department of Commerce, as well as private companies, offered to provide fresh water, diesel fuel, trucks, flat-bottomed boats, aircraft, and law enforcement officers to relieve people's suffering, keep the peace, and aid the rescue effort. Unfortunately, FEMA was incapable of accepting these offers and also had great difficulty coordinating federal relief and rescue efforts with those of the state of Louisiana.

On September 11, 2001, at least thirty-three departments and agencies had responsibility for protecting America's borders, focusing on threats ranging from illegal immigrants and chemical toxins to missiles and electronic sabotage. It is difficult to coordinate so many different agencies, especially when they lack a history of trust and cooperation. Moreover, there are often physical obstacles to cooperation, such as the largely incompatible computer systems of the Immigration and Naturalization Service and the Coast Guard. Once the borders have been breached and an attack has occurred, many other offices get involved in homeland security, including hundreds of state and local agencies.

To coordinate the implementation of a comprehensive national strategy to protect the United States from terrorist threats or attacks, Congress passed a massive reorganization of the government in 2002, including creating a new Department of Homeland Security. The success of this effort is unusual, however. It is difficult to organize government agencies around a single policy area. Broad policies, such as those dealing with environmental protection, are multidimensional and overlap with dimensions of other policies, such as agriculture, transportation, recreation, and energy. Similarly, any terrorist attack cuts across many areas. If people get sick because terrorists spray toxic chemicals on a portion of the food supply, the crime would not only be a case for the FBI but also for the HHS Department, the EPA, the FDA, and the USDA. In the absence of an attack, each of those departments and agencies has other responsibilities that overlap little and provide for less potential for centralization than something as galvanizing as a terrorist attack.

The National Counterterrorism Center's (NCTC's) mission is to gather information from across the government and assess terrorist threats facing the United States and then develop a plan for the government to combat them. To pan these streams of dots (about twelve thousand pieces of information a day) for clues about terrorism, the center's analysts must access at least twenty-eight computer networks maintained by other agencies, mostly through a manual and time-consuming process. They cannot easily conduct dynamic searches, which involve looking for multiple variables and terms that are scattered across databases.

Moreover, the NCTC lacks authority to effectively coordinate counterterrorism policy, and it cannot direct counterterrorism operations. It cannot investigate terrorist suspects in the United States (i.e., the FBI's job), it cannot conduct covert operations overseas (i.e., the CIA's sphere), it cannot intercept foreign communications (i.e., the National Security Agency's domain), and it cannot revoke visas (which is up to the State Department).

In 2004, Congress created the Office of the Director of National Intelligence (DNI) to coordinate the disparate parts of the intelligence community. However, the DNI lacks strict authority over the intelligence agencies because he (or she) does not completely control their budgets. As a result, the agencies still enjoy a large degree of autonomy. Thus, the DNI lacks the authority to compel the agencies to do anything they do not want to do. It is not surprising that the other agencies are still running largely disconnected and incompatible computer systems and that the Senate Select Committee on Intelligence concluded that the intelligence community failed to connect and appropriately analyze the information in its possession prior to December 25, 2009, which would have identified Umar Farouk Abdulmutallab (the "Christmas Day bomber") as a possible terrorist threat to the United States.[142]

Obstacles to Reorganization

If fragmentation is a problem, why not reorganize government? One obstacle to reorganization is Congress. Over the years, Congress has created many separate agencies and has favored categorical grants that assign specific authority and funds to particular agencies in order to oversee more closely and intervene more easily in policy administration. Fragmenting responsibility is especially likely under divided government, when the president's opponents wish to enhance their control over policy implementation.[143]

In addition, dispersing responsibility for a policy area also disperses "turf" to congressional committees. For example, in water resource policy, three committees in the House and three in the Senate have authority over the Army Corps of Engineers, the Soil Conservation Service, and the Bureau of Reclamation, respectively. None of these committees wants to relinquish its hold over these agencies and, therefore, the agencies and programs that deal with a common problem remain divided among three departments.

Like congressional committees, agencies are possessive about their jurisdictions. Usually department or agency heads will vigorously oppose executive branch reorganizations that encroach on their sphere of influence. For example, when Tom Ridge, the director of the White House Office of Homeland Security, proposed consolidating some agencies involved in border security, such as the Immigration and Naturalization Service and the Coast Guard, his proposal was met with a storm of criticism from within the Bush administration, and Ridge had to back off. Similarly, when President Clinton proposed to merge the FBI with the Drug Enforcement Agency (DEA), both of which are units within the Justice Department, DEA officials were fearful of losing their agency identity (and perhaps their jobs) and mobilized sympathetic members of Congress to oppose the move.

Interest groups are a third force supporting fragmentation. They fear that a bureaucratic reorganization would jeopardize the close relationship they have with an agency. Interest groups also develop close working relationships with congressional committees and do not want to lose their special access in a reorganization of committee jurisdictions that might follow an executive branch reorganization.

Often, combinations of interest groups, agencies, or legislative committees oppose reorganization. The Department of Education, which President Carter proposed, is composed almost exclusively of education programs from the old Department of Health, Education, and Welfare. Head Start, Native American education, the school lunch program, GI bill benefits, job training, and some vocational and rehabilitation education programs remained where they were because of opposition to their being moved. For example, the Senate Agriculture Committee opposed any change out of fear of losing oversight responsibility for child nutrition programs, whereas the American Food Service Association opposed any change because it feared nutrition would not be a high priority with educators.

The FBI and CIA resisted having their counterterrorism units placed in the same agency, fearful that the new NCTC, and its director, would rob them of their powers. Civil libertarians, meanwhile, warned that putting the FBI, a domestic law enforcement agency, in such proximity to spies, who labor under fewer and different laws when working abroad, was a recipe for abuse.

Presidential Resources

Presidents have some resources in the battle over reorganization. When they cannot convince Congress to create an administrative agency that they want, presidents may strike out on their own. Over the past six decades, they have created half the new administrative agencies, using executive orders, department orders, and general reorganization authority (which they frequently possessed until the Supreme Court struck down the legislative veto in 1983), such as the National Security Agency, the Peace Corps, and the EPA. These agencies tend to be smaller and less important than agencies that Congress creates with the president, but the president has more control over the personnel in them.[144]

In the past, Congress has often given presidents the right to propose reorganizations that would then receive a quick up or down vote. The polarization of politics in recent times has made such authority less likely. When President Obama asked for this "fast track" authority in 2012, Congress failed to act on his request.

Another approach is the increasingly common practice of presidential appointment of so-called executive branch "czars" in the White House. For example, President Obama appointed officials to oversee economic, health-care reform, energy and climate change, terrorism, nuclear nonproliferation, and urban policies.[145]

Reorganization as a Problem

Sometimes, it is reorganization itself that encourages duplication and bureaucratic turf fights. In the years since the Bureau of Alcohol, Tobacco, Firearms, and Explosives (ATF) was moved into the Department of Justice to better coordinate the fight against terrorism with the FBI, the rival law enforcement agencies have fought each other for control, wasting time and money. The attorney general ordered them to merge their national bomb databases, but the FBI refused. The ATF has long trained bomb-sniffing dogs; the FBI started a competing program.[146]

Not only do such conflicts defeat the purposes of the programs involved but they also force the president's highest-level aides and departmental executives to spend great amounts of time and energy negotiating with one another. This is wasteful, and it may result in compromises representing the lowest common denominators of the officials' original positions. Unfortunately, bold and original ideas may be sacrificed for intragovernmental harmony.

FOLLOW-UP

As a result of all the hindrances to effective policy implementation, it seems reasonable to suggest that implementation would be improved if presidents followed up on their decisions and orders to see that they have been properly implemented.

Aides to George W. Bush were critical that he did not follow through with decisions about postwar Iraq. Success in implementation, they said, requires a president who is engaged and prepared to push the agencies to do what he says.[147]

President Nixon ordered the CIA to destroy its stockpile of biological weapons. CIA Director Richard Helms relayed the president's order to the deputy director for plans (the head of the covert action division), who, in turn, relayed it to a subordinate. Five years later, however, officials discovered two lethal toxins hidden in a secret cache. A mid-level official had disobeyed the president's order and then retired, and his successor had assumed that the storage of the toxins had official approval. When called before Congress, Helms testified that he had undertaken no follow-up check on his own order and when asked who told him the toxins had been destroyed, he replied, "I read it in the newspapers." Indeed, if the official who discovered the toxins had not received a directive from the new CIA director, William Colby, to be on the constant lookout for illegal action, he might not have checked on the legality of the toxins and the cache would still have existed.[148]

Thus, a president must constantly check up on his orders, yet most recent presidents have not followed this advice. On the whole, follow-up has been haphazard. Presidents and their staffs have been too busy with crisis management, electoral politics, or encouraging the passage of legislation to delve into the details involved in monitoring policy implementation. Moreover, they lack systematic information about the performance of agencies. One exception is Donald Trump and immigration policy, in which he is especially interested. He demands regular updates on policy implementation, calling the secretary of Homeland Security several times a week to check in, often with little or no notice.[149]

Some presidents are philosophically opposed to engaging in much follow-up. For example, Ronald Reagan believed that the chief executive should set broad policy goals and general ground rules and then appoint good people to accomplish the goals. He did not believe presidents should constantly monitor their subordinates.[150]

Secrecy

One factor inhibiting follow-up is secrecy. Secretly executed policies, such as those implemented by intelligence agencies, require few reports to Congress or superiors in the executive branch. Consequently, such officials' actions are not routinely monitored. Because members of Congress risk criticism for violating national security if they make public any secret information, they are reluctant to do so and have incentives to forgo their responsibility for the oversight and follow-up of certain secret policies. For example, when President Johnson's fear of leaks regarding decisions on the Vietnam War led him to restrict his direct communications to a few top officials (the Tuesday lunch group), he did so without a prearranged agenda or minutes of the meetings, which would have recorded decisions and made it possible to follow up on them.

Thickening of Government

The increasing number of management layers in government can also hamper follow-up. The thickening of government makes it more difficult to ascertain the locus of responsibility for policy implementation. Accountability is reduced when no one unit or individual can be held responsible for a lack of action or poor communication.

Failing to Report Problems

An organization's personnel may be aware of implementation problems yet fail to report them to the president or other administration officials. There are several reasons for this. An obvious one is that subordinates may fear that reporting implementation failures will reflect poorly on their own performance and also possibly anger their superiors. Additionally, employees may have a natural loyalty to their organization or to others in the organization who might be hurt by their negative reports. Further, the informal norms against reporting negative information may be very strong. Thus, employees may withhold information from their superiors to escape social ostracism in their peer groups. Finally, some bureaucrats may feel that the president is simply too busy to bother with matters of policy implementation.

Organizations may fail to report problems in policy implementation for political reasons, such as the fear of losing public or legislative support for their programs. Also, within some organizations, rivalries between headquarters and field personnel make the latter reluctant to expose themselves to negative reactions to their implementation efforts.

Failing to Use Information

Even when information indicating poor policy implementation is available to the president and other top executive officials, they may fail to use it. Information coming from the field is often fragmentary, circumstantial, inconsistent, ambiguous, and unrepresentative—in sum, it is very often unreliable. In addition, as we have seen, such information may become lost in the huge volume of data circulating in the executive branch. It is very difficult for the president to have a clear idea of how a complex policy is actually implemented.

Increasing Staff

One technique that presidents can use to increase their capacity to follow up on their decisions is to enlarge the size of their personal staffs. Certainly, the executive staff is crucial to the president's ability to put his stamp on policy implementation. As Secretary of State George Shultz put it, "If the president's staff does not support a policy, the policy is not likely to succeed. The president by himself cannot make sure that a policy is being implemented, so the staff has to be brought along."[151]

Relying heavily on the White House staff for policy implementation can create additional burdens for the president, however—even if the staff supports a policy. Because chief executives can personally deal effectively with only a limited number of people, they are forced to relay implementation orders and receive feedback through additional layers of their own staffs. This, in turn, increases both the possibility of communication distortion and the burden of administration, which the staff is supposed to lighten. The more that authority is delegated to people at the top of a hierarchy, the more possibilities there are for inadequate coordination, interoffice rivalries, communication gaps, and other typical administrative problems to arise. Moreover, having a large number of aides with limited access to a top official such as the president increases the chance that they may carry out a presidential order given in anger. Individuals with limited access will be less likely to know the executive well enough or have enough confidence to hold back on implementing their supervisor's instructions.

Having a large implementation staff for a president has another drawback: Only a few people can credibly speak for the president. If too many people begin giving orders in the president's name, for example, they will undermine the credibility of all those claiming to speak for him. Credibility is important for aides trying to help the president implement policies. As one Carter aide explained, "If you are perceived by people in a given agency as being close to the president because you have an office in the West Wing, your phone calls will be returned more rapidly and your requests for information or action will be taken more seriously."[152]

Presidential assistants carry the contingent authority of the president, which is essential to accomplish anything at all because, under the law, presidential assistants have no authority of their own. However, presidential authority is undermined if numerous people attempt to exercise it.

Centralizing Decision Making

Excessively vigorous staff involvement in implementation decisions may cause other problems. For example, some observers of recent presidential administrations have concluded that as larger numbers of bright, ambitious, energetic assistants probe into the activities of departments and agencies, they will bring more issues to the president for decision making, which were formerly decided at lower levels in the bureaucracy. Bureaucrats will begin to pass the buck upward, and the White House must then make increasing numbers of decisions. This can easily make the Executive Office of the President top-heavy and slow. Involvement in the minutiae of government may also divert resources (including time) from the central objectives and major problems of a president's administration. In addition, if White House aides become intimately involved in the management of government programs, they may lose the objectivity necessary to evaluate new ideas regarding "their" programs.

Over-centralization of decision making at the highest levels may have other negative consequences: it may discourage capable people from serving in government posts where their authority is frequently undercut: it may lower morale and engender resentment and hostility in the bureaucracy, which may impede future cooperation; it may decrease respect for lower officials among their subordinates; it may reduce the time bureaucratic officials have for internal management because they must fight to maintain access to and support of the chief executive; and it may weaken the capability of agencies to streamline or revitalize their management. Similarly, too much monitoring of subordinates' behavior may elicit hostility or excessive caution and lack of imagination in administering policy.

CONCLUSION

The president faces many obstacles in implementing public policies. Although the president is the "chief executive," he has not typically been in a position to command the bureaucracy within the executive branch. Moreover, the president operates in an environment of scarce resources and few incentives to devote time and energy to implementation, and he will generally emerge from this process as a facilitator rather than a director.

Improving implementation is difficult, as the roots of most implementation problems are embedded deeply in the fabric of American government and politics. Moreover, as long as presidents remain more concerned with shaping legislation to pass in the Congress than with the implementation of the law after it is passed, persist in emphasizing public relations rather than public policy, and allow "crisis" situations to continue to dominate their time, little progress is likely to be made in improving policy implementation. In addition, until there are more political incentives for officials to devote more attention to policy implementation and to develop better administrative skills, these priorities will probably not change. Given both the low visibility of many policy implementation activities and the lack of interest in them, the prospects for a change in incentives are not very favorable.

DISCUSSION QUESTIONS

1. Since the 1970s, the American public has often supported smaller government in the abstract but no reduction in federal services in practice. How should a president deal with the dilemma of making trade-offs between saving money and providing high-quality public services?

2. Some presidents such as Nixon, Reagan, George W. Bush, and Trump have emphasized bureaucratic responsiveness and made strong efforts to place administration loyalists throughout the bureaucracy. Other presidents, such as George H. W. Bush, Clinton, and Obama have focused on efficiency and emphasized finding the most skilled people to fill administrative positions. Which strategy do you feel is best for the country? Why?

3. In the private sector, businesses and institutions use salary increases and bonuses to encourage effective job performance. Selective bonuses and substantial pay raises are relatively rare in the public sector, however. Should Congress appropriate more funds for the bureaucracy so that the president and his appointees can use economic incentives to make the bureaucracy more responsive to their policies, or would this be a waste of taxpayers' money?

WEB EXERCISES

1. On January 24, 2003, President George W. Bush signed legislation that created the Department of Homeland Security (DHS), the largest department created since 1947. The department's mission is to secure the homeland, and Congress created the department to better coordinate the nation's homeland defenses and to emphasize the war on terrorism among the diverse roles of the department's component agencies. Go to the department's website to learn more about DHS at https://www.dhs.gov. Then, choose areas of DHS responsibility such as securing nuclear power plants or containers arriving by ship and search the Internet to determine whether you are satisfied with DHS's performance.

2. From the *United States Government Manual* (www.usgovernmentmanual. gov), you can obtain a good sense of how the executive branch is organized and some of the implications of the organization of the executive branch for implementing policy. For example, click on the Department of Agriculture. Note that in addition to supporting agricultural research and directly aiding farmers, the department has responsibilities in nutrition, food safety, education, housing, civil rights, conservation, and international trade—areas also covered by other agencies and departments. Go to the *United States Government Manual* and list services that you might not expect in at least three departments. Then, try to determine how well policy in these areas is coordinated in the federal government.

SELECTED READINGS

Aberbach, Joel D., and Bert A. Rockman. *In the Web of Politics: Three Decades of the Federal Executive.* Washington, DC: Brookings Institution, 2000.

Allison, Graham, and Philip Zelikow. *Essence of Decision: Explaining the Cuban Missile Crisis*, 2nd ed. New York: Longman, 1999.

Arnold, Peri E. *Making the Managerial Presidency*, 2nd ed. Princeton, NJ: Princeton University Press, 1996.

Durant, Robert F. *The Administrative Presidency Revisited.* Albany: State University of New York Press, 1992.

Lewis, David E. *Presidents and the Politics of Agency Design.* Stanford, CA: Stanford University Press, 2003.

———. *The Politics of Presidential Appointments.* Princeton, NJ: Princeton University Press, 2008.

Resh, William G. *Rethinking the Administrative Presidency.* Baltimore, MD: Johns Hopkins University Press, 2015.

Vaughn, Justin S., and Jose D. Villalobos. *Czars in the White House.* Ann Arbor: University of Michigan Press, 2015.

Wood, B. Dan, and Richard W. Waterman. *Bureaucratic Dynamics.* Boulder, CO: Westview, 1994.

11

The President and Congress

President Donald Trump addresses a joint session of Congress.

Donald Trump campaigned on bringing major change to public policies on immigration, health care, taxation, spending, environmental protection, and many other areas. Most of the changes he desired required the assent of Congress. He had a broad plan of how to sequence his initiatives and planned to have them finished within the first year, the time of greatest success for new presidents. Yet once in office, the president was stymied—and frustrated. Congress had generally been unsupportive of his major initiatives, including those on immigration, health care, and infrastructure.

If one were to write a job description of the presidency, near the top of the list of presidential responsibilities would be that of working with Congress. According to Lyndon Johnson, "There is only one way for a President to deal with Congress, and that is continuously, incessantly, and without interruption."[1] Because our system of separation of powers is really one of shared powers, presidents can rarely operate independently of Congress. Although they require the cooperation of Congress, they cannot depend on it. Thus, one of the president's most difficult and frustrating tasks is trying to persuade Congress to support his policies.

The differences in our contrasting views of presidential leadership are perhaps most clear in the area of executive–legislative relations. A director president would dominate Congress, reliably obtaining its support for his policies and precluding legislative initiatives he opposes. Facilitators, conversely, would find the going much tougher. They would often fail to achieve their legislative goals and usually have to struggle to win at all. Congress may pass major legislation over their opposition, and frustration and stalemate will characterize such a presidency much of the time.

In this chapter, we examine the president's leadership of Congress. Because it is important to understand the context of presidential-congressional interaction, we begin with a discussion of the president's formal legislative powers and the inevitable sources of conflict between the two branches. We then move to an examination of the potential sources of presidential influence in Congress, including party leadership, public support, and legislative skills. In our discussion, we emphasize both how presidents attempt to persuade members of Congress and the utility of each source of influence.

FORMAL LEGISLATIVE POWERS

Presidents today have a central role in the legislative process. Participants and observers alike expect them to formulate and promote policies. Doing so requires the chief executive to coordinate initiatives within the executive branch, introduce them to Congress, and mobilize support for them on Capitol Hill and, increasingly, with the general public.

These expectations suggest a broad scope of legislative authority for the president. In actuality, however, the constitutional basis for this authority is quite limited. Article II of the Constitution designates only four legislative duties and responsibilities: (1) to inform Congress from time to time on the state of the union, (2) to recommend necessary and expedient legislation, (3) to summon Congress into special session and adjourn it if the two houses cannot agree on adjournment, and (4) to exercise a qualified veto.

With the exception of the veto, these responsibilities stem primarily from the president's unique position within the political system—as the only official other than the vice president who was to have continuous tenure, a national perspective, and the ability to respond quickly and decisively to emergencies. As the framers of the Constitution saw it, these job-related qualifications placed the president in a unique position to inform Congress, recommend legislation, and summon Congress into session if necessary.

The rationale for the veto was different. Justified within the Constitutional Convention as a defensive weapon, the Founders proposed the veto as a device by which the president could prevent the legislature from usurping executive powers. The founders feared that the institutional balance would become undone and that Congress would be the likely perpetrator. We examine later in this chapter the extent to which their fears were justified and how presidents have used the veto as a political and constitutional weapon.

Over the years, presidents have employed their legislative responsibilities to enlarge their congressional influence. The State of the Union address is a good example. In the nineteenth century, it was a routine message dealing primarily with the actions of the executive departments and agencies for the previous year. Beginning with Thomas Jefferson and continuing through William Howard Taft, the White House sent the address to the Congress to be read by the clerk of the House and then distributed to the members. Woodrow Wilson revived the practice of the first two presidents and delivered the speech himself. Subsequently, however, presidents have timed the address to maximize its public exposure, and today it is an important vehicle by which presidents can articulate the legislative goals of their administrations, recite their accomplishments, present their agendas, and try to mobilize support for their programs.

Similarly, presidents have transformed their responsibility to recommend necessary and expedient legislation into an annual agenda-setting function. Although nineteenth-century presidents formulated some legislative proposals and even drafted bills in the White House, it was not until the twentieth century that the practice of presidential programming developed on a regular basis. Theodore Roosevelt, Woodrow Wilson, and Franklin Roosevelt submitted comprehensive legislative proposals to Congress. Harry Truman packaged them in the State of the Union address. With the exception of Dwight Eisenhower in his first year in office, every subsequent president has followed the Truman tradition.

Congress has found the president's legislative initiatives advantageous, and in some cases it has insisted on them. For example, the 1921 Budget and Accounting Act, the 1946 Employment Act, and the 1974 Budget Act require the president to provide Congress with annual reports and an annual executive budget.

The calling of special sessions by the president has fallen into disuse. The length of the current legislative year, combined with changes in the legislative calendar, has made this function largely obsolete. The last special session occurred in 1948. In the past, however, presidents frequently would call special sessions after their inauguration to gain support for their objectives and to initiate "their" Congress. Until the passage of the Twentieth Amendment in 1933, Congress began its session on or around December 1. As a result, every other session of Congress was a "lame duck" session and forced a newly elected president to wait nine months for the newly elected Congress to meet. Between the Lincoln and Franklin Roosevelt administrations, there were nineteen special sessions.[2]

SOURCES OF CONFLICT BETWEEN THE EXECUTIVE AND THE LEGISLATURE

Presidents must influence Congress because they generally cannot act without its consent. Under the constitutional system of separation of powers, Congress must pass legislation and can override vetoes, and the Senate must ratify treaties and confirm presidential appointments to the cabinet, the federal courts, regulatory commissions, and other high offices. The bicameral structure of Congress further complicates the process by requiring the president to build not one but two coalitions from among quite different sets of representatives. In addition, the requirement that the Senate ratify treaties by a two-thirds vote is a constitutional provision that increases the burden of coalition building because it forces the president to achieve a supermajority for ratification. The use of the filibuster in the Senate has a similar effect, requiring sixty votes to stop debate.

However, these overlapping powers and constitutional requirements do not explain the president's need to influence Congress. Theoretically, the two branches could be in agreement. In fact, the president and some members of Congress will always disagree because of their personalities or histories, yet these differences are not the source of systematic conflict. Rather, the source lies in the structure and processes of American politics.

Constituencies

In "The Federalist, No. 46," James Madison focused on the greatest source of conflict between the president and Congress—their different constituencies:

> The members of the federal legislature will likely attach themselves too much to local objects. . . . Measures will too often be decided according to their probable effect, not on the national prosperity and happiness, but on the prejudices, interests, and pursuits of the governments and the people of the individual states.[3]

Only presidents (and their vice presidential running mates) are chosen in a national election. Only a fraction of the populace elects each member. Inevitably, presidents must form a broader electoral coalition in order to win their office than any member of Congress. Moreover, two-thirds of the senators are not elected at the same time as the president. In addition, the Senate overrepresents rural states because each state has two senators regardless of its population. Thus, the whole that the president represents is different from the sum of the parts represented by each legislator. Each member of Congress will give special access to the interests that he or she represents,[4] but Congress as a body has more difficulty in representing the nation as a whole.

It is not true, of course, that the president reliably takes the broadest view of the public good. There is clear evidence that presidents increasingly act to serve their base supporters.[5] It is the case, however, that the president and Congress will define their core constituencies differently.

Internal Structures

The internal structures of the executive and legislative branches also cause differences between the president and Congress. The executive branch is hierarchically organized, facilitating the president examining a broad range of viewpoints on an issue and then weighing and balancing various interests. This structure also helps the president to view the trade-offs among various policies. Because one person, the president, must support all the major policies emanating from the executive branch, he is virtually forced to take a comprehensive view of those policies.

In comparison to the presidency, the houses of Congress are highly decentralized. The party structure is not always sufficient to unify their decision-making processes. Committee memberships are frequently unrepresentative of each chamber,[6] and members of each committee may defer to members of the other committees. Thus, members representing special interests have a disproportionate say over policy regarding those interests.

Although the decentralized structure of Congress ensures that a diversity of views will be heard and that many interests will have access to the legislative process, it does not follow that *each* member will hear all the views and see the proponents of each interest. Indeed, the decentralization of Congress almost guarantees that the information available to it as a whole is not a synthesis of the information available to each legislator. Congress as a whole does not ask questions; individual members do. Thus, not all of its members receive the answers.

One of the functions of decentralizing power and responsibility in Congress is to allow for specialization in various policy areas. However, because of specialization, legislators make decisions about many of the policies with which Congress must deal in form only. In actuality, they tend to rely on the cues of party leaders, state party delegations, relevant committee leaders of their party, and other colleagues to decide how to vote. Members of Congress choose these cue givers because they represent constituencies or ideologies that are similar to their own. Thus, the cue givers do not represent a cross-section of viewpoints.[7]

Besides not considering the full range of available views, members of Congress are not generally in a position to make trade-offs between policies. Because of its decentralization, Congress usually considers policies serially—that is, without reference to other policies. Without an integrating mechanism, members have few means by which to set and enforce priorities and emphasize the policies with which the president is most concerned, especially when the opposition party controls Congress. In addition, Congress has little capability, except within the context of the budget, to examine two policies, such as education and health care, in relation to each other. Not knowing that giving up something on one policy will result in a greater return on another policy, members have little incentive to engage in trade-offs.

Similarly, the decentralization of Congress limits its ability to deal comprehensively with major policy domains. Congress distributes its workload among committees, but committee jurisdictions do not usually cover entire policy areas. For example, no one congressional committee handles health, economic stability, or national security (the last requiring a coordination of defense policy and diplomacy). Conflict with the president may occur because the more centralized nature of the presidency encourages the White House to evaluate legislation in terms of its relationship to related issues in policy domains.

The hierarchical structure of the executive branch, with the president at the pinnacle, forces the president to take responsibility for the entire executive branch. Moreover, when the president exercises power, it is clear who is acting and who should be held accountable. Congress, in contrast, is not responsible for implementing policies, and each member is relatively obscure compared with the president. Because Congress is so decentralized, any member can disclaim responsibility for policies or their consequences. Members of Congress, therefore, can and do make irresponsible or self-serving decisions and then let the president take the blame.

All this can be very frustrating to the president. Gerald Ford, who spent most of his adult life in Congress, wrote the following after leaving the White House:

> When I was in the Congress myself, I thought it fulfilled its constitutional obligations in a very responsible way, but after I became President, my perspective changed. It seemed to me that Congress was beginning to disintegrate as an organized legislative body. It wasn't answering the nation's challenges domestically because it was too fragmented. It responded too often to single-issue special interest groups and it therefore wound up dealing with minutiae instead of attacking serious problems in a coherent way.[8]

Information and Expertise

The different internal structures of the president and Congress influence the amount and quality of the information available to them for decision making, further encouraging the two branches to see issues from different perspectives. Members of Congress rarely have available to them expertise of the quantity and quality that is available to the president.

Aside from the fact that the executive branch includes more than four million civilian and military employees plus hundreds of advisory committees while Congress employs only a few thousand people (many of whom work in supporting agencies, including the Library of Congress), the expertise of the two branches differ. Members of Congress tend to hire generalists, even on committee staffs. Sometimes these individuals develop great expertise in a particular field, but others may only be amateurs compared with their counterparts in the executive branch. Members of Congress select many of their staff to serve their needs and desires that have little to do with policy analysis, and neither house has a merit system, a tenured career service, or a central facility for recruiting the best available talent. Congress is especially at a disadvantage in national security policy where the president relies on classified information that is generally unavailable to Congress.

Time Perspectives

The differences in the length of terms of presidents and members of Congress encourage them to adopt different time perspectives. Presidents fear that their mandates (most presidents feel they obtained one in their election) are short-lived, and they know their tenures will be short. Thus, they can waste no time in pushing for the adoption of their policies. (Presidents, of course, can procrastinate in proposing or reacting to others' solutions to national problems, and they may focus on short-term political gains. The issue is one of institutional tendencies.)

Congress has a different timetable. Its members tend to be careerists and therefore do not have the same compulsion to enact policies rapidly. The decentralization of Congress aggravates this lethargic approach, which ensures that a great deal of negotiating and compromising must take place on all but a few noncontroversial (and usually unimportant) issues. This process can, and often does, take years. President Richard Nixon proposed revenue sharing in 1969; it passed in 1972. President Truman proposed a national health plan in 1948; a limited version (Medicare) was passed in 1965. One consequence of Congress's frequent sluggishness in handling legislation is that the president is not likely to get much of what he wants until later, if at all. A second consequence is that Congress may pass presidential policies too late to become fully effective.

At the same time that differences in tenures encourage the president and Congress to process legislation at different speeds, they also invite them to adopt different time perspectives on policy issues. A president, especially one in his second term, may choose to tackle long-term issues such as Social Security financing or tax reform. They are more worried about their legacies than about providing short-term benefits to voters who will serve electoral needs. Conversely, most members of Congress, especially those in the House, are constantly facing election. As one representative put it during the Reagan presidency, "My neck is on the chopping block—not Reagan's. He can talk about longer-term solutions to interest rates and unemployment. I can't. I need something to tell my people now."[9]

We have seen that the structure of American government exerts strong pressure on the two branches to represent different sets of interests and to view policies differently. These differences set the stage for conflict and virtually compel a president to try to influence Congress.

AGENDA SETTING

Attaining agenda status is a necessary prelude to the passage of a bill, and thus obtaining agenda space for his most important proposals is at the core of every president's legislative strategy. The burdens of leadership are considerably less at the agenda stage than at the floor stage, where the president must try to influence decisions regarding the political and substantive merits of a policy. At the agenda stage, in contrast, the president only has to convince members that his proposals are important enough to warrant attention. The White House generally succeeds in obtaining congressional attention to its legislative proposals.[10] Thus, the agenda-setting stage of the legislative process rarely poses an insurmountable barrier to the president.[11]

PARTY LEADERSHIP

"What the Constitution separates our political parties do not combine."[12] Richard Neustadt wrote these words six decades ago to help explain why presidents could not simply assume support from the members of their party in Congress. The challenge of presidential party leadership in Congress remains just as great and is just as important today as it was when Neustadt wrote his famous treatise on presidential power.

Party Support of the President

Representatives and senators of the president's party are almost always the nucleus of coalitions supporting the president's programs. As one White House aide put it, "You turn to your party members first. If we couldn't move our own people, we felt the opportunities were pretty slim."[13] No matter what other resources presidents may have, without seats in Congress held by their party, they will usually find it very difficult to move their legislative programs through Congress.

As we will see, the opposition party frequently controls one or both houses of Congress. Although important legislation has passed under divided government,[14] presidential initiatives are much more likely to fail under such circumstances.[15] Moreover, the higher the level of partisan polarization, the more the impact of divided government.[16] Thus, leading their party in Congress is the principal task of all presidents as they seek to counter the tendencies of the executive and legislative branches toward conflict inherent in the system of checks and balances.

Tables 11.1 and 11.2 show the party support for the president on contested roll-call votes on which the White House took a stand since 1953, a period covering more than a fourth of the nation's history under the Constitution. Although the presidents of each party varied considerably in their policies, personalities, and political environments, their fellow partisans in Congress gave them considerably more support than they gave presidents of the opposition party. Moreover, the gap between the levels of support from the president's and the opposition parties has been growing since the 1970s, reaching 70 percentage points or more under Barack Obama and about 80 percentage points under Donald Trump.

Table 11.3 shows the same data organized by the party of the president. Several patterns are evident. In the 1950s, President Eisenhower received relatively modest support from his own party, only 63 percent in the House and 69 percent in the Senate. Foreign affairs were the dominant issue of the era, and there was substantial

Table 11.1 Presidential Support in the House*

President	President's Party	Support (%) Republican	Support (%) Democrat	Difference‡
Eisenhower	Republican	63	42	21
Kennedy	Democrat	26	73	47
Johnson	Democrat	27	71	44
Nixon/Ford	Republican	64	39	25
Carter	Democrat	31	63	32
Reagan	Republican	70	29	41
G. H. W. Bush	Republican	73	27	46
Clinton	Democrat	24	75	51
G. W. Bush	Republican	83	19	64
Obama	Democrat	13	88	75
Trump†	Republican	91	13	78

* On roll-call votes on which the winning side was supported by fewer than 80 percent of those voting.
† 2017–2018
‡ Percentage points

Table 11.2 Presidential Support in the Senate*

President	President's Party	Support (%) Republican	Support (%) Democrat	Difference‡
Eisenhower	Republican	69	36	33
Kennedy	Democrat	33	65	32
Johnson	Democrat	44	56	12
Nixon/Ford	Republican	63	33	30
Carter	Democrat	37	63	26
Reagan	Republican	74	31	43
G. H. W. Bush	Republican	75	29	46
Clinton	Democrat	22	83	61
G. W. Bush	Republican	86	18	68
Obama	Democrat	22	92	70
Trump†	Republican	96	15	81

* On roll-call votes on which the winning side was supported by fewer than 80 percent of those voting.
† 2017–2018
‡ Percentage points

diversity of opinion among elected Republican representatives. Many were isolationist and opposed to the president's strong internationalist orientation.[17]

Kennedy and Johnson received somewhat more support from the Democrats in the House than Eisenhower received from his party, but they also received weak support from the Republicans (26 and 27 percent, respectively), who were strongly opposed to many of the liberal initiatives of the New Frontier and the Great Society. The presidents' party support among Senate Democrats was quite modest, reflecting

Table 11.3 Presidential Party Support in Congress*

		House		Senate	
		support			
President	Party	Own Party	Opposition Party	Own Party	Opposition Party
Eisenhower	Republican	63	42	69	36
Kennedy	Democrat	73	26	65	33
Johnson	Democrat	71	27	56	44
Nixon/Ford	Republican	64	39	63	33
Carter	Democrat	63	31	63	37
Reagan	Republican	70	29	74	31
G. H. W. Bush	Republican	73	27	75	29
Clinton	Democrat	75	24	83	22
G. W. Bush	Republican	83	19	86	18
Obama	Democrat	86	13	92	22
Trump[†]	Republican	91	13	96	15

* On roll-call votes on which the winning side was supported by fewer than 80 percent of those voting.
† 2017–2018

the heterogeneity of the Democratic Party and the response of its conservative wing to the same programs. Democrats supported Kennedy about two-thirds of the time. Opposition to civil rights measures was especially strong among the large contingent of Southern Democrats, who supported Lyndon Johnson only 36 percent of the time.[18] The combination of opposition from conservative Democrats and the support of a number of liberal Republican senators resulted in Johnson receiving 44 percent support among Senate Republicans, only slightly less than his 56 percent support among Democrats.

Since the 1970s, there has been a steady increase in the support the president received from his own party in both houses and a corresponding decrease in the support he received from the opposition party. These changes, in turn, have produced the substantial increase in the differences between the support levels of the two parties.

Significantly, presidents of both parties have experienced increasing disparity in support. While George W. Bush received only 19 percent support from House Democrats, Barack Obama received even lower support—13 percent—from House Republicans. Similarly, Bush won 18 percent support from Senate Democrats while Obama achieved 22 percent from Senate Republicans. Donald Trump has fared even worse than Bush among Democrats, 13 percent in the House and 15 percent in the Senate.

With a president of their own in the White House, party members in Congress may alter their voting tendencies. For example, Republicans have a tendency to be more supportive of internationalist foreign policies and are more likely to accept governmental economic activity when a Republican is president. Democrats, in contrast, have a tendency to move in the opposite direction when there is a Republican in the White House. In 1981, with Ronald Reagan, a conservative Republican, as president, many Republicans in Congress shifted to supporting foreign aid and increasing the national debt ceiling, even though they had opposed these policies under the previous Democratic administration of Jimmy Carter. A similar tendency occurred in 2001 when Republican George W. Bush replaced Democrat Bill Clinton. In 2017, when Republican Donald Trump replaced Democrat Barack Obama, many Republicans switched to support for increasing the debt ceiling in response to requests from the administration. Likewise, some members of the president's party who voted for a bill when it was originally passed will switch and vote against the same legislation if their party leader vetoes it.[19]

Although the president receives more support from members of his party than from the opposition, this tendency is not necessarily the result of party affiliation. It is difficult to tell whether a member of the president's party votes for the president's policies because of shared party affiliation, basic agreement with those policies, or some other factor. Undoubtedly, members of the same party share many policy preferences and have similar electoral coalitions supporting them.

The realignment of the parties and the increasing party polarization have been at the core of the divergence in presidential support. The consequences of these dynamics in congressional support for the White House is that the president is more dependent on his party than at any time in at least three generations. His co-partisans are likely to accord him reliable support for his initiatives, while the opposition's response to his proposals will be overwhelmingly negative.

Despite the proclivity of members of Congress to support presidents of their party, all presidents experience at least some slippage in the support of their party in Congress, as we see in tables 11.1–11.3. When constituency opinion and the president's proposals conflict, members of Congress are more likely to vote with their constituents, whom they rely on for reelection. Moreover, if the president is not popular with their constituencies, congressional party members may avoid identifying too closely with the White House. With a bit of exaggeration, Jimmy Carter remarked, "I learned the hard way that there was no party loyalty or discipline when a complicated or controversial issue was at stake—none."[20]

Obstacles to Party Unity

The primary obstacle to party unity is the lack of consensus on policies among party members. Although in recent years the parties in Congress have become more homogeneous (as conservative constituencies increasingly elect Republicans, especially in the House), there is still a substantial range of opinion within each party. This diversity of views often reflects the range of constituencies represented by party members. The frequent defection from support of Democratic presidents by the conservative Southern Democrats, or "boll weevils," was one of the most prominent features of American politics in the twentieth century. More recently, Bill Clinton found it difficult to obtain party support for policies designed to encourage international trade because of the opposition of blue-collar interests, the traditional base of the Democratic Party. Likewise, when Barack Obama negotiated deals with Republicans on taxes in 2010 and spending in 2011, many congressional Democrats voted against him.

Republican presidents often lack stable coalitions as well. George W. Bush received nearly unanimous support from his party for his proposals to reduce taxes, but when it came time to reform Social Security or immigration, things were different. Republicans were not enthusiastic and were sometimes in the forefront of the opposition to these policies. Donald Trump has faced diversity of opinion among Republicans on his priority policies such as immigration, international trade, and health care as well as a range of foreign policies.

Yet other obstacles may confront a president trying to mobilize his party in Congress. If the president's party has just regained the presidency but remains a minority in Congress, its members need to adjust from their past stance as the opposition minority to one of a "governing" minority. Adjustment is not always easily done, however, as Richard Nixon found when he sought Republican votes for budget deficits.

Further difficulties may stem from the fact that the winning presidential candidate may not be the natural leader of the party. Indeed, as in the cases of Jimmy Carter, Donald Trump, and to a lesser extent Bill Clinton, some presidents campaign against the party establishment and do not identify with the traditional stances of their parties. Naturally, when a new president arrives in Washington under these conditions, intraparty harmony is not likely to materialize overnight, and appeals for party loyalty may fall on less than receptive ears.

The constant opposition he faced from the vocal and powerful liberal wing of his own party undermined Carter's ability to promote his policies. In 1980, the president had to deal with the challenge of Senator Edward Kennedy for the Democratic nomination for president. As Carter reflected more than a quarter century after leaving the White House, "The Democratic Party was never mine. . . . I was never able to consolidate support in the Democratic Party, particularly after Kennedy decided to run for president."[21] In the absence of a party consensus on policy, Carter's White House had to rely on forming discrete coalitions.

Because of the president's reliance on his own party, because of slippage in party support, and because he is unlikely to have large majorities in either house of Congress, he needs the support of as much of his party's cohort as possible. What can the White House do to increase the chances of obtaining party support?

Leading the Party

The most straightforward answer to the question of increasing party support is making appeals to co-partisans in Congress. The increasing ideological coherence of the parties has created a substantial overlap in the ideologies of the president and his party's members in Congress. Thus, representatives and senators are inclined to support White House initiatives because they agree with them and may well have advocated them in their campaigns. Moreover, the president and his congressional co-partisans are probably supported by similar electoral coalitions, reinforcing the pull of party ties.

In addition, members of the president's party typically have personal loyalties or emotional commitments to their party and their party leader, which the president can often translate into votes when necessary. Moreover, these officials have a basic distrust of the opposition party, which they quite correctly see as eager to undermine the White House. This perception induces party members to rise to the president's defense.[22] Thus, members of the president's party vote with him when they can, thereby giving him the benefit of the doubt, especially if their own opinion on an issue is weak.

The proclivity for supporting the president increases the effectiveness of other sources of party influence. One of these sources is the desire of members of the presidential party to avoid embarrassing "their" administration. This attitude stems from two motivations. The first is related to the sentiments already discussed, but the second is more utilitarian. Members of the president's party have an incentive to make the president look good because his standing in the public may influence their own chances for reelection and their party's chances of maintaining or regaining a majority. They also want a record of legislative success to take to the voters.[23] In 2003, Republicans overcame their distaste for social welfare programs and supported a prescription drug program under Medicare to show that they could deliver when they had power and to give President George W. Bush a victory to aid his reelection in 2004.

Thus, the willingness of members of Congress to support a policy may depend on who proposes it. Presidential agenda items tend to exacerbate partisan disagreement in Congress. Democrats concurred but Republicans balked in 1993 when Bill Clinton proposed Goals 2000, providing for voluntary testing for students in elementary and secondary schools. In 2001, the parties reversed their stances when George W. Bush proposed a more ambitious educational assessment program.[24]

Presidential leadership, then, demarcates and deepens cleavages in Congress. The differences between the parties and the cohesion within them on floor votes are typically greater when the president takes a stand on issues. When the president adopts a position, members of his party have a stake in his success, while opposition party members have a stake in the president losing. Moreover, both parties take cues from the president that help define their policy views, especially when the lines of party cleavage are not clearly at stake or already well established.[25]

Presidents may also find it easier to obtain party unity behind their programs if their party regains control of one or both houses of Congress at the time of their election. Many new members may feel gratitude for the president's coattails. Moreover, the prospect of exercising the power to govern may provide a catalyst for party loyalty, while the loss of power may temporarily demoralize the opposition party.

Working with Congressional Leaders

Each party has a set of floor and committee leaders in the House and Senate who, in theory, should be a valuable resource for their party's leader in the White House. The president needs both their advice and their resources for making head counts and other administrative chores. Because of their role perceptions, because their reputations for passing legislation give them a clear stake in the president's success, and because they are susceptible to the same sentiments and pressures toward party loyalty as are other members of Congress, floor leaders of the president's party in Congress are usually very supportive of the White House.

Committee leaders of the president's party usually have a similar orientation. Representative Daniel Rostenkowski, chair of the House Ways and Means Committee, told President Clinton, "You send the proposals, and I'll be the quarterback." Senator Daniel Patrick Moynihan, the chair of the Senate Finance Committee, declared, "The most important thing for me coming to the job . . . is that I want to get the president's agenda through."[26]

However, party floor leaders are not always dependable supporters, and they certainly are not simply extensions of the White House. Shortly before Barack Obama's inauguration, House Majority Leader Steny Hoyer dismissed a reporter's suggestion that Democrats would go easy on oversight of the administration. To make his point, he held up a copy of the congressional newspaper *The Hill*, its headline blaring

"I Don't Work for Obama," a reference to a comment by Senate Majority Leader Harry Reid.[27] House Majority Leader Richard Gephardt and House Majority Whip David Bonior broke with President Clinton over several important trade bills and led the opposition to them. The White House can do little in such a situation. Presidents do not lobby for candidates for congressional party leadership positions, and they virtually always remain neutral during the selection process. They have no desire to alienate important members of Congress whose support they will need.

Similarly, seniority usually determines committee chairs and ranking minority members. Furthermore, the chairs always come from the majority party in the chamber, which often is not that of the president. It is unusual for the president to influence who holds these important positions. Moreover, the norm of supporting a president of one's party is weaker for committee leaders than for floor leaders.

Presidents and their staff typically work closely with their party's legislative leaders, meeting weekly for breakfast when Congress is in session. (Sometimes these meetings include the leaders of the opposition party as well.) These gatherings provide opportunities for an exchange of views and for the president to keep communication channels open and maintain morale. The significance of these efforts has varied, however. On one extreme, Richard Nixon's meetings were often pro forma, serving more as a symbolic ritual than a mechanism for leadership. On the other, Lyndon Johnson used them as strategy sessions to integrate congressional leaders into the White House legislative liaison operation.

Equally important as the congressional party leaders' relations with the president are their relations with their party colleagues in Congress. Larger congressional staffs and an explosion in the number of lobbyists, independent policy analysts, and congressional work groups and caucuses have made it easier for members of Congress to inform themselves, challenge the White House (and congressional leadership), and provide alternatives to the president's policies. The increased number of roll-call votes and, thus, the increased visibility of representatives' voting behavior generated more pressure on House members to abandon party loyalty, which made it more difficult for the president to gain passage of legislation. Reforms that opened committee and subcommittee hearings to the public had the same effect. There has also been a heavy turnover in the congressional personnel in recent years, and new members have brought with them new approaches to legislating. They are less likely to adopt the norms of apprenticeship and specialization than were their predecessors in their first terms. Instead, they have eagerly taken an active role in all legislation. They place a heavy emphasis on individualism and showmanship, and usually much less on party regularity.

Thus, congressional party leaders now have more decision makers to influence than they did under, say, Lyndon Johnson in the 1960s. They can no longer rely on dealing with the congressional aristocracy and expect the rest of the members to follow. As Reagan's lobbyist, Kenneth Duberstein, put it, "For most issues you have to lobby all 435 Congressmen and almost all 100 Senators."[28]

Nevertheless, beginning with the Republican takeover of the House in 1995, Speakers of the House of both parties have recentralized some power in the hands of the party leadership. As the party contingents have become more homogeneous, there has been more policy agreement within the parties and thus more party unity in voting on the floor. Increased agreement has made it easier for Speakers to exercise their prerogatives regarding the assignment of bills and members to committees, the rules under which the House considers legislation on the floor, and the use of an expanded whip system—all developments that have enabled the parties to advance an agenda that reflects party preferences and work on behalf of a president of the same party. In addition, the rules in the House make control of the agenda by the majority party much easier than in the more decentralized Senate.

Committee chairs have less discretion than in previous decades because of limits on their terms, and the leadership has placed them on notice that to maintain their positions they have to support the party program. In several instances, the majority party has ignored seniority and named the Speaker's allies as committee chairs, and the leadership has played the predominant role in selecting members to the committees. In addition, to write major legislation, they have sometimes displaced committees with ad hoc task forces of their choosing.

As a result, the House leadership can be quite effective in supporting a president of its party, as it was for George W. Bush in 2001–2006 and Barack Obama in 2009–2010. Conversely, centralized power does little to help the president if the opposition is in the majority, as it frequently is. It only makes opposition to him more effective as when Republicans dominated the agenda-setting process in Congress under Bill Clinton in 1995–2000 and Barack Obama in 2011–2016 or when Democrats had the majority under George W. Bush in 2007–2008 and in the House under Donald Trump in 2019–2020.

Although the party leadership, at least in theory, possesses sanctions that it can exercise to enforce party discipline (including exercising discretion on committee assignments, patronage, campaign funds, trips abroad, and aid with members' pet bills), in reality, this discretion exists primarily on paper. Members of Congress consider most rewards a matter of right, and it is the leadership's job to see that they are distributed equitably. Party leaders usually do not dare to withhold benefits because they fear being overturned by the rank and file. (Senate Majority Leader Robert Dole sometimes termed his position that of "majority pleader.") Threats of sanctions in such a situation are unconvincing and thus rarely occur. When Speaker Newt Gingrich removed a recalcitrant member from a committee, many Republicans rebelled and the Speaker had to compensate the member with a prestigious committee assignment. In addition, few representatives were impressed when Gingrich refused to campaign for those who had failed to provide him reliable support.

Maintaining and Increasing Party Numbers

Because representatives and senators of his party give the president such high levels of support, the best way to improve his chances of obtaining support in Congress as a whole is to increase the number of fellow party members in the legislature. Once members of Congress have been elected, however, they rarely change their party affiliation, and the few instances when they have changed have not resulted from presidential persuasion. (Indeed, under Democrat Bill Clinton, five members of the House and two in the Senate switched from Democrat to Republican.) Thus, if presidents are to alter the party composition of Congress, they must help to elect additional members of their party. Helping incumbents, and thus maintaining the party's cohorts of members of Congress, is also critical.

There are two points at which the White House may act to influence the size of the president's party's contingent in Congress: presidential and midterm elections. Certainly presidents spend considerable time raising money for their parties, and the White House may also be active in encouraging attractive candidates to run for office—and occasionally discouraging less attractive ones.

The most direct potential influence of the president on the outcomes of elections, however, is through their standing with the public. According to Gary Jacobson, in the increasing nationalization of politics, "popular assessments of the president strongly affect how his party is evaluated, perceived, and adopted as an object of identification, which, in turn, helps to account for the president's influence on the electoral fates of his party's candidates."[29]

Presidential Coattails

The presidential coattails effect occurs when voters cast their ballots for congressional candidates of the president's party because those candidates support the president. There is an increasing connection between presidential and congressional voting, with a rise in party loyalty and thus a decline in ticket splitting. Party-line voting reached its highest level ever for House and Senate elections in 2016, with defection rates of 9 percent in House elections and 10 percent in Senate elections. Similarly, 2012 witnessed the lowest incidence of ticket splitting—voting for a Democrat for president and a Republican for US representative or senator, or vice versa—ever: 10 percent for the House and 11 percent for the Senate. Much of this coherence in voting is the result of views about the president.[30]

Coattail victories, whether they bring in new members or preserve the seats of incumbents, can have significant payoffs for the president in terms of support for the administration's programs. Those members of the president's party who won close elections may provide an extra increment of support out of a sense of gratitude for the votes they perceive they received due to presidential coattails or out of a sense of responsiveness to their constituents' support for the president.

However, the president runs *behind* almost every winning congressional candidate of his party. This fact does not in itself prove he has weak coattails, but it hardly provides the basis for inferring them. The lack of competition in nearly all House seats and most Senate seats provides little potential for coattails to determine the winner.[31] So does what seems to be a tendency for politically informed voters to vote for Congress against the party they believe will win the presidency.[32]

It is not surprising that research has found that presidential coattails determine the outcomes of very few congressional races.[33] Winning presidential candidates run behind all but a handful of members of Congress in their states or districts. George W. Bush's Republicans lost four seats in the Senate and two in the House in the elections of 2000, and Donald Trump's Republicans lost two Senate and seven House seats in 2016.

The change in party balance that usually emerges when the electoral dust has settled following a presidential election is strikingly small (table 11.4). In the seventeen presidential elections between 1952 and 2016, the party of the winning presidential candidate gained an average of seven seats (out of 435) per election in the House. In the Senate, the opposition party actually gained seats in eight of the elections (1956, 1960, 1972, 1984, 1988, 1996, 2000, and 2016), and there was no change in 1976 and 1992. The net gain for the president's party in the Senate averaged one seat per election.

Losses for the president's party in presidential elections are nothing new. In 1792, George Washington easily won reelection, but the opposition Democrat-Republicans captured the House of Representatives. Most House seats are too safe for a party, and especially for an incumbent, to have the election outcome affected

Table 11.4 Changes in Congressional Representation of the President's Party in Presidential Election Years

Year	President	House	Senate
1952	Eisenhower	+22	+1
1956	Eisenhower	−2	−1
1960	Kennedy	−22	−2
1964	Johnson	+37	+1
1968	Nixon	+5	+6
1972	Nixon	+12	−2
1976	Carter	+1	0
1980	Reagan	+34	+12
1984	Reagan	+14	−2
1988	G. H. W. Bush	−3	−1
1992	Clinton	−10	0
1996	Clinton	+9	−2
2000	G. W. Bush	−2	−4
2004	G. W. Bush	+3	+4
2008	Obama	+21	+8
2012	Obama	+8	+1
2016	Trump	−6	−2

by the presidential election. Senate elections are more affected by the president's standing with the public, but the president's party typically gains only one seat in a presidential election year.[34]

Thus, presidents cannot expect personally to carry like-minded running mates into office to provide additional support for their programs. On the contrary, rather than being amenable to voting for the president's policies due to shared convictions, representatives are free to focus on parochial matters and respond to narrow constituency interests. Similarly, although we cannot know the extent to which representatives have felt gratitude to presidents for their coattails and thus have given them additional legislative support in the past, we do know that any such gratitude is rarely warranted. The more representatives are aware of the independence of their elections from that of the president, the less likely they are to feel that they must "thank" the president with an additional increment of support.

Midterm Election Campaigning
What about midterm elections? Modern presidents have often taken an active role in midterm congressional elections, and there is evidence that those for whom they campaign show their gratitude in increased support—if they win.[35] Events may constrain the president's campaign efforts, however. In 2014, the White House determined that the president would need to devote time to managing the new bombing campaign against the Islamic State of Iraq and Syria. The president also wanted to avoid the optics of ordering strikes en route to political rallies.[36]

Sometimes presidents are so unpopular that the candidates of their party do not want their support. For example, President Johnson adopted a low profile during the

1966 campaign because of his lack of public support (below 50 percent in the Gallup Poll). Similarly, in 1974, before he resigned, President Nixon wanted invitations to campaign for Republicans to prove that he was not political poison, but he received few offers as the Watergate crisis came to a head. Some candidates asked Ronald Reagan to stay away because of the recession in 1982, with which many voters identified him; in 1994, opposition to Bill Clinton was a primary cause of the Democrats' loss of both houses of Congress; and in 2006, the tables were turned and opposition to George W. Bush was at the core of the Democrats retaking both houses. In 2010, public antagonism toward Barack Obama led to a stinging defeat for Democrats. In 2014, when the Democrats were in a desperate struggle to retain a Senate majority, Barack Obama campaigned in only one state, Michigan, with a competitive Senate race. Instead, he focused his efforts on Democratic states where his approval numbers remained reasonably strong. Donald Trump campaigned vigorously in 2018, but he did so almost exclusively in states he won in 2016.

Ultimately, the president's party typically *loses* seats in midterm elections (table 11.5), sometimes with serious consequences for the president's initiatives. Despite their efforts, presidents often have little impact on the results of congressional elections.[37] For example, in 1986, the Republicans lost eight seats in the Senate, depriving President Reagan of a majority, and in 1994, the Democrats lost eight Senate seats and fifty-two House seats, in the process losing control of both houses. Republicans lost forty House seats—and thus the chamber's majority—2018, making life much more difficult for President Trump.

The president's party is especially likely to lose seats in the House when the president's approval rating is low, as Donald Trump's was in 2018, and when the

Table 11.5 Changes in Congressional Representation of the President's Party in Midterm Elections

Year	President	House	Senate
1954	Eisenhower	−18	−1
1958	Eisenhower	−47	−13
1962	Kennedy	−4	+3
1966	Johnson	−47	−4
1970	Nixon	−12	+2
1974	Ford	−47	−5
1978	Carter	−15	−3
1982	Reagan	−26	0
1986	Reagan	−5	−8
1990	G. H. W. Bush	−9	−1
1994	Clinton	−52	−8
1998	Clinton	+5	0
2002	G. W. Bush	+6	+2
2006	G. W. Bush	−30	−6
2010	Obama	−63	−6
2014	Obama	−13	−9
2018	Trump	+2	−40

party gained a large number of seats in the previous election. Thus, the Democrats suffered huge losses in the 2010 midterm elections, including six seats in the Senate and sixty-three in the House. As a result, Barack Obama found it difficult to win passage of his priority programs. In the 2014 midterms, Democrats lost nine seats in the Senate and thirteen seats in the House. We can trace this phenomenon back further in US history to Woodrow Wilson's midterm campaigning in 1918, which was rewarded by the loss of both houses of Congress. (Even George Washington's Federalists lost seats in the House in the first midterm election, in 1790.)

Recently, there have been exceptions, however. In 1998, the Democrats gained five seats in the House, an election that occurred in the context of the widely unpopular effort by Republicans to impeach Bill Clinton.[38] In 2002, Republicans made small gains in both houses. In this election, George W. Bush engaged in the most active midterm campaigning of any president in history, and the Republican gains were the result of both heavy turnout among Republicans, who responded to the president who was extraordinarily popular in the face of the 9/11 attacks, and favorable redistricting following the 2000 census. In 2006, however, George W. Bush's Republicans lost majorities in both houses of Congress.

Bipartisanship

On July 27, 1981, President Reagan delivered an exceptionally important and effective televised address to the nation seeking the public's support for his tax-cut bill and going to great lengths to present his plan as "bipartisan." It was crucial that he convince the public that this controversial legislation was supported by members of both parties and was therefore, by implication, fair. Thus, he described it as "bipartisan" a full eleven times in the span of a few minutes. No one was to miss the point. The president required the votes of Democrats in the House to pass his bill, and he wanted their constituents to apply pressure on them to support it.

Despite the advantage that presidents have in dealing with members of their party in Congress, they are often forced to solicit bipartisan support. Because the majority party has such tight control over the agenda of the House, it is possible for the White House to win House approval for its initiatives if the president's party has only a small majority, but, as we have seen, a narrow majority is no guarantee of success. Moreover, large majorities are not common. The last time a president's party held 60 percent of House seats was in 1980.

The Senate filibuster rule turns the convenience of a 60 percent majority into a necessity. Presidents generally need at least sixty votes to pass important legislation. Aside from about six months in late 2009 and early 2010, no president has enjoyed a majority of sixty votes since 1978.

The opposition party may control one or both houses of Congress, so even if all members of the president's party supported the administration on its key initiatives, it would not be sufficient. Between 1953 and 1992, Republican presidents faced a Democratic House of Representatives for twenty-six years and a Democratic Senate for twenty years. George W. Bush enjoyed Republican Party control of both houses of Congress for less than five months in 2001 before the Democrats gained a majority in the Senate, and the Democrats had majorities in each house for his last two years in office.

President Clinton faced a Republican House and Senate from 1995 through 2000. Without Republican support, he would not have obtained passage of the North American Free Trade Agreement (NAFTA) and the General Agreement on

Trade and Tariffs (GATT) or the line-item veto. Barack Obama faced a Republican-controlled House in 2011–2016 and a Republican Senate in 2015–2016. Donald Trump had to work with a Democratic House in 2019–2020.

Another reason for bipartisanship is that presidents cannot depend on all the members of their party to support them on all issues. Tables 11.1–11.3 show clearly that members of the president's own party frequently oppose his initiatives. Thus, presidents cannot take party support for granted. Indeed, most legislation that passes, including landmark legislation, does so with a majority of the minority party in support, even under unified government.[39]

Not only do partisan strategies often fail but they also may provoke the other party into a more unified posture of opposition. When there is confrontation, there can be no consensus, and consensus is often required to legislate changes on important issues. In addition, the role expectation of being somewhat above the political fray may constrain presidents in their role as party leader.

Despite the frequent necessity of a bipartisan strategy, it is not without costs. Bipartisanship often creates a strain with the extremes within the president's party, as a Republican president tries to appeal to the left for Democratic votes and a Democratic president to the right for Republican votes. Although it is true that the Republican right wing and Democratic left wing may find it difficult to forge a coalition in favor of alternatives to their own president's policies, it is not true that they must therefore support their president. Instead, they may complicate a president's strategy by joining those who oppose administration policies.

As tables 11.1–11.3 demonstrate, the ultimate limitation on a bipartisan strategy is that the opposition party is generally not a fertile ground for obtaining policy support. Democratic presidents have often been frustrated in their efforts to deal with Republicans. Presidents Clinton and Obama faced virtually unanimous Republican opposition to their economic, budget, and health-care proposals.[40] Republican presidents also face obstacles to obtaining bipartisan support. Only twenty-three House Democrats supported Ronald Reagan on both the important budget and tax votes in 1981, despite the president's persuasive efforts, the perception that the president had a mandate, and the pull of ideology. Similarly, few Democrats supported George W. Bush's tax-cut proposals or the budget on which they were based. Moreover, the president's efforts to exploit bipartisan support for the war on terrorism to increase support for his domestic policies were generally unsuccessful. In 2017, no Democrat in either house supported any version of the Trump White House–backed bills to repeal and replace the Affordable Care Act or the 2017 tax cuts.

The competition for political advantage also inhibits bipartisanship. Since 1980, there has been heavy competition to control each house of Congress. Parties with a president or majority have to focus on legislating while minority parties can focus on political messaging. Representatives and senators believe it is necessary to define and dramatize party differences to energize supporters and persuade undecided voters to support them. To do this, the minority forces roll calls that yield party-line divisions, publicize partisan controversies, raise more campaign money, and make the case for their party to take control. Even when they lose the vote, they may feel they have won politically because they are better positioned in the next election. Unsurprisingly, such adversarial behavior impedes bipartisan cooperation.[41]

Moreover, in times of polarized politics and when well-funded groups and highly ideological media are ready to pounce on any deviation from the ideological line and stir up a party's base, even a hint of opposition party members cooperating with the White House can be detrimental to their political future. Barack Obama explained,

> I have very cordial relations with a lot of the Republican members. We can have really great conversations and arrive at a meeting of the minds on a range of policy issues, but if they think they're going to lose seats or that they're going to lose their own seat because the social media has declared that they sold out the Republican Party, then they won't do it.

As Senate Republican leader Mitch McConnell told the president, "It hurts me just being seen photographed with you." Thus, when working on immigration, the budget, and other issues, the White House stayed behind the scenes so that the Republicans could negotiate with their Democratic counterparts, "because if it looks like they're negotiating with me, it doesn't help."[42]

Despite the challenges of bipartisanship, presidents often cannot ignore the opposition party, and even a few votes may be enough to bring them a majority.

PUBLIC SUPPORT

Although congressional seats held by members of the president's party may be a necessary condition for presidential success in Congress, they are not a sufficient one: The president needs public support as well. In the words of Eisenhower aide and presidential authority Emmet John Hughes, "Beyond all tricks of history and all quirks of Presidents, there would appear to be one unchallengeable truth: the dependence of Presidential authority on popular support."[43]

Public Approval

In his memoirs, President Lyndon Johnson wrote, "Presidential popularity is a major source of strength in gaining cooperation from Congress."[44] Thus, following his landslide electoral victory, he assembled the congressional liaison officials from the various departments and told them that his victory at the polls "might be more of a loophole than a mandate." Moreover, as his popularity could decrease rapidly, they would have to use it to their advantage while it lasted.[45]

President Carter's aides were explicit about the importance of public approval in their efforts to influence Congress. One stated that the "only way to keep those guys [Congress] honest is to keep our popularity high."[46] The president's legislative liaison officials generally agreed that their effectiveness with Congress ultimately depended on the president's ability to influence public opinion. As one of them said, "When you go up to the Hill and the latest polls show Carter isn't doing well, there isn't much reason for a member to go along with him. There's little we can do if the member isn't persuaded on the issue."[47] The Reagan administration was especially sensitive to the president's public approval levels. According to one top aide, "Everything here is built on the idea that the president's success depends on grassroots support."[48]

Why is presidential approval or popularity such an important source of influence in Congress? According to a senior aide to Jimmy Carter:

> When the President is low in public opinion polls, the Members of Congress see little hazard in bucking him. . . . After all, very few Congressmen examine an issue solely on its merits; they are politicians and they think politically. I'm not

saying they make only politically expedient choices. But they read the polls and from that they feel secure in turning their backs on the President with political impunity. Unquestionably, the success of the President's policies bears a tremendous relationship to his popularity in the polls.[49]

The public's evaluations of the president may serve as an indicator of broader opinions on politics and policy. Moreover, members of Congress must anticipate the public's reaction to their decisions to support or oppose the president and his policies. Depending on the president's public standing, they may choose to be close to him or independent from him to increase their chances of reelection. As analyst William Schneider put it, "popularity is power. Members of Congress are all in business for themselves. If a President is popular, they'll support him because they want to be with a winner. If he starts losing popularity, they'll abandon him. Even members of his own party don't want to be associated with a loser."[50]

It is prudent for members of Congress to anticipate voters' reactions to their support for the president. Their constituents hold them accountable for their legislative voting, especially on salient issues such as those on which the president has taken a stand.[51] Strong supporters of unpopular presidents in competitive districts are particularly at risk, because senators and representatives who support the president more than constituents prefer are more likely to lose.[52] In 1994, Democratic candidates were more likely to be defeated in districts where Bill Clinton was weak.[53] Opinions about George W. Bush's job performance and his decision to invade Iraq were exceptionally strong predictors of individual vote choices in the 2006 congressional elections.[54] Nearly 40 percent of voters cast ballots to oppose the president.[55] In 2010, Barack Obama was low in the approval polls, and opposition to his initiatives, particularly health-care reform, cost Democrats their majority in the House and greatly reduced their majority in the Senate.[56]

Members of Congress may also use the president's standing in the polls as an indicator of his ability to mobilize public opinion against his opponents. As Richard Nixon put it, "An even greater incentive for members [of Congress to support the president] is the fear that a popular president may oppose them in the next election."[57]

Public approval operates mostly in the background and sets the limits of what Congress will do for, or to, the president. Widespread support gives a president leeway and weakens resistance to the administration's policies. Moreover, it provides a cover for members of Congress to cast votes to which their constituents might otherwise object, as they can defend their votes as support for the president rather than on substantive policy grounds alone.

Lack of public support strengthens the resolve of those who are inclined to oppose the president and narrows the range in which he receives the benefit of the doubt, as Bill Clinton discovered when his approval ratings dipped into the 35 percent range in mid-1993. In addition, low ratings in the polls may create incentives to attack the president, further eroding an already weakened position. For example, after the arms sales to Iran and the diversion of funds to the Contras became a cause célèbre in late 1986, it became more acceptable in Congress and in the press to raise questions about Ronald Reagan's capacities as president. Disillusionment is a dangerous phenomenon for the White House. As a chief of the White House congressional relations office put it, "When the president's approval is low, it's advantageous and even fun to kick him around."[58]

The impact of presidential approval on presidential support occurs at the margins of coalition building, within the confines of other influences. No matter how low a president's standing in public polls falls or how close it is to the next election, he will still receive support from a substantial number of senators and representatives. Similarly, no matter how high approval levels climb or how large a president's winning percentage of the vote, a significant portion of the Congress may still oppose his policies. Members of Congress are unlikely to vote against the clear interests of their constituents or the firm tenets of their ideology, even out of deference to a widely supported chief executive. George W. Bush's very high approval levels in the months following the 9/11 attacks did not engender similarly high support among Democrats in Congress for his domestic policy proposals.[59] Thus, widespread support should give presidents leeway and weaken resistance to their policies, giving them, at best, leverage but not control.[60] In contrast, when presidents lack popular support, their options are reduced, their opportunities are diminished, and their room for maneuver is checked.

As the most volatile leadership resource, public approval is the factor most likely to determine whether an opportunity for policy change exists. Public approval makes other resources more efficacious. If the chief executive is high in public esteem, the president's party is more likely to be responsive, the public is more easily moved, and legislative skills become more effective. Thus, public approval is the resource that has the most potential to turn a typical situation into one favorable for change, which provides a strong incentive for the president to try to gain popular support. However, as we have seen, the White House cannot easily manipulate presidential approval.

Public approval is a necessary, but not a sufficient, source of influence in Congress. It is most useful in combination with party supporters in each house. If either approval or seats are lacking, the president's legislative program will be in for rough going.

Mandates

Another indicator of the public's opinion of the president is the results of the presidential election. Electoral mandates can be powerful symbols in American politics, as they accord added legitimacy and credibility to the newly elected president's proposals. Moreover, concerns for both representation and political survival will encourage members of Congress to support the president if they feel the people have spoken.[61]

More importantly, mandates change the premises of decisions. Following the 1932 election, the essential question became how government should act to fight the Depression, rather than whether it should act. Similarly, following the 1964 election, the dominant question in Congress was not whether to pass new social programs but, rather, how many to pass and how much to increase spending. In 1981, however, the tables were turned. Ronald Reagan's victory placed a stigma on big government and exalted the unregulated marketplace and large defense efforts. Reagan had won a major victory even before the first congressional vote.

Although presidential elections can structure choices for Congress, merely winning an election does not give a president a mandate. Every election produces a winner, but mandates are much less common. Even large electoral victories such as Richard Nixon's in 1972 and Ronald Reagan's in 1984 carry no guarantee that Congress will interpret the results as mandates from the people to support the president's programs, especially if the voters also elect majorities in Congress from the other party.

The winners in presidential elections usually claim to have been accorded a mandate,[62] of course, but in the absence of certain conditions, few observers accept these assertions at face value. Conditions that promote the perception of a mandate include a large margin of victory, the impression of long coattails, hyperbole in the press analyses of the election results that exaggerates the one-sidedness of the victory, a surprisingly large victory accompanying a change in parties in the White House, a campaign oriented around a major change in public policy, consistency of the new president's program with the prevailing tides of opinion in both the country and his party, or a sense that the public's views have shifted.[63] In 2004, George W. Bush won with less than 51 percent of the vote, lacked substantial coattails, and did not emphasize specific policy proposals in his campaign. Thus, his claims of a mandate lacked credibility—as he soon discovered when the public and Congress were unresponsive to his proposals for reforming Social Security.

Because it is unusual for these conditions to be met, perceptions of mandates are rarely strong. Presidents can do little about these perceptions. Some are simply elected under more favorable conditions for legislative leadership than are others. When mandates do occur or when candidates claim them effectively, the issue becomes one of exploiting the special opportunities they provide. Donald Trump was not fortunate enough to have that option, as you can see in box 11.1.

Box 11.1 ★ Did Trump Win a Mandate?

Donald Trump followed a long tradition of new presidents claiming a mandate from the people. Despite the claims from Trump Tower, however, the president did not receive a mandate. He received only 46 percent of the vote, hardly a landslide. Moreover, he did not win even a plurality of the votes, receiving nearly three million fewer than Hillary Clinton. Trump's party also lost six seats in the House and two in the Senate.

In addition, pre-election polls found that no candidate since 1980 has had a lower percentage of voters saying they planned to cast a vote *for* their candidate. In late October, most Trump voters were voting *against* Hillary Clinton rather than for him.[64] He had the lowest feeling thermometer rating of any major party candidate in the history of the American National Election Study.[65] Immediately after the election, 43 percent of the public had a positive response, but 52 percent were upset or dissatisfied.[66]

Further undercutting any claim to a mandate was the fact that Trump did not emphasize many specific policies during the 2016 campaign—building a wall along the Mexican border and slashing corporate tax rates being the prime exceptions. Instead, he stressed general aspirations, such as making America great again or providing better and less expensive health care. Therefore, there is little evidence to support claims of a mandate for many specific policies, and his election sent no signals to members of Congress that would encourage them to achieve a consensus.

The public seemed to agree. After the election, just 29 percent said Trump had a mandate to carry out the agenda he presented during the campaign, while 59 percent thought he should compromise with Democrats when they strongly disagreed with the specifics of his policy proposals.[67] The first Gallup report on his approval found his initial rating was lower than for any previous president. Moreover, his approval was the most polarized: 90 percent for Republicans but only 14 percent among Democrats.[68]

EVALUATING STRATEGIC POSITION

The first step a new administration should take to ensure success with Congress is to assess its strategic position accurately so it understands the potential for change and will not overreach or underachieve. Presidents must largely play with the hands that the public deals them through its electoral decisions on the presidency and Congress, as well as its evaluations of the chief executive's handling of his job. Presidents are rarely in a position to augment substantially their political capital, especially when just taking office.

The early periods of new administrations most clearly etched on our memories as notable successes were those in which presidents properly identified and exploited conditions for change. When Congress first met in special session in March 1933 after Franklin D. Roosevelt's inauguration, it rapidly passed, at the new president's request, bills to control the resumption of banking, repeal Prohibition, and effect government economies. This is all FDR originally planned for Congress to do; he expected to reassemble the legislature when permanent and more constructive legislation was ready. Yet, the president found a situation ripe for change, and he decided to exploit this favorable environment and strike repeatedly with hastily drawn legislation before sending Congress home. This period of intense activity came to be known as the Hundred Days.

Lyndon Johnson also knew that his personal leadership could not sustain congressional support for his policies. He realized that the assassination of President Kennedy and the election of 1964 provided him a unique chance to pass his Great Society legislation and moved immediately to exploit it. Similarly, the Reagan administration recognized that the perceptions of a mandate and the dramatic elevation of Republicans to majority status in the Senate provided it with a window of opportunity to effect major changes in public policy but that it had to concentrate its focus and move quickly before the environment became less favorable. Moreover, within a week of the March 30, 1981, assassination attempt on Reagan, Michael Deaver convened a meeting of other high-ranking aides at the White House to determine how best to take advantage of the new political capital the shooting had created.

If the White House misreads its strategic position, the president may begin his tenure with embarrassing failures in dealing with Congress. Moreover, the greater the breadth and complexity of the policy change a president proposes, the more opposition it is likely to engender—and thus the stronger the president's strategic position must be to succeed. In an era when a few opponents can effectively tie up bills, the odds are clearly against the White House.

Bill Clinton overestimated the extent of change that a president elected with a minority of the vote could make, especially when the public is dubious and well-organized interest groups are fervently opposed. Nevertheless, the president proposed, without Republican support, perhaps the most sweeping, complex prescriptions for controlling the conduct of state governments, employers, drug manufacturers, doctors, and hospitals, and individuals in American history. The foundation was lacking for change of this magnitude. The consequences of the bill's failure were greater than disappointment, however. Because Clinton declared health-care reform to be the cornerstone of his efforts to change public policy, his handling of the bill became a key indicator of the administration's competency at governing. The bill's death throes occurred only a few months before the 1994 elections, the greatest midterm electoral disaster for the Democrats in the previous fifty years.

George W. Bush faced an especially unusual beginning to his presidency, but he made the most of his situation, Bush was not intimidated by the lack of a plurality in his election, the nature of its resolution, or the loss of Republican seats in both houses of Congress. He ignored those who urged him to strike a bipartisan posture and hold off on his major initiatives. The White House understood that the one policy that both unified and energized Republicans was tax cuts. Although most congressional Democrats would oppose the cuts, a majority of the public, including Independents and even some Democrats, would support or at least tolerate them. Equally important, Congress could consider tax cuts, unlike most other major policies, under rules that prohibited a filibuster. Thus, a united, although slender, majority could—and did—prevail.

Barack Obama campaigned on a platform of major change in policy, enjoyed substantial Democratic majorities in both houses of Congress, and thought his rhetorical skills would allow him to maintain the public's support for his major initiatives. He did get several significant pieces of legislation through Congress, but he also disappointed his supporters by failing to pass reforms of tax policy, immigration, environmental protection and climate change, and other key issues. He had misestimated his ability to win support from the public and congressional Republicans. Like Bill Clinton, he led the Democrats to a major defeat in the 2010 midterm elections, losing his majority in the House.[69]

PRESIDENTIAL LEGISLATIVE SKILLS

Aside from party leadership and public approval, there are other dimensions of White House efforts to persuade members of Congress to support the president's legislative proposals. The president aims some of these activities at building goodwill in the long run and others at obtaining votes from individual members of Congress on specific issues. Whatever the immediate goal, the nature of the legislative process in America demands that presidents apply their legislative skills in a wide range of situations. In the words of one presidential aide:

> Senator A might come with us if Senator B, an admired friend, could be persuaded to talk to him. Senator C wanted a major project out of Chairman D's committee; maybe D, a supporter of our bill, would release it in exchange for C's commitment. Senator E might be reached through people in his home state. If Senator F could not vote with us on final passage, could he vote with us on key amendments? Could G take a trip? Would the President call Senator H?[70]

Congressional Liaison

Although the Constitution establishes separate institutions, the operation of the government requires those institutions to work together. We expect presidents to propose legislation and to get it enacted into law. Clearly, they need all the help they can get. To assist them in these efforts as well as with their other ongoing legislative responsibilities, a White House congressional liaison staff has operated since 1953.

In addition to representing the president's views to members of Congress, the office now caters to the constituency needs of members, gathers intelligence on members' views on legislation, tracks the progress of legislation through the congressional labyrinth, coordinates department and agency legislative efforts, and works closely with the congressional leadership of the president's party. Supplementing these efforts, the White House political office handles patronage and other party-related matters, while the intergovernmental affairs office orchestrates state and local officials behind other administration initiatives.

The White House also established a public liaison office to organize outside groups and community leaders into coalitions behind the administration's proposals.[71] Once established, the White House typically orchestrates these coalitions to mount grassroots efforts directed toward Congress. The public liaison office identifies the positions of members on key issues, targets those who are wavering, and has group representatives from their own constituencies contact them. It also organizes mass letter-writing and telephoning campaigns. The White House designs these constituency-based pressures to make it easier for members of Congress to vote with the president, regardless of their party affiliation, by providing them political cover.

Congressional liaison has developed and expanded because it serves the needs of both the executive and legislative branches. For Congress, it helps integrate legislative views into executive policy making, services constituency needs, forces presidents to indicate their legislative priorities, provides channels for reaching compromises, and helps the leadership to form majority coalitions. For presidents, it enables them to gain a congressional perspective, communicate their views to Congress, mobilize support for their programs, and reach accommodations with the legislature. Such efforts to bridge the constitutional separation have helped to overcome some of the hurdles in the formulation of public policy.

In addition to institutionalized efforts to deal with Congress, presidents and their liaison aides employ particular legislative techniques in their efforts to win support for the administration's proposals on Capitol Hill.

Making Personal Appeals

A special aspect of presidential involvement in the legislative process is the personal appeal for votes. According to presidential scholar Richard Neustadt, "When the chips are down, there is no substitute for the President's own footwork, his personal negotiation, his direct appeal, his voice and no other's on the telephone."[72] Members of Congress are as subject to flattery as other people, and they are equally impressed when the president calls.

Calls from the president must be relatively rare to maintain their usefulness and will have less impact if he (or she) makes them too often. Moreover, members might begin to expect calls, for which the president has limited time, or they might resent the White House applying too much high-level pressure on them. In contrast, they might exploit a call by saying they are uncertain about an issue in order to extract a favor from the president.

Presidents usually become intensely involved only after the long process of lining up votes is almost done and their calls are necessary to win on an important issue (a situation that arises only a few times a year). A good example occurred on the final House vote on President Obama's health-care plan in March 2010. After studying the head counts prepared by the White House congressional liaison and the congressional party whips offices, Obama focused on representatives who were uncommitted or weakly committed in either direction. He engaged in a round-the-clock effort in which he delved into arcane policy discussions, promised favors, and mapped out election strategy. He met with or called dozens of lawmakers,[73] including ninety-two in the week before the final House vote in March 2010.[74] As one Washington reporter put it, "Some fence-sitters nearly drowned in presidential attention."[75] As a result, the president, with the invaluable aid of Speaker Nancy Pelosi, was able to garner enough votes to eke out a narrow victory.

Despite the prestige of their office, their invocations of national interest, and their persuasiveness, presidents often fail in their personal appeals. For example, President Eisenhower liked to depend heavily on charm and reason. In 1953, he tried to persuade Republican chairman Daniel Reed of the House Ways and Means Committee to support the continuance of the excess profits tax and to oppose a tax cut. "I used every possible reason, argument, and device, and every kind of personal and indirect contact," he wrote, "to bring Chairman Reed to my way of thinking." Nonetheless, he failed.[76] Similarly, Lyndon Johnson was renowned for his persuasiveness but nevertheless failed on many issues, ranging from civil rights and education to Medicare and the Panama uprising. "No matter how many times I told Congress to do something," he wrote, "I could never force it to act."[77] If Eisenhower and Johnson often failed in their efforts at persuasion, we should not be surprised that other presidents have failed as well.

In addition, even members of his own party may not want to hear from the president. Donald Trump branded himself as a great "closer" of deals, but he has yet to show he can do so with Congress. He has not been an effective negotiator. His policy stances are often vague and frequently inconsistent, and he lacks command of policy. These characteristics make him an unskilled, unreliable, and untrustworthy negotiator.[78] When the Senate was considering its health-care bill in 2017, the Republican Senate leadership made it known that they would much rather have Vice President Pence negotiate with undecided or recalcitrant senators than have President Trump trying to convince them to support the bill.[79]

Olivier Douliery/dpa/picture alliance/Newscom

Presidents frequently try to persuade members of Congress to support their initiatives. Here President Trump meets with Represent Greg Walden of Oregon.

Bargaining

It is part of the conventional wisdom that the White House regularly "buys" votes through bargains struck with members of Congress. There can be no question that many bargains occur and that they take a variety of forms. Reagan's budget director, David Stockman, recalled, "the last 10 or 20 percent of the votes needed for a majority of both houses [on the 1981 tax cut] had to be bought, period." "The hogs were really feeding," he declared. "The greed level, the level of opportunism, just got out of control."[80] Winning the votes of wavering lawmakers and the support of powerful industries for his ambitious energy and climate-change legislation required the Obama White House to make many compromises and outright gifts. The biggest concessions went to utilities, but rural interests, automakers, steel companies, natural gas drillers, refiners, universities, and real estate agents all got in on the action.[81]

Nevertheless, bargaining, in the form of trading support on two or more policies or providing specific benefits for representatives and senators, occurs less often and plays a less critical role in the creation of presidential coalitions in Congress than one might think. For obvious reasons, the White House does not want to encourage the type of bargaining Stockman described.

The president cannot bargain with Congress as a whole, because it is too large and decentralized for one bargain to satisfy everyone. In addition, the president's time is limited, as are the administration's resources—only a certain number of appointive jobs are available, and the federal budget is restricted. As Barack Obama put it, "one of the things that's changed from the Johnson era obviously is I don't have a postmaster job. Good-government reforms have hamstrung an administration."[82] Moreover, funding for public works projects is in the hands of Congress. Thus, most of the bargains between the president and Congress are implicit. The lack of respectability surrounding bargaining also encourages implicitness.

In addition, if the White House strikes many direct bargains, word will rapidly spread, everyone will want to trade, and persuasive efforts will fail. A good example occurred in 1993 when President Clinton proposed to increase user fees for grazing and mineral rights on federal land. Following protests from Western senators, whose votes he needed for his budget, the president told them he would remove the fees from his budget and deal with them separately in a bill later in the session. His decision opened a Pandora's Box because it signaled to every interest group in Washington that he would cave in to pressure. Member of Congress quickly inundated him with requests to change his budget in other ways. The word was out that the president could be "rolled."

Fortunately for the president, bargaining with everyone in Congress is not necessary. Except on vetoes and treaties, the White House only needs a simple majority of those voting, and thus a large part of Congress can be "written off" on any given vote. Moreover, presidents generally start with a substantial core of party supporters and then add to this number those of the other party who agree with their views on ideological or policy grounds. Others may provide support because of goodwill that a president has generated through White House services, constituency interest, or high levels of public support. Thus, the president needs to bargain only if all these groups fail to provide a majority for crucial votes, and he (or she) need only bargain with enough people to provide that majority.

Because resources are scarce, presidents will usually try to use them for bargaining with powerful members of Congress, such as committee chairs or those whose votes are most important. There is no guarantee senators and representatives will accept a tendered bargain, however. The members may not desire what the president offers, or they may be able to obtain what they want on their own. This is, of course, particularly true of the most powerful members, whose support the president needs most. Sometimes, members of Congress do not want to trade at all because of constituency opinion or personal views. At other times, the president may be unwilling to bargain.

Most of the pressure for bargaining actually comes from Capitol Hill. When the White House calls and asks for support, representatives and senators frequently raise a question regarding some request that they have made. In the words of a presidential aide, "Every time we make a special appeal to a Congressman to change his position, he eventually comes back with a request for a favor ranging in importance from one of the President's packages of matches to a judgeship or cabinet appointment for a 'worthy constituent'."[83]

More general bargains also take place. In the words of Richard Nixon's chief congressional aide, William Timmons, "I think they [members of Congress] knew that we would try our best to help them on all kinds of requests if they supported the President, and we did. It kind of goes without saying." His successor in the Ford administration, Max Friedersdorf, added his assurance that people who want things want to be in the position of supporting the president. This implicit trading on "accounts" is more common than explicit bargaining.[84]

For the White House, a member of Congress indebted to the president is easier to approach and ask for a vote. For the member, previous support increases the chances of the president honoring a request. Thus, officeholders at both ends of Pennsylvania Avenue want to be in each other's favor. The degree of debt determines the strategy used in presidential requests for support. Although services and favors increase the president's chances of obtaining support, presidents do not usually exchange them for votes directly. They are strategic, not tactical, weapons.

Providing Services and Amenities

As a member of Congress who is indebted to the president is easier to approach to ask for a vote, the White House provides many services and amenities for representatives and senators. Although it may bestow these favors on any member of Congress, they actually go disproportionately to members of the president's party. "The White House certainly remembers who its friends are," Lawrence F. O'Brien, head of the congressional liaison office, both warned and promised legislators early in the Kennedy administration.[85] Personal amenities used to create goodwill include social contact with the president, flattery, rides on Air Force One, visits to Camp David, birthday greetings, theater tickets for the presidential box at the Kennedy Center, invitations to bill-signing ceremonies, pictures with the president, briefings, and a plethora of others, the number and variety of which are limited only by the imagination of the president and his staff.

In addition, the White House often helps members of Congress with their constituents. A wide range of services is offered, including greetings to elderly and other "worthy" constituents, signed presidential photographs, presidential tie clasps and other White House memorabilia, reprints of speeches, information about government programs, White House pressure on agencies in favor of constituents, passing the nominations of constituents on to agencies, influence on local editorial writers, ceremonial appointments to commissions, meetings with the president, and arguments to be used to explain votes to constituents. The president may also help members of Congress please constituents through patronage, pork-barrel projects and government contracts, and aid with legislation that is of special interest to particular constituencies. Districts and counties receive systematically more federal outlays when legislators in the president's party represent them.[86]

Campaign aid is yet another service that the White House can provide to party members, and the president may dangle it before them to entice support. This aid may come in various forms, including campaign speeches by the president and executive officials for congressional candidates, funds and advice from the party national committees, presidential endorsements, pictures with the president, and letters of appreciation from the president. Recent presidents have been especially active in directly raising funds for their parties' candidates.

Administrations are not equally active in providing services and amenities for members of Congress. The Johnson and Reagan White Houses fall at the "active" end of this spectrum, while the Nixon and Carter presidencies fall at the other end. However, any such differences are relatively small in comparison with the efforts made by every recent administration to develop goodwill among its party members in Congress. Although this activity is to the advantage of all presidents and may earn them a fair hearing and the benefit of the doubt in some instances, party members consider it their right to receive favors from the White House and are unlikely to be especially responsive to the president's largesse.

Pressuring

Just as presidents can offer the carrot, they can also wield the stick. The increased campaign resources available to the White House in recent years provide increased opportunities to levy sanctions in the form of the withholding of favors. As the deputy chairman of the Republican National Committee said, there is more money than ever "to play hardball with. We're loaded for bear."[87] The threats of such actions are effective primarily with members of the president's party, of course, because members of the opposition party do not expect to receive many favors from the president.

Although sanctions or threats of sanctions are far from an everyday occurrence, they do happen. These may take the form of excluding a member from White House social events, denying routine requests for White House tour tickets, or shutting off access to the president. Each of these personal slights sends a signal of presidential displeasure. More dramatically, after Senator Richard Shelby complained about President Clinton's budget package, the White House announced that it was moving the management team for a space shuttle contract from Alabama to Texas, which constituted a loss of jobs for the senator's state. To add insult to injury, it gave Senator Shelby only one ticket to the White House ceremony honoring the University of Alabama football team; Senator Howell Heflin, Alabama's other senator, received eleven.

Senator James Jeffords of Vermont irritated the George W. Bush administration by his lack of support of some of the president's principal initiatives. The White House did not invite the senator to a ceremony honoring a Vermont teacher, cut Jeffords (chairman of the Senate Education Committee) out of the loop on the administration's education proposal, withheld its support for a Northeastern dairy compact important to him, and passed the word to reporters that Jeffords would learn to rue his rebelliousness.

Heavy-handed pressure is unusual, however, because it can be self-defeating. The White House backtracked on moving the National Aeronautics and Space Administration (NASA) team from Alabama. Nevertheless, Senator Shelby switched parties to fight the president more effectively as a Republican. Similarly, Senator

Jeffords left the Republican Party, costing the president his majority in the Senate. Because of the potential for such responses, presidents generally avoid punishing members of Congress. As Lyndon Johnson's chief congressional liaison aide Lawrence O'Brien put it, the White House sometimes offered positive inducements but "we didn't carry any big stick."[88] You can read about Donald Trump's use of the stick in box 11.2.

Box 11.2 ★ Trump Pressures Members of Congress

Machiavelli argued that it was better to be feared than loved. Donald Trump seems to have taken this advice to heart. Speaking more broadly, he told the *Washington Post*, "Real power is—I don't even want to use the word: 'fear'."[89] It is not surprising, then, that he frequently—and publically—criticized and threatened members of Congress, including congressional Republicans.[90]

As the House was considering its health-care bill in April 2017, Republican Mark Sanford of South Carolina, who was skeptical about the proposal, reported that Trump sent an emissary to tell him that "the president hopes you vote against this because he wants to run somebody against you if you do." Sanford said Trump "has made those kinds of threats to any number of members. . . . But I don't think it's productive to his own legislative agenda. It doesn't make anybody's day when the president of the United States says, 'I want to take you out'."[91]

When it came time for the Senate to vote on its health-care bill in June 2017, America First, a "super PAC" aligned with the president, started an ad campaign against Republican Senator Dean Heller of Nevada, who said he opposed the bill. Republican Majority Leader Mitch McConnell called White House chief of staff Reince Priebus to complain that the attacks were "beyond stupid." McConnell told Priebus that the assault by the group not only jeopardized the bill's prospects but also imperiled Heller's already difficult path to reelection.[92]

Trump and other administration officials also criticized and threatened other Republican senators. The secretary of the Interior even told Lisa Murkowski of Alaska that the administration might change its policy of allowing increased energy exploration in her state if she did not support the president on health care. Nevertheless, she persisted in her opposition.

The *Washington Post* reported that members of Congress regard many of Trump's threats as empty, concluding that crossing the president poses little danger. One senior Republican close to both the White House and many senators called Trump and his political operation "a paper tiger," noting how many GOP lawmakers feel free "to go their own way."[93]

However, the nationalization of politics in recent years has accorded the president some additional influence with members of his party. Donald Trump leveraged his popularity with Republicans in the public to threaten Republicans in Congress with defeats in party primaries if they did not support him. In some cases, his tactics seem to have worked.

There is an inherent limitation to pressuring members of Congress. In his business dealings, Trump's negotiating protocol typically prioritized "take it or leave it offers." That strategy assumes that negotiators can always turn to other bargaining partners to make a different deal. In real estate, for example, Trump liked to keep several balls in the air "because most deals fall out."[94] Unlike business transactions, in which there are many possible deals with many possible partners, he has no alternative but to deal with Congress. Republican Darrell Issa of California said few members of Congress fear permanent retaliation from the president. "He comes from the private sector, where your business partner today isn't always your business partner tomorrow," Issa said. In Washington, "Just because you're one way today doesn't mean you're written off."[95]

Party organizations contribute millions of dollars to House and Senate candidates. However, usually the parties do not use these contributions as incentives to encourage party loyalty. Nor do they withhold funds to punish members who stray from the party line. Instead, the party committees act pragmatically to enhance the prospects of winning elections for all viable candidates, especially those running in competitive districts or states.[96]

Consulting

Consulting with members of Congress on legislation can be advantageous for the White House. Members of Congress appreciate advance warning of presidential proposals, especially those that affect their constituencies directly. No official, especially an elected one, wants to be blindsided. Politicians quite naturally want to be prepared to take credit or avoid blame. Moreover, when a policy fails, members of Congress are unlikely to support the president in the perilous landing of the policy if they are not involved in the take-off.

Consultation before announcing a bill may also be useful in anticipating congressional objections. It may, in fact, be possible to preempt some of the opposition with strategic compromises and to garner some advance commitments. At the very least, members of Congress will feel they have had an opportunity to be heard. They take pride in their work and may be offended if they feel the White House has not taken them seriously.

Despite these advantages, presidential consultation with Congress has often played a modest role in presidential-congressional relations.[97] Consultation is not easy to accomplish. Arriving at a common position within the executive branch may tax the resources and patience of the White House, particularly at a time when other exigencies press on the president and senior staff. Extending the negotiations to the legislature (and thus the public) and broadening the conflict may render the process of policy formulation unmanageable and increase its costs significantly. White House officials often are also concerned with the nature of Congress, which they frequently view as parochial, sieve-like, and prone to transform important matters of state into pork-barrel issues.

Time is an ever-present factor in White House operations, and it influences consultation with Congress as well. If there are severe deadlines on the production of a presidential initiative, consultation may be difficult. In addition, a president with an extensive legislative agenda may send a large number of bills to Congress, restricting the time officials can devote to consulting on any one of them. Donald Trump has a modest legislative agenda and routinely calls some members of Congress. His calls tend to be unfocused, however, and do not concentrate on policy development.[98]

A president with firm ideas on policy or with a proposal that might engender opposition is unlikely to relish consulting with Congress in order to make compromises to satisfy congressional desires. In addition, the White House designs some presidential proposals to assuage constituency groups or fulfill campaign promises, which significantly constrains the possibilities of modifying these bills in response to congressional consultation.

Some observers propose that the White House involve relevant members of Congress in the process of developing the president's legislative program, the rationale being that those who have been involved in formulating a bill are more likely to support it after it is sent to the Hill. This process is not typical, however, because chief executives have found it too cumbersome to include members of Congress, especially those of the opposition party, in writing legislation, and most members of Congress prefer to protect their status as members of an independent branch.

Setting Priorities

An important aspect of a president's legislative strategy can be establishing priorities among legislative proposals. The goal of this effort is to set the congressional agenda. If the president is not able to focus the attention of Congress on his priority programs, these bills may become lost in the complex and overloaded legislative process. Congress needs time to digest what the president sends, to come up with independent analysis, and to schedule hearings and markups of bills. Unless the president gives some indication of what is most important, Congress will simply put the proposals in a queue where they will compete with each other for attention, often with disastrous results for the president.

Queuing is especially likely to be a problem if much of the president's program must go through a single committee, as was the case for Jimmy Carter and the House Ways and Means Committee in 1977. Thus, it may be wise to spread legislative proposals among several committees so that they can work on different parts of the president's agenda at the same time.

Setting priorities is also important because presidents and their staff can lobby effectively for only a few bills at once. Moreover, the president's political capital is inevitably limited, so it is sensible to focus it on the issues the administration cares about most. In 1977, Jimmy Carter spent his political capital on ending pork-barrel water projects, which was not one of his priority items. Similarly, in 1993, Bill Clinton risked losing focus on his economic and health-care programs by proposing a host of controversial policies on abortion, homosexuals in the military, campaign reform, and environmental protection, among others. He initiated many of these policies in response to pressures from segments of his party for action following twelve years of Republican presidents.

Tax cuts, education reform, an overhaul of defense policy, and greater federal support for faith-based social welfare programs were the top priorities of the new George W. Bush administration. The president spoke extensively about each initiative, and the administration went to considerable lengths to focus attention on these priority proposals. The faith-based initiative received attention in the week after the inauguration, followed in successive weeks by education, tax cuts, and defense. Similarly, the president focused on a few initiatives, including reforming Social Security, the tax code, and personal injury lawsuits, in his second term.

Setting priorities in the early weeks of a new administration is also important because, during his first months in office, the president has the greatest latitude in focusing on priority legislation. The White House can put off dealing with the full spectrum of national issues for a period of months at the beginning of the term of a new president, but it cannot do so indefinitely. Eventually it must decide on them. By the second year, the agenda is full and more policies are in the pipeline as the administration attempts to satisfy its constituencies and responds to unanticipated, or simply overlooked, problems, including international crises. These issues affect simultaneously the attention of the public and the priorities of Congress and thus the White House's success in focusing attention on its priority issues.[99]

In addition, presidents themselves may distract from their own legislative priorities. The more the White House tries to do, the more difficult it is to focus the country's attention on a few priority items. As we have seen, presidents have so many demands to speak and decide on issues that it is impossible for White House planners to organize their schedules to focus the attention of Congress and the public for an extended period on their major goals.

Focusing attention on priorities is considerably easier for a president with a short legislative agenda, such as Ronald Reagan's, than it is for one with a more ambitious agenda, such as Barack Obama's. Obama began proposing his large agenda immediately after taking office. Moreover, Democrats had a laundry list of initiatives that George W. Bush had blocked, ranging from gender pay equity and children's health insurance to tougher tobacco regulations and a new public service initiative. In addition, there were recession-related efforts to provide mortgage relief and curb predatory banking practices to complement the president's economic stimulus measure. The more the White House tried to do, the more difficult it was to focus the country's attention on priority issues. Once the administration had put in place policies to deal with the worst of the crises Obama inherited, it moved on to health care, climate change, Afghanistan, and other major initiatives. The result was a perception in the public about a loss of focus on unemployment, prompting a shift back to the economy at the beginning of the president's second year in office.

The president communicates with the public in a congested communications environment clogged with competing messages from a wide variety of sources, through a wide range of media, and on a staggering array of subjects.[100] Congress is quite capable of setting its own agenda and is unlikely to defer to the president for long, especially if the opposition party controls one or both chambers. A year into Barack Obama's tenure, White House communications director Dan Pfeiffer declared, "It was clear that too often we didn't have the ball—Congress had the ball in terms of driving the message."[101]

Moving Quickly

The president must move quickly to exploit the honeymoon atmosphere that typically characterizes the early months of a new administration. First-year proposals have a better chance of passing Congress than do those sent to the Hill later in an administration. Lyndon Johnson explained, "You've got to give it all you can in that first year. . . . You've got just one year when they treat you right."[102] Despite a severely truncated transition because of the disputed election results, George W. Bush lost no time in sending priority bills to Congress. Proposals for a large cut in income taxes, education reform, and increased support for faith-based charities went to Congress in short order. Barack Obama began promoting his economic stimulus program during the transition period so that Congress would be in a position to pass it shortly after he took office.

The failure to be ready to propose priority legislation can be costly. A policy vacuum existed in the approximately ten months between Bill Clinton's inauguration and the arrival of a complete health-care reform proposal on Capitol Hill. In this vacuum, issues of relatively low priority such as the homosexuals in the military issue received disproportionate attention in the press and may have cost the administration vital goodwill that it needed in its search for support for its cornerstone policy. In addition, the president was forced to raise health-care reform in the context of major expenditures of political capital in battles on behalf of his budget and NAFTA.

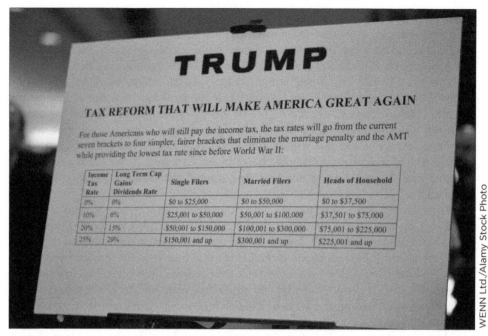

TRUMP

TAX REFORM THAT WILL MAKE AMERICA GREAT AGAIN

For those Americans who will still pay the income tax, the tax rates will go from the current seven brackets to four simpler, fairer brackets that eliminate the marriage penalty and the AMT while providing the lowest tax rate since before World War II:

Income Tax Rate	Long Term Cap Gains/ Dividends Rate	Single Filers	Married Filers	Heads of Household
0%	0%	$0 to $25,000	$0 to $50,000	$0 to $37,500
10%	0%	$25,001 to $50,000	$50,001 to $100,000	$37,501 to $75,000
20%	15%	$50,001 to $150,000	$100,001 to $300,000	$75,001 to $225,000
25%	20%	$150,001 and up	$300,001 and up	$225,001 and up

WENN Ltd./Alamy Stock Photo

Presidents should move quickly to exploit the opportunity to pass legislation early in their terms. President Trump had only the most basic outline of a tax policy, however, delaying consideration for months.

Donald Trump was also not ready to move on his agenda. Although on the campaign trail he promised to reform taxes, spending, health care, immigration, and other major policy areas and to initiate substantial new spending on infrastructure, he was not ready with plans to send to Congress. Indeed, he had no plans. His budget was months late. Thus, he had to wait for Congress to develop policies at its pace, which delayed the process, slowed momentum, and pushed difficult decisions nearer to the 2018 midterm elections. The delays also entangled the legislation with battles over the debt ceiling and the budget.

The danger, of course, is in proposing a policy without thorough analysis in order to exploit this favorable political climate. This hastiness appears to have occurred with the budget cuts that Reagan proposed in early 1981. In this case, the administration kept departments, including cabinet members, and their expertise at a distance in the executive decision-making process. Although taking time to draft proposals does not guarantee that they will be well conceived, it is by no means clear that the rapid drafting of legislation is in the best interests of the nation.

It is easier for a president who has a small agenda with an essentially negative character, such as Ronald Reagan's agenda of cutting taxes or domestic spending, to move rapidly to exploit the honeymoon. It is much more difficult to draft complex legislation rapidly, a problem Jimmy Carter faced in his first year when he tried to deal with issues such as energy, welfare reform, and the containment of health costs. Bill Clinton and Barack Obama faced similar problems with their health-care reform programs. In contrast, Kennedy and Johnson had the advantage of a party program that had been building up during the 1950s when the Democrats were not in the White House.

Structuring Choice

Framing issues in ways that favor the president's programs may set the terms of the debate and thus the premises on which members of Congress cast their votes. The key vote on Ronald Reagan's budget cuts in 1981 was on the rule determining whether there would be a single vote of yea or nay in the House. Once the House adopted the rule, the White House could frame the issue as a vote for or against the popular president, and the broad nature of the reconciliation bill shifted the debate from the losses of individual programs to the benefits of the package as a whole. Although Reagan could not win an important individual vote on cutting a social welfare program, by structuring the choice facing Congress he was required only to win one vote and could avoid much of the potential criticism for specific reductions in spending.

Portraying policies in terms of criteria on which there is a consensus, and playing down divisive issues, are often at the core of efforts to structure choices for Congress. For example, federal aid to education had been a divisive issue for years before President Johnson proposed the Elementary and Secondary Education Act in 1965. To blunt opposition, he successfully changed the focus of debate from teachers' salaries and classroom shortages to fighting poverty and from the separation of church and state to aiding children. This change in the premises of congressional decision making eased the path for the bill.

Although the structuring of choices can be a useful tool for the president, there is no guarantee that it will succeed, and opponents of the president's policies are unlikely to defer to an administration's attempts to structure choices on the issues. On President Clinton's first major legislative proposal—his fiscal stimulus package—Republicans succeeded in defining his economic program in terms of pork-barrel spending instead of increasing employment. In response to his first budget, the Republicans focused public debate on tax increases rather than economic growth or deficit reduction. Clinton attempted to depict his health-care plan in comforting, affordable terms. His opponents did not simply submit, however, and launched an aggressive advertising campaign that characterized the president's plan as expensive, experimental, providing lower-quality and rationed care, costing jobs, and bringing a lot more government and red tape to health care. In the end, public debate focused on the reform's pitfalls. The president's difficulty in defining himself and his policies frustrated him. As Clinton reflected, "The thing that has surprised me most is how difficult it is . . . to really keep communicating what you're about to the American people."[103]

Donald Trump has been no more successful in structuring choice. He promoted taxes as agents of economic growth, but more people saw them as giveaways to the wealthy and a cause of exploding deficits. He advocated restricting immigration in terms of protecting the country from gangs and terrorists, job losses to "illegal aliens," amnesty for lawbreakers, and assaults on American values. Opponents, however, saw unfairness to Dreamers and other "undocumented immigrants," a loss of needed workers, a barrier to uniting families, religious discrimination, and racism.

The Context of Influence

In our discussion of the president's legislative skills, it is important to keep in mind the general context in which a president operates today—a period characterized by congressional assertiveness. The diminished deference to the president by individual members of Congress and the institution as a whole naturally makes presidential influence more problematic.

Stable prices, sustained economic growth, and expansive government characterized the Kennedy-Johnson years. The prosperity of the 1960s provided the federal
government with the funds for implementing new policies with little risk. Officials did
not have to raises taxes or make sacrifices in order to help the underprivileged. The
late 1970s to the late 1990s, however, was a period in which government resources
were scarce—in part because of the continuing cost of the programs enacted in the
1960s. Such a condition made the passage of expensive new programs more difficult. When resources are scarce, presidents face internal competition for them and
the breakdown of supporting coalitions. They must choose between policies rather
than building coalitions for several policies through logrolling.

George W. Bush was the first president in nearly forty years to begin his tenure
with slack resources, easing the path for passage of a large tax cut. Barack Obama
took office under conditions of a financial crisis in which the government was running huge deficits. The desperation of the country, however, created conditions for
the passage of a massive stimulus bill.

The Impact of Legislative Skills

In general, presidential legislative skills must compete, as does public support, with
other, more stable factors that affect voting in Congress, including party, ideology,
personal views and commitments on specific policies, and constituency interests. By
the time a president tries to exercise influence on a vote, most members of Congress
have made up their minds on the basis of these other factors.

Systematic quantitative studies have found that, once we control for the status
of their party in Congress and their standing with the public, presidents renowned
for their legislative skills (such as Lyndon Johnson) are generally no more successful
in winning votes (even close ones) or obtaining congressional support than those,
such as Jimmy Carter, who are considered to have been less adept in dealing with
Congress.[104] Even skilled presidents cannot change the contours of the political landscape and create opportunities for change very much. However, they can recognize
favorable configurations of political forces, such as those that existed in 1933, 1965,
and 1981, which they can effectively exploit to embark on major shifts in public policy. Franklin D. Roosevelt, Lyndon Johnson, and Ronald Reagan were particularly
effective in exploiting their resources in their early years in office; Jimmy Carter, Bill
Clinton, and Donald Trump were not.

It is not necessary to take an extreme position to obtain a better understanding
of the nature of presidential leadership. There are times, of course, when presidents
do persuade some members of Congress to change their votes. A famous example
of apparent large-scale change occurred over the Panama Canal treaties, ratified in
1978. In the fall of 1976, shortly before Jimmy Carter became president, forty-eight
senators introduced a resolution pledging not to approve any change in the existing
treaties regarding the canal. After a full-court press, Carter obtained the two-thirds
vote in the Senate to ratify the new treaties.[105]

The issue is not whether persuasion is *ever* successful in moving a member of
Congress. Instead, the question is whether persuasion is typically the key to presidential success in Congress. Examples such as the Panama Canal treaties are rare.
Whatever the circumstances, the impact of persuasion on the outcome is usually
relatively modest. As Calvin Mouw and Michael MacKuen conclude, "presidential
influence in Congress does not rely on persuasion."[106] Although potentially important, conversion is likely to be at the margins of coalition building rather than at the

core of policy change. Presidential legislative leadership is more useful in exploiting discrete opportunities than in creating broad possibilities for policy change.

THE VETO

Sometimes, presidents not only fail to win passage of their proposals but Congress also passes legislation to which the White House is strongly opposed. Because the legislature must present all bills and joint resolutions, except those proposing constitutional amendments, to the president for approval, he has another opportunity to influence legislation: the veto.

When Congress passes an item and submits it to the president, he has several options. Within ten days (Sundays excepted) of its presentation, the president may (1) sign the measure, in which case it becomes the law of the land; (2) not sign the measure and return it to the house in which it originated with a message stating the reasons for withholding approval; or (3) do nothing.

When the president returns to Congress a bill or joint resolution, he has vetoed it. The legislation can then become law only if each house of Congress repasses it by a two-thirds majority of those present. Congress may override the presidential veto at any time before it adjourns *sine die* (i.e., before the end of that particular Congress).

The veto's origin in America stems from the British colonial experience where the veto served as a means by which colonial governors could protect the interests of the crown. The clashes with the local assemblies that the exercise of the veto produced led the Constitution's framers to qualify the exercise of the veto by allowing two-thirds of both houses to override it.

Early presidents exercised their veto power sparingly; the first six presidents vetoed a total of eight bills. However, the seventh president, Andrew Jackson, vetoed twelve, and his successors have followed his example. Once partisan competition before a broad electorate developed in Jackson's era, there was a greater incentive for presidents to use the veto power to stake out positions and for Congress to take positions by passing legislation it knew the president would veto.[107] The early norm according to which "adversarial" vetoes were considered illegitimate was also less constraining.[108]

The president can veto only an entire bill. Unlike most state governors, presidents do not have an item veto, which would allow them to veto specific provisions of a bill. Because of this constraint, members of Congress use a number of strategies to avoid a possible veto of a particular proposal. For example, Congress may add increased appropriations or riders (i.e., nongermane provisions) that the White House might not want to bills that it otherwise desires, thus forcing the president to decide whether to accept these unattractive provisions in order to gain the legislation. In most such cases, presidents desist from using their vetoes. For example, after President Carter vetoed a bill providing for increased salaries for Public Health Service physicians, Congress added the pay raise to mental health services legislation, a pet project of First Lady Rosalynn Carter, and the president signed the bill.

In 1987, Congress passed the entire discretionary budget of the federal government in one omnibus bill. Consequently, the president had to accept the whole package or else lose appropriations for the entire government. President Reagan frequently called for a constitutional amendment giving the president an item veto, and Presidents Bush and Clinton followed his example. They argued that an item veto would allow the president to stop unnecessary spending within massive appropriations bills and thus help to bring the budget under control.

In 1996, Congress heeded their call with a bill that created an elaborate mechanism for the president to veto specific items in legislation. President Clinton cast eighty-two such vetoes, but opponents challenged the line-item veto in the courts. They charged that Article I of the Constitution vests all legislative power in Congress; the president can only accept or reject bills in their entirety. The new veto, the lawsuits argued, gave the president the power to change a law—or amend it—after he has signed it. In 1998, the Supreme Court agreed, finding the bill to be unconstitutional in *Clinton v. New York City*.

If the president does nothing after receiving a measure from Congress, it becomes law after ten days (Sundays excepted), provided Congress remains in session. If it has adjourned during the ten-day period, thus preventing the president from returning the bill to the house of its origination, the bill is pocket vetoed. A pocket veto kills a piece of legislation just as a regular veto does. Historically, somewhat fewer than half of all vetoes have been pocket vetoes. Table 11.6 presents data on the vetoes by recent presidents.

Presidents have sometimes attempted to use the pocket veto by taking no action on measures sent to them just before Congress went into a temporary recess and claiming that the recess prevented them from returning their veto for congressional consideration. (In 1964, President Johnson pocket vetoed a bill during a congressional recess and then recalled and signed it.) However, in 1976, after the Nixon and Ford White Houses had lost litigation on the issue, the Ford administration promised that the president would not use the pocket veto during congressional recesses as long as Congress designated an official to be on hand to receive his vetoes. Since Congress is in session nearly all year, most people thought that only an adjournment *sine die* would provide the opportunity for a pocket veto.

Ronald Reagan used the pocket veto during a recess at the end of the 1981 session without apparent problems, but thirty-three House Democrats filed suit in

Table 11.6 Regular and Pocket Vetoes

President	Regular Vetoes	Pocket Vetoes	Total Vetoes
Eisenhower	73	108	181
Kennedy	12	9	21
Johnson	16	14	30
Nixon	26	17	43
Ford	48	18	66
Carter	13	18	31
Reagan	39	39	78
G. H. W. Bush	29	15	44
Clinton	37	1	38
G. W. Bush	12	0	12
Obama	12	0	12
Trump*	6	0	6

*As of January 2020.

federal court to challenge his pocket veto during the congressional recess at the end of 1983 of a bill making aid to El Salvador dependent on human rights progress. As a result, in 1984 a federal appeals court ruled against the president. Presidents since Reagan have claimed to have pocket vetoed some bills during congressional recesses, but Congress has treated them like regular vetoes.[109]

The last column in table 11.6 indicates that vetoes are infrequently used (George W. Bush issued no vetoes during his entire first term in office and Barack Obama issued only two). Not only are the absolute numbers low but also less than 1 percent of the bills passed by Congress (which typically number several hundred per session) are vetoed. The table also shows that presidents who face Congresses controlled by the opposition party (Eisenhower, Nixon, Ford, Reagan, and Bush) used more vetoes, as we would expect. Congress was more likely to pass legislation these presidents opposed.

Table 11.7 illustrates another important fact about vetoes—the tendency of Congress to sustain them. Congress does occasionally override a veto, however, especially when the president's party is in the minority in Congress. George W. Bush lost an unusually high percentage of vetoes after the Democrats regained control of Congress in the 2006 election. The legislature has passed some very important legislation over the president's veto. In the post–World War II era, such legislation includes the Taft-Hartley Labor Relations Act (1947), the McCarran-Walter Immigration Act (1952), the McCarran-Wood Internal Security Act (1950), and the War Powers Resolution (1973).

Sometimes presidents choose not to veto a bill, either because they feel that the good in it outweighs the bad or because they do not want Congress to override their veto. Thus, when Congress passed an amendment to a foreign aid authorization bill imposing new sanctions on China by such large margins that it was impossible to sustain a veto, President George H. W. Bush, who was opposed to it, nonetheless reluctantly signed the measure.

When a senator or representative introduces a bill in either house of Congress, the chamber's parliamentarian classifies it as public or private. Generally, public bills

Table 11.7 Vetoes Overridden

President	Regular Vetoes	Vetoes Overridden	Vetoes Overridden (%)
Eisenhower	73	2	3
Kennedy	12	0	0
Johnson	16	0	0
Nixon	26	7	27
Ford	48	12	25
Carter	13	2	15
Reagan	39	9	23
G. H. W. Bush	29	1	3
Clinton	37	2	5
G. W. Bush	12	4	33
Obama	12	1	8
Trump*	6	0	0

*As of January 2020.

relate to public matters and deal with individuals by classifications or categories, such as college students or the elderly. A private bill, in contrast, names a particular individual or entity that is to receive relief, such as through payment of a pension or a claim against the government or the granting of citizenship. Up until 1969, presidents usually vetoed more private than public bills. Recent presidents have vetoed very few private bills, however, reflecting the general decrease in private bills in Congress.

Sometimes the president uses the veto to stop legislation from passing at all. At other times, the White House uses the threat of a veto to shape legislation more to its liking. Presidents frequently threaten to veto bills unless certain provisions are removed or altered, and they usually receive concessions from Congress when they do.[110] For example, George H. W. Bush, a Republican facing large Democratic majorities in Congress, repeatedly made strategic use of the veto to move Congress in his direction. In a typical example, he vetoed a substantial increase in the federal minimum wage in 1989. This encouraged Congress to pass a more modest increase, which was acceptable to the president. President Clinton threatened to veto a large transportation bill in 1998 because it violated his 1997 budget agreement with Congress. Clinton's threatened veto gave leverage to members of Congress who wanted to trim the legislation, and they were successful.

George W. Bush focused his veto threats on appropriations that exceeded his budget and proposals that would alter his key policy initiatives. Usually, his veto threats succeeded in thwarting legislation he opposed, but his reluctance to veto appropriations bills undermined the credibility of his threats on spending measures. Nevertheless, veto threats on appropriations bills generally are effective in bringing the final legislation closer to the president's preferences.[111]

In a more unusual situation, in 1987 President Reagan threatened to veto the omnibus appropriations bill, which contained the money necessary for running the government for the following year, if Congress did not include certain provisions that he favored. Fearing a shutdown of the government, Congress acquiesced. Bill Clinton followed a similar strategy numerous times after he won a major battle with congressional Republicans that led to two unpopular government shutdowns in 1995–1996. Because the president succeeded in assigning to the Republicans culpability for the shutdowns, his threat to veto legislation that did not provide as much funding as he sought provided him important leverage in future budget negotiations.

Signing Statements

For nearly two centuries, presidents have issued *signing statements* addressing constitutional or other legal questions when signing bills into law after failing to convince Congress to modify legislative provisions that they oppose. Often such statements have not been controversial and have been used for rhetorical or hortatory purposes.[112] Yet presidents in the period since the New Deal, especially following the congressional resurgence of the 1970s, have used these statements to attempt to nullify legislative provisions.[113] The White House is most likely to object to a bill when the ideological distance between president and Congress is great.[114]

In *INS v. Chadha* (1983) the Supreme Court held unconstitutional provisions in legislation providing for a veto of executive action by one house of Congress. This decision also voided by implication committee vetoes and reporting requirements that Congress often requires before executive actions can be taken. The Court's decision, however, has not stopped Congress from writing such provisions into legislation and from informally requiring the executive to abide by them. Congress has been particularly active in giving Appropriations committees power over defense and foreign policy issues.[115]

In response to what they see as a violation of the separation powers, presidents, beginning with Reagan, began to identify such provisions and note their "unconstitutionality" when they signed legislation into law.[116] Signing statements function like a dialogue with Congress, routinely addressing general separation of powers themes rather than the substance of a law.[117] Reagan and his successors have also used the statements to keep department and agency officials in line with the president's views on how the law should be implemented.

More generally, recent presidents have used signing statements to challenge congressional provisions that interfered with the president's responsibility "to take care that the laws be faithfully executed" or his constitutional authority in foreign affairs, such as language that directs them in negotiations and discussions with international organizations and foreign governments and prohibits them from performing certain military missions.[118] George W. Bush was particularly active in the use of signing statements,[119] while Barack Obama continued the practice, albeit at a lesser pace. Donald Trump has followed the Bush pattern.[120]

Perhaps the most contentious of Bush's signing statements concerned the 2005 Detainee Treatment Act, which prohibited US personnel from using torture on enemy combatants and other foreign prisoners as a means of exacting information about terrorist activities. The president had opposed a blanket restriction against the use of torture, claiming that US interrogators needed flexibility to extract difficult-to-obtain information necessary to protect the United States against further acts of terrorism. He threatened to veto any legislation that contained such a provision. After Republican leaders in Congress informed Bush that Congress would likely overturn a veto, the president backed off his threat, agreed to some compromise language, and said he would approve the legislation. However, when he did so, Bush reiterated his contention that the part of the legislation that instructed the executive branch on how to execute the law was unconstitutional and therefore unenforceable.[121]

CONCLUSION

Presidents face an uphill battle in dealing with Congress.[122] Their formal powers of recommending legislation and vetoing bills help set the legislature's agenda and prevent some legislation from passing. However, these prerogatives are of only marginal help in obtaining what they want. Conflict between the executive and legislative branches is inherent in the US system of government. The overlapping powers of the two branches, their representation of different constituencies, and the contrast between the hierarchical, expert nature of the executive and the decentralized, generalist Congress guarantee that, except in extraordinary circumstances, conflict between them will remain a central feature of American politics.

The chief executive's assets in dealing with Congress do not provide silver bullets for the White House. Party leadership is a potential source of influence in Congress, and presidents receive considerably more support from members of their party than from the opposition. Much, or even most, of this support is the result of members of the same party sharing similar policy views and political incentives rather than the influence of the president's party leadership. Nevertheless, presidents work closely with their party and its leaders in Congress and tend to gain some increment of support as a result of party loyalty. Party support is undependable, however, as constituency interests, a lack of policy consensus, and other factors intervene and diminish the importance of the party label. Congressional party leaders are often in weak positions to move their troops in the president's direction. Ideally, presidents could influence the election of members of their party to Congress, but presidential coattails are short and midterm campaigning seems to have limited payoffs. Thus, presidents generally have to seek support from opposition party members, but their efforts at bipartisanship, although necessary, may strain relations with the less moderate wing of their own party.

Presidents are more likely to receive support in Congress when they have the public's approval than when they sit low in the polls. However, as we saw in chapter 4, they cannot depend on the public's support nor can they be sure of being able to mobilize new support. Moreover, public approval is usually a necessary but not a sufficient source of influence. Even when presidents are high in the polls, they will find it difficult to pass their programs if their party lacks a majority of congressional seats.

The White House engages in a large-scale legislative liaison effort to create goodwill and influence votes on a more personal level. Presidents consummate bargains, provide services and amenities, twist arms, call members of Congress and consult with them in advance. However, there are severe limits on a president's time and resources. Presidents can increase the chances of their success by moving programs early in their tenure and not letting those programs clog the legislative process. Many find it difficult or impossible to control the congressional agenda so neatly, however. Although presidential legislative skills are crucial in winning some votes, their importance is often exaggerated. Thus, presidents must constantly struggle to succeed in having their policies enacted into law.

Presidential leadership of Congress is at the margins most of the time. In general, successful presidential leadership of Congress has not been the result of the dominant chief executive of political folklore, who reshapes the contours of the political landscape to pave the way for change. Rather than creating the conditions for important shifts in public policy, the effective president is the less heroic figure of the facilitator, who works at the margins of building coalitions by recognizing and exploiting opportunities presented by a favorable configuration of political forces.

DISCUSSION QUESTIONS

1. Some argue that members of the president's party in Congress should simply vote their consciences and pay little attention to party loyalty to their leader. Others say that the only way that election promises can become law, and thus become meaningful to the majority of voters, is for the party to stick together and pass legislation. Should members of Congress defer principally to their party, to the president, or to their constituencies' interests?

2. Many people seem to think that divided government is good for the country because it prevents the president from concentrating too much power in the executive branch. Others view divided government as an obstacle to bringing about change because different parties control the Congress and the White House. What do you think? Is it good for people to split their tickets and vote for a president of one party and members of the House or Senate from the other party? What are the advantages and costs of divided government?

3. What can Donald Trump do to overcome congressional resistance to his major legislative initiatives? Which of the president's legislative activities have been most successful, and why were they successful?

WEB EXERCISES

1. One measure of presidential influence is the extent to which presidents can get Congress to enact bills they support. Go to the OMB website at http://www.whitehouse.gov/omb/public-releases and click on "Statements of Administration Policy" to determine the president's position on pending legislation. Follow the legislation to the relevant congressional committee using the Thomas website at http://Thomas.loc.gov. Determine if congressional committees have held hearings, called administration officials to testify, and marked up the bill and sent it to the floors of their respective houses. Of the legislation that reaches the floor, for which do you think the White House will lobby hardest? Predict whether the president will be successful in passing legislation he supports or stopping legislation he opposes.
2. Every president, including Donald Trump, Barack Obama, and George W. Bush, takes office articulating a desire for bipartisanship. Go to https://voteview.com/parties/all and look at the level of polarization in Congress over time. How much potential is there for President Trump to obtain bipartisanship support for his initiatives? Is he likely to be more successful in some policy areas than in others?
3. One of the hallmarks of the Trump presidency has been numerous investigations of the president's actions, his personal finances, and his administration's policies. Go to https://www.nytimes.com/interactive/2019/05/13/us/politics/trump-investigations.html and review the investigations at all levels of government. The White House's response has been to engage in a long-term strategy to stymie the investigations, refusing to turn over documents or allow administration officials to testify. Is Congress meeting its responsibility to oversee the executive? Should the president be more accommodating to congressional oversight?

SELECTED READINGS

Coleman, John J., and David C. W. Parker. "The Consequences of Divided Government." In *The Oxford Handbook of the American Presidency*, edited by George C. Edwards III and William G. Howell. Oxford, UK: Oxford University Press, 2009.

Edwards, George C., III. *At the Margins: Presidential Leadership of Congress*. New Haven, CT: Yale University Press, 1989.

———. "Presidential Approval as a Source of Influence in Congress." In *The Oxford Handbook of the American Presidency*, edited by George C. Edwards III and William G. Howell. Oxford, UK: Oxford University Press, 2009.

———. *The Strategic President: Persuasion and Opportunity in Presidential Leadership*. Princeton, NJ: Princeton University Press, 2009.

———. *Overreach: Leadership in the Obama Presidency*. Princeton, NJ: Princeton University Press, 2012.

———. *Predicting the Presidency: The Potential of Persuasive Leadership*. Princeton, NJ: Princeton University Press, 2016.

Fisher, Louis. *Constitutional Conflicts between Congress and the President*, 6th ed., rev. Lawrence: University Press of Kansas, 2014.

Grossback, Lawrence J., David A. M. Peterson, James A. Stimson. *Mandate Politics*. Cambridge, UK: Cambridge University Press, 2006.

Jones, Charles O. *The Presidency in a Separated System*, 2nd ed. Washington, DC: Brookings Institution, 2005.

Kriner, Douglas L., and Andrew Reeves. *The Particularistic President*. New York: Cambridge University Press, 2015.

Kriner, Douglas L., and Eric Schickler., *Investigating the President: Congressional Checks on Presidential Power*. Princeton, NJ: Princeton University Press, 2016.

Krutz, Glen S., and Jeffrey S. Peake. *Treaty Politics and the Rise of Executive Agreements*. Ann Arbor: University of Michigan Press, 2009.

Lee, Frances E. *Beyond Ideology: Politics, Principles, and Partisanship in the U.S. Senate*. Chicago, IL: University of Chicago Press, 2009.

———. *Insecure Majorities: Congress and the Perpetual Campaign*. Chicago, IL: University of Chicago Press, 2016.

Neustadt, Richard E. *Presidential Power and the Modern Presidents*. New York: Free Press, 1990.

Rhode, David W., and Meredith Barthelemy. "The President and Congressional Parties in an Era of Polarization." In *The Oxford Handbook of the American Presidency*, edited by George C. Edwards III and William G. Howell. Oxford, UK: Oxford University Press, 2009.

Wayne, Stephen J. "Legislative Skills." In *The Oxford Handbook of the American Presidency*, edited by George C. Edwards III and William G. Howell. Oxford, UK: Oxford University Press, 2009.

12

The President and the Judiciary

President Trump introduces Neil Gorsuch, his first nominee to the Supreme Court.

D onald Trump's first prime-time televised presentation to the American people was introducing his nominee to the Supreme Court, Neil Gorsuch. His most important early initiative was a travel ban on people living in several Middle Eastern countries. Courts blocked two versions of the ban, enraging the president. Courts also struck down actions by the Environmental Protection Agency and the Interior Department to void or weaken regulations protecting the environment, setting back the administration's broad legal strategy for rolling back Obama-era rules. Trump's case illustrates that chief executives have important relationships with the courts. To begin, it is through their nominations to the bench that they have opportunities to influence public policy for years to come. The executive branch, operating through the solicitor general's office, is also a frequent litigant in the federal courts, especially at the Supreme Court level. Such litigation provides another opportunity for the president to influence judicial decisions.

In addition, presidents may end up with responsibility for enforcing court decisions even though they were not directly involved in them. Sometimes, enforcing the law actually means complying with decisions directed at the White House. Although such instances are not common, they may provide moments of high political drama and have important consequences for our political system. Finally, the Constitution gives the president the right to exercise some judicial powers directly through the granting of pardons, amnesty, and clemency for individuals who are accused or convicted of federal crimes.

The distinction between the director and facilitator presidential types is less clear in relationships with the judiciary than with Congress. Although both presidential types would take advantage of the opportunity to nominate compatible judges to the federal bench, it is theoretically possible that dominant presidents would be able to mold the courts more, moving jurists to reach decisions of which they approve and to overturn previous decisions that they oppose. Facilitators will be more constrained in placing their first choices on the bench and will not dominate their judicial decision making. Their victories will result from the views of the judges they nominate to the bench rather than their influence over these judges once they don their judicial robes.

JUDICIAL SELECTION

The president's primary means of exercising leadership of the judicial branch is through the nomination of federal judges. In this section, we examine the process of judicial selection for the federal courts and the types of people who become federal judges.

Selection of Lower-Court Judges

The federal district courts and the courts of appeals include most federal judges and handle most federal cases. The president nominates people to fill these slots for lifetime service, and the Senate must confirm each nomination by a majority vote. Because of the Senate's role, the president's discretion ends up being much less than it appears.

Senatorial Courtesy

Senatorial courtesy is the customary manner in which the Senate disposes of state-level federal nominations for such positions as judgeships and US attorneys.[1] For district court positions, the Senate does not confirm nominees if they are opposed by a senator of the president's party from the state in which the nominee is to serve. To invoke the right of senatorial courtesy, the relevant senator usually simply states a general reason for opposition. Other senators then honor their colleague's views and oppose the nomination, regardless of their personal evaluations of the candidate's merits.

The first instance of senatorial courtesy occurred in 1789, when President George Washington failed to obtain confirmation of Benjamin Fishbourn as naval officer of the port of Savannah because of the opposition of Georgia's two senators, and since that time, senatorial courtesy has become a well-established tradition. By 1840, senators were virtually naming federal district court judges by providing the president with a list of "acceptable" choices from which the administration could choose.

Because of the strength of this informal practice, presidents usually check carefully with the relevant senator or senators ahead of time to avoid making a nomination that the Senate will not confirm. In many instances, this practice is tantamount to giving the power of nomination to these senators. Typically, when there is a vacancy for a federal district judgeship, the relevant senator or senators from the state where the judge will serve suggest one or more names to the attorney general and the president. If neither senator is of the president's party, then the party's state congresspersons or other state party leaders may make suggestions. Other interested senators may also try to influence a selection.[2]

In early 2009, Senate Republicans added a new element to senatorial courtesy when they sent President Obama a letter in which they vowed to prevent the confirmation of judicial nominees in instances where the White House did not properly consult Republican home-state senators. The implication of this letter was that members of the opposition party would have a de facto veto power, something without precedent in the history of judicial selection. Obama did consult with Republican home-state senators and did not nominate judges opposed by these senators,[3] which partly explains why he left office with more than 120 judicial vacancies.

When Donald Trump entered the White House in 2017, Republicans continued the bipartisan application of senatorial courtesy at the district court level. However, they were less likely to defer on courts of appeals nominees. Traditionally, the Senate had confirmed few judges at any level without the support of at least one home-state senator, but the Republicans chose to proceed with circuit court nominations even in the face of the opposition of both home state senators of the opposition party.

The President's Role

The White House, the Department of Justice, and the Federal Bureau of Investigation conduct competency and background checks on persons suggested for judgeships, and the president usually selects a nominee from those who survive the screening process. If a senator to whom senatorial courtesy is due recommended one of these survivors, it is difficult for the president to reject the recommendation in favor of someone else who survived the process. Thus, senatorial courtesy turns the Constitution on its head, and, in effect, the Senate ends up making nominations and the president then approving them.

Presidents possess assets in such a situation, but they rarely will find it worthwhile to fight a senator over a district court judgeship. If they desire to do so, presidents can refuse to nominate anyone to the position in an attempt to pressure a senator into supporting their nominee in order to avoid a backlog of federal cases in the state. Alternately, they may make an appointment during a congressional recess at the end of a session. Although the Senate must confirm such nominees in the next session of Congress, by then they may have had an opportunity to demonstrate such exemplary capabilities on the bench that the Senate will look more favorably on their appointments.

Traditionally, the attorney general asked the Standing Committee on the Federal Judiciary of the American Bar Association (ABA) for its evaluation of potential nominees. However, the George W. Bush and Trump administrations chose not to do so (but the ABA still evaluated candidates after the president nominated them). Other individuals have input in judicial selection as well. The Department of Justice may ask sitting judges, usually at the federal level, to evaluate prospective nominees. Sitting judges may also initiate recommendations to advance or retard someone's chances of being nominated. In addition, candidates for the nomination are often active on their own behalf. They have to alert the relevant parties that they desire the position and orchestrate a campaign of support for themselves. As one appellate judge observed, "People don't get judgeships without seeking them. Anybody who thinks judicial office seeks the man is mistaken. There's not a man on the court who didn't do what he thought needed to be done."[4]

Presidents usually have more influence in the selection of judges to the federal courts of appeals than to federal district courts. Because the decisions of appellate courts are generally more significant than those of lower courts, the president naturally takes a greater interest in appointments to the former. At the same time, individual senators are in a weaker position to determine who the nominee will be because the jurisdiction of an appeals court encompasses several states. Although custom and pragmatic politics require that these judgeships be apportioned among the states, the president has discretion in doing this and therefore has a greater role in recruiting appellate judges than district court judges. Even here, however, senators from the state in which the candidate resides may be able to veto a nomination.

The Reagan White House created an institutional apparatus to ensure that the president's judicial nominees shared the philosophical and policy orientation of the president. The President's Committee on Judicial Selection was a joint White House–Justice Department committee chaired by the White House Counsel, and Reagan's successors have continued to use it. Presidential aides survey candidates' decisions (if they have served on a lower court),[5] speeches, political stands, writings, and other expressions of opinion. They also turn for information to people who know the candidates well. Although it is considered improper to question judicial candidates about upcoming court cases, it is appropriate to discuss broader questions of political and judicial philosophy. The Reagan administration was especially concerned about such matters and had each potential nominee (for all judicial vacancies) fill out a lengthy questionnaire and be interviewed by administration officials.[6] The George H. W. Bush administration, which was also attentive to nominating conservative judges, continued this practice.[7]

When Bill Clinton took office, many supporters hoped he would quickly begin undoing a major legacy from twelve years of Republican control of the White House: a federal judiciary populated with conservative judges. He did not meet these expectations, however. Although Clinton nominated a record number of women and minorities to the federal bench, and although his nominees had impressive credentials, he had little interest in ensuring that his nominees were ideologically liberal. The president was slow to nominate judges and was unwilling to spend political capital to win Senate confirmation for nominees labeled as liberal, especially after the Republicans took control of Congress following the 1994 congressional elections. As a result, Clinton's judges were decidedly less liberal than those of other modern Democratic presidents.[8]

While campaigning for the presidency in 2000, George W. Bush committed himself to naming judges such as Justices Antonin Scalia and Clarence Thomas, two of the most conservative justices on the US Supreme Court. As president, Bush stated bluntly that he was looking to appoint conservatives to the courts.[9] His administration followed through, and almost all of his nominees to the lower federal courts were conservatives who shared the president's judicial philosophy. To an even greater extent than during the Reagan and George H. W. Bush administrations, the White

House Counsel's Office took responsibility for philosophically screening potential candidates, including conducting interviews.[10]

The Obama administration did not see nominating judges as a priority and was slow to send nominees to the Senate. The White House followed Bill Clinton's pattern and was not as rigorous in ideological screening as its Republican predecessors. The president often nominated political moderates to the bench, although not conservative activists or ideologues.[11]

Donald Trump prioritized nominating conservative judges. The Federalist Society played a large role in recommending and vetting candidates for the Supreme Court and other federal judgeships. Nevertheless, the administration's vetting of district court nominees was less than ideal, and it had an unusual number of judges rated as not qualified by the ABA and was forced to withdraw several from consideration.

Success of Recent Presidents

Traditionally, the Senate confirmed lower federal court nominations swiftly and unanimously.[12] However, the polarization of partisan politics in recent years has affected judicial nominations, especially those for the courts of appeals.[13] Increasingly, lower court confirmations have become lengthy and contentious proceedings. Many senators use committee hearings to engage in partisan and ideological position taking.[14] Interest groups opposed to nominations have become more active and encourage senators aligned with them to delay and block nominations.[15] Any senator can now exploit the opportunities for delay and gain influence in the nomination process.[16] As a presidential election nears, the party that controls the Senate has an incentive to delay confirmations in the hope that it will gain control of the White House.[17] As a result, there has been a dramatic increase in the time for confirmation,[18] which has in turn substantially decreased the chances of confirmation.[19] Donald Trump's presidency saw an increase in the conflict over judicial nominations, but the priority the Republican Senate gave to circuit court selections decreased the time for confirmation.

The confirmation process has become more contentious because the trend in judicial selection has been to move away from primarily patronage concerns to concerns about furthering the president's policy agenda through judicial appointments. Since the 1980s, senators have felt free to oppose judicial nominees on policy and judicial philosophical grounds. If the president uses ideological criteria to make nominations,[20] then senators think they are entitled to do the same when considering confirmation of those nominees.[21] The greater the ideological difference between the president and the opposing party, or between the president and the home-state senators, the longer and more contentious the nomination process. Divided party government and the potential for nominees to tip the ideological balance on a circuit court of appeals also contribute to slower and lower confirmation rates.[22]

George H. W. Bush experienced an especially difficult time obtaining the confirmation of lower-court judges from the Democratic-controlled Senate. Bill Clinton suffered even greater frustrations with the Republican Senate after 1995. The Senate confirmed only 61 percent of his nominees to the courts of appeals and only 81 percent of his nominees to the district courts.[23] As a result of Republican obstructionism, Clinton had to negotiate agreements with Republican senators, giving some of them a role in the selection of judges equivalent to that accorded his fellow Democrats. He also made a recess appointment of a court of appeals judge shortly before leaving office. Such appointments are unusual and good only for the remainder of a congressional term.

George W. Bush also faced stiff partisan opposition to some of his nominations and in response made two recess appointments to courts of appeals. Infuriated at what they viewed as a misuse of the recess appointment power and an attempt to bypass the Senate's confirmation responsibilities, Democratic senators shut down the confirmation process for several months in 2004. After the Republicans nearly voted to end the possibility of filibustering judicial nominations,[24] fourteen senators from both parties forged a deal without White House approval that allowed some—but not all—of Bush's stalled judicial nominees to receive floor votes. The White House pledged not to bypass the Senate with any more recess appointments of judges.

Nevertheless, partisan conflict over nominations continued as the Republican minority used secret holds on considering nominees, threats of filibusters, and various Senate procedures to delay and often stymie Barack Obama's judicial nominations, even at the district court level—a new element of the partisan battle. Republican senators frequently invoked senatorial courtesy to oppose nominees and often even failed to make recommendations to the White House, leaving many judicial vacancies unfilled. There was little the White House could do, especially when the Republicans regained the majority in 2015. However, in response to the filibuster threat, in 2013 the Democrats prevailed in changing the Senate's rules to end filibusters for nominations to all but the Supreme Court.

The Republicans extended this rule to the Supreme Court when they retook the majority. In 2019, they also voted to reduce greatly post-cloture debate on federal district court nominees). The priority both the Trump White House and the Republican Senate placed on confirmation of judges resulted in a strong record for the president. He placed more judges on courts of appeals than any other president two years into a term. He also added two justices to the Supreme Court.

Backgrounds of Lower-Court Judges

What type of individual becomes a judge through this process? The data in tables 12.1 and 12.2 show that federal judges are not a representative sample of the American people. They are all lawyers (although this is not a constitutional requirement), and they are overwhelmingly white and male. Only Presidents Obama, Clinton, Carter, and both Bushes have nominated a substantial number of women to the federal bench. Only Obama, Clinton, and Carter, and, to a lesser extent, George W. Bush, have nominated a significant percentage of minorities. Barack Obama's record of nominating women and minorities to the federal bench is in a class by itself. He nominated women and ethnic minorities to a majority of the judicial vacancies during his tenure.[25] Donald Trump has nominated almost no black or Hispanic judges.

Federal judges have also typically held office as judges or prosecutors, and often they have been involved in partisan politics. This involvement is generally what brings them to the attention of senators and the Department of Justice when they seek nominees for judgeships. As Griffin Bell, a former US attorney general and circuit court judge, once remarked,

> For me, becoming a federal judge wasn't very difficult. I managed John F. Kennedy's presidential campaign in Georgia. Two of my oldest and closest friends were two senators from Georgia. And I was campaign manager and special, unpaid counsel for the governor.[26]

Table 12.1 Backgrounds of Recent Federal Appeals Court Judges

	Carter	Reagan	G. H. W. Bush	Clinton	G. W. Bush	Obama	Trump*
			Administration				
No. of nominees	56	78	37	61	59	48	30
Experience (%)							
Judicial	54	60	62	59	61	60	47
Prosecutorial	30	28	30	38	34	52	33
Neither one	39	35	32	30	25	23	30
Party (%)							
Democrat	82	0	3	85	7	88	0
Republican	7	96	89	7	92	0	93
Independent	11	3	8	8	2	13	7
Past party activism (%)	73	67	70	54	68	46	83
Ethnicity or race (%)							
White	79	97	89	74	85	67	90
African American	16	1	5	13	10	19	0
Hispanic	4	1	5	12	5	8	0
Asian American	2	0	0	2	0	6	10
Gender (%)							
Male	80	95	81	67	75	54	80
Female	20	5	19	33	25	46	20
Average age	49	50	49	51	50	52	49

* 2017–2018
Source: Adapted from Elliot Slotnick, Sara Schiavoni, and Sheldon Goldman, "Obama's Judicial Legacy: The Final Chapter," *Journal of Law and Courts* 5 (Fall 2017): 363–423; updated by Sheldon Goldman.

Perhaps the most striking finding in tables 12.1 and 12.2 is the fact that presidents rarely appoint someone to a judgeship who does not share their party affiliation. Merit considerations obviously occur after partisan screening. Judgeships are patronage plums that may serve as rewards for political service to either the president or senators of the president's party, as consolation prizes for unsuccessful candidates, or even to "kick upstairs" an official in order to remove him or her from an executive-branch post. When presidents nominate someone of the other party for a judgeship, it is usually because of ideological congruity with the nominee or to obtain support in a state where his or her party is weak.

Partisanship also plays a role in the creation of judgeships. Because of their keen interest in them, members of Congress are reluctant to create judicial positions to be filled by a president of the minority party in Congress.[27] For example, Democrats in Congress rejected President Dwight Eisenhower's efforts to create new judgeships in every year of his second term (1957–1960), even though he offered to name Democrats to half the new positions. In 1962, however, a similar bill easily passed Congress with Democrat John Kennedy in the White House. This partisan behavior was nothing new. In 1801, the newly elected Jeffersonians repealed a law creating

Table 12.2 Backgrounds of Recent Federal District Court Judges

	Carter	Reagan	G. H. W. Bush	Clinton	G. W. Bush	Obama	Trump*
No. of nominees	202	290	148	305	261	268	53
Experience (%)							
Judicial	54	46	47	52	52	47	38
Prosecutorial	38	44	39	41	47	43	57
Neither one	31	29	32	29	25	31	32
Party (%)							
Democrat	91	5	6	88	8	80	6
Republican	5	92	89	6	83	8	76
Independent	5	3	5	6	9	13	19
Past party activism (%)	61	60	64	50	53	50	55
Ethnicity or race (%)							
White	79	92	89	75	83	63	92
African American	14	2	7	17	6	19	2
Hispanic	7	5	4	6	11	11	2
Asian American	1	1	0	1	1	6	4
Gender (%)							
Male	86	92	80	72	79	59	74
Female	14	8	20	29	21	41	26
Average age	50	49	48	50	50	51	51

* 2017–2018

Source: Adapted from Elliot Slotnick, Sara Schiavoni, and Sheldon Goldman, "Obama's Judicial Legacy: The Final Chapter," *Journal of Law and Courts* 5 (Fall 2017): 363–423; updated by Sheldon Goldman.

separate judges for the circuit courts of appeals passed by the outgoing Federalists a few months earlier.

Although women and people of different ethnicities and religions may desire to have people in their group appointed to the federal bench—at the very least, judgeships have symbolic importance for them[28]—the real question is what, if any, policy differences result. There is some evidence that female judges on the courts of appeals are more likely than male judges to support charges of sex discrimination and sexual harassment, and they seem to influence the male judges deciding the cases with them.[29]

Similarly, racial and ethnic minority judges on these courts are more likely to find for minority plaintiffs in voting rights and affirmative action cases and also to influence the votes of white judges sitting with them,[30] but their voting on employment discrimination cases is more mixed.[31] Republican judges hand out more severe sentences to black defendants than do Democratic judges, but shorter punishments to female defendants.[32]

At the level of the Supreme Court, conservative Justice Antonin Scalia said that Justice Thurgood Marshall "could be a persuasive force just by sitting there. He wouldn't have to open his mouth to affect the nature of the conference and how seriously the conference would take matters of race."[33] It is true, of course, that Justice Clarence Thomas, the second African American justice, is one of the most conservative justices since the New Deal, illustrating that not everyone from a particular background has a particular point of view.

Many members of each party have served, of course, and it appears that Republican judges in general are somewhat more conservative than are Democratic judges, especially on ideologically contested cases.[34] Former prosecutors serving on the Supreme Court have tended to be less sympathetic toward defendants' rights than have other justices. Justices with experience in the executive branch are more likely to defer to the president in separation of powers cases.[35] It seems, then, that background does make some difference,[36] yet for reasons that we examine in the following sections, on many issues party affiliation and other characteristics are imperfect predictors of judicial behavior.

Selection of Supreme Court Justices

As with lower-court judges, a majority of those voting in the Senate must confirm justices of the Supreme Court. There have been no recess appointments to the Court since the Senate voiced its disapproval of the practice in 1960. When the chief justice's position becomes vacant, the president may nominate either someone already on the Court or someone from outside it to fill the position. Usually, presidents choose the latter course in order to widen their range of options, but if they decide to elevate a sitting associate justice, as President Reagan did with William Rehnquist in 1986, he or she must go through a new confirmation by the Senate.

Although many of the same actors are present in the case of Supreme Court nominations, their influence is typically quite different. The president is vitally interested in the Court because of the importance of its work, which includes making decisions on the scope of presidential powers, and will generally be intimately involved in the recruitment process. Unlike the case of federal judges, presidents have been personally acquainted with many of the people they have nominated to the Supreme Court (reflecting their involvement in the selection process), and it is not unusual for an administration official to receive a nomination. Presidents also often rely on White House aides, the attorney general, and the Justice Department to identify and screen candidates for the Court.

There are few matters as important to justices on the Supreme Court as the ideology, competence, and compatibility of their colleagues, and thus it is not surprising that they (especially chief justices) often try to influence nominations to the Court. Chief Justice William Howard Taft, who was a former president, was especially active during his tenure in the 1920s, and Warren Burger played a prominent role in the Richard Nixon administration.[37] Nevertheless, although presidents will listen to recommendations from justices, they feel no obligation to follow them.

Senators play a much less prominent role in the recruitment of Supreme Court justices than in the selection of lower-court judges, especially for the district courts. No senator can claim that the jurisdiction of the Supreme Court falls within the realm of his or her special expertise, interest, or sphere of influence. Thus, presidents typically consult with senators from the state of residence of a nominee after they have decided whom to select. At this point, senators are unlikely to oppose a nomination because they like having their state receive the honor and are well aware that should they reject the nominee, the president can simply select someone from another state. Although home-state senators do not play prominent roles in the selection process for the Court, the Senate as a whole does. In fact, through its Judiciary Committee it may probe a nominee's judicial philosophy in great detail.

Candidates for nomination are also much less likely to play a significant role in the recruitment process. Although there have been exceptions, most notably William Howard Taft, people seldom campaign for a position on the Court. They can accomplish little through such activity, and because of the Court's standing, it might offend those who do play important roles in selecting nominees.

The ABA's Standing Committee on the Federal Judiciary has played a varied, but typically modest, role at the Supreme Court, and the White House usually has asked it to evaluate candidates for the Supreme Court only after the president has nominated them. The committee has never found a nominee unqualified to serve on the Court. In 2001, the Bush administration decided not to ask its advice, the Obama administration revived the practice, and Trump reverted to the Bush policy.

Through 2019, there have been 156 nominations to the Supreme Court and 114 people have served. Of those, four people were nominated and confirmed twice, eight declined appointments or died before beginning service on the Court, and twenty-nine failed to secure Senate confirmation. Presidents, then, have failed 20 percent of the time to appoint the nominees of their choice to the Court—a percentage much higher than that for any other federal position.

For most of the twentieth century, Supreme Court nominations were routine affairs. Of the nine nominees who have failed to receive Senate confirmation since 1900 (see table 12.3), eight have occurred since the presidency of John F. Kennedy. The 1960s were tumultuous times, which bred ideological conflict. Although Kennedy had no trouble with his two nominations to the Court (Byron White and Arthur Goldberg), his successor, Lyndon Johnson, was not so fortunate. He had to withdraw his nomination of Abe Fortas (already serving on the Court) to serve as chief justice, and therefore the Senate never voted on Homer Thornberry, Johnson's nominee to replace Fortas as an associate justice. Richard Nixon, the next president, had two nominees rejected in a row following bruising battles in the Senate.

Table 12.3 Senate Rejections of Supreme Court Nominees since 1900

Nominee	Year	President
John J. Parker	1930	Hoover
Abe Fortas*	1968	Johnson
Homer Thornberry[†]	1968	Johnson
Clement F. Haynsworth Jr.	1969	Nixon
G. Harrold Carswell	1970	Nixon
Robert H. Bork	1987	Reagan
Douglas H. Ginsburg*	1987	Reagan
Harriet Miers*	2005	G. W. Bush
Merrick Garland[†]	2016	Obama

* Nominations were withdrawn. (Fortas was serving on the Court as an associate justice and was nominated to be chief justice.)
[†] The Senate took no action on Thornberry's and Garland's nominations.

The Bork Nomination

Two failed nominations occurred in 1987. On June 26, Justice Lewis Powell announced his retirement from the Supreme Court. President Reagan had already been able to elevate Justice William Rehnquist to chief justice and also had appointed Sandra Day O'Connor and Antonin Scalia. With yet another appointee, he would have a solid bloc of conservative votes on the Court for years to come.

Reagan nominated Judge Robert H. Bork to fill the vacancy. Everyone agreed that Bork was an intelligent and serious legal scholar, and he had also served in the Justice Department. (He was the individual who had fired special prosecutor Archibald Cox in the famous "Saturday Night Massacre" of Watergate fame.) At this point, agreement on his qualifications ended, however.

Bork testified before the Senate Judiciary Committee for twenty-three hours. At the end, his supporters portrayed him as a distinguished scholar who would practice "judicial restraint," deferring to Congress and the state legislatures and adhering to the precedents of the Supreme Court. Conversely, his opponents saw him as an extreme judicial ideologue who would use the Supreme Court to achieve conservative political ends, thus reversing decades of court decisions. A wide range of interest groups entered the fray, mostly in opposition to the nominee, and in the end, following a bitter floor debate, the Senate rejected the president's nomination by a vote of 58 to 42.

Six days after the Senate vote on Bork, the president nominated Douglas H. Ginsburg to the high court. Just nine days later, however, Ginsburg withdrew his nomination following disclosures that he had smoked marijuana at parties while a law professor at Harvard. Not until the spring of 1988 did Reagan finally succeed in filling the vacancy, with Anthony Kennedy.

The Thomas Nomination

In June 1991, at the end of the Supreme Court's term, Associate Justice Thurgood Marshall announced his retirement from the Court. Shortly thereafter, President Bush announced his nomination of another African American federal appeals judge, Clarence Thomas, to replace Marshall. Because Thomas was a conservative, this decision was consistent with the Bush administration's emphasis on placing conservative judges on the federal bench.

The president claimed that he was not employing quotas when he chose another African American to replace the only African American ever to sit on the Supreme Court and argued that Thomas was simply the most qualified person for the job. This placed liberals in a dilemma. On the one hand, they favored having a minority group member serving on the nation's highest court. On the other hand, however, Thomas was unlikely to vote the same way as Thurgood Marshall. Instead, the new justice presented the prospect of strengthening the conservative trend in the Court's decisions. In the end, this ambivalence inhibited spirited opposition to Thomas, who was circumspect about his judicial philosophy in his appearances before the Senate Judiciary Committee, which sent his nomination to the Senate floor on a split vote.

Just as the Senate was about to vote on the nomination, however, charges of sexual harassment leveled against Thomas by University of Oklahoma law professor Anita Hill were made public. Hearings were reopened on the charges in response to criticism that the Senate was sexist for not considering them seriously in the first place. For several days, citizens sat transfixed before their television sets as Professor Hill calmly and graphically described her recollections of Thomas's behavior. Thomas

Anita Hill testifies against the nomination of Clarence Thomas.

then emphatically denied any such behavior and charged the Senate with racism for raising the issue. Ultimately, public opinion polls showed that more people believed Thomas than Hill, and the Senate confirmed him by a vote of fifty-two to forty-eight, the closest vote on a Supreme Court nomination in more than a century.

Clinton Nominations

The Senate's response to President Clinton's nominees harkened back to the Kennedy era. Neither Ruth Bader Ginsburg nor Stephen Breyer caused much controversy. The Clinton administration undertook detailed background checks of potential nominees and floated several names to test public reaction prior to the president's announcements of his choices.[38]

George W. Bush Nominations

The Senate also easily confirmed George W. Bush's nomination of John Roberts as chief justice. Indeed, he was difficult to oppose. His pleasing and professional personal demeanor and his disciplined and skilled testimony before the Senate Judicial Committee gave potential opponents little basis for opposition.

When Justice Sandra Day O'Connor resigned in 2005, Bush nominated White House counsel Harriet Miers replace her. Bush apparently thought Miers's lack of a published record would make it easier to push her nomination through. What looked like an adroit political decision soon turned sour, however. Many of the president's most passionate supporters had hoped and expected that he would make an unambiguously conservative choice to fulfill their goal of clearly altering the Court's balance, even at the cost of a bitter confirmation battle. By instead settling on a loyalist with no experience as a judge and little substantive record on abortion, affirmative action, religion, and other socially divisive issues, the president shied away from a direct confrontation with liberals and in effect asked his base on the right to trust him on his nomination. Many conservatives were bitterly disappointed and highly critical of the president. They demanded a known conservative and a top-flight legal figure. The nomination also smacked of cronyism, with the president selecting a friend and a loyalist rather than someone of obvious merit. The comparison with Roberts only emphasized the thinness of Miers's qualifications. In short order, Miers withdrew from consideration, and the president nominated Samuel Alito.

Alito was clearly a traditional conservative and had a less impressive public presence than Roberts. Response to him followed party lines, but the nominee appeared too well qualified and unthreatening in his confirmation hearings to justify a filibuster, and without one his confirmation was assured. The Senate confirmed Alito by a vote of fifty-eight to forty-two.

Obama Nominations

President Obama made his first nomination to the Court in 2009, selecting Sonia Sotomayor. Although conservatives raised questions about some of her previous statements and decisions, the Senate confirmed her by a vote of sixty-eight to thirty-one, largely along party lines. When she took the oath of office, she became the first Hispanic justice. In 2010, the president nominated Solicitor General Elena Kagan to the Court. She was confirmed by a vote of sixty-three to thirty-seven, once again largely along party lines.

In January 2016, news broke of the sudden death of Antonin Scalia, the outspoken conservative justice. With the eight remaining justices equally split among liberals and conservatives, talk quickly turned to Scalia's replacement. Even before President Obama named his nominee to succeed Scalia, however, Senate Republicans announced that they would not consider any nominee until after the presidential election in November. Refusing to be cowed, President Obama nominated Merrick Garland, a well-respected chief judge on the influential DC Court of Appeals, to take Scalia's vacated seat. The White House argued that the Senate had a constitutional obligation to hold confirmation hearings on Garland's nomination and to cast its votes, yea or nay. Even though fourteen presidents have appointed twenty-one justices during presidential election years, and a half-dozen presidents, classic lame ducks, filled Supreme Court seats even though their successors had been elected, the Senate held no hearings and no votes. Once again, partisanship and the ideological bent of the Supreme Court dominated the process.

Trump Nominations

President Trump often touted his nominations to the Supreme Court as among his greatest accomplishments as president. He introduced both nominees on primetime television and cited them at rallies of his supporters as evidence of his delivering on his promise to put conservatives on the federal bench. You can read about them in box 12.1.

Conditions for Failed Nominations

The history of recent failed nominations indicates that presidents are most likely to run into trouble under certain conditions. Presidents whose parties are in the minority in the Senate or who make a nomination at the end of their term face a

---

Box 12.1 ★ Donald Trump's Supreme Court Nominations

Soon after his inauguration, Donald Trump nominated Neil Gorsuch to fill the seat made vacant by the death of Antonin Scalia. Because Republicans controlled the Senate and because Gorsuch was well-credentialed, his nomination proceeded smoothly. Nevertheless, the Senate confirmed him on a 54–45, party-line vote, nearly as close as the vote on Clarence Thomas.

The next year, the president nominated Brett Kavanaugh to the Supreme Court to replace Anthony Kennedy, who had been in the ideological center for the Court. Because his confirmation would change the balance of the Court, both conservatives and liberals saw the stakes as high. Kavanaugh was well qualified and avoided direct answers to questions about his specific views when he testified before the Judiciary Committee. Shortly before the Senate was to vote, however, several individuals alleged the judge had committed sexual assault and engaged in other improper behavior. After additional acrimonious hearings, the Senate confirmed Kavanaugh by the narrow margin of 50–48.

---

greatly increased probability of substantial opposition. This is also the case for those who have the opportunity to nominate a justice whose confirmation would result in important shifts in the coalitions on the Court and thus affect policy outcomes. Equally important, to defeat a nomination, opponents must usually credibly question a nominee's competence (Carswell and Miers) or ethics (Fortas, Haynsworth, and Carswell) to attract moderate senators to their side and make ideological protests seem less partisan. A charge of scandal will weaken support for a nomination among the president's co-partisans and galvanize the opposition. Opposition based on a nominee's ideology alone is generally not considered a valid reason to vote against confirmation, although ideology is the primary concern of senators.[39] As long as Americans are polarized around social issues and as long as the Court makes critical decisions about these issues, the potential for conflict over the president's nominations is always present.[40]

Characteristics of Justices

Competence and ethical behavior are important to presidents for reasons beyond merely obtaining Senate confirmation of their nominees to the Court. Skilled and honorable justices reflect well on the president and will likely do so for many years. Moreover, they are more effective advocates and thus can better serve the president's interests. In addition, presidents usually have enough respect for the Court and its work that they do not want to saddle it with a mediocre justice. Although the criteria of competence and character screen out some possible candidates, there is still a wide field from which the president may choose. Other characteristics then play prominent roles.

Race, Gender, Religion, and Geography

As with their colleagues on the lower federal courts, Supreme Court justices share many characteristics that are quite unlike those of the typical American. All have been lawyers, and all but six (Thurgood Marshall, nominated in 1967; Sandra Day O'Connor, nominated in 1981; Clarence Thomas, nominated in 1991; Ruth Bader Ginsburg, nominated in 1993; Sonia Sotomayor, nominated in 2009; and Elena Kagan, nominated in 2010) have been white males. Most have been in their fifties

Table 12.4 Supreme Court Justices, 2020

Justice	Birth Year	Previous Position	Nominating President	Year of Appointment
John G. Roberts Jr.	1955	US Court of Appeals	G. W. Bush	2005
Clarence Thomas	1948	US Court of Appeals	G. H. W. Bush	1991
Ruth Bader Ginsburg	1933	US Court of Appeals	Clinton	1993
Stephen G. Breyer	1938	US Court of Appeals	Clinton	1994
Samuel A. Alito Jr.	1950	US Court of Appeals	G. W. Bush	2006
Sonia Sotomayor	1954	US Court of Appeals	Obama	2009
Elena Kagan	1960	US Solicitor General	Obama	2010
Neil M. Gorsuch	1967	US Court of Appeals	Trump	2017
Brett Kavanaugh	1965	US Court of Appeals	Trump	2018

and sixties when they took office, from the upper-middle to upper class, and Protestants. (See table 12.4 for some background information on the current Supreme Court.)

Race and gender have become more salient criteria in recent years. In the 1980 presidential campaign, Ronald Reagan promised to appoint a woman to a vacancy on the Court should he be elected. Geography once was a prominent criterion for selection to the Court but is no longer very important. Presidents do like to spread the slots around, however, as when Richard Nixon decided that he wanted to nominate a southerner. At various times, there have been what some have termed a "Jewish seat" and a "Catholic seat" on the Court, but these are not binding on the president. For example, after a half-century of having a Jewish justice, there was none between 1969 and 1993, until President Clinton nominated Ruth Bader Ginsburg to the Court. She was followed by another Jewish nominee, Stephen Breyer. By 2018, eight of the justices were either Roman Catholic or Jewish, Neil Gorsuch being the exception.

Although presidents have often selected Supreme Court justices at least in part for their symbolic appeal to geographic, gender, racial, and religious interests, such appointees may not actually provide these groups with much policy representation. There is evidence that most symbolic appointees do not vote for their own group's policy attitudes any more than do other members of the Court.[41]

Partisanship

Partisanship remains an important influence on the selection of justices; only 13 of 114 members were nominated by presidents of a different party. Moreover, many of the thirteen exceptions were actually close to the president in ideology, as was the case in Richard Nixon's appointment of Lewis Powell. Herbert Hoover's nomination of Benjamin Cardozo seems to be one of the few cases where partisanship was completely subjugated to merit as a criterion for selection. However, usually about 90 percent of presidents' judicial nominations are of members of their own party.

The role of partisanship is not surprising, even at the level of the highest court. Most of the presidents' acquaintances are in their own party, and there is usually a certain congruity between party and political views. The president may also use

Supreme Court nominations as a reward, as when President Eisenhower nominated Earl Warren as chief justice. As leader of the California delegation to the 1952 Republican convention, Warren had played a crucial role in Eisenhower's successful bid for the Republican nomination for president. Many justices at one time were active partisans, which gave them visibility and helped them obtain the positions from which they moved to the Court.

Previous Position

Typically, justices have held high administrative or judicial positions before moving to the Supreme Court. All but one member of the current Court served on the federal court of appeals (table 12.4), where they created records that the White House could review. Most justices have had some experience as judges, often at the appellate level, and many have worked for the Department of Justice. Some have held high elected office, and a few have had no government service but, rather, have been distinguished attorneys. The fact that not all justices, including many of the most distinguished ones, have had previous judicial experience may seem surprising, but the unique work and environment of the Court renders this background much less important than it might be for other appellate courts.

PRESIDENT–SUPREME COURT RELATIONS

At the top of two complex branches of government stand the president and the Supreme Court. Each has significant powers. In a system of shared powers such as ours, it is not surprising that the president is interested in influencing the Court. In this section, we examine efforts of the White House to mold the Court through filling vacancies, setting its agenda, and influencing and enforcing its decisions. We also look at inter-branch relations that involve advising and other services.

Molding the Court

One of the most significant powers of the president lies in molding the Supreme Court through nominations. In effect, all presidents try to "pack" the courts.[42] They want more than "justice"; they want policies with which they agree. Because justices serve for life, the impact of a president's selections will generally be felt long after that president has left office. As a result, the White House typically makes substantial efforts to ascertain the policy preferences of candidates for the Supreme Court.

As a result of all this effort, presidents are generally satisfied with the actions of their nominees, especially those who had prior judicial experience to examine.[43] Given the discretion that justices often have in making decisions, it is not surprising that consistent patterns related to their values and ideology—to conservative versus liberal positions—are often evident in their decisions.[44] Thus, the right nominations can reinforce, slow, or alter trends in the Court's decisions. Franklin Roosevelt's nominees substantially liberalized the Court, whereas Richard Nixon's choices turned it in a basically conservative direction. Although precedent, legal principles, and even political pressures from the public, Congress, and the White House constrain justices' discretion,[45] justices usually arrive at a decision consistent with their policy preferences.

Nevertheless, it is not always easy to identify the policy inclinations of candidates, and presidents have been disappointed in their selections about a quarter of the time. President Eisenhower, for example, was displeased with the liberal decisions of both Earl Warren and William Brennan. Once, when asked whether he had made any mistakes as president, he replied, "Yes, two, and they are both sitting on the Supreme Court."[46] Earlier, Woodrow Wilson was shocked by the very conservative positions of one of his nominees, James McReynolds. On a more limited scale, Richard Nixon was certainly disappointed when his nominee for chief justice, Warren Burger, authored the Court's decision calling for immediate desegregation of the nation's schools shortly after his confirmation. This did little for the president's "Southern strategy."

There are several reasons presidents may make what, in their view, are errors in nominations to the Court. They and their aides may have done a poor job of probing the views of candidates. Moreover, once on the Court, justices may change their attitudes and values over time because of new insights gained in their position, the normal process of aging, or the influence of other members of the Court. (Virtually all justices between 1801 and 1835 were strongly affected by Chief Justice John Marshall.) Justices are also often constrained by their obligation to follow precedents (when they are clear).

Some presidents have been relatively unconcerned with ideology in their nominations. In periods of relative political and social calm or when there is a solid majority on the Court that shares their views and is likely to persist for several years, presidents might give less weight to policy preferences than to other criteria in choosing justices. In contrast, political polarization led President Clinton to deemphasize ideology in his nominations.

Influencing Vacancies

Presidents cannot have much impact on the Court unless they have vacancies to fill, of course. Although, on the average, there has been an opening on the Supreme Court every two years, there is a substantial variance around this mean.[47] Franklin D. Roosevelt had to wait five years before he could nominate a justice, all the while facing a Court that found much of his New Deal legislation unconstitutional. In more recent years, Jimmy Carter was never able to nominate a justice; indeed, between 1972 and 1984, there were only two vacancies on the Court. George W. Bush did not have the opportunity to nominate a justice in his first term. Conversely, Richard Nixon was able to nominate four justices in his first three years in office.

Sometimes, Congress or the president takes unusual steps to enhance or limit a president's ability to fill vacancies. The legislature altered the size of the Supreme Court many times between 1801 and 1869. In 1801, the Federalists reduced the Court from six to five members, and the Jeffersonians increased it back to six the following year. In 1863, Abraham Lincoln got Congress to increase the number of justices from nine to ten after the Court upheld the legality of measures to fight the Civil War by only a five to four vote.

In 1866, the Radical Republicans in Congress reduced the size of the Court from ten to seven members to prevent Andrew Johnson from nominating new justices. When President Grant took office, Congress increased the number to nine because it had confidence Grant would nominate members to its liking. This number has remained unchanged since then, and it now seems inviolate.

Franklin D. Roosevelt attempted to "pack" the court in 1937, when he proposed to add a justice to the Court for every justice currently serving who was over age seventy and had served ten years. This proposal was an obvious attempt to change the direction of Court decisions on his economic policies and, after a prolonged political battle, Congress refused to approve it. The effort was politically costly to Roosevelt—it marked the end of the New Deal,[48] but the president at least had the satisfaction that the Court was already beginning to approve liberal legislation.

The president's role in Supreme Court judicial selection is not limited to the nomination of justices; it extends to the creation of positions as well. Justices are typically not prone to retirement, but presidents are sometimes frustrated enough at Court decisions to attempt to accelerate the creation of vacancies. Thomas Jefferson and his supporters tried to use impeachment to remove justices and thus gain control of the judiciary, which was largely Federalist (and thus anti-Jeffersonian). They abandoned this strategy, however, when the Senate failed to convict Justice Samuel Chase in 1805, who had made himself vulnerable with his partisan activities off the bench and injudicious remarks on it.

More often, presidents have relied on less direct forms of pressure. Theodore Roosevelt resorted to leaks in the press in an unsuccessful effort to induce two justices to resign. More recently, the Nixon administration orchestrated a campaign to force liberal justice Abe Fortas to resign after he was accused of financial improprieties.

Role of Justices

Justices also play the game of politics, of course, and may try to time their retirements so that a president with compatible views will choose their successor.[49] This is one reason why justices remain on the Court for so long, even when they are clearly infirm. William Brennan and Thurgood Marshall, the most senior justices on the Court in the 1980s, stayed through the Reagan years because their liberal views contrasted sharply with those of the president. William Howard Taft, a rigid conservative, even feared conservative Republican Herbert Hoover naming his successor.

Such tactics do not always succeed. In 1968, Chief Justice Earl Warren submitted his resignation to President Johnson, whom he felt would select an acceptable successor. When Johnson's choice of Abe Fortas failed to win confirmation, however, the opportunity to nominate the new chief justice passed to Warren's old California political rival, newly elected President Richard Nixon.

Arguments in the Courts

The president may influence what cases the courts hear and what arguments judges and justices hear as well as who hears the cases. The Department of Justice has a well-established office for handling appellate litigation in the federal courts.

Solicitor General

The solicitor general is a presidential appointee who must be confirmed by the Senate and who serves in the Department of Justice.[50] It is he or she (not the attorney general) who supervises the litigation of the federal executive branch. In this position, the solicitor general plays a major role in determining the agenda of federal appellate courts. Although able to exercise wide discretion, the solicitor general is subject to the direction of the attorney general and the president, with the latter playing a role in major cases.

The solicitor general decides which of the cases lost by the federal government in the federal district courts or the courts of appeals will be appealed to the next higher court. The courts of appeals must hear properly appealed cases, but the Supreme Court, for all practical purposes, has complete control over its own docket. Thus, it is significant that the Court is far more likely to accept cases that the solicitor general wants to have heard than those from any other source of party to litigation.[51] Moreover, the amount of litigation involved is quite large. In recent years, the federal government has been a party to about half the cases heard in federal courts of appeals and the Supreme Court.

When a case reaches the Supreme Court, the solicitor general supervises the preparation of the government's arguments in support of its position, whether it is a direct party or an amicus. Court decisions often reflect these arguments[52] and thus they become the law of the land. Because the government has participated in almost every major controversy decided by the courts in the past fifty years, the potential influence of the executive branch on public policy through the courts is substantial.

Amicus Curiae

The executive branch also participates in cases to which it is not directly a party. The solicitor general files *amicus curiae* (friend of the court) briefs supporting or opposing the efforts of other parties before the Court.[53] These cases range from affirmative action to abortion rights and equal pay for women. Once again, the Court usually grants the government's request to participate in this way. Indeed, the Court wants to know the president's preferences,[54] although it does not necessarily support them.[55]

Government Success

The solicitor general builds credibility with the Court by not making frivolous appeals and, in a few instances, even by telling the Court that the government should not have won cases in lower courts. For example, during the Obama administration,

Joseph Mirachi/The New Yorker Collection/The Cartoon Bank

"Do you ever have one of those days when every-thing seems unconstitutional?"

Solicitor General Donald Verrilli notified the Supreme Court that the government believed it should not have won a case on immunity for federal prison guards accused of assaulting an inmate and that the Court should overturn the Circuit Court of Appeals decision the government had won.

Equally important, the solicitor general and his or her staff (again, not the attorney general) develop more expertise in dealing with the Court than anyone else because they appear before it more frequently, and they use the resources of the Justice Department to provide the Court with high-quality briefs. In addition, it appears that individual members of the Court are more receptive to the views of the solicitor general when they share general ideological predispositions with him or her.[56]

Traditionally, the federal government won a clear majority of its cases before the Supreme Court, both as a direct party and as an amicus.[57] The solicitor general's office may be losing some of its comparative advantage, however. The emergence of a bar specializing in litigation before the Supreme Court full of former solicitors general and other government lawyers may be offsetting the president's comparative advantage.[58]

Direct Influence

On a very rare occasion, the president may directly attempt to influence a Court decision. James Buchanan, while president-elect, pushed for a decision on the *Dred Scott* case and lobbied a justice to join the Court's southern majority.[59] In a very unusual move in 1969, Department of Justice officials visited Justice Brennan and Chief Justice Warren to alert them that the administration was worried about the outcomes of some wiretapping cases on the Court's agenda. The administration was concerned that the Court's decisions would force the discontinuance of its surveillance of embassies or its prosecutions based on the information obtained from them. According to Warren, this visit had no influence on the Court's decision making.[60]

Not Defending Laws

In rare instances, the president may decide not to defend laws passed by Congress against charges that they are unconstitutional. In 1990, the Bush administration refused to defend a Federal Communications Commission affirmative-action program because it viewed the law as unconstitutional. In 2004, the George W. Bush administration's solicitor general announced that the government would not defend the constitutionality of a law requiring public mass transit agencies, as a condition of receiving federal money, to refuse to accept advertisements urging the legalization of marijuana. Similarly, the Obama administration refused to defend the part of the Defense of Marriage Act that denies federal benefits to gay and lesbian couples married in states that recognize such unions, and it did not defend the constitutionality of statutes blocking same-sex military spouses from receiving marriage benefits—including rights to visitation in military hospitals, survivor benefits, and burial together in military cemeteries. The Trump administration asked the courts to find the entire Affordable Care Act unconstitutional.

Enforcing Court Decisions

Another important relationship between the judicial and executive branches involves enforcing court decisions. Although the executive branch provides the federal courts with US marshals, they are too few and lack sufficient authority to be of systematic aid, especially if a court order is directed against a coordinate branch of government.

Thus, the courts must often rely on the president to enforce their decisions, especially their more controversial ones.

The Constitution is, not surprisingly, ambiguous as to the president's responsibility for aiding the judicial branch. Although it never explicitly discusses the point, it does assign the president the responsibility to "take care that the laws be faithfully executed" (discussed in chapter 2). Typically, presidents have responded to support the courts or, at least, the rule of law. On several occasions, such as during the efforts of President Eisenhower and President Kennedy to integrate educational institutions, presidents have gone so far as to deploy federal troops to ensure compliance with court orders.

Presidents may use the carrot as well as the stick to encourage others to comply with Court decisions. One of the most significant and controversial Supreme Court decisions of this century was *Brown v. Board of Education* (1954), which called for an end to segregation in public schools. Compliance with this decision was a long and tortuous process, but it was aided by the passage of laws that provided federal aid only for school districts that did not segregate and that provided schools with extra funds to help ease the process of desegregation.

In *Worcester v. Georgia* (1832), the Court found that the state of Georgia had no authority over Cherokee Indian lands and that missionaries arrested there by the state should be released. The Court also implied that it was the president's responsibility to enforce its decision. Georgia refused to comply with the decision, however, and President Andrew Jackson took no actions to enforce it. Many students learn that he declared, "Well, [Chief Justice] John Marshall has made his decision, now let him enforce it." Actually, he said no such thing, nor was he responsible for enforcing the decision. Moreover, before the Court could issue its final order, the case became moot; Georgia had settled the litigation.

Other Relationships

In the earliest years of our nation, the line of separation between the executive and judicial branches was vague and was often crossed. President George Washington consulted with the chief justice on a range of matters and received written advisory opinions on matters of law. Washington even used the first two chief justices as diplomats to negotiate with other countries. The chief justice also served on a commission to manage the fund for paying off the national debt.[61]

This inter-branch cooperation did not last long, however. Many critics spoke out against the diplomatic efforts of justices, the Court decided against providing further advisory opinions, and the frequency of informal consultation between the White House and justices declined. The Court also refused to examine pension claims for the secretary of the treasury. Hostility between the president and the judiciary, which was populated primarily by his Federalist political enemies, marked the years of Jefferson's presidency.

In the twentieth century, William Howard Taft often conferred with President Calvin Coolidge and members of his cabinet.[62] The most notable formal exceptions to a strict separation between the two branches have been Justice Owen Roberts's chairing a presidential commission on the attack on Pearl Harbor, Justice Robert Jackson's service as chief American prosecutor at the Nuremberg trials of Nazi leaders following World War II, and Chief Justice Earl Warren's chairmanship of the commission investigating the assassination of President Kennedy. President Johnson turned to Justice Arthur Goldberg[63] and especially Abe Fortas for advice. Fortas received a great deal of criticism for his service as an informal adviser to Johnson on a wide range of issues. While on the Court, in the words of one biographer, "Fortas served as political advisor, speechwriter, crisis manager, administration headhunter, legal expert, war counselor, or just plain cheerleader."[64]

This type of relationship has occurred from time to time, however (principally between justices and the presidents who appointed them), continuing a pattern established before the justice reached the Court. Felix Frankfurter continued to advise Franklin D. Roosevelt after he took his seat on the court, as did Louis Brandeis for Woodrow Wilson,[65] Chief Justice Fred Vinson for Harry Truman,[66] and a number of others throughout US history.

More striking perhaps is the fact that Chief Justice Warren Burger appears to have discussed the Court's internal activities and issues pending before it with President Nixon and other top administration officials.[67] This behavior would seem to be a breach of the separation of powers. Burger also appears to have asked Nixon to use his influence with congressional Republicans to discourage them from proceeding with their attempt to impeach Justice William O. Douglas. Moreover, it is also possible that the chief justice delayed circulating his concurring opinion in *Roe v. Wade* to spare Nixon the embarrassment at his second inauguration.[68]

COMPLYING WITH THE SUPREME COURT

It is one thing for the White House to enforce a court decision against someone else and something quite different for it to comply with an order directed at the president after he has lost a case in the Supreme Court. At that point, interesting constitutional questions arise that have the potential for substantial inter-branch conflict. However, presidents typically do comply with court orders, a task made easier by the general deference of the courts to the chief executive.[69]

The Constitution is ambiguous about which branch shall have the final say in interpreting it. The Supreme Court made some progress in resolving this question in *Marbury v. Madison* (1803), in which it voided an act of Congress for the first time and asserted its right to make the final judgment on the constitutionality of actions of the other branches of government. *Marbury* did not really settle the question of the president's obligation to accept and follow the Court's interpretation of the Constitution, however, because the president could argue that the law the Court had voided actually pertained directly only to the Court's own branch, the judiciary. It was not until *Scott v. Sanford* (1857) that the Court again declared an act of Congress unconstitutional; this time, the law was not directly related to the judiciary.

Several presidents, including Thomas Jefferson, Abraham Lincoln, and Franklin D. Roosevelt, threatened privately to disobey Court decisions that went against them, but in each case defiance was unnecessary because the Court supported them. The most blatant instance of a president's threatening to disobey a Court order occurred in a case in which the Court was asked to enjoin President Andrew Johnson from administering military governments in Southern states following the Civil War. In oral argument before the Court, the president, speaking through his attorney general, let it be known that he would not comply with a decision enjoining him from implementing the laws. The Court, in turn, found in *Mississippi v. Johnson* (1867) that it lacked jurisdiction to stop the president from performing official duties that required executive discretion; consequently, the issue failed to come to a head. We should also note that Johnson had vetoed these bills when Congress passed them, yet once they were passed, the president faced impeachment if he failed to execute them.

Harry Truman

Presidents typically have obeyed Court decisions even when it has been costly to do so. During the Korean War, the United Steelworkers of America gave notice of an industry-wide strike. Concerned about steel production during wartime, President Truman ordered the secretary of commerce to seize and operate the steel mills. The steel companies then asked the courts to find the president's actions unconstitutional. In *Youngstown Sheet and Tube Co. v. Sawyer* (1952), the Supreme Court did so. It found that the president lacked inherent power under the Constitution to seize the steel mills and that Congress had chosen not to give him statutory power to do so. Thus, in a rare occurrence, the Court ordered the president to reverse his actions, and Truman immediately complied.

Richard Nixon

The courts held that President Nixon could not impound funds appropriated by Congress, engage in electronic surveillance without a search warrant, or prevent the publication of the *Pentagon Papers*. He complied with each decision. In 2008 (*Medellin v. Texas*), the Supreme Court declared that President George W. Bush lacked the power to order the state of Texas to reopen the murder case of a Mexican who had been sentenced to death without being told he had a right to contact the Mexican consulate. That decision ended the matter. Similarly, in 2016, a tie on the Supreme Court effectively ended President Obama's program to shield undocumented immigrants who were the parents of citizens or of lawful permanent residents from deportation and to provide them work permits.

The Watergate scandal produced another important case involving presidential prerogatives. The special prosecutor, Leon Jaworski, subpoenaed tapes and documents relating to sixty-four conversations of President Nixon and his aides and advisers. Jaworski needed the material for the prosecution of Nixon administration officials, but the president claimed that executive privilege protected his private conversations with his assistants and refused to produce the subpoenaed material. Thus, the case worked its way quickly to the Supreme Court.

In *United States v. Nixon* (1974), the Court unanimously ordered the president to turn the subpoenaed material over to the special prosecutor. Although Nixon had threatened not to comply with anything less than a "definitive" decision, he obeyed the Court. The Court held that a claim of executive privilege unrelated to military, diplomatic, or national security matters cannot be absolute and in this case must give way to considerations of due process of law in criminal proceedings. Moreover, the justices reaffirmed that it was they, and not the president, who would make the final judgment in such matters. Nixon resigned the presidency about two weeks later.

Bill Clinton

Although the Constitution does not discuss immunity for the president from lawsuits, there has always been a concern that unless executive employees enjoy immunity for their official actions, they would be constantly looking over their shoulders for possible lawsuits and could not administer laws vigorously and effectively. In response, the federal courts have developed a doctrine of official immunity for the president and other executive officials. In 1982, the Supreme Court held that the president is entitled to absolute immunity in civil suits regarding his official acts (*Nixon v. Fitzgerald*).

Paula Jones raised a different issue. She sued Bill Clinton over "abhorrent" sexual advances that she claimed he made to her while he was governor of Arkansas and over punishment that she claimed she received from her supervisors in her state job after she rejected the governor's advances. The White House, fearing a media circus surrounding the embarrassing charges, claimed that while in office, the president was immune from private civil litigation arising out of *unofficial* acts committed in a personal capacity before he took office.

The Supreme Court saw things differently and, in *Clinton v. Jones* (1997), held that the president enjoyed no such immunity. It also opined that the case could move ahead without substantially burdening President Clinton. Preparations for the trial went forward, but the presiding judge dismissed the case as frivolous shortly before it was scheduled to begin in 1998. Jones appealed this decision, and on November 13, 1998, she agreed to accept $850,000 to settle with Clinton.

Nevertheless, the president complied with the Court's decision and provided pre-trial testimony for the Jones case, giving his political opponents, who were funding the case, the opportunity to ask embarrassing questions about his relationship with White House intern Monica Lewinsky (who also provided testimony). Clinton's supporters argued that these questions provided the potential for a perjury trap because the president was naturally reluctant to give complete or fully accurate answers. These responses, in turn, provided the Republicans with ammunition to charge that the president had committed perjury, suborned witnesses, and obstructed justice, leading to the House impeaching him in 1998.

The current Supreme Court. Front row (left to right): Stephen Breyer, Clarence Thomas, John Roberts, Ruth Bader Ginsburg, Samuel Alito. Second row (left to right): Neil Gorsuch, Sonia Sotomayor, Elena Kagan, Brett Kavanaugh.

George W. Bush

The war on terrorism has presented new challenges for judicial oversight of the presidency. The Court limited the president's powers when it found that detainees held in the United States and at the naval base at Guantánamo Bay, Cuba, had the right to challenge their detention before a judge or other neutral decision maker (*Hamdi v. Rumsfeld, Rasul v. Bush,* 2004). In another historic decision, *Hamdan v. Rumsfeld* (2006), the Supreme Court held that the procedures President George W. Bush had approved for trying prisoners at Guantánamo Bay lacked congressional authorization and violated both the Uniform Code of Military Justice and the Geneva Conventions. The flaws the Court cited were the failure to guarantee defendants the right to attend their trial and the prosecution's ability under the rules to introduce hearsay evidence, unsworn testimony, and evidence obtained through coercion. Equally important, the Constitution did not empower the president to establish judicial procedures on his own. The Bush administration followed each of these decisions.

Thomas Jefferson

Presidents are not always compliant with Court decisions, however. In *United States v. Burr* (1807), President Jefferson was subpoenaed to appear at the treason trial of Aaron Burr and to produce a certain letter. Jefferson refused to appear at the trial but he did provide the document, while stressing that he did so voluntarily and not because of judicial writ. Similarly, President James Monroe was subpoenaed as a witness in a trial, but he sent a written response instead.[70]

Abraham Lincoln

The Civil War raised many difficult constitutional questions for the Court and the president. One set of cases found President Abraham Lincoln simply ignoring court orders. The president had suspended the writ of habeas corpus, which requires the government to explain why a person has been detained, and in the most famous of these cases, a citizen named John Merryman who was held prisoner by the military sued for his freedom. Chief Justice Roger Taney ordered his release, but Lincoln refused to give Merryman up to the US marshal sent to bring him into court. The chief justice (on circuit court duty) then held, in *Ex parte Merryman* (1861), that the president had exceeded his constitutional authority (the Constitution seems to give only Congress the power to suspend habeas corpus), but Lincoln simply ignored the decision and Merryman remained under arrest. Lincoln argued that he had not violated the Constitution but that in any case, it would be better for the president to violate a single provision to a limited extent than to incur anarchy because of failure to suppress the rebellion in the South.

DEFERENCE TO THE PRESIDENT

A principal reason why complying with judicial decisions has rarely posed a problem for the president is the small number of instances in which the courts have held presidential actions to be in violation of the Constitution. Rarely have even these decisions interfered significantly with the president's policies (the *Youngstown* case was a major exception). More typically, these cases have dealt with matters such as presidential instructions to customs officials or the suspension of the writ of habeas corpus.

Most presidential actions are not based on the president's prerogatives under the Constitution and therefore do not lend themselves to constitutional adjudication. Effective opposition to most presidential policies must focus on the broader political arena. Moreover, it is especially difficult to prevent the president from acting. Most challenges occur only after the fact. On some occasions, it is possible to oppose the president by challenging the constitutionality of laws he supported and Congress passed. Such efforts are rarely successful, but they were important during the early years of the New Deal. In the end, however, President Roosevelt prevailed.

National Security

In the area of foreign and defense policy, the Court has interpreted the Constitution and statutes to give the president broad discretion to act. In general, the history of litigation regarding challenges to the president's actions in the field of national security policy has been one of avoidance, postponement of action, or deference to the chief executive, particularly during the time frame in which the action occurs. The judiciary has been content to find that discretionary actions of the executive branch were beyond its competence to adjudicate.[71]

Since the Civil War, presidents have been allowed especially broad powers in wartime. During the Civil War, the Supreme Court approved President Lincoln's deployment of troops during hostilities in the absence of a declaration of war and gave the chief executive discretion to determine the extent of force the crisis demanded and when an emergency existed. Similarly, it upheld the president's blockade of the South, the expansion of the army and navy beyond statutory limits, the calling out of the militia, and most of his suspensions of habeas corpus. He spent public funds without appropriations, declared martial law in various areas, ordered people arrested without warrant, tried civilians in military courts, closed the use of the post office for "treasonable" correspondence, seized property, and emancipated slaves—all without interference from the courts.[72]

During World War I, Congress delegated President Woodrow Wilson broad authority to regulate commissions, transportation, and the economy; to draft soldiers; and even to censor criticism—all with the approval of the Court. Franklin D. Roosevelt exercised even broader economic powers during World War II. He ordered the removal of Japanese Americans from the West Coast to relocation centers and confiscated their property, and the Court upheld his action in *Korematsu v. United States* (1944). He also bypassed the courts to establish special military commissions to try Nazi saboteurs, again with the Court's approval in *Ex parte Quirin* (1942).

During the period of US military involvement in Vietnam, no declaration or other formal congressional authorization for the war was ever issued. Many people, including many legal authorities, felt that this country's participation in the war without a formal declaration by Congress was unconstitutional, and several dozen cases were brought in federal court by opponents of the war to challenge various aspects of its legality. However, the Supreme Court simply refused to hear all but one of these cases and never issued a written opinion regarding the war. A combination of deference to the president and pragmatic politics (one wonders what would have happened had the war been declared unconstitutional while troops were engaged in combat) rendered the Court irrelevant to the issue.[73]

Similarly, a district court refused to hear a suit brought by several members of Congress that challenged George Bush's expansion of US forces in the Persian Gulf in 1991 as a prelude to war. In this case, the court simply found that the country was not yet at war and thus there was no basis for the suit. Another court also found the military to be within its rights to inoculate members of the armed forces against biological weapons, even without their permission, to facilitate the preparation for war in the Gulf.

It is interesting that in times in which presidents are most likely to stretch their power (i.e., in wartime), the courts are the least likely to intervene. When they finally do, the war may already be over. For example, following both the Civil War (*Ex parte Milligan*, 1869) and World War II, the Supreme Court held that military tribunals could not try civilians while the civilian courts were open. In each case, however, the president at whom the decision was directed was no longer living.

In the aftermath of the 9/11 terrorist attacks, the FBI detained more than 1,200 people as possible dangers to national security. Of these detainees, 762 were illegal aliens (mostly Arabs and Muslims), and many of them languished in jail for months until cleared by the FBI. For the first time in US history, the federal government withheld the names of detainees, reducing their opportunities to exercise their rights to access to the courts and to counsel. The government argued that releasing the names and details of those arrested would give terrorists a window on the terror investigation. For similar reasons, the president also claimed the right to deny suspected terrorists or captured prisoners normal rights in the judicial process. In 2004, the Supreme Court refused to consider whether the government properly withheld names and other details about these prisoners. However, we have seen that the Court did overrule the president regarding the rights of detainees to challenge their detentions before a neutral official and the procedures for trying prisoners.

During peacetime, the courts have found that presidents also have substantial discretion to act in the areas of foreign affairs and defense. They have broad prerogatives to act in negotiating and executing international agreements, withholding state secrets from the public, allocating international airline routes, terminating treaties, making executive agreements, recognizing foreign governments, using military activities to protect American interests abroad, punishing foreign adversaries, and acquiring and divesting foreign territory.

Domestic Policy

In the domestic sphere, the president's prerogatives are closely linked to maintaining order. Thus, presidents have discretion to declare and terminate national emergencies and even martial law. They may also call out the militia or the regular armed forces to control internal friction and keep the peace.

It is not unusual for courts to find the actions of executive branch officials to be violation of statutes passed by Congress, usually for exceeding the discretionary limits in the law. In these situations, the judiciary generally finds that the law, not the Constitution, must be changed (or perhaps just clarified) before the president's agents can take certain actions. Depending on the prevailing view in Congress, this may pose little problem for the president. At any rate, rarely are the issues involved central to his program.

Donald Trump is an exception. From the earliest days of his presidency, he encountered resistance from the courts on matters central to his administration, as you can see in box 12.2.

Box 12.2 ★ Donald Trump Struggles with the Courts

No policy was more important to Donald Trump than immigration. He acted aggressively to limit both legal and illegal immigration. White House officials claimed the president had almost unlimited discretion to make national security judgments and to control immigration. The courts disagreed.

Federal courts held against the president on his orders to establish travel bans on people from certain countries; to cut funding from cities, sometimes known as "sanctuary cities" that limit cooperation with US immigration authorities; to end the Deferred Action for Childhood Arrivals program that shields from deportation young immigrants brought illegally to the United States as children; to allow long detentions for migrant families; to allow blanket detention of asylum seekers; to swiftly deport asylum seekers who fail an initial screening; require asylum seekers to remain in Mexico while they await a hearing; require asylum seekers to request asylum in countries through which they pass to reach the United States; to hold asylum seekers indefinetly without possibility of a bail hearing; to ask about citizenship in the 2020 census; and to reject asylum claims from migrants entering the United States illegally.

Trump was also assertive in opposing rules designed to protect the environment. Nevertheless, the courts ruled against the administration dozens of times. Examples include orders to delay compliance with rules curbing flaring to burn off leaking methane; reduce asthma-causing ozone pollution; reduce toxic mercury contamination in water supplies; reduce lead in paint; require state transportation departments to monitor greenhouse gas emission levels on national highways and set targets for reducing them; issue new federal coal leases; allow offshore drilling in the Atlantic and Arctic Oceans; lift mining restrictions in Bristol Bay, Alaska; ban the use of some pesticides; speed up the Keystone XL pipeline; and establish renewable-fuel requirements. At least part of the explanation for the administration's losses in the courts was its less than rigorous following of important procedures, leading to poorly crafted legal efforts that risk being struck down in court.[74]

In addition, the courts have voided or delayed the president's orders to ban transgender troops; allow employers with religious or moral objections to opt out of health-care coverage for birth control; make it easier to fire federal employees; add Medicaid work requirements; allow small businesses to set up health insurance plans that skirt requirements of the Affordable Care Act; reduce payments to hospitals for drugs given to Medicare beneficiaries in outpatient clinics; require drug manufacturers to display the price of drugs in advertisements for them; end grants to programs on preventing teen pregnancy; and build a wall along the border with Mexico.

Trump has responded to his losses in the courts with hostility, criticizing them in a bellicose manner. His own nominee to the Supreme Court, Neil Gorsuch, described the president's criticism as "disheartening" and "demoralizing" to independent federal courts. The president's criticism prompted Chief Justice John G. Roberts Jr. to direct a rare and pointed shot at him. "We do not have Obama judges or Trump judges, Bush judges or Clinton judges," Roberts declared. "What we have is an extraordinary group of dedicated judges doing their level best to do equal right to those appearing before them." The statement added, "That independent judiciary is something we should all be thankful for."

Overturning the Courts

If presidents are dissatisfied with Supreme Court decisions, their first thoughts usually are focused on appointing new members with views similar to their own. There are some other options, however. They may join in congressional efforts to remove certain types of cases from the Court's appellate jurisdiction.[75] Congress has succeeded in such an action only once, however—on jurisdiction to hear appeals on certain writ of habeas corpus cases following the Civil War—and in this case (*Ex parte McCardle*, 1869) the president supported the Court.

George W. Bush asked Congress to strip the federal courts of jurisdiction to hear habeas corpus petitions from detainees seeking to challenge their designation as enemy combatants or who were waiting for the government to determine whether they were enemy combatants. This portion of a broader law allowed the US government to detain such aliens indefinitely without prosecuting them in any manner. However, in 2008, the Supreme Court in *Boumediene v. Bush* voided that provision and held that foreign terrorism suspects in custody at Guantánamo Bay have constitutional rights to challenge their detention in US courts. "The laws and Constitution are designed to survive, and remain in force, in extraordinary times," the Court proclaimed. The Court also found that the procedure established for reviewing enemy combatant status failed to offer the fundamental procedural protections of habeas corpus.[76]

Alternatively, presidents might support efforts to pass a constitutional amendment to overturn a Court interpretation of the Constitution, as George H. W. Bush did when the Court held that the burning of the American flag was a form of protected speech. President Reagan supported amendments to allow prayer in public schools and to prohibit abortions. Such efforts rarely succeed, however, and these did not.

In contrast, when the Court has made a statutory interpretation in which it interprets an act of Congress, Congress can reverse the decision simply by changing the law to clarify the intentions of those supporting the policy.[77] In a notable example, in 1953, President Eisenhower supported legislation that deeded federal mineral rights on offshore lands to the states even though the Court had held in 1951 that the federal government owned the rights.

JUDICIAL POWERS

In addition to enforcing court orders, presidents have some judicial instruments of their own. For example, they can issue pardons, commute sentences, grant clemency, and proclaim amnesty. These powers are exclusively theirs. Table 12.5 shows the number of pardon, commutations, and remitted convictions issued by recent presidents.

Over the years, the exercise of this judicial authority by presidents has sparked controversy. Critics accused both Thomas Jefferson and Abraham Lincoln of favoring their friends and Harry S. Truman of avoiding the usual scrutiny of pardons in the Department of Justice. Gerald Ford's unconditional pardon of Richard Nixon in 1974 became a major political issue that adversely affected Ford's electability two years later. Issued prior to a conviction or even an indictment of the former president, the pardon, "for all offenses against the United States which Richard Nixon has committed or may have committed or taken part in during the period from January 20, 1969, through August 9, 1974," precluded any criminal prosecution. Although critics accused Ford of subverting the legal process, they did not dispute his power to issue the pardon.[78] Whether Nixon's acceptance of it amounted to an admission of guilt has also been unclear.

Table 12.5 Presidential Pardons, Commutations, and Rescinded Convictions

President	Years in Office	No. of Pardons, Commutations, and Remitted Convictions
Eisenhower	1953–1961	1,157
Kennedy	1961–1963	575
Johnson	1963–1969	1,187
Nixon	1969–1974	926
Ford	1974–1977	409
Carter	1977–1981	566
Reagan	1981–1989	406
G. H. W. Bush	1989–1993	77
Clinton	1993–2001	459
G. W. Bush	2001–2009	200
Obama	2009–2017	1,927
Trump*	2017–	21

* As of September 2019.
Source: US Department of Justice, "Clemency Statistics."

On December 24, 1992, twelve days before former Secretary of Defense Caspar Weinberger was to go to trial for perjury in the Iran–Contra scandal, George H. W. Bush pardoned him. In issuing pardons to Weinberger and five other Iran–Contra defendants from the Reagan years, President Bush charged that the Independent Counsel's prosecutions represented the "criminalization of policy differences." The other people pardoned included former national security assistant Robert C. McFarlane, former assistant secretary of state Elliott Abrams, and three CIA officials. The Weinberger pardon marked the first time a president had ever pardoned someone in whose trial he might have been called as a witness (the president had knowledge of factual events underlying the case).

In 2007, George W. Bush commuted the sentence of Vice President Dick Cheney's former chief of staff, Scooter Libby, who was found guilty of perjury and obstruction of justice in the case of the leaking the identity of CIA undercover operative Valerie Plame. The president's action was highly controversial and added fuel to the intense political polarization of the time.

In addition to the issuance of unconditional pardons, presidents may grant conditional reprieves. In 1954, the Supreme Court upheld President Eisenhower's commutation of a death sentence, provided that the individual never be paroled; in 1972, President Nixon granted executive clemency to former labor leader James Hoffa on the condition that he refrain from further union activities. In 1999, President Clinton granted clemency to eleven Puerto Rican terrorists on the condition that they renounce the use of violence and that they stay away from each other.

Presidents may also issue general amnesty. George Washington did so for hundreds of participants in the Whiskey Rebellion. Abraham Lincoln exercised this authority in 1863 in an effort to persuade Southern deserters to return to the Union. In order to heal the wounds of the Civil War, his successor, Andrew Johnson, in 1868 granted universal amnesty to all those who had participated in the insurrection. Twentieth-century presidents used this power to pardon those individuals who were convicted of crimes and subsequently served in the military and to prevent the imposition of wartime penalties (still on the books) on those who failed to register for the draft during peacetime. Harry S. Truman pardoned nine thousand people who had been convicted of desertion in peacetime.

The most sweeping and controversial amnesty proclamation in recent times occurred in 1977 when—implementing one of his campaign promises—President Carter pardoned all Vietnam draft resisters and asked the Defense Department to consider, on an individual basis, the cases of military deserters during that war. Congress attempted to undercut Carter's general pardon by prohibiting the use of funds to execute his order but was unsuccessful because the president's directive to the Justice Department did not require a separate appropriation.

President Clinton issued nearly 40 percent of all his pardons on his last day in office in 2001, and several of these pardons raised a storm of controversy. Among those he pardoned were a fugitive on the FBI's Ten Most Wanted list, a crack cocaine drug lord, and a baldness-cure scam artist, whose patrons had paid Clinton's brother-in-law Hugh Rodham $400,000. (Rodham paid it back after the press found out.) The pardon that attracted the most attention, however, was of billionaire Marc Rich, who was accused of tax fraud and illegally doing business with hostile nations. Rich had lived abroad as a fugitive for many years and even renounced his US citizenship, and he employed prominent attorneys with connections to Clinton to make the case for his pardon. Critics charged that in making some of his decisions regarding pardons, the president had circumvented the regular review process in the Department of Justice and responded to inappropriate back-channel lobbying from those who were politically well connected and to some who had made large donations to his presidential library and the Democratic Party.

George W. Bush also granted clemency to several people who circumvented the normal review process. Bush even withdrew one grant of clemency the day after he granted it when more information about the recipient came to light.

Donald Trump issued his first pardon early in his term when he pardoned Joseph Arpaio, the former police chief of Maricopa County, Arizona. Arpaio was convicted of contempt of court when he refused to end racial profiling. In issuing his pardon, the president bypassed the standard White House review process and did not consult the Justice Department. Later, the president pardoned conservative commentator Dinesh D'Souza, convicted of violating campaign finance laws; former Vice President Dick Cheney aide Scooter Libby, convicted of obstruction of justice, perjury, and making false statements regarding the investigation of the leak of the covert identity of Central Intelligence Agency officer Valerie Plame Wilson; and Conrad Black, a personal friend convicted of embezzlement and obstruction of justice who wrote a flattering book about the president. In general, the president has focused his pardons on political figures and been unconcerned with rigorous review of clemency requests.

CONCLUSION

Presidents are involved in vital relationships with the judicial branch, especially with the Supreme Court. They attempt to influence its decisions through the process of selecting judges and justices and through the arguments of their subordinates before the courts. There are strong congressional constraints on them in the selection of judges, however, and presidents sometimes err in their choice of nominees. Although the executive branch has skilled litigators before the federal appellate courts and a clear record of success, the chief executive is ultimately dependent on the judgment of members of a branch of government that is much more autonomous than the legislature. The president is once again a facilitator, not a director, of change.

A judicial decision does not end a president's relationship with the courts on an issue; in the capacity as chief executive, a president may be obliged to enforce judicial decisions (a responsibility that sometimes conflicts with policy goals). Moreover, although the judiciary is generally deferential to presidents, the courts may order a president to comply with a holding against a presidential action. Such decisions do not affect most of what presidents do, but in some instances they do hamper their actions. Thus, both conflict and harmony characterize the president's relations with the courts, and influencing judicial decisions remains an important, but at times frustrating, priority for the White House.

DISCUSSION QUESTIONS

1. Presidents often face considerable opposition to their judicial nominees. What should be the role of the Senate in the confirmation process? Should an opposition-controlled Senate oppose nominees who share the president's views, or should the Senate simply be a check on the nominees' basic qualifications?
2. What criteria should the president employ when choosing judicial nominees? Are race, gender, and partisanship legitimate criteria? What should be the role of ideological considerations, such as whether a nominee believes in judicial activism or restraint?
3. Should the president be immune from civil lawsuits from private individuals while serving in office? Was the Supreme Court correct to state that such suits would not be a drain on the president's time and energy and that there would not be many frivolous suits? Did the Paula Jones suit, followed by the Kenneth Starr investigation, distract President Clinton from his presidential duties and/or encourage him to be more presidential in behavior?

WEB EXERCISES

1. Read the Supreme Court's decision in *United States v. Nixon* (1974). Note how the Court denied the president's claim of executive privilege while at the same time establishing the principle of executive privilege for the first time in a Supreme Court case. Go to https://www.oyez.org/cases/1973/73-1766. What does the case tell us about the relationship between the judiciary and the president?
2. Examine the Supreme Court's decision in *Bush v. Gore.* Go to https://www.oyez.org/cases/2000/00-949. Should the Court have become involved in the Florida election controversy? If so, why? If not, why not? Do you think the Court's prestige increased or decreased as a result of the decision in this matter?

SELECTED READINGS

Abraham, Henry J. *Justices, Presidents, and Senators: A History of U.S. Supreme Court Appointments from Washington to Bush II*, 5th ed. Lanham, MD: Rowman & Littlefield, 2013.

Binder, Sarah A., and Forrest Maltzman. *Advice and Dissent: The Struggle to Shape the Federal Judiciary.* Washington, DC: Brookings Institution, 2009.

Epstein, Lee, and Jeffrey A. Segal. *Advice and Consent*. Oxford, UK: Oxford University Press, 2005.

———. "Nominating Federal Judges and Justices." In *The Oxford Handbook of the American Presidency*, edited by George C. Edwards III and William G. Howell. Oxford, UK: Oxford University Press, 2009.

Fisher, Louis. "Judicial Review of the War Power." *Presidential Studies Quarterly* 35 (September 2005): 466–495.

Goldman, Sheldon. *Picking Federal Judges*. New Haven, CT: Yale University Press, 1997.

Nemacheck, Christine L. "Appointing Supreme Court Justices." In *The Oxford Handbook of U.S. Judicial Behavior*, edited by Lee Epstein and Stefanie A. Lindquist. New York: Oxford University Press, 2017.

Scherer, Nancy. "Appointing Federal Judges." In *The Oxford Handbook of U.S. Judicial Behavior*, edited by Lee Epstein and Stefanie A. Lindquist. New York: Oxford University Press, 2017.

Whittington, Keith E. "Judicial Checks on the President." In *The Oxford Handbook of the American Presidency*, edited by George C. Edwards III and William G. Howell. Oxford, UK: Oxford University Press, 2009.

Yalof, David A. *Pursuit of Justices: Presidential Politics and the Selection of Supreme Court Nominees*. Chicago, IL: University of Chicago Press, 1999.

13

Domestic and Economic Policy Making

★ ★ ★

Office of Management and Budget Director Mick Mulvaney preparing to testify
before Congress about the 2018 budget.

Donald Trump came to office promising to "drain the swamp" and transform
both politics in Washington, DC, and the policies coming out if it. On a full
range of issues—energy, immigration, health care, national defense, international trade, education, criminal justice, infrastructure, tax reform, regulation,
environmental policy—he promised that he would solve problems that previous
presidents could not, or would not. With unified Republican control of the White
House and Congress for the first time in a decade, his supporters expected him to
succeed. Nevertheless, the realities of governing and the limits of the president's
ability to force legislation through a divided Republican majority in Congress frustrated his agenda. His major legislative accomplishments in his first two years were
appointing conservative judges to the federal bench and winning passage of a tax

411

cut. Trump was unable to muster enough congresional support to push through his signature promises to repeal the Affordable Care Act or build a wall on the Mexican border. When he made changes in environmental, immigration, or trade policies, it was through exercising unilateral power.

It is in the nature of the presidency to push for major political change. The public expects the president to articulate and achieve national goals, make good on campaign promises, respond to emergencies, and propose solutions to the country's social, economic, and political ills. Failure to address critical issues and rectify national problems usually results in public criticism, lower job approval, and electoral defeat.

The problem confronting all presidents is that public expectations exceed their institutional and political ability to meet them. Presidents have at their disposal significant policy expertise, but the experts do not always agree on what to do or how to accomplish it. In addition, serious economic, social, and political problems may not be amenable to easy or quick policy solutions. All complex policies involve difficult trade-offs among competing goals, values, and interests. For example, regulations may protect important interests such as health, safety, and economic security, but they may also be costly and inhibit some useful behavior. Finally, presidents cannot depend on the support of those in the other branches of government, much less those outside the government, whose cooperation they require.

THE DEVELOPMENT OF A DOMESTIC POLICY-MAKING ROLE

Presidents have had a limited policy role for much of US history. They recommended measures, took positions, and occasionally even drafted bills, but they rarely formulated domestic policy, which was considered a congressional responsibility. Beginning with Theodore Roosevelt, however, and continuing with Woodrow Wilson, the president's domestic policy-making role became more regularized. Both presidents proposed substantial legislative programs.

Wilson's Republican successors (Harding, Coolidge, and Hoover) did not follow his example. Their conservative philosophy undoubtedly influenced their conception of a more limited presidential role within the domestic policy sphere. From the perspective of the 1920s, the Republican interlude was a return to "normalcy," as Warren Harding termed it, in which Congress proposed and the president disposed. From today's perspective, it was a brief interlude in the growth of the president's domestic expectations and responsibilities.

Franklin D. Roosevelt, more than any other president, enlarged policy-making expectations. Coming into office in the throes of the Great Depression, Roosevelt believed it was essential for the president to take the initiative. He exploited the sizable Democratic majorities during his tenure to pass a large number of policies that addressed the nation's pressing economic problems.

By the end of the Roosevelt era, the president's role as domestic policy maker was firmly established to the point where even Congress expected the president to lead. When Harry S. Truman, Roosevelt's successor, asked Congress for legislation to combat inflation, Republican legislative leaders criticized him for not presenting a draft bill. When Dwight D. Eisenhower failed to propose a comprehensive legislative program during his first year as president, he was criticized from both sides of the aisle. "Don't expect us to start from scratch on what you people want," an irate member of the House Foreign Affairs Committee told an

Eisenhower official. "That's not the way we do things here. You draft the bills and we work them over."[1]

Ever since, the White House has been at the center of domestic policy initiatives. Democratic presidents tend to propose larger and more activist policies, but Republican administrations also have substantial agendas, often promoted as efforts to scale back the scope of government action.

DOMESTIC POLICY UNITS WITHIN THE WHITE HOUSE OFFICE AND THE EOP

Chapter 8 described the growth of the presidential institution, the offices that assist with the monitoring and advisory needs of the president. In addition to these administrative structures, a number of policy-specific advisory units in the White House Office provide substantive policy formulation. These offices develop broad agendas, craft specific proposals, and evaluate plans originating in agencies. These White House structures have become more specialized and entrenched over time.

In 1970, Nixon created a Domestic Council in the White House to oversee policy development and coordination, headed by an Assistant to the President for Domestic Policy. Although the name and internal structure of this unit has changed, presidents have maintained its function as the locus of presidential policy development and for coordinating the policy activities of cabinet agencies. Nixon saw the council as a domestic equivalent to the NSC. Under Donald Trump, its members include the president, two domestic policy advisors, cabinet secretaries, the heads of the OMB, the EPA, and the CEA, and key economic policy officials.

dpa picture alliance/Alamy Stock Photo

National Economic Council Director Larry Kudlow (right) and Treasury Secretary Steven Mnuchin (left).

Generally, presidents have tried to consolidate policy making within the White House and the Executive Office of the President. Deciding issues in the president's immediate orbit offers more control, as key personnel are under direct presidential authority. The influence of these staffs has varied with the operating style and policy goals of presidents, however. Presidents may choose to allow cabinet secretaries more latitude in devising policy, or even delegate key decisions to congressional leadership. Obama, for example, left many legislative details of the Affordable Care Act to Democratic congressional leaders, even in the face of criticism that he had not taken stronger stands on what he would or would not accept in the final bill.[2] On other issues, Obama took more direct control, appointing a number of senior aides as "policy czars" to help him develop initiatives that cut across agency jurisdictions. Obama's proliferation of White House policy units led to complaints from his department and agency heads that they had been left out of the loop and relegated to the policy sidelines.[3]

During the administration of Gerald Ford, the White House staff did not play a major role in policy development until the president began his 1976 election campaign; during Carter's presidency, it did play such a role. The president depended on his domestic policy advisers to detail the principal legislative initiatives he proposed to Congress. Although Ronald Reagan turned to his department secretaries individually and collectively for their advice, he also relied heavily during his first term on his counselor, Edwin Meese, who was responsible for overseeing the implementation of the president's major domestic initiatives. During the Clinton and George W. Bush administrations, the White House staff designed legislative proposals in the areas of health, education, energy, campaign finance, and electoral reform.

Donald Trump has by all accounts a haphazard policy process, centralizing some decisions in the White House, often without clear structures, and delegating other policy decisions to cabinet officials. Some staffers are enormously influential. Stephen Miller is a main driver of the president's hardline immigration policy,[4] and Jared Kushner has an unusually broad portfolio (everything from criminal justice reform, Middle East peace, and trade negotiations to opioid addiction and federal government reorganization).[5] In the Trump White House, longstanding policy units such as the Domestic Policy Council have given way to specific advisors who have the president's ear.[6] At times, the combination of weak policy structures and internal disagreement results in contradictory announcements and rapid policy reversals. For example, after the president met with the Democratic House leadership and announced an agreement to spend $2 trillion on infrastructure, the plan stalled after both acting White House Chief of Staff Mick Mulvaney and Senate Majority Leader Mitch McConnell (R-KY) voiced objections.[7] Daniel Drezner has identified numerous instances in which White House staff walked back Trump's policy announcements or ignored them in the expectation that the president would not follow up.[8]

Growth of White House Policy Staffs

As presidents began exerting more influence over policy initiation, their need for dedicated staff advice grew. Franklin D. Roosevelt, Truman, and Eisenhower had small staffs devoted to policy, often putting issues in the hands of advisors with other responsibilities. (Truman and Kennedy relied on staffers serving as White House Counsel as much for policy work as well as for legal advice.) Kennedy and Johnson set up task forces composed of campaign supporters, academics, and business and labor leaders to investigate problems and devise possible solutions. The large number of task forces brought an expansion in the White House personnel who regularly dealt with domestic policy matters. By the mid-1960s, separate White House staffs had been created in the national security and domestic policy spheres, reflecting the complexity of contemporary issues and the need for more specialization and expertise. President Nixon enlarged and institutionalized these staffs, and they have remained active since then.

The most important domestic policy unit in the White House is the Office of Management and Budget. From its origins as the Bureau of the Budget with responsibility for coordinating budget requests, the office has expanded its role to include additional functions central to the president's ability to monitor and control executive branch activities. These responsibilities have become institutionalized either through presidential practice or by law. In 1970, Nixon reorganized the Bureau of the Budget, acknowledging its broader responsibility over executive branch practices by renaming it the Office of Management and Budget. The OMB now has offices dedicated to financial management, government contracting rules, regulatory review, e-government and information technology policy, and management of government intellectual property.

Policy Roles of the Office of Management and Budget
The OMB's importance in the policy process extends well beyond the preparation of the budget (a major responsibility in its own right).

Legislative Clearance
One key to the OMB's influence remains its central clearance authority. The initial Bureau of the Budget responsibility for reviewing annual agency budget requests was soon extended to all executive branch requests for legislation, regardless of whether money would be expended. In each case, budget officials had to decide whether the proposal was in accordance with the president's program, consistent with the president's objectives, or at the very least not opposed by the president. That review authority was soon extended again to include review of all positions that cabinet officials took on proposed legislation and testimony that officials gave in hearings. Starting in 1947, standing committees of both legislative bodies requested that the BOB indicate the president's position on any legislation that did not originate in the executive departments and agencies.

From the president's perspective, the central clearance process offers a number of benefits: (1) it provides a mechanism for imprinting a presidential seal of approval on those proposals that the administration supports and withholding it from those it opposes; (2) it makes the departments and agencies aware of each other's views; and (3) it helps resolve interagency disputes and promotes internal coordination. For these reasons, central legislative clearance has remained the standard operating procedure for contemporary presidents, despite periodic resistance from agency officials who may view it as an unwelcome constraint.

As part of its coordinative role, the OMB also prepares statements of administration policy (SAPs) on most bills approved by congressional committees and awaiting floor consideration. SAPs, which are drafted by the relevant department or agency or occasionally by the OMB, are then cleared within the executive branch and approved by White House policy and legislative liaison aides. The purpose of such statements is to inform Congress of the administration's position on the legislation, with the ultimate goal of influencing congressional deliberations.[9]

Regulatory Review

Once legislation becomes law, executive branch departments and agencies are charged with its implementation. They typically do so by establishing regulations through which the legislative policy is put into effect. These rules cover everything from environmental standards and workplace safety rules to implementing provisions of the Affordable Care Act that regulate health insurers. These regulations can be controversial, and they became a point of contention by the late 1970s when the cost of environmental regulations in particular triggered opposition.

In 1981, Reagan issued an executive order establishing a regulatory review process designed to reduce the number of regulations that federal agencies promulgate. The process requires that all significant regulations be cleared by a unit of the OMB called the Office of Information and Regulatory Affairs (OIRA). OIRA has the authority to review these rules to make sure that they are necessary, cost effective, and consistent with administration goals. OIRA can require revisions, and can prevent regulations from proceeding further. Reagan's successors have continued this process.

Today, the procedures for reviewing agency regulations begin when an executive department or agency proposes a rule. They then solicit public comments from nongovernmental groups that the rule might affect. Based on these comments, the agencies initiating the regulation may refine it and submit it to the OMB for its review. To justify a proposed regulation to the OMB, federal agencies must provide quantitative data that estimate its costs and benefits. Shortly after taking office, Trump issued an executive order requiring agencies to repeal two regulations for each new rule they propose.[10] It is unclear how well agencies are complying with the order, but the number of new rules has declined.[11]

The regulatory review process has increased the OMB's influence at the expense of the rest of the executive branch and Congress. It circumvents the "iron triangle" relationship that had traditionally existed among the executive branch agencies, the congressional committees that oversee them, and outside interest groups. Regulatory review puts the OMB in a position to negate or modify the political compromises these parties may have made. Working behind the scenes, the OMB has become the presidency's principal naysayer, coordinator, and overseer of executive branch departments and agencies.

MAKING ECONOMIC POLICY

The president's role as an economic manager became permanent in the 1930s with FDR and the New Deal. Prior to that time, presidents initiated or supported proposals to correct specific problems that had arisen within the economy, but they did not assume general responsibility for economic policy. Theodore Roosevelt's trust busting and Woodrow Wilson's labor reforms are two examples of these early forms of presidential involvement.

The depth of the 1930s Depression, the degree of public panic, and Herbert Hoover's resounding 1932 defeat prompted a comprehensive presidential role in economic affairs. No longer could presidents enjoy the luxury of standing on the sidelines. Franklin Roosevelt's activism became the model for his Democratic successors. Even conservative Republicans, such as Ronald Reagan and George W. Bush, found that there was no turning back from public expectations of presidential economic leadership.

Congress expects and even requires this attention. The Employment Act of 1946 obligates the president to strive for maximum employment and production and annually report on the state of the economy to Congress. The Taft-Hartley Act of 1947 authorizes the president to intervene in labor–management disputes that threaten the nation's security and well-being. Congress has not only acknowledged an expanded presidential role but has also created executive agencies to help the executive fulfill it—the Council of Economic Advisers within the White House, the National Labor Relations Board, the Securities and Exchange Commission, and a new agency, the Consumer Financial Protection Bureau, intended to prevent many of the abuses that led to the 2008 financial crisis.

Every president since Roosevelt has strived to meet these expanded expectations. A president's job approval, re-electability, and legacy are closely associated with the state of the economy. Presidents devote more attention to economic matters than to any other policy area, except during noneconomic crises such as war.[12] The bottom line, as far as the president is concerned, is that the economy is usually a salient issue, and during economic downturns, it is *the* issue.

Limits on Control

Despite the centrality of the economy to evaluations of the president, in no other policy sphere are presidential limits more visible and harder to overcome. Although the president can do some things that have short-term economic effects—Trump's imposition of tariffs in 2018 and 2019 is expected to reduce economic growth by anywhere from a few tenths of a percentage point to a full point or more, depending on how long trade disputes last and whether other countries retaliate[13]—most economic factors are beyond the president's control. The business cycle, demographics, technology, oil shocks, international economic events and global growth, and consumer confidence are all beyond the president's immediate reach.[14] Spending levels (see Budget Policy, below) are mostly determined by commitments made in prior years, and are more a function of congressional action than presidential preferences. Presidents may behave as though they can guarantee economic growth, low inflation, low unemployment, and rising incomes through the right policies, but in reality they have neither the authority nor the instruments to do so.

The government agency with the greatest influence over short-term economic performance is the Federal Reserve Board (Fed), which sets interest rates and regulates the money supply. Cutting interest rates may stimulate economic growth but can risk inflationary pressure if growth becomes too fast. Increases in interest rates can reduce inflation and put the brakes on economic growth, but at the cost of short-term economic pain.

Because of the risk that presidents might be tempted to impose political calculations on these decisions, the law purposely insulates the Fed from presidential control. Members of the Board of Governors of the Federal Reserve serve fixed fourteen-year terms, limiting the number of appointments any president can make even over two full terms. In addition, members of the Board can only be removed "for cause." Although there is some dispute over just how effective these structures are, there is a strong norm of Fed independence and resistance to political pressure.[15] As he has in many other areas, Trump is challenging this norm, openly urging the Fed to cut interest rates in 2018 and 2019 and nominating candidates for seats on the Federal Reserve Board of Governors more for political loyalty than economic expertise.[16] Indeed, two of Trump's nominees for Board seats withdrew when Senate resistance emerged over questions about their qualifications and personal behavior.

Long-Term Planning

The politics of economic decision making has made long-range planning more difficult. The White House must consider the election cycle when calculating the effects of policy change. Administrations are likely to try to shape economic outcomes to serve their political benefit, although they rarely succeed.

The impact of politics on economic policy decisions has also made those decisions less stable over time. Unanticipated events and unintended consequences have frequently forced presidents to adjust their economic programs. President Carter had to recant on a promise to provide taxpayers with a $50 rebate as the budget deficit rose. President Reagan had to support a large revenue increase one year after winning a large tax cut from Congress. President George H. W. Bush violated his "read my lips, no new taxes" pledge in 1990; President Clinton was not able to keep his 1992 campaign promise to cut middle-class taxes; President George W. Bush had to support a massive government bailout bill to buttress major banks and other lenders after the financial crisis of 2008; and President Obama was forced to accept major cuts in government spending and a smaller revenue increase than he proposed.

Parochial Concerns

Economic policy making has always been sensitive to outside pressures from Congress, the bureaucracy, and organized interest groups, each of which has its own interests to protect and its own political axes to grind. Members of Congress must consider the economic impact on their constituencies; department and agency heads must be responsive to their clienteles; and organized groups must placate their members and supporters. To the extent that economic decisions require coalition building to become public policy—and most do—presidents must consider these varied interests.

The economic policy decisions of presidents can reap significant benefits for specific groups. Tax proposals, government assistance programs, defense spending, even regulatory activity have consequences for individuals and groups—some benefit, some do not. These outcomes influence evaluations of the president and the party in power and manifest themselves in political contributions and voting behavior.

Political scientists debate the relationship between presidential partisanship and economic performance. Larry Bartels, in his book *Unequal Democracy*, contends that family income rose faster during Democratic administrations than Republican ones from 1948 to 2005, the period of his study. He also found that unemployment was lower and economic inequality less when the Democrats controlled the White House.[17] James Campbell, using similar economic data, attributes the differences in income and unemployment levels to the economic conditions presidents inherited from their predecessors. He argues that Democrats began their presidencies with healthier economies than did Republicans. Taking the previous year's economy into account, Campbell found "no significant differences in the records of Democratic and Republican presidents with respect to economic growth, unemployment, or income inequality."[18] Economists Alan Blinder and Mark Watson found that Democratic presidents had better records than Republican presidents, but they conclude that the differences are more a function of favorable circumstances and international events than of substantive policy choices.[19]

Even the implementation of ongoing programs, in which the executive exercises discretion, can reap political largess. Political scientists Christopher Berry, Barry Burden, and William Howell found that 4 to 5 percent more government funds go to congressional districts represented by a member of the president's party.[20] This spending helps solidify partisan support; it also helps build generic support for presidents running for reelection.[21] Others have found that presidents and their partisan supporters benefit from the distribution of disaster relief and transportation funding.[22]

Economic Policies

The economic policies of presidents have varied. Truman, Kennedy, Reagan, George W. Bush, and Trump supported lower taxes to stimulate economic growth. Clinton advocated increased productivity through subsidies to encourage business to modernize and through tax credits to allow more people to afford additional education or job training. He also sought higher taxes on the wealthiest individuals to help pay for these tax cuts. Obama proposed additional aid for education, especially for improving training in science, technology, and math; expansion of preschool programs; and government grants to stimulate technological innovation; but he also advocated increasing taxes on wealthy individuals and corporations. Trump pushed a major tax cut through Congress in 2017.

Differing fiscal approaches lay at the core of competing presidential policies. A fiscal strategy is a plan to shape government revenue and expenditures to influence economic conditions. Until the mid-1970s, fiscal strategies were predicated on the economic theories of John Maynard Keynes, an eminent British economist who argued that increases in government spending and reductions in government taxes stimulate demand and invigorate the economy during periods of sluggish activity. Such policies also produce budget deficits. Keynes was not worried about these shortfalls, however, because he believed that in the long run a vibrant economy would generate greater revenues, reducing or eliminating the difference between expenditures and income. With the exception of Eisenhower, presidents Truman through Nixon subscribed to Keynes's economic beliefs.

During most of the 1950s and 1960s, sustained economic growth coupled with low unemployment and inflation seemed to confirm the merits of the Keynesian approach. By the 1970s, however, economic conditions began to deteriorate. Budget deficits increased, the rate of economic growth declined, and inflation rose dramatically. Keynesian economics did not offer satisfactory solutions to these problems, prompting economists to propose new theories.

University of Chicago economist Milton Friedman articulated one of these theories. He contended that the supply of money was the key to sound economic growth. Increasing interest rates would reduce the amount of money in circulation, thereby decreasing inflationary pressures and cooling the economy. Lowering interest rates, in contrast, would have the opposite effect, stimulating demand and output by making borrowing cheaper and more money available. In periods of high inflation and an overheated economy, a tight money policy made sense. However, when inflation was high and the economy stagnant, it did not. It was precisely this latter condition in the late-1970s that gave credence to what became known as supply-side economics: an economic theory that tax cuts, particularly at higher income levels, would stimulate investment and increase economic output. The resulting surge in economic production (the "supply" side) would lead to higher economic growth and lower unemployment.

The supply-side philosophy combined the Keynesian approach to generating demand with the regulation of interest rates and the monetary supply. Tax cuts stimulate spending and investment, whereas reducing the supply of money controls inflation. Ronald Reagan and George W. Bush, advocates of supply-side economics, desired to reduce corporate and personal income taxes, which would in theory free up capital for investment. Supporters of supply-side tax cuts argue that although they reduce revenues in the short run, they will increase them in the long term as the economy rebounds. These revenues never fully compensate for the revenues lost, however, and thus tax cuts increase the deficit.[23] Moreover, monetary policy has limits and is more effective at reducing inflation than stimulating long-term economic growth.[24]

The Great Recession

A major economic crisis occurred in the Great Recession of 2007–2008. The financial industry nearly collapsed as a result of the bursting of a real estate bubble. Complex financial instruments tied to mortgages exposed large banks and investment companies to excessive risks. By the fall of 2008, the entire international financial system was close to freezing up, with banks unsure about their ability to make any loans.[25] A breakdown of the system would have led to a global economic catastrophe.

With George W. Bush's support, Congress enacted a $700 billion package, the Troubled Asset Relief Program, designed to shore up bank finances and keep two large auto companies from failing and throwing employees and suppliers out of work and deepening the recession.

One of Barack Obama's first legislative initiatives was a massive fiscal stimulus bill, the $787 billion American Recovery and Reinvestment Act. The Act was designed to stimulate economic growth and help the economy recover. The recovery was slow, however: unemployment reached a thirty-year high, peaking at 10.1 percent; the economy shrank by 2.8 percent in 2009, the largest one-year drop since 1946.[26] The annual deficit grew to over $1.4 trillion in 2009 as revenues shrank from the recession, and it remained above the trillion dollar mark until 2013 (the years 2009–2012 added over $5 trillion to the national debt). Real estate values bottomed out, housing foreclosures increased, and tight credit hampered businesses. Republicans who had overwhelmingly opposed the stimulus bill claimed that the money was not well spent and that tax cuts, not stimulus spending, were the key to generating economic growth. Even as the economy emerged from the recession, annual growth remained modest.

As part of the policy response to the Great Recession, Congress passed the Wall Street Reform and Consumer Protection Act in 2010 (known as the Dodd-Frank bill), imposing new rules on large financial institutions with the goal of preventing another 2008 systemic financial crisis.[27] The legislation has been a lightning rod, with congressional Republicans (and President Trump) insisting that the law imposes burdensome regulations that hurt the financial industry.

With the exception of the health-care debate and the killing of Osama bin Laden, the economy dominated the news for Obama's presidency. Much of the coverage was negative, focusing on people who were out of work, lost their homes, and found their savings depleted. Concern about huge budget deficits and an increasing national debt added to the administration's travails and contributed to the Democrats' defeat in the 2010 midterm elections. Republican control of the House of Representatives and gains in the Senate following the election precluded further economic policy initiatives and placed the president on the political defensive. It took two years of constant campaigning, political brinksmanship, and modest economic recovery for Obama to improve his public standing.

President Obama's experience shows that economic policy takes time to have an impact; the more severe the downturn, the longer it takes to reverse. Yet politics is driven by the here and now, by tangible results and conditions. Presidents bear the consequences of a bad economy, even if they did not cause it and have limited means to correct it.

President Trump proposed a set of economic policies—primarily tax cuts, deregulation, repeal of the Affordable Care Act, trade protectionism, and infrastructure investment—that he insisted would produce economic growth greater than what the country had seen since 2008; the White House claimed that his agenda would produce twenty-five million jobs and 4 percent annual economic growth.[28] A private-sector analysis of his campaign proposal considered the job creation and economic growth goals unrealistic. The gap between promises and actuality is an enduring feature of the president's economic policy role, where optimistic forecasts and assurances usually run into the fact that economic policy is a complex area in which multiple stakeholders exert influence and where presidents have limited leverage.[29]

Trump faces an additional problem that his proposals cut across traditional partisan cleavages. Some of them—tax cuts and deregulation, for example—are core Republican positions. Others, such as tariffs and infrastructure spending, tend to have less support among Republicans in Congress. Although they could hold some appeal to Democrats, there is little evidence of any of the crossover support that the president might need to win passage of his proposals. Moreover, as of 2020, there still is no White House plan for infrastructure spending and little public or congressional support to repeal the Affordable Care Act.

International Trade

One economic policy area in which presidents have more authority is setting the conditions for international trade. While Congress has clear constitutional authority in this area, legislators have delegated much of their power to the president. Beginning with the Reciprocal Trade Act of 1934 and on many occasions since then, Congress has given the president authority to negotiate trade agreements subject to congressional approval and set tariff rates without congressional involvement.

In recent years, presidents have devoted increasing attenti on to international economic issues, especially free trade. The Clinton administration concluded two free trade agreements, the North American Free Trade Agreement (NAFTA) and the World Trade Organization. The George W. Bush and Obama administrations pursued free trade agreements with South Korea, Colombia, and Panama. Obama proposed one with Europe and another with nations on the Pacific Rim, the Trans-Pacific Partnership (TPP). The TPP was an agreement among twelve countries on both sides of the Pacific ocean to lower tariffs and other forms of trade barriers, but it notably excluded China. The Partnership was intended to strengthen US ties to trading partners in Asia and to reduce Chinese economic and strategic influence in the region.[30]

Clinton, Bush, and Obama were not the first presidents to promote international trade. Ever since the Wilson administration, when the United States emerged as a major world power, presidents have sought to lower the barriers to international commerce for American industry. They have met with frequent opposition, however, much of it from organized labor, which fears the loss of American jobs to lower-paid foreign workers, and from small businesses, which fear low-priced foreign competition. Older manufacturing industries, environmentalists, and even consumer advocates have also been critical of such agreements. Big business, in contrast, particularly firms engaged in international commerce, such as high-tech companies and service industries, and most economists tend to be more supportive of a free-trading international environment.

Donald Trump rode into office on a wave of frustration with local economic dislocation, which he blamed on trade deals that allowed foreign imports to undercut domestic production and destroy American jobs. He has used his delegated authority to impose tariffs on many kinds of imports, which he insists will protect American industry. You can read about his strategy in box 13.1.

Box 13.1 ★ Trump and Tariffs

"When a country (USA) is losing many billions of dollars on trade with virtually every country it does business with, trade wars are good and easy to win."[31] This March 2, 2018, tweet summarized the president's view of tariffs and international trade. Tariffs are levies on imported goods, and they are paid by importers, not other countries. Businesses typically pass the cost of tariffs on to consumers.

During the 2016 campaign, Trump promised he would revive American manufacturing and insisted that imports had hurt American businesses and cost American jobs. He argued that the North American Free Trade Agreement (NAFTA), the Trans-Pacific Partnership (TPP), and other trade agreements had catastrophic effects on US manufacturing. One of his first acts as president was to withdraw from the TPP, part of his overall strategy of reversing a decades-long course of encouraging global trade.[32] He also renegotiated NAFTA.

In addition, the president has imposed tariffs on a range of imports, including washing machines, solar panels, steel, and aluminum. Some of these tariffs were specifically targeted at imports from China, America's greatest trade competitor. The president also declared European and Japanese car imports a threat to national security, a step that would permit him to impose tariffs on these products.[33] As of June 2019, the multiple tariffs applied to about 10 percent of US imports ($268 billion), making a modest contribution to the US treasury.

The president claims that tariff pressures give other countries—China in particular—incentives to renegotiate trade agreements on terms more favorable to the United States. So far, these agreements have not materialized. In the meantime, retaliatory tariffs imposed by trading partners can hurt industries that rely on exports. China, for example, has stopped importing soybeans from the United States in response to American tariffs.[34] Most economists predict that a trade war—with reciprocal tariffs imposed by the United States and its trading partners—will stymie economic growth through higher consumer prices and reductions in US exports, even possibly leading to a reession.[35] Withdrawing from the TPP may increase Chinese economic influence in the Pacific Rim, by scaling back US relationships with Asian trading partners.

BUDGETING AND FISCAL POLICY

The federal budget is a document that proposes spending, forecasts revenue, and estimates expenditures of the federal government. It does so for a fiscal year—the twelve-month period beginning October 1 and continuing through the following September 30. The primary purpose of the budget is to allocate limited funds, but that allocation is highly political, as recent confrontations between the Republicans and Democrats and between Congress and the president attest. Moreover, spending is tied closely to tax policy, which generates the revenue needed to fund the government.

Budgets are central to government. Indeed, for many programs, budgeting *is* governing: The amount of money spent on a program determines how many people are served, how well they are served, and how much of something (weapons, vaccines, medical care, and so on) the government can purchase or deliver as services. Public budgets are the supreme example of Harold Lasswell's famous definition of politics as "who gets what, when, and how."[36] It is not surprising that budget battles remain at the center of American politics.

Although the president is a central figure in the budget process, the budget itself is so complicated and affected by so many forces that "the most a president can hope for is to modify the overall budget picture, but doing so is difficult because the budget is an amorphous document that never really exists in one place, nor is it passed at one time. The budget process is a confusing, fragmented, and decentralized process."[37] The law requires the president to deliver a proposed budget to Congress every year, but this is only one step in a multiyear process involving agency negotiations over thousands of budget items, presidential staff decisions about priorities, and congressional deliberations that often ignore what the president has proposed.

Nestled inside the expenditures figures are thousands of policy choices, each prompting plenty of politics. Budget battles are fought over contending interests, ideologies, programs, and agencies. Every political actor has a stake in the budget. Mayors want to keep federal grants-in-aid flowing to their cities, defense contractors like a big defense budget, and scientists push for more funding for the National Science Foundation. Agencies within the government also work to protect their interests. Individual members of Congress act as policy entrepreneurs for new ideas and support constituent benefits, both of which cost money. Presidents try to use budgets to manage the economy and leave their imprint on public policy.

There are a few truisms about budget policy. The first is that demand for spending almost always exceeds the supply, and even a $4.75 trillion budget (the amount proposed by President Trump for fiscal year 2020) cannot satisfy every constituency that wants the federal government to fund favored programs. A second is that taxes—whether from individual income taxes, corporate taxes, or payroll taxes used to fund Social Security and Medicare—are unpopular. A consequence is that, with the exception of 1998–2001, the federal government spent more than it collected in taxes for the last fifty years. The result has been annual deficits that increase the national debt (the total amount of money that the federal government owes), which is now about $23 trillion. Deficit and debt pressures make it difficult for presidents to propose new programs, and congressional budget rules put in place in 2011 limit the amount that spending can increase from one year to the next.

Every year the president must propose a budget, and Congress must appropriate funds. If this process breaks down, the government will come to a virtual standstill as the legal authority to spend money lapses. Although "essential government functions," such as air traffic control or law enforcement continue if appropriations stall, routine government operations are suspended: federal employees are furloughed, offices shut down, national parks closed, and applications for benefits postponed.[38] An impasse over Trump's demand for funding to build a wall on the US-Mexican border, which Congress would not provide, led to a partial federal government shutdown between December 22, 2018, and January 25, 2019; the thirty-five-day shutdown was the longest in US history.

A Brief History

As described in chapter 8, the development of the president's authority to prepare a budget proved crucial in the rise of the presidential institution. Prior to the Budget and Accounting Act of 1921, the president's control over spending was limited to transmitting department budgets to Congress. The president lacked authority to coordinate total revenues and expenditures or revise department requests.[39]

This system worked when the federal government was small, but became unworkable at the start of the twentieth century. Congress recognized that the president needed more control when expenditures and deficits soared during World War I.[40]

The Budget and Accounting Act of 1921 required the president to present an annual executive branch budget. The legislation also established the Bureau of the Budget within the Department of the Treasury to handle these new administrative responsibilities. Acting as a surrogate for the president, the Bureau of the Budget (BOB) organized and ran a process that solicited yearly expenditure estimates from the departments and agencies, evaluated and adjusted them according to the president's policy goals, and combined them into a comprehensive executive budget.

In 1920, federal expenditures totaled $6.4 billion. By 1930 they had been reduced to $3.3 billion. Before the 1930s, most federal spending went directly to the departments and agencies for the costs of running the government. There were relatively few public works projects or benefits programs that required funding.

The Great Depression of the 1930s had a major effect on the budget, increasing demands for government services. Franklin Roosevelt proposed a series of programs that provided jobs, helped protect savings, and, in 1937, led to the creation of the Social Security system. The New Deal constituted a dramatic increase in federal government domestic responsibilities. World War II and then the Cold War with the Soviet Union extended this growth to foreign policy, permanently expanding the US presence in global affairs (and the spending to go along with it). By the mid-1950s, federal spending had risen to 16–17 percent of gross domestic product, up from 3 to 4 percent just before the New Deal.

Lyndon Johnson's Great Society agenda—with new domestic social welfare programs such as Medicare, Medicaid, and anti-poverty programs—added another layer of federal responsibility. By the 1970s, federal spending was 20 percent of GDP, with persistent deficits and sluggish economic growth. This combination has shaped presidential budget engagement ever since.

Richard Nixon provoked a congressional reaction when he both moved funding from one budget category to another not authorized by Congress (reprogramming) and refused to spend money that Congress had appropriated (impoundment). In response, Congress passed the Budget and Impoundment Act of 1974, which limited the president's authority to ignore congressional budget decisions

Ronald Reagan

In the 1980s, the primary objective of presidential budgeting began to change. Seeds of this change were sown in the economic problems of the previous decade: the decline in the nation's productivity and its industrial competitiveness, and the rise in inflation and unemployment. These factors, along with sizable budget deficits and a ballooning debt, led those inside and outside the government to question the wisdom of ever-increasing government expenditures within the domestic sphere.

Reagan took the lead in reordering national priorities, using the budget to achieve his policy goals. He reduced the proportion of the budget devoted to domestic discretionary spending and increased the proportion for defense. Reagan also wanted to cut back on social welfare programs but Congress would not allow him to do so. A major tax cut in 1981 and a serious recession in 1982, triggered by Federal Reserve policies designed to control inflation, resulted in historically unprecedented peacetime budget deficits. The national debt quadrupled over Reagan's two terms, and large deficits became an enduring feature of budget politics.

George H. W. Bush

President George H. W. Bush and the Democratically-controlled Congress tried to halt this growth by agreeing to increase taxes and cut government expenditures in 1990, a compromise that alienated the president's conservative Republican base but contributed greatly to cutting deficits. The 1990 Budget Enforcement Act set deficit targets, placed specific limits on discretionary spending and created new classifications of spending within broad categories: defense, international affairs, and domestic programs. Congress also enacted "pay as you go" provisions in the budget, requiring Congress to pay for any new mandatory program by offsetting budget cuts in existing programs and to pay for any new tax cuts by obtaining additional revenues. The law made a major contribution to limiting what would have been an ever-widening deficit gap, but the debt itself kept increasing.

Bill Clinton

Bill Clinton promised that deficit reduction would be a major priority of his administration, and his initial budget proposed a plan to achieve this through a combination of tax increases and budget cuts. The Democratic Congress modified Clinton's plan, increasing spending cuts and decreasing tax increases, and then enacted it by the barest of margins. Tax increases passed in 1993, and then spending cuts, negotiated with the new Republican congressional majorities, and sustained economic growth combined to improve government finances. In 1998, the federal government ran its first budget surplus since the 1960s.

George W. Bush

When George W. Bush became president, the Congressional Budget Office predicted a huge budget surplus—totaling at least $3 trillion—over the next decade.[41] A major tax cut and the War on Terror quickly turned the surplus into a deficit, however. Increases in farm subsidies, veterans' benefits, and a new Medicare prescription drug benefit added to the red ink. By the end of the final year of the Bush administration, the national debt was almost $10 trillion.

The economy fell into recession in the spring of 2008. In the fall of that year, a major financial crisis, fueled by speculative real estate investments, plunged the country into a severe economic downturn.

Barack Obama

The financial crisis aggravated an already weak economy. Unemployment soared, housing prices collapsed, and the stock market lost almost half of its value over a six-month period. The resulting decline in federal revenues, combined with $1.5 trillion in stimulus spending and efforts to shore up the banking industry, led to historically unprecedented deficits. The 2009 fiscal deficit was $1.4 trillion, more than triple the 2008 level, and the years 2009–2012 added more than $5 trillion to the national debt (see figures 13.1 and 13.2).

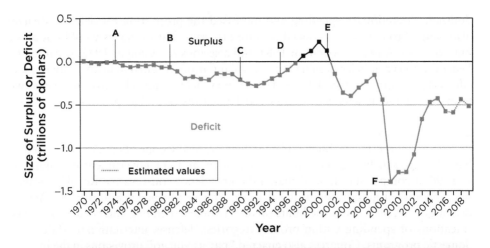

A	1974: The economy declined following the Arab oil embargo, which raised energy prices across the nation. As the economy declined, tax revenues declined correspondingly.
B	1981: Deficits increased sharply after Congress passed the large cuts advocated by President Ronald Reagan.
C	1990: A compromise between President George H. W. Bush and the Democrats in Congress led to expenditure controls and tax increases, beginning a process of bringing the deficit under control.
D	1995: A thriving economy, a tax increase on the wealthy, and tighter controls on expenditures helped the government achieve a balanced budget for 4 years, beginning in 1998 under President Bill Clinton.
E	2001: Congress cut taxes in 2001 and then again in 2003. These revenue losses, along with substantial increases in defense expenditures to fight the war on terrorism, sent deficits skyrocketing.
F	2008: Financial Crisis (the Great Recession), resulting in decreased tax revenues and increased costs to stimulate the economy, explode the size of the deficit.

Figure 13.1 Annual Budget Deficits
Note: Estimates for 2019–2021.
Source: Budget of the United States Government, Fiscal Year 2020: Historical Tables (Washington, DC: US Government Printing Office, 2019), Table 1.3.

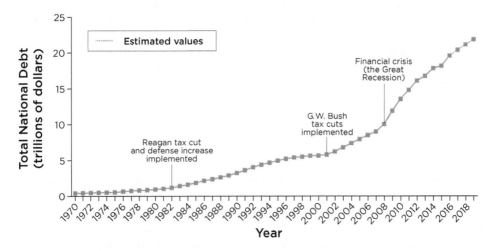

Figure 13.2 Total National Debt
Note: Estimates for 2017–2019.
Source: Budget of the United States Government, Fiscal Year 2020: Historical Tables (Washington, DC: US Government Printing Office, 2019), Table 7.1.

Concern about huge budget deficits and an increasing national debt added to the administration's travails, fueled partisan opposition to the president and negative evaluations of his presidency, and contributed to the Democrats' defeat in the 2010 midterm elections. Republican control of the House produced stalemate on Capitol Hill and brinksmanship on budget and debt-ceiling negotiations. At the same time, the large annual federal deficit was a serious constraint on the president, limiting his ability to propose new programs.

Donald Trump

During the 2016 campaign, Donald Trump promised not only that he would balance the federal budget but also that he would also erase the entire national debt in eight years.[42] The unspecified plan relied on tax cuts, economic growth, and renegotiating trade and military agreements. Observers universally regarded the candidate's promises as wildly unrealistic, as they would have required generating more than $2 trillion in surplus each year out of a budget of roughly $4–$5 trillion. Once Trump was in office, reality proved more complicated. His first budget, for fiscal year 2018, promised to eliminate the annual budget deficit by 2027, although a Congressional Budget Office analysis concluded that this projection was overly optimistic.[43] Two years later, the president's 2020 budget proposal projected deficits of more than $1 trillion from 2021 to 2029. In August 2019, CBO projected that the fiscal year 2019 deficit would be $960 billion as economic growth slowed.[44]

Trump's support for higher defense spending—increasing from $593 billion in fiscal 2016 to a proposed $737 billion in fiscal 2020—increases the deficit even more. In practice, short-term economic growth cannot increase revenues enough to make up for tax cuts and higher big-ticket budget items. Trump's major economic policy was a 2017 tax cut, which you can read about in box 13.2.

Box 13.2 ★ Donald Trump and the 2017 Tax Cuts and Jobs Act

Donald Trump claimed the Tax Cuts and Jobs Act, which he signed in December 2017, would accelerate long-term economic growth and create millions of jobs. The law cut individual income tax rates, doubled the standard deduction (the amount taxpayers can subtract from their total income in calculating their taxes), lowered the corporate tax rate, and changed how the government taxed corporate income earned abroad.

In the short term, tax cuts may stimulate private spending and economic growth by increasing the amount of money corporations and individuals have after paying taxes. The economy seems to have experienced such a stimulus in 2018.

It is the longer term that is of interest to economists, however. If corporations invest their tax reductions in, say, new equipment, they may increase productivity, which can boost economic growth. A stronger economy, in turn, will produce more tax revenue and partially offset the revenue losses of lower tax rates. To this point, corporations have used most of their tax cuts to buy back stock, which may benefit shareholders but does nothing to increase productivity.

Advocates of tax cuts also frequently claim that they will pay for themselves through the increased tax revenue accompanying economic growth. However, the Congressional Budget Office estimates that the tax cut will increase the national debt by $1.9 trillion over 2018–2028, because of lower revenues and higher interest payments on the national debt.[45] The president's 2018 budget, submitted before the tax law passed, estimated deficits of $488 billion in 2020 and $456 billion in 2021. The latest estimates, submitted in 2019, show that deficits will increase to $1.1 trillion in both 2020 and 2021.

Issues in Budgeting

Presidents do not start with a blank sheet when developing a budget. All recent presidents have promised that their budget plans will control deficits and debt and usher in years of economic growth and prosperity. Few have been able to deliver on those promises.

The problem of budgeting is not so much about the procedure as it is about disagreement over how scarce resources should be spent. Presidents have a leadership problem when it comes to the budget, a problem that has been magnified by the persistence of large deficits and the accumulation of debt. Reducing or eliminating the deficit and preventing the debt from getting out of control requires tough decisions that may be unpopular with large constituencies that carry electoral clout. Were presidents able to make these decisions on their own, they might have the courage and will to do so, particularly during their second terms. However, they have not been able to do so effectively because they share budgetary responsibilities with Congress and because past budgetary commitments limit their discretion. Confrontation, negotiation, and compromise, not dictation and domination, describe the relationship between the presidency and Congress on budgetary matters most of the time.

Uncontrollable Expenditures

There are some practical problems as well. About two-thirds of the government's budget does not represent the traditional budget process of the executive asking for money for certain purposes and Congress appropriating funds for those purposes. We often refer to most of the budget as "uncontrollable." Uncontrollable expenditures result from policies that make some groups automatically eligible for some benefits, such as Social Security or veterans' benefits, or from previous obligations of the government, such as interest on the national debt. The government does not decide each year, for example, whether it will pay the interest on the debt or send checks to Social Security recipients. Instead, Congress writes eligibility rules detailing which people are eligible and what their benefits will be. These rules determine how much Congress must spend.

Such policies are called *entitlements*, and they range from agricultural subsidies to veterans' benefits. The biggest uncontrollable expenditure of all is the Social Security system, including Medicare and Medicaid, which in 2019 cost about $2.2 *trillion* dollars, 47 percent of the federal budget. Of course, Congress can, if it desires, cut Social Security benefits or tighten eligibility restrictions. Doing so, however, would provoke a monumental outcry from millions of elderly voters.

Figure 13.3 shows how the budget is divided between discretionary and mandatory expenditures. In fiscal year 2019, mandatory spending accounted for 61 percent of the budget. Most of these expenses were for Social Security, Medicare, and Medicaid. In addition, interest payments on the national debt accounted for nearly 9 percent of the budget. The discretionary portion of the budget, which includes most government programs, makes up the remaining 30 percent of the total. Half of these funds pays for defense policy, and the other half finances everything else the federal government does, from law enforcement to transportation, education to tax collection, scientific research to disaster relief.

Even within the so-called discretionary part of the budget—that is, the part of the budget for which annual appropriations are necessary—many of the expenditures are for big-ticket items, such as the salaries and benefits for civil servants and

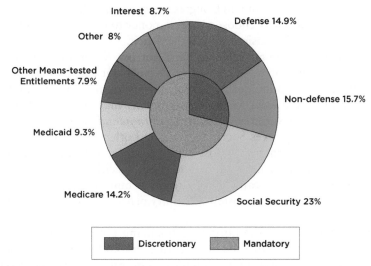

Figure 13.3 Discretionary and Mandatory Expenditures in the Federal Budget
Note: Estimate for 2019; does not include −2.1% in offsetting receipts in mandatory categories.
Source: Budget of the United States Government, Fiscal Year 2020: Historical Tables (Washington, DC: US Government Printing Office, 2019), Table 8.3.

military personnel, scientific research, development and production of intelligence and highly sophisticated communication systems, weapons systems, and construction projects. These costs are difficult to reduce significantly. More importantly, even a drastic cut in this category would have only a marginal effect on the deficit. An immediate across the board discretionary spending cut of 20 percent—a difficult to imagine drop that would entail drastic cutbacks of basic government functions and likely trigger a recession—would save about $300 billion a year but would reduce the annual budget deficit by less than a third.

Because the budget has a direct impact on many people and groups outside the government, constituencies composed of veterans, senior citizens, industries, farmers, labor, and others organize to protect and extend their benefits and exert considerable pressure on those in power to maintain their largesse. Proposals to reduce these expenditures (or eliminate tax breaks) for individuals and groups engender strong opposition. These pressures reduce viable political options for elected government officials. As a consequence the routine needs of government and entitlement programs leave presidents with discretion only over a small portion of the budget.

Deficits

A budget deficit occurs when expenditures exceed revenues in a fiscal year—in other words, when the national government spends more money than it receives in taxes. Americans like low taxes and public benefits, and political leaders are happy to support both. As a result, over the past thirty years, with the exception of 1998–2001, the national government has run up large annual budget deficits (see figure 13.1).

In bad economic times, when tax revenues decrease because fewer people are working, deficits are likely to increase. While revenues diminish, the demands for unemployment insurance, nutrition assistance, and other components of the social safety net increase. The president and Congress may also decide to cut taxes to stimulate the economy, or they may choose to spend money to create jobs, both of which occurred in 2009. All such decisions add to the deficit.

To cover the deficit, the government must borrow. When the federal government wants to borrow money, the Treasury Department sells bonds, guaranteeing to pay interest to bondholders. Citizens, corporations, mutual funds, other financial institutions, and even foreign governments may purchase these bonds. In addition, the federal government has *intragovernmental debt* on its books. This debt is what the Treasury owes Social Security and other trust funds because the government uses for its general purpose revenue collected from social insurance taxes designated to fund Social Security and other specific programs. Most government borrowing is not for capital needs (such as buildings and machinery) but for day-to-day expenses—farm subsidies, military pensions, aid to states and cities, and so on.

Borrowing money shifts the burden of financing government to future taxpayers, who will have to service the debt, with every dollar the government borrows costing taxpayers many more dollars in interest. Dollars spent servicing the debt cannot be spent on health care, education, or infrastructure. Paying the interest on the debt is not optional. Some believe that government borrowing may crowd out private borrowers, both individuals and businesses, from the loan marketplace. Most economists believe that—when the economy is strong—the government's competing to borrow money may lead to increased interest rates, making it more difficult, for example, for businesses to invest in capital expenditures (such as new plants and equipment) that produce economic growth. Higher interest rates also raise the costs to individuals of financing homes or credit card purchases.

Large deficits also make the American government dependent on foreign investors, including other governments, to fund its debt—not a favorable position for a superpower. Foreign investors currently hold a majority of the federal government's public debt. If they stopped lending us money, perhaps to gain leverage in foreign policy, interest rates would rise and the economy would be depressed. Fortunately, to protect their interests, debt holders have an incentive not to harm the US economy.

Sometimes politicians complain that, since families and businesses and even state and local governments balance their budgets, the federal government ought to be able to do the same. However, most families do *not* balance their budgets. They use credit cards to give themselves instant loans, and they go to the bank to borrow money for major purchases such as automobiles and, most important, homes, with mortgages on homes being debts they carry for years. And state and local governments and private businesses differ from the federal government in having a *capital budget*, a budget for expenditures on items that will serve for the long term, such as equipment, roads, and buildings. Thus, for example, when airlines purchase new airplanes or when school districts build new schools, they do not pay for them out of current income. Instead, they borrow money, often through issuing bonds, and these debts do not count against the operating budget. In contrast, when the federal government purchases new jets for the air force or new buildings for medical research, these purchases are counted as current expenditures and run up the deficit.

The National Debt

As a result of the succession of annual deficits, the total national debt rose sharply during the 1980s and then again since 2001, increasing from less than $1 trillion in 1980 to about $22.8 trillion by 2019 (see figure 13.2). About 9 percent of all current budget expenditures go to paying just the interest on this debt.

The need to borrow, in turn, creates an issue in Congress. Since 1917, Congress has enforced the debt ceiling—a statutory limit on the total amount of money the US government can borrow. First imposed during World War I, it was designed initially as an additional check on government spending and providing Congress "a means of expressing views on appropriate fiscal policies."[46] Once the limit is hit, the Treasury Department is prohibited from issuing any new debt, something it does continuously as it issues new obligations to pay back older debt that has come due. This limit can prevent the government from financing, even temporarily, ongoing operations: everything from defense contracts and federal employee salaries to social security or Medicare benefits.[47]

Hitting or exceeding the debt limit would create dire economic consequences. Once the US government was unable to pay back existing debt, it would be in "default" of its obligations. The safety of government securities would be hurt, raising the interest rates that the government had to pay on its borrowing. (Because federal debt is backed by the "full faith and credit of the United States," it is considered one of the safest investments possible. Interest rates for federal bonds are much lower than for other types of borrowing.) In the short term, the inability to borrow could lead to draconian cuts to domestic programs. Stock markets around the world could crash, and another global recession might result. There is widespread consensus that a default would be "devastating."[48]

When Congress is faced with increasing the debt ceiling, the opposition party has an opportunity to criticize the president and use the need to borrow as leverage to extract concessions on other policies. Increasing the debt had been a straightforward process until the Great Recession.[49] Between 1993 and 2010, Congress voted sixteen times to raise the limit, either in standalone bills or language in other budget legislation.[50] However, the absolute need to raise the debt limit gives members of Congress a form of high-stakes bargaining leverage if enough members insist on budget cuts or other policy changes in return for their votes to raise the debt ceiling.

The rapid rise of deficit spending since 2001 and the dramatic increase that occurred after the Great Recession ended this period of relative calm. When the United States approached the limit again in 2011, Obama asked Congress to increase it. This time, however, Republicans in Congress were reluctant to oblige. They insisted that before they agreed to increase the debt limit, the president and the Democrats would have to agree to reduce the debt over time through decreases in spending but not any increases in taxes. In the end, the parties could not agree and Congress passed a temporary solution that raised the debt limit but put off fashioning a long-term solution for two years. As part of the agreement between the White House and Congress, automatic across-the-board cuts (known a "sequestrations"), to be split evenly between defense and domestic spending, were to occur in 2013 if Congress did not agree on how to cut the budget. It did not, and the cuts ensued.

Two years later, Congress and the president dealt with another debt limit crisis. This time, parts of the federal government shut down after the Republican House majority and the president could not agree on a budget. Conservative Republicans attempted to leverage the debt limit vote to force Democrats to swallow unpalatable measures, especially repealing the Affordable Care Act. After the Democratic-controlled Senate and the president rejected such efforts, the government shut down because no budget had been passed. The shutdown lasted sixteen days, and ended just before the United States was set to reach its borrowing limit. Facing public disapproval, congressional Republicans backed down, agreeing to a temporary increase in the debt limit and budget language that reopened the government.[51] The debt ceiling was raised in 2017 and 2018, and will have to be raised several more times during Trump's first term.

CONCLUSION

Presidents have become national policy makers. This role developed primarily in the twentieth century and evolved largely as a consequence of social, economic, and political problems that required solutions by the federal government. With a national perspective, a large staff structure, and the ability to focus public attention and mobilize support, presidents have been placed in the position in which they can initiate policies and then use their institutional and personal resources to push for adoption of those policies. The electoral process has provided them with further incentives to do so. Congress, the executive branch, and the public frequently look to them for leadership.

In budget and economic policy, expectations of presidential performance have grown, but presidents' capacity to affect economic matters has not kept pace. The success or failure of presidents' economic policies depend on many outside factors over which they have little or no control. Directing change under normal conditions is difficult. Under most circumstances the best that presidents can do is to facilitate action.

The diversity of interests within the domestic arena, the impact that domestic policy has on society, and the intensity with which groups fight for their economic and social interests usually make domestic policy making more difficult than foreign policy making for presidents. Domestic policy making tends to be more partisan, requires more compromise, and has shorter-term political consequences; it is the arena where the limits of presidential leadership, and the inefficiencies of the separation of power system, are manifest. These difficulties push presidents to find other ways and other arenas in which to enhance their leadership image.

DISCUSSION QUESTIONS

1. The budget power is often described as the centerpiece of presidential policy influence. But as the text notes, most of the budget is fixed ("mandatory") and most types of spending have constituencies who benefit from it and will fight to protect it. In practical terms, how much influence does the president have in setting budget priorities that will find their way into law?
2. Identify the chief domestic policy advisors in the Trump White House. Can you identify examples of their influence over specific policies? What determines

whether a policy advisor has influence over the president? Is it proximity? Trust? How closely their views align with the president's?

3. Ever since Franklin D. Roosevelt's administration, the president has been expected to be manager of the economy. Can the president really perform this role? What are some of the ways in which presidents can affect the economy, and what are some of their toughest limits? Illustrate your answer with examples from the Trump administration.

WEB EXERCISES

1. There is wide agreement that the budget deficit is too large (although some economists, such as Paul Krugman, argue that interest rates costs are so low that deficit spending produces worthwhile economic benefits). At the same time, it has proven extremely difficult to make the decisions necessary to reduce it. A number of nonpartisan think tanks have budget exercises that allow users to make changes to revenues and expenditures. One such game is called The Fiscal Ship, at http://fiscalship.org/. Go through the exercise and see if you are able to make significant deficit reductions. Were you able to do so? It's possible you had little difficulty. Why do you think it is so difficult for Congress and the president to do this?

2. The president's most recent budget request is available at the Office of Management Budget Web Site: https://www.whitehouse.gov/omb/budget. The first document on this page is the main budget summary, which explains the overall request. Browse the document, and examine the way that budget changes are summarized and defended. What do you observe about the specificity of proposed budget cuts? How does this document compare to the way that the Fiscal Ship game (exercise 1) describes the budget problem?

3. How well do people understand the president's role in managing the economy? Are public expectations of presidential leadership reasonable? If presidents do not have much control over macroeconomic outcomes, why does the public hold them responsible? (The Pew Research Center has polling data on budget and economic policy: http://www.pewresearch.org/topics/economic-policy.)

SELECTED READINGS

Bartels, Larry M. *Unequal Democracy: The Political Economy of the New Gilded Age*. Princeton, NJ: Princeton University Press, 2008.

Berry, Christopher, Barry Burden, and William Howell. "The President and the Distribution of Federal Spending." *American Political Science Review* 104 (November 2010): 783–799.

Edwards, George C., III. *The Strategic Presidency*. Princeton, NJ: Princeton University Press, 2009.

Farrier, Jasmine. *Passing the Buck: Congress, the Budget and Deficits*. Lexington: University of Kentucky Press, 2004.

Fisher, Louis. "Presidential Budgetary Duties." *Presidential Studies Quarterly* 42 (December 2012): 754–790.

Jacobs, Lawrence R., and Theda Skocpol. *Health Reform and American Politics*. New York: Oxford University Press, 2010.

Kriner, Douglas L., and Andrew Reeves. *The Particularistic President: Executive Branch Politics and Political Inequality*. New York: Cambridge University Press, 2015.

Rubin, Irene S. *The Politics of Public Budgeting: Getting and Spending, Borrowing and Balancing*, 8th ed. Washington, DC: CQ Press, 2016.

Schick, Allen. *The Federal Budget: Politics, Policy, Process*, 3rd ed. Washington, DC: Brookings Institution, 2007.

Tomkin, Shelley Lynne. *Inside the OMB*. New York: M. E. Sharpe, 1998.

Warshaw, Shirley Anne. *The Domestic Presidency: Policy Making in the White House*. Boston: Allyn and Bacon, 1997.

Wood, B. Dan. *The Politics of Economic Leadership: The Causes and Consequences of Presidential Rhetoric*. Princeton, NJ: Princeton University Press, 2007.

14

Foreign and Defense Policy

President Trump addresses the nation on the war in Afghanistan.

In the weeks following the terrorist attacks on 9/11, George W. Bush instituted a number of practices designed to protect American security. In November 2001, he issued a military order establishing a system for detaining persons suspected of terrorist activities. The order specified that detainees would be tried by military tribunals instead of civilian courts and that no federal court would have jurisdiction to hear any challenges to the decisions of the tribunals.[1] The following January, Bush announced that members of al-Qaeda were to be considered "unlawful combatants" and as such would not have the protections accorded to prisoners of war under the Geneva Conventions.[2]

Bush also began, and Barack Obama expanded, the practice of covert strikes against suspected terrorists. Under the policy, the United States used "lethal force" against senior al-Qaeda leadership, even if they were US citizens. According to one count, four Americans were killed in drone strikes between 2009 and 2013, including one who was specifically targeted (Anwar al-Awlaki) and three who were killed in raids targeting others. Other strikes killed large numbers of civilians. Despite concerns over due process, neither the federal courts nor Congress have imposed any limits on the president's use of drones.

On April 5, 2017, Donald Trump ordered a missile attack against a Syrian airbase suspected of being used to carry out a chemical weapons attack that killed at least eighty civilians in the city of Khan Sheikoun. Acting on the president's orders, two Navy destroyers launched fifty-nine cruise missiles against the base, in an operation "intended to send a signal to [Syrian President Bashir al] Assad about the United States' intention to use military force if he continues to use chemical weapons."[3]

These three brief examples highlight the reach of presidential power in foreign and defense policy. Presidents, quite literally, hold the power of life and death and operate with a degree of discretion they do not possess in domestic affairs. The two institutions with the greatest ability to check presidential action—Congress and the federal courts—show more deference to the president than they do in domestic affairs. That deference is not unlimited, to be sure; Bush's military tribunal policy was scaled back as a result of several Supreme Court decisions, and several of Trump's initiatives on immigration have been partially blocked by federal courts as well.[4] In addition, Congress mandated new restrictions on the treatment of detainees. Nevertheless, there are fewer checks on national security policy than on domestic policy, a consequence of congressional passivity and a doctrine of presidential supremacy.

In a key respect, however, foreign and defense policy is similar to domestic policy in that expectations of presidential performance exceed the president's ability to meet them. In dealing with other sovereign nations, presidents can find that their ability to persuade (or compel) is limited. And when dealing with adversaries, such as North Korea, the Islamic State of Iraq and Syria (ISIS), or Syria, there may be few good options in trying to achieve policy goals. Box 14.1 notes some of the difficulties the Trump administration is facing in dealing with a nuclear-armed North Korea.

Box 14.1 ★ Donald Trump Confronts the Problem of North Korea

In an August 2017 underground test, North Korea detonated a bomb with a yield large enough to suggest the country might have developed a thermonuclear weapon. At the same time as it developed its nuclear capability, the country has been working on intercontinental ballistic technology, which it claims can deliver a warhead to the continental United States.[5]

The prospect of a "rogue nation" with the ability and expressed intention to launch a nuclear attack on the United States is surely a pressing national security issue. Efforts to induce North Korea to abandon its nuclear weapon and intercontinental ballistic missile programs have gone on since the 1990s, with Presidents Clinton, George W. Bush, and Obama attempting to find diplomatic solutions and offering economic aid in return for an agreement to stop testing. All have failed. Donald Trump has tried personal diplomacy, meeting twice with Kim Jong Un, the North Korean leader. Neither meeting resulted in progress on reducing North Korea's nuclear capacity.

It is not clear whether there are any good options for a US response. The president threatened military action ("fire and fury"), but many military experts are skeptical that any plausible attack could damage North Korea's nuclear capacity, and even a conventional retaliation against Seoul, the capital of the

(continued)

Box 14.1 ★ Continued

US ally South Korea (a city of ten million that is only thirty-five miles from the North Korean border), could result in tens of thousands of causalities. The Trump administration also placed additional sanctions on North Korea, blocking oil and gas exports and freezing its financial assets abroad.[6]

The president has made it clear that he wants China (North Korea's main international supporter) to apply pressure on North Korea. However, China has only limited influence on its neighbor. Moreover, China fears a regime collapse in North Korea would send millions of refugees over its border. Worse, such an event might give the United States and South Korea an excuse to occupy North Korea, an occurrence that China vigorously resists.

North Korea reveals the possible limits of presidential influence over a hostile and uncooperative country with a capacity, and expressed threat, to inflict damage on the United States and its allies.

THE CONSTITUTIONAL DESIGN

Chapter 2 reviewed the Constitution's assignment of powers to the president, noting that some presidential authorities—particularly the power to make treaties and appoint ambassadors—are shared with the Senate. Table 14.1 shows the full constitutional assignments of foreign and defense powers to Congress and the president. At first glance, this list appears to give Congress the bulk of foreign affairs powers: everything from foreign trade and immigration to establishing the military and setting the rules for its functioning.

The framers of the Constitution anticipated a foreign policy-making role for the president, but they did not want the executive to exercise that power alone. Their fear that a president might pursue interests that adversely affected the nation's welfare, as they believed European monarchs had done for centuries, led them to divide and share foreign policy-making responsibilities, just as they had done for domestic and economic matters. The president could initiate treaties with the advice of the

Table 14.1 Constitutional Assignment of Foreign and Defense Powers

Congressional (Article I, Section 8)	Presidential (Article II, Sections 2 and 3)
• Regulate commerce with foreign nations • Establish uniform rule of naturalization • Define and punish piracies on the high seas, and offenses against nations • Declare war • Grant letters of Marque and Reprisal • Make rules concerning captures on land and water • Raise and support armies, provide and maintain a navy, and make rules for the government and regulation of land and naval forces • Provide for organizing and calling forth the militia to repel invasions	• Commander in chief of army and navy, and militia when called into service of the United States • Make treaties (with Senate ratification) • Appoint ambassadors (with Senate confirmation) • Receive ambassadors and other public ministers • Executive power (vesting clause)

Senate; ratification required the concurrence of two-thirds of the upper chamber. Similarly, the president could appoint ambassadors, but that too required Senate approval. The determination of war policy was to be Congress's alone. The president had discretion to act in times of emergency to repel attacks but presumably not to initiate hostilities or in any other way establish permanent war policy. The performance of the ceremonial duties of a head of state and the conduct of foreign policy were seen as executive responsibilities.

In fulfilling these functions, presidents would inevitably make decisions that had policy implications. The framers did not fear this. They anticipated that Congress, by virtue of its power to appropriate money, authorize programs, and regulate commerce, would set the contours of that policy and be able to check presidential initiatives adequately.

Growth of Presidential Power

The president's powers in foreign affairs and national defense have expanded significantly since the time of the framers. Edward S. Corwin described the allocation of national security powers as "an invitation to struggle for the privilege of directing American foreign policy."[7] It is a struggle in which the president has long had the upper hand. In practice, the president dominates in foreign affairs to the point that proponents of executive initiative can cite a 1936 Supreme Court decision, *US v. Curtiss Wright*, which argued that the president has *all* of the nation's foreign affairs power and is the "sole organ" of the federal government in foreign affairs. In upholding the validity of a presidential order that banned certain arms exports, Chief Justice Sutherland pointed to "very delicate, plenary and exclusive power of the President as the sole organ of the federal government in the field of international relations."[8] The White House has cited that doctrine to justify a wide range of presidential initiatives, from a nearly unlimited presidential authority to order military action anywhere in the world to the (now repudiated) view articulated by Department of Justice under George W. Bush that not even statutes prohibiting torture were binding on the president if he concluded that it was necessary to protect national security.[9]

Louis Fisher, a prominent constitutional scholar, argues that the "sole organ" doctrine is an erroneous reading of constitutional language.[10] But there is no question that the president dominates in foreign and defense affairs, in the ability to set policy, determine the US position in international negotiations, manage diplomatic relations, and dominate the agenda.

Presidential influence in foreign affairs is enhanced by the nature of the executive power and the advantages that the president has over Congress and the federal courts in the area. The same dynamic that was described in chapter 2, showing how presidential power grew through precedent, judicial deference, and Congress's frequent inability to push back against presidential action, is present here. It is not an accident that the eighteenth- and nineteenth-century examples of presidential unilateral action all involved foreign policy and national security (the Neutrality Proclamation, the Louisiana Purchase, the Monroe Doctrine, and Lincoln's Civil War actions).

The president's advantages are further reinforced by the *politics* of foreign affairs and the executive's stature as the only elected official with a national constituency. If the country is to have a presence in foreign affairs—and it must—the nature of the presidency, with the ability to act with energy, secrecy, and dispatch, gives it overwhelming advantages over other institutions. No member of Congress has the legitimacy to claim to represent the country, nor does any legislator have the constitutional or political ability to speak authoritatively on the country's behalf.

Those political and constitutional advantages are magnified by a large degree of constitutional delegation of authority to the executive. Even in those areas in which Congress has explicit constitutional powers, it frequently defers to the president. For example, even though Congress has the explicit constitutional authority to set rules for international trade (under its authority to "regulate commerce with foreign nations" in Article I, section 8), legislators have since 1934 delegated much of that authority to the executive branch. The primary motivation in doing has been the recognition that Congress tended to raise tariffs, because doing so benefited specific industries and regions, even though high tariffs were harmful overall to trade and economic growth. Instead of setting tariffs itself, Congress sets overall standards and allows the president to negotiate agreements while retaining a capacity to review the final arrangements.[11]

In making national security policy, the president relies on two primary instruments of authority: diplomacy and, if necessary, the use of force.

DIPLOMACY

The United States has relations with almost every country in the world. Often, representatives of the United States need to negotiate with these nations the issues of trade, borders, human rights, and even the physical security of Americans. Nations also cooperate on matters ranging from crime control to military alliances. The primary way the president manages these relations and conducts negotiations with other countries is through diplomacy.

Treaties

Treaties are written agreements concluded between nations and governed by international law. US relations with many countries are governed by hundreds of treaties, both with one other nation (bilateral) or with many nations (multilateral) (table 14.2). The substance of these treaties includes human rights, arms control, taxation, environmental protection, and intellectual property rights. Domestically, treaties to which the United States is a party are equivalent in status to federal laws, forming part of what the Constitution calls "the supreme law of the land."

The total number of treaties and other international agreements in force increases with time because, once entered into, agreements remain in force until they expire by their own terms or are denounced, replaced, or superseded. Although some international agreements are by their terms temporary or limited to a specific time period, others are intended to be more or less permanent. Still listed among treaties in force with the United Kingdom are the Paris Peace Treaty of 1783, the Jay Treaty of 1794, and the Treaty of Peace and Amity signed at Ghent in 1814.

Only the president can negotiate treaties, although he can appoint whomever he likes to do so on his behalf. In 1799 Congress passed the Logan Act, which prohibits unauthorized citizens from corresponding with foreign governments "relating to controversies or disputes which do or shall exist" between those governments and the United States. The law was enacted after a private citizen, George Logan,

Table 14.2 Treaties and Executive Agreements Approved by the United States, 1789–2019

Year	No. of Treaties	No. of Executive Agreements
1789–1839	60	27
1839–1889	215	238
1889–1929	382	763
1930–1933	49	41
1933–1944 (F. D. Roosevelt)	131	369
1945–1952 (Truman)	132	1,324
1953–1960 (Eisenhower)	89	1,834
1961–1963 (Kennedy)	36	813
1964–1969 (Johnson)	67	1,083
1969–1974 (Nixon)	93	1,317
1974–1977 (Ford)	26	666
1977–1981 (Carter)	79	1,476
1981–1989 (Reagan)	125	2,840
1989–1993 (G. H. W. Bush)	67	1,350
1993–2001 (Clinton)	209	2,048
2001–2009 (G. W. Bush)	163	1,998
2009–2017 (Obama)	14	1,600*
2017– (Trump)[†]	5	188

* Estimate
[†] As of September 2, 2019.
Note: Varying definitions of what comprises an executive agreement and its entry-into-force date make the above numbers approximate.
Source: Congressional Research Service, *Treaties and Other International Agreements: The Role of the United States Senate* (Washington, DC: US Government Printing Office, 2001); Jeffrey S. Peake, "Obama, Unilateral Diplomacy, and Iran: Treaties, Executive Agreements, and Political Commitments," in Richard S. Conley, ed., *Presidential Leadership and National Security: The Obama Legacy* (New York: Routledge Press, 2018); Harold W. Stanley and Richard G. Niemi, *Vital Statistics on American Politics: 2015–2016* (Washington, DC: CQ Press, 2015); US State Department https://www.state.gov/s/l/treaty.

traveled to France and attempted to end the plundering of American merchant ships authorized by the French government. No one has ever been convicted of violating the act, however, and only two persons have been indicted, neither of whom went to trial. Today US citizens often travel abroad and meet with representatives of foreign governments, although without the consent of the president they are not empowered to negotiate treaties or other agreements.

The Constitution vests in the Senate the power to advise and consent to treaties.[12] The latter requires a vote of two-thirds of the senators voting.

Senate Advice

The earliest practice under the Constitution indicates that originally the framers planned for the Senate to advise the president during the treaty-making process as well as to give or withhold consent to the final treaty, but this procedure soon ended. An incident early in the Washington administration soured presidents on seeking the advice of the Senate as a whole.

Official White House Photo by Shealah Craighead

President Trump meets with German chancellor Angela Merkel and British prime minister Theresa May.

On August 22, 1789, President George Washington went to the Senate with Secretary of War Henry Knox to consult on a treaty with Native Americans in western Georgia. Armed with thirteen questions prepared by Knox, Washington explained the proposed treaty and requested the Senate's guidance in the negotiations. While the president, seated in the presiding officer's chair, and Knox waited, the Senate voted to refer these questions to a committee rather than debate the issue in the presence of the revered Washington. Forced to return two days later for what turned out to be insipid advice, Washington decided that, in the future, he would send communications regarding treaties in writing.

Starting with the Jay Treaty in 1994, Washington did not always consult the Senate in advance of negotiations, however. By the time President James K. Polk referred the proposal to divide the Oregon Territory at the 49th parallel to the Senate for its advice prior to signing the Oregon Treaty of 1846, it was a rare practice. Nevertheless, presidents or their secretaries of state have often consulted with individual senators or committees prior to or during the negotiating process in order to enhance the prospects of the final treaty. At the same time, sometimes the Senate takes the initiative and passes resolutions indicating its lack of support for provisions under negotiation.

Presidents have varied in their views toward the participation of individual senators in the treaty process. Some have included senators; others have kept the negotiation of treaties an executive monopoly. President Woodrow Wilson, on one hand, believed that the president should not consult with the Senate and treat it as an equal partner. He applied this theory to the Versailles Treaty, ending World War I, which the Senate twice rejected. On the other hand, presidents such as William McKinley, Warren Harding, Herbert Hoover, and Franklin D. Roosevelt included senators and representatives as members of US delegations that negotiated treaties. When the details of the UN Charter were hammered out at a conference in San Francisco in 1945, half of the eight members of the US delegation came from Congress. The Carter administration consulted with at least seventy Senators during the final phase of the negotiations of the Panama Canal Treaty. During 1977 and 1978, twenty-six senators served in Geneva as official advisers to the Second Round of Strategic Arms Limitation Talks (SALT II) negotiating team.

Senate Consent

When a treaty is submitted to the Senate for approval, the Senate has several options for action. The first is to approve or reject the treaty. A treaty rejection by vote on the floor of the Senate has occurred only twenty-two times in US history (see table 14.3). Three of the treaties, including the Treaty of Versailles ending World War I, were rejected twice. Since 1935, the Senate has rejected just four treaties in this manner: the Convention on the High Seas in 1960; the Montreal Protocol No. 4 regarding air carriers in 1983; the Comprehensive Nuclear Test Ban Treaty in 1999; and the UN Convention for the Rights of the Disabled in 2012.

Sometimes, the Senate formally rejects treaties but keeps them technically alive by adopting or entering a motion to reconsider. Eventually, unapproved treaties have been replaced by other treaties, amended by protocols and then approved, or withdrawn by or returned to the president.

The Senate may make its approval of a treaty conditional by including in its resolution of consent amendments to the text of the treaty—reservations, understandings, interpretations, declarations, or other statements.[13] For example, in early 1978, the Senate consented to two treaties dealing with the Panama Canal but added a reservation to one of them stating that the United States had a right to use military force, if necessary, to keep the canal open. The president and the other countries involved must then decide whether to accept the conditions and changes in the legislation, renegotiate the provisions, or abandon the treaty. The latter is not unusual.

One reason for the low number of rejections is that presidents anticipate rejection and do not forward treaties the Senate will likely vote down. For example, although President Clinton signed the 1997 Kyoto Protocol in 1998, he never submitted it to the Senate, certain that it would be rejected. Presidents may also withdraw treaties if they perceive they stand little chance of passage. Presidents have withdrawn more than 150 treaties since World War II. A prominent example is President Carter's withdrawal of the SALT II Treaty in 1980. Moreover, the Senate has typically chosen not to vote on treaties that its leadership deemed not to have sufficient support for approval.

The Senate may choose to take no definitive action, leaving the treaty pending in the Senate until withdrawn at the request of the president or, occasionally, at the initiative of the Senate.[14] Treaties may languish in the Senate Foreign Relations Committee for extended periods, since there is no requirement for presidents to resubmit treaties at the beginning of each new Congress. There have been instances in which treaties have lain dormant within the committee for years, even decades, without action being taken. President Clinton originally transmitted the UN Convention on the Law of the Sea to the Senate in 1994. It has had support from business groups, energy interests, the US military, President George W. Bush, and President Obama. Despite its significance and substantial domestic support, conservatives in Congress have blocked Senate consideration of the treaty.

Table 14.3 Treaties Rejected by the Senate

Date	Treaty-making Country	Subject	Vote
March 9, 1825	Colombia	Suppression of African Slave Trade	Yeas = 0, Nays = 40
June 11, 1836	Switzerland	Personal and property rights	Yeas = 14, Nays = 23
June 8, 1844	Texas	Annexation	Yeas = 16, Nays = 35
June 15, 1844	German Zollverein	Reciprocity	Yeas = 26, Nays = 18
May 31, 1860	Mexico	Transit and commercial rights	Yeas = 18, Nays = 27
June 27, 1860	Spain	Cuban Claims Commission	*First vote:* Yeas = 25, Nays = 17; *second vote:* Yeas = 24, Nays = 18
April 13, 1869	Great Britain	Arbitration of claims	Yeas = 1, Nays = 54
June 1, 1870	Hawaii	Reciprocity	Yeas = 20, Nays = 19
June 30, 1870	Dominican Republic	Annexation	Yeas = 28, Nays = 28
January 15, 1883; April 20, 1886	Mexico	Mining claims	Yeas = 33, Nays = 20; Yeas = 32, Nays = 26
January 29, 1885	Nicaragua	Interoceanic canal	Yeas = 32, Nays = 23
August 21, 1888	Great Britain	Fishing rights	Yeas = 27, Nays = 30
February 1, 1889	Great Britain	Extradition	Yeas = 15, Nays = 38
May 5, 1897	Great Britain	Arbitration	Yeas = 43, Nays = 26
November 19, 1919; March 19, 1920	Multilateral	Treaty of Versailles	Yeas = 38, Nays = 53; Yeas = 49, Nays = 35
January 18, 1927	Turkey	Commercial rights	Yeas = 50, Nays = 34
March 14, 1934	Canada	St. Lawrence Seaway	Yeas = 46, Nays = 42
January 29, 1935	Multilateral	World Court	Yeas = 52, Nays = 36
May 26, 1960*	Multilateral	Law of the Sea Convention	Yeas = 29, Nays = 30
March 8, 1983†	Multilateral	Montreal Aviation Protocols	Yeas = 50, Nays = 42
October 13, 1999	Multilateral	Comprehensive Nuclear Test Ban Treaty	Yeas = 48, Nays = 51
December 4, 2012	Multilateral	Convention on the Rights of Persons with Disabilities	Yeas = 61, Nays = 38

* Approved on May 26, 1960, with vote of seventy-seven to four; vote immediately followed by motion to reconsider, and on second vote treaty was rejected forty-nine to thirty; second motion to reconsider was introduced on May 27, 1960, but was not taken up; treaty remained on calendar of Committee on Foreign Relations until 2000, when it was returned to the president.

† Rejected on March 8, 1983, with vote of fifty to forty-two; motion to reconsider was entered but not taken up; treaty remained on calendar of Committee on Foreign Relations until 1998, when it was returned to the president as part of the resolution of ratification for Montreal Protocol No. 4.

Source: US Senate, https://www.senate.gov/artandhistory/history/common/briefing/Treaties.htm.

House of Representatives

During House consideration of implementing Jay's Treaty in 1795, George Washington made clear that the Constitutional Convention had rejected the view that the House's assent through implementation was necessary for treaties to become law.[15] Nevertheless, if treaties require implementing legislation or obligate the United States to spend money, then the House of Representatives has a role to play in international agreements. In addition, we will see below that many other types of agreements require the assent of the House, and it is active in holding oversight hearings on international agreements.[16]

Terminating Treaties

The Constitution is silent about terminating treaties. When President Jimmy Carter ended a long-standing defense treaty with the Chinese Nationalists on Taiwan, when George W. Bush announced that the 1972 Anti-Ballistic Missile Treaty was obsolete, and when Donald Trump suspended the 1987 Intermediate-Range Nuclear Forces Treaty with Russia, they did not request approval of the Senate. The Supreme Court dismissed a challenge to Carter's actions,[17] so there is no Court ruling on whether the president has the power to break a treaty without the approval of the Senate.

Only once has Congress terminated a treaty by a joint resolution; that was a mutual defense treaty with France, from which, in 1798, Congress declared the United States "freed and exonerated." In that case, breaking the treaty almost amounted to an act of war; indeed, two days later Congress authorized hostilities against France, which were only narrowly averted.

Presidents also have discretion in their interpretation and reinterpretation of treaties so long as they do not digress from the position that they or their predecessors present to the Senate during the treaty's ratification hearings.[18] The Reagan administration conveniently contended that the ban against space-based missiles in the Anti-Ballistic Missile Treaty, ratified in 1973, did not apply to the development and testing of space-based weapons but only to their deployment. However, in *Hamdan v. Rumsfeld* (2006), the Supreme Court held that the military tribunals set up through executive order by President George W. Bush violated the Geneva Convention, suggesting a role of the courts in treaty interpretation. Moreover, the courts will pay attention to the Senate's intent in interpreting treaties.[19]

Executive Agreements

In addition to treaties, there are other types of international agreements concluded by the executive branch but not submitted to the Senate. These are termed executive agreements. Executive agreements are commonly used to complete consequential international agreements. The US commitments to the security of both Afghanistan and Iraq are governed entirely by executive agreements completed by the Bush and Obama administrations.

Executive agreements have the same legal authority as a treaty under international law. The Supreme Court has also held that the legal status of executive agreements is the same as it is for treaties within the United States.[20] However, although treaties supersede statutes, executive agreements do not. Agreements can be terminated by the executives who negotiated them or by their successors in office.

Executive agreements have been in use since the earliest days of the republic. In 1792 legislation authorized the postmaster general to make arrangements with foreign postmasters for the receipt and delivery of letters and packets. Many executive agreements in the nineteenth century dealt with reciprocal trade agreements under power delegated by Congress.[21]

Increasing Use

As table 14.2 shows, in the first fifty years of US history, twice as many treaties were concluded as executive agreements. In the fifty-year period from 1839 to 1889, executive agreements outnumbered treaties by a small margin. At that point, executive agreements began to greatly outnumber treaties and became the dominant method for completing international agreements in the 1940s. Since World War II, executive agreements have comprised about 95 percent of international agreements.[22]

The increase in the number of nations with which the United States interacts and the increase in international cooperation (as in atomic energy, aviation, commerce, defense, environmental protection, patents, space research, satellites, and taxation) have led to an explosion of international agreements. For example, the United States had more than two hundred international agreements with the United Kingdom in force in 1999, listed under almost sixty different subjects.

Also contributing to the increase in executive agreements has been the passage of legislation authorizing the executive branch to conclude international agreements in areas such as foreign aid, agriculture, and trade.

Finally, norms of treaty use have changed. For most of US history there has been an expectation that the president would use treaties for arms control agreements, human rights accords, multilateral environmental agreements, participation in international organizations, extradition, and bilateral tax, legal assistance, and investment treaties. These norms are changing, however.

How could the executive and legislative branches handle the workload? The president found it took much less time to conclude an executive agreement than a treaty because it did not require obtaining the support of two-thirds of the Senate. In 1952, for instance, the United States signed 14 treaties and 291 executive agreements. This was a larger number of executive agreements than had been reached during the entire century of 1789–1889. It would not have been possible for the president to shepherd all those agreements through the Senate. Moreover, when the Senate is spending time on treaties, it is not spending time on other presidential priorities, so presidents turn to executive agreements even when their party controls the Senate.[23]

The Senate was also concerned about the burden of reviewing the large number of agreements. Submitting all agreements to the Senate as treaties would either overwhelm the Senate with work or force approval to become perfunctory. Moreover, many international agreements are of relatively minor importance and would needlessly overburden the Senate if they were submitted as treaties for advice and consent.[24]

The difficulty of obtaining the Senate's consent has also encouraged presidents to enter into executive agreements.[25] When President John Tyler failed to get the Senate to ratify a treaty annexing Texas, he entered into an executive agreement to do so. The Senate takes an active role in considering treaties, and the preferences of leading senators matter.[26] That is why so many treaties fail to win ratification.

Barack Obama submitted the fewest treaties to the Senate of any modern president (although Donald Trump is on pace to submit even fewer).[27] A primary reason was the difficulty of winning Senate consent. When Secretary of State John Kerry was asked why the 2015 Iran Nuclear Accord was not a treaty, he candidly replied, "frankly, it's become physically impossible. You can't pass a treaty anymore."[28]

Indeed, the arms control agreement (New START) in 2010 was the only major treaty approved by the Senate during the Obama presidency.

One reason for this difficulty is partisan polarization.[29] Because treaties require two-thirds support, the president must be able to build a broad bipartisan coalition—something difficult to do when the parties are highly polarized. Moreover, treaties are clearly seen as presidential initiatives, and opposition party members are reluctant to provide the president with a clear victory.[30]

The obstacle of partisan polarization is not a new phenomenon. The level of polarization most similar to that in the twenty-first century was in the last decades of the nineteenth century. Of the twenty-two explicit Senate rejections of proposed treaties in US history, ten occurred between 1860 and 1897. The Senate rejected every major treaty presented to it between 1869 and 1898.

Despite the utility of executive agreements for both the president and Congress, agreement partners often prefer a treaty to an executive agreement. Treaties send more credible signals of commitment to agreement partners because they require broad domestic political support.[31]

Types

We can divide executive agreements into three categories.[32] The first is congressional-executive agreements and represents the vast majority of executive agreements. These agreements are made pursuant to a previous act of Congress and some may require congressional approval via joint resolution. In some instances Congress provides *ex ante* ("before the event") authorization to the president to complete agreements in a particular policy area. Most recent congressional-executive agreements are of the *ex ante* variety. As an example, the executive branch has concluded numerous defense and base agreements on the basis of the North Atlantic Treaty and other security treaties. In other situations, Congress legislates on a foreign policy matter, instructing the president to verify certain facts before the agreement can take effect.

Finally, the president may need to seek *ex post* ("after the fact") approval by submitting the agreement to Congress (rather than just the Senate) for bicameral approval. This approval requires only majority support from both chambers, rather than the two-thirds Senate majority required by treaties. Major trade agreements, such as the North American Free Trade Agreement, the General Agreement on Tariffs and Trade, and the Central American Free Trade Agreement, are typically completed in this manner, and so are agreements regarding arms transfers, atomic energy cooperation, foreign military and economic assistance, and fisheries.[33]

Congress's participation in approving international agreements can weaken the president's negotiating position if other countries believe that additional conditions may be required before ratification. To rectify this problem Congress has enacted fast-track authority that allows the president to introduce trade agreements for an up-or-down vote.

A second type of executive agreement is one pursuant to an existing treaty. Examples include arrangements and understandings under the North Atlantic Treaty Organization (NATO) and other security treaties. The president's authority to conclude agreements pursuant to treaties seems well established, although controversy occasionally arises over whether particular agreements are within the purview of an existing treaty.

The third category of executive agreement is often referred to as "sole executive agreements" and rest on the authority of the president's constitutional powers. They do not have an underlying explicit or implied authorization by treaty or statute. Chief executives claim as a basis for such agreements the clauses in the Constitution giving the president

- general executive authority;
- power as commander in chief;
- authority to receive ambassadors and other public ministers;
- duty to "take care that the laws be faithfully executed"; and
- the power to negotiate treaties, as agreements might be part of the process of negotiating a treaty.

One of the most famous examples of a sole executive agreement is the Destroyers for Bases Agreement with Britain in 1940. President Franklin D. Roosevelt wanted to help the British, then in desperate straits, and the Senate was unlikely to go along. So he acted on his own authority, despite the fact that he violated two statutes in doing so. FDR also made agreements with Denmark to occupy Greenland and defend Iceland. These actions put the US Navy in direct conflict with German U-boats, resulting in several clashes in the Atlantic. In the end, the president ordered the navy to sink German submarines—months before the United States entered the war.

Courts have indicated that executive agreements based solely on the president's independent constitutional authority can supersede conflicting provisions of state law, but opinions differ regarding the extent to which they can supersede a prior act of Congress. What judicial authority exists seems to indicate that they cannot.

Oversight

In the past, presidents have sometimes entered into executive agreements secretly. Examples include the Yalta Agreement of 1945 and the agreement resolving the Cuban missile crisis in 1962. Even though Congress may not have to approve an executive agreement, legislators do have a right to know about them. In 1969 and 1970, the Senate Foreign Relations Committee discovered that Presidents Lyndon Johnson and Richard Nixon had covertly entered into a number of secret agreements with South Vietnam, South Korea, Thailand, Laos, Ethiopia, Spain, and other countries. In response to these secret pacts, Congress enacted the Case-Zablocki Act in 1972 that requires the secretary of state to transmit the text of any international agreement, other than treaties, to which the United States is a party to Congress within sixty days. If presidents feel publication of the agreement would jeopardize national security, they may transmit the text only to members of the Senate Foreign Relations and House International Relations committees under an injunction of secrecy that only they (or their successors) may remove.

Presidents Richard Nixon and Gerald Ford did not fully comply with this legislation, however. They did not submit some agreements to Congress and were late in submitting others. Consequently, in 1977, Congress passed legislation requiring any department or agency of the US government that enters into any international agreement on behalf of the country to transmit the text to the State Department within twenty days of its signing.

Other Forms of Agreement

There are other types of international agreements besides treaties and executive agreements. The 2015 nuclear accord with Iran (the Joint Comprehensive Plan of

Action) illustrates the point.[34] President Obama brokered a deal with Iran, China, Russia, the United Kingdom, France, and Germany in which Iran agreed to end its efforts to develop nuclear weapons in exchange for the elimination of certain economic sanctions.

The president lacked authority to eliminate or permanently waive sanctions, because statutes require congressional review of nuclear cooperation agreements and only authorized the president to temporarily suspend sanctions against Iran. The president had no authority to complete a binding agreement.

So the White House acted creatively and produced an agreement that was neither a treaty nor an executive agreement but rather a political agreement that relied on existing congressionally delegated presidential authority to grant waivers of sanctions. The president supported congressional efforts to require congressional review of the agreement once it was completed. Congress enacted the Iran Nuclear Agreement Review Act by a bipartisan vote in 2015. The law suspended the president's waiver authority on Iranian sanctions for sixty days while Congress reviewed and debated the agreement. After that time the president could waive sanctions if Congress failed to enact a joint resolution of disapproval.

The president did not require a vote of approval to waive the sanctions, and the agreement would go into effect if Congress voted to approve it or did nothing. Moreover, the president could veto any disapproval resolution. In effect, the president turned the requirement of a vote of two-thirds of the Senate to support a treaty to a requirement of avoiding a veto override by winning just one-third (plus one) of the votes in either chamber of Congress.

In 2015 President Obama also signed the Paris Climate Agreement. Part of the agreement involved the rules for joining and leaving the pact and for reporting progress in reducing pollution. This portion was an executive agreement based on a 1992 treaty authorizing future action. However, the controversial portion of the agreement, the voluntary commitment to reducing emissions, was done as a political agreement without the force of law.

Such agreements are fragile, and Donald Trump pulled the United States out of both the Iranian nuclear agreement and the Paris Climate Agreement early in his presidency.

Recognition of Nations

Another important aspect of presidential diplomacy is initiating or terminating relations with other countries. In 2015 in *Zivotofsky v. Kerry*, the Supreme Court held that the president has the exclusive power of officially recognizing other nations.[35] Although there is evidence to suggest that the framers intended this power to be purely ministerial, presidents have exercised their discretion when using their recognition authority.[36] George Washington was the first to do so when he officially received the representative of the new French Republic in 1789, Citizen Genet. Subsequently, he revoked Genet's credentials after the latter agitated for America to join France in its conflict with England. Washington advocated neutrality.

Presidents have gone so far as to recognize a government that has been removed from power and to acknowledge the rights of a people who lack a state. Following the signing of an agreement between Israel and the Palestine Liberation Organization at the White House in 1993, President Clinton indicated that the United States might grant formal recognition to the Palestine Liberation Organization if it renounced terrorism and recognized Israel's right to exist. Similarly, George W. Bush and Barack

Obama indicated that the United States was prepared to recognize a Palestinian state, if certain conditions were met. In 2008, Bush recognized Kosovo after it declared its independence from Serbia. The Senate has no role in the recognition process other than to consent to the choice of an American ambassador and the establishment of an embassy.

Recognizing countries can be controversial. In 1933, Franklin D. Roosevelt recognized the government of the Soviet Union, fifteen years after it was constituted and functioning. In 1979, Jimmy Carter extended recognition to the People's Republic of China following a period of thirty years of non-recognition. In 1984, Ronald Reagan announced the resumption of formal diplomatic relations with the Vatican. After approving a private visit to the United States in 1995 by the president of Taiwan, an island over which China claims sovereignty, the Clinton administration went to great lengths to indicate to the Chinese that the visit did not imply or portend recognition. Similarly, when the George W. Bush administration allowed the president of Taiwan to visit the United States, it also indicated that the visit was private and did not augur a change in policy toward China. Each of these actions provoked criticism about the merits of the presidents' judgments but not about their authority to make them.

Presidents can also end relations. Before war ensues, it is customary to sever diplomatic ties with adversaries. Events short of war can also result in a disruption of diplomatic activity. The revolutionary activities of Cuba and Iran led Presidents Dwight Eisenhower and Jimmy Carter to cut formal ties with these countries. However, some contact was maintained by an "interests section," which operated out of the embassy of a friendly country. President Obama reinstated full diplomatic relations with Cuba. He also withdrew the United States' recognition of Muammar Qaddafi as the legitimate head of the Libyan government and froze Libya's assets in the United States during the uprising in that country that forced Qaddafi from power. Obama subsequently made those assets available to the rebels who were opposing the Qaddafi regime.

Other Diplomatic Actions

There are other actions that presidents can take to register their disapproval of the policies of other countries. Recalling an ambassador, instituting a trade embargo, and reducing economic or military assistance are all devices that have been employed to sanction the actions and disrupt relations with other countries. The Clinton administration labeled Sudan a terrorist country in 1993 after discovering a tie between two of its representatives at the United Nations and the terrorists who bombed the World Trade Center in New York City. In 2008, Congress identified the Iranian National Guard as a terrorist organization at the urging of the Bush administration. The Obama administration imposed economic sanctions and participated in an international campaign to pressure Iran to halt its nuclear enrichment program. President Trump re-imposed sanctions on Iran after pulling out of the nuclear agreement and his administration increased sanctions on Russia. Presidents can also remove sanctions if the objectionable policy is changed.

COMMANDER IN CHIEF AND THE USE OF FORCE

Diplomacy and other forms of international cooperation are a form of "soft power," in which the United States uses negotiation, persuasion, and economic assistance to shape the international environment. Since the end of World War II, the United

States has been the world's dominant military power, and the president's commander in chief authority places the office at the epicenter of that power. Wars and military actions have long played a central role in the expansion of presidential power, connecting Lincoln's actions at the outset of the Civil War to George W. Bush's assertions of power after 9/11.

War

The Constitution gives Congress the sole power to declare war, a power it has exercised only five times (see table 14.4). Congress can also expressly grant permission for military action through passing resolutions that authorize the use of force, which it has done in eleven other instances (see table 14.5).[37] George H. W. Bush and George W. Bush both claimed that they did not need a congressional resolution to go to war against Iraq, but they requested one to maximize their political support and

Table 14.4 Declarations of War

Year	President	Adversaries
1812	Madison	Great Britain
1846	Polk	Mexico
1898	McKinley	Spain
1917	Wilson	Germany, Austria-Hungary
1941	F. D. Roosevelt	Japan, Germany, Italy, Bulgaria, Hungary, Romania

Source: Jennifer K. Elsea and Matthew C. Weed, "Declarations of War and Authorizations for the Use of Military Force: Historical Background and Legal Implications," Congressional Research Service, April 18, 2014.

Table 14.5 Congressional Authorizations of the Use of Force

Year	President	Purpose
1798	J. Adams	Defend international commerce against France
1802	Jefferson	Defend international commerce against Tripoli
1815	Madison	Defend international commerce against Algeria
1819	Monroe	Defend international commerce against Pirates
1955	Eisenhower	Defend Formosa and Pescadores against the People's Republic of China
1957	Eisenhower	Defend the Middle East against communism
1964	L. Johnson	Defend South Vietnam against North Vietnam
1983	Reagan	Keep peace in Lebanon
1991	G. H. W. Bush	Rollback Iraqi invasion of Kuwait
2001	G. W. Bush	Fight terrorists
2002	G. W. Bush	Remove regime of Saddam Hussein in Iraq

Source: Jennifer K. Elsea and Matthew C. Weed, "Declarations of War and Authorizations for the Use of Military Force: Historical Background and Legal Implications," Congressional Research Service, April 18, 2014.

preclude later partisan opposition in Congress. President Truman fought the Korean War in 1950 under the United Nations Participation Act of 1945, which was ratified by the US Senate, citing resolutions passed by the United Nations Security Council in 1950. Critics have questioned the legality of this use of force ever since.[38]

The White House can also stretch authorization for the use of force beyond recognizable limits. Both the Obama and Trump administrations claimed that the Authorization for the Use of Military Force (AUMF) passed by Congress in September 2001, shortly after the 9/11 attacks, provided authority for them to engage in hostile actions against the Islamic State, including against Syrian troops. Congress wrote the AUMF to respond to whomever "planned, authorized, committed, or aided" the 9/11 attacks, however. Syria had nothing to do with those attacks. Neither did ISIS. Congress refused to pass an authorization for President Obama to use force against Syria after it employed chemical weapons against civilians. When President Trump ordered such a strike on April 6, 2017, the Department of Defense wrote that "the President authorized that strike pursuant to his power under Article II of the Constitution as Commander in Chief and Chief Executive to use this sort of military force overseas to defend important US national interests." Such an assertion would have mystified the Founders.

In addition to congressionally authorized uses of force, presidents have employed forces abroad over two hundred times throughout American history. Table 14.6 lists some examples from the past sixty years. Other instances of the use of force have often involved deployment of US military forces as part of enforcing no-fly zones or other multinational operations associated with NATO or the United Nations, humanitarian interventions, or evacuating Americans from harm's way. In many of these instances, no shots were fired.

Presidential deployment of armed forces in hostile or potentially hostile situations presents a conflict between constitutional theory and practice. As commander in chief, head of state, and head of government, every contemporary president from Truman through Trump has committed the nation to battle. Armed with a near monopoly on first-hand information, an unparalleled potential for engaging public support, and an oath to provide for the common defense, presidents have used their prerogatives to broaden their constitutional powers.

When presidents have used force without legislative authority, they have often claimed self-defense. Jimmy Carter's 1980 attempt to rescue American hostages in Iran, Ronald Reagan's 1986 bombing of Libya after an attack in Germany that killed a US serviceman, and Bill Clinton's 1998 missile strikes against al-Qaeda after the bombing of US embassies in Africa are examples of self-defense. George H. W. Bush explained his 1989 invasion of Panama as a response to Gen. Manuel Antonio Noriega's "reckless threats and attacks upon Americans in Panama [that] created an imminent danger to the 35,000 American citizens" there. Reagan justified his 1983 invasion of Grenada with the rationale that "American lives are at stake."

Presidents have also relied on multilateral support or treaty demands. Reagan, in invading Grenada, was careful to stress that the Organization of Eastern Caribbean States had invited the United States to respond—and that it was doing so in concert with other nations in the region. Similarly, in entering Somalia (1992) and attacking Kosovo (1999) and Libya (2011), US administrations were able to cite both humanitarian concerns and treaty obligations with the United Nations, NATO, or both. Although the War Powers Resolution specifically rules out inferring authority to use force from treaty obligations, international obligations provided the presidents cover.

Table 14.6 Examples of Presidential Use of Force without Declarations of War or Statutory Authority, 1958–2019

Year	President	Purpose
1958	Eisenhower	Troops sent to Lebanon to protect against insurrection
1962	Kennedy	Quarantine of Cuba
1965	Johnson	Troops sent to the Dominican Republic to protect lives and property
1970	Nixon	Invasion of Cambodia to clean out communist sanctuaries
1975	Ford	Attack in Cambodia to rescue crew of *Mayaguez*
1980	Carter	Hostage rescue attempt in Iran
1982–1983	Reagan	Troops sent to Lebanon to restore Lebanese sovereignty
1983	Reagan	Invasion of Grenada to protect lives and restore order
1986	Reagan	Bombing of Libya in response to attacks on US forces
1989–1990	G. H. W. Bush	Invasion of Panama to protect lives, restore democracy, and bring General Noriega to justice
1992–1993	G. H. W. Bush/Clinton	Troops sent to Somalia for humanitarian relief
1993	Clinton	Bombing of Iraq in response to assassination attempt on former president Bush
1994	Clinton	Bombing of Bosnia to prevent Serbian killings
1994	Clinton	Troops sent to Haiti to restore democracy
1998	Clinton	Bombing terrorist camps in Afghanistan and Sudan
1999	Clinton	Bombing Yugoslavia to stop violence against Kosovo Albanians
2011	Obama	Airstrikes against Libya in support of efforts to protect civilians
2017	Trump	Raid on Yemen to gather intelligence and capture terrorists
2017	Trump	Bombing Syria in response to use of chemical weapons

Source: Barbara Salazar Torreon, "Instances of Use of United States Armed Forces Abroad, 1798–2016," Congressional Research Service, October 7, 2016. Updated by authors.

In principle, Congress could have resisted such actions. In practice, it has been unable or unwilling to do so.[39] Congress more commonly tries to avoid blame for unpopular wars than to challenge the executive's right to wage them. The House of Representatives condemned James K. Polk's order to send the Army into disputed territory with Mexico, but only after the Mexican War had been concluded. Congress forced Richard Nixon to end bombing in Cambodia, but only after that action had been carried on for more than two years. During periods of crisis, Congress finds it difficult, if not impossible, to oppose the president. Despite public opposition to the US military presence in Iraq and Afghanistan, Congress was unable to impose a timetable on the withdrawal of American forces. In both cases, it was the administration in consultation with defense department officials that negotiated or established the withdrawal.

Congress faces an enormous difficulty in challenging presidential dominance during wartime. As a majoritarian institution, Congress is famously inefficient, lacks the information and expertise that the executive branch has, would have to confront both a president and military leadership in order to redirect national security policy, and cannot rely on the judiciary to help it check the executive branch. The public tends to rally behind the president during the initial stages of war or during crisis (George H. W. Bush's and George W. Bush's popularity increased from the mid-50s to nearly 90 percent after the first Gulf War and 9/11 respectively. Even the 1979 seizure of American embassy personnel in Tehran, hardly a positive foreign policy event, pushed Jimmy Carter's popularity from the low 30s to nearly 60 percent). Legislators find it politically difficult to challenge a popular president on a national security issue.[40]

War Powers Resolution

The high water mark of congressional assertion of institutional prerogative, the 1973 War Powers Resolution, took place when Nixon was already weakened by Watergate and was enacted over his veto.[41] It requires presidents to (1) consult with Congress before introducing armed forces into hostilities or imminent threat, and (2) submit a written report within forty-eight hours of deploying US armed forces into hostilities or a foreign nation. Congress then has sixty days to approve the action (which is not subject to a presidential veto) or extend the sixty days, unless it cannot meet because of an armed attack on the United States. If Congress does not act, the president must withdraw the troops, although he may extend the use of forces for thirty days if he deems it necessary to protect departing American forces. At any time, Congress can end the use of American armed forces by passing a concurrent resolution.

The law has aroused considerable debate about just what "consultation" means and whether the president could, in sixty days of hostilities, place the United States in a position from which Congress could not extract it. Many uses of armed force have not been approved on the basis of the War Powers Resolution. Moreover, in practically every administration since 1973, there have been instances that could have fallen under the purview of the act but were not reported to Congress.

Institutional rivalry is at the heart of the problem. Presidents believe that the War Powers Resolution unconstitutionally constricts their obligation to provide for the common defense by constraining their powers as commander in chief. Although they have not challenged the constitutionality of the legislation, they have narrowly interpreted its provisions, particularly its consultation and reporting requirements. The White House has also maintained that the president does not need congressional approval to order American forces into situations that may involve combat; presidents claim that they have this authority as commander in chief. In short, the War Powers Resolution has not provided the check Congress had intended.

Nevertheless, in early 2019, both houses of Congress passed a resolution to end US military support for Saudi Arabia's war in Yemen. This action was the first time Congress had passed such a resolution utilizing powers granted under the War Powers Act. President Trump vetoed the resolution, but Congress's bipartisan action was widely viewed as a rebuke of Trump's support for Saudi Arabia despite the killing of the dissident journalist Jamal Khashoggi. It also sent the president a clear signal that there were political costs to his policy.

Is the resolution unworkable? Perhaps. Is it irrelevant? No. In theory, it reasserts congressional authority while acknowledging expanded presidential powers; in practice, it does not prevent presidential initiatives but forces the president to consider the possibility that Congress, through action or inaction, could terminate those initiatives. This consideration reinforces the public and congressional opposition that exists or can develop over time if the operation is not successful. Presidents, particularly those facing reelection, are mindful of the potential political costs of their actions that put American forces in harm's way.

In addition, seeking congressional authorizations for the use of force can bolster support for the president and his foreign policies, particularly if the decision is backed by congressional leaders. Moreover, members of both parties who voted to authorize the use of force are much less willing in the future to vote to curtail it or criticize it publicly than are their co-partisan peers who did not vote for an authorization.[42]

TWO PRESIDENCIES?

In the 1960s, political scientist Aaron Wildavsky argued that presidents are apt to be more successful in crafting foreign policy than domestic policy.[43] Examining congressional action on presidential proposals after World War II, Wildavsky found that presidents had significantly more legislative success in foreign and defense policy than in domestic affairs. He gave several reasons for this institutional dominance:

- Presidents have more expertise in foreign affairs available to them than does Congress.
- Presidents have more constitutional and statutory authority in foreign affairs than for domestic policies.
- By tradition, presidents have assumed a more active role in foreign affairs.
- Presidents can act more quickly and decisively than Congress.
- Because there are fewer interest groups active in the foreign policy arena, presidents have more discretion to act as national leaders.

Wildavsky concluded that there were actually two presidencies, one in foreign affairs and one in the domestic arena, but he completed his analysis after the era of bipartisanship in foreign policy that followed World War II and the onset of the Cold War.[44] Since then, the domestic impact of foreign policy has become more pronounced, blurring the old distinction between foreign and domestic affairs and creating new incentives for Congress to get involved. The old adage that "politics stops at the water's edge" is no longer applicable.

Groups
There are more organized interest groups today that are concerned with the economic, social, and political impact of foreign policy issues than there were in the 1950s, and the groups are more powerful. They have greater resources and technologies to reach and mobilize their members and supporters to pressure government and affect election outcomes. Trade agreements, which can have significant domestic impacts, represent an area in which groups, and thus Congress, have always shown concern and have been the source of considerable political conflict.[45]

The Media
The 24/7 news media cycle and continuous Internet communications are also a constraint on the president. The attention the press gives to certain international events and conditions combined with the more recent flow of pictures and words from around the world on the Internet via YouTube, Twitter, and other social networks has raised public awareness and increased political costs of inaction for presidents.[46] Accounts replete with visual imagery of hunger in Somalia, ethnic cleansing in Kosovo, and repression of popular demonstrations in Libya prompted George H. W. Bush, Bill Clinton, and Barack Obama to order US military forces into these parts of the world, which have very limited strategic value to the United States. In contrast, the failure of the news media to cover the massacres in Rwanda and other civil strife in Africa resulted in little public pressure to do so.[47]

The Public
The public consensus that characterized US foreign policy during World War II and the Cold War has weakened and on some issues ended. Presidents can no longer take public support for granted.

In addition, the public is less deferential to the White House. In general, the more salient the issue and the stronger the public preferences for or against a particular policy outcome, the more likely that presidents will be forced to take a stand and involve the United States in the matter.[48] Although the general public may not be attentive to many of the details of an administration's policy, people do tend to be cognizant of the results, especially if those results fall short of presidential promises, public expectations, or both. The public particularly judges military interventions by their outcomes, regardless of whether a majority supported the president's decision to go to war. Although the presidential decisions to use American military forces in Vietnam (1965–1973), Afghanistan (2001–2014), and Iraq (2003–2012) were initially backed by a majority of the population, over time public opinion turned against these wars when they were not resolved successfully and Americans became more aware of their costs.

Congress
The Framers designed Congress to be the primary check on presidential discretion in national security matters. The record is mixed, however. The partisan composition of Congress affects the exercise of national security powers. Although the two presidencies did flourish under President Eisenhower, the additional support for foreign policy from the opposition party that characterized the two presidencies has been modest since the 1960s and no longer reliably appears. Moreover, the locus of additional support for foreign policy has always been the opposition party. The

president's party in Congress has never provided him with an additional increment of support for his foreign policy proposals.[49]

Contrary to the conventional wisdom, the source of the two presidencies was not congressional bipartisanship or deference in foreign affairs, nor was it the relative advantages of the president in foreign policy making. Instead, the two presidencies appeared to be a natural outgrowth of a president proposing foreign policies, but not domestic policies, that appealed to a substantial segment of the opposition party. When the appeal of a president's foreign policies to the opposition diminish, so do the two presidencies.[50]

William Howell and Jon Pevehouse found that presidents are systematically less likely to exercise military force when their partisan opponents have control of Congress. The partisan composition of Congress, however, matters most for proposed larger military deployments and those directed at less strategically important locales. Moreover, congressional influence is often achieved not through bold legislative action but through public posturing—engaging the media, raising public concerns, and stirring domestic and international doubt about the United States' resolve to see a fight through to the end.[51]

Similarly, Douglas Kriner has shown even in politically sensitive wartime environments, individual members of Congress frequently propose legislation, hold investigative hearings, and engage in national policy debates in the public sphere. These actions influence the president's strategic decisions as he weighs the political costs of pursuing his preferred military course.[52]

Nevertheless, there has been a noticeable reduction in public and secret hearings since the mid-1990s. Committee scrutiny of the wars in Iraq and Afghanistan, for example, fell below levels of oversight in prior major conflicts. The desire of the president's partisans to shield him from public inquiry, growing lack of interest in committee work, and biases among members who join the relevant committees have produced a drop in congressional oversight activity.[53] More broadly, members of Congress seem to defer somewhat to the president on foreign policy votes.[54]

Still, many members of Congress are not disposed to acquiesce quietly to the president's foreign policy initiatives. Donald Trump has experienced an unusual number of congressional rebukes. Congress took the initiative in passing sanctions aimed particularly at punishing Russia. The House also voted to formally disapprove of plans to relax sanctions against companies controlled by Russian oligarch Oleg Deripaska, an ally of Vladimir Putin. Congress passed a resolution to end US support for Saudi Arabia's war in Yemen. The Senate voted unanimously for a resolution officially blaming Saudi Crown Prince Mohammed bin Salman for the killing of journalist Jamal Khashoggi, contrary to the president's views. In response to the president's decision to withdraw all US troops from Syria and Afghanistan, the Senate passed an amendment warning that "the precipitous withdrawal of United States forces from either country could put at risk hard-won gains and United States national security" and arguing that "it is incumbent upon the United States to lead, to continue to maintain a global coalition against terror and to stand by our local partners." Despite Trump's inclinations to withdraw the United States from NATO, the House voted to reaffirm the lawmakers' support for NATO and to specify that no US funds could be spent to withdraw the United States from it. Few of these votes actually altered policies, but they did increase the political cost of persisting in them.

General David Petraeus and Ambassador Ryan Crocker testify before Congress on the war in Iraq.

THE ORGANIZATION OF FOREIGN AND DEFENSE POLICY

A large number of federal agencies are involved in foreign and defense policy; this is hardly surprising given the centrality of the security and international affairs functions of the federal government. Table 14.7 lists the major departments and independent agencies involved. Apart from the agencies that have principal responsibility—the Departments of Defense, State, and Homeland Security—several other agencies have specialized duties. The Department of the Treasury investigates the finances of international terrorism and criminal organizations; the Department of Energy has responsibility for nuclear weapons and nonproliferation; and the Department of Commerce manages export controls and aspects of international trade.

Responsibility for intelligence—the collection and analysis of information necessary for policy making, often done at very high levels of classification—is dispersed among at least seventeen agencies spread across departments or operating as independent offices. Investigations that took place after 9/11 found that intelligence agencies often did not cooperate with each other or share information, which played a role in the failure to discover the terrorist threat and prevent the operation from taking place.[55] A national commission that investigated 9/11 recommended the creation of an office that would coordinate intelligence activities across the organizations involved, and Congress created the Office of the Director of National Intelligence in 2004.[56]

The size and scope of foreign and defense policy pose a problem for presidential leadership. At the same time that presidents have ultimate responsibility for national security policy, the number of agencies involved serves to make central

Table 14.7 Agencies Involved in Foreign and Defense Policy

White House Offices	National Security Council Homeland Security Council Office of the Special Trade Representative
Federal Departments with Primary Responsibility	Department of Defense Department of State Department of Homeland Security
Intelligence Agencies	Office of National Intelligence Central Intelligence Agency National Security Agency Defense Intelligence Agency and thirteen others
Other Agencies	Department of Agriculture (Agricultural Exports/Trade Policy) Department of Commerce (Export Controls) Department of Energy (Nuclear Weapons) Department of Labor (International Labor) Department of Justice (FBI) Department of Treasury (International Financial Crimes) US Agency for International Development (Foreign Aid) Overseas Private Investment Corporation (Foreign Aid)

control challenging (the broad responsibility increases the importance and difficulty of speaking with one voice and presenting a consistent face; see box 14.2). For most of US history, national security policy making "lacked organizational support to integrate national security policies. They relied instead on ad hoc arrangements and informal groups of advisers."[57] The increasing complexity of international affairs, the role of the United States as the world's only superpower, and the breadth of national security issues required new institutional arrangements to make national security policy.

Box 14.2 ★ The Trump Administration Speaks with Many Voices

The idea that the government must speak "with one voice" has a long history: a consistent public position increases the ability of the president to negotiate with other parties (whether members of Congress or foreign adversaries) and reduces uncertainty about what the president intends to do. This principle is even more important in international affairs, where other nations adapt their own policies in response to what they see as US policy.

On January 27, 2017, President Trump issued an executive order banning refugees and prohibiting immigration from seven mostly Muslim countries. In response to an explosion of criticism, his secretary of Homeland Security told the press, "This is not, I repeat, not, a ban on Muslims." Trump then contradicted him by tweeting, "I am calling it what we need and what it is, a TRAVEL BAN!" When a federal court injunction forced the White House to issue a revised order, Trump criticized Attorney General Jeff Sessions and the Justice Department, tweeting that they "should have stayed with the original Travel Ban, not the watered down, politically correct version."

(continued)

Box 14.2 ★ Continued

In a White House meeting with the Russian foreign minister and the ambassador to the United States, Trump revealed sensitive and secret intelligence that might have done serious damage to Israeli operations. His national security adviser, H. R. McMaster, and McMaster's deputy, Dina Powell, told the press that the reports of Trump's discussions were "false." However, Trump undercut his aides' explanations of his revelations when he tweeted, "As President I wanted to share with Russia (at an openly scheduled W. H. meeting) which I have the absolute right to do, facts pertaining to terrorism and airline flight safety."

In early June 2017, Saudi Arabia, Bahrain, the United Arab Emirates, and Egypt accused Qatar of sponsoring terrorist groups, broke off diplomatic relations, and cut off trade. Qatar was home to a US air force base with eleven thousand US troops and an arm of the US Central Command that was crucial to operations against ISIS. Secretary of State Tillerson adopted a conciliatory tone by urging the states to engage in a "calm and thoughtful dialogue" in order to settle their dispute, arguing, "the blockage [of trade] is hindering US military missions in the region and the campaign against ISIS." An hour later, President Trump said that Qatar was a "funder of terror at a very high level." The next day he sided with the Saudi blockade, undercutting Tillerson's attempt to bring the two sides to the negotiation table. Tillerson was forced to admit, "I'm not involved in how the president constructs his tweets, when he tweets, why he tweets, what he tweets."

In August 2017, North Korea successfully tested improved missiles and threatened the United States with their use. Trump declared off the cuff that any threats "will be met with fire and fury like the world has never seen." US foreign policy officials tried to calm a worried public, with Secretary of State Rex Tillerson assuring the public that Americans should "have no concerns about this particular rhetoric of the past few days." The next day Trump declared that his previous rhetoric "wasn't tough enough," contradicting Tillerson's message. In October 2017, Tillerson suggested that the United States should maintain communications with North Korea, but the next day the president tweeted that the secretary of state was "wasting his time" trying to negotiate with the country's leader.

Secretary of State Mike Pompeo demanded "complete, verifiable, irreversible denuclearization" from North Korea, starting with a full accounting of the country's nuclear and missile capabilities. Nevertheless Trump let the North Koreans off the hook by repeatedly declaring he was "in no rush—we just we don't want the testing." In May 2019, after his national security assistant declared that North Korean missile tests violated UN resolutions and that the president would maintain sanctions to pressure the regime to stop them, the president tweeted that he was not bothered by the tests.

When the Treasury Department announced sanctions against two Chinese shipping companies that were accused of facilitating trade with North Korea, Trump ordered the withdrawal of those sanctions the next day.

The United States announced punitive measures against Chinese telecom giant ZTE in response to the company's failure to comply with a settlement of charges for violating sanctions on Iran and North Korea. Shortly thereafter, the president ordered Commerce Secretary Wilbur Ross to save ZTE from collapse, saying the company's failure would cost too many jobs in China. When Ross insisted ZTE would not be a factor in trade talks, Trump contradicted Ross's statement.

The president accused China and Russia of improperly manipulating their currencies in a way that gave them unfair trade advantages, contradicting a report issued by the Treasury Department. After US Trade Representative Robert

(continued)

Box 14.2 ★ Continued

E. Lighthizer announced a "hard deadline" for reaching a trade deal with China, Trump extended the talk deadline. In the Oval Office, the president contradicted Lighthizer in front of Chinese officials on the meaning of "memoranda of understanding." Over four days in August 2019, the president imposed new tariffs on China, called the country's president an "enemy," ordered US companies to leave China, admitted "second thoughts" on the escalating trade war, reversed course hours later to say he only wished he had raised the tariffs higher, called the Chinese president a "great leader," and then vowed that a deal would be coming soon (which it did not).

When top intelligence officials said that Iran was complying with the nuclear deal, Trump contradicted them. After they concluded that Saudi Crown Prince Mohammed bin Salman ordered the assassination of *Washington Post* columnist Jamal Khashoggi, Trump issued a contradictory statement days later: "Maybe he did or maybe he didn't!" When the officials warned of Russian interference in the 2016 election, the president declared that he "didn't see any reason why it would be" Russia who interfered in the 2016 US election. When the president agreed with Russian President Vladimir Putin that Russia was not involved in Venezuela, he contradicted the comments of his secretary of state the previous day, who declared that Russia not only had been involved, it had actually "invaded" Venezuela.

These inconsistent and changing positions make it difficult for other political actors to predict what the government is actually intending to do. According to R. Nicholas Burns, a senior diplomat who served in the Clinton and both Bush administrations, "What matters is what he says."[58] "His administration may have drafted a Russia policy through the interagency process," said Michael A. McFaul, a former American ambassador to Russia, "but Trump seems completely disconnected from it, like he seems to be on many foreign policies."[59] In dealing with adversaries like North Korea, the president's inconsistency increases the likelihood of miscalculation and an eventual crisis.

priorities; to coordinate and integrate domestic, foreign, and military policies; and to suggest specific courses of action, all within the national security sphere:

> The function of the Council shall be to advise the President with respect to the integration of domestic, foreign, and military policies relating to the national security so as to enable the military services and the other departments and agencies of the Government to cooperate more effectively in matters involving the national security.[60]

The authorizing statute (which has been amended several times) now specifies that the president, the vice president, the secretary of state, the secretary of defense, and the secretary of energy are members of the NSC and names the chairman of the Joint Chiefs of Staff as the president's chief military adviser. Presidents, however, can name additional members. Obama specified that the secretaries of the Treasury and Homeland Security, the representative to the United Nations, the national security adviser, and the White House chief of staff were members and included the director of National Intelligence and the chairman of the Joint Chiefs of Staff as advisory participants in all NSC meetings. In addition, other cabinet secretaries and agency heads would attend when an issue fell under their jurisdiction.[61]

President Trump, controversially, added his chief strategist, Stephen K. Bannon, to the Council, a decision that many criticized as politicizing what was intended to be a neutral advisory process.[62] In April 2017, Trump issued a new National Security Memorandum that removed Bannon and added the chairman of the Joint Chiefs of Staff, the director of National Intelligence, and the director of the Central Intelligence Agency as regular attendees.[63] The change was widely attributed to the influence of Trump's second national security adviser, Lt. Gen. H. R. McMaster, who increasingly asserted himself over the flow of national security information in the White House and brought some order to chaotic decision-making processes.[64] Trump soon tired of McMaster, however, replacing him with John Bolton in April 2018.

The head of the NSC staff—the national security adviser, who is not actually mentioned in the 1947 statute but whose position was created by Eisenhower—has become "the president's chief, in-house source of substantive coordination and counsel on foreign policy and national security matters."[65] As described in a transition report written by the White House Transition Project, the contemporary national security adviser's duties encompass acting as the following:

- source of personal advice and counsel to the president;
- focal channel for information during crises;
- conduit for written information to and from the other principals;
- organizer of the president's daily national security briefing;
- provider of day-to-day staff support to the president; and
- watchdog of the president's political interests as they relate to national security matters.

Additionally, the adviser presides over a staff that integrates the views and information of national security organizations into the policy-making process.[66] The position does not require Senate confirmation, although active duty military personnel—such as McMaster—require Senate action to allow them to serve in the office.

The national security adviser has become one of the—if not *the*—most important foreign policy officials in the government. In large part because of their proximity to the president and their ability to focus solely on policy rather than have much of their time devoted to department administration, national security advisers are often more influential than either the secretary of defense or secretary of state. Stephen Hadley, who was George W. Bush's national security adviser from 2005 to 2009, described the position:

> You get to spend more time with the President than any other member of the President's national security team. You are the first to see the President in the morning when the President shows up for work in the Oval Office and the last person to see the President before he or she makes any major foreign policy or national security decision. You are the person most likely to know the President's mind on these issues.[67]

In collecting information from across government, assimilating it into ongoing policy discussions, framing those decisions for the president, and then communicating the results to the national security administrative apparatus for implementation, the NSC serves as the president's "eyes and ears" on national security and the main advisory body within the White House. When the system works well, the process provides the president with the information needed to make decisions, along with considered advice on appropriate options. The adviser acts as an "honest broker" who is fair in assessing alternatives and providing advice.[68]

When the system breaks down, it can limit the information and options the president sees, distorting his view of problems and solutions. Another serious problem occurred in the Reagan administration, when NSC staff became involved in operational affairs and were managing covert operations in Central America without legal authority, triggering a scandal that nearly brought down the presidency in the Iran–Contra affair.[69]

Has the NSC been successful in providing the president with well-grounded and coordinated advice? A 2008 congressionally created commission, the Project for National Security Reform, suggested that it has not. The problem is that the NSC system has not kept up with the scope and breadth of national security policy and, from a purely pragmatic standpoint, since 1990 "the system has failed to achieve desired outcomes more frequently than before."[70] As complex and institutionalized as the NSC system has become, it "cannot manage the national security system as a whole," given the scope and complexity of the problem.[71]

> The US national security system is an enormous aggregate of interacting, interrelated, and interdependent institutions with structural and functional relationships that form a complex whole. For example, during the first year of the George W. Bush administration, the National Security Council (NSC) included six regional committees and eleven policy committees covering diverse topics from counterterrorism to the global environment. The diplomatic community includes 305 embassies, consulates, and diplomatic missions around the globe; the defense community includes seventeen defense agencies, nine unified combatant commands, and seven—field activities—complete with news service and healthcare establishment; the intelligence community includes sixteen separate government agencies; and the department of homeland security encompasses twenty-two formerly separate government agencies and cooperates with tens of thousands of state and local authorities across the country.[72]

The Project recommended replacing the NSC with a new President's Security Council with more flexibility and a broader mandate (particularly with respect to formally including economic and energy matters as national security concerns).[73] The goal is to create a new security planning system that can adapt to an environment where many national security threats are not state-based (as they were during the Cold War) but involve subnational organizations. To this point, there have been no significant changes in the NSC system, and President Trump has shown little interest in building more effective decision-making organizations.

CONCLUSION

The Constitution assigns authority for foreign affairs and defense policy to both Congress and the president. The framers clearly envisioned an important, but limited, role for the president. Today, however, the president dominates national security policy. Presidents are expected to set policy, oversee diplomacy, manage wars, and direct the military. They have almost unfettered discretion to use military force anywhere in the world and have benefited from both congressional delegation and judicial doctrines that make the president, in practice if not in constitutional theory, the primary organ of foreign affairs.

That increased responsibility, authority, and discretion does not necessarily translate into more success, however. The machinery of national security encompasses a large number of institutions and policy makers, creating the same difficult dynamic that the growth of the presidential institution does: as capabilities expand, it becomes more difficult for the president to effectively manage the process.

More importantly, there are no assured ways of compelling foreign leaders to do things they do not want to do—whether making North Korean leader Kim Jong Un abandon his nuclear weapons and ballistic missile programs, renegotiating trade agreements with trading partners, or insisting that other NATO members increase their defense spending. The tools of statecraft—diplomacy, economic assistance, military support, or military force, to name a few—are often blunt instruments, and in many cases there may be no viable options for the United States.

The growth of the NSC apparatus within the White House gives the president greater capacity to coordinate across agencies, but it often fails to work as intended. Staff difficulties can create their own political problems for the president (as Trump found when he was forced to dismiss his first national security adviser, Michael Flynn, after it was revealed that he had held inappropriate and undisclosed meetings with Russian officials).

Thus, although presidential authority and freedom to act may be at their height in foreign affairs, so are the stakes and the consequences of failure. Moreover, an unexpected event or series of events—the Cuban Missile Crisis, the seizure of the American embassy in Teheran in 1979, the Iraqi invasion of Kuwait in 1990, the 9/11 terrorist attack, a Syrian chemical weapons attack, a North Korean nuclear test—can dominate a president's policy agenda and shape the remainder of a presidency.

DISCUSSION QUESTIONS

1. Who controls national security policy in the Trump administration? Think about whether the most influential policy maker is the president, the national security adviser, the secretaries of defense or state, or someone else. Is there evidence that President Trump is more or less reliant on his advisers than previous presidents (e.g., Barack Obama or George W. Bush)? What evidence do you have to support your view?

2. Aaron Wildavsky first advanced his "Two Presidencies" thesis in the 1960s. Thinking about Presidents Trump and Obama, is there evidence from these recent administrations that they continued to have more policy success and congressional support in foreign and national security affairs? Do members of Congress, or other elites, show deference to the White House in foreign affairs?

3. If there were broad support in Congress for restricting the president's ability to use military force without congressional authorization (in effect, passing a law that prohibited the use of force without congressional authorization absent an imminent danger to the United States), what would that legislation look like? Could you fix the problems with the War Powers Resolution? Would this effort be constitutional? How do you think the president might respond?

WEB EXERCISES

1. The Trump White House has not put up much detail on its NSC web page (https://www.whitehouse.gov/nsc). But the Obama White House was active in posting information (https://obamawhitehouse.archives.gov/administration/eop/nsc). How useful is this information, given the very high levels of classification of most of what the NSC does? Is it important for the White House to have a public face for the NSC, or is it not essential to the operation of the office?

2. Select a prominent national security or foreign policy issue (North Korea, ISIS, China, Russia, terrorism, trade, Syria, etc.). Track news coverage over time. Is there evidence that all administrative officials are speaking with one voice and articulating a consistent message and policy? If not, what do you see as the impediments to central White House control of policy and messaging, and what are the consequences of that inconstancy?

SELECTED READINGS

Bohn, Michael K. *Presidents in Crisis: Tough Decisions inside the White House from Truman to Obama*. New York: Arcade, 2016.

Burke, John P. *Honest Broker: The National Security Advisor and Presidential Decision Making*. College Station: Texas A&M University Press, 2009.

Fisher, Louis. *Presidential War Power*, 3rd ed. rev. Lawrence: University Press of Kansas, 2013.

Fowler, Linda. *Watchdogs on the Hill: The Decline of Congressional Oversight of U.S. Foreign Relations*. Princeton, NJ: Princeton University Press, 2015.

Goldsmith, Jack. *Power and Constraint: The Accountable Presidency after 9/11*. New York: W.W. Norton, 2012.

Howell, William, and Jon C. Pevehouse. *When Dangers Gather: Congressional Checks on Presidential War Powers*. Princeton, NJ: Princeton University Press, 2007.

Kriner, Douglas L. *After the Rubicon: Congress, Presidents, and the Politics of Waging War*. Chicago, IL: University of Chicago Press, 2010.

Krutz, Glen S., and Jeffrey S. Peake. *Treaty Politics and the Rise of Executive Agreements: International Commitments in a System of Shared Powers*. Ann Arbor: University of Michigan Press, 2009.

Milner, Helen V., and Dustin Tingley. *Sailing the Water's Edge: The Domestic Politics of American Foreign Policy*. Princeton, NJ: Princeton University Press, 2015.

Priess, David. *The President's Book of Secrets: The Untold Story of Intelligence Briefings of America's Presidents*. New York: Public Affairs Books, 2016.

Project on National Security Reform. *Forging a New Shield*. November 2008.

Schlesinger, Arthur M. Jr. *The Imperial Presidency*. New York: Houghton Mifflin, 1973.

Suri, Jeremi. *The Impossible Presidency: The Rise and Fall of America's Highest Office*. New York: Basic Books, 2017.

Appendix A

Methods for Studying the Presidency

Although political scientists have always been keenly interested in the American presidency, their progress in understanding it has been relatively slow compared to studies of other institutions of government. One reason is their reliance on methods that are either irrelevant or inappropriate to the task of examining the basic relationships in which the presidency is involved. This appendix examines some of the advantages and limitations of methods used by scholars to study the presidency. Throughout, we should remember that methods are not ends in themselves but rather techniques for examining research questions generated by the approaches discussed in chapter 1.

TRADITIONAL METHODS

Studies of the presidency typically describe events, behaviors, and personalities. Journalists[1] or former executive-branch officials who rely on their personal experiences write many of these studies. Many are also written by scholars[2] or journalists who rely primarily on the observations of others—who may be insiders.

Unfortunately, such anecdotal material, although it may be insightful, is generally subjective, fragmentary, and impressionistic. The commentary and reflections of insiders, whether participants or participant-observers, are limited by the insiders' own perspectives. For example, the memoirs of aides to President Lyndon Johnson and President Richard Nixon reveal very different perceptions of the president and his presidency. Henry Kissinger wrote this about the Nixon White House staff,

> It is a truism that none of us really knew the inner man. More significant, each member of his entourage was acquainted with a slightly different Nixon subtly adjusted to the President's judgment of the aide or to his assessment of his interlocutor's background.[3]

Similarly, Dick Morris's account of President Bill Clinton's reelection suggests that the author called all or most of the shots—an account disputed by other White House insiders.[4]

Proximity to power may actually hinder, rather than enhance, an observer's perspective and breadth of view. The reflections of those who have served in government may be colored by the strong positions they advocated in office or a need to justify their decisions and behavior. Faulty memories further cloud such perceptions. Moreover, few insiders are trained to think in analytical terms of generalizations based on representative data and controls for alternative explanations. This is especially true of journalists.[5]

Several examples illustrate the problem. One of the crucial decision points in US involvement in Vietnam occurred during July 1965, when President Johnson committed the United States to large-scale combat operations. In his memoirs, Johnson goes to considerable lengths to show that he considered very carefully all the alternatives available at the time.[6] One of his aides' detailed account of the dialogue between Johnson and some of his advisers shows the president probing deeply for answers, challenging the premises and factual bases of options, and playing the devil's advocate.[7] Other participants and scholars have also concluded that Johnson kept an open mind regarding US intervention in Vietnam during that period.[8] Yet other scholars and participants have concluded that this "debate" was really a charade, staged by the president to lend legitimacy to the decision he had already made.[9]

Another useful example, this one focusing on attributions of influence, is President Johnson's efforts at obtaining the support—or at least the neutrality—of the Senate Finance Committee chair, Harry Byrd of Virginia, for what became the 1964 tax cut. Byrd had resisted a tax cut because of his concern for increasing the budget deficit. Hubert Humphrey reported in his memoirs that Johnson cajoled Byrd into letting the tax bill out of committee, relying on Lady Bird's charm, liquor, and his own famous "treatment."[10] Presidential aide Jack Valenti told a different story, however. He wrote that the president obtained the senator's cooperation by promising to hold the budget under $100 billion.[11] Thus, we have as eyewitnesses two experienced political professionals who knew both Byrd and Johnson very well. Each reported on a different tactic employed by the president and each attributed Senator Byrd's response to the presidential behavior that he observed.

To confuse matters further, Henry Hall Wilson, one of the president's congressional liaison aides, indicated that both eyewitnesses were wrong. According to Wilson, when the president proudly told his chief congressional liaison aide Lawrence O'Brien about his obtaining Byrd's agreement to begin hearings on the tax cut on December 7, O'Brien replied, "You didn't get a thing. I already had a commitment for the seventh."[12] In other words, according to O'Brien, Johnson's efforts were irrelevant and both eyewitnesses were wrong in attributing influence to him.[13]

Even tape recordings of conversations in the Oval Office may be misleading. As Henry Kissinger explains with respect to the Watergate tapes,

> Anyone familiar with Nixon's way of talking could have no doubt he was sitting on a time bomb. His random, elliptical, occasionally emotional manner of conversation was bound to shock, and mislead, the historian. Nixon's indirect style of operation simply could not be gauged by an outsider. There was no way of telling what Nixon had put forward to test his interlocutor and what he meant to be taken seriously; and

no outsider could distinguish a command that was to be followed from an emotional outburst that one was at liberty to ignore—perhaps was even expected to ignore.[14]

Even with a less complex personality than Richard Nixon, it would be difficult years after the event to disentangle the sarcastic from the genuine, the tentative from the serious, the fleeting thought from the careful proposition.[15]

Aside from the difficulty of assessing Nixon's true intentions, the tapes pose other challenges for the researcher. They do not provide a context for the president's remarks or information on who else said what at a different time or place. They also afforded the president and his chief of staff the opportunity to arrange tableaus to enhance the historical record or to provide a basis for shifting blame if policies failed. As Kissinger put it, "Ironically, Nixon's obsession with the historical record came close to destroying the ability of historians to render an accurate account of his presidency."[16]

Problems also arise in studies employing traditional methods when authors make assertions about the behavior of the public. They often fail to look at available systematic data. For example, numerous authors premise analyses of the administration of Ronald Reagan on the president's enjoying substantial support among the public. In reality, as we saw in chapter 4, Reagan's average approval level was an ordinary 53 percent.[17]

When Reagan's pollster found that the public overwhelmingly disapproved of the administration's reductions in aid to education, Michael Deaver—the president's longtime public relations guru—arranged for Reagan to make a series of speeches emphasizing quality education. Deaver later gloated to the *Wall Street Journal* that public approval of the president regarding education "flip-flopped" without any change in policy at all.[18] If public opinion did change as Deaver described, it would indeed have been an impressive performance of presidential persuasion. However, opinion did *not* change. Deaver was referring to the addresses, including national radio addresses, Reagan delivered in the spring and summer of 1983. Yet in Gallup's August poll, only 31 percent of the public approved how Reagan was handling education.[19]

Similarly, in his memoir of the Reagan years, Deaver reports that the president was distressed about the lack of public support for defense spending. According to Deaver,

> Reagan pulled me aside one day; "Mike," he said, "these numbers show you're not doing your job. This is your fault; you gotta get me out of Washington more so I can talk to people about how important this policy is." I did, and he would systematically add his rationale for more military spending to nearly every speech, and eventually his message would get through to the American people.[20]

In fact, however, public opinion on defense spending did not move in the president's direction, as we saw in chapter 6. One does not have to challenge the sincerity of the author's memory to conclude that such commentary contributes to the misunderstanding of presidential leadership.

Although insider accounts have limitations, they often contain useful insights that may guide more rigorous research. They also provide invaluable records of the perceptions of participants in the events of the presidency. As long as the researcher understands the limitations of these works and accepts them as one among many perspectives, they can be of considerable use.

QUANTITATIVE ANALYSES

For several decades, then, research on the presidency often failed to meet the standards of contemporary political science, including the careful definition and measurement of concepts, the rigorous specification and testing of propositions, and the use of empirical theory to develop hypotheses and explain findings. This situation presented a striking irony: The single most important and powerful institution in American politics was the one that political scientists understood the least.

Scholars needed to think theoretically to develop falsifiable propositions about presidential leadership and test these systematically with relevant data and appropriate econometric techniques. They needed to discover generalizations about behavior rather than produce discrete, ad hoc analyses, repeat colorful anecdotes from presidential press clippings, or reach facile conclusions about Lyndon Johnson's skill at swaying members of Congress or Ronald Reagan's ability to mobilize the public behind his proposals. Quantitative analysis has been an extremely useful tool in these endeavors.[21]

Overcoming Obstacles

To gain insight into the nature of presidential leadership, scholars have had to overcome several obstacles that had impeded systematic analysis. Some, but not all, of these hurdles were unique to studying the presidency.

Asking New Questions

The first and most important obstacle, however, was not presidency-centric. To move toward generalizations based on systematic analysis, scholars had to refocus their inquiries. At its core, this effort focused on posing analytical rather than descriptive questions. Discussions of powers and thus the boundaries of appropriate behavior do not explain why actions occur within those boundaries or what their consequences are. Similarly, tracing the persistence and adaptation of organizations and processes over time, such as the Executive Office of the President or central clearance of legislation in the Office of Management and Budget, does not lend itself to explanations of the impact of presidential leadership.

The view that each president (and administration) is relatively unique also impeded rigorous analysis. The personalities of individual presidents and their staffs, the particular events and circumstances of their times in office, and the specific problems and actions of their administrations led scholars to treat each presidency and the times in which it operated as if it were unique. Emphasizing the differences rather than the similarities between presidencies made the identification of patterns and relations more difficult and, in turn, made it more difficult to generalize. Description rather than analysis and speculation rather than generalization were the standard fare. In addition, traditional scholars' heavy reliance on case studies inevitably made the basis of their generalizations rather tenuous.

It is not that all such studies lacked rigor but rather that most of them emphasized description at the expense of explanation. We still know a great deal more about how presidents have organized their White House staffs, for example, than about how these arrangements have affected the kinds of advice they have received. In other words, we know more about the process than about its consequences. Most significantly, little of this research contributed to understanding the central presidential task of leadership.

Richard Neustadt's *Presidential Power* was the first great leap toward a more analytical focus on leadership. His central premise was that presidential leadership was problematic because the president operates in a pluralistic environment in which there are numerous actors with independent power bases and perspectives different from his. In most instances, the president cannot act alone because he shares powers with others. Thus, the president cannot rely on expanding the institution's legal authority or adjusting its support mechanisms. Instead, he must marshal resources to persuade others to do as he wishes.

Neustadt's work encouraged scholars to focus on the people within institutions and their relationships with each other rather than to focus primarily on the institutions themselves and their formalities. As Neustadt saw it, power was a function of personal politics rather than of formal authority or position. It was not the roles of the president but the performance of those roles that mattered. It was not the boundaries of behavior but the actions within those boundaries that warranted the attention of scholars.

Power is a concept that involves relationships among people. By focusing on relationships and suggesting why people respond to the president as they do, Neustadt forced us into a more analytical mode. To understand relationships, we must explain behavior. Describing it is not enough, nor is storytelling about interesting but unrepresentative incidents—a temptation that is only natural when writing about the presidency. Neustadt, however, was concerned with the strategic level of power:

> There are two ways to study "presidential power." One way is to focus on the tactics . . . of influencing certain men in given situations. . . . The other way is to step back from tactics on those "givens" and to deal with influence in more strategic terms: what is its nature and what is its sources? . . . Strategically [for example], the question is not how he masters Congress in a peculiar instance, but what he does to boost his chance for mastery in any instance.[22]

Neustadt, then, was less interested in what causes something to happen in one instance than in what affects the probabilities of something happening in every instance. To think strategically about power, we must search for generalizations and calculate probabilities. Whether we are interested in explaining the consequences of efforts at persuasion or prescribing a strategy to obtain or maintain resources useful in persuasion, the critical questions are, "What is the potential of persuasion"—with Congress, the public, or others? And specifically, "What is the potential of various persuasive resources with those whose support the president needs?" Seeking answers to these questions inevitably leads to explanations and generalizations. Although he employed neither the language nor the methods of modern social science, Neustadt's emphasis on reaching generalizations about presidential power was a significant contribution to research on the presidency.

Increasing the N

The second constraint on presidency research has been the small number of presidents. Only forty-four individuals have served as president—one of whom survived only a few weeks and another only a few months in office. Moreover, the tenure of these presidents spans more than two centuries. How can you generalize from such a small universe of chief executives who have served in such different circumstances?

Scholars overcame the issue of the small universe of presidents when they began viewing the presidency as a set of relationships and asking about interactions between the president and others. Many people are involved in relationships with presidents, including the public, members of Congress, the federal bureaucracy, and world leaders. Employing measures of these interactions produced an enormous amount of data, and analysis of the data provided scholars with a solid foundation for reaching generalizations.

Finding Data

The third obstacle to more systematic and rigorous scholarship on the president was the lack of data. The relatively closed character of the institution contributed to the problem. The presidency is difficult to observe from a distance and, up close, the view may be partial and even biased. Public pronouncements and actions tell only part of what happens and why—and usually only the part that the people in power wish to convey. Inside information is difficult to obtain. Officials' busy schedules, combined with their natural reluctance to reveal information that may be embarrassing, sensitive, or in other ways controversial, often make them unwilling, unresponsive, or unreliable sources.

The key to solving the data problem was posing analytical questions, which naturally led scholars to search for data on the causes and consequences of presidential behavior. Regarding leadership, they typically ask what responses presidents desire from other actors. Among other things, chief executives want support from the public, positive coverage from the media, votes for their programs from members of Congress, sound analysis from their advisers, and faithful policy implementation from the bureaucracy. Thus, scholars employing quantitative analysis develop data on these political actors, whose behavior is usually the dependent variable in their hypotheses—that is, in what we are trying to explain. Similarly, scholars seek data on independent variables, on causes of behavior toward the president, such as the determinants of public opinion, congressional support, bureaucratic faithfulness, and judicial responsiveness.[23]

Scholars have made considerable progress in providing data for students of the presidency. For example, the White House is making a wide range of data available on its website. Lyn Ragsdale published a volume entitled *Vital Statistics on the Presidency*.[24] A number of websites providing useful data are listed at the end of this appendix, and digitized resources from government agencies and private and university repositories allow scholars access to a broader universe of content.[25]

Proper Use of Quantitative Analysis

The proper use of quantitative analysis, as with any other type of analysis, is predicated on a close linkage between the methods scholars employ and the theoretical arguments that underlie the hypotheses they test.[26] A statement that something causes something else to happen is an assertion, not a theoretical argument. A theoretical argument requires an emphasis on explanation on why two variables are related. Quantitative analysis is not an end in itself. Instead, it is a means of rigorously analyzing the components of theoretically meaningful explanations of behavior.

Quantitative analysis is not easy to do, nor is there always consensus on appropriate methods or measures. Inevitably, some authors will employ indicators that lack validity and reliability and tests that are inappropriate. Their conclusions are likely to be controversial and may even be incorrect. In addition, findings can and should be refined as our indicators and tests are improved. In essence, quantitative analysis poses methodological problems precisely because it attempts to measure concepts and to test for relationships carefully. Studies that do not involve such concerns avoid methodological questions, but often at the expense of analytical richness.

Limits to Quantitative Analysis

Despite its utility for investigating a wide range of questions, quantitative analysis is not equally useful for studying all areas of the presidency. It is least useful where there is little change in the variables under study or the subject being examined is at a very high level of abstraction. If the focus of research is just one president and the researcher is concerned not with the president's interactions with others but with how factors such as the president's personality, ideas, values, attitudes, and ideology have influenced his decisions, then quantitative analysis will be of little help. These independent variables are unlikely to vary much during a president's term. Similarly, important elements in the president's environment, such as the federal system or the basic capitalist structure of its economy, change little over time. It is therefore difficult to employ quantitative analysis to gauge their influence on the presidency.

Quantitative analysis is also unlikely to be useful for the legal approach to studying the presidency. There are well-established techniques for interpreting the law, and scholars with this interest will continue to apply them.[27]

Normative questions and arguments have always occupied a substantial percentage of the presidency literature, and rightly so. Can quantitative analysis aid scholars in addressing these concerns? The answer is, "partially." For example, to reach conclusions about whether the presidency is too powerful or not powerful enough (the central normative concern regarding the presidency) requires a three-part analysis. The first is an estimation of just how powerful the presidency is. Quantitative analysis can be useful in measuring and explaining the power of the presidency in a wide range of relationships. For example, it can aid us in understanding the president's ability to influence Congress or the public.

The second step in answering the question of whether the presidency is too powerful or not powerful enough requires an analysis of the consequences of the power of the presidency. In other words, given the power of the presidency, what difference does it make? Are poor people likely to fare better under a weak or a powerful presidency, for example? Are civil rights and civil liberties more or less likely to be abused?

To answer rigorously these and similar questions requires that we correlate levels of power with policy consequences. This analysis does not have to be done quantitatively, of course, but such analyses are likely to be more convincing if we have valid empirical measurements of economic welfare, school integration, wiretapping, military interventions, and other possible consequences of presidential power, as well as measures of mediating variables.

Quantitative analyses will be much less useful in the third part of the analysis: Do we judge the consequences of presidential power to be good or bad? Our values, of course, will determine our evaluation of these consequences. Nevertheless, it is important to remember that quantitative analysis can be very useful in helping us to arrive at the point where our values and not questions of fact dominate our conclusions.

In short, quantitative analysis leads us to examine theoretical relationships, and it has considerable utility in testing and refining them. The question remains, however, whether quantitative analysis is useful for developing theories themselves—that is, basic conceptions of the relationships between variables.

Although quantitative studies cannot replace the sparks of creativity that lie behind conceptualizations, they may produce findings on which syntheses may be built. Conversely, quantitative analysis may also produce findings contrary to the conventional wisdom and thus prod scholars into challenging dominant viewpoints. To this extent, it may also be useful in theory building.

CASE STUDIES

One of the most widely used methods for studying the presidency is the case study of an individual president, a presidential decision, or presidential involvement in a specific area of policy. The case study method offers the researcher several advantages. It is a manageable way to present a wide range of complex information about individual and collective behavior. Because scholars have typically found it difficult to generate quantitative data regarding the presidency, the narrative form often seems to be the only available choice.

Conversely, case studies are widely criticized on several grounds. First, scholars have used them more for descriptive than for analytical purposes, a failing not inherent in the case study. A more intractable problem is the idiosyncratic nature of case studies and the failure of authors to employ common analytical frameworks. This failure makes the accumulation of knowledge difficult because scholars often, in effect, talk past each other. In the words of a close student of case studies,

> The unique features of every case—personalities, external events and conditions, and organizational arrangements—virtually ensure that studies conducted without the use of an explicit analytical framework will not produce findings that can easily be related to existing knowledge or provide a basis for future studies.[28]

Naturally, reaching generalizations about the presidency on the basis of unrelated case studies is a hazardous task.

Despite these drawbacks, case studies can be useful in increasing our understanding of the presidency. For example, analyzing case studies can serve as the basis for identifying problems in decision making[29] or in policy implementation.[30] These in turn may serve as the basis for recommendations to improve policy making. Scholars may also use case studies to test hypotheses or disconfirm theories, such as propositions about group dynamics drawn from social psychology.[31]

Some authors employ case studies to illustrate the importance of looking at aspects of the presidency that have received little scholarly attention, such as presidential influence over interest groups.[32] On a broader scale, Richard Neustadt used several case studies to explicate his influential model of presidential power,[33] and Graham Allison and Philip Zelikow used a case study of the Cuban missile crisis to illustrate three models of policy making.[34]

Writing a case study that has strong analytical content is difficult to do.[35] It requires considerable skill, creativity, and rigor because it is very easy to slip into a descriptive rather than an analytical gear. It is especially important to have an analytical framework in mind before one begins—to provide direction to data gathering and the line of argument. Those who embark on preparing case studies are wise to remind themselves of the pitfalls.

CONCLUSION

Few topics in American politics are more interesting or more important to understand than the presidency. Researching the presidency is not a simple task, however. There are many reasons for this difficulty, including the small number of models to follow and the relative scarcity of research that has applied the approaches and methods of modern political science. But the obstacles to studying the presidency also present researchers with an opportunity. Few questions regarding the presidency are settled, and there is plenty of room for committed and creative researchers to make important contributions to our understanding. The prospects for success will be enhanced if researchers realize the implications of the approaches and methods they employ and choose those that are best suited to shed light on the questions they wish to investigate.

USEFUL WEBSITES

The official White House website: http://www.whitehouse.gov
Essays on White House offices and presidential transitions and interviews with White House officials: http://www.whitehousetransitionproject.org
Data on presidential support in Congress: http://presdata.tamu.edu
Data on presidential approval: http://www.gallup.com/interactives/185273/presidential-job-approval-center.aspx
Executive orders, proclamations, and other presidential documents: http://www.archives.gov/federal-register/publications/index.html
Public papers of the presidents: https://www.archives.gov/federal-register/publications/presidential-papers.html
Information and resources regarding presidential rhetoric: http://www.presidentialrhetoric.com
Information on many aspects of the presidency: http://www.presidency.ucsb.edu
Presidential election results: http://uselectionatlas.org

SELECTED READINGS

Edwards, George C., III, John H. Kessel, and Bert A. Rockman, eds. *Researching the Presidency*. Pittsburgh, PA: University of Pittsburgh Press, 1993.

Edwards, George C., III, and Stephen J. Wayne, eds. *Studying the Presidency*. Knoxville: University of Tennessee Press, 1983.

Howell, William G. "Quantitative Approaches to the Study of the Presidency." In *The Oxford Handbook of the American Presidency*, edited by George C. Edwards III and William G. Howell. Oxford, UK: Oxford University Press, 2009.

Hult, Karen M., Charles E. Walcott, and Thomas Weko. "Qualitative Research and the Study of the U.S. Presidency." *Congress & the Presidency* 26 (Fall 1999): 133–152.

James, Scott C. "Historical Institutionalism, Political Development, and the Presidency." In *The Oxford Handbook of the American Presidency*, edited by George C. Edwards III and William G. Howell. Oxford, UK: Oxford University Press, 2009.

Skowronek, Stephen. "The Paradigm of Development in Presidential History." In *The Oxford Handbook of the American Presidency*, edited by George C. Edwards III and William G. Howell. Oxford, UK: Oxford University Press, 2009.

Nonelectoral Succession, Removal, and Tenure

The Constitution and statutes provide for contingencies that might require the selection, removal, or replacement of a president outside the normal electoral process. In addition to the provisions of Article I ("Impeachment") and Article II ("Impeachment and Succession"), there have been three amendments (numbers 20, 22, and 25) and three laws concerning succession and term of office. This appendix will examine these contingency arrangements. It will also briefly describe the impeachment process and the three most serious attempts to remove a sitting president. The Constitution and statutes provide for methods of succession and removal.

SUCCESSION

The principal reason for creating the vice presidency was to have a position from which the presidency would automatically be filled should it become vacant. Death, resignation, and impeachment constitute clear-cut situations in which this succession mechanism would work. Eight presidents have died in office and one has resigned. In each of the nine instances, the vice president became president.

One contingency the founders did not consider was temporary or permanent disability while in office. On a number of occasions, presidents have become disabled, unable to perform their duties and responsibilities. James Garfield, shot by a disappointed job seeker, lingered for almost three months before he died. Ronald Reagan was hospitalized twice, the first time following an attempt on his life and the other for an operation for cancer of the colon. During both hospital stays, he was unconscious for several hours, and the assassination attempt incapacitated him for several weeks. Other presidents have also been incapacitated. Woodrow Wilson suffered a stroke that disabled him for much of his last year in office, and Dwight Eisenhower's heart attack, ileitis operation, and minor stroke severely limited his presidential activities in 1955, 1956, and 1957.

During none of these periods did vice presidents officially take over. In fact, Chester Arthur and Thomas Marshall, Garfield's and Wilson's vice presidents, respectively, avoided even the appearance of performing presidential duties for fear that their actions would be wrongfully construed. Vice President Richard Nixon did preside at cabinet meetings in Eisenhower's absence but did not assume the president's other responsibilities. Vice President George H. W. Bush, away from the capital at the time Reagan was shot, flew back to Washington immediately to be available if needed. However, to avoid any appearance of impropriety, he had his helicopter land at the vice president's residence even though he was scheduled to meet at the White House with senior presidential aides. By prearrangement with the vice president, President Reagan passed his powers and duties to Bush during the period when he was under the influence of anesthesia during his colon operation in 1985. He reassumed them when he declared himself able to do so several hours after his operation.

It was not until 1967 that procedures were established for the vice president to become acting president in the event of the president's disability. The Twenty-fifth Amendment to the Constitution permits the vice president to exercise the duties and powers of the presidency if the president declares in writing that he is unable to do so or if the vice president and a majority of the principal executive department heads reach that judgment. The president may resume office when he believes that he is able to, unless the vice president and a majority of the principal executive department heads object, in which case Congress must make the final determination. The procedures, however, are weighted in the president's favor. Unless Congress concurs in the judgment that the president is disabled, the president is entitled once again to exercise the duties and powers of the office.

Another important provision of this amendment provides for filling the vice presidency should it become vacant. Prior to 1967, it had been vacant sixteen times. The procedures permit the president to nominate a new vice president, who takes office upon confirmation by a majority of both houses of Congress. Gerald Ford and Nelson Rockefeller were the only two vice presidents who came to office in this manner. Ford was nominated by President Nixon in 1973 after Spiro T. Agnew resigned. After succeeding to the presidency when Nixon resigned, Ford nominated Rockefeller.

Although the presidency and vice presidency have never been vacant at the same time, Congress has provided for such a contingency should it arise by establishing a line of succession. The most recent succession law, enacted in 1947, puts the Speaker of the House next in line, to be followed by the president pro tempore of the Senate and the department heads in chronological order of the creation of their departments, beginning with the secretary of state. The provision for appointing a new vice president, however, makes it less likely that legislative and executive officials would ever succeed to the presidency, barring a catastrophe such as a terrorist attack on the White House or a joint session of Congress or an unlikely set of events that resulted in a president's death before a new vice presidential nomination could be made or confirmed.

REMOVAL

In addition to providing for the president's replacement, the constitutional framers also thought it necessary to provide for the president's removal. They believed that it was too dangerous to wait for the electors' judgment in the case of a president who had abused the authority of the office. Impeachment was considered an extraordinary remedy but one that could be used against executive officials, including the president and vice president, who violated the public trust.

Article II, Section 4, of the Constitution spells out the terms. The president, vice president, and other executive officials can be removed from office for treason, bribery, or other high crimes and misdemeanors. Precisely what actions would be considered impeachable offenses is left for Congress to determine.

The House of Representatives considers the charges against the president. If a majority of the House votes in favor of any of them, a trial is held in the Senate with the chief justice of the Supreme Court presiding. The House presents its case against the president. The latter, who may be represented by outside counsel, defends against the charges. A two-thirds vote of the Senate is required for conviction. A convicted president, who is removed from office, may still be subject to civil or criminal prosecution.

Only two presidents, Andrew Johnson and Bill Clinton, have ever been impeached. Neither was convicted.

The incident that sparked Johnson's impeachment was his removal of Secretary of War Edwin Stanton. Congress had passed a law over Johnson's veto that required appointees to remain in office until the Senate approved their successor. Known as the Tenure of Office Act (1867), it permitted the president some discretion during a congressional recess but required the Senate's advice and consent after Congress reconvened. In the absence of senatorial approval, the office reverted to its previous occupant.

During a congressional recess, Johnson removed Stanton. The Senate refused to concur in his removal upon its return. Under the law, Stanton was entitled to his old job. However, the president once again removed him. When he was removed for a second time, the House of Representatives passed a bill of impeachment against the president. The Senate trial lasted six weeks. In its first vote, the Senate fell one vote short of the required two-thirds. A ten-day recess was called by those favoring Johnson's removal. Extensive lobbying ensued, but when the Senate reconvened, no one's vote changed. Johnson was acquitted. The Tenure of Office Act was subsequently repealed during the administration of Grover Cleveland.

A second attempt to impeach a sitting president occurred in 1973. When Richard Nixon dismissed Archibald Cox, the special prosecutor who had been investigating charges of administrative wrongdoing in the Watergate affair, members of Congress called for Nixon's removal. The Judiciary Committee of the House of Representatives began hearings on the president's impeachment. During the course of these hearings, the committee subpoenaed tapes of conversations that the president had held with aides in the White House, conversations that had been secretly recorded by the president. Claiming that these were privileged communications, Nixon refused to deliver the tapes, although he did send edited transcripts of them to the House committee. Not satisfied with this response, the House took its case to court and won. The Supreme Court ordered Nixon to release the tapes. When he did so, the recordings revealed his early knowledge of the break-in and his participation in the cover-up. This information heightened calls for the president's ouster.

The House Judiciary Committee approved three articles of impeachment against Nixon. It looked as if the full House would vote to impeach him and that the Senate would vote to convict him. Faced with the prospect of a long trial and probable conviction, Nixon resigned on August 9, 1974.

A third attempt to impeach a sitting president was begun in September 1998 when the independent counsel investigating President Clinton's relationship with a White House intern reported to the House of Representatives that the president may have committed eleven possible impeachable offenses. The House sent the report and the White House's responses to its Judiciary Committee, which conducted hearings on whether to recommend four articles of impeachment to the full House: abuse of power, obstruction of justice, and two counts of perjury before the Grand Jury investigating the matter. After a raucous debate, the Republican-controlled House of Representatives voted largely along partisan lines to impeach the president on one count of perjury and one count of obstruction of justice. Democrats were livid, and the president was defiant. The proceedings then moved to the Senate with the chief justice presiding. With forty-five Democratic senators and a two-thirds vote necessary for conviction, the result was never in doubt. After debating the matter with much pomp and eloquence, the Senate voted largely along party lines. Only forty-five senators, but not the two-thirds necessary, supported the count of perjury. The Senate was evenly divided on the other, obstruction of justice. Clinton survived, more popular than he was prior to the whole ordeal, while the Republicans lost Senate seats in the 2000 election. The Republican experience was not lost on the Democratic congressional leadership that came to power in 2007. They nixed impeachment proposals to remove George W. Bush from office on the grounds that he abused executive powers and in doing so violated constitutionally protected rights of American citizens.

The presidency suffered, however. Court decisions weakened the president's claim of executive privilege. Not only was Clinton forced to testify before a grand jury but his top White House aides also were compelled to testify about their conversations with the president, and Secret Service agents were required to testify about the president's movements during this period. Diaries of White House personnel were subject to judicial scrutiny as well.

TENURE

Electoral defeat and impeachment prematurely conclude a presidency—at least from the incumbent's perspective. Initially, the Constitution imposed no limit on the number of times a president could be elected. Indeed, reeligibility was seen as a motive to good behavior. Beginning with Washington, however, an unofficial two-term limit was established. Franklin Roosevelt ended this precedent in 1940 when he ran for a third term and won.

Partially in reaction to Roosevelt's twelve years and one month in office, a Republican-controlled Congress passed and the states ratified the Twenty-second Amendment to the Constitution. It prevents any person from being elected to the office more than twice. Moreover, it limits to one election a president who has succeeded to the office and has served more than two years of his predecessor's term.

Eisenhower was the first president to be subject to the provisions of the amendment; others have included Nixon, Reagan, Clinton, George W. Bush, and Barack Obama.

One of the consequences of this amendment is that it seems to weaken the president in the second term, particularly during the last two years in office. Not being able to run for the presidency again reduces a president's political power and lessens the capacity to mobilize public backing for the administration's programs and policies. Conversely, it may improve the president's ability to mobilize a bipartisan coalition, because political motives may be less subject to suspicion if a president cannot seek reelection.

Another consequence of a term limit is that it encourages presidents to exercise unilateral authority in their second term. Late in his tenure, Bill Clinton approved regulations that imposed more stringent environmental standards. On his last day, he issued 140 pardons and commuted the sentences of thirty-six others.

Provisions of the Constitution of the United States Relating to the Presidency

ARTICLE I

Section 2

(3) [Representatives and direct Taxes[1] shall be apportioned among the several States which may be included within this Union, according to their respective Numbers, which shall be determined by adding to the whole Number of free Persons, including those bound to Service for a Term of Years, and excluding Indians not taxed, three fifths of all other Persons.][2] The actual Enumeration shall be made within three Years after the first Meeting of the Congress of the United States, and within every subsequent Term of ten Years, in such Manner as they shall by Law direct. The Number of Representatives shall not exceed one for every thirty Thousand, but each State shall have at Least one Representative; and until such enumeration shall be made, the State of New Hampshire shall be entitled to choose three, Massachusetts eight, Rhode-Island and Providence Plantations one, Connecticut five, New York six, New Jersey four, Pennsylvania eight, Delaware one, Maryland six, Virginia ten, North Carolina five, South Carolina five, and Georgia three.

(4) When vacancies happen in the Representation from any State, the Executive Authority thereof shall issue Writs of Election to fill such Vacancies.

(5) The House of Representatives shall choose their Speaker and other Officers; and shall have the sole Power of Impeachment.

Section 3

(4) The Vice President of the United States shall be President of the Senate, but shall have no Vote, unless they be equally divided.

(5) The Senate shall choose their other Officers, and also a President pro tempore, in the Absence of the Vice President, or when he shall exercise the Office of President of the United States.

(6) The Senate shall have the sole Power to try all Impeachements. When sitting for that Purpose, they shall be on Oath or Affirmation. When the President of the United States is tried, the Chief Justice shall preside: And no Person shall be convicted without the Concurrence of two thirds of the Members present.

(7) Judgment in Cases of Impeachment shall not extend further than to removal from Office, and disqualification to hold and enjoy any Office of honor, Trust or Profit under the United States: but the Party convicted shall nevertheless be liable and subject to Indictment, Trial, Judgment and Punishment according to Law.

Section 7

(2) Every Bill which shall have passed the House of Representatives and the Senate, shall, before it become a Law, be presented to the President of the United States; If he approve he shall sign it, but if not he shall return it, with his Objections to that House in which it shall have originated, who shall enter the Objections at large on their Journal, and proceed to reconsider it. If after such Reconsideration two thirds of that House shall agree to pass the Bill, it shall be sent, together with Objections, to the other House, by which it shall likewise be reconsidered, and if approved by two thirds of that House, it shall become a Law. But in all such Cases the Votes of both Houses shall be determined by Yeas and Nays, and the Names of the Persons voting for and against the Bill shall be entered on the Journal of each House respectively. If any Bill shall not be returned by the President within ten Days (Sundays excepted) after it shall have been presented to him, the Same shall be a Law, in like Manner as if he had signed it, unless the Congress by their Adjournment prevent its Return, in which Case it shall not be a Law.

(3) Every Order, Resolution, or Vote to which the Concurrence of the Senate and House of Representatives may be necessary (except on a question of Adjournment) shall be presented to the President of the United States; and before the Same shall take Effect, shall be approved by him, or being disapproved by him, shall be repassed by two thirds of the Senate and House of Representatives, according to the Rules and Limitations prescribed in the Case of a Bill.

Section 9

(2) The Privilege of the Writ of Habeas Corpus shall not be suspended, unless when in Cases of Rebellion or Invasion the public Safety may require it.

(8) No Title of Nobility shall be granted by the United States: And no Person holding any Office of Profit or Trust under them, shall, without the Consent of the Congress, accept of any present, Emolument, Office, or Title, of any kind whatever, from any King, Prince, or foreign State.

ARTICLE II

Section 1

(1) The executive Power shall be vested in a President of the United States of America. He shall hold his Office during the Term of four Years, and, together with the Vice President, chosen for the same Term, be elected, as follows:

(2) Each State shall appoint, in such Manner as the Legislature thereof may direct, a Number of Electors, equal to the whole Number of Senators and Representatives to which the State may be entitled in the Congress, but no Senator or Representative, or Person holding an Office of Trust or Profit under the United States, shall be appointed an Elector.

[The Electors shall meet in their respective States, and vote by Ballot for two persons, of whom one at least shall not be an Inhabitant of the same State with themselves. And they shall make a List of all the Persons voted for, and of the Number of Votes for each; which List they shall sign and certify, and transmit sealed to the Seat of the Government of the United States, directed to the President of the Senate. The President of the Senate shall, in the Presence of the Senate and House of Representatives, open all the Certificates, and the Votes shall then be counted. The Person having the greatest Number of Votes shall be the President, if such Number be a Majority of the whole Number of Electors appointed; and if there be more than one who have such Majority, and have an equal Number of Votes, then the House of Representatives shall immediately choose by Ballot one of them for President; and if no Person have a Majority, then from the five highest on the List the said House shall in like Manner choose the President. But in choosing the President, the Votes shall be taken by States, the Representation from each State having one Vote; A quorum for this purpose shall consist of a Member or Members from two thirds of the States, and a Majority of all the States shall be necessary to a Choice. In every Case, after the Choice of the President, the Person having the greatest Number of Votes of the Electors shall be the Vice President. But if there should remain two or more who have equal Votes, the Senate shall choose from them by Ballot the Vice President.][3]

(3) The Congress may determine the Time of choosing the Electors, and the Day on which they shall give their Votes; which Day shall be the same throughout the United States.

(4) No person except a natural born Citizen, or a Citizen of the United States, at the time of the Adoption of this Constitution, shall be eligible to the Office of President; neither shall any Person be eligible to that Office who shall not have attained to the Age of thirty-five Years, and been fourteen Years a Resident within the United States.

(5) In case of the Removal of the President from Office, or of his Death, Resignation, or Inability to discharge the Powers and Duties of the said Office, the same shall devolve on the Vice President, and the Congress may by Law provide for the Case of Removal, Death, Resignation or Inability; both of the President and Vice President, declaring what Officer shall then act as President, and such Officer shall act accordingly, until the Disability be removed, or a President shall be elected.[4]

(6) The President shall, at stated Times, receive for his Services, a Compensation, which shall neither be increased nor diminished during the Period for which he shall have been elected, and he shall not receive within that Period any other Emolument from the United States, or any of them.

(7) Before he enter on the Execution of his Office, he shall take the following Oath or Affirmation:—"I do solemnly swear (or affirm) that I will faithfully execute the Office of President of the United States, and will to the best of my Ability, preserve, protect and defend the Constitution of the United States."

Section 2

(1) The President shall be Commander in Chief of the Army and Navy of the United States, and of the Militia of the several States, when called into the actual Service of the United States; he may require the Opinion in writing, of the principal Officer in each of the executive Departments, upon any subject relating to the Duties of their respective Offices, and he shall have Power to Grant Reprieves and Pardons for Offenses against the United States, except in Cases of Impeachment.

(2) He shall have Power, by and with the Advice and Consent of the Senate, to make Treaties, provided two thirds of the Senators present concur; and he shall nominate, and by and with the Advice and Consent of the Senate, shall appoint Ambassadors, other public Ministers and Consuls, Judges of the supreme Court, and all other Officers of the United States, whose Appointments are not herein otherwise provided for, and which shall be established by Law: but the Congress may by Law vest the Appointment of such inferior Officers, as they think proper, in the President alone, in the Court of Law, or in the Heads of Departments.

(3) The President shall have Power to fill up all Vacancies that may happen during the Recess of the Senate, by granting Commissions which shall expire at the End of their next Session.

Section 3

He shall from time to time give to the Congress Information of the State of the Union, and recommend to their Consideration such Measures as he shall judge necessary and expedient; he may, on extraordinary Occasions, convene both Houses, or either of them, and in Case of Disagreement between them, with Respect to the Time of Adjournment, he may adjourn them to such Time as he shall think proper; he shall receive Ambassadors and other public Ministers; he shall take Care that the Laws be faithfully executed, and shall Commission all the Officers of the United States.

Section 4

The President, Vice President and all civil Officers of the United States, shall be removed from Office on Impeachment for, and Conviction of, Treason, Bribery, or other high Crimes and Misdemeanors.

ARTICLE IV

Section 4

The United States shall guarantee to every State in this Union a Republican Form of Government, and shall protect each of them against Invasion; and on Application of the Legislature, or of the Executive (when the Legislature cannot be convened) against domestic Violence.

ARTICLE VI

(3) The Senators and Representatives before mentioned, and the Members of the several State Legislatures, and all executive and judicial Officers, both of the United States and of the several States, shall be bound by Oath or Affirmation, to support this Constitution; but no religious Test shall ever be required as a Qualification to any Office or public Trust under the United States.

AMENDMENT XII[5]

The Electors shall meet in their respective states and vote by ballot for President and Vice President, one of whom, at least, shall not be an inhabitant of the same state with themselves; they shall name in their ballots the person voted for as President, and in distinct ballots the person voted for as Vice President, and they shall make distinct lists of persons voted for as President, and of all persons voted for as Vice President, and of the number of votes for each, which lists they shall sign and certify, and transmit sealed to the seat of the government of the United States, directed to the President of the Senate;—The President of the Senate shall, in the presence of the Senate and House of Representatives, open all the certificates and the votes shall then be counted;—The person having the greatest Number of votes for President, shall be the President, if such number be a majority of the whole number of Electors appointed; and if no person have such majority, then from the persons having the highest numbers not exceeding three on the list of those voted for as President, the House of Representatives shall choose immediately, by ballot, the President. But in choosing the President, the votes shall be taken by states, the representation from each state having one vote; a quorum for this purpose shall consist of a member or members from two thirds of the states, and a majority of all the states shall be necessary to a choice. [And if the House of Representatives shall not choose a President whenever the right of choice shall devolve upon them, before the fourth day of March next following, then the Vice President shall act as President, as in the case of the death or other constitutional disability of the President.][6]—The person having the greatest number of votes as Vice President, shall be the Vice President, if such number be a majority of the whole number of Electors appointed, and if no person have a majority, then from the two highest numbers on the list, the Senate shall choose the Vice President; a quorum for the purpose shall consist of two thirds of the whole number of Senators, and a majority of the whole number shall be necessary to a choice. But no person constitutionally ineligible to the office of President shall be eligible to that of Vice President of the United States.

AMENDMENT XV[7]

Section 1
The right of citizens of the United States to vote shall not be denied or abridged by the United States or by any State on account of race, color, or previous condition of servitude.

Section 2
The Congress shall have power to enforce this article by appropriate legislation.

AMENDMENT XIX[8]

The right of citizens of the United States to vote shall not be denied or abridged by the United States or by any State on account of sex. Congress shall have power to enforce this article by appropriate legislation.

AMENDMENT XX[9]

Section 1
The terms of the President and Vice President shall end at noon on the 20th day of January, and the terms of Senators and Representatives at noon on the 3rd day of January, of the years in which such terms would have ended if this article had not been ratified; and the terms of their successors shall then begin.

Section 2
The Congress shall assemble at least once in every year, and such meeting shall begin at noon on the 3rd day of January, unless they shall by law appoint a different day.

Section 3
If, at the time fixed for the beginning of the term of the President, the President elect shall have died, the Vice President elect shall become President. If a President shall not have been chosen before the time fixed for the beginning of his term, or if the President elect shall have failed to qualify, then the Vice President elect shall act as a President until a President shall have qualified; and the Congress may by law provide for the case wherein neither a President elect nor a Vice President elect shall have qualified, declaring who shall then act as President, or the manner in which one who is to act shall be selected, and such person shall act accordingly until a President or Vice President shall have qualified.

Section 4
The Congress may by law provide for the case of the death of any of the persons from whom the House of Representatives may choose a President whenever the right of choice shall have devolved upon them, and for the case of the death of any of the persons from whom the Senate may choose a Vice President whenever the right of choice shall have devolved upon them.

Section 5
Sections 1 and 2 shall take effect on the 15th day of October following the ratification of this article.

Section 6
This article shall be inoperative unless it shall have been ratified as an amendment to the Constitution by the legislatures of three fourths of the several States within seven years from the date of its submission.

AMENDMENT XXII[10]

Section 1

No person shall be elected to the office of the President more than twice, and no person who has held the office of President, or acted as President, for more than two years of a term to which some other person was elected President shall be elected to the office of the President more than once. But this Article shall not apply to any person holding the office of President when this Article was proposed by the Congress, and shall not prevent any person who may be holding the office of President, or acting as President, during the term within which this Article becomes operative from holding the office of President or acting as President during the remainder of such term.

Section 2

This article shall be inoperative unless it shall have been ratified as an amendment to the Constitution by the legislatures of three fourths of the several States within seven years from the date of its submission to the States by the Congress.

AMENDMENT XXIII[11]

Section 1

The District constituting the seat of Government of the United States shall appoint in such manner as the Congress may direct:

> A number of electors of President and Vice President equal to the whole number of Senators and Representatives in Congress to which the District would be entitled if it were a State, but in no event more than the least populous State; they shall be in addition to those appointed by the States, but they shall be considered, for the purposes of the election of President and Vice President, to be electors appointed by a State; and they shall meet in the District and perform such duties as provided by the twelfth article of amendment.

Section 2

The Congress shall have power to enforce this article by appropriate legislation.

AMENDMENT XXIV[12]

Section 1

The right of citizens of the United States to vote in any primary or other election for President or Vice President, for electors for President or Vice President, or for Senator or Representative in Congress, shall not be denied or abridged by the United States or any state by reasons of failure to pay any poll tax or other tax.

Section 2

The Congress shall have power to enforce this article by appropriate legislation.

AMENDMENT XXV[13]

Section 1
In case of the removal of the President from office or of his death or resignation, the Vice President shall become President.

Section 2
Whenever there is a vacancy in the office of the Vice President, the President shall nominate a Vice President who shall take office upon confirmation by a majority vote of both Houses of Congress.

Section 3
Whenever the President transmits to the President pro tempore of the Senate and the Speaker of the House of Representatives his written declaration that he is unable to discharge the powers and duties of his office, and until he transmits to them a written declaration to the contrary, such powers and duties shall be discharged by the Vice President as Acting President.

Section 4
Whenever the Vice President and a majority of either the principal officers of the Executive departments or of such other body as Congress may by law provide, transmit to the President pro tempore of the Senate and the Speaker of the House of Representatives their written declaration that the President is unable to discharge the powers and duties of his office, the Vice President shall immediately assume the powers and duties of the office as Acting President.

Thereafter, when the President transmits to the President pro tempore of the Senate and the Speaker of the House of Representatives his written declaration that no inability exists, he shall resume the powers and duties of his office unless the Vice President and a majority of either the principal officers of the executive departments or of such other body as Congress may by law provide, transmit within four days to the President pro tempore of the Senate and the Speaker of the House of Representatives their written declaration that the President is unable to discharge the powers and duties of his office. Thereupon Congress shall decide the issue, assembling within forty-eight hours for that purpose if not in session. If the Congress, within twenty-one days after receipt of the latter written declaration, or, if Congress is not in session, within twenty-one days after Congress is required to assemble, determines by two thirds vote of both houses that the President is unable to discharge the powers and duties of his office, the Vice President shall continue to discharge the same as Acting President; otherwise, the President shall resume the powers and duties of his office.

AMENDMENT XXVI[14]

Section 1
The right of citizens of the United States, who are 18 years of age or older, to vote shall not be denied or abridged by the United States or any state on account of age.

Section 2
The Congress shall have power to enforce this article by appropriate legislation.

Appendix D

2016 Presidential Election Results

State	Popular Vote			Electoral Vote		
	Democratic Party (Clinton/ Kaine)	Republican Party (Trump/ Pence)	Other	Clinton	Trump	Other
Alabama	729,547	1,318,255	75,570		9	
Alaska	116,454	163,387	38,767		3	
Arizona	1,161,167	1,252,401	159,597		11	
Arkansas	380,494	684,872	65,269		6	
California	8,753,788	4,483,810	943,997	55		
Colorado	1,338,870	1,202,484	238,156	9		
Connecticut	897,572	673,215	74,133	7		
Delaware	235,603	185,127	20,860	3		
DC	282,830	12,723	15,715	3		
Florida	4,504,975	4,617,886	297,178		29	
Georgia	1,877,963	2,089,104	147,665		16	
Hawaii	266,891	128,847	33,199	3		1
Idaho	189,765	409,055	91,435		4	
Illinois	3,090,729	2,146,015	299,680	20		
Indiana	1,033,126	1,557,286	144,546		11	
Iowa	653,669	800,983	110,928		6	
Kansas	427,005	671,018	86,379		6	
Kentucky	628,854	1,202,971	92,324		8	
Louisiana	780,154	1,178,638	70,240		8	

(continued)

State	Popular Vote			Electoral Vote		
	Democratic Party (Clinton/ Kaine)	Republican Party (Trump/ Pence)	Other	Clinton	Trump	Other
Maine	357,735	335,593	54,599	3	1	
Maryland	1,677,928	943,169	160,349	10		
Massachusetts	1,995,196	1,090,893	238,957	11		
Michigan	2,268,839	2,279,543	250,902		16	
Minnesota	1,367,705	1,322,949	254,128	10		
Mississippi	485,131	700,714	23,512		6	
Missouri	1,071,068	1,594,511	143,026		10	
Montana	177,709	279,240	37,577		3	
Nebraska	284,494	495,961	63,772		5	
Nevada	539,260	512,058	74,067	6		
New Hampshire	348,526	345,790	49,980	4		
New Jersey	2,148,278	1,601,933	123,835	14		
New Mexico	385,234	319,667	93,418	5		
New York	4,556,142	2,819,557	345,795	29		
North Carolina	2,189,316	2,362,631	189,617		15	
North Dakota	93,758	216,794	33,808		3	
Ohio	2,394,169	2,841,005	261,318		18	
Oklahoma	420,373	949,136	83,481		7	
Oregon	1,002,106	784,403	216,827	7		
Pennsylvania	2,926,441	2,970,733	218,228	20		
Rhode Island	252,525	180,543	31,076	4		
South Carolina	855,373	1,155,389	92,265		9	
South Dakota	117,458	227,721	24,914		3	
Tennessee	870,695	1,522,925	114,407		11	
Texas	3,877,868	4,685,047	406,311		36	2
Utah	310,676	515,231	305,432		6	
Vermont	178,573	95,369	41,125	3		
Virginia	1,981,473	1,769,443	231,836	13		
Washington	1,742,718	1,221,747	352,554	8		4
West Virginia	188,794	489,371	34,886		5	
Wisconsin	1,382,536	1,405,284	188,330		10	
Wyoming	55,973	174,419	25,457		3	
Total	65,677,168	62,692,411	8,417,608	227	304	7

Source: *Statistics of the Presidential and Congressional Election from Official Sources for the Election of November 8, 2016* (Office of the Clerk, US House of Representatives, Washington, DC, February 22, 2017).

Notes

CHAPTER 1

1. Quoted in David McCullough, *Truman* (New York: Simon & Schuster, 1992), pp. 584–585.

2. Bill Simmons, "President Obama and Bill Simmons: The GQ Interview," *GQ*, November 17, 2015.

3. George C. Edwards III and Andrew Barrett, "Presidential Agenda Setting in Congress," in Jon R. Bond and Richard Fleisher, eds., *Polarized Politics: Congress and the President in a Partisan Era* (Washington, DC: CQ Press, 2000).

4. George C. Edwards III and B. Dan Wood, "Who Influences Whom? The President, Congress, and the Media," *American Political Science Review* 93 (June 1999): 327–344.

5. Richard E. Neustadt, *Presidential Power and the Modern Presidents* (New York: Free Press, 1990).

6. Charles O. Jones, *The Presidency in a Separated System* (Washington, DC: Brookings Institution, 1994), p. 1.

7. George C. Edwards III, *Predicting the Presidency: The Potential of Persuasive Leadership* (Princeton, NJ: Princeton University Press, 2016); George C. Edwards III, *Overreach: Leadership in the Obama Presidency* (Princeton, NJ: Princeton University Press, 2012); George C. Edwards III, *The Strategic President: Persuasion and Opportunity in Presidential Leadership* (Princeton, NJ: Princeton University Press, 2009); George C. Edwards III, *On Deaf Ears: The Limits of the Bully Pulpit* (New Haven, CT: Yale University Press, 2003); and George C. Edwards III, *At the Margins: Presidential Leadership of Congress* (New Haven, CT: Yale University Press, 1989). See also Mark A. Peterson, *Legislating Together* (Cambridge, MA: Harvard University Press, 1990); and Jon R. Bond and Richard Fleisher, *The President in the Legislative Arena* (Chicago, IL: University of Chicago Press, 1990).

8. Stephen Skowronek, *The Politics Presidents Make*, rev. ed. (Cambridge, MA: Harvard University Press, 1997).

9. For a more extensive discussion of approaches to studying the presidency, see Stephen J. Wayne, "Approaches," in George C. Edwards III and Stephen J. Wayne, eds., *Studying the Presidency* (Knoxville: University of Tennessee Press, 1983), pp. 17–49.

10. The classic work from the legal perspective is Edward S. Corwin's *The President: Office and Powers,* 4th rev. ed. (New York: New York University Press, 1957). More recent examples include Louis Fisher, *Supreme Court Expansion of Presidential Power: Unconstitutional Leanings* (Lawrence: University Press of Kansas, 2017); Phillip J. Cooper, *By Order of the President,* 2nd ed., rev. and expanded (Lawrence: University Press of Kansas, 2014); Mariah Zeisberg, *War Powers: The Politics of Constitutional Authority* (Princeton, NJ: Princeton University Press, 2013); Louis Fisher, *Presidential War Power,* 3rd ed., rev. (Lawrence: University Press of Kansas, 2013); Mark J. Rozell, *Executive Privilege,* 3rd ed., rev. and updated (Lawrence: University Press of Kansas, 2010); Glen S. Krutz and Jeffrey S. Peake, *Treaty Politics and the Rise of Executive Agreements* (Ann Arbor: University of Michigan Press, 2009); Michael D. Ramsey, *The Constitution's Text in Foreign Affairs* (Cambridge, MA: Harvard University Press, 2007); and Michael J. Glennon, *Constitutional Diplomacy* (Princeton, NJ: Princeton University Press, 1990).

11. See, e.g., Joel K. Goldstein, *The White House Vice Presidency* (Lawrence: University Press of Kansas, 2016); Justin S. Vaughn and Jose D. Villalobos, *Czars in the White House* (Ann Arbor: University

of Michigan Press, 2015); John P. Burke, *Honest Broker? The National Security Advisor and Presidential Decision Making* (College Station: Texas A&M University Press, 2009); Martha Joynt Kumar, *Managing the President's Message: The White House Communications Operation* (Baltimore, MD: Johns Hopkins University Press, 2007); Victoria A. Farrar-Myers, *Scripted for Change* (College Station: Texas A&M University Press, 2007); Charles E. Walcott and Karen M. Hult, *Empowering the White House* (Lawrence: University Press of Kansas, 2004). John P. Burke, *The Institutional Presidency*, 2nd ed. (Baltimore, MD: Johns Hopkins University Press, 2000); Paul C. Light, *The President's Agenda*, 3rd ed. (Baltimore, MD: Johns Hopkins University Press, 1999); Charles E. Walcott and Karen M. Hult, *Governing the White House* (Lawrence: University Press of Kansas, 1995); Thomas J. Weko, *The Politicizing Presidency: The White House Personnel Office, 1948–1994* (Lawrence: University Press of Kansas, 1995); Mark A. Peterson, "The Presidency and Organized Interests: White House Patterns of Interest Group Liaison," *American Political Science Review* 86 (September 1992): 612–625; and Stephen J. Wayne, *The Legislative Presidency* (New York: Harper & Row, 1978).

12. The leading example of this approach to the presidency is Skowronek, *The Politics Presidents Make*. See also Bruce Miroff, *Presidents on Political Ground: Leaders in Action and What They Face* (Lawrence: University Press of Kansas, 2016); Scott C. James, "Historical Institutionalism, Political Development, and the Presidency," in George C. Edwards III and William G. Howell, eds., *The Oxford Handbook of the American Presidency* (Oxford, UK: Oxford University Press, 2009); Stephen Skowronek, "The Paradigm of Development in Presidential History," in George C. Edwards III and William G. Howell, eds., *The Oxford Handbook of the American Presidency* (Oxford, UK: Oxford University Press, 2009); and Richard J. Ellis and Aaron Wildavsky, *Dilemmas of Presidential Leadership: From Washington through Lincoln* (New Brunswick, NJ: Transaction, 1989).

13. See Brandice Canes-Wrone, "Game Theory and the Study of the American Presidency," in George C. Edwards III and William G. Howell, eds., *The Oxford Handbook of the American Presidency* (Oxford, UK: Oxford University Press, 2009).

14. See Brandice Canes-Wrone, *Who Leads Whom?* (Princeton, NJ: Princeton University Press, 2006); William G. Howell, *Politics without Persuasion* (Princeton, NJ: Princeton University Press, 2003); Kenneth R. Mayer, *With the Stroke of a Pen: Executive orders and Presidential Power* (Princeton, NJ: Princeton University Press, 2001); Charles M. Cameron, *Veto Bargaining: Presidents and the Politics of Negative Power* (New York: Cambridge University Press, 2000); Nolan McCarty and Rose Razaghian, "Advice and Consent: Senate Responses to Executive Branch Nominations 1885–1996," *American Journal of Political Science* 43 (October 1999): 1122–1143; Terry Moe, "Presidents, Institutions, and Theory," in George C. Edwards III, Bert A. Rockman, and John H. Kessel, eds., *Researching the Presidency* (Pittsburgh, PA: University of Pittsburgh Press, 1993), pp. 337–386; and Terry M. Moe, "The Politicized Presidency," in John E. Chubb and Paul E. Peterson, eds., *The New Directions in American Politics* (Washington, DC: Brookings Institution, 1985).

15. An exception is John P. Burke and Fred I. Greenstein, *How Presidents Test Reality* (New York: Russell Sage Foundation, 1989).

16. The political power approach is most famously represented in Neustadt, *Presidential Power*.

17. See, e.g., Edwards, *Predicting the Presidency*; Edwards, *Overreach*; Edwards, *The Strategic President*; Edwards, *On Deaf Ears*; and Edwards, *At the Margins*.

18. See, e.g., Gary C. Jacobson, *Presidents & Parties in the Public Mind* (Chicago, IL: University of Chicago Press, 2019); Edwards, *Predicting the Presidency*; Douglas L. Kriner and Eric Schickler, *Investigating the President: Congressional Checks on Presidential Power* (Princeton, NJ: Princeton University Press, 2016); William G. Resh, *Rethinking the Administrative Presidency* (Baltimore, MD: Johns Hopkins University Press, 2015); Edwards, *Overreach*; Edwards, *The Strategic President*; B. Dan Wood, *The Myth of Presidential Representation* (New York: Cambridge University Press, 2009); David E. Lewis, *The Politics of Presidential Appointments* (Princeton, NJ: Princeton University Press, 2008); William G. Howell and Jon C. Pevehouse, *While Dangers Gather: Congressional Checks on Presidential War Powers* (Princeton, NJ: Princeton University Press, 2007); B. Dan Wood, *The Politics of Economic Leadership* (Princeton, NJ: Princeton University Press, 2007); Edwards, *On Deaf Ears*; Jeffrey E. Cohen, *Presidential Responsiveness and Public Policy-Making* (Ann Arbor: University of Michigan Press, 1997); Edwards, *At the Margins*; and Fred I. Greenstein, *The Hidden-Hand Presidency* (New York: Basic Books, 1982).

19. See Bruce Miroff, "Beyond Washington," *Society* 17 (July/August 1980): 66–72.

20. See, e.g., Stephen J. Wayne, *Personality and Politics: Obama for and against Himself* (Washington, DC: CQ Press, 2011); Alexander L. George and Juliette L. George, *Woodrow Wilson and Colonel House: A Personality Study* (New York: Dover, 1964); and Robert Tucker, "The Georges' Wilson Reexamined: An Essay on Psychobiography," *American Political Science Review* 71 (June 1977): 606–618.

21. The most notable example is James David Barber, *The Presidential Character: Predicting Performance in the White House*, 5th ed. (New York: Routledge, 2020). See also Alexander L. George and Juliette L. George, *Presidential Personality and Performance* (Boulder, CO: Westview, 1998), chapter 5.

22. Some relevant studies include Stanley A. Renshon, *In His Father's Shadow: The Transformations of George W. Bush* (New York: Palgrave Macmillan, 2004); Yuen Foong Khong, *Analogies at War* (Princeton, NJ: Princeton University Press, 1993); Richard E. Neustadt and Ernest R. May, *Thinking in Time* (New York: Free Press, 1986); Irving L. Janis, *Groupthink: Psychological Studies of Policy Decisions and Fiascoes*, 2nd ed. (Boston, MA: Houghton Mifflin, 1982); Alexander L. George, *Presidential Decisionmaking in Foreign Policy: The Effective Use of Information and Advice* (Boulder, CO: Westview, 1980); Robert Jervis, *Perception and Misperception in International Politics* (Princeton, NJ: Princeton University Press, 1976); and John D. Steinbruner, *The Cybernetic Theory of Decision* (Princeton, NJ: Princeton University Press, 1974).

23. See George and George, *Presidential Personality and Performance*, chapter 2.

24. Neustadt, *Presidential Power*.

CHAPTER 2

1. Executive order 10340, "Directing the Secretary of Commerce to Take Possession of and Operate the Plants and Facilities of Certain Steel Companies," April 8, 1952.

2. *Youngstown Co. v. Sawyer* (1952), pp. 634–645.

3. Charles L. Black, Jr., "Some Thoughts on the Veto," *Law and Contemporary Problems* 40 (Spring 1976): 87.

4. Kenneth R. Mayer, *With the Stroke of a Pen: Executive orders and Presidential Power* (Princeton: Princeton University Press, 2001), pp. 39–40.

5. Harvey C. Mansfield, Jr., *Taming the Prince: The Ambivalence of Modern Executive Power* (Baltimore: Johns Hopkins University Press, 1993), p. *xxvii*.

6. Richard E. Neustadt, *Presidential Power and the Modern Presidents* (New York: The Free Press, 1990), chapter 1.

7. John Locke, "Second Treatise of Civil Government," in Thomas I. Cook, ed., *Two Treatises of Government* (New York: Hafner, 1956), p. 203.

8. G. Calvin Mackenzie, *The Imperiled Presidency: Leadership Challengers in the Twenty-First Century* (Lanham, MD: Rowman and Littlefield, 2016), p. 7.

9. *Federalist* no. 70.

10. Connecticut delegate Roger Sherman saw the executive as "nothing more than an institution for carrying the will of the Legislature into effect," and believed Congress should decide how many executives should hold office at any time. See Max Farrand, *The Records of the Federal Convention of 1787*, vol. I (New Haven: Yale University Press, 1911), p. 65; cited in Edward S. Corwin, *The President: Office and Powers 1787–1957* (New York: New York University Press, 1957), pp. 10–11.

11. Gordon S. Wood, *The Creation of the American Republic 1776–1787* (Chapel Hill: University of North Carolina Press 1998), pp. 551–552.

12. *Federalist* 51.

13. Charles de Montesquieu, *The Spirit of the Laws*, vol. 1 (New York: Hafner, 1949).

14. Mansfield, *Taming the Prince*, p. 1.

15. US Department of Justice, *Report on the Investigation into Russian Interference in the 2016 Presidential Election*, March 2019, Volume II, p. 2.

16. Office of Legal Counsel, US Department of Justice, *The Amenability of the President, Vice President, and other Civil Officers to Federal Criminal Prosecution while In Office*," September 24, 1973; Office of Legal Counsel, US Department of Justice, *A Sitting President's Amenability to Indictment and Criminal Prosecution*, October 16, 2000.

17. *The Amenability of the President, Vice President, and other Civil Officers to Federal Criminal Prosecution while In Office*," p. 28.

18. Akhil Reed Amar, "On Prosecuting Presidents," *Hofstra Law Review* 27: 671–676, 674 (1998).

19. Office of Legal Counsel, US Department of Justice, *The Amenability of the President, Vice President, and other Civil Officers to Federal Criminal Prosecution while In Office*," September 24, 1973, 26. Even a special counsel such as Robert Mueller, who is independent from direct presidential control, does not resolve the underlying problem. Mueller reported to the Deputy Attorney General, who in turn answered to the president.

20. Ibid, p. 31.

21. Ibid, p. 32.

22. Amar, "On Prosecuting Presidents," p. 674.

23. Lawrence Tribe, "Yes, the Constitution Allows Indictment of the President," *Lawfare*, December 20, 2018.

24. The clause gives Congress the power "To make all laws which shall be necessary and proper for carrying into execution the foregoing powers and all other powers vested by this Constitution in the government of the United States, or in any department or officer thereof."

25. Thach, *The Creation of the American Presidency: A Study in Constitutional History* (Baltimore: Johns Hopkins University Press, 1923), p. 123.

26. Richard Pious, *The Presidency* (Boston: Allyn & Bacon, 1996), p. 33.

27. Steven G. Calabresi and Saikrishna B. Prakash, "The President's Power to Execute the Laws," *Yale Law Journal* 104 (December 1994): 570.

28. Lawrence Lessig and Cass R. Sunstein, "The President and the Administration," *Columbia Law Review* 84 (January 1994): 47–48.

29. Henry P. Monaghan, "The Protective Power of the Presidency," *Columbia Law Review* 93 (January 1993): 22.

30. *In Re Neagle* (1890), holding that the president has the implied authority to appoint a US marshal to protect a Supreme Court Justice, even when there is no statute authorizing such an appointment. The case involved a marshal who shot and killed a man trying to attack the Justice and was arrested and charged with murder by a local prosecutor who argued that the marshal had no authorization under federal statutes.

31. The phrase "Recess of the Senate" is ambiguous, since there are two types of congressional recesses: those that occur between sessions and those that occur within a single session (such as a break over a holiday). Presidents have made recess appointments in both cases. The meaning of this language was not authoritatively interpreted until 2014, when the Supreme Court held that both inter- and intra-session recesses count and that presidents may only make recess appointments when the Senate is, according to its own rules, not in session and unable to transact business. *National Labor Relations Board v. Noel Canning, et al.* (2014).

32. Hamilton, *Federalist 69*.

33. Robert J. Reinstein, "Recognition: A Case Study on the Original Understanding of Executive Power," *University of Richmond Law Review* 45 (March 2011): 862.

34. Lessig and Sunstein, "The President and the Administration," p. 69

35. Calabresi and Praikash, "The President's Power to Execute the Laws," p. 583.

36. Geoffrey P. Miller, "Independent Agencies," *The Supreme Court Review* 1986 (1986): 62–63.

37. T. J. Halstead, *Presidential Signing Statements: Constitutional and Institutional Implications,* Congressional Research Service, RL33667, September 17, 2007, p. 1.

38. Frank H. Easterbrook, "Presidential Review," *Case Western Reserve Law Review* 40 (1989): 907.

39. Mayer, *With the Stroke of a Pen*, p. 117.

40. Easterbrook, "Presidential Review," p. 922.

41. Memorandum Opinion for the General Counsel, Office of Management and Budget, *Application of the Recommendation Clause to Section 802 of the Medicare Prescription Drug, Improvement, and Modernization Act of 2003*. August 25, 2016.

42. A bill of attainder is a legislative action declaring an individual to be a criminal and imposing a punishment, without trial.

43. Easterbrook, "Presidential Review," p. 906.

44. Easterbrook, "Presidential Review," p. 929.

45. Ken Gormley, "Introduction: An Unfinished Presidency," in Ken Gormley, ed., *The Presidents and the Constitution: A Living History* (New York: New York University Press, 2016), pp. 3–4.

46. Cited in Mark J. Rozell, *Executive Privilege: Presidential Power, Secrecy, and Accountability,* 2nd ed. (Lawrence, KS: University Press of Kansas, 2002), p. 28.

47. Fergus M. Bordewich, *The First Congress: How James Madison, George Washington, and a Group of Extraordinary Men Invented the Government* (New York: Simon & Schuster, 2016), p. 47.

48. Ibid, p. 47.

49. Stanley Elkins and Eric McKitrick, *The Age of Federalism: The Early American Republic, 1788–1800* (New York: Oxford University Press, 1993), p. 48.

50. David P. Currie, *The Constitution in Congress: The Federalist Period 1789–1801* (Chicago: University of Chicago Press, 1997), pp. 34–35. Elkins and McKitrick, *The Age of Federalism*, pp. 47–48. Adams's critics in the Senate took to mocking him for his preferences for pretentious titles, dubbing him "His Rotundity."

51. Corwin, *The President: Office and Powers*, p. 54

52. Currie, *The Constitution in Congress: The Federalist Period, 1789–1801*, p. 41.

53. James D. Richardson, *A Compilation of the Messages and Papers of the Presidents, 1789–1902*, vol. VI (New York: Bureau of National Literature and Art, 1897), p. 570.

54. It was a pretext; Johnson's impeachment was part of a broader dispute over the proper course of reconstruction (the readmission of the Confederate states into the United States). Eric Foner, *Reconstruction: America's Unfinished Revolution, 1863–1877* (New York: Harper & Row, 1988), pp. 333–336.

55. Common language includes the restriction on removing the head of the Consumer Financial Protection Bureau, created in 2009: the director can only be removed by the president "for inefficiency, neglect of duty, or malfeasance in office." 12 U.S.C. § 5491 (c)(3)).

56. 12 U.S.C. Chapter 3, Sub chapter II, § 246.

57. Peter M. Shane, "Independent Policymaking and Presidential Power: A Constitutional Analysis," *George Washington University Law Review* 57 (1988–1989): 608–609.

58. Steven G. Calabresi and Christopher S. Yoo, *The Unitary Executive: Presidential Power from Washington to Bush* (New Haven: Yale University Press, 2008), p. 3.

59. Louis Fisher, *Presidential War Power* (Lawrence: University Press of Kansas, 1995), p. 20.

60. *Federalist* 70–77.

61. Fisher, *Presidential War Power*, p. 21.

62. Philip J. Cooper, *By Order of the President: The Use & Abuse of Executive Direct Action* (Lawrence: University Press of Kansas, 2002), p. 124.

63. Joseph Ellis, *American Sphinx: The Character of Thomas Jefferson* (New York: Vintage Books, 1998), p. 243.

64. Thomas E. Cronin, "The President's Executive Power," in Thomas E. Cronin, ed., *Inventing the American Presidency* (Lawrence: University Press of Kansas, 1989), pp. 202–203.

65. Susan Dunn, *Jefferson's Second Revolution: The Election Crisis of 1800 and the Triumph of Republicanism* (Boston: Houghton Mifflin, 2004), p. 240.

66. Gerhard Casper, "Executive-Congressional Separation of Power during the Presidency of Thomas Jefferson," *Stanford Law Review* 47 (February 1995): 495–96.

67. Robert J. Spitzer, "The President's Veto Power," in Cronin, ed., *Inventing the American Presidency*, p. 168.

68. *Federalist* 73.

69. Robert J. Spitzer, *The Presidential Veto: Touchstone of the American Presidency* (Albany, NY: SUNY Press, 1988), p. 35.

70. Joseph Kallenbach, *The American Chief Executive: The President and the Governorship* (New York: Harper & Row, 1966), p. 354.

71. Spitzer, *The Presidential Veto*, pp. 37–38.

72. Charles M. Cameron, *Veto Bargaining: Presidents and the Politics of Negative Power* (New York: Cambridge University Press, 2000).

73. Richard Pious, "Prerogative Power and Presidential Politics," in George C. Edwards III and William G. Howell, eds., *The Oxford Handbook of the American Presidency* (New York: Oxford University Press, 2009).

74. Philip Shaw Paludan, *The Presidency of Abraham Lincoln* (Lawrence, KS: University Press of Kansas1994), p. 71.

75. William H. Rehnquist, *All the Laws But One: Civil Liberties in Wartime* (New York, Vintage Press, 1998), pp. 37–39.

76. Abraham Lincoln, letter to Albert Hodges, April 8, 1964, Roy P. Basler, *Collected Works of Abraham Lincoln*, vol. 7 (New Brunswick, NJ: Rutgers University Press, 1953), p. 282.

77. Special Session Message, July 4, 1861. In Richardson, *Messages and Papers of the President*, vol. VI, p. 25.

78. Clinton Rossiter, *Constitutional Dictatorship: Crisis Government in the Modern Democracies* (Princeton: Princeton University Press, 1948), p. 224.

79. Sanford Levinson and Hack M. Balkin, "Constitutional Dictatorship: Its Dangers and its Design," *Minnesota Law Review* 94 (2009–2010): 1815.

80. 48 Stat. 1

81. Congressional Research Service, *National Emergency Powers*, CRS Report 98–505, February 27, 2019, p. 8–9.

82. The 1976 statute required only a concurrent resolution, which is not subject to a presidential veto. The Supreme Court held in 1983 the that Congress could only overturn an executive action via the

regular statutory process (*INS v. Chadha*). In 1985, Congress amended the National Emergencies Act to require a Joint Resolution to end an emergency, which a president can veto.

83. Catherine Padhi, "Emergencies Without End: A Primer on Federal States of Emergency," *Lawfare*, December 8, 2017.

84. Proclamation 9844, *Declaring a National Emergency Concerning the Southern Border of the United States*, February 15, 2019. 84 *Federal Register* 4949, February 20, 2019; Margaret Taylor, "Declaring a National Emergency: The Statutory Arguments," *Lawfare*, January 7, 2019.

85. Emily Cochrane, "House Fails to Override Trump's Veto, Preserving National Emergency Order," *New York Times*, March 26, 2019.

86. *Sierra Club et al. v. Donald J. Trump et. al.*, case 19-cv-00892-HSG (n.d. Calif), May 24, 2019; Emily Cochrane and Charlie Savage, "House Adds Lawsuit to Challenges Against Trump's Emergency Declaration," *New York Times*, April 4, 2019.

87. Jeanne Whalen, Abha Bhattarai, and Reed Albergotti, "Trump 'Hereby' Orders U.S. Business Out of China. Can He Do That?" *Washington Post*, August 24, 2019.

88. Mark J. Rozell, *Executive Privilege: Presidential Power, Secrecy, and Accountability*, 2nd ed. (Lawrence: University Press of Kansas, 2002), p. 29.

89. Ibid., 31.

90. Kenneth R. Mayer, *With the Stroke of a Pen*, p. 43.

91. Rozell, *Executive Privilege*, p. 46.

92. *United States v. Nixon* (1974).

93. Todd Garvey, *Presidential Claims of Executive Privilege: History, Law, Practice, and Recent Developments*. Congressional Research Service R42670, December 15, 2014, p. 8.

94. Nichals Fandos, "House Panel Approves Contempt for Barr After Trump Claims Privilege Over Full Mueller Report," *New York Times*, May 8, 2019; Rachael Bade, Carol D. Leonnig, and Josh Dawsey, "White House Invokes Executive Privilege to Bar Former Counsel from Turning Over Documents to Congress," *Washington Post*, May 7, 2019.

95. *Historical Statistics of the United States, Colonial Times to 1970*, Part 2, Table Series Y 335–338 (Washington, DC: Bureau of the Census, 1975).

96. Stephen Skowronek, *Building a New American State: The Expansion of State Administrative Capacities*, 1877–1920 (Cambridge: Cambridge University Press, 1982), p. 121.

97. Theodore Roosevelt, *The Autobiography of Theodore Roosevelt* (New York: The MacMillan Company, 1916), p. 372.

98. William Howard Taft, *Our Chief Magistrate and His Powers* (New York: Columbia University Press, 1916), pp. 139–40.

99. Mayer, *With the Stroke of a Pen*, pp. 50, 55. *Youngstown Sheet and Tube v. Sawyer* (1952), p. 655.

100. US Department of Justice, Office of Legal Counsel, Memorandum Opinion for the Deputy Counsel to the President, *The President's Constitutional Authority to Conduct Military Operations Against Terrorists and the Nations Supporting Them*, September 25, 2001, pp. 5–6.

101. US Department of Justice, Office of Legal Counsel, Memorandum for Alberto R. Gonzales, Counsel to the President, *Re: Standards of Conduct for Interrogation under 18 U.S.C §§ 2340–2340A*, August 1, 2002, p. 39.

102. Jack Goldsmith, *The Terror Presidency: Law and Judgment Inside the Bush Administration* (New York: W.W. Norton & Co., 2007), pp. 151, 148.

103. Corwin, *The President: Office and Powers*, p. 307

104. *Trump v. Hawaii* (2018), p. 10.

105. *U.S. v. Midwest Oil Co.* (1915), p. 473.

106. Jared P. Cole, *The Political Question Doctrine: Justiciability and the Separation of Powers*. Congressional Research Service R43834, December 23, 2014.

107. President's Committee on Administrative Management (PCAM), *Report with Special Studies* (Washington, DC: Government Printing Office, 1937), p. 5

108. Hamilton, *Federalist* 70.

109. The first congressional power mentioned Article I section 8 is "To lay and collect Taxes, Duties, Imposts and Excises"; this section also grants Congress the power to "regulate commerce with foreign nations."

110. Timothy Meyer and Ganesh Sitaraman, "The Power to Declare a Trade War," *Lawfare*, March 23, 2018.

111. 50 US Code § 1701(a).

112. Memorandum from Janet Napolitano, Secretary of Homeland Security, *Exercising Prosecutorial Discretion with Respect to Individuals Who Came to the United States as Children*, June 15, 2012.

113. Memorandum from Jeh Johnson, Secretary of Homeland Security, *Exercising Prosecutorial Discretion with Respect to Individuals Who Came to the United States as Children and with Respect to Certain Individuals Who Are the Parents of U.S. Citizens or Permanent Residents*, November 20, 2014.

114. *United States v. Texas* (2016). Adam Liptak and Michael D. Shear, "Supreme Court Tie Blocks Obama Immigration Plan," *New York Times*, June 23, 2016.

115. *Rasul v. Bush* (2004); *Hamdi v. Rumsfeld* (2004); *Hamdan v. Rumsfeld* (2006); *Boumediene v. Bush* (2008).

116. *Trump v. Hawaii* (2018); see Fred Barbash and Deanna Paul, "The Real Reason the Trump Administration is Constantly Losing in Court," *Washington Post*, March 19, 2019.

117. Institute for Policy Integrity, New York University School of Law, https://policyintegrity.org/deregulation-roundup#fn-1-a, accessed May 28, 2019.

118. Terry M. Moe and Scott A. Wilson, "Presidents and the Politics of Structure," *Law and Contemporary Problems* 57 (Spring 1994): 11.

119. GOP Town Hall Event with Voters in South Carolina, February 18, 2016. http://transcripts.cnn.com/TRANSCRIPTS/1602/18/se.01.html.

120. White House Office of the Press Secretary, *President Trump's 100 Days of Historic Accomplishments*, April 25, 2017. https://www.whitehouse.gov/the-press-office/2017/04/25/president-trumps-100-days-historic-accomplishments.

121. Hamilton, *Federalist* 68; see also John Labovitz, *Presidential Impeachment* (New Haven: Yale University Press, 1978), p. 17

122. Lawrence Tribe and Joshua Matz, *To End a Presidency: The Power of Impeachment* (New York: Basic Books, 2018), p. 6.

123. Article I, Section 2.

124. Lawrence H. Tribe, "Defining 'High Crimes and Misdemeanors': Basic Principles," *George Washington Law Review* 67 (1999): 712–734, 713.

125. Gary L. McDowell, "High Crimes and Misdemeanors: Recovering the Intention of the Founders," *George Washington Law Review* 67 (1999): 626–649, 634.

126. Lawrence Tribe and Joshua Matz, *To End a Presidency*, p. 9.

127. United States Senate, *The Impeachment of Andrew Johnson (1868) President of the United States*. https://www.senate.gov/artandhistory/history/common/briefing/Impeachment_Johnson.htm.

128. Tribe and Matz, *To End a Presidency*, pb.55

129. Tribe and Matz, *To End a Presidency*, p. 57.

130. H. Res. 611, 105th Cong., https://www.congress.gov/bill/105th-congress/house-resolution/611.

131. Nicholas Fandos, "Pelosi Urges Caution on Impeachment as Some Democrats Push to Begin," *New York Times*, April 22, 2019.

132. Nicholas Fandos and Sheryl Gay Stolberg, "House Democrats Issue First Subpoena in Impeachment Inquiry," *New York Times*, September 27, 2019.

133. JM Rieger, Kate Rabinowitz, Chris Alcantara, and Kevun Uhrmacher, "Why Now? The Moments that Moved Pelosi and House Democrats Toward Impeachment," *Washington Post*, September 27, 2019.

134. Schlesinger, *The Imperial Presidency*. Boston: Houghton Mifflin, 1973.

135. Louis Fisher, *The Law of the Executive Branch: Presidential Power* (New York: Oxford University Press, 2014), chapter 8.

136. Article I, section 9.

137. There are other general foreign affairs powers that are similarly split. The president negotiates treaties with Senate ratification; appoints ambassadors with Senate confirmation.

138. Corwin, *The President: Office and Powers*, p. 171.

139. Fisher, *Presidential War Power*, p. 8.

140. Fisher, *Presidential War Power*, p. 17.

141. In the *Prize Cases* (1863), the Supreme Court ruled that a declaration of war was not necessary for a state of war to exist and for the president to respond.

142. William G. Howell and John C. Pevehouse, "Presidents, Congress, and the Use of Force," *International Organization* 59 (2005): 209–232.

143. Michael R. Gordon, Helene Cooper, and Michael D. Shear, "Dozens of US Missiles Hit Air Base in Syria," *New York Times*, April 6, 2017.

144. PL 93–148.

145. See Richard Grimmett, *The War Powers Resolution: After Thirty-Six Years*. Congressional Research Service, R41199, April 22, 2010.

146. Robbie Gramer and Amy Mackinnon, "Congress is Finally Done with the War in Yemen," *Foreign Policy*, April 4, 2019.

147. Karoun Dmirjian and Missy Ryan, "Senate Fails to Override Trump's Veto of Resolution Demanding End to U.S. Involvement in Yemen War," *Washington Post*, May 2, 2019.

148. Joseph Story, *Commentaries on the Constitution of the United States*, 5th ed., Melvin Bigelow, ed. (Boston: Little Brown and Co., 1891), p. 280.

149. Jeremi Suri, *The Impossible Presidency: The Rise and Fall of America's Highest Office* (New York: Basic Books, 2017), p. xviii.

CHAPTER 3

1. Stanley Elkins and Eric McKitrick, *The Age of Federalism: The Early American Republic 1788–1800* (New York: Oxford University Press, 1993), p. 515.

2. Lara M. Brown, "The Presidency and the Nomination Process: Aspirants, Parties, and Selections," in Michael Nelson, ed., *The Presidency and the Political System*, 11th ed. (Thousand Oaks, California: CQ Press, 2018), p. 197.

3. Plunkitt was known for his plain-spoken aphorisms—"I seen my opportunities and I took 'em"—and his defense of "honest graft." William Riordan, *Plunkitt of Tammany Hall* (New York: Signet Classic, reprint 1995).

4. Louise Overacker, *The Presidential Primary* (New York: MacMillan Company, 1926), p. 15.

5. James W. Caesar, *Presidential Selection: Theory and Development* (Princeton: Princeton University Press, 1979), pp. 227–228.

6. Elaine Kamarck, *Primary Politics: Everything You Need to Know About How America Nominates Its Presidential Candidates* (Washington, DC: Brookings Institution Press, 2018), p. 9.

7. Stephen J. Wayne, *The Road to the White House 2016* (Boston, MA: Cengage, 2018), pp. 97–98.

8. Byron E. Shafer, *The Quiet Revolution: The Struggle for the Democratic Party and the Shaping of Post-Reform Politics* (New York: Russell Sage Foundation, 1983), p. 28.

9. Report of the Commission on Party Structure and Delegate Selection to the Democratic National Committee. *Mandate for Reform*, Sen George S. McGovern Commission Chairman (Washington, DC: Democratic National Committee, 1970).

10. 1968–1980 data from Lyn Ragsdale, *Vital Statistics on the Presidency* (Thousand Oaks, CA: CQ Press, 2014), tables 2–3; 2016 data from Drew Desilver, "Near-Record Number of Primaries This Year, But Not Quite as Early," *Pew Research Center Fact Tank*, February 17, 2016.

11. Andrew E. Busch, "In Defense of the 'Mixed' System: The Goldwater Campaign & the Role of Popular Movements in the Pre-Reform Presidential Nomination System," *Polity* 24 (1992): 527–594.

12. Brianne Pfannenstiel, "How Democrats Hope to Let Iowans Participate in the Caucuses Without Showing Up in Person," *Des Moines Register,* February 11, 2019.

13. Reid J. Epstein, "Caucuses in Iowa Won't Include Absentee Participation, D.N.C Says," *New York Times*, August 30, 2019.

14. In *Cousins v. Wigoda* 419 US 477 (1975) and *Democratic Party v. La Follette* 450 US 107 (1981), the Supreme Court held that parties could determine their own rules for seating of convention delegates to the national convention.

15. The Green Papers, "Elections 2020: Presidential Primaries, Caucuses and Conventions." https://www.thegreenpapers.com/P20/.

16. Robert J. Huckshorn and John F. Bibby, "National Party Rules and Delegate Selection in the Republican Party," *PS* 14:656–666 (1983).

17. http://www.thegreenpapers.com/.

18. Domenico Montanaro, "Super Tuesday Was Created to Nominate Someone Moderate. It Backfired," NPR.com, February 29, 2016.

19. William G. Mayer, "Superdelegates: Reforming the Reforms Revisited," in Steven S. Smith and Melanie J. Springer, eds., *Reforming the Presidential Nomination Process* (Washington, DC: Brookings Institution Press, 2009), p. 91.

20. The Republicans went through a similar exercise after the 2012 loss, commissioning a study of process, messaging, policy, and proposed primary rules for 2016. Republican National Committee, *Growth and Opportunity Project*, March 2013.

21. David Sides and Natashe Korecki, "Democrats Strip Delegates of Power in Picking Presidential Nominee," *Politico*, August 25, 2018.

22. Beginning in 1976, primary candidates were eligible for public finding that matched the first $250 of each primary contribution. Those accepting the funds had to agree to cap their overall primary spending, as well as the amounts they spent in each state. By the 2000s, the spending limits accompanying public funding were too low for candidates to be competitive. Obama and Clinton declined the primary matching funds in 2008, Obama and Romney declined in 2012, and Trump and Clinton turned them down in 2016.

23. This total includes all disbursements through August 31, 2008.

24. *Citizens United v. Federal Election Commission*, 558 US 310 (2010).

25. Center for Responsive Politics, "2016 Outside Spending By Single Candidate Super PACs." https://www.opensecrets.org/outsidespending/summ.php?cycle=2016&chrt=V&disp=O&type=C.

26. https://www.fec.gov/data/elections/president/2020/.

27. Michael Luo, Jo Becker, and Patrick Healy, "Donors Worried by Clinton Campaign Spending," *New York Times*, February 22, 2008.

28. Nicholas Confessore and Karen Yourish, "$2 Billion Worth of Free Media for Trump" (The Upshot), *New York Times*, March 15, 2016; Peter L. Francia, "Free Media and Twitter in the 2016 Presidential Election: The Unconventional Campaign of Donald Trump," *Social Sciences Computer Review* 36 (2016): 440–455.

29. Aaron Bycoffee and David Wasserman, "Who's on Track for the Nomination?" *FiveThirtyEight*, June 8, 2016.

30. Elisa Shearer and Katerina Eva Matsa, "News Use across Social Media Platforms, 2018," Pew Research Center, 2018.

31. Seth Masket and Julia Azari, "How Parties Took over the Primary Debates," *Vox*, August 30, 2016.

32. Louise Dufresne, "Ronald Reagan's Testy Moment in the 1980 GOP Debate," CBS News, February 11, 2016.

33. Chris Cillizza, "CNBC Presidential Debate: Winners and Losers," *Washington Post*, November 9, 2011.

34. Geoffrey Skelley, "Presidential Primary Debates Can Make—And Break—A Campaign." *FiveThirtyEight*, January 7, 2019.

35. Jonathan Martin, "Republicans Tighten Grip on Debates in 2016 Presidential Race," *New York Times*, May 9, 2014.

36. Dan Balz and Philip Rucker, "RNC Set to Issue Rules to Cut, Regulate Presidential Debates," *Washington Post*, January 15, 2015.

37. Patrick J. Kenney and Karen Shafter. 2007. "Capturing the Power of a Campaign Event: The 2004 Presidential Debate in Tempe," *Journal of Politics* 69: 770–705.

38. Henry Enten, "Scott Walker Blew His Last Chance: The Debate," *FiveThirtyEight*, September 21, 2015.

39. Announced Democratic candidates were Senators Michael Bennet (Colorado), Corey Booker (New Jersey), Kirsten Gillibrand (New York), Kamala Harris (California), Amy Klobuchar (Minnesota), Bernie Sanders (Vermont), and Elizabeth Warren (Massachusetts); Governors Steve Bullock (Montana), John Hickenlooper (Colorado), and Jay Inslee (Washington); Representatives John Delaney (Maryland), Tulsi Gabbard (Hawaii), Seth Moulton (Massachusetts), Tim Ryan (Ohio), and Eric Swalwell (California); former Vice President Joe Biden; former Representative Beto O'Rourke (Texas); Miramar, Florida, Mayor Wayne Messam; New York Mayor Michael de Blasio; San Antonio, Texas, Mayor and former Secretary of Housing and Urban Development Julian Castro; former South Bend, Indiana, Mayor Pete Buttigieg; author Marianne Williamson; and tech entrepreneur Andrew Yang.

40. Lisa Lerer, "Democrats Unveil Plan to Split First 2020 Presidential Debates Over 2 Nights," *New York Times*, February 14, 2019.

41. "Over 2 Million Political Ads Aired this Cycle," Wesleyan Media Project, August 14, 2016. mediaproject.wesleyan.edu/releases/aug-2016/.

42. He raised $40 million, most of it online and by communicating with potential campaign supporters. He and his staff would personally respond to individual queries and suggestions.

43. Michael P. McDonald, "Voter Turnout 2016," US Elections Project. http://www.electproject.org.

44. John Wagner, "Jeb Bush Says Trump Should Face Republican Primary Challenger," *Washington Post*, March 15, 2019

45. Harry Enten, "Why Donald Trump Isn't a Real Candidate, In One Chart," *FiveThirtyEight*, June 16, 2015

46. Nate Silver of *FiveThirtyEight* discounted the relevance of these early polls, "Donald Trump Is Winning the Polls—and Losing the Nomination," *FiveThirtyEight*, August 11, 2015.

47. Philip Rucker and Robert Costa, "The Republican Party's Implosion over Donald Trump's Candidacy Has Arrived," *Washington Post*, February 28,2016.

48. https://twitter.com/jebbush/status/673990065517891584?lang=en.

49. Patrick Healy and Alexander Burns, "Scott Walker Ends His 2016 Presidential Run," *New York Times*, September 21, 2015.

50. Alex Altman, Philip Elliott, and Zeke J. Miller, "Why a Contested GOP Convention Just Got More Likely," *Time*, March 16, 2016.

51. John Sides, Michael Tesler, and Lynn Vavreck, *Identity Crisis: The 2016 Presidential Election and the Battle for the Meaning of America* (Princeton: Princeton University Press, 2018), p. 138.

52. Stephen Battaglio, "TV Viewership for Hillary Clinton's Acceptance Speech Is Smaller than Donald Trump's," *Los Angeles Times*, July 29, 2016.

53. Thomas E. Patterson, "News Coverage of the 2016 National Conventions: Negative News, Lacking Context," Shorenstein Center on Media, Politics, and Public Policy, Harvard University, September 21, 2016

54. Lonna Rae Atkeson, "Divisive Primaries and General Election Outcomes: Another Look at Presidential Campaigns," *American Journal of Political Science* 42 (1998): 256–271.

55. Priscilla Southwell, "The Effect of Nomination Divisiveness on the 2008 Presidential Election," *PS: Political Science and Politics* 43 (2010): 255–258.

56. Sides, Tesler, and Vavreck, *Identity Crisis*, p. 111.

57. Patrick Healy and Jonathan Martin, "Democrats Struggle for Unity on First Day of Convention," *New York Times*, July 25, 2016.

58. Brent Kendall, "Trump Says Judge's Mexican Heritage Presents 'Absolute Conflict'; Republican's Charge that Judge Gonzalo Curiel Has a Conflict of Interest Draws Criticism from Some Legal Observers," *Wall Street Journal*, June 3, 2016.

59. David Weigel, "Ted Cruz Booed by Angry Delegates after Failing to Endorse Trump," *Washington Post*, July 20, 2016. What seemed to be a mid-primary truce between Trump and Cruz collapsed after Trump insulted Cruz's wife and linked his father to Kennedy assassin Lee Harvey Oswald. Cruz responded by calling Trump amoral and a "pathological liar." Aaron Blake, "9 Truly Awful Things Ted Cruz and Donald Trump Said About Each Other," *Washington Post*, September 23, 2016.

60. Sides, Tesler, and Vavreck, *Identity Crisis*, p. 138.

61. Marty Cohen, David Karol, Hans Noel, and John Zaller, "Party versus Faction in the Reformed Presidential Nominating System," *PS: Political Science and Politics* 49 (2016): 701–708.

62. See table 4.6.

CHAPTER 4

1. On the origins of the electoral college, see George C. Edwards III, *Why the Electoral College Is Bad for America*, 3rd ed. (New Haven: Yale University Press, 2019), chapter 5.

2. For more on slavery and the electoral college, see Paul Finkelman, "The Proslavery Origins of the Electoral College," *Cardozo Law Review* 23 (March 2002): 1145–1157.

3. Robert A. Dahl, *On Democracy* (New Haven: Yale University Press, 2000), p. 37. See also Robert A. Dahl, *Democracy and Its Critics* (New Haven: Yale University Press, 1989), p. 110.

4. See Edwards, *Electoral College*, chapter 3.

5. For a discussion of the 1960 election, see Edwards, *Electoral College*, pp. 67–70.

6. The Voter News Service responsible for the exit poll in 2000 reported that 31 percent of Nader's voters said that they would not have voted had Gore and Bush been the only candidates. Of those who said that they would have done so, however, Gore was favored by a two-to-one margin.

7. US Census Bureau, 2010 census results.

8. Jeffrey W. Ladewig and Mathew P. Jasinski, "On the Causes and Consequences of and Remedies for Interstate Malapportionment of the U.S. House of Representatives," *Perspectives on Politics* 6 (March 2008): 89–107.

9. David W. Abbott and James P. Levine, *Wrong Number: The Coming Debacle in the Electoral College* (New York: Praeger, 1991), pp. 82–83.

10. US Census Bureau, 2016 census estimates. Another way to measure the weight of a vote is to compare the voting-age populations of states (rather than the total population) at the time of the election. In a study based on projections of the voting-age populations as of November 7, 2000, William

Frey found that in the 2000 presidential election, an elector represented 471,000 voting-aged persons in Florida but only 119,000 in Wyoming. See William H. Frey, "Regional Shifts in America's Voting-Aged Population: What Do They Mean for National Politics?" Institute for Social Research, University of Michigan, 2000, app. D. The electors in 2000 were allocated on the basis of the 1990 census.

11. See Edwards, *Electoral College*, p. 10, chapter 3.

12. William W. Freehling, *The Road to Disunion: Secessionists at Bay, 1776–1854* (New York: Oxford University Press, 1990), pp. 146–148; James R. Sharp, *American Politics in the Early Republic* (New Haven: Yale University Press, 1993), p. 247; Garry Wills, *"Negro President": Jefferson and the Slave Power* (Boston: Houghton Mifflin, 2003), pp. 2–5, 234; and John Ferling, *Adams v. Jefferson: The Tumultuous Election of 1800* (New York: Oxford University Press, 2004), p. 168.

13. Raymond Tatalovich, "Electoral Votes and Presidential Campaign Trails, 1932–1976," *American Politics Quarterly* 7 (October 1979): 489–497; Scott C. James and Brian L. Lawson, "The Political Economy of Voting Rights Enforcement in America's Gilded Age: Electoral College Competition, Partisan Commitment, and the Federal Election Law," *American Political Science Review* 93 (March 1999): 115–131; Daron R. Shaw, "The Methods behind the Madness: Presidential Electoral College Strategies, 1988–1996," *Journal of Politics* 61 (November 1999): 893–913; and Daron R. Shaw, *The Race to 270* (Chicago, IL: University of Chicago Press, 2007).

14. David Plouffe, *The Audacity to Win* (New York: Viking, 2009), p. 247.

15. See Edwards, *Electoral College*, pp. 4–7, 128–138.

16. Edwards, *Electoral College*, pp. 7, 138–143.

17. *America Goes to the Polls, 2016* (Nonprofit VOTE and US Elections Project, 2017), pp. 12–13.

18. "Mad Money: TV Ads in the 2012 Presidential Campaign," *Washington Post*, November 14, 2012. http://www.washingtonpost.com/wp-srv/special/politics/track-presidential-campaign-ads-2012.

19. *America Goes to the Polls, 2016*, pp. 12–13.

20. Twentieth Century Fund, *Winner Take All* (New York: Holmes & Meier, 1978), chapter 6.

21. Max Farrand, ed., *The Records of the Federal Convention of 1787*, rev. ed., vol. 1 (New Haven: Yale University Press, 1966), p. 483.

22. Ibid., p. 403.

23. James Madison to George Hay, August 23, 1823. In Gaillard Hunt, ed., *The Writings of James Madison*, vol. 9 (New York: G. P. Putnam's Sons, 1900–1910), pp. 47–55.

24. Farrand, *Federal Convention of 1787*, vol. 2, p. 111.

25. Farrand, *Federal Convention of 1787*, vol. 1, pp. 447–449.

26. Voter News Service Exit Polls; Gallup News Service, "Candidate Support by Subgroup," News Release, November 6, 2000 (based on six-day average, October 31–November 5, 2000).

27. See Eric R. A. N. Smithy and Peverill Squire, "Direct Election of the President and the Power of the States," *Western Political Quarterly* 40 (March 1987): 29–44.

28. Keith Melder, *Hail to the Candidate: Presidential Campaigns from Banners to Broadcasts* (Washington, DC: Smithsonian Institution Press, 1992), p. 88.

29. William J. Bryan, *The First Battle* (Port Washington, NY: Kennikat Press, 1971), p. 618.

30. Melder, *Hail to the Candidate*, p. 129.

31. Michael X. Delli Carpini, "Radio's Political Past," *Media Studies Journal* 7: 23–36 (Summer 1993), p. 26.

32. Bureau of the Census, *Historical Statistics of the United States—Colonial Times to 1970*, vol. 2 (Washington DC: Government Printing Office, 1965), p. 796, table R 93–105.

33. Philip Bump, "Donald Trump's Campaign Has Spent More on Hats than on Polling," *Washington Post*, October 25, 2016.

34. Niv M. Sultan, "Election 2016: Trump's Free Media Helped Keep Cost Down, but Fewer Donors Provided More of the Cash," Opensecrets.org, April 13, 2017.

35. Carrie Levine, "Soft Money is Back—and Both Parties are Cashing In," *Politico*, August 6, 2017.

36. "Election 2016: Money Raised as of December 31, 2016," *Washington Post*, February 2018.

37. See Richard L. Hasen, *Plutocrats United: Campaign Money, The Supreme Court, and the Distortion of American Elections* (New Haven: Yale University Press, 2016); and Timothy K. Kuhner, *Capitalism v. Democracy: Money in Politics and the Free Market Constitution* (Stanford: Stanford University Press, 2013). For a contrasting argument opposing restrictions on campaign contributions, see John Samples, *The Fallacy of Campaign Finance Reform* (Chicago: University of Chicago Press, 2006).

38. OpenSecrets.org. https://www.opensecrets.org/pres16/.

39. Erika Franklin Fowler, Travis N. Ridout, and Michael M. Franz, "Political Advertising in 2016: The Presidential Election as Outlier?" *The Forum* 14 (2016).

40. Joshua L. Kalla and David E. Brockman, "The Minimal Persuasive Effects of Campaign Contact in General Elections: Evidence from 49 Field Experiments," *American Political Science Review* 112 (2018): 148–166 ; Christopher Wlezien and Stuart Soroka, "Mass Media and Electoral Preferences during the 2016 Presidential Race," *Political Behavior*, published online June 28, 2018, https://doi.org/10.1007/s11109-018-9478-0; and Andrew Gelman and Gary King, "Why Are American Presidential Election Polls So Variable When Votes Are So Predictable?" *British Journal of Political Science* 23 (1993). Moreover, in the contemporary polarized political environment there are not many independents or cross-pressured voters left. See Samantha Klar and Yanna Krupnikov, *Independent Politics* (New York: Cambridge University Press, 2016).

41. Jill Lepore, "Party Time—Smear Tactics, Skullduggery, and the Debut of American Democracy," *New Yorker*, September 17, 2007.

42. http://www.livingroomcandidate.org/commercials/1964/peace-little-girl-daisy#3983.

43. Robert Mann, *Daisy Petals and Mushrooms: LBJ, Barry Goldwater, and the Ad That Changed American Politics* (Baton Rouge: Louisiana State University Press, 2011).

44. Fowler, Ridout, and. Franz, "Political Advertising in 2016: The Presidential Election as Outlier?"

45. Ibid.

46. Joshua Green, "The Amazing Money Machine," *TheAtlantic.com*, June 2008.

47. Caroline Amia, "Obama Said to Raise $690M through Digital Means," *USA Today*, November 15, 2012.

48. Sean Gallagher, "Inside Team Romney's Whale of an IT Meltdown," *ArsTechnica*, November 9, 2012.

49. Antonio García Martínez, "How Trump Conquered Facebook—Without Russian Ads," *Wired*, February 23, 2018.

50. Tamara Keith, "Commander-In-Tweet: Trump's Social Media Use and Presidential Media Avoidance," NPR.com, November 18, 2016.

51. Joel Winston, "How the Trump Campaign Built an Identity Database and Used Facebook Ads to Win the Election," Medium.com, November 18, 2016.

52. Brian Stelter, "Debate Breaks Record as Most-Watched in U.S. History," *CNNMoney*, September 27, 2016.

53. Jill Serjeant, "Final Trump-Clinton Debate Draws Nearly 72 Million Viewers, Third Largest Ever," Reuters.com, October 20, 2016.

54. Julian Zelizer, "The 8 Biggest Unforced Errors in Debate History," *Politico*, September 24, 2016.

55. CNN/ORC polls, September 16, October 4, October 19, and October 20–23, 2016; ABC News/*Washington Post* poll. October 10–13, 2016; ABC News tracking poll, October 20–22, 2016; Gallup poll, October 20–21, 2016; and Lydia Saad, "Clinton Wins Third Debate, Gains Ground as 'Presidential,'" *Gallup Poll*, October 24, 2016.

56. Abigail Geiger, "16 Striking Findings for 2016," Pew Research Center, December 21, 2016.

57. Michael Barthel and Jeffrey Gottfied, "For Election News, Young People Turned to Some National Papers More than Their Elders," Pew Research Center, February 17, 2017; and Jeffrey Gottfried, Michael Barthel, Elisa Shearer, and Amy Mitchell, "The 2016 Presidential Campaign—a New Event That's Hard to Miss," Pew Research Center, February 4, 2016.

58. Thomas E. Patterson, *News Coverage of the 2016 General Election: How the Press Failed the Voters*, Shorenstein Center on Media, Politics, and Public Policy, Harvard University, December 7, 2016.

59. Ibid.

60. "Low Marks for Major Players in 2016 Election, Including the Winner," Pew Research Center, November 21, 2016.

61. Peverill Squire, "Why the 1936 *Literary Digest* Poll Failed," *Public Opinion Quarterly* 52 (1988): 125–133.

62. Will Lester, "'Dewey Defeats Truman' Disaster Haunts Pollsters," *Los Angeles Times*, November 1, 1998.

63. Nate Cohn, "A 2016 Review: Why Key State Polls Were Wrong about Trump," *New York Times*, May 31, 2017; Five Thirty Eight, "Who Will Win the Presidency?" https://projects.fivethirtyeight.com/2016-election-forecast/.

64. American Association for Public Opinion Research (AAPOR), *An Evaluation of the 2016 Election Polls in the United States*. AAPOR Ad Hoc Committee on 2016 Polling. May 11, 2017.

65. See, e.g., "Debunking Voter Fraud Myth," Brennan Center for Justices, 2017; "The Truth about Voter Fraud," Brennan Center for Justice, 2017; Government Accountability Office, *ELECTIONS: State Laws Addressing Voter Registration and Voting on or before Election Day*, 2012; Eric Lipton and Ian

Urbina, "In 5-Year Effort, Scant Evidence of Voter Fraud," *New York Times,* April 12, 2007; Lorraine C. Minnite, *The Myth of Voter Fraud* (Ithaca, NY: Cornell University Press, 2010); and John S. Ahlquist, Kenneth R. Mayer, and Simon Jackman, "Alien Abduction and Voter Impersonation in the 2012 U.S. General Election: Evidence from a Survey List Experiment," *Election Law Journal* 13 (December 2014): 460–475

66. Executive order 13799, *Establishment of Presidential Advisory Commission on Electoral Integrity,* May 11, 2017. 82 *Federal Register* 22389.

67. Eli Rosenberg, "'The Most Bizarre Thing I've Ever Been a Part Of': Trump Panel Found No Widespread Voter Fraud, Ex-Member Says," *Washington Post,* August 3, 2018.

68. Jan E. Leighley and Jonathan Nagler, *Who Votes Now? Demographics, Issues, Inequality, and Turnout in the United States* (Princeton, NJ: Princeton University Press, 2014).

69. David Leonhardt, "The Democrats' Real Turnout Problem," *New York Times,* November 17, 2016.

70. Sean McElwee, Jesse H. Rhodes, Brian Schaffner, and Bernard L. Fraga, "The Missing Obama Millions," *New York Times,* March 10, 2018.

71. Arthur H. Miller, Martin P. Wattenberg, and Oksana Malanchuk, "Schematic Assessments of Presidential Candidates," *American Political Science Review* 80 (June 1986): 521–540.

72. Pew Research Center, "Low Marks for Major Players in 2016 Election—Including the Winner," November 21, 2016; and Lydia Saad, "Trump and Clinton Finish with Historically Poor Images," *Gallup Poll,* November 8, 2016.

73. ABC News poll, October 20–22, 2016.

74. Nicholas A. Valentino, Carly Wayne, and Marzia Oceno, "Mobilizing Sexism: The Interaction of Emotion and Gender Attitudes in the 2016 Presidential Election," *Public Opinion Quarterly* 82 (2018): 799–821; and John Sides, Michael Tesler, and Lynn Vavreck, *Identity Crisis: The 2016 Presidential Campaign and the Battle for the Meaning of America* (Princeton: Princeton University Press, 2018), pp. 186–189.

75. "Election 2016: Exit Polls," *CNN,* November 23, 2016. http://www.cnn.com/election/results/exit-polls.

76. Diana C. Mutz, "Status Threat, Not Economic Hardship, Explains the Presidential Vote," *Proceedings of the National Academic of Sciences* 115:E4330-E4339 (2018); Tyler T. Reny, Loren Collingwood, and Ali A. Valenzuela, "Vote Switching in the 2016 Election: How Racial and Immigration Attitudes, Not Economics, Explains Shifts in White Voting," *Public Opinion Quarterly* 83 (2019): 91–113; and Gary C. Jacobson, "The Triumph of Polarized Partisanship in 2016: Donald Trump's Improbably Victory," *Political Science Quarterly* 132 (2017): 9–41.

77. Nate Silver, "Why *FiveThirtyEight* Gave Trump a Better Chance than Almost Anyone Else," FiveThirtyEight.com, November 11, 2016; and Josh Katz, "Who Will be President?" *New York Times* (Upshot), November 8, 2016.

78. Sam Wang, "Why I Had to Eat a Bug on CNN," *New York Times,* November 18, 2016.

79. Sides, Tesler, and Vavreck, *Identity Crisis,* 140–141.

80. Jonathan Martin, Maggie Haberman, and Alexander Burns, "Lewd Donald Trump Tape is a Breaking Point for Many in the GOP," *New York Times,* October 8, 2016.

81. Isaac Stanley-Becker, "Roger Stone Wanted Wikileaks Dump to Distract from 'Access Hollywood' Tape, Mueller Witness Says," *Washington Post,* January 29, 2019.

82. Sides, Tesler, and Vavreck, *Identity Crisis,* p. 146.

83. Nate Silver, "The Comey Letter Probably Cost Clinton the Election," *FiveThirtyEight,* May 3, 2017. In contrast, Sides, Tesler, and Vavreck (*Identity Crisis,* pp. 148–149) suggest the effect of Comey's announcement was smaller and, in any event, there is no way to know whether it could have been decisive.

84. Department of Justice, Office of the Special Counsel, *Report on The Investigation into Russian Interference in the 2016 Presidential Election* (Mueller Report), April 2019, p. 1.

85. Intelligence Community Assessment, *Assessing Russian Activities and Intentions in Recent U.S. Elections,* Office of the Director of National Intelligence, ICA 2017-01D, January 6, 2017.

86. Senate Select Committee on Intelligence, *Summary of Initial Findings on Intelligence Community Assessment,* July 3, 2017.

87. Mueller Report, pp. 37–38.

88. Mueller Report, p. 49.

89. Kathleen Hall Jamieson, *Cyber-War: How Russian Hackers and Trolls Helped Elect a President* (New York: Oxford University Press, 2018), pp. 162–172.

90. Mueller Report, p. 66.

91. Young Mie Kim, Jordan Hsu, David Neiman, Colin Kou, Levi Bankston, Soo Yun Kim, Richard Heinrich, Robyn Baragwanath, and Garvesh Raskutti. "The Stealth Media? Groups and Targets behind Divisive Issue Campaigns on Facebook," *Political Communication* 35 (2018): 515–541.

92. Mueller Report, pp. 174–180.

93. Duncan J. Watts and David M. Rothschild. 2017. "Don't Blame the Election on Fake News. Blame it on the Media." *Columbia Journalism Review*, December 5. https://www.cjr.org/analysis/fake-news-media-election-trump.php.

94. Jane Mayer, "How Russia Helped Swing the Election for Trump," *New Yorker*, September 24, 2018.

95. "Full Transcript of Mueller's Statement on Russia Investigation," *New York Times*, May 29, 2019.

96. "Election 2016: Exit Polls," *CNN*, November 23, 2016.

97. https://electionstudies.org/.

CHAPTER 5

1. "First Debate with Stephen A. Douglas, August 21, 1858," in Roy P. Asler, ed., *The Collected Works of Abraham Lincoln* (New Brunswick, NJ: Rutgers University Press, 1953), p. 27.

2. See Stanley Feldman and John Zaller, "The Political Culture of Ambivalence: Ideological Responses to the Welfare State," *American Journal of Political Science* 36 (February 1992): 268–307.

3. See, e.g., Pew Research Center poll, March 29–25, 2019; Politico/Harvard School of Public Health poll, December 4–9, 2018; and NPR/PBS *NewsHour* poll, October 21–23, 2018.

4. See, e.g., Matt Grossmann and David A. Hopkins, *Asymmetric Politics: Ideological Republicans and Group Interest Democrats* (New York: Oxford University Press, 2016), chapter 2.

5. NBC News/*Wall Street Journal* poll, March 23–27, 2019. See also *New York Times* poll, April 1–7, 2019.

6. CBS News/*New York Times* poll, February 5–10, 2010.

7. Bloomberg poll conducted by Selzer & Co., July 9–12, 2010.

8. CBS News/*New York Times* poll, September 10–14, 2010.

9. Bloomberg News National poll, October 24–26, 2010.

10. Public Religion Research Institute, American Values Survey, September 11–October 4, 2015.

11. Bloomberg Politics poll, November 15–17, 2015.

12. Kaiser Health Tracking poll, April 15–20, 2013.

13. Kaiser Family Foundation, "Data Note: 5 Misconceptions Surrounding the ACA," March 21, 2017. See also NPR/Ipsos poll, January 4–5, 2017; and *The Economist*/YouGov poll, December 17–20, 2016.

14. Pew Research Center poll, June 28–July 9, 2012.

15. YouGov poll, June 30–July 2, 2012. See also the Fairleigh Dickinson University poll, December 8–15, 2014. See also *The Economist*/YouGov poll, December 17–20, 2016.

16. Steven Kull, Clay Ramsay, and Evan Lewis, "Misperceptions, the Media, and the Iraq War," *Political Science Quarterly* 118 (Winter 2003–2004): 569–598.

17. YouGov poll, April 26–May 2, 2012. See also the Fairleigh Dickinson University poll, December 8–15, 2014.

18. Benjamin I. Page and Robert Y. Shapiro, *The Rational Public* (Chicago, IL: University of Chicago Press, 1992); and James A. Stimson, *Public Opinion in America: Moods, Cycles, and Swings* (Boulder, CO: Westview, 1991).

19. Ron Chernow, *Washington* (New York: Penguin Press, 2010), pp. 605–608, 654–655; and George C. Edwards III, *On Deaf Ears: The Limits of the Bully Pulpit* (New Haven, CT: Yale University Press, 2003), chapter 5.

20. On the development of White House polling, see Kathryn Dunn Tenpas and James A. McCann, "Testing the Permanence of the Permanent Campaign: An Analysis of Presidential Polling Expenditures, 1977–2002," *Public Opinion Quarterly* 71 (Fall 2007): 349–366; Diane J. Heith, *Polling to Govern: Public Opinion and Presidential Leadership* (Palo Alto, CA: Stanford University Press, 2004); Robert M. Eisinger, *The Evolution of Presidential Polling* (Cambridge, UK: Cambridge University Press, 2003); Shoon Kathleen Murray and Peter Howard, "Variations in White House Polling Operations," *Public Opinion Quarterly* 66 (Winter 2002): 527–558; Lawrence R. Jacobs and Robert Y. Shapiro, "The Rise of Presidential Polling: The Nixon White House in Historical Perspective," *Public Opinion Quarterly* 59 (Summer 1995): 163–195; Lawrence R. Jacobs and Robert Y. Shapiro, "Issues, Candidate Image, and

Priming: The Use of Private Polls in Kennedy's 1960 Presidential Campaign," *American Political Science Review* 88 (September 1994): 527–540; and Bruce Altschuler, *LBJ and the Public Polls* (Gainesville: University of Florida Press, 1990).

21. Morris Levy, Matthew Wright, and Jack Citrin, "Mass Opinion and Immigration Policy in the United States: Re-Assessing Clientelist and Elitist Perspectives," *Perspectives on Politics* 14 (September 2016): 660–680. See also Ariel Edwards-Levy and Grace Sparks, "How Many Americans Support the Travel Ban? Depends on the Poll," *HuffPollster*, February 3, 2017.

22. See Chris Kahn and James Oliphant, "Is the Sky Blue? Depends on What Donald Trump Says," *Reuters*, April 6, 2017.

23. Quoted in Dom Bonafede, "Carter and the Polls—If You Live by Them, You May Die by Them," *National Journal*, August 19, 1978, pp. 1312–1313. See also Mark Blumenthal, "News Flash: Obama Using Polling Data," January 9, 2009, available at http://www.pollster.com/blogs/news_flash_obama_using_polling.php.

24. Interview with Richard Wirthlin, West Point, NY, April 19, 1988; and John Anthony Maltese, *Spin Control* (Chapel Hill: University of North Carolina Press, 1992), p. 185.

25. Diane Heith, "One for All: Using Focus Groups and Opinion Polls in the George H. W. Bush White House," *Congress and the Presidency* 30 (Spring 2003): 81–94.

26. Mark Halperin and John F. Harris, *The Way to Win* (New York: Random House, 2006), pp. 102–103; John F. Harris, *The Survivor: Bill Clinton in the White House* (New York: Random House, 2005), p. 331; Kathryn Dunn Tenpas, "Words vs. Deeds: President George W. Bush and Polling," *Brookings Review* (Summer 2003): 33–35; David Gergen, *Eyewitness to Power: The Essence of Leadership* (New York: Simon & Schuster, 2000), p. 331; Dick Morris, *Behind the Oval Office* (New York: Random House, 1997), pp. 10–11, 83, 338; James Carney, "Playing by the Numbers," *Time,* April 11, 1994, p. 40; James M. Perry, "Clinton Relies Heavily on White House Pollster to Take Words Right Out of the Public's Mouth," *Wall Street Journal*, March 23, 1994, p. A16; Richard L. Berke, "Clinton Adviser Says Polls Had a Role in Health Plan," *New York Times*, December 2, 1993, p. A17; James A. Barnes, "Polls Apart," *National Journal*, July 10, 1993, pp. 1750–1752; and James A. Barnes, "The Endless Campaign," *National Journal*, February 20, 1993, p. 461.

27. Tenpas, "Words vs. Deeds."

28. Sam Stein, "Obama Mocks Polls but Spends More on Them ($4.4M) Than Bush Did," *Huffington Post*, July 29, 2010; and Michael D. Shear, "Poll Results Drive Rhetoric of Obama's Health-Care Message," *Washington Post*, July 30, 2009.

29. Ben Smith, "Meet Obama's Pollsters," *Politico*, April 3, 2009.

30. Shear, "Poll Results Drive Rhetoric of Obama's Health-Care Message."

31. On using polls results for opinion leadership, see Heith, *Polling to Govern*, chapters 3–5.

32. Quoted in Robert Draper, *Dead Certain: The Presidency of George W. Bush* (New York: Free Press, 2007), p. 234.

33. Stanley Kelley, Jr., *Interpreting Elections* (Princeton, NJ: Princeton University Press, 1983), pp. 72–125.

34. Martin P. Wattenberg, *The Rise of Candidate-Centered Politics: Presidential Elections of the 1980s* (Cambridge, MA: Harvard University Press, 1991), chapters 5–6.

35. Brandon Rottinghaus, "Following the 'Mail Hawks': Alternative Measures of Public Opinion on Vietnam in the Johnson White House," *Public Opinion Quarterly* 71 (Fall 2007): 367–391.

36. See, e.g., Herbert G. Klein, *Making It Perfectly Clear* (Garden City, NY: Doubleday, 1980), p. 341; Richard M. Nixon, *RN: The Memoirs of Richard Nixon* (New York: Grosset & Dunlap, 1978), pp. 935, 945; and Saul Pett, "Interview Draws Rare Portrait of Carter," *New Orleans Times-Picayune*, October 23, 1977, sect. 1, p. 13.

37. B. Dan Wood, *The Myth of Presidential Representation* (New York: Cambridge University Press, 2009); and Jeffrey E. Cohen, *Presidential Responsiveness and Public Policy-Making* (Ann Arbor: University of Michigan Press, 1997).

38. George C. Edwards III, *The Bungler: The Leaderhip of Donald Trump* (forthcoming, 2020).

39. Quoted in Tom Matthews, "The Road to War," *Newsweek*, January 28, 1991, p. 65.

40. Quoted in Peter Baker, "Obama Says He'd Rather Be a 'Really Good One-Term President'," *New York Times*, January 25, 2010.

41. Gerald R. Ford, "Imperiled, Not Imperial," *Time*, November 10, 1980, p. 31.

42. Quoted in Kenneth Whyte, *Hoover: An Extraordinary Life in Extraordinary Times* (New York: Knopf, 2017), p. 369.

43. Gallup poll, January 23–28, 2018.

44. Similar results were found for presidents Carter, Reagan, and George W. Bush. See "Early Expectations: Comparing Chief Executives," *Public Opinion*, February/March 1981, p. 39; and Gallup poll, January 15–16, 2001.

45. See *The Polling Report* 5 (January 30, 1989): 2–4; Gallup poll, November 10–11, 1992; Gallup poll, January 15–16, 2001; and Gallup poll, January 9–11, 2009.

46. Gallup poll, January 9–11, 2009.

47. President Carter, quoted in Godfrey Hodgson, *All Things to All Men: The False Promise of the Modern American Presidency* (New York: Simon & Schuster, 1980), p. 25.

48. Frank Newport, "Public Values Vision, Leadership and Economic Stewardship in President," *The Gallup Poll Monthly*, November 1999, pp. 4–6; Pew Research Center for the People and the Press, *Retro-Politics*, November 1999, p. 45; Times Mirror Center for the People and the Press, public opinion survey, October 25–30, 1995; and George C. Edwards III, *The Public Presidency* (New York: St. Martin's, 1983), pp. 189–190.

49. Edwards, *The Public Presidency*, pp. 189–191; and Newport, "Public Values Vision, Leadership and Economic Stewardship in President."

50. "Carter Interview," *Congressional Quarterly Weekly Report*, November 25, 1978, p. 3354.

51. See, e.g., Gallup poll, *Attitudes toward the Presidency*, January 1980, p. 21.

52. Richard C. Waterman, Carol L. Silva, and Hank C. Jenkins-Smith, *The Expectations Gap Thesis: Public Attitudes Concerning the Presidency* (Ann Arbor: University of Michigan Press, 2014); and Edwards, *The Public Presidency*, pp. 193–195.

53. *Washington Post*–ABC News poll, January 21–24, 2019.

54. Wirthlin interview.

55. Stephen J. Adler, Jeff Mason, and Steve Holland, "Exclusive: Trump Says He Thought Being President Would Be Easier Than His Old Life," *Reuters*, April 29, 2017.

56. See, e.g., *The Gallup Poll Monthly*, September 1994, 17, 39, 44; *The Gallup Poll Monthly*, May 1993, p. 13; George Gallup, Jr., and Frank Newport, "Wary Americans Favor Wait and See Posture in Persian Gulf," *The Gallup Monthly Report*, November 1990, p. 14; Jack Dennis, "Dimensions of Public Support for the Presidency" (paper presented at the Annual Meeting of the Midwest Political Science Association, Chicago, April 1975), Tables 4, 8; and Hazel Erskine, "The Polls: Presidential Power," *Public Opinion Quarterly* 37 (Fall 1973): 492, 495.

57. George C. Edwards III, "Presidential Approval and Congressional Support," in *The Oxford Handbook of the American Presidency*, eds. George C. Edwards III and William H. Howell (Oxford, UK: Oxford University Press, 2009); and George C. Edwards III, *At the Margins: Presidential Leadership of Congress* (New Haven, CT: Yale University Press, 1989), chapter 6.

58. Milton Lodge and Charles S. Taber, *The Rationalizing Voter* (New York: Cambridge University Press, 2013); James N. Druckman, Jordan Fein, and Thomas J. Leeper, "A Source of Bias in Public Opinion Stability," *American Political Science Review* 106 (May 2012): 430–454; Rune Slothuus and Claes H. de Vreese, "Political Parties, Motivated Reasoning, and Issue Framing Effects," *Journal of Politics* 72 (July 2010): 630–645; Charles S. Taber, Damon Cann, and Simona Kucsova, "The Motivated Processing of Political Arguments," *Political Behavior* 31 (June 2009): 137–155; Charles S. Taber and Milton Lodge, "Motivated Skepticism in the Evaluation of Political Beliefs," *American Journal of Political Science* 50 (July 2006): 755–769; John T. Jost, "The End of the End of Ideology," *American Psychologist* 61, no. 7 (2006): 651–670; Richard R. Lau and David P. Redlawsk, *How Voters Decide: Information Processing in Election Campaigns* (New York: Cambridge University Press, 2006); Milton Lodge and Charles S. Taber, "The Automaticity of Affect for Political Leaders, Groups, and Issues: An Experimental Test of the Hot Cognition Hypothesis," *Political Psychology* 26 (June 2005): 455–482; David P. Redlawsk, "Hot Cognition or Cool Consideration: Testing the Effects of Motivated Reasoning on Political Decision Making," *Journal of Politics* 64 (November 2002): 1021–1044; Ziva Kunda, "Motivated Inference: Self-Serving Generation and Evaluation of Causal Theories," *Journal of Personality and Social Psychology* 53 (No. 4, 1987): 636–647; Milton Lodge and Ruth Hamill, "A Partisan Schema for Political Information Processing," *American Political Science Review* 80 (June 1986): 505–519; Charles Lord, Lee Ross, and Mark R. Lepper, "Biased Assimilation and Attitude Polarization: The Effects of Prior Theories on Subsequently Considered Evidence," *Journal of Personality and Social Psychology* 37 (November 1979): 2098–2109; Robert P. Abelson, Elliot Ed Aronson, William J. McGuire, Theodore M. Newcomb, Milton J. Rosenberg, and Percy H. Tannenbaum, *Theories of Cognitive Consistency: A Sourcebook* (Chicago: Rand-McNally, 1968); and Leon Festinger, *A Theory of Cognitive Dissonance* (Palo Alto: Stanford University Press, 1957).

59. Donald P. Green, Bradley Palmquist, and Eric Schickler, *Partisan Hearts and Minds* (New Haven, CT: Yale University Press, 2002); and Alan S. Gerber, Gregory A. Huber, and Ebonya Washington, "Party Affiliation, Partisanship, and Political Beliefs: A Field Experiment," *American Political Science Review* 104 (November 2012): 720–744.

60. Jennifer Jerit and Jason Barabas, "Partisan Perceptual Bias and the Information Environment," *Journal of Politics* 74 (July 2012): 672–684.

61. Stephen N. Goggin and Alexander G. Theodoridis, "Seeing Red (or Blue): How Party Identity Colors Political Cognition," *The Forum* 16 (No. 1, 2018): 81–95; Alexander G. Theodoridis, "Me, Myself, and (I), (D), or (R)?"; Stephen N. Goggin and Alexander G. Theodoridis, "Disputed Ownership: Parties, Issues, and Traits in the Minds of Voters," *Political Behavior* 39 (September 2017): 675–702; Jerit and Barabas, "Partisan Perceptual Bias and the Information Environment"; Taber and Lodge, "Motivated Skepticism in the Evaluation of Political Beliefs"; Larry M. Bartels, "Beyond the Running Tally: Partisan Bias in Political Perceptions," *Political Behavior* 24 (June 2002): 117–150; Ziva Kundra and Lisa Sinclair, "Motivated Reasoning with Stereotypes: Activation, Application, and Inhibition," *Psychological Inquiry* 10 (No. 1, 1999): 12–22; and Redlawsk, "Hot Cognition or Cool Consideration?"

62. Gary C. Jacobson, *A Divider, Not a Uniter: George W. Bush and the American Public*, 3rd ed. (New York: Longman, 2011); Brian J. Gaines, James H. Kuklinski, Paul J. Quirk, Buddy Peyton, and Jay Verkuilen, "Same Facts, Different Interpretations: Partisan Motivation and Opinion on Iraq," *Journal of Politics* 69 (November 2007): 957–974; Edwards, *Governing by Campaigning*, chapter 3; and Steven Kull, Clay Ramsay, and Evan Lewis, "Misperceptions, the Media, and the Iraq War," *Political Science Quarterly* 118 (Winter 2003–2004): 569–598.

63. Alan S. Gerber and Gregory A. Huber, "Partisanship, Political Control, and Economic Assessments," *American Journal of Political Science* 54 (January 2010): 153–173; and Suzanna DeBoef and Paul M. Kellstedt, "The Political (and Economic) Origins of Consumer Confidence," *American Journal of Political Science* 48 (October 2004): 633–649.

64. Toby Bolsen, James N. Druckman, and Fay Lomax Cook, "The Influence of Partisan Motivated Reasoning on Public Opinion," *Political Behavior* 36 (June 2014): 235–262.

65. Matthew J. Lebo and Daniel Cassino, "The Aggregated Consequences of Motivated Reasoning and the Dynamics of Partisan Presidential Approval," *Political Psychology* 28 (December 2007): 719–746; and Edwards, *On Deaf Ears*, chapter 9.

66. Kate Kenski and Natalie Jomini Stroud, "Who Watches Presidential Debates? A Comparative Analysis of Presidential Debate Viewing in 2000 and 2004," *American Behavioral Scientist* 49 (October 2005): 213–228; Lee Sigelman and Carol K. Sigelman, "Judgments of the Carter-Reagan Debate: The Eyes of the Beholders," *Public Opinion Quarterly* 48 (January 1984): 624–628; and Sidney Kraus, *The Great Debates: Background, Perspective, Effects* (Bloomington: Indiana University Press, 1962).

67. Nicholas D. Duran, Stephen P. Nicholson, and Rick Dale, "The Hidden Appeal and Aversion to Political Conspiracies as Revealed in the Response Dynamics of Partisans," *Journal of Experimental Social Psychology* 73 (November 2017): 268–278.

68. Paul D. Sweeney and Kathy L. Gruber, "Selective Exposure: Voter Information Preferences and the Watergate Affair," *Journal of Personality and Social Psychology* 46, no. 6 (1984): 1208–1221; and Mark Fischle, "Mass Response to the Lewinsky Scandal: Motivated Reasoning or Bayesian Updating?" *Political Psychology* 21 (March 2000): 135–159.

69. See Howard Lavine, Christopher Johnston, and Marco Steenbergen, *The Ambivalent Partisan* (Oxford, UK: Oxford University Press 2012); Brendan Nyhan and Jason Reifler, *Misinformation and Fact-Checking: Research Findings from Social Science* (Washington, DC: New America Foundation, 2012); Paul Goren, Christopher M. Federico, and Miki Caul Kittilson, "Source Cues, Partisan Identities, and Political Value Expression," *American Journal of Political Science* 55 (October 2009): 805–820; Bartels, "Beyond the Running Tally"; Christopher H. Achen and Larry M. Bartels, "It Feels Like We're Thinking: The Rationalizing Voter and Electoral Democracy," paper delivered at the Annual Meeting of the American Political Science Association, Philadelphia, 2006; and Larry M. Bartels, *Unequal Democracy* (Princeton, NJ: Princeton University Press, 2008), chapter 5.

70. Alison Kodjak, "We Asked People What They Know about Obamacare. See If You Know the Answers," NPR, April 3, 2017; and YouGov.com poll, April 18–20, 2015.

71. CBS News poll, June 15–18, 2917.

72. Steven P. Nawara, "Who Is Responsible, the Incumbent or the Former President? Motivated Reasoning in Responsibility Attributions," *Presidential Studies Quarterly* 45 (March 2015): 110–131. See also Martin Bisgaard, "Bias Will Find a Way: Economic Perceptions, Attributions of Blame, and Partisan-Motivated Reasoning during Crisis," *Journal of Politics* 77 (July 2015): 849–860.

73. Adam J. Berinsky, *In Time of War: Understanding American Public Opinion from World War II to Iraq* (Chicago, IL: University of Chicago Press, 2009), p. 124.

74. See Logan Dancey and Geoffrey Sheagley, "Heuristics Behaving Badly: Party Cues and Voter Knowledge," *American Journal of Political Science* 57 (April 2013): 312–325; and Bisgaard, "Bias Will Find a Way."

75. See, e.g., Jennifer L. Merolla and Elizabeth J. Zechmeister, "Evaluating Political Leaders in Times of Terror and Economic Threat: The Conditioning Influence of Politician Partisanship," *Journal of Politics* 75 (July 2013): 599–612; and Lebo and Cassino, "The Aggregated Consequences of Motivated Reasoning," 719–746.

76. Jacobson, *A Divider, Not a Uniter*, 2nd ed.

77. Gallup poll at www.gallup.com/poll/116479/Barack-Obama-Presidential-Job-Approval.aspx.

78. Gallup poll.

79. Gallup poll.

80. Jeremy Diamond, "Trump: I Could 'Shoot Somebody and I Wouldn't Lose Voters'," CNN.com, January 24, 2016.

81. Douglas Kriner and Lima Schwartz, "Partisan Dynamics and the Volatility of Presidential Approval," *British Journal of Political Science* 39 (July 2009): 609–631.

82. David O. Sears, "Political Socialization," in *Micropolitical Theory*, vol. 2 of *The Handbook of Political Science*, eds. Fred I. Greenstein and Nelson Polsby (Reading, MA: Addison-Wesley, 1975), p. 177.

83. "Remarks of the President at a Meeting with Non-Washington Editors and Broadcasters," *White House Transcript*, September 21, 1979, pp. 11–12.

84. See, e.g., "Trump Has Met the Public's Modest Expectations for His Presidency," Pew Research Center, August 23, 2018.

85. See, e.g., *Gallup Opinion Index*, November 1978, pp. 8–9.

86. See, e.g., The Pew Research Center for the People and the Press survey of January 30–February 2, 1998. See also Gallup poll of March 20–22, 1998.

87. Brian Newman, "Presidential Traits and Job Approval: Some Aggregate-Level Evidence," *Presidential Studies Quarterly*, 34 (June 2004): 437–448; and Brian Newman, "Integrity and Presidential Approval, 1980–2000," *Public Opinion Quarterly* 67 (Fall 2003): 335–367.

88. Gallup poll, July 5–9, 2017. See also HuffPost/YouGov poll, June 29–30, 2017; and *Washington Post*–ABC News poll, July 10–13, 2017.

89. Fox News poll, August 27–29, 2017.

90. See, e.g., HuffPost/YouGov poll, June 29–30, 2017; Pew Research Center polls, August 15–21, 2017, August 8–21, 2017, April 25–May 1, 2018, and July 30–August 12, 2018, and September 18–24, 2018; *Washington Post*–ABC News polls, April 17–20, 2017, January 9–14, 2019, and January 21–24, 2019; and *Washington Post* Fact Checker poll, November 29–December 10, 2018.

91. Jeffrey E. Cohen, "Interest Groups and Presidential Approval," *Presidential Studies Quarterly* 42 (September 2012): 431–454.

92. Philip E. Converse, "The Nature of Belief Systems in Mass Publics," in *Ideology and Discontent*, ed. David Apter (New York: Free Press, 1964), pp. 206–261.

93. Scott Sigmund Gartner, "The Multiple Effects of Casualties on Public Support for War: An Experimental Approach," *American Political Science Review* 102 (March 2008): 95–105.

94. Charles W. Ostrom Jr. and Dennis M. Simon, "The President's Public," *American Journal of Political Science* 32 (November 1988): 1096–1119.

95. Stimson, *Public Opinion in America*, pp. 24–25.

96. Clyde Wilcox and Dee Allsop, "Economic and Foreign Policy as Sources of Reagan Support," *Western Political Quarterly* 44 (December 1991): 941–958; David J. Lanoue, *From Camelot to the Teflon President* (New York: Greenwood Press, 1988); Richard R. Lau, "Two Explanations for Negativity Effect in Political Behavior," *American Journal of Political Science* 29 (February 1985): 119–138; Samuel Kernell, "Presidential Popularity and Negative Voting: An Alternative Explanation of the Midterm Congressional Decline of the President's Party," *American Political Science Review* 71 (March 1977): 44–66; and Howard S. Bloom and H. Douglas Price, "Voter Response to Short-Run Economic Conditions: The Asymmetric Effect of Prosperity and Recession," *American Political Science Review* 69 (December 1975): 1240–1254. However, compare Morris P. Fiorina and Kenneth A. Shepsle, "Is Negative Voting an Artifact?" *American Journal of Political Science* 33 (May 1989): 423–439.

97. Bradley Dickerson, "Economic Perceptions, Presidential Approval, and Causality: The Moderating Role of the Economic Context," *American Politics Research* 44 (November 2016): 1037–1065;

Lanoue, *From Camelot to the Teflon President*; and George C. Edwards III, "Comparing Chief Executives," *Public Opinion*, June/July 1985, p. 54.

98. Ostrom and Simon, "The President's Public."

99. See, e.g., Jon Hurwitz and Mark Peffley, "The Means and Ends of Foreign Policy as Determinants of Presidential Support," *American Journal of Political Science* 31 (May 1987): 236–258.

100. Thomas J. Rudolph, "The Meaning and Measurement of Responsibility Attributions," *American Politics Research* 44 (January 2016): 106–130; Alex I. Ruder, "Agency Design, the Mass Media, and the Blame for Agency Scandals," *Presidential Studies Quarterly* 45 (September 2015): 514–539; Travis M. Johnston and Stephen N. Goggin, "Presidential Confidence in Crisis: Blame, Media, and the BP Oil Spill," *Presidential Studies Quarterly* 45 (September 2015): 467–489; Thomas J. Rudolph, "Who's Responsible for the Economy? The Formation and Consequences of Responsibility Attributions," *American Journal of Political Science* 47 (October 2003): 698–713; Stephen P. Nicholson, Gary M. Segura, and Nathan D. Woods, "Presidential Approval and the Mixed Blessing of Divided Government," *Journal of Politics* 64 (August 2002): 701–720; Shanto Iyengar, *Is Anyone Responsible?* (Chicago, IL: University of Chicago Press, 1992), chapter 8; and Shanto Iyengar, "Television News and Citizens' Explanations of National Affairs," *American Political Science Review* 81 (September 1987): 815–831.

101. Paul Sniderman and Richard A. Brody, "Coping: The Ethic of Self-Reliance," *American Journal of Political Science* 21 (August 1977): 501–522; and Richard A. Brody and Paul Sniderman, "From Life Space to Polling Place," *British Journal of Political Science* 7 (July 1977): 337–360. See also Stanley Feldman, "Economic Self-Interest, and Political Behavior," *American Journal of Political Science* 26 (August 1982): 449–452; and Kay L. Schlozman and Sidney Verba, *Injury to Insult: Unemployment, Class, and Political Response* (Cambridge, MA: Harvard University Press, 1979).

102. Neil Malhotra and Alexander G. Kuo, "Attributing Blame: The Public's Response to Hurricane Katrina," *Journal of Politics* 70 (January 2008): 120–135; K. Jill Kiecolt, "Group Consciousness and the Attribution of Blame for National Economic Problems," *American Politics Quarterly* 15 (April 1987): 203–222; and Iyengar, *Is Anyone Responsible?* p. 80. But see Michael W. Sances, "Attribution Errors in Federalist Systems: When Voters Punish the President for Local Tax Increases," *Journal of Politics* 79 (October 2017): 1286–1301.

103. See Edwards, *The Public Presidency*, chapter 6; George C. Edwards III, *Presidential Approval* (Baltimore, MD: Johns Hopkins University Press, 1990), and sources cited therein; and Martha Joynt Kumar, *Managing the President's Message: The White House Communications Operation* (Baltimore, MD: Johns Hopkins University Press, 2007), p. 8.

104. See, e.g., Michael B. MacKuen, Robert S. Erikson, and James A. Stimson, "Peasants or Bankers? The American Electorate and the U.S. Economy," *American Political Science Review* 86 (September 1992): 597–611; Donald R. Kinder, "Presidents, Prosperity, and Public Opinion," *Public Opinion Quarterly* 45 (Spring 1981): 1–21; Richard Lau and David O. Sears, "Cognitive Links between Economic Grievances and Political Responses," *Political Behavior* 3, no. 4 (1981): 279–302; and Diana C. Mutz, "Mass Media and Depoliticization of Personal Experience," *American Journal of Political Science* 36 (May 1992): 495–496.

105. John E. Mueller, *War, Presidents, and Public Opinion* (New York: Wiley, 1970), pp. 208–213. See also B. Dan Wood, *Presidential Saber Rattling* (New York: Cambridge University Press, 2013).

106. See, e.g., Market Opinion Research, *Americans Talk Security*, no. 12 (January 1989): 31–32, 106.

107. George C. Edwards III and Tami Swenson, "Who Rallies? The Anatomy of a Rally Event," *Journal of Politics* 59 (February 1997): 200–212; and Matthew A. Baum, "The Constituent Foundations of the Rally-Round-the-Flag Phenomenon," *International Studies Quarterly* 46 (2002): 263–298.

108. Jonathan McDonald Ladd, "Predispositions and Public Support for the President during the War on Terrorism," *Public Opinion Quarterly* 71 (Winter 2007): 511–538.

109. Tim Groeling and Matthew A. Baum, "Crossing the Water's Edge: Elite Rhetoric, Media Coverage, and the Rally-Round-the-Flag Phenomenon," *Journal of Politics* 70 (October 2008): 1065–1085.

CHAPTER 6

1. Franklin Roosevelt and Theodore Roosevelt, quoted in Emmett John Hughes, "Presidency vs. Jimmy Carter," *Fortune*, December 4, 1978, pp. 62, 64; italics added for emphasis.

2. One scholar counted only four times when Roosevelt used a fireside chat to discuss legislation under consideration in Congress. See Elmer E. Cornwell, Jr., *Presidential Leadership of Public Opinion* (Bloomington: Indiana University Press, 1965), p. 263.

3. George C. Edwards III, *On Deaf Ears: The Limits of the Bully Pulpit* (New Haven, CT: Yale University Press, 2003), chapters 4–5.

4. John R. Zaller, *The Nature and Origins of Mass Opinion* (New York: Cambridge University Press, 1992), pp. 102–113; and Danielle Shani, "Knowing Your Colors: Can Knowledge Correct for Partisan Bias in Political Perceptions?" (paper presented at the annual meeting of the Midwest Political Science Association, Chicago, 2006).

5. Ryan L. Claassen and Benjamin Highton, "Does Policy Debate Reduce Information Effects in Public Opinion? Analyzing the Evolution of Public Opinion on Health Care," *Journal of Politics* 68 (May 2006): 410–420.

6. Zaller, *The Nature and Origins of Mass Opinion*, p. 48; William G. Jacoby, "The Sources of Liberal–Conservative Thinking: Education and Conceptualization," *Political Behavior* 10 (December 1988): 316–332; Robert C. Luskin, "Measuring Political Sophistication," *American Journal of Political Science* 31 (November 1987): 856–899; W. Russell Neuman, *The Paradox of Mass Politics: Knowledge and Opinion in the American Electorate* (Cambridge, MA: Harvard University Press, 1986); Edward G. Carmines and James A. Stimson, "The Two Faces of Issue Voting," *American Political Science Review* 74 (March 1980): 78–91; and Philip E. Converse, "The Nature of Belief Systems in Mass Publics," in David E. Apter, ed., *Ideology and Discontent* (New York: Free Press, 1964), pp. 206–261.

7. John G. Bullock, "Elite Influence on Public Opinion in an Informed Electorate," *American Political Science Review* 105 (August 2011): 496–515.

8. James N. Druckman, Erik Peterson, and Rune Slothuus, "How Elite Partisan Polarization Affects Public Opinion Formation," *American Political Science Review* 107 (February 2013): 57–79; Geoffrey C. Layman, Thomas M. Carsey, John C. Green, Richard Herrera, and Rosalyn Cooperman, "Activists and Conflict Extension in American Party Politics," *American Political Science Review* 107 (June 2013): 324–346; Gabriel S. Lenz, *Follow the Leader? How Voters Respond to Politicians' Policies and Performance* (Chicago, IL: University of Chicago Press, 2012); and Matthew Levendusky, *The Partisan Sort* (Chicago, IL: University of Chicago Press, 2009). See also Joshua Dyck and Shanna Pearson-Merkowitz, "To Know You Is Not Necessarily to Love You: The Partisan Mediators of Intergroup Contact," *Political Behavior* 36 (September 2014): 553–580.

9. Logan Dancey and Paul Goren, "Party Identification, Issue Attitudes, and the Dynamics of Political Debate," *American Journal of Political Science* 54 (July 2010): 686–699.

10. Howard Lavine, Christopher Johnston, and Marco Steenbergen, *The Ambivalent Partisan* (Oxford, UK: Oxford University Press, 2012).

11. Toby Bolsen, James N. Druckman, and Fay Lomax Cook, "The Influence of Partisan Motivated Reasoning on Public Opinion," *Political Behavior* 36 (June 2014): 235–262; and Michael Bang Petersen, Martin Skov, Søren Serritzlew, and Thomas Ramsøy, "Motivated Reasoning and Political Parties: Evidence for Increased Processing in the Face of Party Cues," *Political Behavior* 35 (December 2013): 831–854.

12. Stephen P. Nicholson, "Polarizing Cues," *American Journal of Political Science* 56 (January 2012): 52–66; and Joanne R. Smith, Deborah J. Terry, Timothy R. Crosier, and Julie M. Duck, "The Importance of the Relevance of the Issue to the Group in Voting Intentions," *Basic and Applied Social Psychology* 27, no. 2 (2005): 163–170.

13. Druckman, Peterson, and Slothuus, "How Elite Partisan Polarization Affects Public Opinion Formation." Party endorsements, particularly under conditions of polarization, do not appear to serve simply as cues people follow. Instead, cues seem to shape how the public views arguments put forth by different sides. See also Bolsen, Druckman, and Cook, "The Influence of Partisan Motivated Reasoning on Public Opinion." But see Cheryl Boudreau and Scott A. MacKenzie, "Informing the Electorate? How Party Cues and Policy Information Affect Public Opinion about Initiatives," *American Journal of Political Science* 58 (January 2014): 48–62.

14. Penny S. Visser, George Y. Bizer, and Jon A. Krosnick, "Exploring the Latent Structure of Strength-Related Attitude Attributes," in Mark P. Zanna, ed., *Advances in Experimental Social Psychology*, vol. 38 (San Diego, CA: Academic Press, 2006).

15. Michael Tesler, "Priming Predispositions and Changing Policy Positions: An Account of When Mass Opinion Is Primed or Changed," *American Journal of Political Science* 59 (October 2015): 806–824; and Lenz, *Follow the Leader?*

16. See Druckman, Peterson, and Slothuus, "How Elite Partisan Polarization Affects Public Opinion Formation."

17. Bolsen, Druckman, and Cook, "The Influence of Partisan Motivated Reasoning on Public Opinion"; Michael Bang Petersen, Martin Skov, Søren Serritzlew, and Thomas Ramsøy, "Motivated Reasoning

and Political Parties: Evidence for Increased Processing in the Face of Party Cues," *Political Behavior* 35 (December 2013): 831–854.

18. Lavine, Johnston, and Steenbergen, *The Ambivalent Partisan.*

19. Donald R. Kinder and Nathan P. Kalmoe, *Neither Liberal Nor Conservative: Ideological Innocence in the American Public* (Chicago, IL: University of Chicago Press, 2017).

20. Michael Barber and Jeremy C. Pope, "Does Party Trump Ideology? Disentangling Party and Ideology in America," *American Political Science Review* 113 (February 2019): 38–54.

21. David Kahneman and Amos Tversky, "Prospect Theory: An Analysis of Decision under Risk," *Econometrica* 47 (March 1979): 263–292; and David Kahneman and Amos Tversky, "Choices, Values, and Frames," *American Psychologist* 39 (April 1984): 341–350.

22. Stuart N. Soroka, *Negativity in Democratic Politics* (New York: Cambridge University Press, 2014); Susan T. Fiske, "Attention and Weight in Person Perception: The Impact of Negative and Extreme Behavior," *Journal of Personality and Social Psychology* 38, no. 6 (1980): 889–906; and David L. Hamilton and Mark P. Zanna, "Differential Weighting of Favorable and Unfavorable Attributes in Impressions of Personality," *Journal of Experimental Research in Personality* 6, nos. 2–3 (1972): 204–212.

23. Richard Lau, "Two Explanations for Negativity Effects in Political Behavior," *American Journal of Political Science* 29 (February 1985): 119–138.

24. See, e.g., David W. Brady and Daniel P. Kessler, "Who Supports Health Reform?" *PS: Political Science and Politics* 43 (January 2010): 1–5; and Michael D. Cobb and James H. Kuklinski, "Changing Minds: Political Arguments and Political Persuasion," *American Journal of Political Science* 41 (January 1997): 88–121.

25. Kevin Arceneaux, "Cognitive Biases and the Strength of Political Arguments," *American Journal of Political Science* 56 (April 2012): 271–285; Michael MacKuen, Jennifer Wolak, Luke Keele, and George E. Marcus, "Civic Engagements: Resolute Partisanship or Reflective Deliberation," *American Journal of Political Science* 54 (April 2010): 440–458; Joanne M. Miller, "Examining the Mediators of Agenda Setting: A New Experimental Paradigm Reveals the Role of Emotions," *Political Psychology* 28 (December 2007): 689–717; George E. Marcus, *The Sentimental Citizen* (University Park: Pennsylvania State University Press, 2002); George E. Marcus, W. Russell Neuman, and Michael MacKuen, *Affective Intelligence and Political Judgment* (Chicago, IL: University of Chicago Press, 2000); Michael MacKuen, Jennifer Wolak, Luke Keele, and George E. Marcus, "Civic Engagements: Resolute Partisanship or Reflective Deliberation," *American Journal of Political Science* 54 (April 2010): 440–458; and Cobb and Kuklinski, "Changing Minds: Political Arguments and Political Persuasion."

26. See George C. Edwards III, *The Bungler: The Leadership of Donald Trump* (forthcoming, 2020), chapter 4.

27. James H. Kuklinski, Paul J. Quirk, Jennifer Jerit, David Schwieder, and Robert F. Rich, "Misinformation and the Currency of Democratic Citizenship," *Journal of Politics* 62 (August 2000): 790–816. See also Brendan Nyhan, "Why the 'Death Panel' Myth Wouldn't Die: Misinformation in the Health Care Reform Debate," *Forum* 8, no. 1 (2010). Accessed at www.bepress.com/forum/vol8/iss1/art5.

28. Brendan Nyhan and Jason Reifler, "When Corrections Fail: The Persistence of Political Misperceptions," *Political Behavior* 32 (June 2010): 303–330; and David P. Redlawsk, Andrew J. W. Civettini, and Karen M. Emmerson, "The Affective Tipping Point: Do Motivated Reasoners Ever 'Get It'?" *Political Psychology* 31 (August 2010): 563–593.

29. Logan Dancey and Paul Goren, "Party Identification, Issue Attitudes, and the Dynamics of Political Debate," *American Journal of Political Science* 54 (July 2010): 686–699; Martin Bisgaard, "Bias Will Find a Way: Economic Perceptions, Attributions of Blame, and Partisan-Motivated Reasoning during Crisis," *Journal of Politics* 77 (July 2015): 849–860.

30. Ruth Mayo, Yaacov Schul, and Eugene Burnstein, "'I Am Not Guilty' vs 'I Am Innocent': Successful Negation May Depend on the Schema Used for Its Encoding," *Journal of Experimental Social Psychology* 40 (July 2004): 433–449.

31. Norbert Schwarz, Lawrence J. Sanna, Ian Skurnik, and Carolyn Yoon, "Metacognitive Experiences and the Intricacies of Setting People Straight: Implications for Debiasing and Public Information Campaigns," *Advances in Experimental Social Psychology* 39 (2007): 127–161; and Ian Skurnik, Carolyn Yoon, Denise C. Park, and Norbert Schwarz, "How Warnings about False Claims Become Recommendations," *Journal of Consumer Research* 31 (March 2005): 713–724.

32. John Bullock, "Experiments on Partisanship and Public Opinion: Party Cues, False Beliefs, and Bayesian Updating" (PhD dissertation, Stanford University, 2007).

33. Jeffrey J. Mondak, "Source Cues and Public Approval: The Cognitive Dynamics of Public Support for the Reagan Administration," *American Journal of Political Science* 37 (February 1993): 186–212.

34. On the importance of source credibility, see James N. Druckman, "On the Limits of Framing Effects: Who Can Frame?" *Journal of Politics* 63 (November 2001): 1041–1066; James N. Druckman, "Using Credible Advice to Overcome Framing Effects," *Journal of Law, Economics, and Organization* 17, no. 1 (2001): 62–82; Joanne M. Miller and Jon A. Krosnick, "News Media Impact on the Ingredients of Presidential Evaluations: Politically Knowledgeable Citizens Are Guided by a Trusted Source," *American Journal of Political Science* 44 (April 2000): 301–315; James H. Kuklinski and Norman Hurley, "On Hearing and Interpreting Messages: A Cautionary Tale of Citizen Cue-Taking," *Journal of Politics* 56 (August 1994): 729–751; and Zaller, *The Nature and Origins of Mass Opinion,* pp. 42–48.

35. James N. Druckman and Toby Bolsen, "Framing, Motivated Reasoning, and Opinions about Emergent Technologies," *Journal of Communication* 61 (August 2011): 659–688.

36. Lenz, *Follow the Leader?*

37. Marc J. Hetherington and Thomas J. Rudolph, *Why Washington Won't Work* (Chicago, IL: University of Chicago Press, 2015).

38. See, e.g., Markus Prior, *Post-Broadcast Democracy: How Media Choice Increases Inequality in Political Involvement and Polarizes Elections* (New York: Cambridge University Press, 2007); Neuman, *The Paradox of Mass Politics,* pp. 170, 172, 177–178, 186.

39. Joe S. Foote, "Ratings Decline of Presidential Television," *Journal of Broadcasting and Electronic Media* 32 (Spring 1988): 225; A. C. Nielsen, *Nielsen Newscast* (Northbrook, IL: Nielson, 1975); Edwards, *On Deaf Ears,* chapter 8; George C. Edwards III, *Governing by Campaigning,* 2nd ed. (New York: Longman, 2007), pp. 86–94.

40. Jeffrey E. Cohen, *The Presidency in the Era of 24-Hour News* (Princeton, NJ: Princeton University Press, 2008); and Matthew A. Baum and Samuel Kernell, "Has Cable Ended the Golden Age of Presidential Television?" *American Political Science Review* 93 (March 1999): 99–114.

41. Markus Prior, "News vs. Entertainment: How Increasing Media Choice Widens Gaps in Political Knowledge and Turnout," *American Journal of Political Science* 49 (July 2005): 577–592; and Baum and Kernell, "Has Cable Ended the Golden Age of Presidential Television?"; "Changing Channels: Americans View Just 17 Channels Despite Record Number to Choose From," Nielsen Company, May 6, 2014.

42. Edwards, *On Deaf Ears,* chapter 6.

43. See Lori Cox Han, "New Strategies for an Old Medium: The Weekly Radio Addresses of Reagan and Clinton," *Congress & the Presidency* 33 (Spring 2006): 25–45.

44. Beverly Horvit, Adam J. Schiffer, and Mark Wright, "The Limits of Presidential Coverage of the Weekly Radio Address," *Press/Politics* 13, no. 1 (2008): 8–28.

45. Scott Rasmussen, "60 Percent of U.S. Adults Underestimate Size of Personal Tax Cuts," *Ballotpedia,* September 21, 2018.

46. HuffPost/YouGov poll, February 5–7, 2018.

47. Pew Research Center poll, March 7–14, 2018.

48. Martha Joynt Kumar, *Managing the President's Message: The White House Communications Operation* (Baltimore, MD: Johns Hopkins University Press, 2007), p. 9; and James N. Druckman and Lawrence R. Jacobs, *Who Governs? Presidents, Public Opinion, and Manipulation* (Chicago, IL: University of Chicago Press, 2015), chapter 5.

49. Dennis Chong and James N. Druckman, "Dynamic Public Opinion: Communication Effects over Time," *American Political Science Review* 104 (November 2010): 663–680; Douglas A. Hibbs Jr., "Implications of the 'Bread and Peace' Model for the 2008 Presidential Election," *Public Choice* 137 (October 2008): 1–10; Seth J. Hill, James Lo, Lynn Vavreck, and John Zaller, "The Duration of Advertising Effects in the 2000 Presidential Campaign" (paper presented at the 2008 Annual Meeting of the American Political Science Association, Boston); Dennis Chong and James N. Druckman, "A Theory of Framing and Opinion Formation in Competitive Elite Environments," *Journal of Communication* 57 (February 2007): 99–118; Alan Gerber, James G. Gimpel, Donald P. Green, and Daron R. Shaw, "The Influence of Television and Radio Advertising on Candidate Evaluations: Results from a Large-Scale Randomized Experiment" (paper presented at the 2007 Annual Meeting of the Midwest Political Science Association, Chicago); Diana C. Mutz and Byron Reeves, "The New Videomalaise: Effects of Televised Incivility on Political Trust," *American Political Science Review* 99 (February 2005): 1–15; Claes H. de Vreese, "Primed by the Euro," *Scandinavian Political Studies* 27 (March 2004): 45–65; James N. Druckman and Kjersten R. Nelson, "Framing and Deliberation: How Citizens' Conversations Limit Elite Influence," *American Journal of Political Science* 47 (October 2003): 729–745; and David Tewksbury,

Jennifer Jones, Matthew W. Peske, Ashlea Raymond, and William Vig, "The Interaction of News and Advocate Frames: Manipulating Audience Perceptions of a Local Public Policy Issue," *Journalism and Mass Communication Quarterly* 77 (December 2000): 804–829.

50. On the importance of repetition in strengthening and increasing confidence in attitudes, see James N. Druckman and Toby Bolsen, "Framing, Motivated Reasoning, and Opinions about Emergent Technologies," *Journal of Communication* 61 (August 2011): 659–688; Wesley G. Moons, Diane Mackie, and Teresa Garcia-Marques, "The Impact of Repetition-Induced Familiarity on Agreement with Weak and Strong Arguments," *Journal of Personality and Social Psychology* 96 (January 2009): 32–44; Michele P. Claibourn, "Making a Connection: Repetition and Priming in Presidential Campaigns," *Journal of Politics* 70 (October 2008): 1142–1159; Richard Johnston, Michael G. Hagen, and Kathleen Hall Jamieson, *The 2000 Presidential Election and the Foundations of Party Politics* (New York: Cambridge University Press, 2004); Daron R. Shaw, "The Effect of TV Ads and Candidate Appearances on Statewide Presidential Votes, 1988–96," *American Political Science Review* 93 (June 1999): 345–361; Prashant Malaviya and Brian Sternthal, "The Persuasive Impact of Message Spacing," *Journal of Consumer Psychology* 6, no. 3 (1997): 233–255; Ida E. Berger, "The Nature of Attitude Accessibility and Attitude Confidence," *Journal of Consumer Psychology* 1, no. 2 (1992): 103–123; and John T. Cacioppo and Richard E. Petty, "Effects of Message Repetition on Argument Processing, Recall, and Persuasion," *Basic and Applied Social Psychology* 10, no. 1 (1989): 3–12.

51. David Gergen, *Eyewitness to Power: The Essence of Leadership* (New York: Simon & Schuster, 2000), pp. 54, 186. Also see Kumar, *Managing the President's Message*, chapters 2–3.

52. "Remarks by President Bush in a Conversation on Strengthening Social Security," Greece, New York, March 24, 2005.

53. See George C. Edwards III, *The Strategic President: Persuasion and Opportunity in Presidential Leadership* (Princeton, NJ: Princeton University Press, 2009), pp. 96–104.

54. Mark Hertsgaard, *On Bended Knee: The Press and the Reagan Presidency* (New York: Farrar, Straus, and Giroux, 1988), pp. 107–108; Larry Speakes, *Speaking Out* (New York: Scribner's, 1988), p. 301; James A. Baker III, *"Work Hard, Study … and Keep Out of Politics!"* (New York: G. P. Putnam's Sons, 2006), pp. 132–133, 136–137, 148, 171; and Lou Cannon, *President Reagan: The Role of a Lifetime* (New York: Simon & Schuster, 1991), pp. 163, 344.

55. Bill Clinton, *My Life* (London: Hutchison, 2004), p. 467.

56. Quoted in Dan Balz, "For Obama, a Tough Year to Get the Message Out," *Washington Post*, January 10, 2010.

57. Daniel Pfeiffer, *Yes We (Still) Can* (New York: Twelve, 2018), p. 79.

58. George Packer, "Obama's Lost Year," *New Yorker*, March 15, 2010, p. 46.

59. See, e.g., Matthew Eshbaugh-Soha and Jeffrey S. Peake, *Breaking through the Noise* (Stanford, CA: Stanford University Press, 2011); and Matthew Eshbaugh-Soha and Thomas Miles, "Presidential Speeches and the Stages of the Legislative Process," *Congress & the Presidency* 38 (September–December 2011): 301–321.

60. Gergen, *Eyewitness to Power*, p. 54.

61. Ibid.

62. Christopher Olds, "Assessing Presidential Agenda-Setting Capacity: Dynamic Comparisons of Presidential, Mass Media, and Public Attention to Economic Issues," *Congress & the Presidency* 40 (September–December 2013): 255–284; and Jeffrey E. Cohen, *Presidential Responsiveness and Public Policy-Making* (Ann Arbor: University of Michigan Press, 1997).

63. B. Dan Wood, *The Politics of Economic Leadership* (Princeton, NJ: Princeton University Press, 2007), chapter 3; and Kim Quaile Hill, "The Policy Agendas of the President and the Mass Public: A Research Validation and Extension," *American Journal of Political Science* 42 (October 1998): 1328–1334.

64. They may also direct public attention to popular policy stances to increase their general public support. See Druckman and Jacobs, *Who Governs?*

65. Brandice Canes-Wrone, *Who Leads Whom? Presidents, Policy, and the Public* (Princeton, NJ: Princeton University Press, 2006), p. 80, chapters 3–4.

66. See, e.g., Arthur Lupia, "Shortcuts versus Encyclopedias: Information and Voting Behavior in California Insurance Reform Elections," *American Political Science Review* 88 (March 1994): 63–76; Samuel L. Popkin, *The Reasoning Voter* (Chicago, IL: University of Chicago Press, 1991); Paul M. Sniderman, Richard Brody, and Philip E. Tetlock, *Reasoning and Choice* (New York: Cambridge University Press, 1991); Daniel Kahneman, Paul Slovic, and Amos Tversky, *Judgment under Uncertainty: Heuristics and Biases* (New York: Cambridge University Press, 1982); and Herbert A. Simon, "A Behavioral Model of Rational Choice," *Quarterly Journal of Economics* 69 (February 1955): 99–118.

67. Richard R. Lau, "Construct Accessibility and Electoral Choice," *Political Behavior* 11 (March 1989): 5–32; Thomas K. Srull and Robert S. Wyer, Jr., *Memory and Cognition in Their Social Context* (Hillsdale, NJ: Erlbaum, 1989); Robert S. Wyer Jr., and Jon Hartwick, "The Recall and Use of Belief Statements as Bases for Judgments," *Journal of Experimental Social Psychology* 20 (January 1984): 65–85; E. Tory Higgins and Gary A. King, "Accessibility of Social Constructs: Information-Processing Consequences of Individual and Contextual Variation," in N. Cantor and J. F. Kihlstrom, eds., *Personality, Cognition, and Social Interaction* (Hillsdale, NJ: Erlbaum, 1981); Thomas K. Srull and Robert S. Wyer, Jr., "Category Accessibility and Social Perception: Some Implications for the Study of Person Memory and Interpersonal Judgments," *Journal of Personality and Social Psychology* 38, no. 6 (1980): 841–856; and Thomas K. Srull and Robert S. Wyer, Jr., "The Role of Category Accessibility in the Interpretation of Information about Persons: Some Determinants and Implications," *Journal of Personality and Social Psychology* 37, no. 10 (1979): 1660–1672.

68. See, e.g., Donald R. Kinder and Lynn M. Sanders, *Divided by Color: Racial Politics and Democratic Ideals* (Chicago, IL: University of Chicago Press, 1996); Zhongdang Pan and Gerald M. Kosicki, "Framing Analysis: An Approach to News Discourse," *Political Communication* 10, no. 1 (1993): 55–75; William A. Gamson, *Talking Politics* (Cambridge, UK: Cambridge University Press, 1992); William A. Gamson and Andre Modigliani, "Media Discourse and Public Opinion on Nuclear Power: A Constructionist Approach," *American Journal of Sociology* 95 (July 1989): 1–37; and William A. Gamson and Andre Modigliani, "The Changing Culture of Affirmative Action," in Richard D. Braungart, ed., *Research in Political Sociology*, vol. 3 (Greenwich, CT: JAI Press, 1987), p. 143.

69. There is some evidence that the president's rhetoric can prime the criteria on which the public evaluates him. See James N. Druckman and Justin W. Holmes, "Does Presidential Rhetoric Matter? Priming and Presidential Approval," *Presidential Studies Quarterly* 34 (December 2004): 755–778.

70. Quoted in Gerald M. Boyd, "'General Contractor' of the White House Staff," *New York Times*, March 4, 1986, sec. A, p. 22.

71. For the view that framing does not work by altering the accessibility to different considerations, see James N. Druckman, "On the Limits of Framing Effects: Who Can Frame?" *Journal of Politics* 63 (November 2001): 1041–1066. See also Thomas E. Nelson, Rosalee A. Clawson, and Zoe M. Oxley, "Media Framing of a Civil Liberties Conflict and Its Effect on Tolerance," *American Political Science Review* 91 (September 1997): 567–584; and Joanne M. Miller and Jon A. Krosnick, "News Media Impact on the Ingredients of Presidential Evaluations: Politically Knowledgeable Citizens Are Guided by a Trusted Source," *American Journal of Political Science* 44 (April 2000): 301–315.

72. Over the past generation, the research on public opinion has produced a large number of studies showing the impact of priming and framing on people's opinions. For evidence of the impact of framing effects, see John Sides, "Stories or Science? Facts, Frames, and Policy Attitudes," *American Politics Research* 44 (May 2016): 387–414; Samara Klar, "The Influence of Competing Identity Primes on Political Preferences," *Journal of Politics* 75 (October 2013): 1108–1124; Dan Cassino and Cengiz Erisen, "Priming Bush and Iraq in 2008: A Survey Experiment," *American Politics Research* 38 (March 2010): 372–394; Nicholas J. G. Winter, "Beyond Welfare: Framing and the Racialization of White Opinion on Social Security," *American Journal of Political Science* 50 (April 2006): 400–420; Nicholas A. Valentino, Vincent L. Hutchings, and Ismail K. White, "Cues that Matter: How Political Ads Prime Racial Attitudes during Campaigns," *American Political Science Review* 96 (March 2002): 75–90; Thomas E. Nelson, "Policy Goals, Public Rhetoric, and Political Attitudes," *Journal of Politics* 66 (May 2004): 581–605; Valentino, Hutchings, and White, "Cues that Matter"; William G. Jacoby, "Issue Framing and Public Opinion on Government Spending," *American Journal of Political Science* 44 (October 2000): 750–767; Thomas E. Nelson and Zoe M. Oxley, "Issue Framing Effects on Belief Importance and Opinion," *Journal of Politics* 61 (November 1999): 1040–1067; Joseph N. Cappella and Kathleen Hall Jamieson, *Spiral of Cynicism: The Press and the Public Good* (New York: Oxford University Press, 1997); Thomas E. Nelson, Rosalee A. Clawson, and Zoe M. Oxley, "Toward a Psychology of Framing Effects," *Political Behavior* 19 (September 1997): 221–246; Nelson, Clawson, and Oxley, "Media Framing of a Civil Liberties Conflict and Its Effect on Tolerance"; Donald R. Kinder and Lynn M. Sanders, *Divided by Color: Racial Politics and Democratic Ideals* (Chicago, IL: University of Chicago Press, 1996); Thomas E. Nelson and Donald R. Kinder, "Issue Frames and Group-Centrism in American Public Opinion," *Journal of Politics* 58 (November 1996): 1055–1078; Dennis Chong, "How People Think, Reason, and Feel about Rights and Liberties," *American Journal of Political Science* 37 (August 1993): 867–899; W. Russell Neuman, Marion K. Just, and Ann N. Crigler, *Common Knowledge: News and the Construction of Political Meaning* (Chicago, IL: University of Chicago Press, 1992); John Zaller and Stanley Feldman, "A Simple Theory of the Survey Response: Answering Questions versus Revealing Preferences," *American Journal of Political*

Science 36 (August 1992): 579–616; Stanley Feldman and John Zaller, "The Political Culture of Ambivalence: Ideological Responses to the Welfare State," *American Journal of Political Science* 36 (February 1992): 268–307; Donald R. Kinder and Lynn M. Sanders, "Mimicking Political Debate with Survey Questions: The Case of White Opinion on Affirmative Action for Blacks," *Social Cognition* 8, no. 1 (1990): 73–103; Jon A. Krosnick and Donald R. Kinder, "Altering the Foundations of Support for the President through Priming," *American Political Science Review* 84 (June 1990): 497–512; John H. Aldrich, John Sullivan, and Eugene Borgida, "Foreign Affairs and Issue Voting: Do Presidential Candidates Waltz before a Blind Audience?" *American Political Science Review* 83 (March 1989): 123–141; Daniel Kahneman and Amos Tversky, "Rational Choice and the Framing of Decisions," in Hillel J. Einhorn and Robin M. Hogarth, eds., *Rational Choice: The Contrast between Economics and Psychology* (Chicago, IL: University of Chicago Press, 1987); Daniel Kahneman and Amos Tversky, "Choices, Values, and Frames," *American Psychologist* 39 (April 1984): 341–350; and Amos Tversky and Daniel Kahneman, "The Framing of Decisions and the Psychology of Choice," *Science* 211 (January 30, 1981): 453–458.

73. Druckman and Jacobs, *Who Governs?*, chapter 5.

74. For a good discussion of this point, see Lawrence R. Jacobs and Robert Y. Shapiro, *Politicians Don't Pander* (Chicago, IL: University of Chicago Press, 2000), pp. 49–52.

75. See Druckman and Jacobs, *Who Governs?*

76. "Remarks by the President on the Importance of Passing a Historic Energy Bill," White House Transcript, June 25, 2009.

77. See, e.g., William B. Riker, *The Art of Political Manipulation* (New Haven, CT: Yale University Press, 1986); William B. Riker, *The Strategy of Rhetoric: Campaigning for the American Constitution* (New Haven, CT: Yale University Press, 1996); and William B. Riker, "The Heresthetics of Constitution Making: The Presidency in 1787, with Comments on Determinism and Rational Choice," *American Political Science Review* 78 (March 1984): 1–16.

78. Byron E. Shafer and William J. M. Claggett, *The Two Majorities: The Issue Context of Modern American Politics* (Baltimore, MD: Johns Hopkins University Press, 1995). See also James N. Druckman, Lawrence R. Jacobs, and Eric Ostermeier, "Candidate Strategies to Prime Issues and Image," *Journal of Politics* 66 (November 2004): 1180–1202.

79. John R. Petrocik, "Divided Government: Is It All in the Campaigns?" in Gary W. Cox and Samuel Kernell, eds., *The Politics of Divided Government* (Boulder, CO: Westview, 1991); and John R. Petrocik, "Issue Ownership in Presidential Elections, with a 1980 Case Study," *American Journal of Political Science* (August 1996): 825–850.

80. Andrew Gelman and Gary King, "Why Are American Presidential Election Campaign Polls So Variable When Votes Are So Predictable?" *British Journal of Political Science* 23 (Part 4, 1993): 409–451.

81. See, e.g., Carl Albert, interview by Dorothy Pierce McSweeny, April 13, 1969, interview 3, transcript, pp. 8–9, Lyndon Johnson Library, Austin, Texas.

82. See, e.g., Richard P. Nathan et al., *Revenue Sharing: The Second Round* (Washington, DC: Brookings Institution, 1977).

83. Gergen, *Eyewitness to Power*, p. 348.

84. See Bryan D. Jones and Frank R. Baumgartner, *The Politics of Attention: How Government Prioritizes Problems* (Chicago, IL: University of Chicago Press, 2005), chapter 3; Bryan D. Jones, *Reconceiving Decision-Making in Democratic Politics* (Chicago, IL: University of Chicago Press, 1994), chapter 4; and E. E. Schattschneider, *The Semi-Sovereign People: A Realist's View of Democracy in America* (New York: Holt, Rinehart and Winston, 1960).

85. Quoted in Steven V. Roberts, "Return to the Land of the Gipper," *New York Times*, March 9, 1988, p. A28.

86. Ronald Reagan, *Where's the Rest of Me? The Autobiography of Ronald Reagan* (New York: Karz, 1965), p. 138.

87. Dennis Chong and James N. Druckman, "Counterframing Effects," *Journal of Politics* 75 (January 2013): 1–16; James N. Druckman, Jordan Fein, and Thomas J. Leeper, "A Source of Bias in Public Opinion Stability," *American Political Science Review* 106 (May 2012): 430–454; Adam J. Berinsky, "Assuming the Costs of War: Events, Elites, and American Public Support for Military Conflict," *Journal of Politics* 69 (November 2007): 975–997; Paul M. Sniderman and Sean M. Theriault, "The Structure of Political Argument and the Logic of Issue Framing," in Willem E. Saris and Paul M. Sniderman, eds., *Studies in Public Opinion: Attitudes, Nonattitudes, Measurement Error and Change* (Princeton, NJ: Princeton University Press, 2004); James N. Druckman and Kjersten R. Nelson, "Framing and Deliberation: How Citizens' Conversations Limit Elite Influence," *American Journal of Political Science* 47 (October 2003): 729–745; James N. Druckman, "Political Preference Formation: Competition, Deliberation, and the (Ir)

relevance of Framing Effects," *American Political Science Review* 98 (November 2004): 671–686; Paul M. Sniderman, "Taking Sides: A Fixed Choice Theory of Political Reasoning," in Arthur Lupia, Mathew D. McCubbins, and Samuel L. Popkin, eds., *Elements of Reason: Understanding and Expanding the Limits of Political Rationality* (New York: Cambridge University Press, 2000); John R. Zaller, "Elite Leadership of Mass Opinion: New Evidence from the Gulf War," in W. Lance Bennett and David L. Paletz, eds., *Taken by Storm: The Media, Public Opinion, and U.S. Foreign Policy in the Gulf War* (Chicago, IL: University of Chicago Press, 1994), pp. 186–209; and Zaller, *The Nature and Origins of Mass Opinion*, p. 99, chapter 9. But see Dennis Chong and James N. Druckman, "Framing Public Opinion in Competitive Democracies," *American Political Science Review* 101 (November 2007): 637–655.

88. Zaller, "Elite Leadership of Mass Opinion," pp. 186–209.

89. James N. Druckman, Jordan Fein, and Thomas J. Leeper, "A Source of Bias in Public Opinion Stability," *American Political Science Review* 106 (May 2012): 430–454.

90. See Jean-Christophe Boucher and Cameron G. Thies, "'I Am a Tariff Man': The Power of Populist Foreign Policy Rhetoric under President Trump," *Journal of Politics* 81 (April 2019): 712–722; Ethan C. Busby, Joshua R. Gubler, and Kirk A. Hawkins, "Framing and Blame Attribution in Populist Rhetoric," *Journal of Politics* 81 (April 2019): 616–630; Chelsea M. Coe, Kayla S. Canelo, Kau Vue, Matthew V. Hibbing, and Stephen P. Nicholson, "The Physiology of Framing Effects: Threat Sensitivity and the Persuasiveness of Political Arguments," *Journal of Politics* 79 (October 2017): 1465–1468; Dennis Chong and James N. Druckman, "Counterframing Effects," *Journal of Politics* 75 (January 2013): 1–16; James N. Druckman and Kjersten R. Nelson, "Framing and Deliberation: How Citizens' Conversations Limit Elite Influence," *American Journal of Political Science* 47 (October 2003): 729–745; James N. Druckman, "Using Credible Advice to Overcome Framing Effects," *Journal of Law, Economics, and Organization* 17 (April 2001): 62–82; Donald P. Haider-Markel and Mark R. Joslyn, "Gun Policy, Opinion, Tragedy, and Blame Attribution: The Conditional Influence of Issue Frames," *Journal of Politics* 63 (May 2001): 520–543; Gregory A. Huber and John S. Lapinski, "The 'Race Card' Revisited: Assessing Racial Priming in Policy Contests," *American Journal of Political Science* 50 (April 2006): 421–40.

91. Daniel J. Hopkins, "The Exaggerated Life of Death Panels: The Limits of Framing Effects in the 2009–2012 Health Care Debate." Available at SSRN: http://ssrn.com/abstract=2163769; and Frank R. Baumgartner, Jeffrey M. Berry, Marie Hojnacki, Beth L. Leech, and David C. Kimball, *Lobbying and Policy Change: Who Wins, Who Loses, and Why* (Chicago, IL: University of Chicago Press, 2009), chapter 9.

92. Gregory A. Huber and Celia Paris, "Assessing the Programmatic Equivalence Assumption in Question Wording Experiments: Understanding Why Americans Like Assistance to the Poor More Than Welfare," *Public Opinion Quarterly* 77 (January 2013): 385–397; and Gabriel S. Lenz, "Learning and Opinion Change, Not Priming: Reconsidering the Priming Hypothesis," *American Journal of Political Science* 53 (October 2009): 821–837.

93. Erik Peterson and Gabor Simonovits, "The Electoral Consequences of Issue Frames," *Journal of Politics* 80 (October 2018): 1283–1296.

94. See, e.g., Prior, *Post-Broadcast Democracy*.

95. Converse, "The Nature of Belief Systems in Mass Publics"; William G. Jacoby, "The Sources of Liberal-Conservative Thinking: Education and Conceptualization," *Political Behavior* 10 (Winter 1988): 316–32; Luskin, "Measuring Political Sophistication"; Neuman, *The Paradox of Mass Politics*; Carmines and Stimson, "The Two Faces of Issue Voting"; and Zaller, *The Nature and Origins of Mass Opinion*, p. 48.

96. See Brian J. Gaines, James H. Kuklinski, Paul J. Quirk, Buddy Peyton, and Jay Verkuilen, "Same Facts, Different Interpretations: Partisan Motivation and Opinion on Iraq," *Journal of Politics* 69 (November 2007): 957–974; Edwards, *On Deaf Ears*, chapter 9; and Larry Bartels, "Beyond the Running Tally: Partisan Bias in Political Perceptions," *Political Behavior* 24 (June 2002): 117–150.

97. See Hans Noel, "The Coalition Merchants: The Ideological Roots of the Civil Rights Realignment," *Journal of Politics* 74 (January 2012): 156–173; Mark A. Smith, *The Right Talk: How Conservatives Transformed the Great Society into the Economic Society* (Princeton, NJ: Princeton University Press, 2007); and Edward G. Carmines and James A. Stimson, *Issue Evolution: Race and the Transformation of American Politics* (Princeton, NJ: Princeton University Press, 1989).

98. See, e.g., David Remnick, "A Conversation with Maggie Haberman, Trump's Favorite Foe," *New Yorker*, July 21, 2017; and Boucher and Thies, "'I Am a Tariff Man'." See also Busby, Gubler, and Hawkins, "Framing and Blame Attribution in Populist Rhetoric."

99. Edwards, *The Bungler*, chapter 4.

100. A key source on these activities is Kumar, *Managing the President's Message*. See especially pp. 4–5.

101. An analysis of President Johnson's public statements on Vietnam shows that he varied their content—that is, their "hawkishness"—depending on the audience he was addressing. Lawrence C. Miller

and Lee Sigelman, "Is the Audience the Message? A Note on LBJ's Vietnam Statements," *Public Opinion Quarterly* 42 (Spring 1978): 71–80. See also Malcolm Goggin, "The Ideological Content of Presidential Communications," *American Politics Quarterly* 12 (July 1984): 361–384.

102. Michael K. Deaver, *Behind the Scenes* (New York: William Morrow, 1987), p. 73; see also pp. 126–127, 135.

103. Laurence I. Barrett, *Gambling with History* (New York: Penguin, 1983), p. 442.

104. See, e.g., Karen Hughes, *Ten Minutes from Normal* (New York: Viking, 2004), pp. 85–86, 219–220.

105. Donald J. Trump, *The Art of the Deal* (New York: Random House, Ballantine Books, 1987, pp. 39–40.

106. Quoted in Michael Baruch Grossman and Martha Joynt Kumar, *Portraying the President: The White House and the News Media* (Baltimore, MD: Johns Hopkins University Press, 1981), p. 29.

107. Juliet Eilperin, "Behind Closed Doors, Trump Signs Bill Allowing States to Strip Federal Family Planning Funds from Abortion Providers," *Washington Post*, April 13, 2017.

108. Matthew R. Miles, "The Bully Pulpit and Media Coverage: Power without Persuasion," *International Journal of Press/Politics* 19 (January 2014): 66–84.

109. Cannon, *President Reagan*, p. 453.

110. See Richard Ellis, *Presidential Lightning Rods: The Politics of Blame Avoidance* (Lawrence: University Press of Kansas, 1994); and Fred I. Greenstein, *The Hidden-Hand Presidency: Eisenhower as Leader* (New York: Basic Books, 1982), pp. 90–92.

111. Bob Woodward, *Bush at War* (New York: Simon & Schuster, 2002), p. 13.

112. See Donald T. Regan, *For the Record* (San Diego, CA: Harcourt Brace Jovanovich, 1988), pp. 247–249.

113. Deaver, *Behind the Scenes,* p. 141.

114. Elisabeth Bumiller, "Keepers of Bush Image Lift Stagecraft to New Heights," *New York Times*, May 16, 2003, pp. A1, A8.

115. Ibid.

116. Quoted in Rich Jaroslovsky, "Manipulating the Media Is a Specialty for the White House's Michael Deaver," *Wall Street Journal*, January 5, 1984, p. 44.

117. Speakes, *Speaking Out*, p. 220.

118. Virginia Heffernan, "The YouTube Presidency—Why the Obama Administration Uploads So Much Video," *New York Times*, April 12, 2009; Brian Stelter, "Obama to Field Questions Posted by YouTube Users," *New York Times*, February 1, 2010.

119. Julie Hirschfeld Davis, "The Ripple Effect of a Trump Tweetstorm," *New York Times*, October 23, 2018.

120. Andy McDonald, "Former White House Adviser Reveals 'Meticulous' Way Trump Dictates His Tweets," HuffPost, November 26, 2018.

121. Interview with Tucker Carlson on Fox News, March 15, 2017.

122. Gallup poll, May 1–13, 2018.

123. HuffPost/YouGov poll, October 16–17, 2018.

124. Gallup poll, May 1–13, 2018.

125. HuffPost/YouGov poll, October 16–17, 2018.

126. Fox News poll, March 12–14, 2017.

127. ABC News–*Washington Post* poll, July 10–13, 2017; NBC News–*Wall Street Journal* poll, September 14–18, 2017; ABC News–*Washington Post* poll, January 15–18, 2018.

128. CNN poll, August 3–6, 2017.

129. McClatchy polls, February 15–19, 2017, and March 22–27, 2017; NPR-*PBS NewsHour* poll, June 21–25, 2017; and Marist College poll, August 8–12, 2017. See also CNN poll, August 3–6, 2017.

130. CNN poll, August 3–6, 2017; Marist College poll, October 15–17, 2017; NPR-PBS NewsHour poll, December 4–7, 2017.

131. *Economist*-YouGov poll, July 3–4, 2017.

132. Philip Bump, "The White House Had a Coordinated Message This Month. Trump Didn't," *Washington Post*, June 30, 2017.

133. See, e.g., Quinnipiac University poll, August 9–13, 2018 (registered voters).

134. ABC News–*Washington Post* poll, January 15–18, 2018.

135. Pew Research Center, *Mapping Twitter Topic Networks: From Polarized Crowds to Community Clusters*, February 20, 2014.

136. Scott McClellan, *What Happened: Inside the Bush White House and Washington's Culture of Deception* (New York: Public Affairs, 2008), p. 229.

137. Spencer Ackerman and John B. Judis, "The First Casualty," *New Republic*, June 30, 2003, pp. 17–18.

138. Bob Woodward, *State of Denial* (New York: Simon & Schuster, 2006), pp. 337, 471, 480, 491.

139. Juliet Eilperin, "Under Trump, Inconvenient Data Is Being Sidelined," *Washington Post*, May 15, 2017; and Chris Mooney and Juliet Eilperin, "EPA Website Removes Climate Science Site from Public View after Two Decades," *Washington Post*, April 29, 2017; Alan Zibel, "Inconvenient Information: How the Trump Administration Squelches Data, Uses Psuedo-Statistics, Stifles Expert Views and Cancels Important Studies," Public Citizen, March 13, 2018, https://corporatepresidency.org/inconvenient/; and Silencing Science Tracker, Columbia Law School, http://columbiaclimatelaw.com/resources/silencing-science-tracker/

140. Burgess Everett and Josh Dawsey, "White House Orders Agencies to Ignore Democrats' Oversight Requests," *Politico*, June 2, 2017.

141. Gordon M. Goldstein, *Lessons in Disaster: McGeorge Bundy and the Path to War in Vietnam* (New York: Holt, 2008), pp. 169–170, 173, 197–198.

142. Edwin E. Moise, "Lyndon Johnson's War Propaganda," *New York Times*, November 20, 2017.

143. See, e.g., James S. Robbins, *This Time We Win: Revisiting the Tet Offensive* (New York: Encounter Books, 2010).

144. Fred I. Greenstein, "Eisenhower as an Activist President: A Look at New Evidence," *Political Science Quarterly* 94 (Winter 1979–1980): 588–590.

145. See, e.g., Howard Kurtz, *Spin Cycle* (New York: Free Press, 1998), pp. 300–301.

146. David Stockman, *The Triumph of Politics* (New York: Harper & Row, 1986), p. 173; see also pp. 132, 353.

147. For other budgetary distortions, see Tim Muris, "Budget Manipulations," *The American Enterprise*, May/June 1993, pp. 24–28.

148. Quoted in Joseph C. Goulden, *Truth Is the First Casualty* (Chicago, IL: Rand McNally, 1969), p. 160. See also Edwin E. Moise, *Tonkin Gulf and the Escalation of the Vietnam War* (Chapel Hill: University of North Carolina Press, 1996); and Goldstein, *Lessons in Disaster*, pp. 122–128, 133–134.

149. Donald Trump, "Remarks by President Trump in Joint Address to Congress," February 28, 2017, White House. https://www.whitehouse.gov/the-press-office/2017/02/28/remarks-president-trump-joint-address-congress.

150. John E. Mueller, *War, Presidents, and Public Opinion* (New York: Wiley, 1973), pp. 112–113.

151. For a more complete discussion, see George C. Edwards III, *The Public Presidency* (New York: St. Martin's, 1983), pp. 60–64; and James P. Pfiffner, *The Character Factor* (College Station: Texas A&M University Press, 2004). See also Speakes, *Speaking Out*, pp. 141, 160–162, 172.

152. Kurtz, *Spin Cycle*, pp. xxi–xxii.

153. James P. Pfiffner, "Did President Bush Mislead the Country in His Arguments for War with Iraq?" *Presidential Studies Quarterly* 34 (March 2004): 25–46.

154. See, e.g., Barton Gellman, *Angler: The Cheney Vice Presidency* (New York: Penguin Press, 2008), pp. 149, 217–222.

155. See, e.g., PolitiFact.com, *Washington Post* Fact Checker, *New York Times* Fact Checks.

156. Glenn Kessler, "A Year of Unprecedented Deception: Trump Averaged 15 False Claims a Day in 2018," *Washington Post*, December 30, 2018.

157. Glenn Kessler, Salvador Rizzo, and Meg Kelly, "President Trump Made 8,158 False or Misleading Claims in His First Two Years," *Washington Post*, January 21, 2019.

158. Maggie Haberman, "A President Who Believes He Is Entitled to His Own Facts," *New York Times*, October 18, 2018.

159. Blake, "President Trump's Full *Washington Post* Interview Transcript, Annotated."

160. See, e.g., Aaron Blake, "Rex Tillerson on Trump: 'Undisciplined, Doesn't Like to Read' and Tries to Do Illegal Things," *Washington Post*, December 7, 2018; and Bob Woodward, *Fear: Trump in the White House* (New York: Simon and Schuster, 2018), pp. 271, 276.

161. Maggie Haberman and Mark Landler, "A Week after the Midterms, Trump Seems to Forget the Caravan," *New York Times*, November 13, 2018; and Philip Rucker and Josh Dawsey, "From Dire Warnings to Happy Talk: Trump Changes His Tune after the Midterms," *Washington Post*, November 19, 2018.

162. Julie Hirschfeld Davis, "In a Fox-Inspired Tweetstorm Trump Offers a Medley of Falsehoods and Misstatements," *New York Times*, July 3, 2018; Josh Dawsey, Damian Paletta, and Erica Werner, "In Fundraising Speech, Trump Says He Made up Trade Claim in Meeting with Justin Trudeau," *Washington Post*, March 15, 2018.

163. *Washington Post*–ABC News poll, April 17–20, 2017.

164. Pew Research Center poll, September 18–24, 2018. See also ABC News–*Washington Post* poll, January 21–24, 2019.

165. *Washington Post* Fact Checker poll, November 29–December 10, 2018. See also Pew Research Center poll, January 9–14, 2019.

166. *USA Today*–Suffolk University poll, December 11–16, 2018 (registered voters).

167. See, e.g., CBS News–*New York Times* poll, October 30, 1986, Table 29.

168. See, e.g., William Schneider, "Opinion Outlook," *National Journal*, November 29, 1986, pp. 2908–2909; and Edwards, *Governing by Campaigning*, chapter 4.

169. On presidents' success in leading the public, see Edwards, *The Bungler*; George C. Edwards III, *Predicting the Presidency: The Potential of Persuasive Leadership* (Princeton, NJ: Princeton University Press, 2016); George C. Edwards III, *Overreach: Leadership in the Obama Presidency* (Princeton, NJ: Princeton University Press, 20012); Edwards, *The Strategic President*, pp. 96–104; Edwards, *Governing by Campaigning*, chapter 3; and Edwards, *On Deaf Ears*, chapters 4–5.

170. See Edwards, *On Deaf Ears*, chapter 5.

171. Edwards, *The Strategic President*, pp. 25–34, 193–195; and Edwards, *On Deaf Ears*, pp. 93–94, 99–100.

172. Ronald Reagan, *An American Life* (New York: Simon & Schuster, 1990), pp. 459, 471.

173. This discussion is based on Edwards, *On Deaf Ears*, chapter 3.

174. William G. Mayer, *The Changing American Mind* (Ann Arbor: University of Michigan Press, 1992), p. 127.

175. Quoted in R. W. Apple, "Bush Sure-Footed on Trail of Money," *New York Times*, September 29, 1990, p. 8.

176. Edwards, *Governing by Campaigning*, pp. 98–111; and Frank Newport, "Public Wants Congressional and U.N. Approval before Iraq Action," Gallup poll, News Release, September 6, 2002.

177. Stanley Feldman, Leonie Huddy, and George E. Marcus, *Going to War in Iraq: When Citizens and the Press Matter* (Chicago, IL: University of Chicago Press, 2015).

178. Barack Obama, *Dreams from My Father* (New York: Crown Publishers, 1995), p. 106.

179. Pfeiffer, *Yes We (Still) Can*, pp. 96–98.

180. See Edwards, *Overreach*, pp. 89–99.

181. Edwards, *The Bungler*, chapter 4.

182. Ibid.

183. Ibid.

184. James Stimson, *Public Opinion in America: Moods, Cycles, and Swings*, 2nd ed. (Boulder, CO: Westview Press, 1999).

185. Benjamin I. Page and Robert Y. Shapiro, T*he Rational Public: Fifty Years of Trends in Policy Preferences* (Chicago, IL: University of Chicago Press, 1992).

186. Benjamin I. Page with Marshall M. Bouton, *The Foreign Policy Disconnect: What Americans Want from Our Leaders but Don't Get* (Chicago, IL: University of Chicago Press, 2006).

187. See also Druckman and Jacobs, *Who Governs?* chapter 6.

CHAPTER 7

1. Quoted in Bob Woodward, *The Agenda: Inside the Clinton White House* (New York: Simon & Schuster, 1994), p. 313.

2. Martha Joynt Kumar, "The White House Beat at the Century Mark," *Press/Politics* 2 (Summer 1997): 10–30.

3. Doris A. Graber, *Mass Media and American Politics*, 7th ed. (Washington, DC: CQ Press, 2006), pp. 271–275; Elmer E. Cornwell Jr., "Presidential News: The Expanding Public Image," *Journalism Quarterly* 36 (Summer 1959): 275–283; Alan P. Balutis, "The Presidency and the Press: The Expanding Presidential Image," *Presidential Studies Quarterly* 7 (Fall 1977): 244–251; *Media Monitor,* July/August 1994, pp. 1–2; *Media Monitor,* September/October 1994, pp. 1–2; and *Media Monitor,* May/June 1995, pp. 1–2.

4. Rich Noyes and Mike Ciandella, "2017: The Year the News Media Went to War against a President," Media Research Center, January 16, 2018; Echelon Insights, *The Year in News 2017*, December 27, 2017; and Thomas E. Patterson, "News Coverage of Donald Trump's First 100 Days," Shorenstein Center, Harvard University, May 18, 2017.

5. James E. Pollard, *Presidents and the Press* (New York: Macmillan, 1947), p. 14; and Richard Harris, "The Presidency and the Press," *New Yorker*, October 1, 1973, p. 122.

6. Quoted in Harris, "The Presidency and the Press," p. 122; and see Peter Forbath and Carey Winfrey, *The Adversaries: The President and the Press* (Cleveland: Regal Books, 1974), p. 5.

7. Quoted in Joseph P. Berry Jr., *John F. Kennedy and the Media: The First Television President* (Lanham, MD: Rowman & Littlefield, 1987), p. 66.

8. See Jann S. Wenner and William Greider, "President Clinton," *Rolling Stone*, December 9, 1993, p. 81.

9. Philip Rucker, Josh Dawsey, and Ashley Parker, "Venting about Press, Trump Has Repeatedly Sought to Ban Reporters over Questions," *Washington Post*, July 27, 2018.

10. Quoted in Lesley Stahl, "Trump Admitted Mission to 'Discredit' Press," *CBS News*, May 23, 2018.

11. David Nakamura, "Trump's Insults toward Black Reporters, Candidates Echo 'Historic Playbooks' Used against African Americans, Critics Say," *Washington Post*, November 9, 2018.

12. Philip Rucker, Josh Dawsey, and Ashley Parker, "Venting about Press, Trump Has Repeatedly Sought to Ban Reporters over Questions," *Washington Post*, July 27, 2018.

13. Aaron Blake, "Trump Claims His Intelligence Chiefs Said They Were 'Totally Misquoted.' They Spoke in Public," *Washington Post*, January 31, 2019; and Shane Harris, "Intelligence Officials Were 'Misquoted' after Public Hearing, Trump Claims," *Washington Post*, January 31, 2019.

14. Seung Min Kim, "Trump Falsely Accuses the *New York Times* of Making Up a Source. It Was an Official Who Briefed Reporters," *Washington Post*, May 26, 2018.

15. Philip Bump, "Trump Blames the Media for Not Asking Questions. The Blame Lies with the White House," *New York Times*, February 20, 2019.

16. See also Monmouth University poll, March 2–5, 2018.

17. A key source on these activities is Martha Joynt Kumar, *Managing the President's Message: The White House Communications Operation* (Baltimore, MD: Johns Hopkins University Press, 2007).

18. Marlin Fitzwater, *Call the Briefing* (New York: Times Books, 1995), p. 4.

19. Daniel Pfeiffer, *Yes We (Still) Can* (New York: Twelve, 2018), p. 66; and Dylan Byers, "President Obama, Off the Record," *Politico*, November 1, 2013.

20. There is some question as to whether the summary was an accurate representation of the news. See Christopher F. Karpowitz, "What Can a President Learn from the News Media? The Instructive Case of Richard Nixon," *British Journal of Political Science* 39 (October 2009): 755–780.

21. Quoted in "Press Secretaries Explore White House News Strategies," *APIP Report* 1 (January 1991): 2.

22. On the number and type of press conferences, see Kumar, *Managing the President's Message*, chapter 7. Professor Kumar has updated these data.

23. John Wagner, "Trump Says He Directed Sarah Sanders 'Not to Bother' with White House Press Briefings," *Washington Post*, January 22, 2019.

24. Ken Auletta, "Non-Stop News," *New Yorker*, January 25, 2010, p. 41.

25. Doris A. Graber, *Mass Media and American Politics*, 6th ed. (Washington, DC: CQ Press, 2002), p. 291.

26. Michael Baruch Grossman and Martha Joynt Kumar, *Portraying the President: The White House and the News Media* (Baltimore, MD: Johns Hopkins University Press, 1981), pp. 59–60, 63–64, 280–281.

27. Mark J. Rozell, "Presidential Image-Makers on the Limits of Spin Control," *Presidential Studies Quarterly* 25 (Winter 1995): 77.

28. Interview by author with Peter Jennings, New York, October 18, 1987.

29. Byers, "President Obama, Off the Record"; and Auletta, "Non-Stop News," p. 42.

30. Ben Schreckinger and Hadas Gold, "Trump's Fake War on the Fake News," *Politico Magazine*, May/June 2017; and John Harris, "How Trump Is Like JFK," *Politico Magazine*, March 8, 2019.

31. Jeffrey E. Cohen, *Going Local: Presidential Leadership in the Post-Broadcast Age* (New York: Cambridge University Press, 2010); Jeffrey S. Peake and Matthew Eshbaugh-Soha, "The Presidency and Local Media: Local Newspaper Coverage of President George W. Bush," *Presidential Studies Quarterly* 38 (December 2008): 609–630; and Andrew W. Barrett and Jeffrey S. Peake, "When the President Comes to Town: Examining Local Newspaper Coverage of Domestic Presidential Travel," *American Politics Research* 35 (January 2007): 3–31.

32. Pew Research Center, "Local TV News Fact Sheet," July 12, 2018.

33. Kumar, *Managing the President's Message*, p. 42.

34. Paul Brace and Barbara Hinckley, *Follow the Leader: Opinion Polls and the Modern Presidents* (New York: Basic Books, 1992), chapter 3.

35. Dom Bonafede, "The Washington Press: It Magnifies the President's Flaws and Blemishes," *National Journal,* May 1, 1982, pp. 267–271.

36. Graber, *Mass Media and American Politics,* 6th ed., p. 285.

37. Quoted in David L. Paletz and Robert M. Entman, *Media–Power–Politics* (New York: Free Press, 1981), pp. 55–56.

38. Brian Stelter, "Fox's Volley with Obama Intensifying," *New York Times,* October 12, 2009; and Jim Rutenberg, "Behind the War between White House and Fox," *New York Times,* October 23, 2009.

39. Auletta, "Non-Stop News," p. 47.

40. Michael M. Grynbaum, "White House Bars *Times* and Other News Outlets from Briefing," *New York Times,* February 24, 2017; and Julie Hirschfeld Davis and Michael M. Grynbaum, "Trump Intensifies His Attacks on Journalists and Condemns F.B.I. 'Leakers'," *New York Times,* February 24, 2017.

41. Peter Baker and Cecilia Kang, " Trump Threatens NBC over Nuclear Weapons Report," *New York Times,* October 11, 2017.

42. Howard Kurtz, *Spin Cycle* (New York: Free Press, 1998), p. 134.

43. Jonathan Alter, *The Promise: President Obama, Year One* (New York: Simon and Schuster, 2010), pp. 154–156, 386.

44. Remarks by President Trump in Press Conference, White House, February 16, 2017.

45. William Safire, *Before the Fall: An Inside View of the Pre-Watergate White House* (New York: Doubleday, 1975), p. 373; and Henry Kissinger, *Years of Upheaval* (Boston, MA: Little, Brown, 1981), p. 116.

46. Lyndon Johnson quoted in George Christian, *The President Steps Down: A Personal Memoir of the Transfer of Power* (New York: Macmillan, 1970), p. 203.

47. Gerald S. Strober and Deborah H. Strober, *"Let Us Begin Anew": An Oral History of the Kennedy Presidency* (New York: HarperCollins, 1993), p. 156.

48. "The U.S. vs. William Colby," *Newsweek,* September 28, 1981, p. 30.

49. "The Tattletale White House," *Newsweek,* February 25, 1980, p. 21.

50. Robert T. Hartmann, *Palace Politics: An Inside Account of the Ford Years* (New York: McGraw-Hill, 1980), p. 38.

51. William J. Lanouette, "The Washington Press Corps: Is It All That Powerful?" *National Journal,* June 2, 1979, p. 898.

52. Kurtz, *Spin Cycle,* p. 92.

53. "Power Couple," *Newsweek,* October 31, 1994, p. 6.

54. James A. Baker III, *The Politics of Diplomacy* (New York: Putnam, 1995), p. 520; see also pp. 34, 154.

55. Dick Morris, *Behind the Oval Office* (New York: Random House, 1997), pp. 101–102.

56. Henry Kissinger, *Years of Renewal* (New York: Simon & Schuster, 1999), pp. 79, 83.

57. Lou Cannon, *President Reagan: The Role of a Lifetime* (New York: Simon & Schuster, 1991), p. 452.

58. Donald T. Regan, *For the Record: From Wall Street to Washington* (San Diego, CA: Harcourt Brace Jovanovich, 1988), p. xiv.

59. Morris, *Behind the Oval Office,* p. 122.

60. Sharon LaFraniere, "Math behind Leak Crackdown: 153 Cases, 4 Years, 0 Indictments," *New York Times,* July 20, 2013.

61. Charlie Savage and Leslie Kaufman, "Phone Records of Journalists Seized by U.S.," *Washington Post,* May 13, 2013.

62. Schreckinger and Gold, "Trump's Fake War on the Fake News."

63. Woodrow Wilson quoted in William Small, *To Kill a Messenger: Television News and the Real World* (New York: Hastings, 1970), p. 221.

64. President Carter, quoted in Michael Baruch Grossman and Martha Joynt Kumar, "Carter, Reagan, and the Media: Have the Rules Really Changed or the Poles of the Spectrum of Success?" (Paper presented at the Annual Meeting of the American Political Science Association, New York, September 3–6, 1981), p. 8.

65. Amy Chozick, "Obama Is an Avid Reader, and Critic, of the News," *New York Times,* August 3, 2012; and Auletta, "Non-Stop News," p. 47.

66. Thomas E. Patterson, *Doing Well and Doing Good* (Cambridge, MA: Shorenstein Center, 2000), pp. 2–5. See also Stephen J. Farnsworth and S. Robert Lichter, "News Coverage of US Presidential Campaigns: Reporting on Primaries and General Elections, 1988–2012," in William Benoit, ed., *The Praeger Handbook of Political Campaigning in the United States*, vol. 1 (Santa Barbara, CA: Praeger, 2016), pp. 233–253; and Thomas E. Patterson, "News Coverage of the 2016 General Election: How the Press Failed the Voters," Shorenstein Center, December 7, 2016.

67. Sam Donaldson, quoted in "Washington Press Corps," *Newsweek*, May 25, 1981, p. 90.

68. Quoted in Grossman and Kumar, *Portraying the President*, p. 43.

69. Ari Fleischer, *Take Heat* (New York: William Morrow, 2005), pp. 43, 76, 86, 276; and Scott McClellan, *What Happened: Inside the Bush White House and Washington's Culture of Deception* (New York: Public Affairs, 2008), pp. 124, 125, 158.

70. Elisabeth Bumiller, "The White House without a Filter," *New York Times*, June 4, 2006.

71. John G. Geer, "The News Media and the Rise of Negativity in Presidential Campaigns," *PS: Political Science & Politics* 45 (July 2012): 422–427.

72. Howard Kurtz, "Journalists, Left Out of the Debate: Few Americans Seem to Hear Health Care Facts," *Washington Post*, August 24, 2009.

73. See "1998 Year in Review," *Media Monitor* 13 (January/February 1999).

74. Project for Excellence in Journalism, "How the Press Covered Health Care Reform," June 21, 2010; Kathleen Hall Jamieson and Joseph N. Capella, "The Role of the Press in the Health Care Reform Debate of 1993–1994," in Doris Graber, Denis McQuail, and Pippa Norris, eds., *The Politics of News, The News of Politics* (Washington, DC: CQ Press, 1998), pp. 118–119; and Lawrence R. Jacobs and Robert Y. Shapiro, *Politicians Don't Pander* (Chicago, IL: University of Chicago Press, 2000), chapters 5–6. See also Farnsworth and Lichter, "News Coverage of US Presidential Campaigns"; Patterson, "News Coverage of the 2016 General Election"; and Pfeiffer, *Yes We (Still) Can*, pp. 100–101.

75. Sam Donaldson, *Hold On, Mr. President* (New York: Random House, 1987), pp. 196–197.

76. Ibid, p. 26.

77. Quoted in Auletta, "Non-Stop News," p. 42.

78. More broadly, see Amber E. Boydstun, *Making the News* (Chicago, IL: University of Chicago Press, 2013).

79. Dan Rather, quoted in Hoyt Purvis, ed., *The Presidency and the Press* (Austin, TX: Lyndon B. Johnson School of Public Affairs, 1976), p. 56.

80. See Patterson, "News Coverage of the 2016 General Election"; John Sides and Lynn Vavreck, *The Gamble: Choice and Chance in the 2012 Presidential Election* (Princeton, NJ: Princeton University Press, 2013); David D'Alessio and Mike Allen, "Media Bias in Presidential Elections: A Meta-Analysis," *Journal of Communication* 50 (2000): 133–156; Maria Elizabeth Grabe and Erik Page Bucy, *Image Bite Politics: News and the Visual Framing of Elections* (New York: Oxford University Press, 2009); and George C. Edwards III, *The Public Presidency (New York: St. Martin's, 1983)*, p. 156, and sources cited therein.

81. Larry Speakes, quoted in Eleanor Randolph, "Speakes Aims Final Salvos at White House Practices," *Washington Post*, January 31, 1987, p. A3.

82. Lanny J. Davis, *Truth to Tell* (New York: Free Press, 1999), p. 252.

83. McClellan, *What Happened*, pp. 156–158.

84. John P. Robinson, "The Press as King-Maker: What Surveys from Last Five Campaigns Show," *Journalism Quarterly* 51 (Winter 1974): 587–594, 606.

85. Kathleen Hall Jamieson and Joseph N. Cappella, *Echo Chamber: Rush Limbaugh and the Conservative Media Establishment* (Oxford, UK: Oxford University Press, 2008).

86. Ángela Fonseca Galvis, James M. Snyder Jr., and B. K. Song, "Newspaper Market Structure and Behavior: Partisan Coverage of Political Scandals in the United States from 1870 to 1910," *Journal of Politics* 78, no. 2 (April 2016): 368–381; and Riccardo Puglisi and James M. Snyder Jr., "Newspaper Coverage of Political Scandals," *Journal of Politics* 73 (July 2011): 931–950.

87. Taylor Adams, Jessia Ma, and Stuart A. Thompson, "Trump Loves 'Fox & Friends.' Here's Why," *New York Times*, November 1, 2017; Philip Bump, "The Pattern Continues: Fox News Spends Far Less Time Discussing Trump's Law-breaking Allies," *Washington Post*, September 18, 2018; and Philip Bump, "Up to Speed on the Stormy Daniels Story? If You Watch Fox, Probably Not." *Washington Post*, March 19, 2019.

88. Jane Mayer, "The Making of the Fox News White House," *New Yorker*, March 11, 2019.

89. Gregory J. Martin and Joshua McCrain, "Local News and National Politics," *American Political Science Review* 113 (May 2019): 372–384.

90. Yochai Benkler, Robert Faris, Hal Roberts, and Ethan Zuckerman, "Ecosystem Altered Broader Media Agenda," *Columbia Journalism Review*, March 2, 2017.

91. Brent Cunningham, "Re-Thinking Objectivity," *Columbia Journalism Review* 4 (July–August 2003).

92. W. Lance Bennett, Regina G. Lawrence, and Steven Livingston, *When the Press Fails* (Chicago, IL: University of Chicago Press, 2007), chapters 1–2. See also Daniel C. Hallin, *The "Uncensored War": The Media and Vietnam* (New York: Oxford University Press, 1986); Jonathan Mermin, *Debating War and Peace: Media Coverage of U.S. Intervention in the Post-Vietnam Era* (Princeton, NJ: Princeton University Press, 1999); and John Zaller and Dennis Chiu, "Government's Little Helper: U.S. Press Coverage of Foreign Policy Crises, 1945–1991," *Political Communication* 13, no. 4 (1996): 385–405.

93. Bill D. Moyers, "The Press and Government: Who's Telling the Truth?" in Warren K. Agee, ed., *Mass Media in a Free Society* (Lawrence: University Press of Kansas, 1969), p. 19.

94. Brendan Nyhan, "Scandal Potential: How Political Context and News Congestion Affect the President's Vulnerability to Media Scandal," *British Journal of Political Science* 45 (April 2014): 435–466.

95. See Mark J. Rozell, *The Press and the Ford Presidency* (Ann Arbor: University of Michigan Press, 1992).

96. Thomas E. Patterson, *Out of Order* (New York: Knopf, 1993), chapter 3; Matthew Robert Kerbel, *Edited for Television* (Boulder, CO: Westview, 1994), pp. 60–64, 88; and S. Robert Lichter and Richard E. Noyes, *Good Intentions Make Bad News*, 2nd ed. (Lanham, MD: Rowman & Littlefield, 1996), chapters 6–7.

97. Patterson, *Out of Order*, pp. 16–21, 113–115; Kerbel, *Edited for Television*, pp. 111–112; Kevin G. Barnhurst and Catherine A. Steele, "Image-Bite News: The Visual Coverage of Elections on U.S. Television, 1968–1992," *Press/Politics* 2, no. 1 (1997): 40–58; Lichter and Noyes, *Good Intentions Make Bad News*, pp. 116–126; Richard Nadeau, Richard G. Niemi, David P. Fah, and Timothy Amato, "Elite Economic Forecasts, Economic News, Mass Economic Judgments, and Presidential Approval," *Journal of Politics* 61 (February 1999): 109–135; and "Campaign 2000 Final: How TV News Covered the General Election Campaign," *Media Monitor* 14 (November/December 2000). See also Jennifer Kavanagh, William Marcellino, Jonathan S. Blake, Shawn Smith, Steven Davenport, and Mahlet G. Tebeka, *News in a Digital Age: Comparing the Presentation of News Information over Time and across Media Platforms* (Santa Monica, CA: RAND Corporation, 2019).

98. Paul Farhi, "We Have Reached Peak Punditry," *Washington Post*, June 2, 2016.

99. Patterson, "News Coverage of the 2016 General Election"; Lawrence R. Jacobs, "Lord Bryce's Curse: The Costs of Presidential Heroism and the Hope of Deliberative Incrementalism," *Presidential Studies Quarterly* 43 (December 2013): 732–752; Patterson, *Doing Well and Doing Good*, pp. 10, 12; "Campaign 2000 Final: How TV News Covered the General Election Campaign," *Media Monitor* 14 (November/December 2000); Patterson, *Out of Order*, pp. 3–27; "Clinton's the One," *Media Monitor* 6 (November 1992): 3–5; and Lichter and Noyes, *Good Intentions Make Bad News*, chapters 6–7, esp. pp. 288–299. See also Stuart N. Soroka, "The Gatekeeping Function: Distributions of Information in Media and the Real World," *Journal of Politics* 74 (April 2012): 514–528.

100. Marc Trussler and Stuart Soroka, "Consumer Demand for Cynical and Negative News Frames," *International Journal of Press/Politics* 19 (July 2014): 360–379.

101. Tim Groeling and Matthew A. Baum, "Crossing the Water's Edge: Elite Rhetoric, Media Coverage, and the Rally-Round-the-Flag Phenomenon," *Journal of Politics* 70 (October 2008): 1074.

102. *Media Monitor*, May/June 1995, pp. 2–5; and Thomas E. Patterson, "Legitimate Beef: The Presidency and a Carnivorous Press," *Media Studies Journal* 8 (Spring 1994): 21–26. However, compare Andras Szanto, "In Our Opinion ...: Editorial Page Views of Clinton's First Year," *Media Studies Journal* 8 (Spring 1994): 97–105; and Lichter and Noyes, *Good Intentions Make Bad News*, p. 214.

103. Stephen J. Farnsworth and S. Robert Lichter, *The Mediated Presidency: Television News and Presidential Governance* (Lanham, MD: Rowman & Littlefield, 2006), pp. 40–45, chapter 4; and Stephen J. Farnsworth and S. Robert Lichter, *The Nightly News Nightmare: Television's Coverage of U.S. Presidential Elections, 1988–2004*, 3rd ed. (Lanham, MD: Rowman & Littlefield, 2011), chapter 4. See also Cohen, *The Presidency in the Era*, chapters 5–6.

104. Stephen J. Farnsworth and S. Robert Lichter, "The Return of the Honeymoon: Television News Coverage of New Presidents, 1981–2009," *Presidential Studies Quarterly* 41 (September 2011): 590–603.

105. Pew Research Center's Project for Excellence in Journalism, "How the Press Covered Health Care Reform," June 21, 2010; and Pew Research Center's Project for Excellence in Journalism, "Stimulus News Seen as More Negative than Positive," February 11, 2009.

106. Pew Research Center's Project for Excellence in Journalism, *Winning the Media Campaign 2012*, November 2, 2012.

107. Patterson, "News Coverage of the 2016 General Election."

108. Thomas E. Patterson, *News Coverage of Donald Trump's First 100 Days*, Shorenstein Center on Media, Politics, and Public Policy, May 18, 2017; Amy Mitchell, Jeffey Gottfried, Galen Stocking, Katerina Matsa, and Elizabeth M. Grieco, *Covering President Trump in a Polarized Media Environment*, Pew Research Center, October 2, 2017; and Noyes and Ciandella, "2017: The Year the News Media Went to War against a President."

109. Jimmy Carter, *Keeping Faith: Memoirs of a President* (New York: Bantam, 1982), pp. 179–180.

110. "The Invisible Man: TV News Coverage of President Bill Clinton, 1993–1995," *Media Monitor* 12 (May/June 1995); Patterson, "Legitimate Beef"; "Sex, Lies, and TV News," *Media Monitor* 12 (September/October 1998); and "TV News Coverage of the 1998 Midterm Elections," *Media Monitor* 12 (November/December 1998). However, compare Szanto, "In Our Opinion …"; and Lichter and Noyes, *Good Intentions Make Bad News*, p. 214. See also Tim Groeling and Samuel Kernell, "Is Network News Coverage of the President Biased?" *Journal of Politics* 60 (November 1998): 1063–1087.

111. See Edward Jay Epstein, *News from Nowhere: Television and the News* (New York: Vintage, 1973), pp. 215–220; Herbert J. Gans, *Deciding What's News* (New York: Vintage, 1979), pp. 68–69, 187; Stephen Hess, *The Washington Reporters* (Washington, DC: Brookings Institution, 1981), p. 88; Patterson, *Out of Order,* chapter 2; and Kerbel, *Edited for Television,* p. 116.

112. Quoted in Dana Milbank, "Rove's Reading: Not So Liberal as Leery," *Washington Post,* April 20, 2005, p. A4.

113. Grossman and Kumar, *Portraying the President,* pp. 255–259, 270–271, 274–279; Grossman and Kumar, "Carter, Reagan, and the Media," p. 13; and Hess, *The Washington Reporters,* p. 98.

114. For an overview, see Cliff Zukin, "Mass Communication and Public Opinion," in Dan D. Nimmo and Keith R. Sanders, eds., *The Handbook of Political Communication* (Beverly Hills, CA: Sage, 1981), pp. 359–390. See also Diana C. Mutz and Joe Soss, "Reading Public Opinion: The Influence of News Coverage on Perceptions of Public Sentiment," *Public Opinion Quarterly* 61 (Fall 1997): 431–451. Compare Russell J. Dalton, Paul A. Beck, and Robert Huckfeldt, "Partisan Cues and the Media: Information Flows in the 1992 Presidential Election," *American Political Science Review* 92 (March 1980): 111–126; and Paul M. Kellstedt, *The Mass Media and the Dynamics of American Racial Attitudes* (Cambridge, UK: Cambridge University Press, 2003). But see Susanna Dilliplane, "Activation, Conversion, or Reinforcement? The Impact of Partisan News Exposure on Vote Choice," *American Journal of Political Science* 58 (January 2014): 79–94.

115. Graber, *Mass Media and American Politics*, 7th ed., p. 189.

116. Benjamin I. Page and Robert Y. Shapiro, *The Rational Public* (Chicago, IL: University of Chicago Press, 1992), pp. 12–13.

117. Ashley Muddiman, Nathalie J. Stroud, and M. McCombs, "News Media Fragmentation, Attribute Agenda Setting, and Political Beliefs about Iraq," *Journal of Broadcasting and Electronic Media* 58, no. 2 (2014): 215–233; Stuart N. Soroka, "Media, Public Opinion, and Foreign Policy," *Press/Politics* 8 (Winter 2003): 27–48; Jeffrey S. Peake, "Presidential Agenda Setting in Foreign Policy," *Political Research Quarterly* 54 (March 2001): 69–86; Maxwell McCombs and George Estrada, "The News Media and the Pictures in Our Heads," in Shanto Iyengar and Richard Reeves, eds., *Do the Media Govern? Politicians, Voters, and Reporters in* America (Thousand Oaks, CA: Sage, 1997); William Gonzenbach, *The Media, the President, and Public Opinion: A Longitudinal Analysis of the Drug Issue, 1984–1991* (Mahwah, NJ: Lawrence Erlbaum Associates, 1996); James W. Dearing and Everett M. Rogers, *Agenda Setting* (Thousand Oaks, CA: Sage, 1996); Maxwell McCombs and Donald Shaw, "The Evolution of Agenda Setting Research: Twenty-five Years in the Marketplace of Ideas," *Journal of Communication* 43, no. 2 (1993): 58–67; David L. Portess and Maxwell McCombs, eds., *Agenda Setting: Readings on Media, Public Opinion, and Policymaking* (Hillsdale, NY: Lawrence Erlbaum Associates, 1991); Fay Lomax Cook, Tom R. Tyler, and Edward G. Goetz, "Media and Agenda-Setting: Effects on the Public, Interest Group Leaders, Policy Makers, and Policy," *Public Opinion Quarterly* 47 (Spring 1983): 16–35; Shanto Iyengar, Mark D. Peters, and Donald R. Kinder, "Experimental Demonstrations of the 'Not-So-Minimal' Consequences of Television News Programs," *American Political Science Review* 76 (December 1982): 848–858; James P. Winter and Chaim H. Eyal, "Agenda-Setting for the Civil Rights Issue," *Public Opinion Quarterly* 45 (Fall 1981): 376–383; Michael Bruce MacKuen and Steven Lane Coombs, *More than News* (Beverly Hills, CA: Sage 1981), chapters 3–4; and Doris A. Graber, "Agenda-Setting: Are There Women's Perspectives?" in Laurily Epstein, ed., *Women and the News* (New York: Hastings House, 1978), pp. 15–37.

118. Graber, *Mass Media and American Politics,* 7th ed., p. 194.

119. Matthew Eshbaugh-Soha and Jeffrey S. Peake, *Breaking through the Noise: Presidential Leadership, Public Opinion, and the News Media* (Stanford, CA: Stanford University Press, 2011).

120. Shanto Iyengar, *Is Anyone Responsible?* (Chicago, IL: University of Chicago Press, 1991), p. 2. See also Scott L. Althaus and Young Mie Kim, "Priming Effects in Complex Information Environments: Reassessing the Impact of News Discourse on Presidential Approval," *Journal of Politics* 68 (November 2006): 960–976; Iyengar, Peters, and Kinder, "Experimental Demonstrations"; Dhavan V. Shah, Mark D. Watts, David Domke, David P. Fan, and Michael Fibison, "News Coverage, Economic Cues, and the Public's Presidential Preferences, 1984–1996," *Journal of Politics* 61 (November 1999): 914–943; and Larry M. Bartels, "Messages Received: The Political Impact of Media Exposure," *American Political Science Review* 87 (June 1993): 267–285. But see Neil Malhorta and Jon A. Krosnick, "Retrospective and Prospective Performance Assessments during the 2004 Election Campaign: Tests of Mediation and News Media Priming," *Political Behavior* 29 (June 2007): 249–278. There is also evidence that presidential approval is influenced by elite opinion, as brought to the public's attention in the mass media. See Richard A. Brody, *Assessing the President* (Stanford, CA: Stanford University Press, 1991).

121. Austin Hart and Joel A. Middleton, "Priming under Fire: Reverse Causality and the Classic Media Priming Hypothesis," *Journal of Politics* 76 (April 2014): 581–592; and Kevin Arceneaux and Martin Johnson, *Changing Minds or Changing Channels?* (Chicago, IL: University of Chicago Press, 2013).

122. Jon A. Krosnick and Donald R. Kinder, "Altering the Foundations of Support for the President through Priming," *American Political Science Review* 84 (June 1990): 497–512; and Iyengar, *Is Anyone Responsible?* chapter 8.

123. Jon A. Krosnick and Laura A. Brannon, "The Impact of the Gulf War on the Ingredients of Presidential Evaluations: Multidimensional Effects of Political Involvement," *American Political Science Review* 87 (December 1993): 963–975. See also Shanto Iyengar and Adam Simon, "News Coverage of the Gulf Crisis and Public Opinion," in W. Lance Bennett and David L. Paletz, eds., *Taken by Storm* (Chicago, IL: University of Chicago Press, 1994).

124. George C. Edwards III, Andrew Barrett, and Reed Welch, "Explaining Presidential Approval: The Significance of Issue Salience," *American Journal of Political Science* 39 (February 1995): 108–134.

125. Shanto Iyengar and Donald R. Kinder, *News That Matters* (Chicago, IL: University of Chicago Press, 1987).

126. Iyengar, Peters, and Kinder, "Experimental Demonstrations." See also Larry M. Bartels, "Messages Received: The Political Impact of Media Exposure," *American Political Science Review* 87 (June 1993): 267–285.

127. Frederick T. Steeper, "Public Response to Gerald Ford's Statements on Eastern Europe in the Second Debate," in George F. Bishop, Robert G. Meadow, and Marilyn Jackson-Beeck, eds., *The Presidential Debates: Media, Electoral, and Public Perspectives* (New York: Praeger, 1978), pp. 81–101.

128. Michael J. Robinson, "News Media Myths and Realities," in Kay Lehman Schlozman, ed., *Elections in America* (Boston, MA: Allen and Unwin, 1987), p. 149.

129. Thomas E. Patterson, *The Mass Media Election: How Americans Choose Their President* (New York: Praeger, 1980), pp. 84–86, 98–100, 105, chapter 2; Doris A. Graber, "Personal Qualities in Presidential Images: The Contribution of the Press," *Midwest Journal of Political Science* 16 (February 1972): 295; Graber, *Mass Media and American Politics*, 6th ed., pp. 240–243; and Barry C. Burden and Anthony Mughan, "The International Economy and Presidential Approval," *Public Opinion Quarterly* 67 (Winter 2003): 555–578.

130. Gerald R. Ford, *A Time to Heal: The Autobiography of Gerald R. Ford* (New York: Harper & Row, 1979), p. 289; see also pp. 343–344.

131. Katherine Graham, *Personal History* (New York: Vintage, 1998).

132. See, e.g., *Media Monitor*, June/July 1998.

133. Douglas M. McLeod and Dhavan V. Shah, *News Frames and National Security: Covering Big Brother* (New York: Cambridge University Press, 2015); and Adam J. Berinsky and Donald R. Kinder, "Making Sense of Issues through Media Frames: Understanding the Kosovo Crisis," *Journal of Politics* 68 (August 2006): 640–656.

134. Pew Research Center's Project for Excellence in Journalism, "How the Press Covered Health Care Reform," June 21, 2010. See also Jacobs and Shapiro, *Politicians Don't Pander*, pp. 176–182, 214–215; and Kathleen Hall Jamieson and Joseph N. Cappella, "The Role of the Press in the Health Care Reform Debate of 1993–1994," in Doris A. Graber, Denis McQuail, and Pippa Norris, eds., *The Politics of News: The News of Politics* (Washington, DC: CQ Press, 1998), pp. 110–131, on Bill Clinton's healthcare proposal in 1993–1994.

135. Jacobs and Shapiro, *Politicians Don't Pander*, pp. 232–255.

136. Joseph M. Capella and Kathleen Hall Jamieson, *Spiral of Cynicism: The Press and the Public Good* (New York: Oxford University Press, 1997). Apparently, people, especially those with higher levels of political engagement, are drawn to stories on the horserace and strategy. See Shanto Iyengar, Helmut Norpoth, and Kyu S. Hahn, "Consumer Demand for Election News: The Horserace Sells," *Journal of Politics* 66 (February 2004): 157–175.

137. Matthew Levendusky, *How Partisan Media Polarize America* (Chicago, IL: University of Chicago Press, 2013).

138. See James H. Kuklinski, Paul J. Quirk, Jennifer Jerit, David Schwieder, and Robert F. Rich, "Misinformation and the Currency of Democratic Citizenship," *Journal of Politics* 62 (August 2000): 790–816.

139. Joshua P. Darr and Johanna L. Dunaway, "Resurgent Mass Partisanship Revisited: The Role of Media Choice in Clarifying Elite Ideology," *American Politics Research* 46 (November 2018): 943–970; Jennifer Jerit, "Understanding the Knowledge Gap: The Role of Experts and Journalists," *Journal of Politics* 71 (April 2009): 442–456; and Jason Barabas and Jennifer Jerit, "Estimating the Causal Effects of Media Coverage on Policy-Specific Knowledge," *American Journal of Political Science* 53 (January 2009): 73–89. See also Stuart N. Soroka, Dominik A. Stecula, and Christopher Wlezien, "It's (Change in) the (Future) Economy, Stupid: Economic Indicators, the Media, and Public Opinion," *American Journal of Political Science* 59 (April 2015): 457–474.

140. Pew Research Center for the People & the Press poll, August 14–17, 2009. See also NBC News poll, August 15–17, 2009.

141. Public Mind poll from Fairleigh Dickinson University Poll, December 8–15, 2014.

142. Public Mind poll from Fairleigh Dickinson University Poll, December 8–15, 2014; Steven Kull, Clay Ramsay, and Evan Lewis, "Misperceptions, the Media, and the Iraq War," *Political Science Quarterly* 118 (Winter 2003–2004): 569–598.

143. Steve Rendell and Tara Broughel, "Amplifying Officials, Squelching Dissent," *Extra!* (May/June 2003), Fairness and Accuracy in Reporting, http://www.fair.org/extra/0305/warstudy.html.

144. Muddiman, Stroud, and McCombs, "News Media Fragmentation."

145. David C. Barker, *Rushed to Judgment: Talk Radio, Persuasion, and American Political Behavior* (New York: Columbia University Press, 2002). But see Diana Owen, "Talk Radio and Evaluations of President Clinton," *Political Communication* 14, no. 3 (1997): 333–353.

146. Gregory J. Martin and Ali Yurukogluyz, "Bias in Cable News: Persuasion and Polarization," *American Economic Review* 107, no. 9 (2017): 2565–2599.

147. Michael P. Olson, "The Print Media and the American Party System: Evidence from the 2016 US Presidential Election," *Quarterly Journal of Political Science* 13, no.4 (2018): 405–426.

148. Mathew A. Baum, *Soft News Goes to War: Public Opinion and American Foreign Policy in the New Media Age* (Princeton, NJ: Princeton University Press, 2003).

149. George C. Edwards III and B. Dan Wood, "Who Influences Whom? The President, Congress, and the Media," *American Political Science Review* (June 1999): 327–344. See also B. Dan Wood and Jeffrey S. Peake, "The Dynamics of Foreign Policy Agenda Setting," *American Political Science Review* 92 (March 1998): 173–184; and Matthew Eshbaugh-Soha and Jeffrey S. Peake, "Presidents and the Economic Agenda," *Political Research Quarterly* 58 (March 2005): 127–138.

150. Jacobs and Shapiro, *Politicians Don't Pander*, chapters 5–6; and Edwards and Wood, "Who Influences Whom?"

151. Baker, *Politics of Diplomacy*, p. 103. See also Eytan Gilboa, "Television News and U.S. Foreign Policy," *Press/Politics* 8 (Fall 2003): 97–113.

152. Quoted in Morris, *Behind the Oval Office*, pp. 197, 245.

153. Carl M. Cannon, "From Bosnia to Kosovo," *National Journal*, April 3, 1999, p. 881.

154. Colin Powell, *My American Journey* (New York: Ballantine, 1995), pp. 550, 573.

155. Quoted in Powell, *My American Journey*, p. 507. See also Richard N. Haass, *War of Necessity, War of Choice: A Memoir of Two Iraq Wars* (New York: Simon & Schuster, 2009), pp. 129, 143.

156. Powell, *My American Journey*, p. 418.

157. Travis M. Johnston and Stephen N. Goggin, "Presidential Confidence in Crisis: Blame, Media, and the BP Oil Spill," *Presidential Studies Quarterly* 45 (September 2015): 467–489; and Alex I. Ruder, "Agency Design, the Mass Media, and the Blame for Agency Scandals," *Presidential Studies Quarterly* 45 (September 2015): 514–539.

158. Kim L. Fridkin, Patrick J. Kenney, and Sarah Allen Gershon, "Spinning Debates: The Impact of the News Media's Coverage of the Final 2004 Presidential Debate," *Press/Politics* 13, no. 1 (2008): 29–51; Dwight F. Davis, Lynda Lee Kaid, and Donald L. Singleton, "Information Effects of Political

Commentary," *Experimental Study of Politics* 6 (June 1977): 45–68; and Lynda Lee Kaid, Donald L. Singleton, and Dwight F. Davis, "Instant Analysis of Televised Political Addresses: The Speaker versus the Commentator," in Brent D. Ruben, ed., *Communication Yearbook I* (New Brunswick, NJ: Transaction Books, 1977), pp. 453–464.

159. Paletz and Entman, *Media–Power–Politics,* p. 70.

160. Patterson, *Out of Order,* p. 22, chapter 2.

161. Cappella and Jamieson, *Spiral of Cynicism.*

162. Kevin Quealy, "We Avoid News We Don't Like: Some Trump-Era Evidence," *New York Times,* February 21, 2017; Arceneaux and Johnson, *Changing Minds or Changing Channels?*; Nathalie J. Stroud, *Niche News: The Politics of News Choice* (New York: Oxford University Press, 2011); and Doris A. Graber, *Processing the News,* 2nd ed. (New York: Longman), pp. 90–93.

163. See, e.g., *Perceived Accuracy and Bias in the News Media,* A Gallup/Knight Foundation Survey, 2018, based on a Gallup poll, February 5–March 11, 2018.

164. Monmouth University poll, March 2–5, 2018.

165. Interview by author with Leslie Stahl, West Point, NY, 1986. See also James N. Druckman, "The Power of Televised Images: The First Kennedy-Nixon Debate Revisited," *Journal of Politics* 65 (May 2003): 559–571.

166. Matthew A. Baum and Philip B. K. Potter, *War and Democratic Constraint: How the Public Influences Foreign Policy* (Princeton, NJ: Princeton University Press, 2015).

167. Stanley Feldman, Leonie Huddy, and George E. Marcus, *Going to War in Iraq: When Citizens and the Press Matter* (Chicago, IL: University of Chicago Press, 2015), chapters 5–6.

CHAPTER 8

1. Nelson W. Polsby, "The Institutionalization of the U.S. House of Representatives," *American Political Science Review* 62 (1968); and James G. March and Johan P. Olsen, "Institutional Perspectives on Political Institutions," *Governance: An International Journal of Policy and Administration* 9 (1996).

2. Terry M. Moe, "The New Economics of Organization," *American Journal of Political Science* 28 (1984).

3. US Congress, House Committee on Post Office and Civil Service, Subcommittee on Employee Ethics and Utilization, *Presidential Staffing—A Brief Overview,* 95th Cong., 2d sess., Committee Print 95–17, July 25, 1978, p. 18.

4. *American State Papers,* Senate, 2nd cong., 2nd session, 1793, pp. 57–58.

5. Leonard White, *The Federalists: A Study in Administrative History* (New York: MacMillan Company, 1961), p. 255.

6. Ibid., p. 476.

7. Ibid., p. 473.

8. Stephen Skowronek, *Building a New American State: The Expansion of National Administrative Capacities 1877–1920* (New York: Cambridge University Press, 1982), p. 23.

9. White, *The Federalists: A Study in Administrative History,* p. 31.

10. Leonard White, *The Jeffersonians: A Study in Administrative History 1801–1829* (New York: The MacMillan Company, 1951), p. 72.

11. *Presidential Staffing—A Brief Overview,* pp. 4–6.

12. William C. Spragens, "White House Staffs, 1789–1974," in Bradley D. Nash et al., eds., *Organizing and Staffing the Presidency* (New York: Center for the Study of the Presidency, 1980), pp. 20–21.

13. Charles E. Walcott and Karen M. Hult, "White House Structure and Decision Making: Elaborating the Standard Model," *Presidential Studies Quarterly* 35 (2005): 303–318, p. 304.

14. 5 U.S. Code §101—Executive Departments.

15. The Presidential Succession Act, 3 U.S. Code § 19 defines the line of succession in case of a presidential and vice presidential vacancy. After the Speaker of the House and the President Pro Tem of the Senate, succession continues with cabinet Secretaries in order of the original establishment of the agency; as new cabinet agencies are created, Congress also modifies this list. The Twenty-Fifth Amendment allows a majority vote of the vice president and cabinet secretaries to remove a president who is unable to carry out the duties of office.

16. Richard F. Fenno, Jr., "President-Cabinet Relations: A Pattern and a Case Study," *American Political Science Review* 52 (1958): 388-405, p.390.

17. *Presidential Staffing—A Brief Overview,* p. 19.

18. Lindsay M. Chervinsky, "The Historical Presidency: George Washington and the First Presidential Cabinet," *Presidential Studies Quarterly* 48 (2018): 139–152, p. 147.

19. *Presidential Staffing—A Brief Overview*, p. 21.

20. The secretaries of certain department heads, the so-called inner cabinet—state, defense, justice, and the treasury—have tended to have closer and more collaborative relationships with the president than the secretaries of the other departments. Thomas E. Cronin, *The State of the Presidency* (Boston: Little, Brown, 1980), p. 283.

21. Nathaniel Rakich, "Two Years In, Turnover in Trump's Cabinet Is Still Historically High," *FiveThirtyEight*, January 9, 2019.

22. *Historical Statistics of the United States, Colonial Times to 1970*, Part 2, Table Series Y 308–317 and Y 335–338 (Washington, DC: Government Printing Office, 1975).

23. Much of the following discussion in this section comes from Kenneth R. Mayer, *With the Stroke of a Pen: Executive orders and Presidential Power* (Princeton, NJ: Princeton University Press, 2001), chapter 4.

24. James L. Sundquist, *The Decline and Resurgence of Congress* (Washington, DC: Brookings Institution, 1981), p. 39.

25. *The Need for a National Budget: Message from the President of the United States Transmitting the Report of the Commission on Economy and Efficiency on the Subject of the Need for a National Budget*, 62d Cong., 2d sess., 1912, House Document 854, p. 10.

26. Larry Berman, *The Office of Management and Budget and the Presidency, 1921–1979* (Princeton, NJ: Princeton University Press, 1979), p. 4.

27. Robert Jackson, *The Struggle for Judicial Supremacy* (New York: Alfred A. Knopf, 1949), pp. 90–91.

28. President's Committee on Administrative Management (PCAM), *Report with Special Studies* (Washington, DC: Government Printing Office, 1937), p. 5.

29. John Hart, *The Presidential Branch* (New York: Pergamon Press, 1987), p. 26.

30. The Committee proposed reorganizing the entire executive branch, placing the hundred or so individual units into twelve cabinet-level departments. This portion of the report was never implemented.

31. Hart, *The Presidential Branch*, p. 34.

32. Philip Rucker, Josh Dawsey,and Damian Paletta, "Trump Slams Fed Chair, Questions Climate Change and Threatens to Cancel Putin Meeting in Wide-Ranging Interview with *The Post*," *Washington Post*, November 27, 2018.

33. Steve Holland, "Advisors Lighthizer, Mnuchin Opposed Trump's Tariff's over Immigration: Sources," *Reuters*, May 31, 2019.

34. Jeffrey H. Birnbaum, *Madhouse: The Private Turmoil of Working for the President* (New York: Times Books, 1996), p. 7.

35. Fred I. Greenstein, *The Hidden Hand President* (New York: Basic Books, 1982).

36. For analysis of recent chiefs of staff, see David B. Cohen, Karen M. Hult, and Charles E. Walcott, "White House Evolution and Institutionalization: The Office of Chief of Staff since Reagan," *Presidential Studies Quarterly* 46 (2016): 4–29.

37. Charles E. Walcott, Shirley Anne Warshaw, and Stephen J. Wayne, "The Office of Chief of Staff," in Martha Joynt Kumar and Terry Sullivan, eds., *White House World: Transitions, Organizations, and Office Operations* (College Station: Texas A&M University Press, 2003), p. 11.

38. Walcott and Hult, "White House Structure and Decision Making: Elaborating the Standard Model," p. 310.

39. See Chris Whipple, *The Gatekeepers: How the White House Chiefs of Staff Define Every Presidency* (New York: Crown, 2017).

40. James P. Pfiffner, "Organizing the Trump Presidency," *Presidential Studies Quarterly* 48 (2018); and Bob Woodward, *Fear: Trump in the White House* (New York: Simon and Schuster, 2018).

41. Martha Joynt Kumar, *White House Staff and Organization: Ten Observations*. White House Transition Project, Report 2017–10 (2017): 2.

42. Michael D. Shear, Glenn Thrush, and Maggie Haberman, "John Kelly, Asserting Authority, Fires Anthony Scaramucci," *New York Times*, July 31, 2017.

43. Eliana Johnson and Nancy Cook, "Kelly Moves to Control the Information Trump Sees," *Politico*, August 24, 2017.

44. Andrew deGrandpre, "John Kelly, Trump's New Chief of Staff, 'Won't Suffer Idiots and Fools'," *Washington Post*, July 29, 2017; and Ron Nixon and Michael D. Shear, "John Kelly, New Chief of Staff, Is Seen as Beacon of Discipline," *New York Times*, July 28, 2017.

45. Elaina Plott and Peter Nicholas, "Trump's Chief of Staff Says He's Having a Ball," *The Atlantic*, April 24, 2019.

46. Annie Karni and Maggie Haberman, "John Kelly to Step Down as Trump, Facing New Perils, Shakes Up Staff," *New York Times*, December 8, 2018.

47. Michael Tackett and Maggie Haberman, "Trump Names Mick Mulvaney Acting Chief of Staff," *New York Times*, December 14, 2018.

48. Peter Baker and Maggie Haberman, "Mick Mulvaney Tries Letting Trump be Trump," *New York Times*, April 9, 2019.

49. Katie Dunn Tenpas, "In Search of a Third Chief of Staff, Trump Sets a Record," Brookings Institution, December 10, 2018. https://www.brookings.edu/blog/fixgov/2018/12/10/in-search-of-a-third-chief-of-staff-trump-sets-a-record/.

50. Katie Dunn Tenpas and Karen Hult, *The Office of the Staff Secretary*, White House Transition Project Report 2017–23 (2017): 9.

51. Josh Dawsey, Beth Reinhard, and Elise Viebeck, "Senior White House Official to Resign After Ex-Wives' Allegations of Abuse," *Washington Post*, February 7, 2018.

52. Geoffrey Hodgson, *Woodrow Wilson's Right Hand: The Life of Colonel Edward M. House* (New Haven: Yale University Press, 2008): 8–9.

53. Justin S. Vaughn and José D. Villalobos, *Czars in the White House: The Rise of Policy Czars as Presidential Management Tools* (Ann Arbor: University of Michigan Press, 2015).

54. Congressional Research Service, *The Federal Anti-Nepotism Statute: Limits on Appointing, Hiring, and Promoting Relatives*, CRS Legal Sidebar, December 1, 2016.

55. Memorandum Opinion for the Counsel to the President, *Application of the Anti-Nepotism Statute to a Presidential Appointment in the White House*, Department of Justice, Office of Legal Counsel, January 20, 2017.

56. Ryan Lizza, "Anthony Scaramucci Called Me to Unload about White House Leakers, Reince Priebus, and Steve Bannon," *New Yorker*, July 27, 2017.

57. Ian Schwartz, "Acosta vs. Huckabee Sanders: Shouldn't You have the Guts to Name Which Journalists are the Enemy of the People?" *Real Clear Politics*, October 29, 2019.

58. James P. Pfiffner, "White House Staff vs. the Cabinet: Centripetal and Centrifugal Roles," *Presidential Studies Quarterly* 16 (1986): 675–676.

59. Jeremy Rabkin, "At the President's Side: The Role of the White House Counsel in Constitutional Policy," *Law and Contemporary Problems* 56 (1993).

60. Maryanne Borelli, Karen Hult, and Nancy Kassop, "The White House Counsel's Office," in Martha Joynt Kumar and Terry Sullivan, eds. *The White House World: Transitions, Organization, and Office Operations* (College Station: Texas A&M University Press, 2003), p. 197.

61. Jack Goldsmith, *The Terror Presidency: Law and Judgment inside the Bush Administration* (New York: W.W. Norton & Co., 2007), pp. 64, 180.

62. US Department of Justice, *Report on the Investigation into Russian Interference in the 2016 Presidential Election*, March 2019, Volume II, pp. 113–118.

63. Michael S. Schmidt and Maggie Haberman, "Trump Wanted to Order Justice Department to Prosecute Comey and Clinton," *New York Times*, November 20, 2018.

64. Bradley H. Patterson Jr., *To Serve the President: Continuity and Innovation in the White House Staff* (Washington, DC: Brookings Institution Press, 2008), p. 265.

65. Graham Allison and Philip Zelikow, *Essence of Decision: Explaining the Cuban Missile Crisis*, 2nd ed. (New York: Addison Wesley, 1999), p. 110. The Ex Com convened on occasion for the rest of Kennedy's Administration.

66. Executive order 13228, "Establishing the Office of Homeland Security and the Homeland Security Council," October 8, 2001,

67. Executive order 13199, "Establishment of White House Office of Faith-Based and Community Initiatives," January 29, 2001.

68. Clinton T. Brass, *Office of Management and Budget: A Brief Overview*, Congressional Research Service RS21665, February 14, 2005, p. 3.

69. Letter for the Heads of Executive Departments and Agencies, "Guidance on Compliance with the Congressional Review Act," Office of Management and Budget, April 19, 2019.

70. Mark M. Lowenthal, *The National Security Council: Organizational History*, Congressional Research Service 78–104F, June 27, 1978, p. 2.

71. See John P. Burke, *Honest Broker? The National Security Advisor and Presidential Decision Making* (College Station: Texas A&M University Press, 2009).

72. Executive order 13228, "Establishing the Office of Homeland Security and the Homeland Security Council," October 8, 2001.

73. Homeland Security Act of 2002, PL 107–296, November 25, 2002.

74. Jordan Brunner, "NSPM 2—Organization of the National Security Council and the Homeland Security Council: A Summary," *Lawfare*, January 28, 2017.

75. PL 79–304, Section 2, February 20, 1946.

76. Patterson, *The White House Staff*, p. 91.

77. Dan Diamond, "Trump Budget Would Effectively Kill Drug Control Office," *Politico*, May 5, 2017.

78. Executive order 11075, "Administration of the Trade Expansion Act of 1962," January 15, 1963.

79. Office of the United States Special Trade Representative, *History of the United States Trade Representative*. https://ustr.gov/about-us/history.

80. Executive order 11514, "Protection and Enhancement of Environmental Quality," March 5, 1970.

81. Terry M. Moe, "The Politicized Presidency," in John Chubb and Paul E. Peterson, eds., *New Directions in American Politics* (Washington, DC: Brookings Institution, 1985).

82. David E. Lewis, *The Politics of Presidential Appointments* (Princeton, NJ: Princeton University Press, 2008), pp. 202–219.

83. Andrew Rudalevige, *Managing the President's Program* (Princeton, NJ: Princeton University Press, 2002), p. 114.

84. Hart, *The Presidential Branch*, p. 217.

85. An agency's ability to do this is built in with Civil Service protections that make it difficult to fire most federal employees.

86. Samuel Kernell, "The Creed and Reality of White House Management," in Samuel Kernell and Samuel L. Popkin, eds., *Chief of Staff: Twenty Five Years of Managing the Presidency* (Berkeley: University of California Press, 1986), p. 200.

87. Robert Costa, Philip Rucker, and Elise Viebeck, "Pence Replaces Christie as Leader of Trump Transition Effort," *Washington Post*, November 11, 2016.

88. John Adams, *The Works of John Adams*, vol. 1, ed. C. F. Adams (Boston: Little, Brown, 1850), p. 289.

89. Thomas Jefferson, *The Writings of Thomas Jefferson*, vol. 1, ed. P. L. Ford (New York: Putnam, 1896), pp. 98–99.

90. Woodrow Wilson, *Congressional Government* (New York: Meridian Books, 1956; originally printed in 1885), p. 162.

91. Bradley H. Patterson, Jr., *The Ring of Power* (New York: Basic Books, 1988), p. 287.

92. Doris Kearns, *Lyndon Johnson and the American Dream* (New York: Harper and Row, 1976), p. 164.

93. Joel K. Goldstein, "The Rising Power of the Modern Vice Presidency," *Presidential Studies Quarterly* 38 (September 2008): 374-389.

94. Patterson, *To Serve the President*, pp. 238–239.

95. Joel K. Goldstein, "The Contemporary Presidency: Cheney, Power, and the War on Terror," *Presidential Studies Quarterly* 40 (March 2010): 102-139.

96. Josh Rogin, "Pence Takes Power in Foreign Policy," *Washington Post*, March 6, 2017.

97. Michael D. Shear, "How the White House Explains Waiting 18 Days to Fire Michael Flynn," *New York Times*, May 9, 2017.

98. Andrew Hanna, "Pence Insists U.S. is Committed to Article 5 in Speech Honoring NATO Leader," Politico.com, June 5, 2017.

99. Gabby Orr, "Pence Takes Trumpism Abroad," *Politico*, February 21, 2019.

100. Joel Goldstein, "Mike Pence Has Lasted Two Years as Trump's VP. That May be His Main Accomplishment." *Washington Post* (Monkey Cage), January 18, 2019.

101. Paul Kane. "Pence, a Man of the House, Becomes Trump's Eyes and Ears in the Senate," *Washington Post*, February 8, 2017.

102. Adams had cast sixteen over the equivalent period of April 30,1789–October 30, 1791. United States Senate Historical Office, *Occasions When Vice Presidents Have Voted to Break Tie Votes in the Senate*, December 21, 2018; Senate Historical Office, "Tie Votes," https://www.senate.gov/pagelayout/reference/four_column_table/Tie_Votes.htm, accessed May 29, 2019.

103. Gene Smith, *When the Cheering Stopped: The Last Years of Woodrow Wilson* (New York: William Morrow, 1964).

104. Doris Kerns Goodwin, *No Ordinary Time: Franklin and Eleanor Roosevelt: The Home Front in World War II* (New York: Simon & Schuster, 1994).

105. Hillary Clinton attended cabinet meetings as well. Robert P. Watson, *The President's Wives: Reassessing the Office of First Lady* (Boulder, CO: Lynne Rienner, 2000), p. 56.

106. Betty Boyd Caroli, *First Ladies: The Ever Changing Role from Martha Washington to Melania Trump* (New York: Oxford University Press 2019), p. 348.

107. Kate Bennett, "One Year of Melania Trump's 'Be Best': Big Ideas, Little Progress," CNN.com, May 6, 2019.

108. James Wilson as quoted in Madison's journal and as appears in Max Farrand, ed., *Records of the Federal Convention*, vol. I (New Haven, CT: Yale University Press, 1921), p. 66.

CHAPTER 9

1. Mark Landler, "Obama Warns U.S. Faces Diffuse Terrorism Threats," *New York Times*, May 28, 2014.

2. Quoted in John C. Donovan, *The Politics of Poverty*, 2nd ed. (Indianapolis, IN: Pegasus, 1973), p. 111.

3. On continuity in foreign policy despite changes in the occupant of the presidency, see William J. Dixon and Stephen M. Gardner, "Presidential Succession and the Cold War: An Analysis of Soviet-American Relations, 1948–1988," *Journal of Politics* 54 (February 1992): 156–175.

4. Quoted in Paul C. Light, *The President's Agenda: Domestic Policy Choice from Kennedy to Carter* (Baltimore, MD: Johns Hopkins University Press, 1982), p. 179.

5. Richard E. Neustadt, *Presidential Power and the Modern Presidents* (New York: Free Press, 1990), pp. 121–122; and Dean Acheson, *Present at the Creation: My Life in the State Department* (New York: Norton, 1969), pp. 466–468.

6. James A. Baker III, *The Politics of Diplomacy* (New York: Putnam, 1995), p. 263.

7. Quoted in Burt Solomon, "Clinton Tinkers with His Staff … to Counter His Own Failings," *National Journal*, May 15, 1995, p. 1193.

8. National Commission on Terrorist Attacks on the United States, *The 9/11 Commission Report* (New York: Norton, 2004), pp. 185–186, 208, 212–213; Richard A. Clarke, *Against All Enemies: Inside America's War on Terror* (New York: Free Press, 2004), pp. 26, 228, 230–231, 234–235, 237, 242–243, 254; and Bob Woodward, *Plan of Attack* (New York: Simon & Schuster, 2004), pp. 80, 254.

9. Amy B. Zegart, *Spying Blind: The CIA, the FBI, and the Origins of 9/11* (Princeton, NJ: Princeton University Press, 2009), pp. 3–5.

10. George Tenet, *At the Center of the Storm: My Years at the CIA* (New York: HarperCollins, 2007), pp. 322–323.

11. Bob Woodward, *State of Denial* (New York: Simon & Schuster, 2006), pp. 149–150; and Donald Rumsfeld, *Known and Unknown* (New York: Penguin, 2011), p. 485.

12. Quoted in William Greider, "The Education of David Stockman," *Atlantic Monthly*, December 1981, p. 34.

13. Alexander L. George, "The Case for Multiple Advocacy in Making Foreign Policy," *American Political Science Review* 66 (September 1972): 766. See also John P. Burke, "Organizational Structure and Presidential Decision Making," in George C. Edwards III and William G. Howell, eds., *The Oxford Handbook of the American Presidency* (Oxford, UK: Oxford University Press, 2009), pp. 501–527; and Daniel E. Ponder, *Good Advice: Information and Policy Making in the White House* (College Station: Texas A&M Press, 2000).

14. Bryce Harlow, quoted in Emmet John Hughes, *The Living Presidency: The Resources and Dilemmas of the American Presidential Office* (Baltimore, MD: Penguin, 1973), p. 345.

15. Henry Kissinger, *White House Years* (Boston, MA: Little, Brown, 1979), p. 47; see also p. 1455.

16. Roger B. Porter, "Gerald Ford: A Healing Presidency," in Fred I. Greenstein, ed., *Leadership in the Modern Presidency* (Cambridge, MA: Harvard University Press, 1988), pp. 199–227. See also Alejandro Bonvecchi, "Crises, Structures and Managerial Choice in Economic Policymaking: Presidential Economic Advisory Agencies and the Management of Macroeconomic Policy in Argentina and the United States, 1944–2009," *Presidential Studies Quarterly* 46 (September 2016): 507–530; William W. Newmann, "Searching for the Right Balance? Managing Foreign Policy Decisions under Eisenhower and Kennedy," *Congress & the Presidency* 42 (May–August 2015): 119–146; and David Mitchell, "Does

Context Matter? Advisory Systems and the Management of Foreign Policy Decision-Making Process," *Presidential Studies Quarterly* 40 (December 2010): 631–659.

17. Theodore C. Sorensen, *Decision-Making in the White House: The Olive Branch or the Arrows?* (New York: Columbia University Press, 1963), p. 3. See also Patrick J. Haney, *Organizing for Foreign Policy Crises* (Ann Arbor: University of Michigan Press, 1997).

18. President Ford wrote about this problem in *A Time to Heal: The Autobiography of Gerald R. Ford* (New York: Harper & Row, 1979), p. 147; see also p. 186.

19. President Gerald Ford's interview with Martha Kumar, "Presidency Research Group's 2000 Transition Project," October 10, 2000.

20. Jimmy Carter, *White House Diary* (New York: Farrar, Straus and Giroux, 2010), p. 60.

21. See, e.g., David Remnick, "A Conversation with Maggie Haberman, Trump's Favorite Foe," *New Yorker*, July 21, 2017; David E. Lewis, Patrick Bernhard, and Emily You, "President Trump as Manager: Reflections on the First Year," *Presidential Studies Quarterly* 48 (September 2018): 480–501; James P. Pfiffner, "Organizing the Trump Presidency," *Presidential Studies Quarterly* 48 (March 2018): 153–167; Andrew Rudalevige, "Will a New White House Chief of Staff Matter? Not Unless Trump Wants Change," *Washington Post*, December 12, 2018; John P. Burke, "Struggling with Standard Order: Challenges and Performance of the Trump National Security Council System," *Presidential Studies Quarterly* 48 (December 2018): 640–666; and Bob Woodward, *Fear: Trump in the White House* (New York: Simon and Schuster, 2018), pp. xviii, xix, 141–145, 156, 158, 189–191, 205–206, 211–212, 233, 236, 261–265.

22. Woodward, *Fear*, pp. 262.

23. Susan B. Glasser, "John Kelly, Scott Pruitt, and the Epic Turnover of the Trump Administration," *New Yorker*, July 6, 2018.

24. Kathryn Dunn Tenpas "Tracking Turnover in the Trump Administration," Brookings Institution, January 2019; and Kathryn Dunn Tenpas, "White House Staff Turnover in Year One of the Trump Administration: Context, Consequences, and Implications for Governing," *Presidential Studies Quarterly* 48 (September 2018): 502–516. .

25. Clark Clifford, *Counsel to the President* (New York: Random House, 1991), p. 636.

26. See Kissinger, *White House Years*, pp. 40, 602.

27. Interview with Henson Moore, White House Interview Program, October 15, 1999. See also Karl Rove, *Courage and Consequence* (New York: Threshold Editions, 2010), p. 226.

28. Hamilton Jordan, *Crisis: The Last Year of the Carter Presidency* (New York: Putnam, 1982), p. 42.

29. Jim Rasenberger, *The Brilliant Disaster: JFK, Castro, and America's Doomed Invasion of Cuba's Bay of Pigs* (New York: Scribner, 2011), p. 127.

30. David Priess, *The President's Book of Secrets* (New York: Public Affairs, 2016), pp. 265–266; Tenet, *At the Center of the Storm*, pp. 310, 315–316, 327–328, 334–335, 354, 358, 370; Thomas E. Ricks, *Fiasco: The American Military Adventure in Iraq* (New York: Penguin Press, 2006), pp. 54–55; and Paul R. Pillar, *Intelligence and U.S. Foreign Policy: Iraq, 9/11, and Misguided Reform* (New York: Columbia University Press, 2011), pp. 36, 142–143.

31. Sorensen, *Decision-Making in the White House*, p. 62.

32. Quoted in Light, *The President's Agenda*, p. 200.

33. On Obama, see Jonathan Alter, *The Promise: President Obama, Year One* (New York: Simon & Schuster, 2010), pp. 178, 194, 196, 198–199, 204–205, 218, 220, 315; Bob Woodward, *Obama's Wars* (New York: Simon & Schuster, 2010), pp. 168, 236–238, 258, 278–280, 298, 322; and Ron Suskind, *Confidence Men: Wall Street, Washington, and the Education of a President* (New York: Harper, 2011), pp. 228, 279, 301–302, 323, 355–356, 364.

34. Kissinger, *White House Years*, p. 996.

35. See John P. Burke, "The Neutral/Honest Broker Role in Foreign-Policy Decision Making: A Reassessment," *Presidential Studies Quarterly* 35 (June 2005): 229–258.

36. Neustadt, *Presidential Power and the Modern Presidents*, chapters 6–7.

37. Robert M. Gates, *Duty* (New York: Knopf, 2014), p. 300

38. Suskind, *Confidence Men*, pp. 148–153, 214, 228, 277, 315–318, 340, 348, 377, 389; and Alter, *The Promise*, pp. 190, 204–205, 207, 216, 218.

39. Richard N. Haass, *War of Necessity, War of Choice: A Memoir of Two Iraq Wars* (New York: Simon & Schuster, 2009), pp. 5–6, 212–216, 220, 234, 272; Bob Woodward, *The War Within* (New York: Simon & Schuster, 2008), pp. 28, 50; Woodward, *State of Denial*, p. 381; Michael Isikoff and David Corn, *Hubris: The Inside Story of Spin, Scandal, and the Selling of the Iraq War* (New York: Crown, 2006), p. 310; and Ivo Daalder and I. M. Destler, "In the Shadow of the Oval Office," *Foreign Affairs*, January/February 2009, pp. 125–126.

40. Rumsfeld, *Known and Unknown*, pp. 318–319, 327, 329, 485, 491–492, 494, 498, 510–511, 517–519, 523, 525, 602; Douglas J. Feith, *War and Decision: Inside the Pentagon at the Dawn of the War on Terrorism* (New York: Harper, 2008), pp. 245, 273; Tenet, *At the Center of the Storm*, p. 308; Ron Suskind, *The One Percent Doctrine* (New York: Simon & Schuster, 2006), p. 224; Woodward, *State of Denial*, pp. 379–380, 404, 408, 455; and Ron Suskind, *The Price of Loyalty* (New York: Simon & Schuster, 2004), pp. 121, 125–126, 144–149, 156, 273.

41. Rumsfeld, *Known and Unknown*, pp. 318–327.

42. Suskind, *The One Percent Doctrine*, p. 111; and Barton Gellman, *Angler: The Cheney Vice Presidency* (New York: Penguin Press, 2008), chapters 11–12.

43. Condoleezza Rice, *No Higher Honor: A Memoir of My Years in Washington* (New York: Crown, 2011), pp. 105–106; Gellman, *Angler*, pp. 81–90, 135–139, 162–173, 351; James P. Pfiffner, "Policy Making in the Bush White House," *Presidential Studies Quarterly* 39 (June 2009): 363–384; and Peter Baker, *Days of Fire: Bush and Cheney in the White House* (New York: Doubleday, 2013), pp. 95–97, 174–175.

44. Tenet, *At the Center of the Storm*, pp. 347, 356–358, 373; James Risen, *State of War: The Secret History of the CIA and the Bush Administration* (New York: Free Press, 2006), pp. 75–76; David L. Phillips, *Losing Ground* (Boulder, CO: Westview, 2005), pp. 60–61, 73, chapter 7; Gellman, *Angler*, pp. 222–225, 247; and Jane Mayer, *The Dark Side: The Inside Story of How the War on Terror Turned into a War on American Ideals* (New York: Doubleday, 2008), p. 5.

45. Risen, *State of War*, pp. 64–65; and Stephen Benedict Dyson, "What Really Happened in Planning for Postwar Iraq?" *Political Science Quarterly* 128, no. 3 (2013): 465.

46. Rumsfeld, *Known and Unknown*, p. 323.

47. Rumsfeld, *Known and Unknown*, pp. 319, 326–327, 329, 485, 491–492, 494, 498, 510–511, 517–519, 523, 525, 602; Woodward, *State of Denial*, pp. 109, 190–191, 249, 241, 267; Risen, *State of War*, pp. 63–64, 66; Feith, *War and Decision*, pp. 143–144, 245, 250, 283–284, 439; Gellman, *Angler*, pp. 340–342; Mayer, *The Dark Side*, pp. 186–188; and Peter W. Rodman, *Presidential Command* (New York: Knopf, 2009), pp. 249–251, 256, 262–271.

48. Elizabeth N. Saunders, "No Substitute for Experience: Presidents, Advisers, and Information in Group Decision-Making," *International Organization* 71, no. 1 (2017): 219–247.

49. Woodward, *Obama's Wars*, pp. 158–162.

50. Ronald Reagan, *An American Life* (New York: Simon & Schuster, 1990), pp. 540–541.

51. Bob Woodward, *Bush at War* (New York: Simon & Schuster, 2002), pp. 136–137, 145, 168, 342. See also Suskind, *The Price of Loyalty*, pp. 165–166.

52. Gates, *Duty*, p. 94; Woodward, *The War Within*, pp. 431, 433; Suskind, *The Price of Loyalty*, pp. 165–166; and Scott McClellan, *What Happened: Inside the Bush White House and Washington's Culture of Deception* (New York: Public Affairs, 2008), pp. 127, 145, 203, 208. But see Rove, *Courage and Consequence*, p. 124.

53. Suskind, *The Price of Loyalty*, pp. 57–60, 107–109, 126, 148–149, 153, 295–306. A number of Bush's close associates thought the president asked probing questions. See Karen Hughes, *Ten Minutes from Normal* (New York: Viking, 2004), pp. 93, 282; Rumsfeld, *Known and Unknown*, pp. 319, 694; and Rove, *Courage and Consequence*, pp. 168, 171. Robert Gates, who joined the administration at the end of 2006, provides a more mixed view. See Gates, *Duty*, p. 94.

54. Clarke, *Against All Enemies*, pp. 243–244; McClellan, *What Happened*, p. 145; Suskind, *The One Percent Doctrine*, p. 79; and Pillar, *Intelligence and U.S. Foreign Policy*, p. 13.

55. See National Commission on Terrorist Attacks on the United States, *The 9/11 Commission Report*, pp. 260–262; and Woodward, *Plan of Attack*, p. 80.

56. Woodward, *Plan of Attack*, pp. 249–250; Woodward, *State of Denial*, p. 188; and Pillar, *Intelligence and U.S. Foreign Policy*, p. 32. Bush did, however, ask his national security assistant to review the intelligence again. See Rice, *No Higher Honor*, p. 200.

57. George W. Bush, *Decision Points* (New York: Crown, 2010), p. 242.

58. Pillar, *Intelligence and U.S. Foreign Policy*, pp. 14, 36, 41–42, 53–59.

59. Woodward, *State of Denial*, pp. 226, 237, 336–337, 419; Woodward, *Plan of Attack*, pp. 80, 149, 151; Isikoff and Corn, *Hubris*, p. 357; Suskind, *The Price of Loyalty*, pp. 57–60, 107–109, 126, 144–149, 153, 170–171, 295–306; and Woodward, *The War Within*, p. 106.

60. Isikoff and Corn, *Hubris*, p. 310.

61. Haass, *War of Necessity, War of Choice*, pp. 5–6, 212–216, 220, 234, 272; and Pillar, *Intelligence and U.S. Foreign Policy*, pp. 13–14.

62. Rumsfeld, *Known and Unknown*, p. 456; Woodward, *Plan of Attack*, p. 251–252, 272, 416–417; Woodward, *State of Denial*, p. 90; and Woodward, *The War Within*, p. 28. But see Baker, *Days of Fire*, p. 241.

63. Bush, *Decision Points*, p. 251.

64. Woodward, *Plan of Attack*, p. 295; and Ricks, *Fiasco*, p. 42.

65. Bush, *Decision Points*, pp. 199, 367.

66. Paul R. Pillar, "Intelligence, Policy, and the War in Iraq," *Foreign Affairs*, March/April 2006, pp. 24–25; Woodward, *Plan of Attack*, p. 139; Woodward, *The War Within*, pp. 106–107; and Woodward, *State of Denial*, p. 260.

67. Rumsfeld, *Known and Unknown*, pp. 515–519; Rice, *No Higher Honor*, p. 238; Feith, *War and Decision*, p. 433; Woodward, *State of Denial*, pp. 197–198, 442; Woodward, *The War Within*, pp. 49–50; Tenet, *At the Center of the Storm*, pp. 426–428, 431, 437; Risen, *State of War*, p. 3; Michael R. Gordon, "Fateful Choice on Iraq Army Bypassed Debate," *New York Times*, March 17, 2008; Michael R. Gordon and Bernard E. Trainor, *Cobra II: The Inside Story of the Invasion and Occupation of Iraq* (New York: Pantheon Books, 2006), pp. 482–483; and Edmund Andrews, "Envoy's Letter Counters Bush on Dismantling of Iraqi Army," *New York Times*, September 4, 2007; Ricks, *Fiasco*, p. 158.

68. Mayer, *The Dark Side*, pp. 34, 41–43, 52, 55, 64, 68–70, 80–89, 123–124, 186–188, 220–221, 234–236, 265, 268–269.

69. Bush, *Decision Points*, pp. 259–260.

70. Woodward, *The War Within*, p. 433.

71. Bush, *Decision Points*, p. 268.

72. Priess, *The President's Book of Secrets*, pp. 267–269.

73. Bush, *Decision Points*, pp. 371, 378.

74. Elisabeth Bumiller, "Casualty of Firestorm: Outrage, Bush and FEMA Chief," *New York Times*, September 10, 2005; and Eric Lipton, "Hurricane Investigators See 'Fog of War' at White House," *New York Times*, January 28, 2006.

75. Woodward, *The War Within*, pp. 106, 320; and Ricks, *Fiasco*, pp. 73, 99, 101.

76. Aaron Blake, "Rex Tillerson on Trump: 'Undisciplined, Doesn't Like to Read' and Tries to Do Illegal Things," *Washington Post*, December 7, 2018; Julian E. Barnes and Michael S. Schmidt, "To Woo a Skeptical Trump, Intelligence Chiefs Talk Economics Instead of Spies," *New York Times*, March 3, 2019; Carol D. Leonnig, Shane Harris, and Greg Jaffe "Breaking with Tradition, Trump Skips President's Written Intelligence Report and Relies on Oral Briefings," *Washington Post*, February 9, 2018; and Woodward, *Fear*, pp. 271–276.

77. Remnick, "A Conversation with Maggie Haberman, Trump's Favorite Foe"; Ashley Parker, David Nakamura, and Philip Rucker, "Trump's Wall: The Inside Story of How the President Crafts Immigration Policy," *Washington Post*, July 19, 2017; and Maggie Haberman and Glenn Thrush, "Trump Reaches beyond West Wing for Counsel," *New York Times*, April 22, 2017.

78. Woodward, *Fear*, p. 231; Remnick, "A Conversation with Maggie Haberman, Trump's Favorite Foe"; Parker, Nakamura, and Rucker, "Trump's Wall"; and Haberman and Thrush, "Trump Reaches beyond West Wing for Counsel."

79. Burke, "Struggling with Standard Order"; and Woodward, *Fear*, pp. xviii, xix, 141–145, 156, 158, 189–191, 205–206, 211–212, 233, 236, 261–265.

80. Mark Landler and Helene Cooper, "Bolton Walked Back Syria Statement: His Disdain for Debate Helped Produce It," *New York Times*, January 7, 2019; Karen DeYoung, Greg Jaffe, John Hudson, and Josh Dawsey, "John Bolton Puts His Singular Stamp on Trump's National Security Council," *Washington Post*, March 4, 2019; and Hal Brands, "Trump's True Foreign Policy: Chaos," Bloomberg, August 20, 2019.

81. Coral Davenport, "In the Trump Administration, Science Is Unwelcome. So Is Advice." *New York Times*, June 9, 2018.

82. Quoted in Philip Bump, "Objective Information Has Less of a Place in an Intuition-Based Presidency," *Washington Post*, March 13, 2018.

83. Woodward, *Fear*, p. 138.

84. Woodward, *Fear*, p. 133

85. David Rohde, "Is Trump Trying to Bully America's Intelligence Agencies Into Silence?" *New Yorker*, January 31, 201; and Eileen Sullivan, "Trump Calls His Intelligence People 'Naive'," *New York Times*, January 30, 2019.

86. Philip Rucker, Josh Dawsey, and Damian Paletta, "Trump Slams Fed Chair, Questions Climate Change and Threatens to Cancel Putin Meeting in Wide-Ranging Interview with *The Post*," *Washington Post*, November 27, 2018. See also Blake, "Rex Tillerson on Trump."

87. See, e.g., Julie Hirschfeld Davis and Helene Cooper, "Trump Says Transgender People Will Not Be Allowed in the Military," *New York Times*, July 26, 2017, p. 76; Kim Soffen and Darla Cameron, "How Trump's Travel Ban Broke from the Normal executive order Process, *Washington Post*, February 9,

2017; and Josh Rogin, "Inside the White House-Cabinet Battle over Trump's Immigration Order," *Washington Post*, February 4, 2017; Woodward, *Fear*. pp. 146–147, 191, 202–203, 223–4, 230; Antony J. Blinken, "No People. No Process. No Policy." *New York Times*, January 28, 2019; and Stephanie Ruhle, "Trump Was Angry and 'Unglued' When He Started a Trade War, Officials Say," NBC News, March 3, 2018.

88. Chester L. Cooper, *The Lost Crusade: America in Vietnam* (New York: Dodd, Mead, 1970), p. 223.

89. See, e.g., Gordon M. Goldstein, *Lessons in Disaster: McGeorge Bundy and the Path to War in Vietnam* (New York: Holt, 2008), pp. 183, 202–204. See also H. R. McMaster, *Dereliction of Duty: Lyndon Johnson, Robert McNamara, the Joint Chiefs of Staff, and the Lies that Led to Vietnam* (New York: Harper Perennial, 1998).

90. Jonathan Alter, *The Promise: President Obama, Year One* (New York: Simon & Schuster, 2010), pp. 219, 222.

91. Ford, *A Time to Heal*, pp. 187–188. See also Reagan, *An American Life*, p. 536.

92. Melvyn P. Leffler, *For the Soul of Mankind* (New York: Hill & Wang, 2007), p. 232; Andrew Preston, *The War Council: McGeorge Bundy, the NSC, and Vietnam* (Cambridge, MA: Harvard University Press, 2006), p. 181; Robert Dallek, *Flawed Giant: Lyndon Johnson and His Times, 1961–1973* (New York: Oxford University Press, 1998), p. 253; and Goldstein, *Lessons in Disaster*, p. 162.

93. George E. Reedy, *The Twilight of the Presidency* (New York: New American Library, 1970).

94. Richard N. Goodwin, *Remembering America: A Voice from the Sixties* (Boston, MA: Little, Brown, 1988), pp. 176–177.

95. Pillar, "Intelligence, Policy, and the War in Iraq," p. 23; Woodward, *State of Denial*, pp. 224–225, 328, 370–371, 383; Tenet, *At the Center of the Storm*, pp. 317, 343; and Risen, *State of War*, pp. 128–130, 145–147.

96. Ricks, *Fiasco*, pp. 99–100.

97. The Commission on the Intelligence Capabilities of the United States Regarding Weapons of Mass Destruction, *Report to the President of the United States* (Washington, DC, 2005), p. 11 ff; Pillar, *Intelligence and U.S. Foreign Policy*, chapter 6; Richard K. Betts, *Enemies of Intelligence: Knowledge and Power in American National Security* (New York: Columbia University Press, 2007), pp. 94–95; Risen, *State of War*, pp. 23–25, 106, 110–119, 128–130, 145–147; Isikoff and Corn, *Hubris*, pp. 4–5, 61, 138–140, 410–411; Tenet, *At the Center of the Storm*, p. 302; and Suskind, *The One Percent Doctrine*, pp. 189–190. But see Tenet, *At the Center of the Storm*, pp. 336, 342, 344; Gordon and Trainor, *Cobra II*, p. 127; and Robert Jervis, *Why Intelligence Fails* (Ithaca, NY: Cornell University Press, 2010), p. 134. Also see Jack Davis, "Intelligence Analysts and Policymakers: Benefits and Dangers of Tensions in the Relationship," *Intelligence and National Security* 21 (December 2006): 1007–1009.

98. Dean Rusk, quoted in Leon V. Sigal, *Reporters and Officials: The Organization and Politics of Newsmaking* (Lexington, MA: Heath, 1973), p. 147.

99. Irving Janis, *Groupthink*, 2nd ed. (Boston, MA: Houghton Mifflin, 1982).

100. Larry Speakes, *Speaking Out* (New York: Scribner's, 1988), pp. 244–245.

101. Ryan Lizza, "Anthony Scaramucci Called Me to Unload about White House Leakers, Reince Priebus, and Steve Bannon," *New Yorker*, July 27, 2017; Peter Baker and Maggie Haberman, "Anthony Scaramucci's Uncensored Rant: Foul Words and Threats to Have Priebus Fired," *New York Times*, July 27, 2017; and Jenna Johnson, Philip Rucker, and David Nakamura, "White House Tensions Flare in the Open as Scaramucci Rips Priebus in Vulgar Tirade," *Washington Post*, July 27, 2017.

102. Interview with Dean Rusk, "Mr. Secretary: On the Eve of Emeritus," *Life,* January 17, 1969, p. 62B.

103. Jack Valenti, *A Very Human President* (New York: Norton, 1975), pp. 115–116.

104. Woodward, *The War Within*, pp. 106–107.

105. Rice, *No Higher Honor*, pp. 16, 21; Woodward, *Plan of Attack*, pp. 148–152; and Rumsfeld, *Known and Unknown*, p. 323.

106. Ashley Parker, "Snubs and Slights Are Part of the Job in Trump's White House," *Washington Post*, May 29, 2017.

107. Marc Fisher, "Trump's Tools of Persuasion—from Tough Talk to Polite Cajoling," *Washington Post*, June 7, 2017.

108. Peter Baker, Michael S. Schmidt, and Maggie Haberman, "Citing Recusal, Trump Says He Wouldn't Have Hired Sessions," *New York Times*, July 19, 2017.

109. Michael C. Bender, "Trump Won't Say If He Will Fire Sessions," *Wall Street Journal*, July 25, 2017.

110. John P. Burke and Fred I. Greenstein, *How Presidents Test Reality: Decisions on Vietnam, 1954 and 1965* (New York: Russell Sage Foundation, 1989); Robert S. McNamara, *In Retrospect: The Tragedy and Lessons of Vietnam* (New York: Times Books, 1995); and Goldstein, *Lessons in Disaster*, p. 291.

111. See, e.g., Elizabeth N. Saunders, *Leaders at War: How Presidents Shape Military Interventions* (Ithaca, NY: Cornell University Press, 2013).

112. Richard K. Betts, *Surprise Attack: Lessons for Defense Planning* (Washington, DC: Brookings Institution, 1982).

113. Baker, *The Politics of Diplomacy*, p. 274. See also Haass, *War of Necessity, War of Choice*, pp. 272–273.

114. Jervis, *Why Intelligence Fails*, pp. 142, 176–177.

115. Tenet, *At the Center of the Storm*, p. 45.

116. Betts, *Surprise Attack*, pp. 68–80; and Chaim Herzog, *The War of Atonement: October 1973* (Boston, MA: Little, Brown, 1975).

117. Gates, *Duty*, pp. 115–116; Rumsfeld, *Known and Unknown*, pp. 464, 480–481, 517, 664; Haass, *War of Necessity, War of Choice*, pp. 237, 254–258, 272–273; Woodward, *Plan of Attack*, pp. 415–416; Woodward, *State of Denial*, p. 455; Suskind, *The One Percent Doctrine*, pp. 62, 254; and Mayer, *The Dark Side*, pp. 4–5.

118. Baker, *Days of Fire*, p. 334.

119. Bush, *Decision Points*, p. 229; Rice, *No Higher Honor*, p. 198; Feith, *War and Decision*, pp. 238–239, 245–246, 274; Tenet, *At the Center of the Storm*, pp. 308–309, 322, 395; Suskind, *The Price of Loyalty*, pp. 76, 86, 96–97; Gordon and Trainor, *Cobra II*, pp. 14, 126; and Ricks, *Fiasco*, pp. 42–43.

120. Pillar, "Intelligence, Policy, and the War in Iraq," p. 18; Haass, *War of Necessity, War of Choice*, pp. 5–6, 212–216, 220, 231, 234, 272; and Baker, *Days of Fire*, p. 207.

121. Pillar, "Intelligence, Policy, and the War in Iraq," p. 18.

122. Isikoff and Corn, *Hubris*, pp. 32, 137, 295–296.

123. Kevin Woods, James Lacey, and Williamson Murray, "Saddam's Delusions: The View from the Inside," *Foreign Affairs*, May/June 2006.

124. Bush, *Decision Points*, pp. 224, 242, 245.

125. Haass, *War of Necessity, War of Choice*, p. 245.

126. Tenet, *At the Center of the Storm*, pp. 45–46, 330–332.

127. Leslie H. Gelb and Richard K. Betts, *The Irony of Vietnam: The System Worked* (Washington, DC: Brookings Institution, 1979), pp. 190, 353–354, 365–367. See also Robert McNamara, *In Retrospect: The Tragedy and Lessons of Vietnam* (New York: Times Books, 1995); and Goldstein, *Lessons in Disaster*, pp. 172–190, 215–218, 226.

128. John F. Harris and Dan Balz, "A Question of Balance," *Washington Post*, April 29, 2001, pp. A1, A6.

129. Kenneth T. Walsh, "Commander in Chief," *U.S. News and World Report*, December 31, 1990–January 7, 1991, p. 24.

130. Harding once complained to a friend:John, I can't make a damn thing out of this tax problem. I listen to one side and they seem right, and then God! I talk to the other side and they seem just as right, and there I am where I started. I know somewhere there is a book that would give me the truth, but hell, I couldn't read the book. I know somewhere there is an economist who knows the truth, but I don't know where to find him and haven't the sense to know him and trust him when I did find him. God what a job!

Warren Harding, in William Allen White, *Masks in a Pageant* (New York: Macmillan, 1928), pp. 422–423.

131. George P. Schultz, *Turmoil and Triumph* (New York: Scribner's, 1933), pp. 263, 819.

132. Gates, *Duty*, p. 94.

133. Clarke, *Against All Enemies*, pp. 243–244.

134. O'Neill describes the president in meetings as silent and expressionless, uninformed, and unengaged: "The only way I can describe it is that, well, the President is like a blind man in a room of deaf people.," quoted in Suskind, *The Price of Loyalty*, pp. 114, 149.

135. Woodward, *Fear*, pp. 220, 223, 232.

136. See, e.g., Rumsfeld, *Known and Unknown*, pp. 221, 665, 667, 720; and Haass, *War of Necessity, War of Choice*, pp. 272–273.

137. Rice, *No Higher Honor*, pp. 506–507.

138. Doris Kearns, *Lyndon Johnson and the American Dream* (New York: Harper & Row, 1976), pp. 252–253.

139. George W. Bush, "Address," October 7, 2002.

140. Schultz, *Turmoil and Triumph*, pp. 263, 1133.

141. See, e.g., Goldstein, *Lessons in Disaster*, pp. 172–173, 179–180, 186, 188–190, 215, 226.

142. Yuen Foong Khong, *Analogies at War: Korea, Munich, Dien Bien Phu, and the Vietnam Decisions of 1965* (Princeton, NJ: Princeton University Press, 1992).

143. Goldstein, *Lessons in Disaster*, pp. 138–140.

144. H. R. Haldeman, *The Ends of Power* (New York: Times Books, 1978), p. 34.

145. James David Barber, *The Presidential Character: Predicting Performance in the White House*, 4th ed. (New York: Pearson, 2009).

146. The most notable example can be found in Alexander L. George and Juliette L. George, *Presidential Personality and Performance* (New York: Westview, 1998), chapter 2.

147. See, e.g., the contrast between Barber's view of Dwight Eisenhower and that of Fred I. Greenstein, *The Hidden-Hand Presidency* (New York: Basic Books, 1982).

148. See Mark W. Huddleston and William W. Boyer, *The Higher Civil Service in the United States: Quest for Reform* (Pittsburgh, PA: University of Pittsburgh Press, 1996).

149. Richard M. Nixon, *Public Papers of the Presidents: Richard Nixon, 1972* (Washington, DC: Government Printing Office, 1974), p. 1150.

150. Graham Allison and Philip Zelikow, *Essence of Decision*, 2nd ed. (New York: Addison Wesley Longman), pp. 299–300.

151. Harry McPherson, *A Political Education* (Boston, MA: Little, Brown, 1972), p. 298.

152. Gates, *Duty*, pp. 127–135; Mayer, *The Dark Side*, pp. 24–25; Thom Shanker, "Gates Wants to Shift $1.2 Billion to Bolster War Surveillance," *New York Times*, July 26, 2008; and Thom Shanker, "Sharpened Tone in Debate over Culture of Military," *New York Times*, April 23, 2008.

153. Gates, *Duty*, pp. 120–121, 135–143, 306; and Thom Shanker, "Defense Chief Criticizes Bureaucracy at the Pentagon," *New York Times*, September 30, 2008.

154. National Commission on Terrorist Attacks on the United States, *The 9/11 Commission Report*, pp. 76–78.

155. Quoted in Haldeman, *The Ends of Power*, p. 107.

156. Goldstein, *Lessons in Disaster*, p. 43.

157. Rasenberger, *The Brilliant Disaster*.

158. Rice, *No Higher Honor*, pp. 105–106.

159. Baker, *The Politics of Diplomacy*, p. 68.

160. Laurence E. Lynn Jr. and David deF. Whitman, *The President as Policymaker: Jimmy Carter and Welfare Reform* (Philadelphia, PA: Temple University Press, 1981), pp. 116, 269.

161. Morton H. Halperin and Priscilla A. Clapp, *Bureaucratic Politics and Foreign Policy*, 2nd ed. (Washington, DC: Brookings Institution, 2006), pp. 85–86.

162. See, e.g., Leon Panetta, *Worthy Fights* (New York: Penguin Press, 2014), pp. 252–253.

163. Betts, *Enemies of Intelligence*, pp. 23–24, 80–81, and sources cited therein.

164. National Commission on Terrorist Attacks on the United States, *The 9/11 Commission Report*, pp. 79, 91–92, 181–182, 267–269, 272–277, 352, 358, 400, 417; and Mayer, *The Dark Side*, pp. 15–16, 112, 138.

165. Ibid.

166. National Commission on Terrorist Attacks on the United States, *The 9/11 Commission Report*, pp. 263–265.

167. Amy Zegart, *Spying Blind*, pp. 3–5.

168. National Commission on Terrorist Attacks on the United States, *The 9/11 Commission Report*, p. 263.

169. Ibid, p. 180.

170. McNamara, *In Retrospect*, pp. 211–212; and Andrew F. Krepinevich Jr., *The Army and Vietnam* (Baltimore, MD: Johns Hopkins University Press, 1986). For an exception, see Timothy J. McKeown, "Plans and Routines, Bureaucratic Bargaining, and the Cuban Missile Crisis," *Journal of Politics* 63 (November 2001): 1163–1190.

171. National Commission on Terrorist Attacks on the United States, *The 9/11 Commission Report*, p. 350.

CHAPTER 10

1. See, e.g., Richard P. Nathan, *The Administrative Presidency* (New York: John Wiley and Sons, 1983); and Terry M. Moe, "The Politicized Presidency," in James P. Pfiffner, ed., *The Managerial Presidency*, 2nd ed. (College Station: Texas A&M University Press, 1999).

2. President Carter quoted in G. Calvin Mackenzie, "Personnel Appointment Strategies in Post-War Presidential Administrations" (paper presented at the Annual Meeting of the Midwest Political Science Association, Chicago, April 1980), introductory page.

3. Quoted in Paul C. Light, *The President's Agenda: Domestic Policy Choice from Kennedy to Carter* (Baltimore, MD: Johns Hopkins University Press, 1982), p. 145.

4. On this point, see Eileen Burgin, "Congress, Policy Sustainability, and the Affordable Care Act: Democratic Policy Makers Overlooked Implementation, Post-Enactment Politics, and Policy Feedback Effects," *Congress & the Presidency* 45 (September–December 2018): 279–314; Martha Derthick, *Agency under Stress* (Washington, DC: Brookings Institution, 1990), esp. pp. 66, 184; and Elaine C. Kamarck, *Why Presidents Fail* (Washington, DC: Brookings Institution, 2016).

5. Quoted in Derthick, *Agency under Stress*, p. 152.

6. David Gergen quoted in "How Much Can Any Administration Do?" *Public Opinion* (December/January 1982): 56.

7. Among the many studies of this issue, see Michael R. Gordon and Bernard E. Trainor, *Cobra II: The Inside Story of the Invasion and Occupation of Iraq* (New York: Pantheon Books, 2006); and Thomas E. Ricks, *Fiasco: The American Military Adventure in Iraq* (New York: Penguin Press, 2006). See also Condoleezza Rice, *No Higher Honor: A Memoir of My Years in Washington* (New York: Crown Publishers, 2011), pp. 189–190.

8. David L. Phillips, *Losing Ground* (Boulder, CO: Westview, 2005), p. 156.

9. Al Gore, *From Red Tape to Results: Creating a Government That Works Better and Costs Less* (New York: Times Books, 1993).

10. Quoted in Shawn Zeller, "Performance Anxiety for 'New' Federal Standards," *CQ Weekly*, March 30, 2009, pp. 708–709.

11. National Commission on Terrorist Attacks on the United States, *The 9/11 Commission Report* (New York: Norton, 2004), pp. 40–44; and Philip Shenon and Christopher Marquis, "Panel Says Chaos in Administration Was Wide on 9/11," *New York Times*, June 18, 2004.

12. *The 9/11 Commission Report*, pp. 14–31.

13. See, e.g., William Safire, *Before the Fall: An Inside View of the Pre-Watergate White House* (New York: Doubleday, 1975), pp. 112–113, 285–287, 353, 566–567; and H. R. Haldeman, *The Ends of Power* (New York: Times Books, 1978), pp. 58–59, 111–112, 185–187.

14. Bob Woodward, *Fear: Trump in the White House* (New York: Simon and Schuster, 2018), pp. 146–147; Aaron Blake, "Trump Says 'Nobody Disobeys My Orders.' Here Are 15 Recorded Instances of Exactly That," *Washington Post*, April 22, 2019; S. V. Date, "Trump's Agencies Are Learning to Ignore Their Boss," *HuffPost*, August 10, 2017.

15. Special Counsel Robert S. Mueller, III, *Report on The Investigation into Russian Interference in The 2016 Presidential Election* Volume II, Washington, DC, March 2019, pp. 157–158.

16. David Lewis and Mark Richardson, *Survey on the Future of Government Service*, Center for the Study of Democratic Institutions, 2015. See also Gary J. Miller and Andrew B. Whitford, *Above Politics: Bureaucratic Discretion and Credible Commitment* (New York: Cambridge University Press, 2016).

17. Bob Woodward, *Obama's Wars* (New York: Simon & Schuster, 2010), pp. 385–390.

18. Paul C. Light, *Thickening Government* (Washington, DC: Brookings Institution, 1995), p. 86.

19. George P. Shultz, *Turmoil and Triumph* (New York: Scribner's, 1993), pp. 228–229. See also Donald Rumsfeld, *Known and Unknown* (New York: Penguin, 2011), p. 15.

20. See, e.g., Henry Kissinger, *White House Years* (Boston, MA: Little, Brown, 1979), pp. 26, 28–29, 45–46, 48, 141–142, 158–159, 264, 482, 729, 806, 879, 887, 900, 909, 917, 994.

21. Ibid, pp. 28–29, 264, 900.

22. See Ted Sorensen, *Counselor: A Life on the Edge of History* (New York: HarperCollins, 2008), p. 341, regarding John F. Kennedy using press conferences to speak to his own administration, especially those in middle and lower ranks.

23. Jane Mayer, *The Dark Side: The Inside Story of How the War on Terror Turned into a War on American Ideals* (New York: Doubleday, 2008), chapter 10.

24. Douglas J. Feith, *War and Decision: Inside the Pentagon at the Dawn of the War on Terrorism* (New York: Harper, 2008), pp. 436–440. See also Ricks, *Fiasco*, pp. 174–182; and Stephen Benedict Dyson, "What Really Happened in Planning for Postwar Iraq?" *Political Science Quarterly* 128, no. 3 (2013): 455–493.

25. Dyson, "What Really Happened in Planning for Postwar Iraq?" pp. 486–487.

26. Morton H. Halperin and Priscilla A. Clapp, *Bureaucratic Politics and Foreign Policy*, 2nd ed. (Washington, DC: Brookings Institution, 2006), p. 243.

27. Dyson, "What Really Happened in Planning for Postwar Iraq?"

28. Lyndon Johnson quoted in Doris Kearns, *Lyndon Johnson and the American Dream* (New York: Harper & Row, 1976), p. 137.

29. Halperin and Clapp, *Bureaucratic Politics and Foreign Policy*, pp. 244, 250.

30. James Q. Wilson, Bureaucracy: *What Government Agencies Do and Why They Do It* (New York: Basic Books, 1989), p. 158.

31. See Amy Goldstein and Juliet Eilperin, "HealthCare.gov: How Political Fear Was Pitted against Technical Needs," *Washington Post*, November 2, 2013; and Todd S. Purdum, "The Obamacare Sabotage Campaign," *Politico*, November 1, 2013.

32. United States Office of Personnel Management, *2018 Federal Workforce Priorities Report*, February 2018.

33. See, e.g., B. Dan Wood and James E. Anderson, "The Politics of U.S. Antitrust Regulation," *American Journal of Political Science* 37 (February 1993): 1–39; B. Dan Wood and Richard W. Waterman, *Bureaucratic Dynamics* (Boulder, CO: Westview, 1994), chapter 4; and Evan J. Ringquist, "Political Control and Policy Impact in EPA's Office of Water Quality," *American Journal of Political Science* 39 (May 1995): 336–363.

34. Robert F. Durant, *The Administrative Presidency Revisited* (Albany: State University of New York Press, 1992).

35. See, e.g., Daniel W. Drezner, "Present at the Destruction: The Trump Administration and the Foreign Policy Bureaucracy," *Journal of Politics* 81 (April 2019): 723–730.

36. United States Office of Personnel Management, *2018 Federal Workforce Priorities Report*; and Lewis and Richardson, *Survey on the Future of Government Service*.

37. Ahmed Rashid, *Descent into Chaos: The United States and the Failure of Nation Building in Pakistan, Afghanistan, and Central Asia* (New York: Viking, 2008), p. 194.

38. *The 9/11 Commission Report*, pp. 80–83.

39. United States Government Accountability Office, *Unaccompanied Children*, Washington, DC, October 2018.

40. See Lewis and Richardson, *Survey on the Future of Government Service*.

41. Goldstein and Eilperin, "HealthCare.gov."

42. Paul C. Light, *The True Size of Government* (Washington, DC: Brookings Institution, 1999), pp. 1, 44.

43. Paul C. Light, "Obama Has a Chance to Reverse Long Erosion of the Federal Service," *Washington Post*, November 19, 2008, p. A19.

44. Paul C. Light, "The True Size of Government," The Volcker Alliance, October 5, 2017.

45. Project on Government Oversight, *Bad Business: Billions of Taxpayer Dollars Wasted on Hiring Contractors* (Washington, DC: Project on Government Oversight, 2011).

46. Melinda N. Ritchie and Hye Young You, "Legislators as Lobbyists," *Legislative Studies Quarterly* 44 (February 2019): 65–95; Scott R. Furlong, "Political Influence on the Bureaucracy: The Bureaucracy Speaks," *Journal of Public Administration Research and Theory* 8 (January 1998): 39–65.

47. Terry M. Moe, "Control and Feedback in Economic Regulation: The Case of the NLRB," *American Political Science Review* 79 (December 1985): 1094–1116; Shep Melnick, *Regulation and the Courts: The Case of the Clean Air Act* (Washington, DC: Brookings Institution, 1983); George A. Krause, "Federal Reserve Policy Decision Making: Political and Bureaucratic Influences," *American Journal of Political Science* 38 (February 1994): 124–144; Richard W. Waterman, Amelia Rouse, and Robert Wright, "The Venues of Influence: A New Theory of Political Control of the Bureaucracy," *Journal of Public Administration Research and Theory* 8 (January 1998): 13–38; Richard W. Waterman and Kenneth J. Meier, "Principal-Agent Models: An Expansion?" *Journal of Public Administration Research and Theory* 8 (April 1998): 173–202; and Jeff Worsham, Marc Allen Eisner, and Evan J. Ringquist, "Assessing the Assumptions: A Critical Analysis of Agency Theory," *Administration and Society* 28 (February 1997): 419–440.

48. See, e.g., Ringquist, "Political Control and Policy Impact."

49. Andrew B. Whitford, "The Pursuit of Political Control by Multiple Principals," *Journal of Politics* 67 (February 2005): 29–49; and Richard A. Harris and Sidney M. Milkis, *The Politics of Regulatory Change: A Tale of Two Agencies* (New York: Oxford University Press, 1989), p. 276.

50. Adam O'Neal, "How to Prevent Another HealthCare.gov," *RealClearPolitics*, November 25, 2013.

51. On administrative discretion, see Lewis and Richardson, *Survey on the Future of Government Service*; and Gary S. Bryner, *Bureaucratic Discretion* (New York: Pergamon Press, 1987).

52. See Lawrence R. Jacobs and Robert Y. Shapiro, *Politicians Don't Pander* (Chicago, IL: University of Chicago Press, 2000), pp. 88–89, on how the Clinton administration distrusted civil servants in developing their health-care reform plan in 1993.

53. Mark W. Huddleston, *The Government's Managers* (New York: Priority Press, 1987), p. 61.

54. See, e.g., Rosemary O'Leary, "The Bureaucratic Politics Paradox: The Case of Wetlands Legislation in Nevada," *Journal of Public Administration Research and Theory* 4, no. 4 (1994): 443–467.

55. David Lowery, "The Presidency, the Bureaucracy, and Reinvention: A Gentle Plea for Chaos," *Presidential Studies Quarterly* 30 (March 2000): 93.

56. Quoted in Carl M. Brauer, *Presidential Transitions: Eisenhower through Reagan* (New York: Oxford University Press, 1986), p. 150.

57. Gerald R. Ford, "Imperiled, Not Imperial," *Time*, November 10, 1980, p. 30.

58. See, e.g., Joel D. Aberbach and Bert A. Rockman, "Clashing Beliefs within the Executive Branch: The Nixon Administration Bureaucracy," *American Political Science Review* 70 (June 1976): 456–468; Richard L. Cole and David A. Caputo, "Presidential Control of the Senior Civil Service: Assessing the Strategies of the Nixon Years," *American Political Science Review* 73 (June 1979): 399–413; Robert Maranto, "Still Clashing after All These Years: Ideological Conflict in the Reagan Executive," *American Journal of Political Science* 37 (August 1993): 681–698; Marissa Martino Golden, "Exit, Voice, Loyalty, and Neglect: Bureaucratic Responses to Presidential Control during the Reagan Administration," *Journal of Public Administration Research and Theory* 2 (January 1992): 29–62; Robert A. Maranto, *Politics and Bureaucracy in the Modern Presidency: Careerists and Appointees in the Reagan Administration* (Westport, CT: Greenwood Press, 1993); and Judith E. Michaels, *The President's Call: Executive Leadership from FDR to George Bush* (Pittsburgh, PA: University of Pittsburgh Press, 1997).

59. John Brehm and Scott Gates, *Working, Shirking, and Sabotage: Bureaucratic Responses to a Democratic Republic* (Ann Arbor: University of Michigan Press, 1997), p. 73, chapter 5.

60. Quoted in Morton H. Halperin and Priscilla A. Clapp, *Bureaucratic Politics and Foreign Policy*, 2nd ed. (Washington, DC: Brookings Institution, 2006), p. 254. See also Joshua B. Kennedy, "'Do This! Do That!' and Nothing Will Happen': Executive orders and Bureaucratic Responsiveness," *American Politics Research* 43 (January 2015): 59–82.

61. See, e.g., Rachel Augustine Potter, "Slow-Rolling, Fast-Tracking, and the Pace of Bureaucratic Decisions in Rulemaking," *Journal of Politics* 79 (July 2017): 841–855; and Hugh Heclo, *A Government of Strangers* (Washington, DC: Brookings Institution, 1977), pp. 171–172, 224–232.

62. B. Dan Wood, "Principals, Bureaucrats, and Responsiveness in Clean Air Enforcements," *American Political Science Review* 82 (March 1988): 213–234; B. Dan Wood and Richard W. Waterman, "The Dynamics of Political-Bureaucratic Adaptation," *American Journal of Political Science* 37 (May 1993): 497–528; and Wood and Waterman, *Bureaucratic Dynamics*.

63. Golden, "Exit, Voice, Loyalty, and Neglect."

64. "I Am Part of the Resistance Inside the Trump Administration," *New York Times*, September 5, 2018.

65. Gates, *Duty*, p. 340.

66. Yu Ouyang, Evan T. Haglund, and Richard W. Waterman, "The Missing Element: Examining the Loyalty-Competence Nexus in Presidential Appointments," *Presidential Studies Quarterly*, 47 (March 2017): pp. 62–91; and David E. Lewis and Richard W. Waterman, "The Invisible Presidential Appointments: An Examination of Appointments to the Department of Labor, 2001–11," *Presidential Studies Quarterly* 43 (March 2013): 35–57.

67. Kevin Parsneau, "Politicizing Priority Departments: Presidential Priorities and Subcabinet Experience and Loyalty," *American Politics Research* 41 (May 2013): 443–470.

68. Robert Maranto and B. Douglas Skelley, "Neutrality: An Enduring Principle of the Civil Service," *American Review of Public Administration* 22 (September 1992): 173–188.

69. Francis Rourke, "Bureaucracy in the American Constitutional Order," *Political Science Quarterly* 102 (Summer 1987): 219.

70. Francis E. Rourke, "Grappling with the Bureaucracy," in Arnold J. Meltsner, ed., *Politics and the Oval Office: Towards Presidential Governance* (San Francisco, CA: Institute for Contemporary Studies, 1981), p. 137.

71. Wilson, *Bureaucracy*, p. 275. See also Colin Campbell and Donald Naulls, "The Limits of the Budget-Maximizing Theory: Some Evidence from Officials' Views of Their Roles and Careers," in Andre Blais and Stephane Dion, eds., *The Budget-Maximizing Bureaucrat: Appraisals and Evidence* (Pittsburgh, PA: University of Pittsburgh Press, 1991), pp. 85–118.

72. Terry M. Moe, "Regulatory Performance and Presidential Administration," *American Journal of Political Science* 26 (February 1982): 97–224; Moe, "Control and Feedback in Economic Regulation"; Wood, "Principals, Bureaucrats, and Responsiveness in Clean Air Enforcements"; Wood and Anderson, "The Politics of U.S. Antitrust Regulation"; B. Dan Wood and Richard W. Waterman, "The Dynamics of

Political Control of the Bureaucracy," *American Political Science Review* 85 (September 1991): 801–828; Wood and Waterman, "The Dynamics of Political-Bureaucratic Adaptation"; Wood and Waterman, *Bureaucratic Dynamics*; Ringquist, "Political Control and Policy Impact"; Patricia W. Ingraham, "Political Direction and Policy Change in Three Federal Departments," in James P. Pfiffner, ed., *The Managerial Presidency*, 2nd ed. (College Station: Texas A&M University Press, 1999), pp. 209–211; Steven D. Stehr, "Top Bureaucrats and the Distribution of Influence in Reagan's Executive Branch," *Public Administration Review* 57 (January/February 1997): 75–82; and Marissa Martino Golden, *What Motivates Bureaucrats?* (New York: Columbia University Press, 2000), chapter 7.

73. Richard W. Waterman and Kenneth J. Meier, "Principal–Agent Models: An Expansion?" *Journal of Public Administration Research and Theory* 8 (April 1998): 173–202.

74. Joel D. Aberbach and Bert A. Rockman, with Robert M. Copeland, "From Nixon's Problem to Reagan's Achievement: The Federal Executive Reexamined," in Larry Berman, ed., *Looking Back on the Reagan Presidency* (Baltimore, MD: Johns Hopkins University Press, 1990); Joel D. Aberbach and Bert A. Rockman, "The Political Views of U.S. Senior Federal Executives, 1970–1992," *Journal of Politics* 57 (August 1995): 838–852; Joel D. Aberbach, "The Federal Executive under Clinton," in Colin Campbell and Bert A. Rockman, eds., *The Clinton Presidency: First Appraisals* (Chatham, NJ: Chatham House Publishers, 1996); and Joel D. Aberbach, "The President and the Executive Branch," in Colin Campbell and Bert A. Rockman, eds., *The Bush Presidency: First Appraisals* (Chatham, NJ: Chatham House Publishers, 1991).

75. James P. Pfiffner, *The Strategic Presidency*, 2nd ed. (Lawrence: University Press of Kansas, 1996), pp. 78–81; and James P. Pfiffner, "Political Appointees and Career Executives: The Democracy-Bureaucracy Nexus in the Third Century," *Public Administration Review* 47 (January/February 1987): 57–65. See also Paul C. Light, "When Worlds Collide: The Political-Career Nexus," in G. Calvin Mackenzie, ed., *The In-and-Outers: Presidential Appointees and Transient Government in Washington* (Baltimore, MD: Johns Hopkins University Press, 1987); and Robert Maranto, "Does Familiarity Breed Acceptance? Trends in Career-Noncareer Relations in the Reagan Administration," *Administration and Society* 23 (August 1991): 247–266.

76. Light, "When Worlds Collide," p. 166.

77. Michaels, *The President's Call*, pp. 234–235.

78. Brehm and Gates, *Working, Shirking, and Sabotage*, p. 202. They also found that federal employees do not shirk and are hard workers, chapter 5.

79. Joel D. Aberbach and Bert A. Rockman, "Mandates or Mandarins?" in James P. Pfiffner, ed., *The Managerial Presidency* (College Station: Texas A&M University Press, 1999), p. 168.

80. David E. Lewis, *The Politics of Presidential Appointments* (Princeton, NJ: Princeton University Press, 2008), chapter 7.

81. William G. Resh, *Rethinking the Administrative Presidency* (Baltimore, MD: Johns Hopkins University Press, 2015).

82. Light, "When Worlds Collide," p. 160.

83. See, e.g., Wood and Waterman, *Bureaucratic Dynamics*, chapter 3; and Ringquist, "Political Control and Policy Impact."

84. See, e.g., John Hudak, *Presidential Pork: White House Influence over the Distribution of Federal Grants* (Washington, DC: Brookings, 2014).

85. Partnership for Public Service, 2019.

86. See Emily H. Moore, "Polarization, Excepted Appointments, and the Administrative Presidency," *Presidential Studies Quarterly* 48 (March 2018): 72–92; David Lewis and Richard W. Waterman, "The Invisible Presidential Appointments: An Examination of PAS, Schedule C, and SES Appointments to the Department of Labor, 2001–2011," *Presidential Studies Quarterly* 43 (March 2013): 35–57.

87. Fox News, February 28, 2017.

88. David Lewis, "Trump's Slow Pace of Appointments Is Hurting Government—and His Own Agenda," *Washington Post*, August 3, 2017; David Lewis, "So Far, Trump Is Really Struggling as a Chief Executive," *Washington Post*, April 27, 2017; and David Lewis, "Deconstructing the Administrative State," *Journal of Politics* 81 (July 2019): 767–789.

89. Gary E. Hollibaugh and Lawrence S. Rothenberg, "The When and Why of Nominations: Determinants of Presidential Appointments," *American Politics Research* 45 (March 2017): 280–303.

90. Hollibaugh and Rothenberg, "The When and Why of Nominations"; Gary E. Hollibaugh, Jr., "Vacancies, Vetting, and Votes: A Unified Dynamic Model of the Appointments Process," *Journal of Theoretical Politics* 27, no. 2 (2015): 206–236; and Nolan McCarty and Rose Razaghian, "Advice and

Consent: Senate Responses to Executive Branch Nominations, 1885–1996," *American Journal of Political Science* 43 (October 1999): 1122–1143.

91. Fang-Yi Chiou and Lawrence S. Rothenberg, "Executive Appointments: Duration, Ideology, and Hierarchy," *Journal of Theoretical Politics* 26, no. 3 (2014): 496–517; Joel D. Aberbach and Bert A. Rockman, "The Appointments Process and the Administrative Presidency," *Presidential Studies Quarterly* 39 (March 2009): 38–59; McCarty and Razaghian, "Advice and Consent"; and Glen S. Krutz, Richard Fleisher, and Jon R. Bond, "From Abe Fortas to Zöe Baird: Why Some Presidential Nominations Fail in the Senate," *American Political Science Review* 92 (December 1998): 871–881.

92. Gary E. Hollibaugh Jr., Gabriel Horton, and David E. Lewis, "Presidents and Patronage," *American Journal of Political Science* (October 2014): 1024–1042. See also Gary E. Hollibaugh, "Patronage Appointments and Agency Independence," *Journal of Politics* 80 (October 2018): 1411–1416.

93. John F. Kennedy quoted in Kenneth P. O'Donnell and David F. Powers, *Johnny, We Hardly Knew Ye: Memories of John Fitzgerald Kennedy* (New York: Pocket Books, 1972), p. 270.

94. Jonathan Alter, *The Promise: President Obama, Year One* (New York: Simon & Schuster, 2010), p. 45.

95. Ron Chernow, *Washington* (New York: Penguin Press, 2010), p. 735.

96. Andrew Rudalevige quoted in Charlie Savage, "For White House, Hiring Is Political," *New York Times*, July 31, 2008.

97. On techniques for politicizing the bureaucracy, see Lewis, *The Politics of Presidential Appointments*, pp. 26–43.

98. White House Transition Project, http://whitehousetransitionproject.org/appointments accessed April 24, 2019.

99. Ibid.; John P. Burke, "'It Went Off the Rails': Trump's Presidential Transition and the National Security System," *Presidential Studies Quarterly* 48 (December 2018): 832–844; and David E. Lewis, Patrick Bernhard, and Emily You, "President Trump as Manager: Reflections on the First Year," *Presidential Studies Quarterly* 48 (September 2018): 480–501.

100. Heather Ba and Terry Sullivan, "The Senate 'Went Nuclear'—but That Won't Speed Things Up Much," *Washington Post*, April 24, 2019.

101. See, e.g., Tim Kraft quoted in Dom Bonafede, "Carter Sounds Retreat from 'Cabinet Government'," *National Journal*, November 18, 1978, pp. 1852–1857. See also "Rafshoon and Co.," *Newsweek*, January 29, 1979, p. 23.

102. George A. Krause and Anne Joseph O'Connell, "Experiential Learning and Presidential Management of the U.S. Federal Bureaucracy: Logic and Evidence from Agency Leadership Appointments," *American Journal of Political Science* 60 (October 2016): 914–931.

103. Ian Ostrander, "Powering Down the Presidency: The Rise and Fall of Recess Appointments," *Presidential Studies Quarterly* 45 (September 2015): 558–572.

104. Juliet Eilperin, Josh Dawsey, and Seung Min Kim, "'It's Way Too Many': As Vacancies Pile Up in Trump Administration, Senators Grow Concerned," *Washington Post*, February 4, 2019.

105. See Light, *Thickening Government*; and Moe, "The Politicized Presidency."

106. Light, "When Worlds Collide." See also Paul C. Light and Virginia L. Thomas, *The Merit and Reputation of an Administration: Presidential Appointees on the Appointments Process* (Washington, DC: Brookings Institution and Heritage Foundation, 2000), p. 19; and Laurence E. Lynn, Jr., "The Reagan Administration and the Renitent Bureaucracy," in Lester M. Salamon and Michael S. Lund, eds., *The Reagan Presidency and the Governing of America* (Washington, DC: Urban Institute, 1985).

107. See, e.g., Wood and Anderson, "The Politics of U.S. Antitrust Regulation"; Wood and Waterman, *Bureaucratic Dynamics*, chapter 4; and Ringquist, "Political Control and Policy Impact."

108. Robert F. Durant, *The Administrative Presidency Revisited* (Albany: State University of New York Press, 1992).

109. David M. Cohen, "Amateur Government," *Journal of Public Administration Research and Theory* 8 (October 1998): 450–497.

110. See Heclo, *A Government of Strangers*; Carolyn Ban and Patricia Ingraham, "Short-Timers: Political Appointee Mobility and Its Impact on Political-Career Relations in the Reagan Administration," *Administration and Society* 22 (May 1990): 106–124; Maranto, *Politics and Bureaucracy in the Modern Presidency*; and Michaels, *The President's Call*.

111. See, e.g., Ingraham, "Political Direction and Policy Change in Three Federal Departments," pp. 212–213.

112. Timothy B. Clark and Marjorie Wachtel, "The Quiet Crisis Goes Public," *Government Executive*, June, 1988, p. 28.

113. Ibid., p. 211.

114. Ron Chernow, *Washington* (New York: Penguin Press, 2010), pp. 735, 744.

115. Melvin Laird quoted in Seymour M. Hersh, *The Price of Power: Kissinger in the Nixon White House* (New York: Summit, 1983), pp. 235–236.

116. Robert C. McFarlane, *Special Trust* (New York: Cadell & Davies, 1994), pp. 270–271.

117. Tweet on December 7, 2018.

118. See, e.g., Woodward, *Fear*, pp. 124–125, 159–160, 214, 216, 223–226, 249, 256.

119. John F. Harris, *The Survivor: Bill Clinton in the White House* (New York: Random House, 2005), p. 280.

120. Richard M. Nixon, *RN: The Memoirs of Richard Nixon* (New York: Grosset & Dunlap, 1978), pp. 472–473, 513.

121. See, e.g., Richard L. Cole and David A. Caputo, "Presidential Control of the Senior Civil Service: Assessing the Strategies of the Nixon Years," *American Political Science Review* 73 (June 1979): 399–413.

122. Lewis and Richardson, *Survey on the Future of Government Service*.

123. Jimmy Carter quoted in "Civil Service Reform," *Congressional Quarterly Weekly Report*, March 11, 1978, p. 660.

124. Kathleen M. Doherty, David E. Lewis, and Scott Limbocker, "Controlling Agency Choke Points: Presidents and Regulatory Personnel Turnover" (paper presented at the Center for the Study of Democratic Institutions, Vanderbilt University, 2015).

125. Brehm and Gates, *Working, Shirking, and Sabotage*, chapters 4–5.

126. Jimmy Carter quoted in "Press Conference Text," *Congressional Quarterly Weekly Report*, March 11, 1978, p. 655.

127. Gore, *From Red Tape to Results*, p. 11.

128. William T. Gormley, *Taming the Bureaucracy: Muscles, Prayers, and Other Strategies* (Princeton, NJ: Princeton University Press, 1989); Paul C. Light, *The Tides of Reform: Making Government Work, 1945–1995* (New Haven, CT: Yale University Press, 1997); Peri Arnold, *Making the Managerial Presidency: Comprehensive Reorganization Planning, 1905–1996* (Lawrence: University Press of Kansas, 1998); and William F. West, *Controlling the Bureaucracy* (Armonk, NY: M. E. Sharpe, 1995).

129. Joseph Cooper and William F. West, "Presidential Power and Republican Government: The Theory and Practice of OMB Review of Agency Rules," *Journal of Politics* 50 (November 1988): 864–895; and William F. West, "The Institutionalization of Regulatory Review: Organizational Stability and Responsive Competence at OIRA," *Presidential Studies Quarterly* 35 (March 2005): 76–93.

130. Patrick J. Wolf, "Why Must We Reinvent the Federal Government? Putting Historical Developmental Claims to the Test," *Journal of Public Administration Research and Theory* 7 (July 1997): 353–388.

131. See Donald F. Kettl, *Sharing Power: Public Governance and Private Markets* (Washington, DC: Brookings Institution, 1993); and Thad E. Hall and Laurence J. O'Toole, "Structures for Policy Implementation: An Analysis of National Legislation, 1965–1966 and 1993–1994," *Administration and Society* 31 (January 2000): 667–686.

132. Franklin D. Roosevelt quoted in M. S. Eccles, *Beckoning Frontiers* (New York: Knopf, 1951), p. 336.

133. Quoted in Deborah Shapely, *Promise and Power* (Boston, MA: Little, Brown, 1993), p. 177. For a slightly different version of this confrontation, see Dino A. Brugioni, *Eyeball to Eyeball* (New York: Random House, 1991), p. 474. See also Michael Dobbs, *One Minute to Midnight: Kennedy, Khrushchev, and Castro on the Brink of Nuclear War* (New York: Knopf, 2008), pp. 71–72.

134. *The 9/11 Commission Report*, pp. 17–18.

135. Robert M. Gates, *Duty* (New York: Knopf, 2014), pp. 135–142.

136. Ted Sorensen, *Counselor: A Life on the Edge of History* (New York: HarperCollins, 2008), p. 305. See also Dobbs, *One Minute to Midnight*, pp. 94, 303.

137. DOD Commission on Beirut International Airport Terrorist Act, October 23, 1983, *Report of the DOD Commission on Beirut International Airport Terrorist Act*, October 23, 1983 (Washington, DC: Government Printing Office, December 20, 1983), p. 133.

138. Gates, *Duty*, pp. 116–135, 306.

139. Donald Trump, "Remarks by the President Signing an executive order to Reorganize the Executive Branch," White House, March 13, 2017.

140. "Carter Criticizes Federal Bureaucracy," *Congressional Quarterly Weekly Report*, June 3, 1978, p. 1421.

141. *The 9/11 Commission Report*, p. 401.

142. Senate Select Committee on Intelligence, *Report on the Attempted Terrorist Attack on Northwest Airlines Flight 253*, May 18, 2010.

143. Sean Farhang and Miranda Yaver, "Divided Government and the Fragmentation of American Law," *American Journal of Political Science* 60 (March 2016): 401–417.

144. William G. Howell and David E. Lewis, "Agencies by Presidential Design," *Journal of Politics* 64 (November 2002): 1095–1114.

145. See, e.g., Justin S. Vaughn and Jose D. Villalobos, *Czars in the White House* (Ann Arbor: University of Michigan Press, 2015); and Mark J. Rozell and Mitchel A. Sollenberger, "Obama's Executive Branch Czars: The Constitutional Controversy and a Legislative Solution," *Congress & the Presidency* 39 (January–April 2012): 74–99.

146. Jerry Markon, "FBI, ATF Battle for Control of Cases; Cooperation Lags Despite Merger," *Washington Post*, May 2008.

147. Dyson, "What Really Happened in Planning for Postwar Iraq?" p. 487.

148. William Colby, *Honorable Men: My Life in the CIA* (New York: W. W. Norton, 1975), pp. 440–441; and "Intelligence Failures, CIA Misdeeds Studied," *Congressional Quarterly Weekly Report*, September 20, 1975, p. 2025.

149. Ashley Parker, David Nakamura, and Philip Rucker, "Trump's Wall: The Inside Story of How the President Crafts Immigration Policy," *Washington Post*, July 19, 2017.

150. Ronald Reagan, *An American Life* (New York: Simon & Schuster, 1990), p. 161.

151. Shultz, *Turmoil and Triumph*, p. 166.

152. Quoted in Stephen J. Wayne, "Working in the White House: Psychological Dimensions of the Job" (paper presented at the annual meeting of the Southern Political Science Association, New Orleans, November 1977), pp. 16–17.

CHAPTER 11

1. Lyndon Johnson quoted in Doris Kearns, *Lyndon Johnson and the American Dream* (New York: Harper & Row, 1976), p. 226.

2. Occasionally, Congress may continue its session after the elections. The 103rd Congress did that in 1994 in order to consider the General Agreement on Tariffs and Trade (GATT). The president supported GATT, but some members of Congress did not wish to vote on it until after the midterm elections. In 2008, Congress reconvened after the presidential election to attempt to deal with the financial crisis. Special sessions occur only after Congress has adjourned.

3. James Madison, "The Federalist, No. 46," in *The Federalist* (New York: Modern Library, 1937), p. 307.

4. See, e.g., Rebecca U. Thorpe, *The American Warfare State: The Domestic Politics of Military Spending* (Chicago, IL: University of Chicago Press, 2014).

5. Barry Edwards, "Does the Presidency Moderate the President?" *Presidential Studies Quarterly* 47 (March 2017): 5–26; Douglas L. Kriner and Andrew Reeves, *The Particularistic President* (New York: Cambridge University Press, 2015); Douglas L. Kriner and Andrew Reeves, "Presidential Particularism and Divide-the-Dollar Politics," *American Political Science Review* 109 (February 2015): 155–171; Adam M. Dynes and Gregory A. Huber, "Partisanship and the Allocation of Federal Spending: Do Same-Party Legislators or Voters Benefit from Shared Party Affiliation with the President and House Majority?" *American Political Science Review* 109 (February 2015): 172–186; John Hudak, *Presidential Pork* (Washington, DC: Brookings Institution, 2014); Matthew Eshbaugh-Soha and Brandon Rottinghaus, "Presidential Position Taking and the Puzzle of Representation," *Presidential Studies Quarterly* 43 (March 2013): 1–15; Christopher R. Berry, Barry C. Burden, and William G. Howell, "The President and the Distribution of Federal Spending," *American Political Science Review* 104 (November 2010): 783–799; and B. Dan Wood, *The Myth of Presidential Representation* (New York: Cambridge University Press, 2009).

6. E. Scott Adler and John S. Lapinski, "Demand-Side Theory and Congressional Committee Composition: A Constituency Characteristics Approach," *American Journal of Political Science* 41 (July 1997): 895–918; William T. Bianco, "Reliable Source or Usual Suspects? Cue-Taking, Information Transmission, and Legislative Committees," *Journal of Politics* 59 (August 1997): 913–924; Tim Groseclose, "Testing Committee Composition Hypotheses for the U.S. Congress," *Journal of Politics* 56 (May 1994): 440–458; Christopher J. Deering and Steven S. Smith, *Committees in Congress,* 3rd ed. (Washington, DC: Congressional Quarterly Press, 1997); Richard L. Hall and Bernard Grofman, "The Committee

Assignment Process and the Conditional Nature of Committee Bias," *American Political Science Review* 84 (December 1990): 1149–1166; John Londregan and James M. Snyder, "Comparing Committee and Floor Preferences," *Legislative Studies Quarterly* 19 (May 1994): 233–266; Geoffrey D. Peterson and J. Mark Wrighton, "The Continuing Puzzle of Committee Outliers: A Methodological Reassessment," *Congress & the Presidency* 25 (Spring 1998): 67–78; Kenneth A. Shepsle, *The Giant Jigsaw Puzzle: Democratic Committee Assignments in the Modern House* (Chicago, IL: University of Chicago Press, 1978); and James M. Snyder, "Artificial Extremism in Interest Group Ratings," *Legislative Studies Quarterly* 17 (August 1992): 319–345. But see Keith Krehbiel, "Are Congressional Committees Composed of Preference Outliers?" *American Political Science Review* 84 (March 1991): 149–163; and Keith Krehbiel, "Deference, Extremism, and Interest Group Ratings," *Legislative Studies Quarterly* 19 (February 1994): 61–77.

7. See, e.g., John W. Kingdon, *Congressmen's Voting Decisions,* 3rd ed. (Ann Arbor: University of Michigan Press, 1989); and Donald R. Matthews and James A. Stimson, *Yeas and Nays* (New York: Wiley, 1975).

8. Gerald R. Ford, *A Time to Heal: The Autobiography of Gerald R. Ford* (New York: Harper & Row, 1979), p. 150.

9. Quoted in Norman J. Ornstein, "Assessing Reagan's First Year," in Norman J. Ornstein, ed., *President and Congress: Assessing Reagan's First Year* (Washington, DC: American Enterprise Institute, 1982), pp. 102–103.

10. George C. Edwards III and Andrew Barrett, "Presidential Agenda Setting in Congress," in Jon R. Bond and Richard Fleisher, eds., *Polarized Politics: Congress and the President in a Partisan Era* (Washington, DC: CQ Press, 2000).

11. See, however, George C. Edwards III and B. Dan Wood, "Who Influences Whom? The President, Congress, and the Media," *American Political Science Review* (June 1999): 327–344.

12. Richard E. Neustadt, *Presidential Power and the Modern Presidents* (New York: Free Press, 1990), p. 29.

13. Quoted in Paul C. Light, *The President's Agenda: Domestic Policy Choice from Kennedy to Carter* (Baltimore, MD: Johns Hopkins University Press, 1982), p. 135.

14. David R. Mayhew, *Divided We Govern: Party Control, Lawmaking, and Investigations, 1946– 2002* (New Haven, CT: Yale University Press, 2005).

15. George C. Edwards III, Andrew Barrett, and Jeffrey Peake, "The Legislative Impact of Divided Government," *American Journal of Political Science* 41 (April 1997): 545–563.

16. Tyler Hughes and Deven Carlson, "Divided Government and Delay in the Legislative Process: Evidence from Important Bills, 1949–2010," *American Politics Research* 43 (September 2015): 771–792.

17. See George C. Edwards III, *At the Margins: Presidential Leadership of Congress* (New Haven, CT: Yale University Press, 1989), chapter 4.

18. Ibid, p. 178.

19. See Keith Krehbiel, *Pivotal Politics: A Theory of U.S. Lawmaking* (Chicago, IL: University of Chicago Press, 1998); Terry Sullivan, "Bargaining with the President: A Simple Game and New Evidence," *American Political Science Review* 84 (December 1990): 1167–1196; and Glen Biglaiser, David J. Jackson, and Jeffrey S. Peake, "Back on Track: Support for Presidential Trade Authority in the House of Representatives," *American Politics Research* 32 (November 2004): 679–697, concerning party members switching to support the president of their party.

20. Jimmy Carter, *Keeping Faith* (New York: Bantam, 1982), p. 80.

21. George C. Edwards III, "Interview with President Jimmy Carter," *Presidential Studies Quarterly* 38 (March 2008): 2, 5–6.

22. Kingdon, *Congressmen's Voting Decisions,* pp. 172–173.

23. Gregory Koger and Matthew J. Lebo, *Strategic Party Government: Why Winning Trumps Ideology* (Chicago, IL: University of Chicago Press, 2016); and Matthew J. Lebo and Andrew J. O'Green, "The President's Role in the Partisan Congressional Arena," *Journal of Politics* 73 (July 2011): 718–734.

24. Francis Lee, "Dividers, Not Uniters: Presidential Leadership and Senate Partisanship, 1981– 2004," *Journal of Politics* 70 (October 2008): 914–928.

25. Frances E. Lee, *Beyond Ideology: Politics, Principles, and Partisanship in the U.S. Senate* (Chicago, IL: University of Chicago Press, 2009), chapter 4.

26. Moynihan quoted in "Recasting Senate Finance: Moynihan to Take Helm," *Congressional Quarterly Weekly Report,* December 12, 1992, p. 3796.

27. Shailagh Murray and Paul Kane, "Democratic Congress Shows Signs It Will Not Bow to Obama," *Washington Post,* January 11, 2009, p. A5.

28. Quoted in Steven R. Weisman, "No. 1, the President Is Very Result Oriented," *New York Times*, November 12, 1983, pp. 10, 85. See also Shirley Elder, "The Cabinet's Ambassadors to Capitol Hill," *National Journal*, July 29, 1978, p. 1196.

29. Gary C. Jacobson, "The President's Effect on Partisan Attitudes," *Presidential Studies Quarterly* 42 (December 2012): 683–718. More broadly, see Gary C. Jacobson, *Presidents & Parties in the Public Mind* (Chicago, IL: University of Chicago Press, 2019).

30. ANES 2016, face-to-face sample. A good review of the data for 2012 can be found in Gary C. Jacobson, "Barack Obama and the Nationalization of Electoral Politics in 2012," *Electoral Studies* 40 (December 2015): 471–481; and Gary C. Jacobson, "Partisan Polarization in American Politics," *Presidential Studies Quarterly* 43 (December 2013): 688–708.

31. James E. Campbell and Joe A. Sumners, "Presidential Coattails in Senate Elections," *American Political Science Review* 84 (June 1990): 513–524; and George C. Edwards III, *The Public Presidency* (New York: St. Martin's, 1983), pp. 83–93.

32. Robert S. Erikson, "Congressional Elections in Presidential Years: Presidential Coattails and Strategic Voting," *Legislative Studies Quarterly* 41 (August 2016): 551–574.

33. Edwards, *The Public Presidency*, pp. 83–93; Gregory N. Flemming, "Presidential Coattails in Open-Seat Elections," *Legislative Studies Quarterly* 20 (May 1995): 197–212; and Barry C. Burden and David C. Kimball, *Why Americans Split Their Tickets* (Ann Arbor: University of Michigan Press, 2002).

34. Campbell and Sumners, "Presidential Coattails in Senate Elections"; and Alan I. Abramowitz and Jeffrey A. Segal, *Senate Elections* (Ann Arbor: University of Michigan Press, 1992), pp. 121, 233, 238.

35. Paul Herrnson, Irwin Morris, and John McTague, "The Impact of Presidential Campaigning for Congress on Presidential Support in the U.S. House of Representatives," *Legislative Studies Quarterly* 36 (February 2011): 99–122.

36. Edwards-Isaac Dovere, "President Obama Plays the Campaign Calendar Blues," Politico.com, September 24, 2014.

37. For evidence of the impact of the president's campaigning in midterm elections, see Jeffrey E. Cohen, Michael A. Krassa, and John A. Hamman, "The Impact of Presidential Campaigning on Midterm U.S. Senate Elections," *American Political Science Review* 85 (March 1991): 165–178. On the president's effect on congressional elections more broadly, see James E. Campbell, *The Presidential Pulse of Congressional Elections* (Lexington: University Press of Kentucky, 1993).

38. Benjamin Highton, "Bill Clinton, Newt Gingrich, and the 1998 House Elections," *Public Opinion Quarterly* 66 (Spring 2002): 1–17.

39. James M. Curry and Frances E. Lee, "Non-party Government: Bipartisan Lawmaking and Party Power in Congress," *Perspectives on Politics* 17 (March 2019): 47–65.

40. See Edwards, *Overreach*, chapters 4–6, for Obama's efforts to obtain bipartisan support and his lack of success in doing so.

41. Francis E. Lee, *Insecure Majorities: Congress and the Perpetual Campaign* (Chicago, IL: University of Chicago Press, 2016).

42. Jonathan Chait, "Five Days that Shaped His Presidency," *New York Times Magazine*, October 2, 2016.

43. Emmet John Hughes, *The Living Presidency* (Baltimore, MD: Penguin, 1974), p. 68.

44. Lyndon B. Johnson, *The Vantage Point: Perspectives of the Presidency, 1963–1969* (New York: Popular Library, 1971), p. 443.

45. Ibid, p. 323.

46. Quoted in "Run, Run, Run," *Newsweek,* May 2, 1977, p. 38.

47. Quoted in "Carter Seeks More Effective Use of Departmental Lobbyists' Skills," *Congressional Quarterly Weekly Report,* March 4, 1978, p. 585.

48. Quoted in Sidney Blumenthal, "Marketing the President," *New York Times Magazine,* September 13, 1981, p. 110.

49. Quoted in Dom Bonafede, "The Strained Relationship," *National Journal,* May 19, 1979, p. 830.

50. William, Schneider, "It's Payback Time for GOP and Press," *National Journal*, March 19, 1994, p. 696.

51. Brandice Canes-Wrone, David W. Brady, and John F. Cogan, "Out of Step, Out of Office: Electoral Accountability and House Members' Voting," *American Political Science Review* 96 (March 2002): 127–140.

52. Paul Gronke, Jeffrey Koch, and J. Matthew Wilson, "Follow the Leader? Presidential Approval, Presidential Support, and Representatives' Electoral Fortunes," *Journal of Politics* 65 (August

2003): 785–808; Burden and Kimball, *Why Americans Split Their Tickets*; David W. Brady, Brandice Canes-Wrone, and John F. Cogan, "Differences between Winning and Losing Incumbents," in David W. Brady, John F. Cogan, and Morris P. Fiorina, eds., *Change and Continuity in House Elections* (Stanford, CA: Stanford University Press, 2000); and David W. Brady, John F. Cogan, Brian Gaines, and R. Douglas Rivers, "The Perils of Presidential Support: How the Republicans Captured the House," *Political Behavior* 18 (December 1996): 345–368.

53. Brady et al., "The Perils of Presidential Support."

54. Gary C. Jacobson, "The War, the President, and the 2006 Midterm Congressional Elections" (paper delivered at the Annual Meeting of the Midwest Political Science Association, April 12–15, 2007).

55. Pew Research Center for the People & the Press, "October 2006 Survey on Electoral Competition: Final Topline October 17–22, 2006."

56. See Edwards, *Overreach*, chapter 7.

57. Richard M. Nixon, *In the Arena: A Memoir of Victory, Defeat and Renewal* (New York: Simon & Schuster, 1990), p. 282.

58. Memorandum from William E. Timmons to Richard Nixon, December 31, 1973, p. 3. See also George W. Bush, *Decision Points* (New York: Crown, 2010), p. 330.

59. Michael S. Rocca, "9/11 and Presidential Support in the 107th Congress," *Congress & the Presidency* 36, no. 2 (2009): 272–296.

60. Stephen A. Borrelli, J. Mark Wrighton, and Chad Bryan, "Policy-Specific Approval Ratings and Presidential Success on Roll Calls: An Exploration," *American Review of Politics* 19 (Fall 1998): 267–282; and George C. Edwards III, "Aligning Tests with Theory: Presidential Approval as a Source of Influence in Congress," *Congress & the Presidency* 24 (Fall 1997): 113–130.

61. Lawrence J. Grossback, David A. M. Peterson, and James A. Stimson, *Mandate Politics* (New York: Cambridge University Press, 2006).

62. Patricia Heidotting Conley, *Presidential Mandates* (Chicago, IL: University of Chicago Press, 2001).

63. Edwards, *At the Margins*, chapter 8; and Lawrence J. Grossback and David A. M. Peterson, "Comparing Competing Theories on the Causes of Mandate Perceptions," *American Journal of Political Science* 49 (April 2005): 406–419.

64. ABC News poll, October 20–22, 2016.

65. 2016 American National Election Study.

66. HuffPost/YouGov poll, November 10–14, 2016.

67. *Washington Post*–Schar School poll, November 11–14, 2016.

68. Gallup poll, January 20–22, 2017.

69. See Edwards, *Overreach*.

70. Harry McPherson, *A Political Education* (Boston: Little, Brown, 1972), p. 192.

71. On the office's organization of outside groups, see Mark A. Peterson, "The Presidency and Organized Interests: White House Patterns of Interest Group Liaison," *American Political Science Review* 86 (September 1992): 612–625.

72. Richard E. Neustadt, "Presidency and Legislation: Planning the President's Program," in Aaron Wildavsky, ed., *The Presidency* (Boston: Little, Brown, 1969), p. 596.

73. Sandhya Somashekhar and Paul Kane, "Democrats Yet to Decide on Health-Care Bill Bear the Weight of Washington," *Washington Post*, March 18, 2010; Sheryl Gay Stolberg, Jeff Zeleny, and Carl Hulse, "The Long Road Back," *New York Times*, March 21, 2010; and Jonathan Alter, *The Promise: President Obama, Year One* (New York: Simon & Schuster, 2010), pp. 409, 432.

74. Brien Friel et al., "So, Who Won?" *National Journal*, March 27, 2010, p. 20.

75. These examples come from Ceci Connolly, "How Obama Revived His Health-Care Bill," *Washington Post*, March 23, 2010.

76. Dwight D. Eisenhower, *Mandate for Change, 1953–1956* (New York: Signet, 1963), pp. 254–255.

77. Johnson, *The Vantage Point*, p. 40.

78. George C. Edwards III, *The Bungler: The Leadership of Donald Trump* (forthcoming, 2020), chapter 8.

79. Jake Sherman and Anna Palmer, *The Hill to Die On: The Battle for Congress and the Future of Trump's America* (New York: Crown, 2019), pp. 150–153; Jonathan Martin and Glenn Thrush, "As Trump's Tactics Fall Short, Pence Takes Lead on Health Care Bill," *New York Times*, June 27, 2017; Sean Sullivan, Robert Costa, and Kelsey Snell, "Trump Joins the Effort to Pass a Health-care Bill, but Another GOP Senator Is Opposed," *Washington Post*, June 23, 2017; Robert Costa and Sean Sullivan,

"The Trump-McConnell Bond Is Being Tested. So Is the GOP Agenda," *Washington Post*, June 27, 2017; Glenn Thrush and Jonathan Martin, "On Senate Health Bill, Trump Falters in the Closer's Role," *New York Times*, June 27, 2017; and Philip Rucker, Robert Costa and Ashley Parker, "Who's Afraid of Trump? Not Enough Republicans—at Least for Now," *Washington Post*, June 27, 2017.

80. David Stockman, *The Triumph of Politics* (New York: Harper & Row, 1986), pp. 251, 253, 260–261, 264–265; see also William Greider, "The Education of David Stockman," *Atlantic Monthly*, December 1981, p. 51.

81. John M. Broder, "With Something for Everyone, Climate Bill Passed," *New York Times*, July 1, 2009.

82. Chait, "Shaped His Presidency."

83. Quoted in Gary W. Reichard, *The Reaffirmation of Republicanism: Eisenhower and the Eighty-Third Congress* (Knoxville: University of Tennessee Press, 1975), p. 173.

84. William Timmons and Max Friedersdorf quoted in "Turning Screws: Winning Votes in Congress," *Congressional Quarterly Weekly Report*, April 24, 1976, pp. 952–953.

85. Quoted in Neil McNeil, *Forge of Democracy* (New York: McKay, 1963), p. 260.

86. Kriner and Reeves, *The Particularistic President*; Berry, Burden, and Howell, "The President and the Distribution of Federal Spending"; Hudak, *Presidential Pork*; and Dynes and Huber, "Partisanship and the Allocation."

87. Quoted in "Turning Screws," pp. 952–953.

88. Lawrence O'Brien, in Robert L. Hardesty, ed., *The Johnson Years: The Difference He Made* (Austin, TX: Lyndon B. Johnson School of Public Affairs, 1993), p. 75.

89. Bob Woodward and Robert Costa, "Transcript: Donald Trump Interview with Bob Woodward and Robert Costa," *Washington Post*, April 2, 2016.

90. Edwards III, *The Bungler*, chapter 9.

91. Marc Fisher, "Trump's Tools of Persuasion—from Tough Talk to Polite Cajoling," *Washington Post*, June 7, 2017.

92. Martin and Thrush, "As Trump's Tactics Fall Short, Pence Takes Lead on Health Care Bill."

93. Quoted in Rucker, Costa, and Parker, "Who's Afraid of Trump?"

94. Donald J. Trump, *Trump: The Art of the Deal* (New York: Random House, 1987), p. 35.

95. Quoted in Rucker, Costa, and Parker, "Who's Afraid of Trump?"

96. Timothy P. Nokken, "Ideological Congruence versus Electoral Success: Distribution of Party Organization Contributions in Senate Elections, 1990–2000," *American Politics Research* 31 (January 2003): 3–26; David F. Damore and Thomas G. Hansford, "The Allocation of Party Controlled Campaign Resources in the House of Representatives, 1989–1996," *Political Research Quarterly* 52 (June 1999): 371–385; and David M. Cantor and Paul S. Herrnson, "Party Campaign Activity and Party Unity in the U.S. House of Representatives," *Legislative Studies Quarterly* 22, no. 3 (August 1997): 393–415.

97. See Mark A. Peterson, *Legislating Together* (Cambridge, MA: Harvard University Press, 1990).

98. Sherman and Palmer, *The Hill to Die On*, pp. 48–49, 215–216, 224; Seung Min Kim and Josh Dawsey, "'He Just Picks Up': Trump and the Lawmakers He Loves to Talk to on the Phone," *Washington Post*, February 19, 2019.

99. See an interview with Bill Clinton by Jack Nelson and Robert J. Donovan, "The Education of a President," *Los Angeles Times Magazine*, August 1, 1993, p. 39. See also Bill Clinton, *My Life* (New York: Knopf, 2004), p. 556.

100. See George C. Edwards III, *The Strategic President: Persuasion and Opportunity in Presidential Leadership* (Princeton, NJ: Princeton University Press, 2009), pp. 96–104.

101. Quoted in Michael D. Shear, "White House Revamps Communications Strategy," *Washington Post*, February 15, 2010.

102. Quoted in McPherson, *A Political Education,* p. 268.

103. Clinton quoted in Bob Woodward, *The Agenda: Inside the Clinton White House* (New York: Simon & Schuster, 1994), p. 313.

104. Edwards, *At the Margins*, chapter 9. See also Richard Fleisher, Jon R. Bond, and B. Dan Wood, "Which Presidents Are Uncommonly Successful in Congress?" in Bert Rockman and Richard W. Waterman, eds., *Presidential Leadership: The Vortex of Presidential Power* (New York: Oxford University Press, 2007; and Krehbiel, *Pivotal Politics*, chapters 7–8.

105. For Carter's description of this process, see George C. Edwards III, "Interview with President Jimmy Carter," *Presidential Studies Quarterly* 38 (March 2008): 7–8, 12.

106. Calvin Mouw and Michael MacKuen, "The Strategic Configuration, Personal Influence, and Presidential Power in Congress," *Western Political Quarterly* 45 (September 1992): 598.

107. Nolan McCarty, "Presidential Vetoes in the Early Republic: Changing Constitutional Norms or Electoral Reform?" *Journal of Politics* 71 (April 2009): 369–384.

108. Trevor Latimer, "Vetoes in the Early Republic: A Defense of Norms," *Presidential Studies Quarterly* 47 December 2017): 665–694.

109. Robert J. Spitzer, "The Historical Presidency: Growing Executive Power: The Strange Case of the 'Protective Return' Pocket Veto," *Presidential Studies Quarterly* 42 (September 2012): 637–655.

110. Charles M. Cameron, *Veto Bargaining: Presidents and the Politics of Negative Power* (New York: Cambridge University Press, 2000). See also Rebecca E. Deen and Laura W. Arnold, "Veto Threats as a Policy Tool: When to Threaten?" *Presidential Studies Quarterly* 32 (March 2002): 44.

111. Hans J. G. Hassell and Samuel Kernell, "Veto Rhetoric and Legislative Riders," *American Journal of Political Science* 60 (October 2016): 845–859.

112. Christopher S. Kelley and Bryan W. Marshall, "The Last Word: Presidential Power and the Role of Signing Statements," *Presidential Studies Quarterly* 38 (June 2008): 248–267.

113. Richard S. Conley, "The Harbinger of the Unitary Executive? An Analysis of Presidential Signing Statements from Truman to Carter," *Presidential Studies Quarterly* 41 (September 2011): 546–569; and Kevin A. Evans, "Looking before Watergate: Foundations in the Development of the Constitutional Challenges within Signing Statements, FDR–Nixon," *Presidential Studies Quarterly* 42 (June 2012): 390–405.

114. Andrew B. Whitford, "Signing Statements as Bargaining Outcomes: Evidence from the Administration of George W. Bush," *Presidential Studies Quarterly* 42 (June 2012): 343–362. See also Kevin Evans, "Challenging Law: Presidential Signing Statements and the Maintenance of Executive Power," *Congress & the Presidency* 38, no. 2 (2011): 217–234.

115. See Michael J. Berry, *The Modern Legislative Veto* (Ann Arbor: University of Michigan Press, 2016).

116. Michael J. Berry, "Controversially Executing the Law: George W. Bush and the Constitutional Signing Statement," *Congress & the Presidency* 36, no. 2 (2009): 244–271.

117. Ian Ostrander and Joel Sievert, "What's So Sinister about Presidential Signing Statements?" *Presidential Studies Quarterly* 43 (March 2013): 58–80.

118. Go to *The American Presidency Project*, University of California at Santa Barbara, http://www.presidency.ucsb.edu/signingstatements.php?year=2010&Submit=DISPLAY#axzz282wCwcpS, to see examples of signing statements.

119. Phillip J. Cooper, "George W. Bush, Edgar Allan Poe, and the Use and Abuse of Presidential Signing Statements," *Presidential Studies Quarterly* 35 (September 2005): 515–532.

120. http://www.coherentbabble.com/listDJTall.htm.

121. James P. Pfiffner, *Power Play: The Bush Presidency and the Constitution* (Washington, DC: Brookings Institution, 2008), pp. 159–160. More broadly, see Christopher S. Kelley and Bryan W. Marshall, "Assessing Presidential Power: Signing Statements and Veto Threats as Coordinated Strategies," *American Politics Research* 37 (May 2009): 508–533.

122. See David R. Mayhew, *Partisan Balance: Why Political Parties Don't Kill the U.S. Constitutional System* (Princeton, NJ: Princeton University Press, 2011), pp. 57–79.

CHAPTER 12

1. See Sarah A. Binder and Forrest Maltzman, *Advice and Dissent: The Struggle to Shape the Federal Judiciary* (Washington, DC: Brookings Institution, 2009), on the history and procedures regarding judicial nominations.

2. Sarah Binder and Forrest Maltzman, "The Limits of Senatorial Courtesy," *Legislative Studies Quarterly* 29 (February 2004): 5–22. Michael A. Sollenberger, "The Blue Slip: A Theory of Unified and Divided Government, 1979–2009," *Congress & the Presidency* 37 (May–August 2010): 125–156; and Brandon Rottinghaus and Chris Nicholson, "Counting Congress In: Patterns of Success in Judicial Nomination Requests by Members of Congress to Presidents Eisenhower and Ford," *American Politics Research* 38 (July 2010): 691–717.

3. Sheldon Goldman, Elliot Slotnick, and Sara Schiavoni, "Obama's Judiciary at Midterm," *Judicature* 94 (May–June 2011): 262–303.

4. Quoted in J. Woodford Howard Jr., *Courts of Appeals in the Federal Judicial System* (Princeton, NJ: Princeton University Press, 1981), p. 101.

5. One study found, however, that judicial experience is not related to the congruence of presidential preferences and the justices' decisions on racial equality cases. See John Gates and Jeffrey Cohen,

"Presidents, Supreme Court Justices, and Racial Equality Cases: 1954–1984," *Political Behavior* 10, no. 1 (1988): 22–35.

6. David M. O'Brien, "The Reagan Judges: His Most Enduring Legacy?" in Charles O. Jones, ed., *The Reagan Legacy* (Chatham, NJ: Chatham House, 1988), pp. 60–101.

7. Sheldon Goldman, "The Bush Imprint on the Judiciary: Carrying on a Tradition," *Judicature* 74 (April/May 1991): 294–306.

8. See David M. O'Brien, "Judicial Legacies: The Clinton Presidency and the Courts," in Colin Campbell and Bert A. Rockman, eds., *The Clinton Legacy* (New York: Seven Bridges Press, 2000).

9. Elisabeth Bumiller, "Bush Vows to Seek Conservative Judges," *New York Times*, March 29, 2002, p. A24.

10. Sheldon Goldman, "Do We Have a Crisis in Judicial Selection?" in George C. Edwards III, ed., *Presidential Politics* (Belmont, CA: Wadsworth, 2005), pp. 337–354.

11. Sheldon Goldman, Elliot Slotnick, and Sara Schiavoni, "Obama's Judiciary at Midterm," *Judicature* 94 (May–June 2011): 262–303.

12. Binder and Maltzman, *Advice and Dissent*, chapters 1–2.

13. Scott Basinger and Mark Maxwell, "The Changing Politics of Federal Judicial Nominations," *Congress & the Presidency* 37 (May–August 2010): 157–175; Sollenberger, "The Blue Slip"; and Ryan C. Black, Anthony J. Madonna, and Ryan J. Owens, "Obstructing Agenda-Setting: Examining Blue Slip Behavior in the Senate," *The Forum* 9, no. 4 (2011).

14. Logan Dancey, Kjersten R. Nelson, and Eve M. Ringsmuth, "Individual Scrutiny or Politics as Usual? Senatorial Assessment of U.S. District Court Nominees," *American Politics Research* 42 (September 2014): 784–814.

15. Nancy Scherer, Brandon L. Bartels, and Amy Steigerwalt, "Sounding the Fire Alarm: The Role of Interest Groups in the Lower Federal Court Confirmation Process," *Journal of Politics* 70 (October 2008): 1026–1039.

16. Sarah A. Binder and Forrest Maltzman, "The Limits of Senatorial Courtesy," *Legislative Studies Quarterly* 29 (February 2004): 5–22.

17. Wendy L. Martinek, Mark Kemper, and Steven R. Van Winkle, "To Advise and Consent: The Senate and Lower Federal Court Nominations, 1977–1998," *Journal of Politics* 64 (May 2002): 337–361.

18. Barry J. McMillion, "President Obama's First-Term U.S. Circuit and District Court Nominations: An Analysis and Comparison with Presidents since Reagan," Congressional Research Service, May 2, 2013; Binder and Maltzman, *Advice and Dissent*, pp. 4–6, chapters 2, 4; Jon R. Bond, Richard Fleisher, and Glen S. Krutz, "Malign Neglect: Evidence That Delay Has Become the Primary Method of Defeating Presidential Appointment," *Congress & the Presidency* (Fall 2009): 226–243; and Lauren Cohen Bell, "Senatorial Discourtesy: The Senate's Use of Delay to Shape the Federal Judiciary," *Political Research Quarterly* 55 (September 2002): 589–607.

19. McMillion, "President Obama's First-Term U.S. Circuit and District Court Nominations"; and Binder and Maltzman, *Advice and Dissent*, pp. 2–4, chapter 4.

20. On this point, see Elisha Carol Savchak, Thomas G. Hansford, Donald R. Songer, Kenneth L. Manning, and Robert A. Carp, "Taking It to the Next Level: The Elevation of District Court Judges to the U.S. Court of Appeals," *American Journal of Political Science* 50 (April 2006): 478–493.

21. Goldman, "Do We Have a Crisis in Judicial Selection?"

22. Binder and Maltzman, *Advice and Dissent*, chapters 3–4.

23. Elizabeth Palmer, "For Bush's Judicial Nominees, A Tough Tribunal Awaits," *CQ Weekly*, April 28, 2001, pp. 898–902.

24. On the role of filibusters, see Edward H. Stiglitz, "Appointment Politics and the Ideological Composition of the Judiciary," *Legislative Studies Quarterly* 39 (February 2014): 27–54.

25. Sheldon Goldman, Elliot Slotnick, and Sara Schiavoni, "Obama's First Term Judiciary," *Judicature* 96 (July/August 2013): 7–47.

26. Griffin Bell quoted in Nina Totenberg, "Will Judges Be Chosen Rationally?" *Judicature* 60 (August/September 1976): 93.

27. See Binder and Maltzman, *Advice and Dissent*, chapter 5; and Jon R. Bond, "The Politics of Court Structure: The Addition of New Federal Judges, 1949–1978," *Law and Policy Quarterly* 2 (April 1980): 181–188.

28. See, e.g., the important role that African American support played in the confirmation of Clarence Thomas even though he was likely to vote against the wishes of leading civil rights organizations. L. Marvin Overby, Beth M. Henschen, Julie Walsh, and Michael H. Strauss, "Courting Constituents:

An Analysis of the Senate Confirmation Vote on Justice Clarence Thomas," *American Political Science Review* 86 (December 1992): 997–1003.

29. Christina L. Boyd, Lee Epstein, and Andrew D. Martin, "Untangling the Causal Effects of Sex on Judging," *American Journal of Political Science* 54 (April 2010): 389–411; and Jennifer L. Peresie, "Female Judges Matter: Gender and Collegial Decisionmaking in the Federal Appellate Courts," *Yale Law Journal* 114 (May 2005): 1759–1790. See also Thomas G. Walker and Deborah J. Barrow, "The Diversification of the Federal Bench: Policy and Process Ramifications," *Journal of Politics* 47 (May 1985): 596–617.

30. Jonathan P. Kastellec, "Racial Diversity and Judicial Influence on Appellate Courts," *American Journal of Political Science* 57 (January 2013): 167–183; and Adam B. Cox and Thomas J. Miles, "Judging the Voting Rights Act," *Columbia Law Review* 108 (January 2008): 1–54.

31. Jason L. Morin, "The Voting Behavior of Minority Judges in the U.S. Courts of Appeals: Does the Race of the Claimant Matter?", *American Politics Research* 42 (January 2014): 34–64. See also Walker and Barrow, "The Diversification of the Federal Bench."

32. Alma Cohen and Crystal S. Yang, "Judicial Politics and Sentencing Decisions," *American Economic Journal: Economic Policy* 11 (February 2019): 160–191.

33. Quoted in Adam Liptak, "The Waves Minority Judges Always Make," *New York Times*, May 1, 2009.

34. Cass R. Sunstein, David Schkade, Lisa M. Ellman, and Andres Sawicki, *Are Judges Political?* (Washington, DC: Brookings Institution, 2006); Robert A. Carp, Donald Songer, C. K. Rowland, Ronald Stidham, and Lisa Richey-Tracy, "The Voting Behavior of Judges Appointed by President Bush," *Judicature* 76 (April/May 1993): 298–302; C. K. Rowland and Bridget Jeffery Todd, "Where You Stand Depends on Who Sits: Platform Promises and Judicial Gatekeeping in the Federal District Courts," *Journal of Politics* 53 (February 1991): 175–185; C. K. Rowland, Donald R. Songer, and Robert A. Carp, "Presidential Effects on Criminal Justice in the Lower Federal Courts: The Reagan Judges," *Law and Society Review* 22, no. 1 (1988): 191–200; Timothy B. Tomasi and Jess A. Velona, "All the President's Men? A Study of Ronald Reagan's Appointments to the U.S. Courts of Appeals," *Columbia Law Review* 87 (May 1987): 766–793; and John Gottschall, "Reagan Appointments to the United States Court of Appeals: The Continuation of a Judicial Revolution," *Judicature* (June/July 1986): 48–54 and sources cited therein.

35. Rob Robinson, "Executive Branch Socialization and Deference on the U.S. Supreme Court," *Law and Society Review* 46 (December 2012): 889–901.

36. For the impact of a highly specific aspect of background, see Adam N. Glynn and Maya Sen, "Identifying Judicial Empathy: Does Having Daughters Cause Judges to Rule for Women's Issues?" *American Journal of Political Science* 59 (January 2015): 37–54.

37. See John W. Dean, *The Rehnquist Choice* (New York: Free Press, 2001).

38. See John Anthony Maltese, *The Selling of Supreme Court Nominees* (Baltimore, MD: Johns Hopkins University Press, 1995).

39. See Robert J. McGrath and James A. Rydberg, "The Marginality Hypothesis and Supreme Court Confirmation Votes in the Senate," *Congress & the Presidency* 43 (September–December 2016): 324–351; Lee Epstein, René Lindstädt, Jeffrey A. Segal, and Chad Westerland, "The Changing Dynamics of Senate Voting on Supreme Court Nominees," *Journal of Politics* 68 (May 2006): 296–307; John Massaro, *Supremely Political* (Albany: State University of New York Press, 1992); Charles M. Cameron, Albert D. Cover, and Jeffrey A. Segal, "Senate Voting on Supreme Court Nominees: A Neoinstitutional Model," *American Political Science Review* 84 (June 1990): 525–534; Jeffrey Segal, "Senate Confirmation of Supreme Court Justices: Partisan and Institutional Politics," *Journal of Politics* 49 (November 1987): 998–1015; and P. S. Ruckman Jr., "The Supreme Court, Critical Nominations, and the Senate Confirmation Process," *Journal of Politics* 55 (August 1993): 793–805.

40. See also Charles M. Cameron, Jonathan P. Kastellec, and Jee-Kwang Park, "Voting for Justices: Change and Continuity in Confirmation Voting 1937–2010," *Journal of Politics* 75 (April 2013): 283–299; Scott Basinger and Maxwell Mak, "The Changing Politics of Supreme Court Confirmations," *American Politics Research* 40 (July 2012): 737–763; and Charles R. Shipan and Megan L. Shannon, "Delaying Justice(s): A Duration Analysis of Supreme Court Confirmations," *American Journal of Political Science* 47 (October 2003): 654–668.

41. Thomas R. Marshall, "Symbolic versus Policy Representation on the U.S. Supreme Court," *Journal of Politics* 55 (February 1993): 140–150.

42. See Bryon J. Moraski and Charles R. Shipan, "The Politics of Supreme Court Nominations: A Theory of Institutional Constraints and Choices," *American Journal of Political Science* 43 (October

1999): 1069–1095; and David Cottrell, Charles R. Shipan, and Richard J. Anderson, "The Power to Appoint: Presidential Nominations and Change on the Supreme Court," *Journal of Politics* 81 (July 2019): 1057–1068.

43. Robert Scigliano, *The Supreme Court and the Presidency* (New York: Free Press, 1971). This is also true for nominees to the courts of appeals. See Ashlyn Kuersten and Donald Songer, "Presidential Success through Appointments to the United States Courts of Appeals," *American Politics Research* 31 (March 2003): 107–137; Donald R. Songer and Martha Humphries Ginn, "Assessing the Impact of Presidential and Home State Influences on Judicial Decisionmaking in the United States Courts of Appeals," *Political Research Quarterly* 55 (June 2002): 299–328; and Micheal W. Giles, Virginia A. Hettinger, and Todd Peppers, "Picking Federal Judges: A Note on Policy and Partisan Selection Agendas," *Political Research Quarterly* 54 (September 2001): 623–641.

44. See, e.g., Jeffrey A. Segal and Harold J. Spaeth, *The Supreme Court and the Attitudinal Model* (Cambridge, UK: Cambridge University Press, 1993); Jeffrey A. Segal and Albert O. Cover, "Ideological Values and the Votes of U.S. Supreme Court Justices," *American Political Science Review* 83 (June 1989): 557–566; Tracey E. George and Lee Epstein, "On the Nature of Supreme Court Decision Making," *American Political Science Review* 86 (June 1992): 323–337; and Jeffrey A. Segal and Harold J. Spaeth, "The Influence of *Stare Decisis* on the Votes of United States Supreme Court Justices," *American Journal of Political Science* 40 (November 1996): 971–1003.

45. Michael A. Bailey and Forrest Maltzman, *The Constrained Court: Law, Politics, and the Decisions Justices Make* (Princeton, NJ: Princeton University Press, 2011); Brandon L. Bartels, "Choices in Context: How Case-Level Factors Influence the Magnitude of Ideological Voting on the U.S. Supreme Court," *American Politics Research* 39 (January 2011): 142–175; and Brandon L. Bartels, "The Constraining Capacity of Legal Doctrine on the U.S. Supreme Court," *American Political Science Review* 103 (August 2009): 474–495.

46. Dwight Eisenhower quoted in Henry J. Abraham, *Justices, Presidents, and Senators: A History of U.S. Supreme Court Appointments from Washington to Clinton* (Lanham, MD: Rowman & Littlefield, 1999), p. 200.

47. See Gary King, "Presidential Appointments to the Supreme Court: Adding Systematic Explanation to Probabilistic Description," *American Politics Quarterly* 15 (July 1987): 373–386.

48. See George C. Edwards III, *The Strategic President: Persuasion and Opportunity in Presidential Leadership* (Princeton, NJ: Princeton University Press, 2009), pp. 193–195.

49. On the importance of ideology and partisanship considerations in judicial retirement and resignation decisions, see Ross Stolzenberg and James Lindgren, "Retirement and Death in Office of U.S. Supreme Court Justices," *Demography* 47 (No. 2, 2010): 269–298; Kjersten R. Nelson and Eve M. Ringsmuth, "Departures from the Court: The Political Landscape and Institutional Constraints," *American Politics Research* 37 (May 2009): 486–507; Deborah J. Barrow and Gary Zuk, "An Institutional Analysis of Turnover in the Lower Federal Courts, 1900–1987," *Journal of Politics* 52 (May 1990): 457–476; and Gary Zuk, Gerard S. Gryski, and Deborah J. Barrow, "Partisan Transformation of the Federal Judiciary, 1869–1992," *American Politics Quarterly* 21 (October 1993): 439–457.

50. See Ryan C. Black and Ryan J. Owens, *The Solicitor General and the United States Supreme Court: Executive Branch Influence and Judicial Decisions* (New York: Cambridge University Press, 2012); Rebecca Mae Salokar, *The Solicitor General* (Philadelphia, PA: Temple University Press, 1992); and Lincoln Caplan, *The Tenth Justice: The Solicitor General and the Rule of Law* (New York: Random House, 1987).

51. On the Court's acceptance of cases, see Black and Owens, *The Solicitor General and the United States Supreme Court*; H. W. Perry, Jr., *Deciding to Decide: Agenda Setting in the United States Supreme Court* (Cambridge, MA: Harvard University Press, 1991); Doris Marie Provine, *Case Selection in the United States Supreme Court* (Chicago, IL: University of Chicago Press, 1980); and Stuart H. Teger and Douglas Kosinski, "The Cue Theory of Supreme Court Certiorari Jurisdiction: A Reconsideration," *Journal of Politics* 42 (August 1980): 834–846.

52. Michael A. Bailey and Forrest Maltzman, *The Constrained Court: Law, Politics, and the Decisions Justices Make* (Princeton, NJ: Princeton University Press, 2011), chapters 6–7; and James F. Spriggs and Paul J. Wahlbeck, "Amicus Curiae and the Role of Information in the Supreme Court," *Political Research Quarterly* 50 (June 1997): 365–386.

53. Chris Nicholson and Paul M. Collins, Jr., "The Solicitor General's Amicus Curiae Strategies in the Supreme Court," *American Political Research* 36 (May 2008): 382–415.

54. See Timothy R. Johnson, "The Supreme Court, the Solicitor General, and the Separation of Powers," *American Politics Research* 31 (July 2003): 426–451.

55. Rebecca E. Deen, Joseph Ignagni, and James Meernik, "Executive Influence on the U.S. Supreme Court: Solicitor General *Amicus* Cases, 1953–1997," *American Review of Politics* 22 (Spring 2001): 3–26.

56. Michael A. Bailey, Brian Kamoie, and Forrest Maltzman, "Signals from the Tenth Justice: The Political Role of the Solicitor General in Supreme Court Decision Making," *American Journal of Political Science* 49 (January 2005): 72–85.

57. On the solicitor general's success, see Jeffrey A. Segal, "Courts, Executives, and Legislatures," in John B. Gates and Charles A. Johnson, eds., *The American Courts* (Washington, DC: Congressional Quarterly Press, 1991), pp. 376–382.

58. Adam Liptak, "Why Obama Struggled at Court, and Trump May Strain to Do Better," *New York Times*, January 23, 2017.

59. Burt Solomon, *FDR v. The Constitution* (New York: Walker, 2009), p. 10.

60. Earl Warren, *The Memoirs of Chief Justice Earl Warren* (Garden City, NY: Doubleday, 1971), pp. 337–342.

61. William Castro, *The Supreme Court in the Early Republic* (Columbia, SC: University of South Carolina Press, 1995), chapter 6.

62. Solomon, *FDR v. The Constitution*, p. 10.

63. Robert A. Caro, *The Passage of Power* (New York: Knopf, 2012), pp. 368, 407.

64. Bruce Allen Murphy, *Fortas* (New York: William Morrow, 1988), p. 235. Murphy chronicles the Johnson–Fortas relationship in great detail. See also Joseph A. Califano, Jr., *The Triumph and Tragedy of Lyndon Johnson* (New York: Simon & Schuster, 1991), pp. 95–96, 118, 120, 153–154, 161–163, 189, 191, 205, 213–218, 298, 306, 312–315.

65. Bruce Allen Murphy, *The Brandeis/Frankfurter Connection: The Secret Political Activities of Two Supreme Court Justices* (New York: Oxford University Press, 1982).

66. See Clark Clifford, *Counsel to the President* (New York: Random House, 1991), p. 215; and David McCullough, *Truman* (New York: Simon & Schuster, 1992), p. 897.

67. John Ehrlichman, *Witness to Power: The Nixon Years* (New York: Simon & Schuster, 1982), p. 133.

68. Linda Greenhouse, *Becoming Justice Blackmun* (New York: Times Books, 2005), pp. 99–100, 127.

69. But see Ryan J. Owens, "The Separation of Powers and Supreme Court Agenda Setting," *American Journal of Political Science* 54 (April 2010): 412–427.

70. Grant, Nixon, Ford, Carter, and Clinton also responded to court orders to provide testimony and other information.

71. See, e.g., Craig R. Ducat and Robert L. Dudley, "Federal District Judges and Presidential Power during the Postwar Era," *Journal of Politics* 51 (February 1989): 98–118.

72. Forrest McDonald, *The American Presidency: An Intellectual History* (Lawrence: University Press of Kansas, 1994), pp. 398–402.

73. Anthony A. D'Amato and Robert M. O'Neil, *The Judiciary and Vietnam* (New York: St. Martin's, 1972); and Louis Fisher, "Judicial Review of the War Power," *Presidential Studies Quarterly* 35 (September 2005): 466–495.

74. Institute for Policy Integrity, New York University School of Law https://policyintegrity.org/deregulation-roundup.

75. Congress has succeeded in such an action only once, however—on jurisdiction to hear appeals on certain writ of habeas corpus cases following the Civil War—and in this case, the president supported the Court. The case was *Ex parte McCardle* (1828).

76. Congress has frequently passed legislation to strip lower court jurisdiction. See Dawn M. Chutkow, "Jurisdiction Stripping: Litigation, Ideology, and Congressional Control of the Courts," *Journal of Politics* 70 (October 2008): 1053–1064.

77. William N. Eskridge, "Overriding Supreme Court Statutory Interpretation Decisions," *Yale Law Journal* 101 (1991): 331–455; and Joseph Ignagni and James Meernik, "Explaining Congressional Attempts to Reverse Supreme Court Decisions," *Political Research Quarterly* 10 (June 1994): 353–372. See also R. Shep Melnick, *Between the Lines: Interpreting Welfare Rights* (Washington, DC: Brookings Institution, 1994).

78. There were many allegations of a deal between the two men, and some observers even accused Ford of having agreed to the pardon prior to his nomination as vice president by Nixon. However, in sworn testimony before the House Judiciary Committee in 1974, Ford vehemently denied that he had made such an agreement.

CHAPTER 13

1. Richard E. Neustadt, "Presidency and Legislation: Planning the President's Program," *American Political Science Review* 49 (1955): 980–1021, p. 1015.

2. Lawrence R. Jacobs and Theda Skocpol, *Health Care Reform and American Politics: What Everyone Needs to Know,* revised ed. (New York: Oxford University Press, 2012), p. 54.

3. Justin S. Vaughn and José D. Villalobos, *Czars in the White House: The Rise of Policy Czars as Presidential Management Tools* (Ann Arbor: University of Michigan Press, 2015).

4. Gabby Orr and Andrew Restuccia, "How Stephen Miller Made Immigration Personal," *Politico*, April 22, 2019.

5. Peter Baker, Glenn Thrush, and Maggie Haberman, "Jared Kushner and Ivanka Trump: Pillars of Family-Driven West Wing," *New York Times*, April 15, 2017.

6. Nancy Cook and Daniel Lippman, "Kushner Makes White House Power Play," *Politico*, November 27, 2018.

7. Seung Min Kim, Josh Dawsey, and Mike DeBonis, "Trump's Bipartisan Infrastructure Plan Already Imperiled as Mulvaney, GOP Lawmakers Object to Cost," *Washington Post*, May 4, 2019.

8. Daniel W. Drezner, "The #ToddlerinChief Thread is Now the Age of a Toddler. Here's What I've Learned," *Washington Post*, April 25, 2019; and Eliana Plott, "Ignoring Trump's Orders, Hoping He'll Forget," *The Atlantic*, May 15, 2019.

9. https://www.whitehouse.gov/omb/statements-of-administration-policy/.

10. Executive order 13771, "Reducing Regulation and Controlling Regulatory Costs," January 30, 2017.

11. Connor Raso, "How Has Trump's Deregulatory Order Worked in Practice?" *Brookings Institution Series on Regulatory Process and Perspective*, September 6, 2018.

12. B. Dan Wood, *The Politics of Economic Leadership: The Causes and Consequences of Presidential Rhetoric* (Princeton, NJ: Princeton University Press, 2007), p. xiii.

13. Congressional Budget Office, *The Budget and Economic Outlook: 2019–2029*, January 2019, pp. 26–28; and Jeanna Smialek, Jim Tankersley, and Mark Lander, "Trump's Trade War Escalation Will Exact Economic Pain, Adviser Says," *New York Times*, May 12, 2019.

14. Alan S. Blinder and Mark W. Watson, "Presidents and the U.S. Economy: An Econometric Exploration," *American Economic Review* 106 (2016): 1015–1045.

15. Peter Conti-Brown, "The Institutions of Federal Reserve Independence," *Yale Journal on Regulation* 32 (2015): 257–310.

16. Jeanna Smialek, "Fed Likely to Leave interest Rates Unchanged as Trump Calls for Cut," *New York Times*, April 30, 2019.

17. Larry Bartels, *Unequal Democracy: Political Economy of the New Gilded Age* (Princeton, NJ: Princeton University Press, 2008), chapter 2.

18. James E. Campbell, "The Economic Records of the Presidents, Party Differences, and Inherited Economic Conditions," *Forum* 9, art. 7 (2011), p. 15; and James E. Campbell, "The President's Economy: Parity in Presidential Party Performance," *Presidential Studies Quarterly* 42 (2012): 811–818.

19. Blinder and Watson, "Presidents and the U.S. Economy: An Econometric Exploration," p. 1043.

20. Christopher Berry, Barry Burden, and William Howell, "The President and the Distribution of Federal Spending," *American Political Science Review* 104 (2010): 783–799.

21. Douglas L. Kriner and Andrew Reeves, "The Influence of Federal Spending on Federal Elections," *American Political Science Review* 106 (2012): 348–366.

22. John T. Gasper and Andrew Reeves, "Make It Rain: Retrospection and the Attentive Electorate in the Context of Natural Disasters," *American Journal of Political Science* 55 (2011): 340–355; Andrew J. Healy and Neil Malhotra, "Myopic Voters and Natural Disaster Policy," *American Political Science Review* 103 (2009): 387–406; and Andrew Reeves, "Political Disaster: Unilateral Powers, Electoral Incentives, and Presidential Disaster Declarations," *Journal of Politics* 73 (2011): 1142–1151.

23. The economic literature on this question is vast. A good summary is Thomas L. Hungerford, *Taxes and the Economy: An Economic Analysis of the Top Tax Rates since 1945* (Updated), Congressional Research Service R42729, December 12, 2012.

24. Neel Kashkari, "The Role and Limits of Monetary Policy," Federal Reserve Bank of Minneapolis, May 9, 2016.

25. Andrew Ross Sorkin, Diana B. Henriques, Edmund L. Andrews, and Joe Nocera, "As Credit Crisis Spiraled, Alarm Led to Action," *New York Times*, October 2, 2008.

26. Data from the Federal Reserve Bank of St. Louis. https://fred.stlouisfed.org/series/A191RL1A225NBEA.

27. Baird Webel, *The Dodd-Frank Wall Street Reform and Consumer Protection Act: Background and Summary*, Congressional Research Service R-41350, April 21, 2017.

28. https://www.whitehouse.gov/bringing-back-jobs-and-growth.

29. Mark Zandi, Chris Lafakis, Dan White, and Adam Ozimek, *The Macroeconomic Consequences of Mr. Trump's Economic Policies*. Moody's Analytics, June 2016.

30. James McBride and Andrew Chatzky, "What is the Trans-Pacific Partnership? *Council on Foreign Relations Backgrounder*, January 4, 2019.

31. https://twitter.com/realDonaldTrump/status/969525362580484098.

32. Yian Q. Mui, "Withdrawal from Trans-Pacific Partnership Shifts U.S. Role in World Economy," *Washington Post*, January 23, 2017.

33. Brock R. Williams, *Escalating U.S. Tariffs Timeline*, Congressional Research Service IN10943, June 5, 2019; Presidential Proclamation 9888, "Adjusting Imports of Automobiles and Automobile Parts into the United States," May 17, 2019.

34. Chris Mills Rodrigo, "China Halts US Soy Purchases amid Trade War," *The Hill*, May 30, 2019.

35. Jim Tankersley, "Trump's Tariffs Could Nullify Tax Cut, Clouding Economic Picture," *New York Times*, June 3, 2019; Mary Amiti, Stephen J. Redding, and David Weinstein, "The Impact of the 2010 Trade War on Prices and Welfare," Discussion Paper DP 13564, Centre for Economic Policy Research (London), March 2, 2019; and Olivia Paschal, "The Unexpected Side Effects of Trump's Trade War," *The Atlantic*, March 19, 2019.

36. Harold G. Lasswell, *Politics: Who Gets What, When, and How* (New York: McGraw-Hill, 1936).

37. Lyn Ragsdale, *Vital Statistics on the Presidency*, 4th ed. (Thousand Oaks, CA: CQ Press, 2014), pp. 476–477.

38. Clinton T. Brass et al., *Shutdown of the Federal Government: Causes, Processes, and Effects*, Congressional Research Service RL 34680, May 5, 2017.

39. For a discussion of the budgetary process during this early period, see Louis Fisher, *The Politics of Shared Power: Congress and the Executive* (Washington, DC: Congressional Quarterly, 1992), pp. 177–178; and Louis Fisher, "Presidential Budget Duties," *Presidential Studies Quarterly*, 42 (2012): 761.

40. The national debt increased from about $1 billion in 1916 to over $25 billion by 1919. Fisher, "Presidential Budget Duties," p. 763.

41. Congressional Budget Office, *The Budget and Economic Outlook 2001–2010*, January 2000.

42. Bob Woodward and Robert Costa, "In a Revealing Interview, Trump Predicts a 'Massive Recession' but Intends to Eliminate the National Debt in 8 years," *Washington Post*, April 2, 2016.

43. Congressional Budget Office, *An Analysis of the President's 2018 Budget*, July 2017.

44. Congressional Budget Office, *An Update to the Budget and Economic Outlook: 2019 to 2029*, August 21, 2019.

45. John McClelland and Jeffrey Werling, "How the 2017 Tax Act Affects CBO's Projections," Congressional Budget Office, April 20, 2018.

46. D. Andrew Austin, *The Debt Limit since 2011*, Congressional Research Service R43389, August 9, 2017.

47. United States Department of the Treasury, *Monthly Treasury Statement of Receipts and Outlays of the United States Government for Fiscal Year 2017*, October 2016.

48. Steven L. Schwarcz, "Rollover Risk: Ideating a U.S. Debt Default," *Boston College Law Review* 55:1-37 (2014): 1.

49. Linda K. Kowlalcky and Lance T. LaLoup, "Congress and the Politics of Statutory Debt Limitation," *Public Administration Review* 53 (1993): 14–27, p. 13.

50. D. Andrew Austin, *The Debt Limit: History and Recent Increases*, Congressional Research Service RL31967, November 2, 2015, p. 12, Table 2.

51. Jonathan Weisman and Ashley Parker, "Republicans Back Down, Ending Crisis over Shutdown and Debt Limit," *New York Times*, October 16, 2013.

CHAPTER 14

1. Military Order of November 13, 2001, "Detention, Treatment, and Trial of Certain Non-Citizens in the War against Terrorism," *66 Federal Register* 222 (November 16, 2001): 57833–57836.

2. Fact Sheet, "Status of Detainees at Guantanamo," White House Press Office, February 7, 2002. http://www.presidency.ucsb.edu/ws/index.php?pid=79402&st=&st1.

3. Michael R. Gordon, Helene Cooper, and Michael D. Shear, "Dozens of U.S. Missiles Hit Air Base in Syria," *New York Times*, April 6, 2017.

4. In *Hamdi v. Rumsfeld* (2006), the Supreme Court held that detainees had due process rights to challenge their status as enemy combatants and that the president did not have the constitutional authority to prevent federal courts from hearing those challenges.

5. David E. Sanger and Choe Sang-Hun, "North Korean Nuclear Test Draws U.S. Warning of 'Massive Military Response'," *New York Times*, September 2, 2017.

6. Anne Gearan and Emily Rauhala, "Trump Renews Threat of Force against North Korea over Nuclear Weapons," *Washington Post*, September 7, 2017.

7. Edward S. Corwin, *The President: Office and Powers, 1787–1957* (New York: New York University Press, 1957), p. 171.

8. *United States v. Curtiss Wright Export Corporation*, 299 US 304 (1936), 320.

9. "Congress can no more interfere with the President's conduct of the interrogation of enemy combatants than it can dictate strategic or tactical decisions on the battlefield. Just as statutes that order the President to conduct warfare in a certain manner or force specific goals would be unconstitutional, so too are laws that seek to prevent the President from gaining the intelligence he believes necessary to prevent attacks upon the United States." *Standards of Conduct for Interrogation under 18 U.S.C. §§ 2340–2340A*, Office of Legal Counsel, US Department of Justice, August 1, 2002. Reprinted in Karen J. Greenberg and Joshua L. Dratel, eds., *The Torture Papers: The Road to Abu Ghraib* (New York: Cambridge University Press, 2005), p. 207.

10. Louis Fisher, *Supreme Court Expansion of Presidential Power: Unconstitutional Leanings* (Lawrence: University Press of Kansas, 2017).

11. Caitlain Devereaux Lewis, *Presidential Authority over Trade: Imposing Tariffs and Duties*, Congressional Research Service R44707, December 9, 2016.

12. For a detailed report on the Senate and international agreements, see Congressional Research Service, *Treaties and Other International Agreements: The Role of the United States Senate* (Washington, DC: US Government Printing Office, 2001).

13. David Auerswald and Forrest Maltzman, "Policymaking through Advice and Consent: Treaty Consideration by the United States Senate," *Journal of Politics* 65 (November 2003): 1097–1110.

14. See Brandon C. Prins and Bryan W. Marshall, "Senate Influence or Presidential Unilateralism? An Examination of Treaties and Executive Agreements from Theodore Roosevelt and George W. Bush," *Conflict Management and Peace Science* 26, no. 2 (2009): 191–208.

15. Noah Feldman, *The Three Lives of James Madison: Genius, Partisan, President* (New York: Random House, 2017), pp. 402–403.

16. Glen S. Krutz and Jeffrey S. Peake, *Treaty Politics and the Rise of Executive Agreements: International Commitments in a System of Shared Powers* (Ann Arbor: University of Michigan Press, 2009), chapter 6.

17. *Goldwater v. Carter* (1979).

18. When debating the Intermediate Range Nuclear Forces Treaty in 1988, the Senate declared that any digression from the "common understanding" of the treaty at the time of ratification would require joint action by Congress and the president. Louis Fisher, *The Politics of Shared Power: Congress and the Executive* (Washington, DC: Congressional Quarterly, 1993), p. 156.

19. *United States v. Stuart* (1983).

20. *United States v. Belmont* (1937); and *United States v. Pink* (1942).

21. Such delegations of the commerce power upheld in *Field v. Clark* (1892).

22. Kiki Caruson and Victoria A. Farrar-Myers, "Promoting the President's Foreign Policy Agenda: Presidential Use of Executive Agreements as Policy Vehicles," *Political Research Quarterly* 60 (December 2007): 631–634.

23. Judith G. Kelley and Jon C. W. Pevehouse, "An Opportunity Cost Theory of US Treaty Behavior," *International Studies Quarterly* 59, no. 3 (2015): 531–543; and Krutz and Peake, *Treaty Politics and the Rise of Executive Agreements*, chapter 3.

24. Ibid.

25. Krutz and Peake, *Treaty Politics and the Rise of Executive Agreements*, chapter 5; and Prins and Marshall, "Presidential Unilateralism?"

26. Krutz and Peake, *Treaty Politics and the Rise of Executive Agreements*, chapters 4–5.

27. Jeffrey S. Peake, "Obama, Unilateral Diplomacy, and Iran: Treaties, Executive Agreements, and Political Commitments," in Richard S. Conley, ed., *Presidential Leadership and National Security: The Obama Legacy and Trump Trajectory* (New York: Routledge Press, 2018).

28. Tim Hains, "John Kerry Explains Why Iran Deal Is Not Legally a Treaty: 'You Can't Pass a Treaty Anymore'," *RealClearPolitics*, July 29, 2015.

29. Peake, "Obama, Unilateral Diplomacy, and Iran"; Jeffrey S. Peake, "The Domestic Politics of U.S. Treaty Ratification: Bilateral Treaties from 1949 to 2012," *Foreign Policy Analysis* 13 (October 2017): 832-853; and Krutz and Peake, *Treaty Politics and the Rise of Executive Agreements*, pp. 33–34.

30. Frances E. Lee, *Beyond Ideology: Politics, Principles, and Partisanship in the U.S. Senate* (Chicago, IL: University of Chicago Press, 2009), chapter 4.

31. Lisa L. Martin, "The President and International Commitments: Treaties as Signaling Devices," *Presidential Studies Quarterly* 35 (September 2005): 440–465; and Lisa L. Martin, *Democratic Commitments: Legislatures and International Cooperation* (Princeton, NJ: Princeton University Press, 2000).

32. Oona A. Hathaway, "Presidential Power over International Law: Restoring the Balance," *Yale Law Journal* 119 (November 2009): 210–215.

33. Bruce A. Ackerman and David Golove, *Is NAFTA Constitutional?* (Cambridge, MA: Harvard University Press, 1995).

34. On this accord, see Peake, "Obama, Unilateral Diplomacy, and Iran"; and Jack Goldsmith, "The Contributions of the Obama Administration to the Practice and Theory of International Law," *Harvard International Law Journal* 57 (Spring 2016): 1–19.

35. On this decision, see Mark Rush, "*Zivotofsky v. Kerry*: An Unnecessary Decision Grounded on Weak Precedents," *Presidential Studies Quarterly* 46 (December 2016): 911–924.

36. David Gray Adler, "The President's Recognition Power: Ministerial or Discretionary?" *Presidential Studies Quarterly* 25 (Spring 1995): 267–286.

37. There are some practical differences between an Authorization to Use Military Force (an AUMF) and a declaration of war. A declaration of war triggers some specific consequences under international law (relating to the treatment of prisoners of war and noncombatants) and some specific domestic legal powers that the president can exercise. See Jennifer K. Elsea and Richard E. Grimmett, *Declarations of War and Authorizations for the Use of Military Force: Historical Background and Legal Implications*, Congressional Research Service RL31133, March 17, 2011.

38. See, e.g., Louis Fisher, "The Korean War: On What Legal Basis Did Truman Act?" *American Journal of International Law* 89 (April 1995): 21–39.

39. See Christopher Deering, "Foreign Affairs and War," in Paul Quirk and Sarah Binder, eds., *The Legislative Branch* (New York: Oxford University Press, 2005); and Louis Fisher, *Congressional Abdication on War and Spending* (College Station: Texas A&M University Press, 2000).

40. Data taken from the Gallup Presidential Approval Center, http://www.gallup.com/interactives/185273/presidential-job-approval-center.aspx.

41. The resolution was first passed in July 1973 and vetoed by the president. In November 1973 both the House and Senate overrode in bipartisan votes. By then, Nixon's approval was in the high 20s and low 30s.

42. Douglas L. Kriner, "Obama's Authorization Paradox: Syria and Congress's Continued Relevance in Military Affairs," *Presidential Studies Quarterly* (June 2014): 309–327.

43. See Aaron Wildavsky, "The Two Presidencies," in Steven A. Shull, ed., *The Two Presidencies: A Quarter-Century Assessment* (Chicago, IL: Nelson-Hall, 1991), pp. 11–25.

44. Ibid.

45. Helen Milner and B. B. Rosendorff, "Democratic Politics and International Trade Negotiations: Elections and Divided Government as Constraints on Trade Liberalization," *Journal of Conflict Resolution* 41 (February 1997): 117–146; and David Karol, "Divided Government and Trade Policy: Much Ado about Nothing?" *International Organization* 54 (September 2000): 825–844.

46. Douglas L. Kriner, "Presidents, Domestic Politics, and the International Arena," in George C. Edwards III and William G. Howell, eds., *The Oxford Handbook of the American Presidency* (Oxford, UK: Oxford University Press, 2009), p. 684; and Piers Robinson, *The CNN Effect: The Myth of News, Foreign Policy, and Intervention* (New York: Routledge, 2002).

47. Matthew Baum, "Going Private: Public Opinion, Presidential Rhetoric, and the Domestic Politics of Audience Costs in U.S. Foreign Policy," *Journal of Conflict Resolution* 48 (October 2004): 603–631.

48. Thomas Knecht, *Paying Attention to Foreign Affairs: How Public Opinion Affects Presidential Decision Making* (University Park: The Pennsylvania State University Press, 2010), p. 205.

49. George C. Edwards III, *At the Margins: Presidential Leadership of Congress* (New Haven, CT: Yale University Press, 1989), chapter 4.

50. Ibid.

51. William G. Howell and Jon C. Pevehouse, *While Dangers Gather: Congressional Checks on Presidential War Powers* (Princeton, NJ: Princeton University Press, 2007).

52. Douglas L. Kriner, *After the Rubicon: Congress, Presidents, and the Politics of Waging War* (Chicago, IL: University of Chicago Press, 2010).

53. Linda Fowler, *Watchdogs on the Hill: The Decline of Congressional Oversight of U.S. Foreign Relations* (Princeton, NJ: Princeton University Press, 2015).

54. Eric Paul Svensen, "Structured-Induced Deference or Equal and Coordinate Actor: Congressional Influence on American Foreign Policy," *American Politics Research* 47 (January 2019): 88–118.

55. The National Commission on Terrorist Attacks on the United States, *The 9/11 Commission Report* (New York: W.W. Norton, 2004).

56. Intelligence Reform and Terrorism Prevention Act of 2004, PL 108–458, December 17, 2007.

57. Richard A. Best Jr., *The National Security Council: An Organizational Assessment*, Congressional Research Service RL30840, December 28, 2011, p. 1.

58. Quoted in Mark Landler and Julie Hirschfeld Davis, "Trump Opens His Arms to Russia. His Administration Closes Its Fist." *New York Times*, July 14, 2018.

59. Quoted in Mark Landler, "Trump's Tweets on Syria, Russia and China: The Triumph of Contradiction," *New York Times*, April 11, 2018.

60. National Security Act of 1947, Title 1, sec. 101 PL 80–253, July 26, 1947.

61. Presidential Policy Directive PPD-1, *Organization of the National Security Council System*, February 13, 2009.

62. Presidential National Security Memorandum NSM-2, *Organization of the National Security Council and the Homeland Security Council*, January 28, 2017.

63. Presidential National Security Memorandum NSM-4, *Organization of the National Security Council, the Homeland Security Council, and Subcommittees*, April 4, 2017.

64. Robert Costa and Abby Phillips, "Stephen Bannon Removed from National Security Council," *Washington Post*, April 5, 2017.

65. John P. Burke, *Honest Broker: The National Security Advisor and Presidential Decision Making* (College Station: Texas A&M University Press, 2009), p. 1.

66. John P. Burke, *The National Security Advisor and Staff*, White House Transition Project, Report 2017–24, 2017, p. 11.

67. Stephen J. Hadley, *The Role and Importance of the National Security Advisor*, Scowcroft Paper No. 1, Scowcroft Institute of Public Affairs, Bush School of Government and Public Service, Texas A&M University, April 26, 2016, p. 2.

68. Burke, *Honest Broker*.

69. See US Senate, Select Committee on Secret Military Assistance to Iran and the Nicaraguan Opposition, *Report of the Congressional Committees Investigating the Ira–Contra Affair*, November 17, 1987. S. Rept. No. 100–216, 100th Cong., 1st Session.

70. Project on National Security Reform, *Forging a New Shield*, November 2008, p. 100.

71. Ibid., p. 137.

72. Ibid., p. 23.

73. Ibid., Part VI.

APPENDIX A

1. The most prominent examples are the books of Bob Woodward, including, most recently, *Fear: Trump in the White House* (New York: Simon & Schuster, 2018); *The Price of Politics* (New York: Simon & Schuster, 2012); and *The War Within: A Secret White House History 2006–2008* (New York: Simon & Schuster, 2008).

2. An outstanding and rare example of direct observation from the inside by a scholar is Martha Kumar, *Managing the President's Message: The White House Communications Operation* (Baltimore, MD: Johns Hopkins University Press, 2007).

3. Henry Kissinger, *Years of Upheaval* (Boston, MA: Little, Brown, 1982), p. 1182.

4. Dick Morris, *Behind the Oval Office* (New York: Random House, 1997).

5. Excellent studies of the misperceptions of participants in presidential policy making include Richard E. Neustadt, *Alliance Politics* (New York: Columbia University Press, 1970); and Fred I. Greenstein and Richard H. Immerman, "What Did Eisenhower Tell Kennedy about Indochina? The Politics of Misperception," *Journal of American History* 79 (September 1992): 568–587.

6. Lyndon B. Johnson, *The Vantage Point: Perspectives of the Presidency, 1963–1969* (New York: Popular Library, 1971), pp. 144–153.

7. Jack Valenti, *A Very Human President* (New York: Norton, 1975), pp. 317–319, 358.

8. See George W. Ball, *The Past Has Another Pattern* (New York: Norton, 1982), p. 399; and George McT. Kahin, *Intervention: How America Became Involved in Vietnam* (New York: Knopf, 1986), pp. 366–390.

9. Gordon M. Goldstein, *Lessons in Disaster: McGeorge Bundy and the Path to War in Vietnam* (New York: Holt, 2008), pp. 204–218; Larry Berman, *Planning a Tragedy: The Americanization of the War in Vietnam* (New York: Norton, 1982), pp. 105–121; Chester Cooper, *The Lost Crusade: America in Vietnam* (Greenwich, CT: Dodd, Mead, 1970), pp. 284–285; and US Department of Defense, *United States–Vietnam Relations, 1945–1967*, vol. 3 (Washington, DC: Government Printing Office, 1971), p. 475.

10. Hubert H. Humphrey, *The Education of a Public Man: My Life and Politics* (Garden City, NY: Doubleday, 1976), pp. 290–293.

11. Valenti, *A Very Human President*, pp. 196–197. See also Russell D. Renka, "Bargaining with Legislative Whales in the Kennedy and Johnson Administration" (paper presented at the annual meeting of the American Political Science Association, Washington, DC, August 1980), p. 20.

12. Transcript, Henry Hall Wilson Oral History Interview, April 11, 1973, by Joe B. Frantz, p. 16, Lyndon B. Johnson Library, Austin, Texas.

13. For another example of the unreliability of "eyewitness" accounts, see Robert Dallek, *An Unfinished Life: John F. Kennedy, 1917–1963* (Boston, MA: Little, Brown, 2003), pp. 318–319.

14. Kissinger, *Years of Upheaval*, pp. 111–112. Recently, transcripts of tapes from several presidents have been published. These include Ernest R. May and Philip D. Zelikow, *The Kennedy Tapes* (Cambridge, MA: Belknap Press, 1997); Michael R. Beschloss, ed., *Taking Charge: The Johnson White House Tapes, 1963–1964* (New York: Simon & Schuster, 1997); and Stanley I. Kutler, ed., *Abuse of Power: The New Nixon Tapes* (New York: Free Press, 1997).

15. Henry Kissinger, *Years of Renewal* (New York: Simon & Schuster, 1999), pp. 63–64.

16. Kissinger, *Years of Renewal*, p. 67.

17. See George C. Edwards III, *Presidential Approval* (Baltimore, MD: Johns Hopkins University Press, 1990), p. 175.

18. Quoted in Rich Jaroslovsky, "Manipulating the Media Is a Specialty for the White House's Michael Deaver," *Wall Street Journal*, January 5, 1984, p. 44.

19. Gallup poll, August 5–8, 2003. In a Gallup poll of January 28–29, 1987, only 32 percent of the public felt the Reagan administration had made progress in solving the problems of education.

20. Michael K. Deaver, *A Different Drummer: My Thirty Years with Ronald Reagan* (New York: HarperCollins, 2001), p. 154.

21. For a more extensive discussion of quantitative analysis of the presidency, see George C. Edwards III, "Quantitative Analysis," in George C. Edwards III and Stephen J. Wayne, eds., *Studying the Presidency* (Knoxville: University of Tennessee Press, 1983), pp. 99–124; Gary King, "The Methodology of Presidency Research," in George C. Edwards III, Bert A. Rockman, and John H. Kessel, eds., *Researching the Presidency* (Pittsburgh, PA: University of Pittsburgh Press, 1993), pp. 387–412; and William G. Howell, "Quantitative Approaches to the Study of the Presidency," in George C. Edwards III and William G. Howell, eds., *The Oxford Handbook of the American Presidency* (Oxford, UK: Oxford University Press, 2009).

22. Richard E. Neustadt, *Presidential Power and the Modern Presidents* (New York: Free Press, 1990), p. 4.

23. Recent examples of quantitative studies of the presidency include Gary C. Jacobson, *Presidents & Parties in the Public Mind* (Chicago: University of Chicago Press, 2019); Douglas L. Kriner and Eric Schickler, *Investigating the President: Congressional Checks on Presidential Power* (Princeton, NJ: Princeton University Press, 2016); George C. Edwards III, *Predicting the Presidency: The Potential of Persuasive Leadership* (Princeton, NJ: Princeton University Press, 2016); Douglas L. Kriner and Andrew Reeves, *The Particularistic President* ((New York: Cambridge University Press, 2015); Richard Waterman, Carol Silva, and Hank Jenkins-Smith, *The Presidential Expectations Gap: Public Attitudes Concerning the Presidency* (Ann Arbor: University of Michigan Press, 2014); William G. Howell, Saul P. Jackman, and Jon C. Rogowski, *The Wartime President: Executive Influence and the Nationalizing Politics of Threat* (Chicago, IL: University of Chicago Press, 2014); George C. Edwards III, *Overreach: Leadership in the Obama Presidency* (Princeton, NJ: Princeton University Press, 2012); Douglas L. Kriner, *After the Rubicon: Congress, Presidents, and the Politics of Waging War* (Chicago, IL: University of Chicago Press, 2010); B. Dan Wood, *The Myth of Presidential Representation* (Cambridge, UK: Cambridge University Press, 2009); George C. Edwards III, *The Strategic President: Persuasion and Opportunity in Presidential Leadership* (Princeton, NJ: Princeton University Press, 2009); Frances E. Lee, *Beyond Ideology: Politics, Principles and Partisanship in the U.S. Senate* (Chicago, IL: University of Chicago Press, 2009); Jeffrey E. Cohen, *The Presidency in the Ear of 24-Hour News* (Princeton, NJ: Princeton University Press, 2008); David E. Lewis, *The Politics of Presidential Appointments* (Princeton, NJ: Princeton University Press, 2008); B. Dan Wood, *The Politics of Economic Leadership* (Princeton, NJ: Princeton University Press, 2007); William G. Howell and Jon C. Pevehouse, *While Dangers Gather: Congressional Checks on Presidential War Powers* (Princeton, NJ: Princeton University Press, 2007); Brandice Canes-Wrone, *Who*

Leads Whom? (Princeton, NJ: Princeton University Press, 2006); Lawrence J. Grossback, David A. M. Peterson, and James A. Stimson, *Mandate Politics* (Cambridge, NY: Cambridge University Press, 2006); George C. Edwards III, *On Deaf Ears: The Limits of the Bully Pulpit* (New Haven, CT: Yale University Press, 2003); William G. Howell, *Power without Persuasion: The Politics of Direct Presidential Action* (Princeton, NJ: Princeton University Press, 2003); and Andrew Rudalevige, *Managing the President's Program* (Princeton, NJ: Princeton University Press, 2002).

24. Lyn Ragsdale, *Vital Statistics on the Presidency*, 4th ed. (Washington, DC: CQ Press, 2014).

25. Lisa Deluca and Robert Pallitto, "Digital Resources to Support Quantitative Scholarship in Presidential Studies," *Presidential Studies Quarterly* 48 (September 2018): 537–551.

26. See, e.g., George C. Edwards III, "Presidential Approval as a Source of Influence in Congress," in George C. Edwards III and William G. Howell, eds., *The Oxford Handbook of the American Presidency* (Oxford, UK: Oxford University Press, 2009).

27. For more on legal analysis of the presidency, see Louis Fisher, "Political Scientists and the Public Law Tradition," in George C. Edwards III and William G. Howell, eds., *The Oxford Handbook of the American Presidency* (Oxford, UK: Oxford University Press, 2009); and Louis Fisher, "Making Use of Legal Sources," in Edwards and Wayne, eds., *Studying the Presidency,* pp. 182–198.

28. Norman C. Thomas, "Case Studies," in Edwards and Wayne, eds., *Studying the Presidency*, p. 52.

29. See, e.g., Alexander L. George, "The Case for Multiple Advocacy in Making Foreign Policy," *American Political Science Review* 66 (September 1972): 765–781; John P. Burke and Fred I. Greenstein, *How Presidents Test Reality* (New York: Russell Sage Foundation, 1989); Ryan J. Barilleaux, *The President and Foreign Affairs* (New York: Praeger, 1985); and Patrick J. Haney, *Organizing for Foreign Policy Crises* (Ann Arbor: University of Michigan Press, 1997).

30. See, e.g., Robert F. Durant, *The Administrative Presidency Revisited* (Abany: State University of New York Press, 1992).

31. See Irving L. Janis, *Groupthink*, 2nd ed. (Boston, MA: Houghton Mifflin, 1982).

32. See, e.g., Bruce Miroff, "Presidential Leverage over Social Movements: The Johnson White House and Civil Rights," *Journal of Politics* 43 (February 1981): 2–23.

33. Neustadt, *Presidential Power*.

34. Graham T. Allison and Philip Zelikow, *Essence of Decision: Explaining the Cuban Missile Crisis*, 2nd ed. (New York: Longman, 1999).

35. Examples of work focusing on a single president in an insightful and analytical fashion include Charles O. Jones, *The Trusteeship Presidency* (Baton Rouge: Louisiana State University Press, 1988); Lawrence R. Jacobs and Robert Y. Shapiro, "Issues, Candidate Image, and Priming: The Use of Private Polls in Kennedy's 1960 Presidential Campaign," *American Political Science Review* 88 (September 1994): 527–540; and Roger B. Porter, "Gerald R. Ford: A Healing Presidency," in Fred I. Greenstein, ed., *Leadership in the Modern Presidency* (Cambridge, MA: Harvard University Press, 1988), pp. 199–227.

APPENDIX C

1. The Sixteenth Amendment replaced this with respect to income taxes.
2. Repealed by the Fourteenth Amendment.
3. This paragraph was superseded in 1804 by the Twelfth Amendment.
4. Changed by the Twenty-fifth Amendment.
5. Adopted in 1804.
6. Superseded by the Twentieth Amendment, section 3.
7. Adopted in 1870.
8. Adopted in 1920.
9. Adopted in 1933.
10. Adopted in 1951.
11. Adopted in 1961.
12. Adopted in 1964.
13. Adopted in 1967.
14. Adopted in 1971.

Index

Note: Page numbers in italics indicate figures, tables, and boxes.